SECURITY AND HUMAN

This is the second edition of the acclaimed *Secu* published in 2007. Reconciling issues of security with a respect for fundamental human rights has become one of the key challenges facing governments throughout the world. The first edition broke the disciplinary confines in which security was often analysed before and after the events of 11 September 2001. The second edition continues in this tradition, presenting a collection of essays from leading academics and practitioners in the fields of criminal justice, public law, privacy law, international law, national security law, critical social theory, political theory and human rights law. The collection offers genuinely multidisciplinary perspectives on the relationship between security and human rights. In addition to exploring how the demands of security might be reconciled with the protection of established rights, *Security and Human Rights* provides fresh insight into the broader legal and political challenges that lie ahead as states attempt to control crime, prevent terrorism, and protect their citizens. The volume features a set of new essays that engage with the most pressing questions facing security and human rights in the twenty-first century and is essential reading for all those working in the area.

Volume 6 in Hart Studies in Security and Justice

Hart Studies in Security and Justice
Series editors: Liora Lazarus and Ben Saul

The interplay between security and justice has always featured prominently in legal scholarship, but it has taken on a particular urgency since the new Millennium. The new scholarly questions that arise are theoretical, doctrinal and empirical, cutting across a range of traditional sub-disciplines within the legal academy. They address some of the most pressing legal issues of our time, such as the legal status of the 'the war on terror', the nature of states of exception, targeted killing, preventive pre-trial detention, mass surveillance and the numerous other threats that security poses to human rights, the rule of law and liberal democracy.

The purpose of this series is to engage with security and justice scholarship broadly conceived, and to promote a sophisticated and complex understanding of the important challenges it faces. The series is inclusive, promoting new and established scholars from a range of disciplines. It covers doctrinal, empirical, historical and theoretical work, as well as studies which focus on domestic, comparative and international dimensions of emerging security and justice fields. The series also strives to promote the most inclusive range of politics and methodologies, scrutinising received wisdom and established paradigmatic approaches, and promoting an intellectual dialogue between its authors and the wider field of law as a whole.

Recent titles in this series:

Surveillance, Privacy and Trans-Atlantic Relations
Edited by David Cole, Federico Fabbrini and Stephen Schulhofer

Parliament's Secret War
Veronika Fikfak and Hayley J Hooper

Permanent States of Emergency and the Rule of Law
Alan Greene

The National Security Constitution
Paul F Scott

The Constitutional Structure of Europe's Area of 'Freedom, Security and Justice' and the Right to Justification
Ester Herlin-Karnell

Security and Human Rights

Second Edition

Edited by
Benjamin J Goold
and
Liora Lazarus

•HART•
OXFORD • LONDON • NEW YORK • NEW DELHI • SYDNEY

HART PUBLISHING

Bloomsbury Publishing Plc

Kemp House, Chawley Park, Cumnor Hill, Oxford, OX2 9PH, UK

HART PUBLISHING, the Hart/Stag logo, BLOOMSBURY and the Diana logo are trademarks of Bloomsbury Publishing Plc

First published in Great Britain 2019

A catalogue record for this book is available from the British Library.

Library of Congress Cataloging-in-Publication data

Names: Goold, B. J. (Benjamin Jervis), 1970- editor. | Lazarus, Liora, editor.

Title: Security and human rights / edited by Benjamin J. Goold and Liora Lazarus.

Description: Second edition. | Oxford ; Chicago, Illinois : Hart, an imprint of Bloomsbury, 2019. | Series: Hart studies in security and justice ; volume 6 | Includes bibliographical references and index.

Identifiers: LCCN 2019021092 (print) | LCCN 2019022295 (ebook) | ISBN 9781849467308 (paperback) | ISBN 9781509917785 (ePDF) | ISBN 9781509917778 (EPub)

Subjects: LCSH: Civil rights. | National security—Law and legislation. | National security—Philosophy. | Terrorism—Prevention—Law and legislation. | BISAC: LAW / Civil Rights. | POLITICAL SCIENCE / Political Freedom & Security / International Security. | POLITICAL SCIENCE / Political Freedom & Security / Human Rights.

Classification: LCC K3240 .S43 2019 (print) | LCC K3240 (ebook) | DDC 342.08/5—dc23

LC record available at https://lccn.loc.gov/2019021092

LC ebook record available at https://lccn.loc.gov/2019022295

ISBN: PB: 978-1-84946-730-8
ePDF: 978-1-50991-778-5
ePub: 978-1-50991-777-8

Typeset by Compuscript Ltd, Shannon
Printed and bound in Great Britain by CPI Group (UK) Ltd, Croydon CR0 4YY

Acknowledgements

THIS BOOK IS a collaborative project, and we would like to express our gratitude to all the authors, particularly for their patience as the book process evolved. The collection is stronger because of Lisa Gourd's outstanding attention to the arguments of each chapter and to the overarching structure of the book itself. We are both extremely grateful for her meticulous approach to every part of the volume. Further thanks must go to Alix de Zitter for his excellent translation work, and we are also indebted to Christopher Boulle for his on-demand translation skills at key moments. As with any long project, we have inevitably relied on the patient support of our partners (Kim Stern and Lisa Gourd) and children (Sophia and Theo Goold), and we are eternally grateful to them. Finally, we would like to thank Bill Asquith (formerly General Editor of Hart/Bloomsbury Publishing) and Richard Hart for encouraging us to embark on a second edition of this collection, and to Rosamund Jubber, Kate Whetter, and Linda Staniford of Hart Publishing for their ongoing support.

Benjamin J Goold and Liora Lazarus
Vancouver and Oxford
March 2019

Contents

Acknowledgements ...... *v*
About the Contributors ...... *ix*

1. *Security and Human Rights: Finding a Language of Resilience and Inclusion* *1*
Liora Lazarus and Benjamin J Goold

PART I
RELIGION, IDENTITY, AND CITIZENSHIP

2. *Torture and Othering* *27*
Natasa Mavronicola

3. *Their Bodies, Ourselves: Muslim Women's Clothing at the Intersection of Rights, Security, and Extremism* *53*
Rumee Ahmed and Ayesha S Chaudhry

4. *The Uses of Religious Identity, Practice, and Dogma in 'Soft' and 'Hard' Counterterrorism* *77*
Aziz Z Huq

5. *Curtailing Citizenship Rights as Counterterrorism* *99*
Lucia Zedner

6. *Trusted Travellers and Trojan Horses: Security, Privacy, and Privilege at the Border* *125*
Benjamin J Goold

PART II
RIGHTS, ACCOUNTABILITY, AND THE STATE

7. *Secrecy as a Meta-paradigmatic Challenge* *147*
Liora Lazarus

8. *Accountability Mechanisms for Transnational Counterterrorism* *179*
Kent Roach

9. *Security and Human Rights after the Nationalist Backlash* *211*
Victor V Ramraj

10. *The Demise of Rights as Trumps* 233
Robert Diab

11. *Violence, Human Rights, and Security* 259
Chetan Bhatt

PART III
PRIVACY, ANONYMITY, AND DISSENT

12. *Privacy versus Security: Regulating Data Collection and Retention in Europe* 275
Arianna Vedaschi

13. *Anonymity for Victims at the Special Tribunal for Lebanon: Security and Human Rights at Work in International Criminal Justice* 297
Juan-Pablo Pérez-León-Acevedo

14. *The Legal Death of Rebellion: Counterterrorism Laws and the Shrinking Legal Freedom of Violent Political Resistance* 323
Ben Saul

15. *Indirectly Inciting Terrorism? Crimes of Expression and the Limits of the Law* 343
Helen Duffy and Kate Pitcher

PART IV
EXCEPTIONALISM, RISK, AND PREVENTION

16. *Oversight of the State of Emergency in France* 389
Marc-Antoine Granger

17. *Bounded Factuality: The Targeted Killing of Salah Shehadeh and the Legal Epistemology of Risk* 421
Shiri Krebs

18. *Countering Terrorism and Violent Extremism: The Security–Prevention Complex* 455
Andreas Armborst

19. *Security and Human Rights in the Context of Forced Migration*........... 473
David Irvine and Travers McLeod

Index 499

About the Contributors

Rumee Ahmed is the Associate Dean in the Faculty of Arts and Associate Professor of Islamic Law at the University of British Columbia. His writing and research span religion, law, theology, philosophy, and hermeneutics, and he is a regular commentator for multiple international policy organisations. He is the author of *Sharia Compliant: A User's Guide to Hacking Islamic Law* (Stanford University Press, 2018) and *Narratives of Islamic Legal Theory* (Oxford University Press, 2012) and is co-editor of the *Oxford Handbook of Islamic Law* (Oxford University Press, 2018) and *The Objectives of Islamic Law* (Lexington Books, 2018).

Andreas Armborst is a criminologist and head of the National Center for Crime Prevention in Germany, a think tank for evidence-based practices in criminal policy and counter-radicalisation. In 2015 he was Marie Curie Postdoctoral Fellow at the University of Leeds School of Law. His doctorate research at the Max-Planck-Institute for Foreign and International Criminal Law examined the ideological origins of religiously inspired violence, and he has been involved in projects on fear of crime, punitive attitudes, urban security, and international security.

Chetan Bhatt is a Professor of Sociology at the London School of Economics and Political Science. He is a member of LSE Human Rights and works and teaches on several human rights areas, including political violence, the international far-right, the religious right, and areas related to women's and minority rights. He is involved in several research and academic projects, including caste-based discrimination and violence in India, the regulation of Palestinian everyday life, and religious right violence against writers and activists in Bangladesh.

Ayesha S Chaudhry is the Canada Research Chair in Religion, Law, and Social Justice and an Associate Professor of Islamic Studies and Gender Studies at the University of British Columbia, where she has served on the Board of Governors. In 2018, she was named a Pierre Elliott Trudeau Fellow and a Member of the College of the Royal Society of Canada. She was a 2016–17 Wall Scholar at the Peter Wall Institute for Advanced Study at UBC, and she was the 2015–16 Rita E Hauser Fellow at the Radcliffe Institute for Advanced Study at Harvard University. She is the author of *Domestic Violence and the Islamic Tradition: Ethics, Law, and the Muslim Discourse on Gender* (Oxford University Press, 2014).

Robert Diab is an Associate Professor in the Faculty of Law at Thompson Rivers University and the author *The Harbinger Theory: How the Post-9/11 Emergency Became Permanent and the Case for the Reform* (Oxford University Press, 2015) and *Guantanamo North: Terrorism and the Administration of Justice in Canada* (Fernwood, 2008). His recent publications focus on national security, police powers, and issues involving technology and rights.

Helen Duffy is Gieskes Professor of International Humanitarian Law and Human Rights at Leiden University. Her areas of research include human rights litigation, the interplay of human rights and humanitarian law, and issues related to counterterrorism, human rights, and the rule of law.

Benjamin J Goold is a professor at the Peter A Allard School of Law, University of British Columbia. He was formerly a Fellow of Somerville College and Lecturer in Law at the University of Oxford. His major research interests include privacy rights, the use of surveillance technologies by the police and intelligence communities, and human rights at the border. He has served as Specialist Legal Advisor to the House of Lords Constitution Committee and as a member of the British Columbia Information and Privacy Commissioner's External Advisory Board. He is the author of *CCTV and Policing: Public Area Surveillance and Police Practices in Britain* (Oxford University Press, 2004) and co-editor (with Liora Lazarus) of *Security and Human Rights* (Hart Publishing, 2007).

Marc-Antoine Granger is a lecturer in public law at the University of Bourgogne Franche-Comté. He has also taught at Panthéon-Sorbonne University (Paris 1), University of Pau, and University of Versailles; and has worked in the legal department of the *Conseil constitutionnel*. His research focuses on the public law of security and the police. He is a member of the *Association française de droit de la sécurité et de la défense*, part of the editorial team for internal security law at Dalloz, and author of *Constitution et sécurité intérieure: Essai de modélisation juridique* (winner of the 2011 *Conseil constitutionnel* Thesis Prize).

Aziz Huq is the Frank and Bernice J Greenberg Professor of Law at the University of Chicago. His scholarship focuses on how the design of constitutions influences individual rights and liberties. He has published in leading US law reviews and peer-reviewed journals in the areas of empirical legal studies, criminology, and social psychology. His book *How to Save a Constitutional Democracy* (with Tom Ginsburg) was published by the University of Chicago Press in October 2018.

David Irvine is Chair of the Australian Foreign Investment Review Board and an Adjunct Professor at Charles Sturt University. He served as Australian High Commissioner to Papua New Guinea (1996–99) and as Australian Ambassador to the People's Republic of China, Mongolia, and the Democratic People's Republic of Korea (concurrently, 2000–03). He has published two books on

Indonesia and is a Fellow of the Australian Institute of International Affairs and a member of the Advisory Council of the National Archives of Australia. He was appointed an Officer of the Order of Australia (AO) in 2005 for service to the country in the promotion of Australia's international relations.

Shiri Krebs is a Senior Lecturer and Director of Higher Degrees by Research at Deakin Law School. Her research focuses on legal fact-finding at the intersection of law, politics, and social psychology. She has also served as legal advisor on international law to the Chief Justice of the Israeli Supreme Court. She has been recognised by the American Society of International Law New Voices in International Law (2016) and been the recipient of the Franklin International Law Award (2015), the Goldsmith Award in Dispute Resolution (2012), the Block Civil Liberties Award (2011), and the Hebrew University Dean's Junior Faculty Award (2007).

Liora Lazarus is an Associate Professor in Law, a Fellow of St Anne's College, and Head of Research at the Bonavero Institute of Human Rights at the University of Oxford. In 2012–13, she held a British Academy Mid-career Fellowship. Liora balances her academic research on human rights and security with public interest work, cofounding Oxford Pro Bono Publico and producing reports for the UK Ministry of Justice, UK Stern Review on Rape Complaints, UK Parliamentary Modern Slavery Bill Committee, the Basque Working Group on Treatment of Political Detainees, and the European Union Parliament. She is the author of *Contrasting Prisoners' Rights* (Oxford University Press, 2004) and co-editor (with Christopher McCrudden and Nigel Bowles) of *Reasoning Rights* (Hart Publishing, 2014).

Natasa Mavronicola is a Senior Lecturer in Law at the University of Birmingham Law School. Her research and teaching focus on human rights, public law, and legal theory, particularly the interplay between counterterrorism and human rights. She currently serves as Special Advisor to the United Nations Special Rapporteur on Torture. She has conducted research for the Council of Europe and the Irish legislature and has published in numerous journals, including the *Human Rights Law Review* and *Modern Law Review*.

Travers McLeod is chief executive of the Centre for Policy Development (CPD), an Australian think tank, and founder of the second-track Asia Dialogue on Forced Migration. He is a board member of the Victorian Foundation for Survivors of Torture and an Honorary Fellow at both the School of Social and Political Sciences at the University of Melbourne and the Faculty of Law at the University of Western Australia. He was previously a policy adviser for the Oxford Martin School at the University of Oxford, where he remains an Associate. He studied at Oxford University as a Rhodes Scholar and is author of *Rule of Law in War: International Law and United States Counterinsurgency in Iraq and Afghanistan* (Oxford University Press, 2015).

Juan-Pablo Pérez-León-Acevedo is a Postdoctoral Research Fellow at PluriCourts, Faculty of Law, University of Oslo, where he also lectures on international criminal law, international human rights law, and international humanitarian law. He has held positions at the University of Oxford, Max Planck Institute for Foreign and International Criminal Law, University of Luxemburg, Åbo Akademi (Finland), and the University of Pretoria. He has also served at the International Criminal Court, the International Criminal Tribunal for the former Yugoslavia, the UN Office of Legal Affairs, and the Peruvian Ministry for Foreign Affairs.

Kate Pitcher has a Masters of Advanced Studies in Public International Law *cum laude* from Leiden University, where her thesis focused on United Nations Security Council Resolution 2178 (2014) and foreign fighters under international law. She is coauthor (with Christophe Paulussen) of 'Prosecuting (Potential) Foreign Fighters: Legislative and Practical Challenges', a research paper for the International Centre for Counter-Terrorism (2018); and coauthor of contributions to the 2015 and 2016 *Yearbook of International Humanitarian Law*. She has previously worked at the TMC Asser Institute and the International Criminal Court and as an editorial assistant for the *Yearbook of International Humanitarian Law* and the *Leiden Journal of International Law*.

Victor V Ramraj a Professor in the Faculty of Law and Chair in Asia-Pacific Legal Relations at the University of Victoria in British Columbia, Canada. Since 2017, he has served as the Director of the of the Centre for Asia-Pacific Initiatives. He has also worked at the National University of Singapore and was twice seconded to the Centre for Transnational Legal Studies in London. His recent research interests and publications focus on comparative constitutional and administrative law, transnational regulation, and the regulatory challenges arising from the state–company relationship. He has edited and co-edited several volumes, including *Emergency Powers in Asia* (Cambridge University Press, 2010).

Kent Roach is a Professor of Law at the University of Toronto, where he holds the Prichard Wilson Chair in Law and Public Policy. He is the author of fourteen books, including *The 9/11 Effect* (Cambridge University Press, 2011) and *Comparative Counter-Terrorism* (Cambridge University Press, 2015). He has also worked with several Canadian inquiries on accountability and national security.

Ben Saul is the Challis Chair of International Law at the University of Sydney, the former Chair of Australian Studies at Harvard University, and an Associate Fellow of Chatham House. He has published twenty books, including *Defining Terrorism in International Law* (Oxford University Press, 2006) and (with David Kinley and Jacqueline Mowbray) *Oxford Commentary on the International Covenant on Economic, Social and Cultural Rights* (Oxford University Press, 2014), which was awarded a Certificate of Merit by the American Society of International Law. He has been advisor to the United Nations, governments, and NGOs and served on various international and national bodies.

Arianna Vedaschi is Full Professor of Comparative Public Law at Bocconi University, Milan. She is the author of *Istituzioni europee e tecnica legislativa* (Giuffré, 2001) and *À la guerre comme à la guerre? La disciplina della guerra nel diritto costituzionale comparato* (Giappichelli, 2007). She is co-editor (with David Cole and Federico Fabbrini) of *Secrecy, National Security and the Vindication of Constitutional Law* (Elgar Publishing, 2013). In addition to articles and chapters on counterterrorism law, national security, and human rights, she has published most recently on mass surveillance and passenger name record (PNR) data. She is the Coordinator of the International Academy for Constitutional Law Research Group on Constitutional Responses to Terrorism and is a member of the Europol Platform for Experts.

Lucia Zedner is a Senior Research Fellow at All Souls College, Professor of Criminal Justice in the Faculty of Law, and a member of the Centre for Criminology at the University of Oxford. She is also a Conjoint Professor in the Faculty of Law, University of New South Wales, a Fellow of the British Academy, and an Overseas Fellow of the Australian Academy of Law. Her recent books include *Prevention and the Limits of the Criminal Law* (Oxford University Press, 2013), co-edited with Andrew Ashworth and Patrick Tomlin; *Preventive Justice* (Oxford University Press, 2014), with Andrew Ashworth; and *Changing Contours of Criminal Justice* (Oxford University Press, 2016), co-edited with Mary Bosworth and Carolyn Hoyle.

1

Security and Human Rights: Finding a Language of Resilience and Inclusion

LIORA LAZARUS AND BENJAMIN J GOOLD

SECURITY AND HUMAN *Rights* was first published in 2007, six years after the events of 9/11. We argued then that liberal democracies, if they were to withstand growing calls for exceptionalism, needed to find a way to reconcile the demands of security with a respect for fundamental human rights. With the benefit of hindsight, and having witnessed the steady rise of populism over the last ten years, this call now appears both prophetic and increasingly urgent. Today there is little doubt that populism constitutes a central challenge to liberal democratic norms, preying as it does on existential fear while promoting nationalist paranoia and stoking racial and religious division.[1] In this 'politics of fear', the threat of insecurity has been hyper-inflated and exploited to justify a pernicious authoritarianism.[2] It is against this backdrop that many academics, policy actors, and human rights activists have found themselves vilified as out-of-touch elitists or naïve experts and their calls for a thoughtful balance between security and rights dismissed as mere 'virtue-signalling' rhetoric.

The threat of this security populism is now so profound that core values of human rights, constitutionalism, and tolerance are under acute pressure in democracies throughout the world. At the time of writing, the signs of this pressure are all around us. The withdrawal of the United States from the

[1] D Runciman, *How Democracy Ends* (London, Profile Books, 2018); Y Mounk, *The People vs Democracy: Why Our Freedom is in Danger and How to Save it* (Cambridge, MA, Harvard University Press, 2018); WA Galston, *Anti-Pluralism: The Populist Threat to Liberal Democracy* (New Haven, Yale University Press, 2018); T Snyder, *The Road to Unfreedom: Russia, Europe, America* (London, Bodley Head, 2018); S Levitsky and D Ziblatt, *How Democracies Die: What History Reveals about Our Future* (London, Penguin Random House, 2018).

[2] K Roth, 'Twin Threats: How the Politics of Fear and the Crushing of Civil Society Imperil Global Rights' in Human Rights Watch (ed), *Human Rights Watch World Report 2016*, available at https://www.hrw.org/world-report/2016 (accessed 15 March 2019).

UN Human Rights Council, the support of the US Supreme Court for President Donald Trump's travel ban, the separation of children from their parents at the US border, the purging of the Polish Constitutional Court, the undermining of the rule of law and academic freedom in Hungary, Russia's constitutional amendment undermining the status of decisions from the European Court of Human Rights (ECtHR), the consolidation of emergency power in Turkey, the continuing rejection by the Right in the United Kingdom of the legitimacy of the European human rights regime, and the increasing political strength globally of anti-immigrant and racist right-wing populism are only a few examples of this dramatic and disturbing trend. Almost every day we hear news of another executive action aimed at rolling back the human rights advances of the last half century. As David Rieff has argued, 'the global balance of power has tilted away from governments committed to human rights norms and toward those indifferent or actively hostile to them.'[3]

There is no denying, however, that the erosion of fundamental rights and the consolidation of executive power in pursuit of security took (and takes) place under the watch of self-identified 'liberal' leaders. While the state of emergency in France was initiated in 2015 after attacks in Paris, it continued for six months after Emmanuel Macron came to power in 2017, and the issues of emergency powers and lethal force have recently arisen again in response to the *gilets jaunes* protests.[4] Austria, France, Belgium, and Denmark have all banned religious dress covering the face,[5] while the US targeted killing programme expanded significantly during the presidency of Barack Obama. The contradictions within 'liberalism', whether expressed through the pursuit of security at the expense of rights or as a blunt ideological commitment to secularism, have served only to exacerbate a pre-existing scepticism towards the liberal project in countries across Europe and in the United States. These contradictions are nothing new: the counternarratives of slavery and colonialism have long been sublimated alongside celebrations of so-called liberal values.[6] Defending

[3] D Rieff, 'The End of Human Rights? Learning from the Failure of the Responsibility to Protect and the International Criminal Court', *Foreign Policy* (9 April 2018), https://foreignpolicy.com/2018/04/09/the-end-of-human-rights-genocide-united-nations-r2p-terrorism/. For discussion of the effects of populism on liberal constitutional norms and democratic institutions, see a recent special double issue of the *German Law Journal* (2019) 20(2&3); and T Ginsburg and AZ Huq, *How to Save a Constitutional Democracy* (Chicago, University of Chicago Press, 2019).

[4] G Koenig, 'Emmanuel Macron is on a Slippery Slope towards "Democratic Despotism"', *Financial Times* (10 March 2019). See also News Wires, 'UN Calls for Probe into "Excessive" Force by French Police at Yellow Vests Protests', *France 24* (6 March 2019), https://www.france24.com/en/20190306-un-france-investigate-excessive-force-yellow-vests. Regarding Europe more broadly, see Amnesty International, 'Dangerously Disproportionate: The Ever-Expanding National Security State in Europe', EUR 01/5342/2017 (17 January 2017).

[5] See the further discussion below, as well as the chapter in this volume by Rumee Ahmed and Ayesha S Chaudhry.

[6] The whitewashing of European colonialism is the subject of the European Parliament Resolution of 26 March 2019 on fundamental rights of people of African descent in Europe (2018/2899 RSP). See also R Drayton, *Whose Constitution? Law, Justice and History in the Caribbean*, 6th Distinguished Jurist Lecture (Port of Spain, Judicial Education Institute of Trinidad and Tobago, 2016); C Elkins, *Imperial Reckoning: The Untold Story of Britain's Gulag in Kenya* (New York, Henry Holt, 2005).

liberalism in the face of both its historical legacy and its more recent failure to balance security with rights, remains a fundamental challenge for human rights advocates.

In times of such pressure, there is a strong temptation to jettison human rights, or even constitutionalism, as a failed paradigm,[7] on the grounds that it is little more than a liberal façade or a thin veil of legality behind which the dirty work of security is carried out.[8] As in the months immediately following 9/11, there are increasing signs that human rights proponents are experiencing profound self-doubt.[9] During such moments, however, it is imperative for those engaged in the promotion and protection of human rights to return to fundamental values. While critical evaluation is essential and is certainly present in this volume, it is also important to remind ourselves of what human rights stand for, as well as the achievements of human rights and the constitutional paradigm.

While many states continue to undermine human rights norms, their efforts have thankfully been met with stubborn resistance, sometimes resulting in successful appeals to justice. Recently, the UK Parliamentary Intelligence and Security Committee published a report damning British intelligence agencies and the Foreign Secretary for their involvement in the torture and kidnap of terrorist suspects after 9/11.[10] This report is the most recent of a series of inquiries across jurisdictions and institutions[11] and key judicial decisions[12] relating to the use of CIA-led torture and kidnapping as part of extraordinary

[7] PJ Deneen, *Why Liberalism Failed* (New Haven, Yale University Press, 2018). By 'constitutionalism' we mean a belief in constitutional government, or government limited by laws. See W Waluchow, 'Constitutionalism' in EN Zalta et al (eds), *Stanford Encyclopedia of Philosophy* (Stanford, Stanford Center for the Study of Language and Information, 2017), https://plato.stanford.edu/entries/constitutionalism/.

[8] M Neocleous, 'Security, Liberty and the Myth of Balance: Towards a Critique of Security Politics' (2007) 6 *Contemporary Political Theory* 131–49.

[9] Rieff (above n 3); and K Roth, 'The Dangerous Rise of Populism: Global Attacks on Human Rights Values' in Human Rights Watch (ed), *Human Rights Watch World Report 2017*, available at https://www.hrw.org/world-report/2017 (accessed 15 March 2019).

[10] Intelligence and Security Committee of Parliament (UK), 'Detainee Mistreatment and Rendition: Current Issues' (2018, HC 1113), https://fas.org/irp/world/uk/isc-detainee2.pdf.

[11] D Marty (Special Rapporteur), 'Secret Detentions and Illegal Transfers of Detainees Involving Council of Europe Member States: Second Report', Council of Europe Parliamentary Assembly report (7 June 2007), http://assembly.coe.int/CommitteeDocs/2007/EMarty_20070608_NoEmbargo.pdf; Senate Select Committee on Intelligence (USA), 'Committee Study of the Central Intelligence Agency's Detention and Interrogation Program', Senate Report 113–288 (9 December 2014), https://www.intelligence.senate.gov/sites/default/files/documents/CRPT-113srpt288.pdf; Commission of Inquiry into the Actions of Canadian Officials in Relation to Maher Arar ('Arar Commission'), 'Report of the Events Relating to Maher Arar' (2006), available at http://publications.gc.ca/site/eng/9.688875/publication.html. See also the chapter in this volume by Kent Roach.

[12] *El-Masri v Former Yugoslav Republic of Macedonia* (2013) 57 EHRR 25; *Al Nashiri and Husayn v Poland* (2015) 60 EHRR 16; *Nasr and Ghali v Italy* (2016) ECHR 2010; *Al Nashiri v Romania* (2018) App No 33234/12); *Belhaj and Rahmatullah v Straw and Ministry of Defence* [2017] UKSC 3; *Khaled El-Masri v United States*, Inter-Am CHR Case 419.08, Report No 21/16 (15 April 2016). But see *El-Masri v Tenet*, 437 F Supp 2d 530, 539; and *El-Masri v United States*, 479 F3d 296, 300 (4th Cir 2007), cert denied, 552 US 947 (2007).

rendition processes post-9/11. While exposure of these practices came far too slowly for rendition victims, and impunity in respect of those actors who committed torture remains a serious concern,[13] there is little doubt that the absolute prohibition on torture under international and domestic human rights law played a part in this process and will continue to have ramifications for those involved in the years to come.[14] Similarly, protections against arbitrary detention have enabled courts to gradually overturn laws that sought to allow for indefinite detention without trial in the United States and Britain in the wake of 9/11. In many ways, the right to *habeas corpus* has grown in stature thanks to its role in the dismantling of the early regimes at Guantanamo Bay and Belmarsh.[15] Talk of a *jus cogens* status for the right against arbitrary detention is now even being acknowledged in UK courts.[16]

On the other hand, some human rights protections have shown a disturbing elasticity when confronted with novel security measures. Just as the right to a fair trial has 'adapted' to allow for the admission of certain forms of secret evidence,[17] privacy jurisprudence has shown considerable flexibility in the face of steady expansions in state surveillance.[18] Similarly, there has been a notable rise in the use of immigration law as a weapon of counterterrorism, with citizenship deprivation at the most extreme end of these policies.[19] Set outside the procedural safeguards of the criminal law and the full jurisdictional protections of human and constitutional rights, immigration law is a fertile ground for human rights

[13] See Joint Committee on Human Rights (UK), 'Closing the Impunity Gap: UK Law on Genocide (and Related Crimes) and Redress for Torture Victims' (2008–09, HL 153 HC 553); and L Lazarus and J Blackbourn, 'Intelligence and the Criminal Law in England and Wales' in M Dyson and B Vogel (eds), *The Limits of Criminal Law* (Cambridge, Intersentia, 2018). But see recent movements toward greater accountability: O Bowcott, 'Police Investigating Role of UK Officers in Torture of al-Qaida Suspect', *Guardian* (31 March 2019).

[14] See the chapter in this volume by Natasa Mavronicola.

[15] *Rasul v Bush* 542 US 466 (2004); *Hamdi v Rumsfeld* 542 US 507 (2004); *Hamdan v Rumsfeld* 548 US 557 (2006); *Boumediene v Bush* 553 US 723 (2008); and *A v Secretary of State for the Home Department* [2004] UKHL 56.

[16] *Belhaj v Straw* and *Rahmatullah v Ministry of Defence* [2017] UKSC 3, paras 270–71.

[17] The accommodation process has been at its most evident within ECHR jurisprudence. See E Nanopoulos, 'European Human Rights and the Normalisation of the "Closed Material Procedure": Limit or Source?' (2015) 78(6) *Modern Law Review* 913–44; *A v United Kingdom* (2009) 49 EHRR 29; *Sher v United Kingdom* (2016) 63 EHRR 24; *Al Dulimi v Switzerland* (2016) 42 BHRC 163; and *Home Secretary v AF* [2009] UKHL 28. UK common law has shown itself to be more resistant: *Al Rawi v The Security Service* [2011] UKSC 34; and *Bank Mellat v HM Treasury (No 1)* [2013] UKSC 38. For fair trial rights in the context of the Special Tribunal for Lebanon, see the chapter in this volume by Juan Pablo Pérez-León-Acevedo.

[18] See S Chesterman, 'Terrorism, Surveillance, and Privacy' in B Saul (ed), *Research Handbook on International Law and Terrorism* (Cheltenham, Edward Elgar, 2014). For a recent account of the steady expansion in state surveillance, see D Lyon, *The Culture of Surveillance* (Cambridge, Polity Press, 2018). See also the chapter in this volume by Arianna Vedaschi.

[19] The recent deprivation of Shamima Begum's citizenship and the death of her newborn baby in a refugee camp shortly after this decision was made have raised widespread public criticism; the decision is also the subject of a pending challenge. See V Dodd, 'Shamima Begum Family Challenge Javid's Citizenship Decision', *Guardian* (20 March 2019). See also the chapter in this volume by Lucia Zedner.

limitations, and courts have been alarmingly slow to intervene when individuals have been left without the 'protections of nationality'.[20] Indeed, the tendency of supposed liberal democracies to 'export' the dirty work of counterterrorism is a major concern.[21]

Similarly concerning is the erosion of the right to life through the continued use of targeted killing programmes. Here the reach for legal justification by democratic states, most notably Israel and the United States, has stretched international law paradigms relating to armed conflict and the proportionality of lethal force.[22] In this pursuit, President Obama did little to constrain the executive power awarded to the Presidency by his hawkish predecessors. Targeted killing, as with extraordinary rendition and indefinite detention, radically undermines any claim to the moral high ground by the United States and its allies purporting to uphold 'Western' democratic values.[23] The stain of this programme remains indelible, especially as the victims' families have had almost no human rights recourse or vindication. Notwithstanding vocal condemnation by human rights institutions such as the Special Rapporteurs and NGOs[24] and the recent condemnation of the North Rhine Westphalia Higher Administrative

[20] L Zedner, 'Citizenship Deprivation, Security and Human Rights' (2016) 18(2) *European Journal of Migration and Law* 222–42, 230.

[21] The recent decision of the UK High Court in *El Gizouli v Secretary of State for the Home Department* [2019] EWC 60 (Admin) is a particularly egregious example of judicial deference in this respect. The Court held that the Secretary of State was entitled to authorise mutual legal assistance to the United States to assist in a criminal investigation that was likely to lead to the death penalty upon conviction, without seeking any diplomatic assurances to the contrary.

[22] See C Heyns, D Akande, L Hill-Cawthorne, and T Chengeta, 'The International Law Framework Regulating the Use of Armed Drones' (2016) 65(4) *International and Comparative Law Quarterly* 791–827; R Goodman, 'Why the Laws of War Apply to Drone Strikes Outside "Areas of Active Hostilities": A Memo to the Human Rights Community', *Just Security* (4 October 2017), https://www.justsecurity.org/45613/laws-war-apply-drone-strikes-areas-active-hostilities-a-memo-human-rights-community; M Milanovic, 'On Whether IHL Applies to Drone Strikes Outside "Areas of Active Hostilities": A Response to Ryan Goodman', *EJIL: Talk!* (5 October 2017), https://www.ejiltalk.org/on-whether-ihl-applies-to-drone-strikes-outside-areas-of-active-hostilities-a-response-to-ryan-goodman; N Modirzadeh, 'Reframing the Debate: A Response to Ryan Goodman's Memo to the Human Rights Community', *Lawfare* (9 October 2017), https://www.lawfareblog.com/reframing-debate-response-ryan-goodmans-memo-human-rights-community; and S Bachmann, 'Targetted Killings: Contemporary Challenges, Risks and Opportunities' (2013) 18(2) *Journal of Conflict and Security Law* 259–88. See also the chapter in this volume by Shiri Krebs.

[23] L Lazarus, B Goold, and C Goss, 'Control without Punishment: Understanding Coercion' in J Simon and R Sparks (eds), SAGE *Handbook of Punishment and Society* (London, Sage, 2013).

[24] P Alston, 'Report of the Special Rapporteur on Extrajudicial, Summary or Arbitrary Executions: Addendum', Human Rights Council, UN Doc A/HRC/14/24/Add.6 (28 May 2010); B Emmerson, 'Report of the Special Rapporteur on the Promotion and Protection of Human Rights and Fundamental Freedoms while Countering Terrorism', UN General Assembly, UN Doc A/68/389 (18 September 2013); B Emmerson, 'Report of the Special Rapporteur on the Promotion and Protection of Human Rights and Fundamental Freedoms while Countering Terrorism', Human Rights Council, A/HRC/25/59 (11 March 2014); and C Heyns, 'Report of the Special Rapporteur on Extrajudicial, Summary or Arbitrary Executions', UN General Assembly, UN doc A/68/382 (13 September 2013).

Court on the legality of drone operations conducted in Germany,[25] no effective remedy is available to those communities that have lost innocent lives.[26]

Along with the erosion of fundamental rights across the globe, there has been a corresponding movement to make security the object of human rights protections. National security concerns, once seen in tension with fundamental rights, have come to be embodied within new 'coercive human rights', which centre on the protective obligations of states in relation to victims or potential victims of private violence – rather than being understood as a limitation on state action.[27] The turn to security from within human rights discourse is indicative of a broader shift towards securitisation, whereby even the concept of the rule of law and the ambition of economic development are seen as mere preconditions to the security of individuals rather than as substantive goods in themselves.[28] While two decades ago we might have referred to a 'right to food' we now speak of 'food security'; while the 'rule of law' used to refer to the absence of arbitrary state power, it is now gradually being replaced by 'security, law, and order' rhetoric.[29]

This shift towards protection or coercion can be viewed in a variety of ways. On the one hand, it can be argued that this move runs counter to the ever-growing perception or caricature that human rights and the rule of law limit the pursuit of order and security; and the elision of human rights with security is an appropriate response to the increasing threat of private violence. On the other hand, it also signals the corrosive influence of security politics within international political discourse. Ultimately, what these trends signal is the capacity of human

[25] The Court concluded that 'the German Federal Government's present assumption that there are no indications of violations of German or international law by the USA through the USA's activities in Germany is based on an insufficient investigation of the facts and is ultimately not legally sustainable.' *Faisal bin Ali Jaber and Others v the Federal Republic of Germany*, North Rhine-Westphalia Higher Administrative Court, 4 A 1361/15 (19 March 2019), https://www.ecchr.eu/fileadmin/Juristische_Dokumente/OVG_Muenster_oral_declaration_of_judgment_19_March_2019_EN.pdf (translation).

[26] American Civil Liberties Union (ACLU) and Amnesty International et al, 'Joint Letter to President Obama on US Drone Strikes and Targeted Killings' (11 April 2013), available at https://www.hrw.org/news/2013/04/11/joint-letter-president-obama-us-drone-strikes-and-targeted-killings (accessed 20 March 2019). See also the Human Rights Watch webpage on 'Targeted Killings and Drones', https://www.hrw.org/topic/terrorism-counterterrorism/targeted-killings-and-drones (accessed 20 March 2019).

[27] L Lazarus, 'Positive Obligations and Criminal Justice: Duties to Protect or Coerce?' in J Roberts and L Zedner (eds), *Principled Approaches to Criminal Law and Criminal Justice: Essays in Honour of Professor Andrew Ashworth* (Oxford, Oxford University Press, 2012); L Lavrysen, 'Human Rights in a Positive State: Rethinking the Relationship between Positive and Negative Obligations under the European Convention on Human Rights' (Cambridge, Intersentia, 2016); and N Mavronicola, 'Taking Life and Liberty Seriously: Reconsidering Criminal Liability under Article 2 of the ECHR' (2017) 80(6) *Modern Law Review* 1026–51.

[28] L Lazarus, 'The Right to Security: Securing Rights or Securitising Rights?' in R Dickinson, E Katselli, C Murray, and OW Pedersen (eds), *Examining Critical Perspectives on Human Rights* (Cambridge, Cambridge University Press, 2012); and L Lazarus, 'Doing Violence to the Rule of Law' (April 2018), available at https://ssrn.com/abstract=3170649 (accessed 20 March 2019).

[29] Lazarus, 'Doing Violence to the Rule of Law' (ibid).

rights to be co-opted and transformed by national and international narratives about security. The adaptability of rights discourse may be both its most significant protection and its most dangerous threat.

While human rights have shown themselves both adaptable and vulnerable to the pressures associated with the pursuit of security, the landscape of security has also evolved significantly since the first edition of this book, with many of the 'threats' targeted by hawkish states showing signs of persistence and intractability. There is little doubt that security interventions and rights violations have themselves helped to entrench the very threats to security that states have sought to counter: one need only look at the rise of ISIS after the illegal invasion of Iraq to find a clear example of how security overreach can undermine its stated objective. The cycle of terrorism has thus continued, with fatalities rising globally.[30]

In the Global North, the response to recent terrorist attacks has been complex. Despite encouraging signs that the centrist public is growing tired of securitised rhetoric and instead turning to discourses of resilience,[31] terrorism in some metropolitan cities in Europe has resulted in the application of emergency conditions[32] and led to a surge in Islamophobic rhetoric and violence.[33] The uneven nature of political reactions and media treatment of different types of violence and aggression has itself become a point of contention.[34] Certainly, the immediate and unequivocal labelling of the Christchurch mosque massacres as 'terrorism' by New Zealand Prime Minister Jacinda Adern stood in sharp contrast to the denialism of President Donald Trump when he has been queried about the actions of white supremacists and other right-wing extremists. In many ways, the manner in which security threats are named and explained has now become a conscious political marker in an increasingly polarised environment.

One clear point we can draw from the last decade is that governments that suggest they can 'end' insecurity, 'terminate' threats, or 'bring this carnage to an end today' are unlikely ever to deliver on their promises.[35] Far more likely is

[30] Data shows that after 2007, fatalities from terrorist attacks globally were in decline, but this trend was sharply reversed in 2010, after which fatalities rose from 7727 to 43,566. By far the greatest number of terrorism-related fatalities have occurred in Iraq (13,000 in 2014 and 12,187 in 2016) and Afghanistan (6,119 in 2016). M Roser, M Nagdy, and H Ritchie, 'Terrorism', OurWorldInData website (January 2018), https://ourworldindata.org/terrorism.

[31] S Jenkins, 'Media Hype about the Westminster Attacks Will Only Encourage Others', *Guardian* (24 March 2017); and S Jenkins, 'How Our Politicians and Media Are Helping Terrorists Win', *Spectator* (9 April 2016).

[32] See the chapter in this volume by Marc-Antoine Granger.

[33] S Marsh, 'Record Number of Anti-Muslim Attacks Reported in UK Last Year', *Guardian* (20 July 2018). See also chapters in this volume by Aziz Z Huq; and Rumee Ahmed and Ayesha S Chaudhry.

[34] A Serwer, 'The Terrorism that Doesn't Spark a Panic', *Atlantic* (28 January 2019); A Batrawy, 'Is it Terrorism? Post-NZ Attack, Muslims See Double Standard', *Washington Post* (24 March 2019). See also interview with Ayesha Chaudhry, *CTV News* (15 March 2019), available at https://www.ctvnews.ca/video?clipId=1637407 (accessed 27 March 2019).

[35] D Trump, 'Inaugural Address', White House (20 January 2017), https://www.whitehouse.gov/briefings-statements/the-inaugural-address.

that such governments will play the politics of security, just as they have always done, to shore up their own political power. This security populism, which is premised on the vilification of outsider groups and has increasingly relied on systemic Islamophobia, is now showing its real face. Instead of more security, right-wing terrorism has risen, with devastating effects.[36] While the shock of the recent attacks in Christchurch is still reverberating around the globe, right-wing terrorist violence has also occurred over the last three years in Quebec, Ajaccio, Munich, Dresden, Duma, Zurich, London, Portland, Jefferstown, and Pittsburgh. These are only a few examples of a clear trend that also encompasses increasingly open expressions of anti-semitism. As the Anti-Defamation League has reported in the context of the United States, 'extremist-related murders in 2018 were overwhelmingly linked to right-wing extremists'.[37] As a consequence, there have been signs that such threats are now on the radar of counterterrorism efforts in the United States and elsewhere.[38]

As the years since 9/11 have repeatedly shown, the claim that greater security can be achieved if we are willing to accept an erosion of rights is clearly false. Yet human rights and security continue to be placed in opposition to one another, as proponents of both rights and security are repeatedly drawn into the interstices of an intractable campaign against a permanent threat. In this complex and interrelated world, human rights are increasingly tested by populists who both grossly underplay the gains to be made by safeguarding human rights and seriously underestimate the harms to security that result from their breach. Similarly, the inevitably of risk in a free and globalised society has been downplayed in favour of unrealistic claims about achieving security in order to justify nationalism and autarchism, which in turn are inherently connected to the vilification of others.

Balancing security and human rights will thus require a compelling counternarrative that appeals to the values of inclusion, resilience, and realism, and recognises that risk is the unavoidable concomitant of freedom. The case must be made, clearly and widely, that human rights are capable of accommodating security pursuits while simultaneously requiring security pursuits to be necessary, realistic, grounded in the particularities of the local contexts in which they are placed, and sensitive to the lived realities of those whose rights are engaged. In this way, human rights can constitute a moderating framework in which resilient and tolerant societies can survive and thrive.

[36] J Cassidy, 'It's Time to Confront the Threat of Right-Wing Terrorism', *New Yorker* (16 March 2019); and J Freedland and M Hasan, 'Muslims and Jews Face a Common Threat from White Supremacists. We Must Fight It Together', *Guardian* (3 April 2019).

[37] Anti-Defamation League (ADL), 'Murder and Extremism in the United States in 2018' (January 2019), https://www.adl.org/murder-and-extremism-2018.

[38] C Hawkins, 'Counter-Terrorism Operations against Right-Wing Extremism in Western Europe Increase 191% in 24 Months', *IHS Markit* (7 December 2018), https://ihsmarkit.com/research-analysis/counterterrorism-operations-against-right-wing-extremism.html; D Sandford, 'Far-Right Terror Threat "Growing" in UK as Four Plots Foiled', *BBC* (26 February 2018); BBC, 'Far-Right Groups Could Exploit Brexit Tensions – Police', *BBC News* (23 January 2019); and W Cai and S Landon, 'Attacks by White Extremists are Growing. So Are Their Connections', *New York Times* (3 April 2019).

I. IDENTITY, RELIGION, AND CITIZENSHIP

Shortly after 9/11, Jeremy Waldron warned that the common image of balancing rights and security sublimates a pernicious distributive bias.[39] His instincts that the rights of marginalised minorities would be traded off in favour of the interests of the homogenous majority have since been vindicated. In many senses, the challenge for human rights defenders today is how best to confront the asymmetrical impact of rights-limiting 'emergency' measures, as well as the ways in which security populism has associated human rights with the protection of vilified 'outsider' groups.

It is telling that in the years since the first edition of *Security and Human Rights* was published, issues of identity, religion, and citizenship have moved to the forefront of discussions about security and rights, as more and more examples of the trade-off Waldron warned of have become reality. Put simply, matters of identity – be they religious, ethnic, socioeconomic, national, sexual, or gender – have now become inexorably linked with assessments of risk, calls for increasingly intrusive state surveillance, and demands for institutional discrimination and exclusion. Perhaps even more seriously, in the ongoing rhetorical assault on human rights, the linking of identity with security has become an accepted part of mainstream debates about the future of rights, as the scapegoating and othering of key groups, most notably Muslim and migrant communities, have become increasingly normalised.

In Part I of this book, we see an effort to grapple with these issues. While some of the authors question whether individualised and supposedly 'neutral' human rights reasoning is capable of confronting the broader systemic inequalities in the distribution of coercive power, together the chapters make clear that the dialectic between security and rights must be expanded to include a recognition of the inextricable links with wider social and personal processes of identity formation and contestation.

In her chapter, Natasa Mavronicola identifies the moral wrong of torture in the radical othering that it entails and compounds, and situates it within the 'othering continuum', which poses an existential threat to human rights more broadly. Building on existing accounts for the absolute prohibition of torture as 'the archetype of the human rights edifice' and as an affront to human dignity, Mavronicola confronts the gap between the absolute prohibition of torture in law and moral theory and its continuing prevalence in practice. Pointing to the othering behaviour that populists such as Trump use to demarcate 'the border of humanity', Mavronicola argues that this practice 'both drives and is central to the act of torture' and in turn 'lies on a continuum with other ways in which the essence of human rights is undermined in the name of security'. Torture, for Mavronicola, is thus an extreme case of the more 'banal' or 'acceptable mechanics

[39] J Waldron, 'Security and Liberty: The Image of Balance' (2003) 11(2) *Journal of Political Philosophy* 191–210.

and expressions of othering that pervade counterterrorism'. This broader othering narrative is 'not only incidental but integral to the "trade-off" underpinning the pursuit of security at the expense of human rights'. For Mavronicola, much of the crisis of faith in human rights that has consequently ensued is thus not a rejection of the merits of human rights themselves but rather a rejection of 'the human rights of others'. She concludes by arguing that rather than a pragmatic move to condone the distinction between 'deserving' and 'underserving' rights-bearers, this threat to human rights can be met only by a profound reaffirmation of human dignity and by respecting a dynamic integrity of law.

This concern with the implications of 'othering' for the protection of minority rights also lies at the heart of the next two chapters. Taking the burkini and efforts to ban it in parts of Austria, France, and Germany as their starting point, Rumee Ahmed and Ayesha S Chaudhry examine the ways in which rights and security narratives have been deployed in relation to Muslim women. Depicted in both religious and secular contexts as 'non-ideal females', Muslim women are frequently portrayed as a threat to the security of 'ideal citizens' – in Western democratic states as well as in religious autocracies like Afghanistan, Iran, and Saudi Arabia. As such, the regulation of their appearance and dress is a focal point not just for religious extremists. As Ahmed and Chaudhry demonstrate, it has also become a flashpoint for likewise extremist secular discourses that 'weaponise' the language of human rights. This unwillingness to see Islam in anything other than reductive terms, coupled with a denial of the fact that Muslim women can maintain multiple identities that cut across religious and secular boundaries, has led to efforts to ban the burkini and thus to criminalise the choices of an already marginalised group. More significantly, Ahmed and Chaudhry argue, rather than being recognised as holders of rights that should protect them, Muslim women are constructed as a threat to other citizens, becoming the object of state policing instead.

Echoing some of the themes explored by Ahmed and Chaudhry, Aziz Huq in his chapter looks at how conceptions of Islam and the Muslim influence the development and application of counterterrorism laws and policies. While Islam and Muslim identity are frequently used as 'criteria of suspicion' in the context of counterterrorism, Huq argues that these concepts are mobilised in variety of other, often less obvious ways. In particular, aspects of Islam and Muslim identity are deliberately singled out in public debates with a view to juxtaposing 'the moral legitimacy of the liberal state with the perceived normative bankruptcy of Islam'. As Huq rightly notes, counterterrorism policies that target Muslims not only have consequences for the promotion and protection of individual rights but also raise questions of distributive justice. Observing that 'the costs of security are borne by Muslims' – not only in the form of stigma and private violence but also in terms of 'economic exclusion' – Huq draws our attention to the ways in which the pursuit of security has exacerbated and entrenched existing forms of anti-Muslim discrimination. Although he notes in his conclusion that Muslim civil society organisations have begun to resist the steady securitisation of Islam, given the law's inability to curb the worst excesses of security, Huq is pessimistic about the future, especially if the political landscapes of Europe and the United States continue to be dominated by right-wing populists.

In the next chapter, Lucia Zedner turns to another aspect of identity that has been transformed in the years since 9/11, namely citizenship. She focuses in particular on the mobility rights that citizenship entails and the ways they have been transformed by terrorism and the pursuit of security. Harking back to her chapter in the first edition of *Security and Human Rights*, which explored how preventive measures implemented in the wake of 9/11 had eroded fundamental rights and due process protections, Zedner argues here that efforts to limit the citizenship rights of individuals held to be 'enemies of the state' represent an even greater challenge to our commitment to fundamental rights. Noting that in some cases these measures have the potential to leave individuals stateless, Zedner contends that 'the rights enjoyed by all citizens are today more precarious and their protection less secure'. In this regard, she echoes the concerns of many of the other contributors to this volume: namely, that the relentless drive towards ever-more restrictive security measures has transformed the way we think about what were once stable ideas of national identity and citizenship, with the result that we now live in a world that in which human rights are increasingly denied to those deemed to be a threat by the state.

Changing conceptions of citizenship, particularly at the border, are also the focus of Benjamin Goold's chapter. Using 'trusted traveller' schemes such as the UK Registered Traveller Service and the US–Canada NEXUS programme as a point of focus, Goold invites us to think about the ways in which we are encouraged by the state to accept and internalise new forms of identity that do not rely merely on the traditional citizen/noncitizen binary. Under the aegis of 'security' but also in exchange for convenience and privilege at the border, many states have induced travellers to hand over large amounts of personal information in order to join the ranks of a new class that is deemed 'safe' or 'trusted'. Drawing on research that sees borders as sites of social sorting, Goold highlights how the proliferation of such programmes enables 'trusted travellers' to maintain a range of existing privileges that centre around race, ethnicity, language, education, and socioeconomic status and mirror those that perpetuate inequalities well beyond the border. The foil of these 'trusted travellers' is simultaneously constructed as groups of 'undesirable' or 'high-risk' travellers, whose plight is more easily dismissed by those who can take advantage of (and pay for) streamlined security and 'fast-track' immigration procedures. As Goold points out, this process of social sorting has been swept up into a wider neoliberal narrative that casts 'trusted travellers' as good consumer-citizens but downplays the lack of status and mobility of others. Goold therefore concludes that the emergence of 'trusted traveller' schemes does not simply pose a danger to individual privacy; such programmes also risk exacerbating existing forms of discrimination and contributing to a fractured politics that sees questions of security and immigration only in terms of 'us' and 'them'.

II. RIGHTS, ACCOUNTABILITY, AND THE STATE

Rights are traditionally understood to be held by individuals to protect them from the overweening power of the state. Yet the covertness surrounding most national security endeavours makes it difficult for courts, lawyers, legal academics, and journalists to access even basic information about the surveillance and counterterrorism activities of governments, and even more difficult to determine whether such activities are being carried out in a manner that is consistent with domestic and international law. Given the scope that modern states have for intruding into the lives of their citizens and the insulation from critical scrutiny that can result from state secrecy doctrines, the question of what it means to hold a state accountable for transgressions inevitably animates many of the chapters in this collection.

In the face of consistent efforts by states to keep their activities secret, Liora Lazarus argues in her chapter for a principle of retrospective accountability. Noting that academics must recognise the critical role they play in holding knowledge accountable, she contends that legal academics in particular have responsibilities to the rule of law that are fundamentally challenged by state secrecy. Drawing on David Pozen's categories of 'shallow' and 'deep' secrets, Lazarus points out the ways that both kinds of secrecy undermine the capacity of legal scholars to evaluate legal proceedings and state activities, thus preventing them from fulfilling one of their core functions as dialogic participants in the creation of law. According to Lazarus, the solution lies in part with a consideration of the temporality of both academic scrutiny and legal accountability. While it may take many years to unravel the secrets surrounding sensitive government activities such as counterterrorism operations, it is essential that academics impose a degree of retrospective accountability. Drawing on the right to truth and the principle of open justice in developing principles of retrospective accountability, Lazarus argues that academics have a role to play in ensuring that governments are subject to scrutiny in the future. By making it clear to state officials and judges that secret decisions can and will be scrutinised later, a system of future scrutiny would thus serve both scholarship and the rule of law.

For Kent Roach, a challenge arises from a lack of agreement about what exactly it means to hold states and governments to account. As Roach notes, if we take a narrow view of the meaning of accountability and confine ourselves to a focus on 'control, sanction, and redress', it is hard not to be disheartened by the failure of courts and legislative bodies to punish state actors for human rights abuses arising from extraordinary rendition, detention and torture at secret prisons, and other transnational counterterrorism measures. If, however, we take a broader view of accountability – one that encompasses the various efforts of the media, civil society, and academics to expose rights violations arising from the pursuit of security – then the picture is less bleak. While Roach acknowledges that much of what we have learned about the security activities of states since 9/11 has come from whistleblowers and investigative journalists – and that the flow of such information is precarious and unsteady – the combined efforts of state and non-state actors have ensured at least a limited degree of accountability over the last fifteen years.

Notwithstanding these opportunities for optimism, it is increasingly apparent that rights as a limit on state power are under attack. Both Victor Ramraj and Robert Diab observe in their respective chapters that there are reasons to worry that the collective commitment to rights – both in terms of the interests they seek to protect and their legal status – has been significantly eroded in recent years. For Ramraj, human rights have come under particular assault from the rising tide of nationalism in many liberal democratic states. He points out the ways that this nationalism both privileges national security over the interests of vulnerable groups such as refugees and asylum seekers and is hostile to the role played by international institutions such as the ECtHR, the Court of Justice of the European Union (CJEU), and the UN Security Council.

In contrast, Diab argues that one of the challenges for rights comes from the fact that their status has come to be widely questioned in an era when the threat of mass terrorism looms large in the public and political imagination. He traces the evolution of the notion of rights as trumps since Ronald Dworkin first formulated it in 1970's and notes especially the changes that occurred in the security and human rights debate after 9/11. According to Diab, that watershed event not only led many to question the value of rights but also prompted a reimagining of the idea of (in)security. While rights may have, in principle at least, retained their status as trumps in most liberal democracies, security has also acquired something akin to a trump status. While Roach and Ramraj suggest that there are reasons to be optimistic about the future of rights, in large part due to the growing role of non-state actors in the promotion and protection of such rights, Diab is less positive. We have, he argues, reached a critical impasse in the history of human rights, during which fears of mass terror dominate news cycles and political debates, and the currency of rights has been significantly devalued.

If we are to find our way out of the crisis identified by Diab, one possible approach may lie with a re-examination of our idea of rights and their relationship to notions of the political. As Chetan Bhatt notes, at the heart of liberal conceptions of the relationship between security and rights are assumptions about the distinction between legitimate and illegitimate violence. Although Hobbes is rarely evoked in contemporary discussions of security, his ideas about the state of nature, sovereign power, and the economy of fear continue to inform the ways in which we talk about the limits of the state. For Bhatt, it is important to remember that threats to sovereign power – and to the life of the state – are forbidden in the Hobbesian conception of the state because they raise the prospect of a descent into civil war and chaos. Looked at in this way, it becomes clear that the challenge of reconciling a commitment to rights with the reality of state violence (against its own citizens as well as against those on the 'outside') is hardly new. Indeed, Bhatt suggests that far from being oppositional, security and rights are deeply intertwined: their relationship reflects 'a deeper relationship between politics and violence' that lies at the heart of the liberal state. While Locke and his successors may have succeeded in expanding the liberal conception of rights – and at the same time helped to define the boundaries of the state – the Hobbesian-inspired fear of the state of nature continues to underpin many of the arguments that privilege security over rights.

III. PRIVACY, ANONYMITY, AND DISSENT

Since the publication of the first edition of *Security and Human Rights,* where Goold warned about the potential of surveillance to reconstitute the relationship between individuals and the state, there has been an exponential increase in the use of sophisticated and (often secret) surveillance technologies by (and between) governments around the world. Although the steady expansion of mass surveillance, communications monitoring, and data collection since 9/11 has long worried privacy activists, academics, and journalists, recent disclosures of secret surveillance mechanisms operating transnationally have also resulted in more widespread public outcries about the intrusiveness of state surveillance.

What do we risk each time we hand new surveillance powers to the state in the name of security? For Arianna Vedaschi, the key to answering these questions lies with our understanding of privacy and the legal structures that exist to protect it. In her chapter, she reflects on how the CJEU has approached the difficult task of balancing a commitment to privacy with the ongoing efforts of EU Member States to expand their electronic surveillance and data collection capacities. As she points out, the Court clearly accepts that national governments have a legitimate interest in collecting and retaining certain types of electronic data for the purposes of combatting terrorism, but it has affirmed that such activity must also be proportionate and subject to meaningful procedural safeguards. By both invalidating the former Data Retention Directive and declaring the US Safe Harbour Agreement inconsistent with Articles 7 and 8 of the Charter of Fundamental Rights of the European Union, the Court sent a clear message to Member States that privacy rights must be taken seriously.[40] Yet as Vedaschi notes, recent efforts by the United Kingdom and France suggest that some states have continued to try to minimise their obligations under the Convention by

[40] These developments led to the abandonment of the US Safe Harbour Agreement and the establishment of the EU–US Privacy Shield Framework in July 2016, which the European Commission subsequently declared was sufficient under EU law to enable data transfers to the United States. See European Commission, 'EU Commission and United States Agree on New Framework for Transatlantic Data Flows', EU-US Privacy Shield press release (2 February 2016), http://europa.eu/rapid/press-release_IP-16-216_en.htm; and Commission Implementing Decision (EU) 2016/1250 of 12 July 2016 pursuant to Directive 95/46/EC of the European Parliament and of the Council on the adequacy of the protection provided by the EU-US Privacy Shield (notified under document C(2016) 4176) (Text with EEA relevance), available at https://eur-lex.europa.eu/legal-content/EN/TXT/?uri=uriserv%3AOJ.L_.2016.207.01.0001.01.ENG.

developing increasingly intrusive mechanisms of data collection and retention. While Vedaschi suggests that national courts and legislatures should commit themselves to the privacy principles that underlie the recent decisions of the CJEU, it remains to be seen whether EU states will continue to collect, process, and share large amounts of personal data in the name of security.[41]

While Vedaschi focuses on judicial efforts to protect the privacy of citizens from state surveillance, in his chapter, Juan Pablo Pérez-León-Acevedo considers the ways in which anonymity has been used by courts to protect the identity of victims and witnesses. Focusing on the proceedings for *Ayyash et al* at the Special Tribunal for Lebanon (STL),[42] he develops a framework for the reconciliation of the right to anonymity of victims/witnesses and the rights of defendants within international criminal processes based on 'contextual and particular personal circumstances', human rights standards, national and international criminal law standards, and 'practical considerations'. Emphasising the importance within international criminal justice of the determination of truth and the establishment of historical record, he questions the complete and pre-emptive exclusion of anonymous victim participants (as opposed to witnesses) at the STL. While recognising the inadmissibility of 'anonymous witnesses' as a necessary safeguard of fair trial rights of the accused, Pérez-León-Acevedo further suggests that additional and alternative measures may be introduced to reconcile the opposing interests of fair trial rights and witness security. As he demonstrates, the unique status of the STL, means that the Tribunal's ongoing attempts in *Ayyash et al* to achieve this balance between the security rights of victim/witnesses and the fair trial rights of defendants may become an influential source for national and international courts when dealing with terrorism-related cases.

Criminal law is also the subject of analysis for the next two chapters, but the authors shift focus by highlighting some of the ways that states have employed the authority of the criminal law as a means of indirectly supressing public debate and political dissent while ostensibly aiming to combat terrorism. Ben Saul details the ways in which overly broad and vague counterterrorism laws have been used to criminalise political resistance and substantially reduce the possibility of even nonviolent protest in many countries. Central to Saul's analysis is the observation that some states, despite warnings from international

[41] Despite the apparent advances recently introduced by the General Data Protection Regulation (Regulation (EU) 2016/679 of 27 April 2016 on the protection of natural persons with regard to the processing of personal data and on the free movement of such data, and repealing Directive 95/46/EC) the courts have yet to provide definitive and specific guidance on more permissive EU instruments that deal with data protection in the context of law enforcement and security, including, for example, the Police Directive (Directive (EU) 2016/680 of 27 April 2016 on the protection of natural persons with regard to the processing of personal data by competent authorities for the purposes of the prevention, investigation, detection or prosecution of criminal offences or the execution of criminal penalties, and on the free movement of such data, and repealing Council Framework Decision 2008/977/JHA).

[42] *Prosecutor v Ayyash et al* (STL-11-01) See the STL webpage for details about the ongoing case: https://www.stl-tsl.org/en/the-cases/stl-11-01.

bodies such as the International Committee of the Red Cross (ICRC), have substantially expanded their domestic definitions of terrorism. Saul is especially concerned by the use of International Humanitarian Law (IHL) as a means of justifying these increasingly restrictive counterterrorism laws and legitimising efforts to apply such laws extraterritorially. He notes that while the diminishment of unregulated space for political resistance is unevenly experienced across jurisdictions, it in many cases leads to stigmatisation and criminalisation of all forms of resistance as 'terrorism' and, more fundamentally, can be seen as part of a 'mutual transnational consolidation of state authority'.

Echoing some of the themes that are central to Saul's chapter, Helen Duffy and Kate Pitcher likewise raise an alarm regarding what they describe as a 'global trend' towards the criminalisation of the expression of ideas. They survey a proliferation of 'expansive offences' that are enforced across a range of international, regional, and national jurisdictions, against individuals who share or make available ideas and opinions deemed 'dangerous to society'. As Duffy and Pitcher point out, it is not only direct incitement, instigation, and inducement to violence offences that have been criminalised; recent prosecutions have employed indirect incitement offences that include even speech acts which have no aim of supporting acts of violence. Such moves run counter to the well-established criminal law principles of harm and remoteness, as well as the basic rule-of-law requirements of necessity, proportionality, and foreseeability. While a turn to criminal law might be welcomed as an antidote to the exceptionalist tendency to 'define out' terrorism and hence as a means of bringing state counterterrorism into the fold of criminal law restraints on state overreach, Duffy and Pitcher rightly ask how far the criminal law can stretch in pursuit of terrorism prevention. Drawing together criminal principles and international human rights standards, the authors advocate for coherent and consistent guidance from international courts on the issue of freedom of expression and the *ultima ratio* basis of the criminal law as a preventive tool.

IV. EXCEPTIONALISM, RISK, AND PREVENTION

In the first edition of *Security and Human Rights*, we pointed to the rise of a global culture of exceptionalism, most notably in jurisdictions with avowed commitments to human rights and constitutionalism. Many of the scholars in that volume sought to grapple with the question of how the rule of law could be reconciled with claims to exceptional powers within a state of emergency.[43]

[43] See in particular D Dyzenhaus and M Hunt, 'Deference, Security and Human Rights' in BJ Goold and L Lazarus (eds), *Security and Human Rights*, 1st edn (Oxford, Hart Publishing, 2007); and VV Ramraj, 'Between Idealism and Pragmatism: Legal and Political Constraints on State Power in Times of Crisis' in BJ Goold and L Lazarus (eds) (above).

At the time, a key issue was whether courts could oversee the use of derogations or states of emergency and whether these powers could be reconciled with a culture of justification rather than simply lending extraordinary powers a 'veneer of legality'.

Twelve years later, the debate surrounding the role of the judiciary in emergency conditions continues, evolving through richer, and often contradictory, experience. Some senior members of the judiciary showed themselves to be capable of facing down the most extreme emergency measures of the early years post-9/11, with the UK *Belmarsh* case and US *Boumediene* case becoming yardsticks for upholding a basic minimum of rights guarantees in the face of state claims to exceptionalism. In many ways, however, these decisions sit in stark contrast with a number of other judgments that have allowed for the accommodation of counterterrorism measures within the normal frameworks of human right law.[44]

Amidst the global intensification of security challenges, the judicialisation of emergencies has proven to be a crucial development. No jurisdiction is more central to this discussion than France, which returned to the use of emergency powers for two years after Paris suffered terrorist attacks in November 2015. The chapter by Marc Antoine Granger is a granular analysis of the judicial and non-judicial oversight frameworks which applied during that time. Granger explains that while administrative courts have some attenuated powers to review declarations and extensions of the state of emergency, their 'actual capacity to rule on these highly political decisions is questionable'. Far more powerful are the extensive judicial powers to review and control administrative measures adopted as part of the state of emergency, which included powers to order home searches and raids anywhere and at any time, powers to limit freedom of movement of people and vehicles, powers of house arrest, and powers of temporary closure of theatres pubs and meeting places. Alongside judicial mechanisms, Granger points to the success of parliamentary controls through the activity of Parliamentary Law Commissions and the Rights Defender which has proved to be a strong 'counter-power' to executive overreach during the state of emergency. The web of controls surveyed by Granger lead him to the conclusion that while 'ultimately the state of emergency does not operate outside the rule of law', its continuation over two years requires serious interrogation and has wide effect on the French legal system even after its termination, resulting in a 'lite' state of emergency that is restrictive of freedoms within the normal law.

In the first edition, we argued that any engagement with the question of security and human rights would necessitate an engagement with the language of risk. The modalities of security prevention over the past twelve years have vindicated the predictions of authors in the first edition, most notably

[44] For examples in the context of secret intelligence material, see above n 17. See also the chapter in this volume by Liora Lazarus.

Lucia Zedner and Bernard Harcourt, who drew urgent attention to the capacity for sophisticated risk technologies to legitimate pre-emptive intervention. Undoubtedly, the relationship between human rights and security is integrally bound up with what Shiri Krebs refers to in her chapter as 'the epistemology of risk'. There are few more iconic examples of the dominance of the technology and discourse of risk over the counterterrorism terrain than targeted killing, and Kreb's chapter is a critical engagement with the modalities of risk-based decision-making used in evaluating the potential collateral damage of targeted killing operations.

Focusing on the Israeli Special Investigatory Commission Report on the collateral damage caused by the killing of Salah Shehadeh in 2002, Krebs highlights the fundamental vulnerabilities of the decision-making process regarding such risks, as well as the challenges to public scrutiny of these decisions. Using the concept of 'bounded factuality', Krebs shows how biases occur in the assessment of facts when applying international law safeguards (such as the principle of precaution) to the use of lethal force. Through her analysis of the Shehadeh Commission Report and associated primary documentation, Krebs concludes that political oversight mechanisms are susceptible to the simplifications that are inherent to national security narratives and therefore unlikely to bring such complex biases to light. The Commission's failure to explore whether intelligence errors constituted a violation of the IHL principles of proportionality and precaution prompts her to formulate a set of proposals for going forward, based on an acknowledgment of the limitations on legal fact-finding during conditions of armed conflict.

The epistemology of risk is certainly not confined to the extreme case of lethal force, as it can now be said to have transformed the criminal law and criminal justice system.[45] In his chapter, Andreas Armborst explores the recent rise of programmes aimed at countering violent extremism within broader civil society, arguing that these have been implemented to 'creatively circumvent' the structural limitations of the criminal justice system. Situating these prevention programmes alongside similar moves in a range of jurisdictions, Armborst points to the European Programme Preventing Terrorism and Countering Violent Extremism and Radicalization and the UN Plan of Action to Prevent Violent Extremism as examples of a shift at the international level.[46] He raises concerns about the potential of the turn to 'pre-prevention' or 'hyperpreventionalism' to 'securitise everything', especially where programmes engage actors within civil society beyond the traditional boundaries of the criminal justice

[45] A Ashworth and L Zedner, *Preventive Justice* (Oxford, Oxford University Press, 2014).

[46] Organization for Security and Co-operation in Europe (OSCE), 'Preventing Terrorism and Countering Violent Extremism and Radicalization that Lead to Terrorism: A Community-Policing Approach' (March 2014), available at https://www.osce.org/atu/111438; and UN General Assembly, 'Plan of Action to Prevent Violent Extremism', A/70/674 (24 December 2015), available at https://www.un.org/counterterrorism/ctitf/en/plan-action-prevent-violent-extremism.

and security sector. The German 'Strategy to Prevent Extremism and Promote Democracy'[47] operates under the aegis of the Ministry for Family Affairs, and like the UK Prevent programme, it engages NGOs, communities, and the education sector. Although these measures appear less coercive than those often employed by criminal law and the police, they are not necessarily less intrusive and indeed risk reifying the divisions they seek to address. Armborst concludes by asking whether programmes aimed at countering violent extremism will be moderated by the 'approaches, mentalities, and professional skills' of civic society actors tasked with their implementation, or whether such programmes will result in a securitisation of these sectors.

Over-securitisation is also at the heart of the chapter by David Irvine and Travers McLeod. Taking forced migration as their focus, Irvine and McLeod argue that many of the problems associated with mass human displacement are the result of insufficient resources being devoted to the processing and resettlement of refugees, poor co-ordination between countries, and inadequate systems of identification. On this last point, Travers and McLeod argue that while a 'necessary condition for governments to attend effectively to these issues is the ability to determine who is in their country', existing approaches to the identification and registration of forced migrants are in desperate need of reform. Going further, they suggest that the problems of forced migration are not the product of some irreconcilable conflict between security and human right but rather a failure on the part of governments to take the challenges of resettlement sufficiently seriously. Community cohesion, the maintenance of security, and the protection of individual rights can all be achieved simultaneously, provided we are willing to provide refugees with sufficient opportunities on arrival and devote adequate resources to ensuring their 'successful absorption into the national fabric of settlement countries'.

V. CONCLUSION

When the first edition of this collection was published in 2007, many scholars were struggling with the question of whether it is possible to reconcile a commitment to human rights with the demands of security in a post-9/11 world. More than a decade later, this fundamental tension remains at the heart of many discussions about the relationship between security and human rights. But in the

[47] Federal Ministry for Family Affairs, Senior Citizens, Women and Youth (Germany), 'Strategy to Prevent Extremism and Promote Democracy' (adopted July 2016), available in English at https://www.bmfsfj.de/blob/115448/cc142d640b37b7dd76e48b8fd9178cc5/strategie-der-bundesregierung-zur-extremismuspraevention-und-demokratiefoerderung-englisch-data.pdf. See also BT Said and H Fouad, 'Countering Islamist Radicalisation in Germany: A Guide to Germany's Growing Prevention Infrastructure', International Centre for Counter-terrorism (ICCT) Policy Brief (September 2018), https://icct.nl/publication/countering-islamist-radicalization-in-germany-a-guide-to-germanys-growing-prevention-infrastructure.

twelve years that have passed since the first edition, we have also seen the re-emergence of nationalism and xenophobia, a hardening of attitudes towards migrants, and a dramatic increase in Islamophobia in populist security discourse. Combined, these trends mean that the liberal order underpinning the international human rights framework since World War II is now under threat. For those who seek to defend human rights and the idea that states must always, no matter how serious the emergency, be committed to the rule of law, the challenge is to make sense of these interconnected trends and to speak to the concerns of those who see rights as nothing more than a hurdle to addressing real and perceived problems of immigration, crime, and terrorism.

This will not be an easy task. While some of the most egregious attacks on rights and the rule of law have either been repelled or rolled back by courts in recent years, as many of the authors included in this collection note, politicians around the world continue to play on insecurity and demand that fundamental freedoms give way in the face of security threats. Moreover, the rise of right-wing populism and the revival of nationalistic rhetoric in democratic countries suggest that the assault on human rights is becoming even more aggressive and divisive.

There are, however, reasons to be optimistic about the future of rights and the capacity of liberal constitutionalism to provide a brake on the worst excesses of security populism. As many of the contributions in this volume demonstrate, in the years since the first edition of *Security and Human Rights* was published, both the academy and civil society have come to recognise that falling back on conventional arguments and assumptions about rights will only take us so far. Two shifts may be necessary in order to reinvigorate an effective defence of rights in the face of security mandates. First, defenders of human rights must directly and critically engage with emotive claims of insecurity and unrealistic promises of security. Rather than reacting with similarly reductive narratives, we should seek to develop a discourse of sober resilience – one that provides a serious account of the risks to security while acknowledging both the inherent constraints on democratic states in achieving security and the wider security benefits to be gained from protecting rights. Ultimately, this narrative will need to build on a recognition, even a celebration, of the risk that comes with a free society.

The second, related shift involves meaningful acknowledgment of the role that liberalism has played in the historical and continued oppression of vulnerable groups. By addressing the ways in which the law in supposedly liberal democracies has been co-opted in the name of security, we help to lay bare flaws in the individualistic liberal vision of rights and the disconnect between abstract claims of universality and lived experiences on the ground. This process of exposure should not be seen as a step towards the abandonment of the liberal human rights project but rather as part of an attempt to revive it and make it relevant to those who have, in Huq's words, borne the 'costs of security'.

The scope and variety of the chapters in this volume serve as a reminder that though they are writ large, law and security are iterative – socially, politically, and even personally. If security populism (like terrorism) seeks to annihilate difference,[48] then to combat it we must recommit ourselves at every level to the values that lie at the heart of human rights. As a touchstone for engaging with difference, these values provide not only a means to bridge the divides that security populists so often seek to exploit but also a set of shared personal and political commitments that will help us to navigate the challenges to democracy that the pursuit of security inevitably presents.

REFERENCES

Alston, P, 'Report of the Special Rapporteur on Extrajudicial, Summary or Arbitrary Executions: Addendum', Human Rights Council, UN Doc A/HRC/14/24/Add.6 (28 May 2010).

American Civil Liberties Union (ACLU) and Amnesty International et al, 'Joint Letter to President Obama on US Drone Strikes and Targeted Killings' (11 April 2013), available at https://www.hrw.org/news/2013/04/11/joint-letter-president-obama-us-drone-strikes-and-targeted-killings (accessed 20 March 2019).

Amnesty International, 'Dangerously Disproportionate: The Ever-Expanding National Security State in Europe', EUR 01/5342/2017 (17 January 2017), https://www.amnesty.org/en/documents/eur01/5342/2017/en/.

Anti-Defamation League (ADL), 'Murder and Extremism in the United States in 2018' (January 2019), https://www.adl.org/murder-and-extremism-2018.

Ashworth, A and Zedner, L, *Preventive Justice* (Oxford, Oxford University Press, 2014).

Bachmann, S, 'Targetted Killings: Contemporary Challenges, Risks and Opportunities' (2013) 18(2) *Journal of Conflict and Security Law* 259–88.

Bowcott, O, 'Police Investigating Role of UK Officers in Torture of al-Qaida Suspect', *Guardian* (31 March 2019).

Cai, W and Landon, S, 'Attacks by White Extremists are Growing. So Are Their Connections', *New York Times* (3 April 2019).

Cassidy, J, 'It's Time to Confront the Threat of Right-Wing Terrorism', *New Yorker* (16 March 2019).

Chaudhry, AS, 'Interview on Islamophobia and the Christchurch, NZ Attacks', *CTV News* (15 March 2019), available at https://www.ctvnews.ca/video?clipId=1637407 (accessed 26 April 2019).

Chesterman, S, 'Terrorism, Surveillance, and Privacy' in B Saul (ed), *Research Handbook on International Law and Terrorism* (Cheltenham, Edward Elgar, 2014).

Commission of Inquiry into the Actions of Canadian Officials in Relation to Maher Arar ('Arar Commission'), 'Report of the Events Relating to Maher Arar' (2006), available at http://publications.gc.ca/site/eng/9.688875/publication.html (accessed 26 April 2019).

Deneen, PJ, *Why Liberalism Failed* (New Haven, Yale University Press, 2018).

Dodd, V, 'Shamima Begum Family Challenge Javid's Citizenship Decision', *Guardian* (20 March 2019).

[48] This thought is inspired by Suzanne Moore's insight: 'Terrorism sees difference and wants to annihilate it. Ardern sees difference and wants to respect it, embrace it, and connect with it.' S Moore, 'Jacinda Adern Is Showing the World What Real Leadership Is: Sympathy, Love and Integrity', *Guardian* (18 March 2019).

Drayton, R, *Whose Constitution? Law, Justice and History in the Caribbean*, 6th Distinguished Jurist Lecture (Port of Spain, Judicial Education Institute of Trinidad and Tobago, 2016).

Dyzenhaus, D and Hunt, M, 'Deference, Security and Human Rights' in BJ Goold and L Lazarus (eds), *Security and Human Rights*, 1st edn (Oxford, Hart Publishing, 2007).

Emmerson, B, 'Report of the Special Rapporteur on the Promotion and Protection of Human Rights and Fundamental Freedoms while Countering Terrorism', UN General Assembly, UN Doc A/68/389 (18 September 2013).

——, 'Report of the Special Rapporteur on the Promotion and Protection of Human Rights and Fundamental Freedoms while Countering Terrorism', Human Rights Council, A/HRC/25/59 (11 March 2014).

European Commission, 'EU Commission and United States Agree on New Framework for Transatlantic Data Flows', EU-US Privacy Shield press release (2 February 2016), http://europa.eu/rapid/press-release_IP-16-216_en.htm.

Freedland, J and Hasan, M, 'Muslims and Jews Face a Common Threat from White Supremacists. We Must Fight It Together', *Guardian* (3 April 2019).

Galston, WA, *Anti-Pluralism: The Populist Threat to Liberal Democracy* (New Haven, Yale University Press, 2018).

Ginsburg, T and Huq, AZ, *How to Save a Constitutional Democracy* (Chicago, University of Chicago Press, 2019).

Goodman, R, 'Why the Laws of War Apply to Drone Strikes Outside "Areas of Active Hostilities": A Memo to the Human Rights Community', *Just Security* (4 October 2017), https://www.justsecurity.org/45613/laws-war-apply-drone-strikes-areas-active-hostilities-a-memo-human-rights-community.

Goold, BJ and Lazarus, L (eds), *Security and Human Rights*, 1st edn (Oxford, Hart Publishing, 2007).

Hawkins, C, 'Counter-Terrorism Operations against Right-Wing Extremism in Western Europe Increase 191% in 24 Months', *IHS Markit* (7 December 2018), https://ihsmarkit.com/research-analysis/counterterrorism-operations-against-right-wing-extremism.html.

Heyns, C, 'Report of the Special Rapporteur on Extrajudicial, Summary or Arbitrary Executions', UN General Assembly, UN doc A/68/382 (13 September 2013).

Heyns, C, Akande, D, Hill-Cawthorne, L, and Chengeta, T, 'The International Law Framework Regulating the Use of Armed Drones' (2016) 65(4) *International and Comparative Law Quarterly* 791–827.

Intelligence and Security Committee of Parliament (UK), 'Detainee Mistreatment and Rendition: Current Issues', HC 1113 (2018), https://fas.org/irp/world/uk/isc-detainee2.pdf.

Jenkins, S, 'How Our Politicians and Media Are Helping Terrorists Win', *Spectator* (9 April 2016).

——, 'Media Hype about the Westminster Attacks Will Only Encourage Others', *Guardian* (24 March 2017).

Joint Committee on Human Rights (UK), 'Closing the Impunity Gap: UK Law on Genocide (and Related Crimes) and Redress for Torture Victims' (2008–09, HL 153 HC 553).

Koenig, G, 'Emmanuel Macron is on a Slippery Slope towards "Democratic Despotism"', *Financial Times* (10 March 2019).

Lavrysen, L, *Human Rights in a Positive State: Rethinking the Relationship between Positive and Negative Obligations under the European Convention on Human Rights* (Cambridge, Intersentia, 2016).

Lazarus, L, 'Doing Violence to the Rule of Law' (April 2018), available at https://ssrn.com/abstract=3170649 (accessed 20 March 2019).

——, 'Positive Obligations and Criminal Justice: Duties to Protect or Coerce?' in J Roberts and L Zedner (eds), *Principled Approaches to Criminal Law and Criminal Justice: Essays in Honour of Professor Andrew Ashworth* (Oxford, Oxford University Press, 2012).

——, 'The Right to Security: Securing Rights or Securitising Rights?' in R Dickinson, E Katselli, C Murray, and OW Pedersen (eds), *Examining Critical Perspectives on Human Rights* (Cambridge, Cambridge University Press, 2012).

Lazarus, L and Blackbourn, J, 'Intelligence and the Criminal Law in England and Wales' in M Dyson and B Vogel (eds), *The Limits of Criminal Law* (Cambridge, Intersentia, 2018).

Lazarus, L, Goold, B, and Goss, C, 'Control without Punishment: Understanding Coercion' in J Simon and R Sparks (eds), *SAGE Handbook of Punishment and Society* (London, Sage, 2013).

Levitsky, S and Ziblatt, D, *How Democracies Die: What History Reveals about Our Future* (London, Penguin Random House, 2018).

Lyon, D, *The Culture of Surveillance* (Cambridge, Polity Press, 2018).

Marsh, S, 'Record Number of Anti-Muslim Attacks Reported in UK Last Year', *Guardian* (20 July 2018).

Marty, D (Special Rapporteur), 'Secret Detentions and Illegal Transfers of Detainees Involving Council of Europe Member States: Second Report', Council of Europe Parliamentary Assembly report (7 June 2007), http://assembly.coe.int/CommitteeDocs/2007/EMarty_20070608_NoEmbargo.pdf.

Mavronicola, N, 'Taking Life and Liberty Seriously: Reconsidering Criminal Liability under Article 2 of the ECHR' (2017) 80(6) *Modern Law Review* 1026–51.

Milanovic, M, 'On Whether IHL Applies to Drone Strikes Outside "Areas of Active Hostilities": A Response to Ryan Goodman', *EJIL: Talk!* (5 October 2017), https://www.ejiltalk.org/on-whether-ihl-applies-to-drone-strikes-outside-areas-of-active-hostilities-a-response-to-ryan-goodman.

Ministry for Family Affairs, Senior Citizens, Women and Youth (Germany), 'Federal Strategy to Prevent Extremism and Promote Democracy' (adopted July 2016), available in English at https://www.bmfsfj.de/blob/115448/cc142d640b37b7dd76e48b8fd9178cc5/strategie-der-bundesregierung-zur-extremismuspraevention-und-demokratiefoerderung-englisch-data.pdf.

Modirzadeh, N, 'Reframing the Debate: A Response to Ryan Goodman's Memo to the Human Rights Community', *Lawfare* (9 October 2017), https://www.lawfareblog.com/reframing-debate-response-ryan-goodmans-memo-human-rights-community.

Moore, S, 'Jacinda Adern Is Showing the World What Real Leadership Is: Sympathy, Love and Integrity', *Guardian* (18 March 2019).

Mounk, Y, *The People vs Democracy: Why Our Freedom is in Danger and How to Save it* (Cambridge, MA, Harvard University Press, 2018).

Nanopoulos, E, 'European Human Rights and the Normalisation of the "Closed Material Procedure": Limit or Source?' (2015) 78(6) *Modern Law Review* 913–44.

Neocleous, M, 'Security, Liberty and the Myth of Balance: Towards a Critique of Security Politics' (2007) 6 *Contemporary Political Theory* 131–49.

News Wires, 'UN Calls for Probe into "Excessive" Force by French Police at Yellow Vests Protests', *France 24* (6 March 2019), https://www.france24.com/en/20190306-un-france-investigate-excessive-force-yellow-vests.

Organization for Security and Co-operation in Europe (OSCE), 'Preventing Terrorism and Countering Violent Extremism and Radicalization that Lead to Terrorism: A Community-Policing Approach' (March 2014), available at https://www.osce.org/atu/111438.

Ramraj, VV, 'Between Idealism and Pragmatism: Legal and Political Constraints on State Power in Times of Crisis' in BJ Goold and L Lazarus (eds), *Security and Human Rights*, 1st edn (Oxford, Hart Publishing, 2007).

Rieff, D, 'The End of Human Rights? Learning from the Failure of the Responsibility to Protect and the International Criminal Court', *Foreign Policy* (9 April 2018), https://foreignpolicy.com/2018/04/09/the-end-of-human-rights-genocide-united-nations-r2p-terrorism/.

Roser, M, Nagdy, M, and Ritchie, H, 'Terrorism', *OurWorldInData* website (January 2018), https://ourworldindata.org/terrorism.

Roth, K, 'The Dangerous Rise of Populism: Global Attacks on Human Rights Values' in Human Rights Watch (ed), *Human Rights Watch World Report 2017*, available at https://www.hrw.org/world-report/2017 (accessed 15 March 2019).

——, 'Twin Threats: How the Politics of Fear and the Crushing of Civil Society Imperil Global Rights' in Human Rights Watch (ed), *Human Rights Watch World Report 2016*, available at https://www.hrw.org/world-report/2016 (accessed 15 March 2019).

Runciman, D, *How Democracy Ends* (London, Profile Books, 2018).

Said, BT and Fouad, H, 'Countering Islamist Radicalisation in Germany: A Guide to Germany's Growing Prevention Infrastructure', International Centre for Counter-terrorism (ICCT) Policy Brief (September 2018), https://icct.nl/publication/countering-islamist-radicalization-in-germany-a-guide-to-germanys-growing-prevention-infrastructure.

Senate Select Committee on Intelligence (USA), 'Committee Study of the Central Intelligence Agency's Detention and Interrogation Program', Senate Report 113–288 (9 December 2014), https://www.intelligence.senate.gov/sites/default/files/documents/CRPT-113srpt288.pdf.

Serwer, A, 'The Terrorism that Doesn't Spark a Panic', *Atlantic* (28 January 2019).

Snyder, T, *The Road to Unfreedom: Russia, Europe, America* (London, Bodley Head, 2018).

Trump, D, 'Inaugural Address', White House (20 January 2017), https://www.whitehouse.gov/briefings-statements/the-inaugural-address.

UN General Assembly, 'Plan of Action to Prevent Violent Extremism', A/70/674 (24 December 2015), available at https://www.un.org/counterterrorism/ctitf/en/plan-action-prevent-violent-extremism.

Waldron, J, 'Security and Liberty: The Image of Balance' (2003) 11(2) *Journal of Political Philosophy* 191–210.

Waluchow, W, 'Constitutionalism' in EN Zalta et al (eds), *Stanford Encyclopedia of Philosophy* (Stanford, Stanford Center for the Study of Language and Information, 2017), https://plato.stanford.edu/entries/constitutionalism/.

Part I

Religion, Identity, and Citizenship

2

Torture and Othering

NATASA MAVRONICOLA

I. INTRODUCTION

WE UNDERSTAND TORTURE to be a unique moral and legal wrong. Its absolute prohibition at international law has endured the 'war on terror', and it is widely defended by legal scholars and philosophers worldwide. Nonetheless, violations of the prohibition of torture continue to be documented across the world, and the non-negotiability of the prohibition has been challenged on a number of fronts. In this chapter, I reaffirm the absolute character of the prohibition on torture; at the same time, moving beyond the framing of torture as an exceptional or unique wrong, I consider connections and continuities between the wrong of torture and a prevailing theme at the intersection between security and human rights: othering.

I take othering to be not the denial of sameness but rather the denial of equivalent moral status. I argue that the wrong of torture is a form of radical othering. I propose that it is thus indelibly connected to what Jeremy Waldron has subtly called 'difficulties with distribution' in the 'image of balance' between security and liberty; to the way that the war on terror amplifies 'us' and 'them' narratives; and to contemporary mainstream gaps in human rights 'buy-in'. In light of this, I argue that exploring how the prohibition of torture is theorised, debated, and indeed flouted, can illuminate some of the foundational challenges faced by human rights and the imperative of responding to them with integrity.

II. THE ABSOLUTE CHARACTER OF THE PROHIBITION OF TORTURE IN HUMAN RIGHTS LAW

The absolute character of the prohibition of torture as a matter of international human rights law has survived the war on terror, in spite of some political figures and jurists who would have it otherwise.[1] In the aftermath of a cascade of revelations regarding the use of torture by US agents and their collaborators after 9/11 and the exposure of the infamous legal manoeuvres found in the 'Torture Memos',[2] the prohibition of torture has been reaffirmed in a spate of statements and court judgments.[3] Space does not permit a comprehensive defence of the absolute character of the prohibition here, but it has been adeptly defended in both moral and legal terms in an array of recent writings.[4] I have also made a case elsewhere for the absolute prohibition of torture in relation to international human rights law in particular.[5]

My focus in this chapter is the positioning of this prohibition within human rights law and at the intersection between security and human rights. In my view, the most compelling account of the character and significance of the prohibition of torture within human rights law is its depiction as an archetype of the human rights edifice.[6] An 'archetype', according to Waldron, is

> ... a particular provision in a system of norms which has a significance going beyond its immediate normative content, a significance stemming from the fact that it sums up or makes vivid to us the point, purpose, principle, or policy of a whole area of law ... a rule or positive law provision that operates not just on its own account, and does not just stand simply in a cumulative relation to other provisions, but that also operates in a way that expresses or epitomizes the spirit of a whole structured area of doctrine, and does so vividly, effectively, publicly ...[7]

[1] For a critical overview of the special challenge posed to the prohibition of torture by US practice and legal argument after 9/11, see WB Wendel, 'The Torture Memos and the Demands of Legality' (2009) 12 *Legal Ethics* 107–23.

[2] See, among many writings on the subject, P Sands, *Torture Team: Deception, Cruelty and the Compromise of Law* (London, Allen Lane, 2008); and D Cole (ed), *The Torture Memos: Rationalizing the Unthinkable* (New York, New Press, 2009). See also Senate Select Committee on Intelligence (USA), 'Committee Study of the Central Intelligence Agency's Detention and Interrogation Program' (2012), declassified version (3 December 2014) available at https://www.amnestyusa.org/pdfs/sscistudy1.pdf.

[3] See, for instance, ZJ Miller, 'Obama: "We Tortured Some Folks"', *TIME* (1 August 2014). Note too the UN Human Rights Council, 'Report of the UN Special Rapporteur on Torture and Other Cruel, Inhuman or Degrading Treatment or Punishment' (14 February 2017), UN doc A/HRC/34/54, paras 16 and 18–19. Judgments concerning the use of torture in violation of relevant human rights or constitutional rights provisions include *El-Masri v Former Yugoslav Republic of Macedonia* (2013) 57 EHRR 25 (European Court of Human Rights); and *Binyam Mohamed v Secretary of State for Foreign and Commonwealth Affairs* [2010] EWCA Civ 158.

[4] See, among others, H Shue, *Fighting Hurt* (Oxford, Oxford University Press, 2016) chs 2–6; M Farrell, *The Prohibition of Torture in Exceptional Circumstances* (Cambridge, Cambridge University Press, 2013); and D Luban, 'Liberalism, Torture, and the Ticking Bomb' (2005) 91(6) *Virginia Law Review* 1425–61.

[5] See N Mavronicola, 'Is the Prohibition against Torture and Cruel, Inhuman and Degrading Treatment Absolute in International Human Rights Law? A Reply to Steven Greer' (2017) 17(3) *Human Rights Law Review* 479–98.

[6] See J Waldron, 'Torture and Positive Law: Jurisprudence for the White House' (2005) 105(6) *Columbia Law Review* 1681–750. See also J Waldron, *Torture, Terror and Trade-Offs: Philosophy for the White House* (Oxford, Oxford University Press, 2012). For a nuanced, critical look at Waldron's 'archetype' thesis, see Farrell (above n 4).

[7] Waldron, *Torture, Terror and Trade-Offs* (ibid) 228.

Torture's absolute prohibition is a norm without which the commitment to the elevated and equal moral status of all persons, which is foundational to human rights, crumbles. This elevated and equal moral status is 'human dignity',[8] to which ample reference is made in human rights instruments. This argument encompasses both a moral account of the norm against torture and of the foundations of human rights, and the imperative that human rights law must reflect that moral position. Moreover, it is premised on locating the wrong of torture in a dehumanisation that, as I argue below, amounts to a form of radical othering and is accordingly an 'affront to human dignity'.[9] The discussion below builds on these starting points to illuminate the continuum of othering within counterterrorism and beyond, the existential threat that this othering continuum continues to pose both to the prohibition of torture and to human rights more broadly, and the response it therefore demands.

Torture is prohibited in unqualified terms in international law, with no room for displacement of the prohibition even in circumstances of war or public emergency threatening the life of the nation; and it protects everyone, irrespective of what they have done or been suspected of doing, be they criminals or innocent children. I wish nonetheless briefly to address three key challenges raised in regard to the absolute character of the prohibition of torture in human rights law. These concern (a) the norm's effectiveness, (b) its position within a conflict of rights, and (c) its contested contours.

The 'effectiveness challenge' can be summed up as suggesting that in theory, the prohibition of torture is absolute; but in practice, for a range of reasons, including sheer ignorance and culpable defiance, the prohibition is frequently flouted and/or left without redress.[10] It is both necessary and chastening to acknowledge that the enduring absoluteness of the prohibition at human rights law by no means entails universal compliance: as Michelle Farrell has commented, '[torture's] prevalence is a conspicuous reminder of the gap between the norm and its realisation.'[11] Across the world, every day, far too many people are subjected to torture and other ill treatment.[12] Nonetheless, that the norm has not been accompanied by the eradication of the wrong it proscribes does

[8] This builds on J Tasioulas, 'Human Dignity and the Foundations of Human Rights' in C McCrudden (ed), *Understanding Human Dignity* (Oxford, Oxford University Press, 2013) 305; and the notion of 'intrinsic worth' demanding acts consistent with respecting this worth as set out in C McCrudden, 'Human Dignity and Judicial Interpretation of Human Rights' (2008) 19(4) *European Journal of International Law* 655–724, 679. On dignity as rank, see J Waldron, *Dignity, Rank, and Rights* (Oxford, Oxford University Press, 2012).

[9] S Levinson, 'In Quest of a "Common Conscience": Reflections on the Current Debate about Torture' (2005) 1 *Journal of National Security Law and Policy* 231–52, 232.

[10] See, for example, N Grief and M Addo, 'Some Practical Issues Affecting the Notion of Absolute Right in Article 3 ECHR' (1998) 23 *European Law Review* 17–30.

[11] Farrell (above n 4) 6.

[12] See, for example, the most recent observation by the United Nations Special Rapporteur on Torture: 'Torture and other cruel, inhuman or degrading treatment or punishment are still rampant in most, if not all, parts of the world.' UN Human Rights Council (above n 3) para 14.

not alter the norm's non-displaceable character as a matter of human rights law,[13] much like the non-eradication of murder does not alter the character of the prohibition of murder. This does not, of course, mean that we should not be concerned about the gap between the prohibition and the eradication of torture. The limitations on the norm's effective enforcement have been addressed in a range of studies, and vital work continues towards assessing, strengthening, and building further safeguards towards the more effective prevention of torture.[14] Human rights law carries considerable potential in preventing and redressing torture, including through the elaboration of positive obligations on states to protect persons from torture, which courts such as the European Court of Human Rights (ECtHR) have tied specifically to effectiveness.[15] Nonetheless, it is vital to acknowledge the limits of (human rights) law in this regard and the significance of the wider context in which respect for the norm, or lack thereof, is embedded. My account of the continuum between torture and (other forms of) othering alludes to aspects of that wider context.

The position of the prohibition of torture within an alleged conflict of rights has been the focal point of challenges to the absolute character of the prohibition in the moral domain for decades,[16] framed frequently in terms of 'the ticking time bomb scenario'.[17] The notion of a conflict of rights has been the focus of a recent challenge by Steven Greer to the absolute character of the prohibition as a matter of human rights law.[18] In his account, Greer suggests that the scenario in *Gäfgen v Germany*,[19] in which a child's kidnapper, Gäfgen, was threatened with torture to reveal the child's (Jakob's) whereabouts under time-pressured conditions, encapsulates a conflict of rights. In this conflict, Greer has argued:

> [T]he right of a kidnap victim to be spared the torture, cruel, inhuman or degrading treatment and the risk of death caused by the kidnapping, should constitute an exception to the suspected kidnapper's right not to be threatened with torture in an attempt to facilitate rescue.[20]

[13] See N Mavronicola, 'What Is an "Absolute Right"? Deciphering Absoluteness in the Context of Article 3 of the European Convention on Human Rights' (2012) 12(4) *Human Rights Law Review* 723–58, 735.

[14] See, for example, L Oette, 'Implementing the Prohibition of Torture: The Contribution and Limits of National Legislation and Jurisprudence' (2012) 16(5) *International Journal of Human Rights* 717–36; and R Carver and L Handley, *Does Torture Prevention Work?* (Liverpool, Liverpool University Press, 2016).

[15] See, for example, D Shelton and A Gould, 'Positive and Negative Obligations' in D Shelton (ed), *The Oxford Handbook of International Human Rights Law* (Oxford, Oxford University Press, 2013) 569.

[16] Consider, for instance, the way Gewirth grapples with the idea of a conflict of rights in A Gewirth, 'Are There Any Absolute Rights?' (1981) 31 *Philosophical Quarterly* 1–16, 9.

[17] Discrediting this scenario, see H Shue, 'Torture in Dreamland: Disposing of the Ticking Bomb (2006) 37(2) *Case Western Reserve Journal of International Law* 231–39.

[18] S Greer, 'Is the Prohibition against Torture, Cruel, Inhuman and Degrading Treatment Really "Absolute" in International Human Rights Law?' (2015) 15 *Human Rights Law Review* 101–37.

[19] *Gäfgen v Germany* (2011) 52 EHRR 1.

[20] Greer (above n 18) 105.

As I have argued elsewhere, Greer has miscast the issue and glossed over important aspects.[21] While it makes sense in philosophical terms to describe the situation as one in which the kidnapped child's right has been violated by the kidnapper, this does not involve a conflict of rights: Jakob's right is violated by Gäfgen, whereas Greer has proposed that Gäfgen's right not to be subjected to proscribed ill treatment ought to be infringed by the state. The duty-bearers are distinct, so the idea of Jakob's right 'trumping' Gäfgen's right is misplaced, as the two rights demand acts or forbearances from different actors – they are not, as such, in conflict.

In the alternative, Greer may be alluding to the rights of both the kidnapper and the kidnapped child as against the state – but on this account, while the duty-bearer is the same, distinct types of duties are at play. As concerns the kidnapped child's rights, the correlative state duty is the positive obligation to take all reasonable measures to protect individuals from being subjected to torture or other proscribed ill treatment at the hands of non-state actors.[22] This positive obligation is not boundless: it is constrained by considerations of reasonableness and, indeed, legality.[23] There is no *duty to torture* within such a positive obligation to take reasonable measures.[24] This important in the context of counterterrorism: the state's positive duties to protect the lives of persons within its jurisdiction do not extend to duties to torture or inflict cruel, inhuman, or degrading treatment.

Lastly, it is worth considering the argument that the prohibition of torture amounts to the 'absolute prohibition of a relative term'.[25] In brief, the argument suggests that whilst the non-displaceable prohibition at law is accepted, what it proscribes is deeply contested and arguably indeterminate or relative, in the sense of being in the eye of the beholder. This is something the infamous Torture Memos exploited. This also underpins an argument put forward by Greer to the effect that the contours of the prohibition are a matter of 'interpretation, choice and attribution rather than necessity and inescapable prescription'.[26] For Greer, this supposed malleability can accommodate carving exceptions to the prohibition on the basis of 'moral choice'.[27] This is inapposite. The prohibition of torture proscribes a particular moral wrong. Its morally loaded terms are not

[21] Mavronicola, 'A Reply to Steven Greer' (above n 5).

[22] Henry Shue has classified duties under basic rights as duties of restraint, duties to protect, and duties to provide. See H Shue, *Basic Rights: Subsistence, Affluence, and US Foreign Policy*, 2nd edn (Princeton, New Jersey, Princeton University Press, 1996) 35. See also S Fredman, 'Human Rights Transformed: Positive Duties and Positive Rights' (2006) *Public Law* 498–520, 500.

[23] See the contribution by Liora Lazarus to the first edition of this volume: L Lazarus, 'Mapping the Right to Security' in BJ Goold and L Lazarus (eds), *Security and Human Rights* (Oxford, Hart Publishing, 2007) 342.

[24] See Mavronicola, 'What Is an "Absolute Right"?' (above n 13) 732.

[25] O Ze'ev Bekerman, 'Torture – The Absolute Prohibition of a Relative Term: Does Everyone Know What Is in Room 101?' (2005) 53 *American Journal of Comparative Law* 743–83.

[26] Greer (above n 18) 111–12.

[27] Ibid, 125.

empty canvases that contain no express rights and on which subjective preferences can, without further ado, simply be imposed. Their interpretation does not entail an all-encompassing moral choice: it does not accommodate displacement through the back door, by allowing extraneous considerations to distort the way the wrongs at issue are understood and applied. Rather, the interpretation of the prohibition of torture and other ill treatment should proceed on a principled understanding of the wrong(s) proscribed.[28] Waldron has instructively distinguished *interpretation* of terms such as torture, inhumanity and degradation from *displacement* in the following way:

> We are certainly not permitted to follow … a realist logic proceeding on the basis of *modus tollens*:
>
> 1. If X is inhuman then X is prohibited;
> 2. But because X is necessary, it is unthinkable that X should be prohibited;
> 3. Therefore, (3) X cannot be regarded as inhuman.[29]

My affirmation of the absolute prohibition of torture at human rights law is thus anything but a dismissal of the complexities and contestation surrounding it, some of which I have explored elsewhere. Acknowledging the complexity and contestation in this area and in human rights more broadly is vital to ensuring that (support for) the norm does not ossify and that those who support the absolute prohibition do not become unduly complacent. The present piece reflects a commitment to confronting this complexity in a dynamic manner.

These initial reflections on the absolute character of the prohibition of torture would be incomplete without mention of the pro-torture stance adopted by the current President of the United States, Donald Trump.[30] His position was set out during his electoral campaign in the following terms:

> You look at the Middle East, they're chopping off heads, they're chopping off the heads of Christians and anybody else that happens to be in the way. They're drowning people in steel cages, and now we're talking about waterboarding … It's fine, and if we want to go stronger, I'd go stronger too. Because frankly, that's the way I feel. Can you imagine these people, these animals, over in the Middle East that chop off heads, sitting around talking and seeing that we're having a hard problem with waterboarding? We should go for waterboarding and we should go tougher than waterboarding.[31]

Trump's statements encapsulate an 'equality of arms' argument for cruelty; as it has been put (not approvingly, it should be said) elsewhere, 'To eschew such tools [as waterboarding] is to fight terrorism with one hand tied behind your back.'[32]

[28] See Waldron, *Torture, Terror and Trade-Offs* (above n 6) esp ch 9. See also Mavronicola, 'What Is an "Absolute Right"?' (above n 13) 746–47.

[29] Waldron, *Torture, Terror and Trade-Offs* (above n 6) 297.

[30] See T Miles, 'Experts Warn Donald Trump Policy on Torture Could Be "Catastrophic"', *Independent* (31 January 2017).

[31] T Berenson, 'Donald Trump Defends Torture at Republican Debate', *TIME* (3 March 2016).

[32] *Economist*, 'The Real Price of Freedom: Civil Liberties under Threat', *Economist* (20 September 2007).

Yet Trump's stance is also premised on a demarcation of the border of humanity: the prospective victims of torture, 'these people', become 'these animals', branded as lesser creatures that are unworthy (for Trump) of protection from torture and indeed, that deserve our inhumanity.[33] The argument put forward in the remainder of this chapter is that the othering found in Trump's statement both drives and is central to the act of torture; in turn, it lies on a continuum with other ways in which the essence of human rights is undermined in the name of security.

III. TORTURE AND OTHERING

Torture is both a (sadly) frequent phenomenon and a profound wrong. Philosophical perspectives serve to illuminate precisely 'what's wrong with torture', as David Sussman has asked in a memorable piece (to which I return below).[34]

Torture evokes enduring images and acts, old and new, that form what we may call the paradigm of torture. Focusing on the paradigm case, David Luban has suggested that torture, through the exercise of control and the infliction of pain and suffering, isolates,[35] terrorises and humiliates the victim.[36] He has provided a communicative account of torture, as follows:

> Torture of someone in the torturer's custody or physical control is the assertion of unlimited power over absolute helplessness, communicated through the infliction of severe pain or suffering on the victim that the victim is meant to understand as the display of the torturer's limitless power and the victim's absolute helplessness.[37]

On this paradigm, torture involves the infliction of pain or suffering on someone in the torturer's control so as to communicate the total subordination of the victim to the torturer.[38] The paradigm does not exhaust the wrong's manifestations, however.[39] Luban's account allows for situations in which the torturer has failed to attain the total subordination of the victim.

[33] It is worth noting that this also reflects the Bush Administration position that terrorist suspects did not warrant protection under the Geneva Conventions. See Office of the Assistant Attorney General (USA), 'Memorandum for Alberto R Gonzales, Counsel to the President, and William J Haynes II, General Counsel of the Department of Defense' ('The Bybee Memo'), US Department of Justice (22 January 2002), available at http://www.washingtonpost.com/wp-srv/nation/documents/012202bybee.pdf?noredirect=on; and GW Bush (White House), 'Humane Treatment of al Qaeda and Taliban Detainees', memorandum (7 February 2002), available at https://www.aclu.org/legal-document/presidential-memo-feb-7-2002-humane-treatment-al-qaeda-and-taliban-detainees.

[34] D Sussman, 'What's Wrong with Torture?' (2005) 33(1) *Philosophy and Public Affairs* 1–33.

[35] Elaine Scarry famously suggested that 'in serious pain the claims of the body utterly nullify the claims of the world'. E Scarry, *The Body in Pain: The Making and Unmaking of the World* (Oxford, Oxford University Press, 1985) 33.

[36] D Luban, *Torture, Power, and Law* (Cambridge, Cambridge University Press, 2014) 48–50.

[37] Ibid, 128.

[38] Ibid.

[39] Ibid, 130.

Luban's account of torture builds on Sussman's, which portrays chiefly interrogational torture as forcing its victim 'into the position of colluding against himself through his own affects and emotions, so that he experiences himself as simultaneously powerless and yet is actively complicit in his own violation'.[40] The goal of such torture is for its victim to be so thoroughly subordinated as to be rendered a puppet in the hands of the torturer. This subordination of the will is what we might call, in Colin Dayan's words, 'spirit thievery',[41] a form of domination that 'recalls the debilitation of slavery'.[42] Luban has highlighted the 'directionality' of the pain and suffering, which form a 'fanfare' underpinning the torturer's sovereignty over the victim.[43] Jay Bernstein, while examining the moral *injury* of torture, has also emphasised that pure torture is 'torture *for the sake of breaking the victim*, and hence a torture whose point is the asymmetry and non-reversibility of position between torturer and victim, the establishment of the absolute *authority* of the torturer'.[44] In Luban's account, this tyrannisation of a defenceless victim's body and spirit[45] makes torture entirely inimical to the antitotalitarian vision that underpins human rights.[46]

The moment of ('successful') torture is one of total domination, indeed of enslavement of a person's body and spirit. Whether the goal is to elicit information or a confession, or to intimidate or punish, it is the (attempted) dehumanisation of another person that is central to the wrong. As Michelle Farrell has put it, torture is 'the reduction of the human … to the status of less than human'.[47] Torture is thus a form of radical othering: it actively and intently takes aim at the equal and elevated status ascribed within the human rights edifice to all human persons over and above objects and animals, to which we often refer as 'human dignity'. Torture fundamentally wrongs the person subjected to it, but it also strikes more broadly at this very foundation of human rights.

Indeed, the act of torture not only radically others but tends to occur within a cycle of othering. Victims of torture often find themselves in the hands of torturers because society has vilified, marginalised, or abandoned them. Nigel Rodley has argued this aptly:

> [W]hen [torture] is part of an institutional practice … the victim is – must be – dehumanised, seen as an object. This is the traditional and inevitable means of considering 'the enemy', be it a class enemy, a race enemy, a religious enemy, or a foreign enemy.

[40] Sussman (above n 34) 4.

[41] C Dayan, *The Law Is a White Dog* (Princeton, Princeton University Press, 2011) 21–22.

[42] Ibid, 22.

[43] Luban, *Torture, Power, and Law* (above n 36) 129.

[44] JM Bernstein, *Torture and Dignity: An Essay on Moral Injury* (Chicago, University of Chicago Press, 2015) 163 (emphasis in original).

[45] Luban, *Torture, Power, and Law* (above n 36) 48; and H Shue, 'Torture' (1978) 7(2) *Philosophy & Public Affairs* 124–43, 125 and 129–30.

[46] See also the 'archetype' thesis in Waldron, *Torture, Terror and Trade-Offs* (above n 6) 232.

[47] Farrell (above n 4) 246.

> Whatever the group, its members must be stripped of their inherent dignity as human beings in order to mobilise the rest against them.[48]

On this account, torture thrives in a context of systematic or systemic othering. The perpetrator's empathy towards the victim is blunted or extinguished through the victim's otherness. As Patrick Lenta has highlighted in the context of US torture practices post-9/11, these were underpinned by a stark 'othering' of the 'enemy':

> [O]nce the identity of those that the United States designates as its enemies has been constructed as a wholly negative, uncivilized other, torture will appear to the US soldiers who inflict it on Iraqis as morally unobjectionable and even heroic.[49]

Torture is also the culmination of othering. In his sharp and devastating account of torture at the hands of the Nazi regime, Jean Améry argued that 'torture was not an accidental quality of this Third Reich, but its very essence'.[50] In torture, Améry located the obliteration of mercy, the 'negation'[51] of one's fellow man. This, he avowed, represented the 'apotheosis'[52] of Nazism, which 'hated the word "humanity" like the pious man hates sin, and [thus] spoke of "sentimental humanitarianism"'.[53] In both rupturing any relational ties of empathy between perpetrator and victim and seeking to possess and subvert the victim's human faculties, torture therefore radically others in a way that cuts to the core of the humanist, egalitarian vision of human rights.[54] Yuval Ginbar has affirmed this cycle of othering in the context of torturing suspected terrorists: 'torturing suspected terrorists may both be encouraged by prejudice and encourage such prejudice further.'[55]

There is little that is aberrant or new in this link between torture and othering. Darius Rejali has highlighted the prevalence of torture in ancient republics and points out that it was inflicted 'exclusively on noncitizens: slaves, barbarians and foreigners'.[56] Page DuBois has brought the othering involved in torture full circle, reflecting on the othering function of torture in ancient Greece:

> As an instrument of demarcation, [torture] delineates the boundary between slave and free, between the untouchable bodies of free citizens and the torturable bodies of slaves. The ambiguity of slave status, the difficulty of sustaining an absolute sense

[48] N Rodley, *The Treatment of Prisoners under International Law* (Oxford, Oxford University Press, 1999) 14–15.

[49] P Lenta, 'Waiting for the Barbarians after September 11' (2006) 42(1) *Journal of Postcolonial Writing* 71–83, 73.

[50] J Améry, *At the Mind's Limits: Contemplations by a Survivor on Auschwitz and Its Realities* (Bloomington, Indiana University Press, 1980) 24.

[51] Ibid, 35.

[52] Ibid, 30.

[53] Ibid, 31.

[54] This is exemplified in Art 1 of the Universal Declaration of Human Rights.

[55] Y Ginbar, *Why Not Torture Terrorists?* (Oxford, Oxford University Press, 2008) 142.

[56] D Rejali, *Torture and Democracy* (Princeton, New Jersey, Princeton University Press, 2007) 56.

> of differences, is addressed through this practice of the state, which carves the line between slave and free on the bodies of the unfree.[57]

Applicable in ancient Greece and other contexts in which torture and slavery have intersected, DuBois' account locates (the scars of) torture as a physical 'marker' of lesser status. Looking at more recent practices of torture, Rejali has identified torture as a 'civic marker' demarcating those deemed worthy of being treated as fully human from those deemed less worthy:

> Today, torture victims include not simply terrorists and criminals, but street children, vagrants, loiterers, and illegal immigrants. We may not speak of them as slaves, but they fall into a class of quasi citizens that is perceived as vicious.[58]

In the experience of torture, people deemed 'lesser' in society learn the contours of their more limited citizenship: '[w]hether one can go here or there without fear of being beaten, whether one can travel in one's car without being pulled over or electrified, these are experiences constitutive of citizenship'.[59] Torture, in Rejali's view, thus operates to '[remind] lesser citizens who they are and where they belong'.[60]

Torture is an absolute wrong because of the total subordination or 'spirit thievery' it seeks or attains. It is an especially stark form of othering, entirely inimical to the human rights project because of the inhumanity it so completely embodies, but it is also part of a continuum and a cycle of othering. Once we have recognised the othering that lies at the heart of this archetypal wrong, it is imperative that we also squarely confront the othering that is endemic to counterterrorism and to our securitised states more broadly.

IV. COUNTERTERRORISM, OTHERING, AND THE 'HUMAN' IN HUMAN RIGHTS

In this section, I trace the othering continuum in some of the prevalent challenges to human rights, particularly in the context of security and counterterrorism. I link this to the othering found in torture and in attacks on the absolute prohibition of torture.

A. 'Difficulties with Distribution'

The relationship between counterterrorism and human rights has tended to attract variations of the argument that we must strike a balance between security

[57] P DuBois, *Torture and Truth* (Abingdon, Routledge, 1991) 63.
[58] Rejali (above n 56) 57.
[59] Ibid, 58.
[60] Ibid.

and human rights, a normative idea that has been critically interrogated by numerous scholars.[61] In his examination of the 'image of balance' between security and liberty, for example, Waldron has highlighted the imperative of paying close attention to 'the distributive character of the changes that are proposed and to the possibility that the change involves, in effect, a proposal to trade off the liberties of a few against the security of the majority'.[62] David Cole has put this in starker terms: '*their* liberty, *our* security'.[63] Many of the instances of interference with human rights in the counterterrorism context boil down to the sacrifice of the rights of the few for the security – or perceived security – of the many, bolstered by the unspoken motto of 'do unto the rights of others whatever it takes to make me feel more secure', as Luban has framed it.[64]

The dichotomy between 'our' (perceived) security and 'their' human rights captures the distributive skew reflected in an array of counterterrorism devices. Such devices have included the preventive detention of suspected terrorists, 'enemies' of foreign background, or those associated with one identifiable part of the community, as, for example, in Northern Ireland;[65] but they have also included the rendition and torture of 'high-value detainees' in the US war on terror.[66] Indeed, the very concept of 'terrorism', as deployed within obscure and/or overbroad legal contours for the purposes of – *inter alia* – surveillance, stop and search, arrest and detention, and prosecution, duly elicits parallels to Carl Schmitt's 'friend'/'enemy' distinction.[67] Since 9/11, the chief 'suspect community'[68] facing the worst excesses of counterterrorism measures have been persons (suspected to be)

[61] See, for instance, L Lazarus and BJ Goold, 'Introduction: Security and Human Rights – The Search for a Language of Reconciliation' in Goold and Lazarus (eds) (above n 23) 16–17; A Ashworth, 'Security, Terrorism, and the Value of Human Rights' in Goold and Lazarus (eds) (above n 23); and L Zedner, 'Seeking Security by Eroding Rights: The Side-Stepping of Due Process' in Goold and Lazarus (eds) (above n 23). See also R Dworkin, 'The Threat to Patriotism', *New York Review of Books* (28 February 2002); and J Waldron, 'Security and Liberty: The Image of Balance' (2003) 11(2) *Journal of Political Philosophy* 191–210.

[62] Waldron, 'Security and Liberty' (ibid) 194.

[63] D Cole, *Enemy Aliens* (New York, New Press 2003) 17 (emphasis in original).

[64] D Luban, 'Eight Fallacies About Liberty and Security' in R Ashby Wilson (ed), *Human Rights in the 'War on Terror'* (Cambridge, Cambridge University Press, 2005) 243. See also Ashworth (above n 61) 209.

[65] See R Daniels, *Prisoners Without Trial: Japanese Americans in World War II* (New York, Hill and Wang, 2004); R Dove (ed), *'Totally Un-English'? Britain's Internment of 'Enemy Aliens' in Two World Wars* (Leiden, Brill, 2005); K McEvoy, *Paramilitary Imprisonment in Northern Ireland: Resistance, Management, and Release* (Oxford, Oxford University Press, 2001); F de Londras, *Detention in the War on Terror: Can Human Rights Fight Back?* (Cambridge, Cambridge University Press, 2006).

[66] See M Satterthwaite, 'Rendered Meaningless: Extraordinary Rendition and the Rule of Law' (2007) 75 *George Washington Law Review* 1333–420.

[67] See J Friedrichs, 'Defining the International Public Enemy: The Political Struggle Behind the Legal Debate on International Terrorism' (2006) 19(1) *Leiden Journal of International Law* 69–91, 70, citing C Schmitt, *Der Begriff des Politischen* (Berlin, Duncker & Humblot, 1932) 26. On the hegemonic capture of the term 'terrorist', see also C Gearty, 'Terrorism and Morality' (2003) *European Human Rights Law Review* 377–83.

[68] See P Hillyard, *Suspect Community: People's Experience of the Prevention of Terrorism Acts in Britain* (London, Pluto Press, 1993).

of Muslim background.[69] More broadly, Cole's observation in 2003 that '[t]he war on terrorism has been waged largely through anti-immigrant measures'[70] strikes a particularly poignant note amidst the brutal securitisation of 'suspect communities' seeking asylum or simply a better life in Europe and across the world.[71] There is ample reason therefore for considering othering to be not only incidental but integral to the 'trade-off' underpinning the pursuit of security at the expense of human rights in the context of counterterrorism.

B. 'Us' and 'Them' Narratives

The distribution issue has not been a dimension of merely the legal measures impinging on human rights in the name of 'balance' between security and liberty. The notion of sacrificing 'their' rights for 'our' security has entered the political vernacular and been openly embraced in the context of counterterrorism.[72] The practices of counterterrorism, as Marie Breen-Smyth has suggested, 'witnessed by the public and represented in the media, create and consolidate a suspect community in the public eye'.[73] At the same time, the rhetoric of othering is used to create and bolster the conditions for these practices to develop and culminate in warfare and atrocity. As Didier Bigo and Elspeth Guild have highlighted in relation to torture in particular, 'prisoners [in the war on terror] have been labelled "unlawful combatants", "terrorists of the worst kind" and "pure evil" in order to negate their humanity'.[74] Similarly, Richard Jackson has argued:

> Constructing a large-scale project of political violence such as a global counter-terrorist war requires an extremely powerful process of demonisation and dehumanisation to overcome the natural reticence over the destruction of human life for political reasons.[75]

[69] See C Pantazis and S Pemberton, 'From the "Old" to the "New" Suspect Community: Examining the Impacts of Recent UK Counter-Terrorist Legislation' (2009) 49 *British Journal of Criminology* 646–66; T Choudhury and H Fenwick, 'The Impact of Counter-terrorism Measures on Muslim Communities', Equality and Human Rights Commission Research Report 72 (2011); and the chapter in this volume by Aziz Z Huq.

[70] Cole, *Enemy Aliens* (above n 63) 21.

[71] An illustrative account of the brutality and death faced by migrants is offered in UN Special Rapporteur on Extrajudicial, Summary or Arbitrary Executions, 'Unlawful Death of Refugees and Migrants', Report to the UN General Assembly, UN doc A/72/335 (15 August 2017). On the securitisation of migration, see P Bourbeau, *The Securitization of Migration: A Study of Movement and Order* (Abingdon, Routledge, 2011).

[72] See R Jackson, *Writing the War on Terrorism: Language, Politics and Counter-terrorism* (Manchester, Manchester University Press, 2005) ch 3; and S Talbot, '"Us" and "Them": Terrorism, Conflict and (O)ther Discursive Formations' (2008) 13(1) *Sociological Research Online* 17.

[73] M Breen-Smyth, 'Theorising the "Suspect Community": Counterterrorism, Security Practices and the Public Imagination' (2013) 7(2) *Critical Studies on Terrorism* 223–40.

[74] D Bigo and E Guild, 'The Worst-Case Scenario and the Man on the Clapham Omnibus' in Goold and Lazarus (eds) (above n 23) 111.

[75] Jackson (above n 72) 60.

Indeed, in November 2001, Patricia Williams aptly observed a dichotomy central to the American public's readiness to contemplate righteous torture:

> Torture is an investment in the right to be all-knowing, in the certitude of what appears 'obvious.' It is the essence of totalitarianism. Those who justify it with confident proclamations of 'I have nothing to hide, why should they?' overlap substantially with the class of those who have never been the persistent object of suspect profiling, never been harassed, never been stigmatized just for the way they look.[76]

Williams accordingly advised the US public to be 'wary of persecuting those who conform to our fears'.[77]

More broadly, 'us' and 'them' narratives have played a key role within recent shifts in the legal and political landscape of numerous states and regions across the world, underpinned by what we might term the 'politics of othering'.[78] This othering is normative in slant: it boils down to a form of dehumanisation that simultaneously 'uncovers' – or rather constructs – and amplifies the (perceived) danger posed by the 'Other', obscures their suffering, and advances or condones their marginalisation.[79] As I argue below, this othering also plays an important role in the crisis in human rights 'buy-in'; confronting its role in this crisis should inform the way forward in defending human rights.

C. The Crisis in Human Rights 'Buy-In'

It would be naive and simplistic to present the crisis of faith in human rights as monolithic. Critique and scepticism towards human rights come in many different forms and represent a variety of grievances and shades of the political spectrum. I wish to argue nonetheless that a key aspect of the current mainstream political crisis of faith in human rights is othering.

Today, this othering crisis in human rights is nowhere more starkly exposed than in the treatment of 'the stranger' at the border. Consider, for example, the plight of those who have found themselves on Europe's geographic and moral fringes: the persons caught up in Europe's self-branded 'refugee crisis'. The EU's widely publicised[80] commitment to human rights is belied by its readiness to employ a variety of techniques to deny full human rights protection to thousands of vulnerable people at risk of persecution, torture, or other

[76] P Williams, 'By Any Means Necessary', *Nation* (26 November 2001).

[77] Ibid.

[78] See G Lazaridis, G Campani, and A Benveniste (eds), *The Rise of the Far Right in Europe: Populist Shifts and 'Othering'* (Basingstoke, Palgrave Macmillan, 2016).

[79] On manifestations of such othering in policing Muslim women's clothing, see the chapter in this volume by Rumee Ahmed and Ayesha S Chaudhry.

[80] See, for example, the European Union's own website: https://europa.eu/european-union/topics/human-rights_en.

ill treatment.[81] Such policies are boosted or condoned by sentiments of the 'not in my backyard' variety, apathy, or overt racism within Member State populations.[82] Indeed, as predicted in 1991 by Joseph Weiler, it is hard to deny that the advent of EU citizenship has played a role in deeply and perhaps irreparably othering the non-EU citizen:

> Nationality as referent for interpersonal relations, and the human alienating effect of Us and Them are brought back again, simply transferred from their previous intra-Community context to the new intercommunity one. We have made little progress if the Us becomes European (instead of German or French or British) and the Them becomes those outside the Community or those inside who do not enjoy the privileges of citizenship.[83]

In the United Kingdom and elsewhere, the crisis in human rights 'buy-in' has often found expression in arguments of varied force launched against the alleged 'activism' of supranational human rights courts engaged in interpreting human rights instruments, in the face of opposition by state structures, a matter that is particularly prominent in Europe as regards the ECtHR.[84] The Conservative Party in the United Kingdom has attacked what it labels the 'mission creep' of the ECtHR, citing in particular its dynamic interpretation of the European Convention on Human Rights (ECHR) as regards the protection of prisoners and foreigners – groups that have been perennially othered. A clear case in point is a 2014 Conservative Party publication that laid out grievances against the UK Human Rights Act 1998 and the ECHR.[85] It explicitly targeted the judgments in a number of ECtHR cases concerning the rights of prisoners and foreign criminals,[86] including *Vinter v UK*, in which the Grand Chamber of the ECtHR found irreducible whole-life sentences to be contrary to Article 3 ECHR.[87]

[81] For a good overview, see J Borg-Barthet and C Lyons, 'The European Union Migration Crisis' (2016) 20(2) *Edinburgh Law Review* 230–35. On the EU–Turkey deal, see Amnesty International, 'A Blueprint for Despair: Human Rights Impact of the EU–Turkey Deal' (2017), http://www.amnesty.eu/content/assets/Reports/EU-Turkey_Deal_Briefing_Formatted_Final_P4840-3.pdf. On its operation in Greece, see M Gkliati, 'The EU–Turkey Deal and the Safe Third Country Concept before the Greek Asylum Appeals Committees' (2017) 3(2) *Movements: Journal for Critical Migration and Border Regime Studies* 213–24.

[82] M Tiessink, 'Not in My Backyard: The European Refugee Crisis', *Euractiv* (8 September 2015), http://www.euractiv.com/section/global-europe/opinion/not-in-my-backyard-the-european-refugee-crisis/.

[83] J Weiler, 'The Transformation of Europe' (1991) 100(8) *Yale Law Journal* 2403–83, 2482.

[84] For some of the arguments raised in relation to the ECtHR, see R Spano, 'Universality or Diversity of Human Rights?' (2014) 14(3) *Human Rights Law Review* 487–502.

[85] Conservative Party, 'Protecting Human Rights in the UK: The Conservatives' Plans for Changing Britain's Human Rights Laws' (2014), https://www.conservatives.com/~/media/files/downloadable%20files/human_rights.pdf.

[86] Ibid, 3.

[87] On *Vinter*, see N Mavronicola, 'Inhuman and Degrading Punishment, Dignity, and the Limits of Retribution' (2014) 77(2) *Modern Law Review* 292; D van Zyl Smit, P Weatherby, and S Creighton, 'Whole Life Sentences and the Tide of European Human Rights Jurisprudence: What Is to Be Done?' (2014) 14(1) *Human Rights Law Review* 59–84. But see the Grand Chamber's recent reassessment of the compatibility of UK law with Art 3 ECHR in *Hutchinson v United Kingdom* App No 57592/08, Judgment of 17 January 2017.

Thus, in the political arena, the UK Conservative Party attack against the ECtHR has predominantly revolved around the beneficiaries of human rights. By focusing on the protection of those deemed unworthy of even *human* rights,[88] this anti-human rights politics galvanises the public against human rights, harnessing and further fuelling dominant media representations in the process. As Lieve Gies has astutely observed, othering is central to attacks on human rights in the media: 'the media separate out the deserving and the undeserving in relation to human rights claims, constructing what are effectively victim hierarchies.'[89] In declarations that the Human Rights Act is a 'charter for criminals and parasites', there is a discernible attack on the 'human' in human rights.[90] The principle that human rights protect *everyone*, especially those who fall through the cracks of the political process, is the central object of challenge.

Accordingly, much of the ongoing mainstream crisis in human rights 'buy-in' may be read not as brazen dismissal by a substantial portion of the public of the merits of having one's privacy and liberty protected, or of being safe from torture or from extrajudicial killings in the name of a seemingly global and unending war, but as a lack of buy-in to *the human rights of others*. At best, there is in this a misguided disregard of the value of human rights by the 'haves' vis-à-vis the 'have-nots'. At worst, it is premised on a (re)configuration of humanity. On both readings, the politics of othering plays a central role.

The academe is not immune from the politics of othering, which emerge in force in John Finnis' rejection of the non-refoulement dimension of Article 3 ECHR. Finnis has attacked the obligation not to expel people to places where they face a real risk of torture or related ill treatment, casting it as an example of dangerous judicial activism:

> [T]his, the Court insists in its usual bland, inexplicit way, is an exceptionless rule, an absolute, from which there can be no derogation even if the life of the nation were to be certainly imperilled by the importation of ebola or other plague, or of uncountable numbers of terrorists, or others, intent on overthrowing by force, or numbers, the state and the Convention …[91]

The dehumanisation inherent in the dichotomy Finnis draws between those who are imperilled and those who imperil is palpable. The net is cast wide, with the othering of the foreigner at its centre: 'terrorists, or others, intent on overthrowing by force, or numbers'. The argument attests both to the othering that

[88] I emphasise the 'human' in human rights because I consider that the forfeiture argument is inapplicable in relation to *human* rights.

[89] L Gies, 'Human Rights, the British Press and the Deserving Claimant' in KS Ziegler, E Wicks, and L Hodson (eds), *The UK and European Human Rights: A Strained Relationship?* (Oxford, Hart Publishing, 2015) 474.

[90] See M Elliott, 'A Damp Squib in the Long Grass: The Report of the Commission on a Bill of Rights' (2013) *European Human Rights Law Review* 137–51, 140–41.

[91] J Finnis, 'Judicial Power: Past, Present and Future', Policy Exchange Lecture, Gray's Inn Hall (21 October 2015), http://judicialpowerproject.org.uk/wp-content/uploads/2015/10/John-Finnis-lecture-20102015.pdf.

has pervaded discourse and practice on counterterrorism and to the metastatic potential of such discourses and practices.

The continuum of othering outlined above is not and cannot be ahistorical. Rather, unpacking it illuminates and makes it all the more imperative to acknowledge the othering central to colonial history and, indeed, to the history of human rights. In his magisterial account of the use and evolution of torture techniques, Rejali has exposed the 'long, unbroken, though largely forgotten history of torture in democracies at home and abroad', not least within colonial practices[92] and, as highlighted above, the role of othering within such torture.[93] Frantz Fanon sharply illuminated the continuum of othering culminating in torture in the context of French colonialism and torture in Algeria:

> In reality, the attitude of the French troops in Algeria fits into a pattern of police domination, of systematic racism, of dehumanization rationally pursued. Torture is inherent in the whole colonialist configuration.[94]

In acknowledging the continuum that runs from the politics of othering to the brutal denial of another's humanity encompassed by torture, we must also thus confront the extent to which states that have often availed of the (problematic) label 'civilised' have in fact shaped and occupied the whole of this continuum of othering and continue to do so. Indeed, the legacy of colonialism forms the undercurrent of inhumanity that haunts the egalitarian underpinnings of human rights. Over the course of the twentieth century and the growth of the human rights project, as Upendra Baxi has highlighted, 'large masses of colonized peoples were not regarded as sufficiently human or even as potentially human.'[95]

These conclusions entail that those of us who consider ourselves proponents of human rights must unswervingly trace the fault lines in the way the egalitarian vision of human rights encapsulated by human dignity has been articulated and given effect in practice. This may lead us to see the human rights project as unsalvageable. I opt for a more optimistic view: I suggest that there is scope for redeeming the egalitarian vision of human rights, but it cannot come about through concessions to the politics and practices of othering.

V. RESPONDING TO THE CHALLENGE WITH INTEGRITY: (RE)AFFIRMING HUMAN DIGNITY

Attacks on human rights cut to the very core of human rights when they deny or effectively (seek to) dismantle the equal moral status of all persons: their

[92] Rejali (above n 56) 4. See also M Lazreg, *Torture and the Twilight of Empire: From Algiers to Baghdad* (Princeton, Princeton University Press, 2008). In relation to British torture, see I Cobain, *Cruel Britannia: A Secret History of Torture* (London, Portobello Books, 2013).

[93] Rejali (above n 56) 56–58.

[94] F Fanon, *Toward the African Revolution*, H Chevalier (trans) (New York, Grove Press, 1967) 64.

[95] U Baxi, *The Future of Human Rights* (Oxford, Oxford University Press, 2008) 48.

human dignity. While such denials are exemplified by wrongs such as torture, they are manifest in an array of other attacks on human rights that ultimately cast certain persons as the 'have-nots' of human rights. Such challenges may be prominent in the counterterrorism context, but they are also manifested in the politics of othering that pervade our securitised states. Defending human rights demands recognising and responding head-on to the dehumanising processes and discourses that so deeply undermine them, with a view to (re)affirming the equal moral status ascribed to all persons under human rights. This requires the (re)interpretation and (re)assertion of the demands of human rights in a way that coheres with the egalitarian, humanist essence of human rights.

My aims in this chapter have been twofold: the first has been to expose and confront the connection between what many present as an exceptional wrong on the one hand and the pervasive othering that we may be readier to tolerate on the other, both of which cut to the core of human rights. The second has been to highlight the need for a morally coherent response to the politics of othering undermining human rights, so that the fight to defend human rights is not fought at the expense of what they fundamentally stand for. This section focuses on this second aim.

To concretise my argument, I propose to reflect briefly on one dimension of the crisis facing the ECHR and, notably, the ECtHR. In Brexit UK, leaving the ECHR remains a possibility,[96] and it would be the culmination of a defiance with clear contagion potential.[97] The end of the ECHR would be an unwelcome development – to say the least – for those of us who believe that it embodies an invaluable bulwark against atrocity and oppression. Thus, some of the ECtHR's pragmatic supporters may be tempted to argue that the Court must temper its activism to appease contracting states and secure its continued survival.[98] Insofar as such arguments may be brought to bear on human rights cases concerning violations of the rights of persons whose vindication seems politically unsustainable, there is a risk that restraint may mean deferring to the politics of othering.

[96] See W Worley, 'Theresa May "Will Campaign to Leave the European Convention on Human Rights in 2020 Election"', *Independent* (29 December 2016).

[97] On this, see P Leach and A Donald, 'Russia Defies Strasbourg: Is Contagion Spreading?' *EJIL: Talk!* (European Journal of International Law blog) (19 December 2015), https://www.ejiltalk.org/russia-defies-strasbourg-is-contagion-spreading/; L Mälksoo, 'Russia's Constitutional Court Defies the European Court of Human Rights' (2016) 12 *European Constitutional Law Review* 377–95; and recently, 'Russian Court Rejects ECHR Order on $2bn Yukos Compensation', *RT* (19 January 2017), https://www.rt.com/politics/374197-russian-court-rules-echr-order/.

[98] There are elements of this, for example, in M Bossuyt, 'Is the European Court of Human Rights on a Slippery Slope?' in S Flogaitis, T Zwart, and J Fraser (eds), *The European Court of Human Rights and its Discontents: Turning Criticism into Strength* (Cheltenham, Edward Elgar, 2013). For a distinct, nuanced perspective on subsidiarity and appeasement in the context of the UK relationship with the ECtHR in particular, see H Fenwick, 'Enhanced Subsidiarity and a Dialogic Approach – Or Appeasement in Recent Cases on Criminal Justice, Public Order and Counter-Terrorism at Strasbourg Against the UK?' in Ziegler, Wicks, and Hodson (eds) (above n 89).

In 2012, for example, Joshua Rozenberg applauded the ECtHR findings in *Ahmad v UK*,[99] in which the Court, through dubious legal reasoning,[100] allowed the extradition of a number of terrorist suspects to the United States to face trial and likely long-term or whole-life imprisonment in supermax-security prisons.[101] He commented, 'No human rights court would last very long if it took the view that mass murderers and other convicted terrorists should not be locked up for a very long time indeed.'[102] Such statements risk trading the vital and complex function of the anti-torture norm in protecting prisoners[103] with a pragmatic 'how not to' shortcut to survival, guided by a clear sense of the victim hierarchy alluded to by Gies.[104]

In brief, I would advocate against deploying a pragmatism that distinguishes or condones the distinction between the deserving and the undeserving beneficiaries of human rights; or that accepts the setting apart of a category of persons whose human rights may be treated as collateral, to be sacrificed in the name of the long-term survival of human rights. It is fundamentally contradictory to pursue the long-term survival of human rights at the expense of their essence. The (predicted) popularity of (the beneficiaries of) judgments should not determine the supranational interpretation of human rights.

In the recent ECtHR Grand Chamber judgment in *Hutchinson v UK*,[105] one might locate hints of such problematic pragmatism. The finding of the majority of the Grand Chamber that whole-life sentences are *de jure* and *de facto* reducible under the relevant UK law is difficult to square with the statements of principle and conclusions of the Grand Chamber on the same issue in 2013 in *Vinter v UK*, subsequently applied in a number of cases.[106] In a strongly worded dissent, Judge Pinto de Albuquerque lamented the prospect that the Court's attempt at appeasing the UK government at the expense of prisoners' rights 'leaves the door wide open for certain governments to satisfy their electoral base and protect their favourite vested interests … [which] is not what the Convention is all about'.[107]

[99] *Ahmad v UK* (2013) 56 EHRR 1.

[100] See the criticism in N Mavronicola and F Messineo, 'Relatively Absolute? The Undermining of Article 3 ECHR in *Ahmad v UK*' (2013) 76(3) *Modern Law Review* 589–603.

[101] The finding in *Ahmad* that whole-life imprisonment without parole is Art 3-compatible has now been overtaken by the Grand Chamber judgment in *Vinter v UK* (2016) 63 EHRR 1. See Mavronicola, 'Inhuman and Degrading Punishment, Dignity, and the Limits of Retribution' (above n 87) 302 and 306.

[102] J Rozenberg, 'European Court Makes the Right Call on Abu Hamza', *Guardian* (10 April 2012).

[103] See, for example, N Rodley and M Pollard, *The Treatment of Prisoners under International Law*, 3rd edn (Oxford, Oxford University Press, 2009). On Art 3 ECHR and punishment, see N Mavronicola, 'Crime, Punishment and Article 3 ECHR: Puzzles and Prospects of Applying an Absolute Right in a Penal Context' (2015) 15(4) *Human Rights Law Review* 721–43.

[104] Gies (above n 89) 474.

[105] *Hutchinson v UK* (above n 87).

[106] See, for example, *Trabelsi v Belgium* (2015) 60 EHRR 21; and *Murray v Netherlands* (2017) 64 EHRR 3.

[107] *Hutchinson v UK* (above n 87) dissenting opinion of Judge Pinto de Albuquerque, para 38.

The challenge that the politics of othering poses to human rights demands a principled response, which we can refer to as 'integrity'.[108] Integrity in human rights law requires, at base, that the equal moral status of all persons is never abandoned. It demands that those determining human rights questions oppose rather than absorb the politics of othering. An integrity that rests on human dignity thus requires that the absolute character of the anti-torture norm is affirmed and more effectively secured, alongside similarly vital norms such as the prohibition of slavery. It also necessitates ensuring that any measures impinging on qualified rights in the name of security are not *de jure* or *de facto* discriminatory[109] and do not extinguish the core of any person's or group of persons' rights[110] in the name of a crude balancing act. Judgments that exemplify such integrity include *Gillan v UK*, which concerned overbroad stop-and-search powers capable of being exercised in an arbitrary and discriminatory manner,[111] and *A v UK*, which involved direct discrimination in the imposition of detention without trial on foreign terrorist suspects, as well as impingement of the core of the right to a fair hearing under Articles 5 and 6 ECHR in the closed proceedings preceding such orders of detention.[112]

Is integrity enough? One of the most potent challenges levied against Ronald Dworkin's integrity relates to its undue default adherence to the status quo[113] – a status quo inescapably shaped and tarnished by hegemonic practices of othering. Yet a focus on the archetypes and fundamentals of human rights unlocks the dynamic potential of integrity. A dynamic rather than 'reactionary' integrity may well reveal that principled coherence in human rights law demands a substantial reconsideration or even subversion of the way key principles have so far been concretised. To put it in simpler terms, dynamic integrity requires norm-interpreters and norm-appliers to countenance the prospect that 'we have been getting human dignity wrong (on X)'. This may come about especially through foregrounding the views of the maligned and/or marginalised 'Other'

[108] See R Dworkin, *Law's Empire* (first published 1986) (Oxford, Hart Publishing, 1998) esp chs 2 and 3. See also R Dworkin, *Freedom's Law: The Moral Reading of the American Constitution* (Cambridge, MA, Harvard University Press, 1996) 103, where Dworkin speaks of an 'integrity of principle'.

[109] The non-discrimination requirement is highlighted in numerous articles on counter-terrorism measures; see, for example, F de Londras, 'Can Counter-Terrorist Internment Ever be Legitimate?' (2011) 33(3) *Human Rights Quarterly* 593–619. Note too the non-discrimination proviso in many human rights instruments' derogation clauses, such as Art 4 of the International Covenant on Civil and Political Rights (ICCPR).

[110] On the minimum core or essence of a right, see, for example, *Ashingdane v United Kingdom* (1985) 7 EHRR 528, para 57.

[111] See *Gillan v United Kingdom* (2010) 50 EHRR 45, paras 76–87.

[112] See *A and Others v Secretary of State for the Home Department* [2004] UKHL 56; and *A v United Kingdom* (2009) 49 EHRR 29. In relation to the core of the right to a fair hearing, note the violation of Art 5(4) found in relation to a number of the applicants in *A v UK*, paras 202–24.

[113] See, for example, R West, 'Integrity and Universality: A Comment on Dworkin's *Freedom's Law*' (1997) 65 *Fordham Law Review* 1313–34. See also S Levinson, 'Hercules, Abraham Lincoln, the United States Constitution, and the Problem of Slavery' in A Ripstein (ed), *Ronald Dworkin* (Cambridge, Cambridge University Press, 2007).

in shaping and applying human rights standards.[114] A dynamic integrity can accommodate – indeed, support – a radical departure from the way certain human rights have been specified in particular contexts – for example, from the ECtHR case law on headscarf bans, which is premised on a 'neutrality' that, as William Simmons has put it, 'cauterises' the voice of the 'Other'.[115]

VI. CONCLUSION

Torture paradigmatically embodies the denial of a person's humanity. Its absolute prohibition reflects the egalitarian foundation of human rights – human dignity – on the basis of which all persons are accorded an equally elevated moral status demanding certain minimum protections. At the same time, the inhumanity we locate in torture lies on a continuum of othering. This continuum encompasses what might sometimes be considered the more 'banal' or acceptable mechanics and expressions of othering that pervade counterterrorism and underpin prominent challenges to human rights. Just as the prohibition of torture must be vigorously defended by proponents of human rights, so too must the politics of othering be confronted and resisted rather than absorbed, through an integrity that not only protects but foregrounds those who are pervasively dehumanised through systematic or systemic othering.

REFERENCES

Améry, J, *At the Mind's Limits: Contemplations by a Survivor on Auschwitz and Its Realities* (Bloomington, Indiana University Press, 1980).

Amnesty International, 'A Blueprint for Despair: Human Rights Impact of the EU–Turkey Deal' (2017), http://www.amnesty.eu/content/assets/Reports/EU-Turkey_Deal_Briefing_Formatted_Final_P4840-3.pdf.

Ashworth, A, 'Security, Terrorism, and the Value of Human Rights' in BJ Goold and L Lazarus (eds), *Security and Human Rights* (Oxford, Hart Publishing, 2007).

Baxi, U, *The Future of Human Rights* (Oxford, Oxford University Press, 2008).

Berenson, T, 'Donald Trump Defends Torture at Republican Debate', *TIME* (3 March 2016).

Bernstein, JM, *Torture and Dignity: An Essay on Moral Injury* (Chicago, University of Chicago Press, 2015).

[114] See W Simmons, *Human Rights Law and the Marginalized Other* (Cambridge, Cambridge University Press, 2011) 220–27.

[115] Ibid, ch 2. See also J Marshall, 'Conditions for Freedom? European Human Rights Law and the Islamic Headscarf Debate' (2008) 30 *Human Rights Quarterly* 631–54. For the Court's approach on this, see, for example, *Şahin v Turkey* (2007) 44 EHRR 5. On the topic of 'burkini bans' in Europe, see also the chapter in this volume by Rumee Ahmed and Ayesha S Chaudhry.

Bigo, D and Guild, E, 'The Worst-Case Scenario and the Man on the Clapham Omnibus' in BJ Goold and L Lazarus (eds), *Security and Human Rights* (Oxford, Hart Publishing, 2007).

Borg-Barthet, J and Lyons, C, 'The European Union Migration Crisis' (2016) 20(2) *Edinburgh Law Review* 230–35.

Bossuyt, M, 'Is the European Court of Human Rights on a Slippery Slope?' in S Flogaitis, T Zwart, and J Fraser (eds), *The European Court of Human Rights and its Discontents: Turning Criticism into Strength* (Cheltenham, Edward Elgar, 2013).

Bourbeau, P, *The Securitization of Migration: A Study of Movement and Order* (Abingdon, Routledge, 2011).

Breen-Smyth, M, 'Theorising the "Suspect Community": Counterterrorism, Security Practices and the Public Imagination' (2013) 7(2) *Critical Studies on Terrorism* 223–40.

Bush, GW (White House), 'Humane Treatment of al Qaeda and Taliban Detainees', memorandum (7 February 2002), available at https://www.aclu.org/legal-document/presidential-memo-feb-7-2002-humane-treatment-al-qaeda-and-taliban-detainees.

Carver, R and Handley, L, *Does Torture Prevention Work?* (Liverpool, Liverpool University Press, 2016).

Choudhury, T and Fenwick, H, 'The Impact of Counter-terrorism Measures on Muslim Communities', Equality and Human Rights Commission Research Report 72 (2011).

Cobain, I, *Cruel Britannia: A Secret History of Torture* (London, Portobello Books, 2013).

Cole, D, *Enemy Aliens* (New York, New Press 2003).

—— (ed), *The Torture Memos: Rationalizing the Unthinkable* (New York, New Press, 2009).

Conservative Party, 'Protecting Human Rights in the UK: The Conservatives' Plans for Changing Britain's Human Rights Laws' (2014), https://www.conservatives.com/~/media/files/downloadable%20files/human_rights.pdf.

Daniels, R, *Prisoners Without Trial: Japanese Americans in World War II* (New York, Hill and Wang, 2004).

Dayan, C, *The Law Is a White Dog* (Princeton, Princeton University Press, 2011).

de Londras, F, 'Can Counter-Terrorist Internment Ever be Legitimate?' (2011) 33(3) *Human Rights Quarterly* 593–619.

——, F, *Detention in the War on Terror: Can Human Rights Fight Back?* (Cambridge, Cambridge University Press, 2006).

Dove, R (ed), *'Totally Un-English'? Britain's Internment of 'Enemy Aliens' in Two World Wars* (Leiden, Brill, 2005).

DuBois, P, *Torture and Truth* (Abingdon, Routledge, 1991).

Dworkin, R, *Freedom's Law: The Moral Reading of the American Constitution* (Cambridge, MA, Harvard University Press, 1996).

——, *Law's Empire* (first published 1986) (Oxford, Hart Publishing, 1998).

——, 'The Threat to Patriotism', *New York Review of Books* (28 February 2002).

Economist, 'The Real Price of Freedom: Civil Liberties under Threat', *Economist* (20 September 2007).

Elliott, M, 'A Damp Squib in the Long Grass: The Report of the Commission on a Bill of Rights' (2013) *European Human Rights Law Review* 137–51.

Fanon, F, *Toward the African Revolution*, H Chevalier (trans) (New York, Grove Press, 1967).

Farrell, M, *The Prohibition of Torture in Exceptional Circumstances* (Cambridge, Cambridge University Press, 2013).

Fenwick, H, 'Enhanced Subsidiarity and a Dialogic Approach – Or Appeasement in Recent Cases on Criminal Justice, Public Order and Counter-Terrorism at Strasbourg Against the UK?' in KS Ziegler, E Wicks and L Hodson (eds), *The UK and European Human Rights: A Strained Relationship?* (Oxford, Hart Publishing, 2015).

Finnis, J, 'Judicial Power: Past, Present and Future', Policy Exchange Lecture, Grey's Inn Hall (21 October 2015), http://judicialpowerproject.org.uk/wp-content/uploads/2015/10/John-Finnis-lecture-20102015.pdf.

Fredman, S, 'Human Rights Transformed: Positive Duties and Positive Rights' (2006) *Public Law* 498–520.

Friedrichs, J, 'Defining the International Public Enemy: The Political Struggle Behind the Legal Debate on International Terrorism' (2006) 19(1) *Leiden Journal of International Law* 69–91.

Gearty, C, 'Terrorism and Morality' (2003) *European Human Rights Law Review* 377–83.

Gewirth, A, 'Are There Any Absolute Rights?' (1981) 31 *Philosophical Quarterly* 1–16.

Gies, L, 'Human Rights, the British Press and the Deserving Claimant' in KS Ziegler, E Wicks, and L Hodson (eds), *The UK and European Human Rights: A Strained Relationship?* (Oxford, Hart Publishing, 2015).

Ginbar, Y, *Why Not Torture Terrorists?* (Oxford, Oxford University Press, 2008).

Gkliati, M, 'The EU–Turkey Deal and the Safe Third Country Concept before the Greek Asylum Appeals Committees' (2017) 3(2) *Movements: Journal for Critical Migration and Border Regime Studies* 213–24.

Greer, S, 'Is the Prohibition against Torture, Cruel, Inhuman and Degrading Treatment Really "Absolute" in International Human Rights Law?' (2015) 15 *Human Rights Law Review* 101–37.

Grief, N and Addo, M, 'Some Practical Issues Affecting the Notion of Absolute Right in Article 3 ECHR' (1998) 23 *European Law Review* 17–30.

Hillyard, P, *Suspect Community: People's Experience of the Prevention of Terrorism Acts in Britain* (London, Pluto Press, 1993).

Jackson, R, *Writing the War on Terrorism: Language, Politics and Counter-terrorism* (Manchester, Manchester University Press, 2005).

Lazaridis, G, Campani, G, and Benveniste, A (eds), *The Rise of the Far Right in Europe: Populist Shifts and 'Othering'* (Basingstoke, Palgrave Macmillan, 2016).

Lazarus, L, 'Mapping the Right to Security' in BJ Goold and L Lazarus (eds), *Security and Human Rights* (Oxford, Hart Publishing, 2007).

Lazarus, L and Goold, BJ, 'Introduction: Security and Human Rights – The Search for a Language of Reconciliation' in BJ Goold and L Lazarus (eds), *Security and Human Rights* (Oxford, Hart Publishing, 2007).

Lazreg, M, *Torture and the Twilight of Empire: From Algiers to Baghdad* (Princeton, Princeton University Press, 2008).

Leach, P and Donald, A, 'Russia Defies Strasbourg: Is Contagion Spreading?' *EJIL: Talk!* (European Journal of International Law blog) (19 December 2015), https://www.ejiltalk.org/russia-defies-strasbourg-is-contagion-spreading/.

Lenta, P, 'Waiting for the Barbarians after September 11' (2006) 42(1) *Journal of Postcolonial Writing* 71–83.

Levinson, S, 'Hercules, Abraham Lincoln, the United States Constitution, and the Problem of Slavery' in A Ripstein (ed), *Ronald Dworkin* (Cambridge, Cambridge University Press, 2007).

——, 'In Quest of a "Common Conscience": Reflections on the Current Debate about Torture' (2005) 1 *Journal of National Security Law and Policy* 231–52.

Luban, D, 'Eight Fallacies About Liberty and Security' in R Ashby Wilson (ed), *Human Rights in the 'War on Terror'* (Cambridge, Cambridge University Press, 2005).

——, 'Liberalism, Torture, and the Ticking Bomb' (2005) 91(6) *Virginia Law Review* 1425–61.

——, *Torture, Power, and Law* (Cambridge, Cambridge University Press, 2014).

Mälksoo, L, 'Russia's Constitutional Court Defies the European Court of Human Rights' (2016) 12 *European Constitutional Law Review* 377–95.

Mälksoo, L (ed), *Russia and European Human Rights Law: The Rise of the Civilizational Argument* (Leiden, Brill Nijhoff, 2014).

Marshall, J, 'Conditions for Freedom? European Human Rights Law and the Islamic Headscarf Debate' (2008) 30 *Human Rights Quarterly* 631–54.

Mavronicola, N, 'Crime, Punishment and Article 3 ECHR: Puzzles and Prospects of Applying an Absolute Right in a Penal Context' (2015) 15(4) *Human Rights Law Review* 721–43.

——, 'Inhuman and Degrading Punishment, Dignity, and the Limits of Retribution' (2014) 77(2) *Modern Law Review* 292.

——, 'Is the Prohibition against Torture and Cruel, Inhuman and Degrading Treatment Absolute in International Human Rights Law? A Reply to Steven Greer' (2017) 17(3) *Human Rights Law Review* 479–98.

——, 'What Is an "Absolute Right"? Deciphering Absoluteness in the Context of Article 3 of the European Convention on Human Rights' (2012) 12(4) *Human Rights Law Review* 723–58.

Mavronicola, N and Messineo, F, 'Relatively Absolute? The Undermining of Article 3 ECHR in *Ahmad v UK*' (2013) 76(3) *Modern Law Review* 589–603.

McEvoy, K, *Paramilitary Imprisonment in Northern Ireland: Resistance, Management, and Release* (Oxford, Oxford University Press, 2001).

McCrudden, C, 'Human Dignity and Judicial Interpretation of Human Rights' (2008) 19(4) *European Journal of International Law* 655–724.

Miles, T, 'Experts Warn Donald Trump Policy on Torture Could Be "Catastrophic"', *Independent* (31 January 2017).

Miller, ZJ, 'Obama: "We Tortured Some Folks"', *TIME* (1 August 2014).

Oette, L, 'Implementing the Prohibition of Torture: The Contribution and Limits of National Legislation and Jurisprudence' (2012) 16(5) *International Journal of Human Rights* 717–36.

Office of the Assistant Attorney General (USA), 'Memorandum for Alberto R Gonzales, Counsel to the President, and William J Haynes II, General Counsel of the Department of Defense' ('The Bybee Memo'), US Department of Justice (22 January 2002), available at http://www.washingtonpost.com/wp-srv/nation/documents/012202bybee.pdf.

Pantazis, C and Pemberton, S, 'From the "Old" to the "New" Suspect Community: Examining the Impacts of Recent UK Counter-Terrorist Legislation' (2009) 49 *British Journal of Criminology* 646–66.

Rejali, D, *Torture and Democracy* (Princeton, New Jersey, Princeton University Press, 2007).

Rodley, N, *The Treatment of Prisoners under International Law* (Oxford, Oxford University Press, 1999).

Rodley, N and Pollard, M, *The Treatment of Prisoners under International Law*, 3rd edn (Oxford, Oxford University Press, 2009).

Rozenberg, J, 'European Court Makes the Right Call on Abu Hamza', *Guardian* (10 April 2012).

RT, 'Russian Court Rejects ECHR Order on $2bn Yukos Compensation', *RT* (19 January 2017), https://www.rt.com/politics/374197-russian-court-rules-echr-order/.

Sands, P, *Torture Team: Deception, Cruelty and the Compromise of Law* (London, Allen Lane, 2008).

Satterthwaite, M, 'Rendered Meaningless: Extraordinary Rendition and the Rule of Law' (2007) 75 *George Washington Law Review* 1333–420.

Scarry, E, *The Body in Pain: The Making and Unmaking of the World* (Oxford, Oxford University Press, 1985).

Schmitt, C, *Der Begriff des Politischen* (Berlin, Duncker & Humblot, 1932).

Senate Select Committee on Intelligence (USA), 'Committee Study of the Central Intelligence Agency's Detention and Interrogation Program' (2012), declassified version (3 December 2014), available at https://www.amnestyusa.org/pdfs/sscistudy1.pdf.

Shelton, D and Gould, A, 'Positive and Negative Obligations' in D Shelton (ed), *The Oxford Handbook of International Human Rights Law* (Oxford, Oxford University Press, 2013).

Shue, H, *Basic Rights: Subsistence, Affluence, and US Foreign Policy*, 2nd edn (Princeton, New Jersey, Princeton University Press, 1996).

——, *Fighting Hurt* (Oxford, Oxford University Press, 2016).

——, 'Torture' (1978) 7(2) *Philosophy & Public Affairs* 124–43.

——, 'Torture in Dreamland: Disposing of the Ticking Bomb (2006) 37(2) *Case Western Reserve Journal of International Law* 231–39.

Simmons, W, *Human Rights Law and the Marginalized Other* (Cambridge, Cambridge University Press, 2011).

Spano, R, 'Universality or Diversity of Human Rights?' (2014) 14(3) *Human Rights Law Review* 487–502.

Sussman, D, 'What's Wrong with Torture?' (2005) 33(1) *Philosophy and Public Affairs* 1–33.

Talbot, S, '"Us" and "Them": Terrorism, Conflict and (O)ther Discursive Formations' (2008) 13(1) *Sociological Research Online* 17.

Tasioulas, J, 'Human Dignity and the Foundations of Human Rights' in C McCrudden (ed), *Understanding Human Dignity* (Oxford, Oxford University Press, 2013).

Tiessink, M, 'Not in My Backyard: The European Refugee Crisis', *Euractiv* (8 September 2015), http://www.euractiv.com/section/global-europe/opinion/not-in-my-backyard-the-european-refugee-crisis/.

UN Human Rights Council, 'Report of the UN Special Rapporteur on Torture and Other Cruel, Inhuman or Degrading Treatment or Punishment', UN doc A/HRC/34/54 (14 February 2017).

UN Special Rapporteur on Extrajudicial, Summary or Arbitrary Executions, 'Unlawful Death of Refugees and Migrants', Report to the UN General Assembly, UN doc A/72/335 (15 August 2017).

van Zyl Smit, D, Weatherby, P, and Creighton, S, 'Whole Life Sentences and the Tide of European Human Rights Jurisprudence: What Is to Be Done?' (2014) 14(1) *Human Rights Law Review* 59–84.

Waldron, J, *Dignity, Rank, and Rights* (Oxford, Oxford University Press, 2012).
——, 'Security and Liberty: The Image of Balance' (2003) 11(2) *Journal of Political Philosophy* 191–210.
——, 'Torture and Positive Law: Jurisprudence for the White House' (2005) 105(6) *Columbia Law Review* 1681–750.
——, *Torture, Terror and Trade-Offs: Philosophy for the White House* (Oxford, Oxford University Press, 2012).
Weiler, J, 'The Transformation of Europe' (1991) 100(8) *Yale Law Journal* 2403–83.
Wendel, WB, 'The Torture Memos and the Demands of Legality' (2009) 12 *Legal Ethics* 107–23.
West, R, 'Integrity and Universality: A Comment on Dworkin's Freedom's Law' (1997) 65 *Fordham Law Review* 1313–34.
Williams, P, 'By Any Means Necessary', *Nation* (26 November 2001).
Worley, W, 'Theresa May "Will Campaign to Leave the European Convention on Human Rights in 2020 Election"', *Independent* (29 December 2016).
Ze'ev Bekerman, O, 'Torture – The Absolute Prohibition of a Relative Term: Does Everyone Know What Is in Room 101?' (2005) 53 *American Journal of Comparative Law* 743–83.
Zedner, L, 'Seeking Security by Eroding Rights: The Side-Stepping of Due Process' in BJ Goold and L Lazarus (eds), *Security and Human Rights* (Oxford, Hart Publishing, 2007).

3

Their Bodies, Ourselves: Muslim Women's Clothing at the Intersection of Rights, Security, and Extremism

RUMEE AHMED AND AYESHA S CHAUDHRY

I. SECULAR AND RELIGIOUS EXTREMISMS

LET'S BEGIN THIS chapter with a story. In 2004, an Australian woman named Aheda Zanetti noticed that her niece was not enjoying the water sports and beach culture so popular in Australia for a reason that seemed simple and easily addressable (ha!): she was uncomfortable in the water sport and beach attire available to her.[1] In fact, she was participating in water sports, but the clothes she was wearing got heavy and cumbersome when wet. Zanetti worried that her niece might be discouraged from participating in water sports unless she found outfits she would be more comfortable wearing. This Australian woman, who is also Muslim and Lebanese, saw that her niece was trying to negotiate her national, cultural, and religious identities. Rather than pressing her niece to arrange these identities hierarchically – either by asking her to wear less clothing or by telling her to stop playing water sports – Zanetti tried to facilitate her niece's negotiations so that she could carry all of her identities lightly, with ease, without any one identity being burdensome and cumbersome.

Zanetti went online and searched for water sport outfits that were less revealing, more concealing, but made from lightweight fabric that was water friendly. To her surprise, she couldn't find anything, so she set about designing an ideal outfit for her niece. As she designed an outfit that covered the body but also allowed for comfortable water sport activity, it occurred to Zanetti that

[1] 'Bukini Swimsuits Spark Anti-Muslim Outrage – and Fast Sales', *Newsweek* (8 August 2016), http://www.newsweek.com/2016/08/19/burkini-swimsuits-spark-anti-muslim-outrage-sales-488138.html.

this problem was likely not unique to her niece. Rather, it was likely that many women around the world might not be able to enjoy water sports and beach culture because of the limited dress options available to them. Seeing an opportunity to serve women with various relationships to their bodies – relationships mediated by and filtered through social, cultural, religious expectations and standards for female beauty and virtue – Zanetti designed an outfit that would offer an alternative to the bikinis and one-pieces that dominated and still dominate the women's swimwear market.

Seeing this also for the entrepreneurial opportunity that it was – How had no one done this already? – Zanetti designed a lightweight, water-friendly prototype that was loose fitting rather than tight fitting, covered the entire body with the exception of the hands and feet, and came with an optional headpiece that covered all but the face. Brilliantly, she combined the words 'bikini' and 'burqa' and named her product the 'burkini'. The bikini and the burqa are heavy with political meaning; both items of clothing represent opposing ideas about ideal femininity, opposing ideas about the correct standard for measuring the 'civilization' of a people or nation; both politicise women's bodies by making them measures for progressiveness or backwardness; both elicit strong emotional responses; both can reduce women's bodies to objects, texts that are read and that articulate the virtue and moral righteousness of various communities; and both are used by women the world over to express agency and control, liberation and freedom.[2] Read in this way, the burkini could be a site of resistance, a middle ground, offering women a space between two politicised kinds of clothing – a third option.

The burkini was immediately popular, one of those creations whose time had arrived before it appeared. The world was already hungry for the burkini, and within a decade, the Australian company founded by Zanetti was valued at several million dollars. The burkini is now carried internationally by large department stores, including Marks and Spencer, where it is often on back order. Zanetti's hunch in 2004 had been correct: the burkini's appeal crossed religious and cultural boundaries, proving those boundaries to be porous, soft, undefined. While the product was popular for Muslim women, an estimated thirty-five to forty-five per cent of the sales were made to non-Muslim women.[3] Women were attracted to burkinis for various reasons, including health, body consciousness, religion, and culture. The burkini meant they could participate in water sports and beach culture in dedicated beach attire and swimwear while being free from

[2] The political resonances of the burqa and the burkini, both independently and in relation to one another, have been well-documented and theorised. See, for example, T Hefferman, *Veiled Figures: Women, Modernity and the Spectres of Orientalism* (Toronto, University of Toronto Press, 2016) 119–44; PK Mingati, 'Burqinis, Bikinis and Bodies: Encounters in Public Pools in Italy and Sweden' in E Tarlo and A Moors (eds), *Islamic Fashion and Anti-Fashion: New Perspectives from Europe and North America* (London, Bloomsbury, 2013) 33–54; and C Schmidt, *The Swimsuit: Fashion from Poolside to Catwalk* (London, Berg, 2012) especially ch 2.

[3] 'Bukini Swimsuits Spark Anti-Muslim Outrage' (above n 1).

the social pressure of baring themselves beyond their comfort level. It expanded women's range of options.[4]

The story of Zanetti is a story of ingenuity and entrepreneurship, risk-taking and innovation. The story of the burkini is a story of female empowerment, of the best that multiple identities and pluralism has to offer. This is a story of a Muslim woman creating, marketing, and selling a product that serves the needs of diverse women, worldwide – a product that crosses religious and cultural boundaries, facilitates the management of multiple identities, some of which might seem in tension with each other or might feel contradictory. The burkini is, at its best, a bridge, a language, a passageway that makes it possible to embrace and hold several values at once: the right of women to wear what they want, the right of women to occupy public spaces, the right of women to engage in leisurely public activities, the right of women to have agency in the kind of femininity they perform.

It is also a story that checks every box in the celebratory narratives of the 'free', 'independent', 'liberated' woman, while also turning the conventional script for Muslim women on its head. There is no familiar trope for a middle-class Australian-Lebanese Muslim woman who goes on to own a multimillion dollar company that markets to diverse populations around the world. Yet it is precisely Zanetti's various identities that allowed her successfully to navigate a path through integration and pluralism. As such, her story defies and exposes the false binary between 'the West' and 'Islam'. Insofar as the story of the burkini is the story of a Muslim woman – as opposed to, say, an Australian woman (which she is, and can you really separate the two identities in a person?) – this story subverts every caricatured imagine of Muslim women. Zanetti's various identities work together to make her successful: they do not hold her back but rather push her forward.

So it is puzzling that instead of this story being celebrated as the epitome of pluralism, feminism, human rights, and multiculturalism – ideals of liberal democracies the world over – the burkini has become a symbol of misogyny, anti-assimilation, anti-pluralism, racism, xenophobia, and Islamophobia.[5] How did the ascribed meaning of the burkini flip from one that increases women's choices and agency over their own bodies while facilitating integration to one that decreases women's agency and choices, prevents women from enjoying the

[4] The burkini is regularly discussed in relation to the ideas of 'choice' and 'options' in scholarly articles (eg, S Limoochi and J Le Clair, 'Reflections on the Participation of Muslim Women in Disability Sport: Hijab, Burkini®, Modesty and Changing Strategies' (2011) 14(9) *Sport in Society* 1300–9) and in popular articles (eg, A Ibtisam, 'Bikini to Burkini: The Choice is Yours', *South Asian Generation Next* (3 February 2010), http://www.sagennext.com/2010/02/03/bikini-to-burkini-%E2%80%93-the-choice-is-yours/.

[5] I Ajala, 'From Islamic Dress and Islamic Fashion to Cool Islam: An Exploration of Muslim Youth Hybrid Identities in the West' (2017) 12(3) *International Journal of Interdisciplinary Cultural Studies* 1–11; S Tang, *Disrobed: How Clothing Predicts Economic Cycles, Saves Lives, and Determines the Future* (Lanham, MD, Rowman and Littlefield, 2017) 111.

beach, and ostracises those who are unwilling to don specific outfits to enjoy the beach?

The emergence of the burkini as a site of contestation rather than celebration became apparent in the summer of 2016, when several towns and cities in France, Austria, and Germany instituted burkini bans, forbidding women from wearing burkinis. The bans were justified in the name of women's freedom and resistance against patriarchy, the claim being that the burkini oppresses women, is anti-feminist, and is a hygiene risk.[6]

In banning the burkini, these European towns mimicked the very institutions and people they were critiquing, aping the actions and rhetoric of the very particular expressions of religion they claimed to find abominable.[7] The European bans used the language of security, public order, hygiene, and purity in order to justify their control of and restrictions on women's sartorial choices, making it difficult for some of them to be in public spaces without compromising their comfort and safety.[8] Muslim women were singled out as burkini-wearers (despite the fact that many non-Muslim women also wear burkinis), and they were made to feel unsafe through the language of safety. In other words, their security was jeopardised in the name of security.[9]

In the face of the story of Aheda Zanetti and the burkini ban, let us consider some images that were widely circulated in the summer of 2016.[10] The setting is a sunny beach in Nice, France, filled with swimmers, sunbathers, and sand. A woman is lying on her side in a relaxed pose, wearing a long black tunic, tights, and a blue cap on her head. Then she is surrounded by four police officers, all white, all male, their weapons – guns and batons – clearly on display, threatening physical violence. The officers, two of whom are themselves covered from head to toe with the exception of their arms, hands, and heads, demand

[6] C Jung, 'Criminalization of the Burkini' (2016) 37(5) *Harvard International Review* 6–7; and S Tayyen, 'From Orientalist Sexual Object to Burkini Terrorist Threat: Muslim Women through Evolving Lens' (2017) 4(1) *Islamophobia Studies Journal* 101–14.

[7] P Baehr and D Gordon, 'From the Headscarf to the Burqa: The Role of Social Theorists in Shaping Laws against the Veil' (2013) 42(2) *Economy and Society* 249–80; and G Gustavsson, J van der Noll, and R Sundberg, 'Opposing the Veil in the Name of Liberalism: Popular Attitudes to Liberalism and Muslim Veiling in the Netherlands' (2016) 39(10) *Ethnic and Racial Studies* 1719–37.

[8] M Abdelaal, 'Extreme Secularism vs. Religious Radicalism: The Case of the French Burkini' (2017) 23(3) *ILSA Journal of International and Comparative Law* 443–68; S Laegaard, 'Burqa Ban, Freedom of Religion and "Living Together"' (2015) 16(3) *Human Rights Review* 203–19; and S Kovach-Orr, 'Banning the Burka: Indicative of a Legitimate Aim or a Thinly-Veiled Attempt to Legislate Religious and Cultural Intolerance' (2016) 18(1) *Rutgers Journal of Law and Religion* 89–100.

[9] H Afshar, 'The Politics of Fear: What Does It Mean to Those Who Are Otherized and Feared?' (2013) 36(1) *Ethnic and Racial Studies* 9–27; L Berg and M Lundahl, 'Un/veiling the West: Burkini-Gate, Princess Hijab and Dressing as Struggle for Postsecular Integration' (2016) 8(3) *Culture Unbound* 263–83; and C Hopkins, 'Social Reproduction in France: Religious Dress Laws and *Laïcité*' (2015) 48 *Women's Studies International Forum* 154–64.

[10] B Quinn, 'French Police Make Woman Remove Clothing on Nice Beach Following Burkini Ban', *Guardian* (24 August 2016), https://www.theguardian.com/world/2016/aug/24/french-police-make-woman-remove-burkini-on-nice-beach.

the woman remove her clothing, and in a series of shots, you see her removing her shirt, then her cap, as someone outside of the frame takes photos. We can see other bathers, white people in bathing suits and bikinis, watching. They are not smiling. Their gaze is unkind. We later learn that some of them encouraged the officers, clapping for them and berating the woman by shouting 'Go home!' Her daughter was crying. No one attempted to stop the officers or protect the vulnerable woman on the ground who was being forced to disrobe, to strip in the public gaze, as four white men towered over her, circled her, peered down at her. And then she was fined. Not the officers. The woman. Apparently, her outfit is what was threatening, what compromised security – not the officers, not her forced public disrobing.

The picture of white male police officers compelling a covered woman to disrobe recalls and inverts another kind picture that is familiar in our media, another kind of policing of the Muslim female body: the picture of bearded brown men in Iran, Afghanistan, Saudi Arabia, forcing women to cover, compelling women to cover, to pull the chador more closely around their necks, be sure to catch all the hair, to not leave an ankle or a wrist exposed. This threat of violence against the exposed female body for the sake of protecting the female body, for protecting society, for fear of social chaos – this threat too is made against Muslim women in the language of security. Here, too, Muslim women's bodies are perceived to threaten security, and thus their own security is jeopardised in the name of security.

The striking similarity between secular language and religious language about Muslim women's bodies demonstrate that, despite the claims of both 'religious' and 'secular' people and despite the performance of the two as binaries, religion and secularism are not actually binaries. They are both contested categories, they both offer moral narratives of how the world ought to work, and they flow from each other; they are formed in relation to each other. So it should come as no surprise that there are extremist, intolerant forms of secularism, just as there are such forms of religiosity; and on the flip-side, there are pluralistic, tolerant forms of religion, just as there are such forms of secularism.

Similarities between the ways that both religion and secularism operate abound because humans are not so original as to create entirely unique moral narratives. Rather, we recycle old ideas in new language. Hence, the reliance on ideas of 'hygiene' when banning the burkini.[11] Hygiene is another word for purity. Purity, which must be carried by the female body for us, by the silent Muslim female body, so that we can feel purer ourselves, so our self-narratives

[11] 'Hygiene' as term of inclusion and exclusion in security discourses has been most authoritatively theorised in A Bashford, *Imperial Hygiene: A Critical History of Colonialism, Nationalism and Public Health* (New York, Springer, 2004); and in several essays in A Bashford (ed), *Medicine at the Border: Disease, Globalization and Security, 1850–Present* (New York, Springer, 2007) esp chs 1 and 2.

are not ruptured, so we can remain liberal, and feminist, and progressive, even as we ban women's clothing, restrict their choices, prevent them from wearing clothes we do not wish to see, demand they contort their bodies so our sight is untroubled, so we are pleased.[12]

Claims of purity then, become rallying cries for security. Any threat to purity is a pollution, and pollution threatens chaos.[13] It becomes easy, in the face of maintaining purity, to strip people – literally and figuratively – of their civil liberties, including the freedom of religious expression and the right of women to wear what they like. In this discourse, 'security' comes to mean the opposite of its plain-sense meaning; instead of protecting human rights, it comes to justify stripping citizens of their human rights. And hence the scenario in which four male officers can demand a woman who is deemed to be wearing too much clothing to remove her tunic, her cap, and whatever else is too threatening for the beach. In this and in all security conversations, we must ask: who is making claims of providing protection? Who is being protected from whom? And by what means?

Around the globe today, in religious and secular contexts, the female Muslim body has come to serve as the lynchpin for justifying the securitised state – a state in which various rights and liberties are removed from citizens in service of the 'security' of the state. In Saudi Arabia, Muslim women must wear face veils in public. The Taliban and ISIS likewise demand that Muslim women conceal their entire bodies, including their faces, or else be punished. They make these arguments in the name of 'protecting' society from social chaos. Covered women are less likely to be harassed, they say; covered women are protected from the ravenous male gaze. They are also protected from the corrupting influence of 'the West', which seeks to colonise Muslim women's bodies, turning them into Trojan horses that will destroy 'Islam' from within. Muslim women who cover are touted as purer, as preserving the honour of the state. The purity of the state's intentions and adherence to 'Islam' is demonstrated, enacted upon and through the bodies of Muslim women, so that the state is the ventriloquist and Muslim women's bodies mere puppets. Muslim women are required to wear the correct uniform, the right garb, to ensure they project a certain image of the men who claim them.

[12] The notion that these bans represent a kind of 'negative mirror' has been theorised in works such as A al-Saji, 'The Racialization of Muslim Veils: A Philosophical Analysis' (2010) 36(8) *Philosophy and Social Criticism* 875–902; and Á Ramírez, 'Control over Female "Muslim" Bodies: Culture, Politics and Dress Code Laws in Some Muslim and non-Muslim Countries' (2015) 22(6) *Identities: Global Studies in Culture and Power* 671–86. These works are often grounded in the theories of F Fanon, *Peau Noire, Masques Blancs* (Paris, Seuil, 1971); and M Douglas, *Purity and Danger* (London, Routledge, 1966).

[13] There are also economic concerns that intersect with political and social concerns linking purity to social cohesion, political progress, and economic strength. See L Malkki, *Purity and Exile: Violence, Memory, and National Cosmology among Hutu Refugees in Tanzania* (Chicago, University of Chicago Press, 1995); and A McClintock, 'Soft-Soaping Empire: Commodity Racism and Imperial Advertising' in J Bird et al (eds), *Traveller's Tales: Narratives of Home and Displacement* (London, Routledge, 1994).

These visions of Islam are of course contested. Other Muslim-majority nations have no official dress codes for Muslim women: for example, Egypt, Indonesia, Bangladesh, and Nigeria. At the other end of the spectrum, countries like Iran under the Shah and Turkey until recently prohibited Muslim women from wearing veils in public and denied them education and jobs if they did not adhere to a 'secular' dress code. These Muslim-majority states adhered to extremism as well – not religious extremism, but secular extremism. And this secular extremism is the same demonstrated in French towns and cities that banned the burkini, despite their bans being overturned as unconstitutional by the federal government.[14] Advocates for the bans argued that they were trying to 'save' Muslim women in Europe, as well as 'save' Europeans from the corrupting influences of Islam. They were trying to preserve their culture and traditions by forcing women to reveal their bodies more fully, and they also cast Muslim women as Trojan horses who challenge the purity of secularism both literally and figuratively by the imagined hygiene risk posed by the burkini (notwithstanding the lack of evidence of such risk) and by raising children who would never be truly 'French' but rather 'Muslim' first and only.

II. SECURITY AND THE SUPRARATIONAL

These are, to say the least, very strange reactions to clothing. Both secular and religious extremisms place a curious emphasis on the extent to which Muslim women's bodies are covered or uncovered in their security conversations. Why is it that the Muslim female body and its state of (un)dress is so central to security conversations the world over, such that discussions of 'safety', 'purity', and 'protection' inevitably centre on Muslim women? One would think that, assuming a rational-actor analysis, Muslim women would be but one group of individuals whose human rights should be balanced in the quest for security, and that their centrality in security discussions should be relative only to their power and potential to harm.

But security conversations, of which law is only a subset, notoriously resist rational analysis.[15] 'Security', conceived broadly, is itself a concept built upon our deepest anxieties,[16] and instead of rational logic, security operates

[14] D Almeida, 'Marianne at the Beach: The French Burkini Controversy and the Shifting Meanings of Republican Secularism' (2018) 39(1) *Journal of Intercultural Studies* 20–34; E Chabal, 'From the *Banlieue* to the Burkini: The Many Lives of French Republicanism' (2017) 25(1) *Modern and Contemporary France* 68–74.

[15] See the essays in M Brown et al (eds), *Rational Choice and Security Studies: Stephen Walt and His Critics*, (Cambridge, MIT Press, 2000).

[16] We are using the term 'security' here in the broad sense of Giddens' 'ontological security', which, following Wittgenstein, links security to a sense of order and stability in current and future personal and societal states. A Giddens, *Modernity and Self-Identity: Self and Society in the Late Modern Age* (Stanford, Stanford University Press, 1991). See also R van Kriekan, 'Reassembling Civilization: State-Formation, Subjectivity, Security, Power' in A Yeatman and M Zolkos (eds), *State, Security,*

according to what philosophers call 'suprarational' logic.[17] This is a type of logic that describes a reality that transcends and even defies rationality. It is only within this suprarational framework of 'security' that the inordinate attention given to Muslim women makes any sense at all.

Security conversations, whether in a secular or religious context, are bound to operate in a suprarational space because 'security' itself is an impossible ideal. The precariousness of human life, the contingency of human existence, and the irremediable unpredictability of autonomous others ensures that individuals and societies will never achieve perfect security. Instead, we live in a state of perpetual insecurity, such that insecurity is perhaps the defining characteristic of human existence.[18] Despite – or perhaps because of – this fact, humans preoccupy themselves with constructing elaborate ideas about how to achieve complete security. There are innumerable theories on how to do so, including renouncing the world, serving others, returning to nature, installing benevolent dictators, and providing humans with a baseline of rights. Such security theories have internal languages and shared assumptions, and they debate and challenge rival theories. Security theories are developed and argued with passion and care precisely because security is so elusive, and the perennial lack of security feeds a seemingly constant human anxiety.[19]

Security discourses work to ameliorate this primal anxiety by imagining an ideal, secure world in which insecurity is abolished.[20] Humans are drawn to different notions of this secure world and, by extension, advocate different methods for achieving it. Whereas some are drawn to spiritual approaches, others are drawn to legalistic ones. The secure world that we find appealing says a great deal about us, as does the method that we advocate for realising that world. It speaks to the root of our anxiety and to our underlying beliefs about an ideal society. Sometimes those beliefs are noble – like that all humans should be treated equally – and sometimes they are ugly, betraying tribal and

and Subject Formation (London, Bloomsbury, 2010); and D Staniševski, 'Fear Thy Neighbor' (2011) 33(1) *Administrative Theory and Praxis* 62–79.

[17] The idea of the suprarational is prevalent in religious literature, though it was popularised as a philosophical term of art by German philosophers like Schleiermacher and Weber and has since been theorised in a number of different ways. In this chapter, suprarationality is used in its religio-pragmatic sense, following William James and Charles S Peirce. See P Ochs, 'Charles Peirce's Unpragmatic Christianity: A Rabbinic Appraisal' (1988) 9(1/2) *American Journal of Theology and Philosophy* 41–73.

[18] Weldes et al have argued that especially in the context of the modern state, 'insecurity and identity are produced in a mutually constitutive process.' Weldes et al, 'Introduction: Constructing Insecurity' in J Weldes et al (eds), *Cultures of Insecurity: States, Communities, and the Production of Danger* (Minneapolis, University of Minnesota Press, 1999) 11.

[19] For a succinct review of the relevant literature, see A Shreve-Neiger, 'Religion and Anxiety: A Critical Review of the Literature' (2004) 24(4) *Clinical Psychology Review* 379–97.

[20] E Griffin, 'In Violence and in Peace: The Role of Religion and Human Security' in J Wellman, Jr and C Lombardi (eds), *Religion and Human Security: A Global Perspective* (New York, Oxford University Press, 2012); and C Kinnvall, 'Globalization and Religious Nationalism: Self, Identity, and the Search for Ontological Security' (2004) 25(5) *Political Psychology* 741–67.

punitive predilections. We express our beliefs using (un)sophisticated discourses that reflect how we think the impossible, secure state is best achieved, and the very act of expressing our beliefs generates meaning and approximates some measure of control in a fundamentally insecure world.

Both secular and religious actors engage in this suprarational activity, which helps explain their extreme and irrational reactions to Muslim women's bodies. Understanding the suprarational logic that both religious and secular actors engage in will help us understand why Muslim women play such a prominent role in contemporary security debates. It's easier to spot in religious discourse, which is unabashedly suprarational, whereas secular discourse masks its suprarational nature in the seemingly rational language of human rights and law. That language is designed to appear logical and dispassionate, hiding the anxieties and suprarational logic animating the discourse itself. Uncovering it is most easily done by first examining how suprarational security logic works in religious discourses, especially in religious law, and then examining its parallels and resonances in secular ones.

III. SUPRARATIONALITY IN RELIGIOUS AND SECULAR LAWS

Since we are discussing Muslim women, it makes sense to explain suprarational religious security discourses using examples from Islamic religious literature. Within this literature, Muslim religious scholars from vastly diverse contexts demonstrate a constant preoccupation with security theories. The term for 'security' (*aman*) is a foundational Islamic concept and is a primary concern for Muslim religious scholars of all eras and backgrounds. Many Islamic scholars point out that the Arabic word for 'security' shares the same linguistic root as the word for 'belief' (*iman*), and so, they reason, true religious belief leads to security. But even likeminded Muslims have had trouble agreeing on how exactly to achieve such security, and scholars have gone to great lengths to describe their ideal versions of personal and societal security.[21]

Sufis, for instance, famously disagree about security. Some hold that the world is irremediably profane, and so one must look within in order to find the security one seeks. If one is secure within oneself, then the world falls away, and the renunciant transcends the world, which is the only way to achieve true security. Other Sufis argue that the world is a reflection of God, so one must learn to see God in all things. Once that is done, one achieves a kind of union with the world, and with that comes security. Yet other Sufis say that life is inherently insecure, and peace during life is impossible; however, if one embraces

[21] For an overview of security theories in Muslim scholarly thought and for many of the positions recounted below, see H Hanafi, 'Security Conceptualization in Arab Philosophy and Ethics and Muslim Perspectives' in H Brauch et al (eds), *Globalization and Environmental Challenges: Reconceptualizing Security in the 21st Century* (New York, Springer, 2008).

that inescapable insecurity and dedicates one's life to God, one will live in total security in the life hereafter. Each of these paths to security comes with attendant ideas about the self, about society, and about how to lead a good life.[22]

Some Islamic scholars feel that the best way to achieve security is to engage in a close study of law and rights. They believe that peace and security is possible if societies follow certain laws and if individuals live according to clearly delineated rights and responsibilities. To this end, they compose extensive tomes containing thousands of laws on everything from personal hygiene to inheritance to commerce to governance to marriage and divorce. These legal scholars debate minute points of law, spending lifetimes trying to convince one another of their positions in a bid to describe a legal world of perfect security.[23]

They do this not because they are engaged in legislation or security policy but because describing an ideal, secure world is itself a meaning-generating practice. Most Islamic legal scholars do not work for the state. Today, as throughout much of Muslim history, most Islamic legal scholars have no hard power; they live and work at the mercy of patronage networks and are rarely consulted by either the executive or the judiciary. And even when Islamic legal scholars are consulted, their opinions are rarely captured in legal codes or statutes, and there is no concept of judicial precedent in Islamic law, so that laws fluctuate, serving the beliefs, needs, and desires of the powerful. Yet Islamic legal scholars nonetheless dedicate their lives to the study of law, not because they are trying to influence state policy per se but because their legal discourse speaks to an anxiety about the relentless insecurity of the world, allowing them to express their beliefs about an ideal world and an ideal society that would provide citizens security in this life, if not the next, using legal language.

These scholars describe vastly different notions of an ideal society through the language of Islamic law. Some scholars argue for a strong, authoritarian state that privileges security over individual rights; others describe a quasi-secular state that has limited power to intervene in the lives of its residents. Yet other legal scholars describe a state in which the judiciary is the most powerful entity, mediating between a sovereign, to whom they confer executive authority, and the laity, whom they characterise as dependent on the judiciary for guidance. There are many more theories about an ideal, secure state that are highly detailed, using sophisticated legal discourse, championed by some scholars against others.[24]

None of these ideal scenarios actually exist, and it is in fact impossible for them to ever come to pass. That is because these ideal, secure worlds are highly

[22] These different Sufi theories and their political implications and contexts are described in detail in A Karamustafa, *Sufism: The Formative Period* (Edinburgh, Edinburgh University Press, 2007) esp 56–112.

[23] R Ahmed, *Sharia Compliant: A User's Guide to Hacking Islamic Law* (Stanford, Stanford University Press, 2018) 44–58; and W Hallaq, *An Introduction to Islamic Law* (Cambridge, Cambridge University Press, 2009) esp pt II.

[24] R Ahmed, 'Jurisprudence and Political Philosophy in Islam' in L Farjeat and R Taylor (eds), *The Routledge Companion to Islamic Philosophy* (New York, Routledge, 2016).

structured and require people to act in idealised ways that are constant, predictable, and restricted. People, however, are inherently unpredictable and act in ways that we would characterise sometimes as rational and sometimes as irrational. That reality does not deter Islamic legal thinkers though, since their interest is in the suprarational. In the face of the irremediable insecurity and unpredictability of the world, Islamic law as a genre confers meaning upon those working within and consuming it. Islamic legal texts describe how society *should* work, how people *should* act, and how laws *should* be articulated in order for society to attain perfect harmony, with the full knowledge that the world is not, nor ever will be, in perfect harmony.[25] The process of talking about how the world should work in order to achieve security generates meaning for groups and individuals, regardless of whether that reality is realised or indeed even possible.

It is therefore meaningful for Islamic legal scholars to use the discourse of law to describe a perfect world as if it existed, even though it does not and never will. With this mindset, they write books of Islamic law to describe ideal worlds, according citizens rights and responsibilities necessary for the proper functioning of their ideal, secure society, as though citizens act in idealised, predictable ways.[26] Of course, these ideal worlds only exist in the minds of scholars, as do the rights and responsibilities that they discuss. Thus, Islamic legal texts and the assumptions that they make about ideal worlds and ideal individuals tell us more about the minds of their authors than they do about any lived reality.

When reading these texts, we might find scholars interpreting technical legal terms native to Islamic legal discourse to suggest that the world is a scary place and that citizens need a strong sovereign to keep them in check. Or perhaps they might interpret those technical terms to describe a world in which power corrupts, and brave citizens are required to resist the evil tendencies of the powerful. Either way, their legal texts describe groups of people – citizens, foreigners, rulers, children – in caricature, such that they play roles that must be kept in balance in order to mitigate conflict and make the world secure.[27] Laws exist only to describe that ideal world and to assign people their proper roles. The laws are not ends unto themselves but are means for getting to an ideal, secure world, which is itself the ultimate goal. In fact, Muslim legal scholars write extensively about how the law should be suspended if any idealised characters were to overstep their bounds and threaten security,[28] which suggests that they believe that the law is mutable, whereas security is not.

[25] R Ahmed, *Narratives of Islamic Legal Theory* (Oxford, Oxford University Press, 2012) 152–53.
[26] AS Chaudhry, 'Domestic Violence and Idealized Cosmologies' in M Birkel (ed), *Qur'an in Conversation* (Waco, Baylor University Press, 2014).
[27] On how scholars constructed categories of persons in caricature, see A Emon, *Religious Pluralism and Islamic Law: Dhimmis and Others in the Empire of Law* (Oxford, Oxford University Press, 2012) 33–76. See also with respect to female subjects in Islamic law, H Azam, *Sexual Violation in Islamic Law: Substance, Evidence, and Procedure* (Cambridge, Cambridge University Press, 2015).
[28] S Tabassum, 'Combatants, Not Bandits: The Status of Rebels in Islamic Law' (2011) 93(881) *International Review of the Red Cross* 121–39.

So, let's say that a jurist uses legal language to describe an ideal world as a quasi-secular state in which the executive has limited authority to intervene in the lives of the laity. In this case, the ideal laity is described as generally competent, functioning best when left alone by the executive. Executives in turn are viewed with suspicion for their potential to corrupt the laity. In this world, the jurist uses Islamic law to maximise individual freedoms and to identify and neutralise any imposition from the executive upon the laity. The jurist would discuss all laws according to this dynamic, including, say, ideal zoning laws that would give maximum discretion to residents and minimal power to city planners. In this narrative, the normative citizen is a non-state actor who must be protected from encroachment by the state. This citizen is presented as a vulnerable character type, invariably male, who must be empowered against the state. State actors in this ideal world are likewise presented in caricature, in the persons of overzealous judges and power-hungry mayors who threaten the security and flourishing of municipalities. These state and non-state characters play scripted roles in the legal scholar's overall vision of a secure state, and they tell us more about the scholar's conception of the ideal world than they do about actual citizens, judges, mayors, and others.[29]

To take the converse example, legal scholars who favour authoritarianism are wary of individual rights and devise laws that expand the rights of state actors and limit the powers of lay citizens. Citizens, in this narrative, are always seen as potential threats to the social order who would, if empowered, ruin society. Again, the characters in this ideal world are one-dimensional and inherently unrealistic, interesting only insofar as they contribute to or detract from the scholar's vision of a secure state. This is of necessity. In order for the ideal world to work, individuals have to fulfil their ideal roles; and so, the more meticulously defined the ideal world, the more individuals have to conform to predefined caricatures.

This is how idealised discourses work, whether in a religious or a secular context. And whereas Islamic legal scholars might engage in this discourse in the language of Islamic law, secular legal scholars might engage in it using a language like human rights law.[30] Though often unacknowledged, human rights language is itself rooted in religious concepts[31] and accords people rights

[29] AS Chaudhry, *Domestic Violence and the Islamic Tradition: Ethics, Law, and the Muslim Discourse on Gender* (Oxford, Oxford University Press, 2014) 11–13.

[30] See many of the essays in AM Emon, M Ellis, and B Glahn (eds), *Islamic Law and International Human Rights Law* (Oxford, Oxford University Press, 2012). Nils Bubandt has similarly argued that we should understand 'security' as a discursive, contextually-based practice based in localised discourses rather than as a consistent, ontological concept: N Bubandt, 'Vernacular Security: The Politics of Feeling Safe in Global, National and Local Worlds' (2005) 36(3) *Security Dialogue* 275–96.

[31] A An-Na'im, 'The Interdependence of Religion, Secularism, and Human Rights: Prospects for Islamic Societies' (2005) 11(1) *Common Knowledge* 56–80; MR Ishay, *The History of Human Rights: From Ancient Times to Globalization* (Berkeley, University of California Press, 2008) 18ff; and J Witte, Jr, 'Law, Religion, and Human Rights' (1996) 28(1) *Columbia Human Rights Law Review* 11ff.

and responsibilities that, in an ideal world, all human beings should possess. These rights are described as intrinsic and inevitable, using technical terms and ideas that make 'human rights' an area of inquiry unto itself. This discourse is always aspirational, in that it describes how humans *should* be treated in order to achieve security. That is, it describes a secure, suprarational, impossible world using universal, legalistic language, and the act of promoting a particular conception of human rights generates meaning for those so engaged. The human rights discourse provides a path for achieving security in an insecure world and promises a universalist ethic across hard national and, by extension, legal boundaries. The purported function of human rights – to achieve perfect security – is an impossible ideal; yet discussing it and promoting it despite the inescapable insecurity of the world is considered a good in and of itself.

We most clearly see how the concept of human rights is used as an idealised discourse for describing a secure society in the work of the United Nations, whose Universal Declaration of Human Rights (UDHR) is often used as a starting point in such conversations. The UDHR aims to fulfill the mandate of the United Nations, which, according to the first article in its Charter, is designed:

> To maintain international peace and security, and to that end: to take effective collective measures for the prevention and removal of threats to the peace, and for the suppression of acts of aggression or other breaches of the peace, and to bring about by peaceful means, and in conformity with the principles of justice and international law, adjustment or settlement of international disputes or situations which might lead to a breach of the peace.[32]

To that end, the UDHR begins with the premise that 'recognition of the inherent dignity and of the equal and inalienable rights of all members of the human family is the foundation of freedom, justice and peace in the world' and warns that 'disregard and contempt for human rights have resulted in barbarous acts which have outraged the conscience of mankind'.[33] These statements have all the hallmarks of an ideal, secure world seen earlier in Islamic legal discourse.

The UN also aims at an impossible goal: international peace and security. In the pursuit of this impossible goal, the UN has developed a list of rights and responsibilities that describe how people in an idealised world would attain that impossible goal. State actors, nongovernmental organisations (NGOs), and human rights theorists then use the technical terms related to those rights and responsibilities named in the UDHR and elsewhere to construct different narratives to describe an ideal and secure world.

Terms like 'peaceful assembly', 'arbitrary interference', and 'impartial tribunal', for example, are deployed and interpreted to describe the ways in

[32] United Nations, *Charter of the United Nations* (26 June 1945), available at http://www.un.org/en/charter-united-nations/.

[33] United Nations General Assembly, 'Universal Declaration of Human Rights', 10 December 1948, 217 A (III), available at http://www.un.org/en/universal-declaration-human-rights/.

which a secure state should work. Regimes can interpret those terms to argue that women should have unfettered freedom of association; or they can interpret them, as many do, to argue that women should be protected from corrupting influences. The same human rights can be interpreted to protect the right to peaceful protest or to justify a government crackdown on groups that are seen as pernicious. The fact that human rights can be interpreted in vastly different ways is not news, and it is also not the point here; as a discourse, human rights of course follows the same rules as any idealised discourse, in which terms bend according to context. What is important for our purposes is to understand that *however* human rights are interpreted, they speak to larger, suprarational ideas about a secure world and to the roles of individuals within it.

IV. IDEAL MEN, NON-IDEAL WOMEN, AND THE SECURE STATE

Contemporary debates over Muslim women's right to dress as they please, whether in Muslim-majority or Muslim-minority contexts, exemplify how human rights language is employed to describe an ideal, secure, suprarational world. This is certainly true in Azerbaijan, France, Kosovo, and Turkey, where Muslim women are forbidden from wearing headscarves in government institutions; and also in Austria, Belgium, Bulgaria, Holland, Morocco, Syria, and Tunisia, where Muslim women are forbidden from wearing face-veils in public.

Each of these countries, though using slightly different wording and legal reasoning, justifies their bans on the twin foundations of 'human rights' and 'security'. That is to say that Muslim women, when they wear something on their head or face, are presumed to be either victims of human rights violations or violating others' human rights, and they are thought to undermine the notion of an ideal, secure state. For instance, in 1989 Turkey rejected a landmark petition that argued, on the basis of human rights and freedom of religion, that women should be allowed to wear headscarves in public buildings.[34] The Turkish Constitutional Court, in rejecting the petition, argued:

> The headscarf and the particular style of clothing that accompanies it, which lacks a modern appearance, is not an exemption but a tool of segregation.... Using democratic principles to challenge secularism is the abuse of freedom of religion.[35]

Here, we see the Turkish court pitting one human right against another, arguing that as a 'tool of segregation', the freedom to engage in this particular religious expression violates freedom of association. This, despite the fact that many Muslim women claim that the hijab actually facilitates desegregation by

[34] Cited in VK Vojdik, 'Politics of the Headscarf in Turkey: Masculinities, Feminism, and the Construction of Collective Identities' (2010) 33 *Harvard Journal of Law & Gender* 669.

[35] Ibid, citing to fn 55, Anayasa Mahkemesi, 7 March 1989, Esas No 1989/1, Karar No 1989/12, (TC Resmi Gazete, 1989, No 20216).

allowing them to be in public spaces while maintaining their religious beliefs about modesty. Thus, in this case, two human rights were in conflict: freedom of association and freedom of religion. Which human right should take precedence over the other hinged on the Court's conception of an ideal, secure world in which citizens are expected to adopt clothing of 'modern appearance'. This is an ideal worldview that is desperately trying to transcend its past, in which certain historical vestiges are seen as threats to the secure, theoretical world that is being aimed at through a hierarchy of rights. The Court described Muslim women who wear the headscarf as victims – presumably of unenlightened men – who are forced to wear the headscarf as a tool of segregation. Here, certain Muslim men and women are presented in caricature, serving a role in the articulation of a theoretical world in which some citizens are ideal and some less so.

Also in 1989, France's highest court, the *Conseil d'État*, came to a strikingly similar conclusion regarding the types of religious symbols permissible for display, differentiating between religious symbols that are supposedly 'discreet' and those that are 'ostentatious'.[36] The former are seen as innocuous, whereas the latter are seen as threats that are active means of 'pressure, provocation, proselytising, or propaganda'.[37] Based on this ruling, the French education minister issued a memorandum, known as the 'Bayrou Memo', claiming that Muslim women who wear headscarves are engaged in 'ostentatious' symbol-bearing, since 'their meaning is precisely to take certain pupils outside the rules for living together [*vie commune*] in the school.'[38] Such behaviour was seen to violate the human rights of other students and to threaten the ability of the school community to live in peace and security. The memorandum states:

> School is the space which more than any other involves education and integration where all children and all youth are to be found, learning to live together and respect one another. If in this school there are signs of behaviour which show that they cannot conform to the same obligations or attend the same courses and follow the same programs, it negates this mission. All discrimination should stop at the school gates, whether it is sexual, cultural, or religious discrimination.[39]

Here again, we see that human rights are defined in relation to perceived threats to the ideal social order. In this case, instead of Muslim women being

[36] Consel d'État, Assemblée générale (Section de l'intérieur), 27 Novembre 1989. See also E Beller, 'The Headscarf Affair: The Conseil D'état on the Role of Religion and Culture in French Society' (2004) 39 Texas International Law Journal 589–623. See also the 2012 school guidelines released by the French Ministry of Education, 'Orientations et instructions pour la préparation de la rentrée 2012', circular n ° 2012-056 (27 March 2012), http://www.education.gouv.fr/pid25535/bulletin_officiel.html?cid_bo=59726 (accessed 5 December 2018).

[37] S Benhabib, *The Rights of Others: Aliens, Residents, and Citizens* (Cambridge, Cambridge University Press, 2004) 189.

[38] François Bayrou, Circulaire no 1649 du Septembre 1994. See also JR Bowen, *Why the French Don't Like Headscarves: Islam, the State, and Public Space* (Princeton, Princeton University Press, 2007) 89ff.

[39] C Laborde, *Critical Republicanism: The Hijab Controversy and Political Philosophy* (Oxford, Oxford University Press, 2008) 52.

caricatured as victims of segregationists as in Turkey, they are caricatured as pernicious agents who are trying to disrupt French school communities. This caricature works within a larger narrative of an ideal, secure society, in light of which human rights are interpreted and articulated. For the caricature to work, the 'female Muslim headscarf-wearing student' character must operate within a larger cast of characters. These include 'female Muslim non-headscarf wearer', 'male religious Muslim', 'male non-religious Muslim', 'female secularist non-Muslim', 'male religious non-Muslim', 'schoolteacher', 'pupil', 'community', and many more. These individuals are understood in caricature as well, such that the 'non-Muslim French student' is a helpless mark who must be protected by the state from the machinations of the 'female Muslim headscarf-wearing student', and 'schoolteachers' are cast as frontline protectors of vulnerable 'non-Muslim French students' and, indeed, of secure French society itself.

Working backwards from the 'female Muslim headscarf-wearing student', we can reconstruct the ideal world that is assumed by the Bayrou Memo and similar edicts, and flesh out the ideal state, ideal citizens, non-ideal citizens, and the interactions between and among them that result in a secure state. In doing so, we find that, even though the non-ideal 'female Muslim headscarf-wearer' is consistently singled out in clothing bans, these bans are not actually about her at all. That is, these bans are not designed to protect her from the state and its ideal citizens but rather to protect the state and its ideal citizens from her. Whenever we see restrictions on women's clothing, whether they must wear something or must not wear something, we find that the main concern of the restriction is to protect ideal citizens and the state from the threat posed by non-ideal women.

A preoccupation with articulating laws that police women's clothing – whether in secular or religious language – suggests that in both religious and secular contexts, the secure state is imagined with certain ideal citizens in mind, in relation to whom certain female non-ideal citizens are threats. A threat to the ideal citizens of the state is, by extension, a threat to the security of the state itself, and so it must be protected against, even if that means curtailing the rights of non-ideal citizens.

When instituting clothing requirements or bans for women, state officials are often explicit in describing just how non-ideal women compromise the security of the state, and in the process they tell us about how they imagine ideal citizens. The Turkish court ruling, for instance, warns of the female whose outward appearance and inner worldview is informed by premodern ideas, suggesting that the ideal citizen is the opposite – that is, a male whose outward appearance and inner worldview is informed by certain secular, modern mores. Similar headscarf bans in countries like Morocco and Tunisia warn of women who are either malevolent or unwitting agents beholden to 'foreign elements', 'political Islam', 'salafisation', 'extremism', and the like, and each time they presume an ideal citizen who embodies the antithesis of these.

The same dynamic is at work in the headscarf bans of countries like Afghanistan, Iran, and Saudi Arabia, in which women are banned from *not* wearing headscarves. In the language of these bans, women who do not cover their hair are threats to the 'public morality',[40] introducing 'modern corruptions'[41] and 'Western cultural influence' into society.[42] These mirror the laws that ban rather than require headscarves, and we see their proponents using similar language. Tunisia's ex-President, for instance, warned in 2006 that the headscarf 'does not fit with Tunisia's cultural heritage',[43] and Kosovar officials explained that their country's ban is necessary because 'the scarf in Kosovo is not an element of our identity',[44] much like the mayor of Cannes, the first French town to ban the burkini, insisted that the burkini represented the 'salafisation of our society'.[45]

In all of these bans, whether against wearing the headscarf or against removing it, women are the purported subjects because they, as non-ideal citizens to begin with, introduce corruptions and alien influences into ideal society and pose a potential threat to ideal, male citizens. It is therefore no accident that in vastly different countries around the world, women and their dress are contested areas for legal control; they function as foils for idealised males and are centered precisely because they are not central.

In all of these diverse contexts, human rights language is deployed, and Muslim women are caricatured in service of a suprarational narrative of a secure society that allows a particular ideal male to thrive. The more detailed that narrative and the more precisely defined the ideal male in the minds of lawmakers, the more threatening is the non-ideal woman, and the more she is reduced to caricature. This is of necessity: if the non-ideal female is thought to be a particular threat to the ideal male, then she must embody the opposite attributes

[40] *Islamic Penal Code of Iran: English Translation* (Islamabad, Iran–Pakistan Institute of Persian Studies, 1986) art 638.

[41] N Dupree, 'Afghan Women under the Taliban' in W Maley (ed), *Fundamentalism Reborn? Afghanistan and the Taliban* (New York, New York University Press, 2001) 145. Dupree explains that the Afghan ordinances were written with the intention of creating 'secure environments where the chasteness and dignity of women may once again be sacrosanct'.

[42] The phrase 'Western cultural influences' is common in defence of existing clothing restrictions, though it is not found in the wording of the laws themselves.

[43] Cited in S Hawkins, 'Who Wears Hijab with the President: Constructing a Modern Islam in Tunisia' (2001) 41(1) *Journal of Religion in Africa* 36.

[44] M Lowen, 'Headscarf Ban Sparks Debate over Kosovo's Identity', *BBC News* (24 August 2010), http://www.bbc.com/news/world-europe-11065911. For more on Kosovo's ban, see T Perkins, 'Unveiling Muslim Women: The Constitutionality of Hijab Restrictions in Turkey, Tunisia and Kosovo' (2012) 30 *Boston University International Law Journal* 558–62; and B Sadriu, 'Rhetorical Strategies of Kosovo's Imams in the Fight for "Women's Rights"' in A Elbasani and O Roy (eds), *The Revival of Islam in the Balkans: From Identity to Religiosity* (New York, Palgrave MacMillan, 2015).

[45] Cited by A Chrisafis, 'French Mayors Refuse to Lift Burkini Ban Despite Court Ruling', *Guardian* (28 August 2016), https://www.theguardian.com/world/2016/aug/28/french-mayors-burkini-ban-court-ruling.

of the ideal male. In other words, the more precisely defined the ideal world, the less space there is for idealised characters to step outside of their assigned roles without becoming threats to the secure state. When the ideal citizen and the secure state are tightly circumscribed, citizens, both ideal and non-ideal, function only at the extremes of caricature. Extremism, then, is the natural result of narrowly and restrictively defined ideas about ideal citizens and the secure state, and it is realised on a state level whenever lawmakers have the power to implement those ideas using legal language.

It is within this conceptual framework that 'secularism' and 'religion' operate in the current debate over the burkini. In contexts where the ideal male is highly secular, the idealised non-ideal female must be visibly and politically religious. In contexts where the ideal male is culturally homogenous, the idealised non-ideal female must be foreign. The more meticulously defined the ideal male, the more the non-ideal female must fit into a certain oppositional box. This mode of thinking, in which citizens accord to carefully defined characteristics, is the very core of extremism, and it can come in an 'Islamic' flavour, just as it can come in a 'secular' flavour. An extremist narrative needs its citizens to contribute to a particular suprarational ideal society, and it needs different extremisms against which to define its ideal citizens.

It should therefore come as no surprise that in extremist regimes across the world, in which males are invariably the ideal citizens, women's dress becomes the focus of debates on human rights and security. The descriptors 'Muslim', 'secular', 'woman', 'headscarf-wearer', and the like, are potent tools for clarifying extreme conceptions of the ideal male citizen. Extreme conceptions of the ideal male need extreme conceptions of the non-ideal female to work as foils, just as extreme conceptions of secularism need extreme conceptions of religiosity, and vice versa. In this discourse, Muslim women are the character type that is defined – or sacrificed – to better define the suprarational, ideal, secure world that, in each case that we have seen, allows a certain ideal male to function and thrive. The burkini challenges this meaning-generating drive to define security, and whenever it encounters an extremism, it is seen as undermining security. The burkini cannot be neutral in an extremist context; so long as those with power promote a suprarational world that works to protect male-dominated homogeneity, the burkini will be a flashpoint for debates on security and human rights.

V. CONCLUSION

The burkini ban and its revocation in France demonstrates that secularism and religion are as contested in France as they are today in, for example, Turkey, where the covered Muslim woman's body is making a resurgence as the ideal 'Turkish' woman, after decades of women being prohibited from wearing hijabs in public institutions like schools, universities, and Parliament. And Muslim women's bodies have become the site for this battle between intolerant, extremist versions of secularism and Islam, and more tolerant and pluralistic versions of both. This is not an accident: extremist visions of secularism and Islam are constructed against each other, they rely on each other, they are reflections of each other, in symmetry with each other, and they are the raison d'être for each other.

Extremist secularism and extremist Islam can imagine the other only as extreme, intolerant, and supersessionist, and in the face of the other as such, they imagine themselves as holders of the only correct, moral narrative of the world, see themselves as the most virtuous, the most righteous. They see the other – whether 'Islam' or 'secularism' – as manifesting the opposite of what they believe themselves to stand for, even though they are only opposite to each other as the image of oneself in the mirror. Both extremist secularism and extremist Islam disregard and discount as "inauthentic" more tolerant, pluralistic versions of Islam and secularism. Acknowledging the legitimacy of more tolerant versions of secularism and Islam compromises the moral superiority offered by extremism, the moral superiority that justifies intolerance. Tolerant and pluralistic versions of Islam and extremism rupture the self-narrative of extremism. Any extremist ideology must create an extremist enemy as a foil for itself; and this foil must be extreme in order to preserve the extremism of the imaginer. Tolerance, pluralism, and multiculturalism threaten extremism by threatening the security of extremist views, and so the language of security is deployed to criminalise them. It is logically consistent then that the burkini, an expression of pluralism, is seen as a threat to extreme secularism and that extreme secularists therefore seek its criminalisation.

The burkini resists the binaries of Islam and secularism as mutually exclusive ideologies, instead facilitating the performance of multiple identities at once. It is therefore read as a threat by extremists, both Islamic and secular. The inability to accept the burkini for what it is, the ability to see the burkini as something that must be banned and criminalised – these are the result of secular extremism's inability to accept the legitimate existence of a pluralistic, tolerant, and perhaps even secular (gasp!) Islam. It is the direct result of secular extremism's inability to hold multiple identities at once, to be self-reflective and self-critical, to be honest, even about the history of the bikini itself, which was banned in Europe when it first appeared almost a century ago. The burkini bans result from the failures of secular extremism, a failure of its imagination, a failure to meet its own ideals of liberty, freedom, and human dignity as goods in and of themselves, apart from the religious. Instead, in this discourse, human rights language is weaponised against the most marginalised citizens of the state, and rather than protecting them, it is used to police them. And this is the result of seeing secularism and religion as binaries, when far more unites them than divides them.

REFERENCES

Abdelaal, M, 'Extreme Secularism vs Religious Radicalism: The Case of the French Burkini' (2017) 23(3) *ILSA Journal of International and Comparative Law* 443–68.

Afshar, H, 'The Politics of Fear: What Does It Mean to Those Who Are Otherized and Feared?' (2013) 36(1) *Ethnic and Racial Studies* 9–27.

Ahmed, R, 'Jurisprudence and Political Philosophy in Islam' in L Farjeat and R Taylor (eds), *The Routledge Companion to Islamic Philosophy* (New York, Routledge, 2016).

—— *Narratives of Islamic Legal Theory* (Oxford, Oxford University Press, 2012).

—— *Sharia Compliant: A User's Guide to Hacking Islamic Law* (Stanford, Stanford University Press, 2018).

Ajala, I, 'From Islamic Dress and Islamic Fashion to Cool Islam: An Exploration of Muslim Youth Hybrid Identities in the West' (2017) 12(3) *International Journal of Interdisciplinary Cultural Studies* 1–11.

al-Saji, A, 'The Racialization of Muslim Veils: A Philosophical Analysis' (2010) 36(8) *Philosophy and Social Criticism* 875–902.

Almeida, D, 'Marianne at the Beach: The French Burkini Controversy and the Shifting Meanings of Republican Secularism' (2018) 39(1) *Journal of Intercultural Studies* 20–34.

An-Na'im, A, 'The Interdependence of Religion, Secularism, and Human Rights: Prospects for Islamic Societies' (2005) 11(1) *Common Knowledge* 56–80.

Azam, H, *Sexual Violation in Islamic Law: Substance, Evidence, and Procedure* (Cambridge, Cambridge University Press, 2015).

Baehr, P and Gordon, D, 'From the Headscarf to the Burqa: The Role of Social Theorists in Shaping Laws against the Veil' (2013) 42(2) *Economy and Society* 249–80.

Bashford, A, *Imperial Hygiene: A Critical History of Colonialism, Nationalism and Public Health* (New York, Springer, 2004).

Bashford, A (ed), *Medicine at the Border: Disease, Globalization and Security, 1850–Present* (New York, Springer, 2007).

Beller, E, 'The Headscarf Affair: The Conseil D'état on the Role of Religion and Culture in French Society' (2004) 39 *Texas International Law Journal* 589–623.

Benhabib, S, *The Rights of Others: Aliens, Residents, and Citizens* (Cambridge, Cambridge University Press, 2004).

Berg, L and Lundahl, M, 'Un/veiling the West: Burkini-Gate, Princess Hijab and Dressing as Struggle for Postsecular Integration' (2016) 8(3) *Culture Unbound* 263–83.

Bowen, JR, *Why the French Don't Like Headscarves: Islam, the State, and Public Space* (Princeton, Princeton University Press, 2007).

Brown, M, Coté Jr, O, Lynn-Jones, S, and Miller, S, *Rational Choice and Security Studies: Stephen Walt and His Critics* (Cambridge, MA, Massachusetts Institute of Technology Press, 2000).

Bubandt, N, 'Vernacular Security: The Politics of Feeling Safe in Global, National and Local Worlds' (2005) 36(3) *Security Dialogue* 275–96.

Chabal, E, 'From the Banlieue to the Burkini: The Many Lives of French Republicanism' (2017) 25(1) *Modern and Contemporary France* 68–74.

Chaudhry, AS, 'Domestic Violence and Idealized Cosmologies' in M Birkel (ed), *Qur'an in Conversation* (Waco, Baylor University Press, 2014).

—— *Domestic Violence and the Islamic Tradition: Ethics, Law, and the Muslim Discourse on Gender* (Oxford, Oxford University Press, 2014).

Chrisafis, A, 'French Mayors Refuse to Lift Burkini Ban Despite Court Ruling', *Guardian* (28 August 2016), https://www.theguardian.com/world/2016/aug/28/french-mayors-burkini-ban-court-ruling.

Douglas, M, *Purity and Danger* (London, Routledge, 1966).

Dupree, N 'Afghan Women under the Taliban' in W Maley (ed), *Fundamentalism Reborn? Afghanistan and the Taliban* (New York, New York University Press, 2001).

Emon, A, *Religious Pluralism and Islamic Law: Dhimmis and Others in the Empire of Law* (Oxford, Oxford University Press, 2012).

Emon, AM, Ellis, M, and Glahn, B (eds), *Islamic Law and International Human Rights Law* (Oxford, Oxford University Press, 2012).

Fanon, F, *Peau Noire, Masques Blancs* (Paris, Seuil, 1971).

Giddens, A, *Modernity and Self-Identity: Self and Society in the Late Modern Age* (Stanford, Stanford University Press, 1991).

Griffin, E, 'In Violence and in Peace: The Role of Religion and Human Security' in J Wellman, Jr and C Lombardi (eds), *Religion and Human Security: A Global Perspective* (New York, Oxford University Press, 2012).

Gustavsson, G, van der Noll, J, and Sundberg, R, 'Opposing the Veil in the Name of Liberalism: Popular Attitudes to Liberalism and Muslim Veiling in the Netherlands' (2016) 39(10) *Ethnic and Racial Studies* 1719–37.

Hallaq, W, *An Introduction to Islamic Law* (Cambridge, Cambridge University Press, 2009).

Hanafi, H, 'Security Conceptualization in Arab Philosophy and Ethics and Muslim Perspectives' in H Brauch et al (eds), *Globalization and Environmental Challenges: Reconceptualizing Security in the 21st Century* (New York, Springer, 2008).

Hawkins, S, 'Who Wears Hijab with the President: Constructing a Modern Islam in Tunisia' (2001) 41(1) *Journal of Religion in Africa* 36.

Hefferman, T, *Veiled Figures: Women, Modernity and the Spectres of Orientalism* (Toronto, University of Toronto Press, 2016).

Hopkins, C, 'Social Reproduction in France: Religious Dress Laws and Laïcité' (2015) 48 *Women's Studies International Forum* 154–64.

Ibtisam, A, 'Bikini to Burkini: The Choice is Yours', *South Asian Generation Next* (3 February 2010), http://www.sagennext.com/2010/02/03/bikini-to-burkini-%E2%80%93-the-choice-is-yours/.

Ishay, MR, *The History of Human Rights: From Ancient Times to Globalization* (Berkeley, University of California Press, 2008).

Islamic Penal Code of Iran: English Translation (Islamabad, Iran–Pakistan Institute of Persian Studies, 1986).

Jung, C, 'Criminalization of the Burkini' (2016) 37(5) *Harvard International Review* 6–7.

Karamustafa, A, *Sufism: The Formative Period* (Edinburgh, Edinburgh University Press, 2007).

Kinnvall, C, 'Globalization and Religious Nationalism: Self, Identity, and the Search for Ontological Security' (2004) 25(5) *Political Psychology* 741–67.

Kovach-Orr, S, 'Banning the Burka: Indicative of a Legitimate Aim or a Thinly-Veiled Attempt to Legislate Religious and Cultural Intolerance' (2016) 18(1) *Rutgers Journal of Law and Religion* 89–100.

Laborde, C, *Critical Republicanism: The Hijab Controversy and Political Philosophy* (Oxford, Oxford University Press, 2008).

Laegaard, S, 'Burqa Ban, Freedom of Religion and "Living Together"' (2015) 16(3) *Human Rights Review* 203–19.

Limoochi, S and Le Clair, J, 'Reflections on the Participation of Muslim Women in Disability Sport: Hijab, Burkini®, Modesty and Changing Strategies' (2011) 14(9) *Sport in Society* 1300–9.

Lowen, M, 'Headscarf Ban Sparks Debate over Kosovo's Identity', *BBC News* (24 August 2010), http://www.bbc.com/news/world-europe-11065911.

Malkki, L, *Purity and Exile: Violence, Memory, and National Cosmology among Hutu Refugees in Tanzania* (Chicago, University of Chicago Press, 1995).

McClintock, A, 'Soft-Soaping Empire: Commodity Racism and Imperial Advertising' in J Bird et al (eds), *Traveller's Tales: Narratives of Home and Displacement* (London, Routledge, 1994).

Mingati, PK, 'Burqinis, Bikinis and Bodies: Encounters in Public Pools in Italy and Sweden' in E Tarlo and A Moors (eds), *Islamic Fashion and Anti-Fashion: New Perspectives from Europe and North America* (London, Bloomsbury, 2013).

Ministry of Education (France), 'Orientations et instructions pour la préparation de la rentrée 2012', circular n ° 2012-056 (27 March 2012), http://www.education.gouv.fr/pid25535/bulletin_officiel.html?cid_bo=59726 (accessed 5 December 2018).

Ochs, P, 'Charles Peirce's Unpragmatic Christianity: A Rabbinic Appraisal' (1988) 9(1/2) *American Journal of Theology and Philosophy* 41–73.

Perkins, T, 'Unveiling Muslim Women: The Constitutionality of Hijab Restrictions in Turkey, Tunisia and Kosovo' (2012) 30 *Boston University International Law Journal* 558–62.

Quinn, B, 'French Police Make Woman Remove Clothing on Nice Beach Following Burkini Ban', *Guardian* (24 August 2016), https://www.theguardian.com/world/2016/aug/24/french-police-make-woman-remove-burkini-on-nice-beach.

Ramírez, Á, 'Control over Female "Muslim" Bodies: Culture, Politics and Dress Code Laws in Some Muslim and non-Muslim Countries' (2015) 22(6) *Identities: Global Studies in Culture and Power* 671–86.

Sadriu, B, 'Rhetorical Strategies of Kosovo's Imams in the Fight for "Women's Rights"' in A Elbasani and O Roy (eds), *The Revival of Islam in the Balkans: From Identity to Religiosity* (New York, Palgrave MacMillan, 2015).

Schmidt, C, *The Swimsuit: Fashion from Poolside to Catwalk* (London, Berg, 2012).

Shreve-Neiger, A, 'Religion and Anxiety: A Critical Review of the Literature' (2004) 24(4) *Clinical Psychology Review* 379–97.

Staniševski, D, 'Fear Thy Neighbor' (2011) 33(1) *Administrative Theory and Praxis* 62–79.

Tabassum, S, 'Combatants, Not Bandits: The Status of Rebels in Islamic Law' (2011) 93(881) *International Review of the Red Cross* 121–39.

Tang, S, *Disrobed: How Clothing Predicts Economic Cycles, Saves Lives, and Determines the Future* (Lanham, MD, Rowman and Littlefield, 2017).

Tayyen, S, 'From Orientalist Sexual Object to Burkini Terrorist Threat: Muslim Women through Evolving Lens' (2017) 4(1) *Islamophobia Studies Journal* 101–14.

United Nations, Charter of the United Nations (26 June 1945), available at http://www.un.org/en/charter-united-nations/.

United Nations General Assembly, 'Universal Declaration of Human Rights', 10 December 1948, 217 A (III), available at http://www.un.org/en/universal-declaration-human-rights/.

van Kriekan, R, 'Reassembling Civilization: State-Formation, Subjectivity, Security, Power' in A Yeatman and M Zolkos (eds), *State, Security, and Subject Formation* (London, Bloomsbury, 2010).

Vojdik, VK, 'Politics of the Headscarf in Turkey: Masculinities, Feminism, and the Construction of Collective Identities' (2010) 33 *Harvard Journal of Law and Gender* 669.

Weldes, J, Laffey, M, Gusterson, H, and Duvall, R (eds), *Cultures of Insecurity: States, Communities, and the Production of Danger* (Minneapolis, University of Minnesota Press, 1999).

Witte, J, 'Law, Religion, and Human Rights' (1996) 28(1) *Columbia Human Rights Law* Review 11.

4

The Uses of Religious Identity, Practice, and Dogma in 'Soft' and 'Hard' Counterterrorism

AZIZ Z HUQ*

WHAT ROLE SHOULD religious identity, practice, and dogma play in security-related policies and laws trained upon organisations such as the Islamic State (IS) and al Qaeda? Today, this question is centrally about Islamic dogma and the identity-related practices of those perceived to be Muslim. It is also as contested today as it was more than a decade and a half ago, when al Qaeda burst onto the global geopolitical stage. Today, faith is no longer weaponised by violent terrorist groups alone. States too have realised that Islam can be deployed under a security banner in a variety of ideological and practical ways. At the same time, a fractious wave of right-of-centre populism has crashed over northern Europe and the United States with demands for newly restrictive rules for the citizenship and migration of Muslims.[1] The result of these trends is continued, sharp contestation over the uses of Islam in counterterrorism and coterminous policy fields.

In the first decade of the twenty-first century, the normative and human rights implications of religion's intersection with national security turned on the narrow question of whether religious identity could lawfully be used

* I would like to thank the editors, Benjamin Goold and Liora Lazarus, for their terrific substantive suggestions; and the copyeditor, Lisa Y Gourd, for her insightful edits.

[1] F Yılmaz, 'Right-Wing Hegemony and Immigration: How the Populist Far-Right Achieved Hegemony through the Immigration Debate in Europe' (2012) 60 *Current Sociology* 368. The magnitude of new restrictions on immigration varies widely, and at least until now, marginal changes to immigration policy have been small. T Akkerman, 'Immigration Policy and Electoral Competition in Western Europe: A Fine-Grained Analysis of Party Positions over the Past Two Decades' (2015) 21 *Party Politics* 54.

as an effective criterion for investigation or coercive action.[2] Now, religious identity and practice play more complex and ambiguous roles across a range of both 'hard' coercive actions and 'soft,' more regulatory counterterrorism interventions. Islam is no longer solely a signal and proxy of risk but also an object for reform or an object for extirpation. At security policy's periphery, pejorative conceptions of Islam exercise a gravitational pull on contiguous policy domains such as immigration – a pull amplified by partisan mobilisation and exogenous shocks such as financial recessions and refugee crises. As Didier Bigo perceptively framed the matter more than a decade ago, those contiguous policy domains have become thoroughly 'securitised'.[3]

My aim in this chapter is to map the ways in which the interrelated concepts of Islam and the Muslim are employed in the context of counterterrorism law and policy. These intersections are increasingly complex, and a narrow focus on religious discrimination as reflected by religious profiling is no longer apposite.[4] To be sure, larger strategic and partisan trends have sustained and expanded religious profiling. But they have also motivated a novel mobilisation of ideas about Islam and Muslims in the service of security-related policies. By illustrating three distinct ways in which Islamic identity and practice now do work in counterterrorism law and policy – as proxy for risk, object for reform, and object of extirpation – I hope to clear space for new legal and normative inquiries. These underscore the value of considering the dynamic, political effects of regulation that uses faith as a salient criterion for coercive intervention and further regulation that takes faith itself not as a trigger for action but rather as the object of governmental scrutiny and reform.[5]

I. WHY ARE MUSLIMS STILL THE PROBLEM?

In the immediate aftermath of the 2001 attacks on the eastern American seaboard, the 2004 attack on Madrid's Atocha station, and the 2005 London attacks, security policymakers in affected jurisdictions faced a situation of uncertainty rather than risk. They did not know who was a security concern.

[2] A Huq, 'The New Counterterrorism: Investigating Terror, Investigating Muslims' in RC Leone and G Anrig (eds), *Liberty under Attack: Reclaiming Our Freedoms in an Age of Terror* (New York, Public Affairs, 2007).

[3] D Bigo, 'Security and Immigration: Toward a Critique of the Governmentality of Unease' (2002) 27 *Alternatives: Global, Local, Political* 63.

[4] For an excellent study of the profiling question, see B Harcourt, 'Muslim Profiles Post 9/11: Is Racial Profiling an Effective Counter-terrorism Measure and Does It Violate the Right to be Free from Discrimination?' in BJ Goold and L Lazarus (eds), *Security and Human Rights* (Oxford, Hart Publishing, 2007).

[5] I have considered in other work the question of why Muslims have been targeted for opprobrium in Europe, the Americas, and Asia. See A Huq, 'What is the Case against Muslims?' in M Nussbaum, Z Hasan, A Huq, and V Verma (eds), *'The Empire of Disgust': Prejudice, Stigma, and Discrimination in India and the US* (Delhi, Oxford University Press, 2018).

Nor did they know the magnitude of the aggregate risk. Given al Qaeda's putative inspiration in Islamic doctrine, it was disappointing, although not especially surprising, that a first generation of investigative and preventive measures used Muslim identity as a predicate for investigation.[6]

But time passed. New attacks did not proliferate after 2001, or at least they did not occur as fast as many feared. The notion that sleeper cells were strewn willy-nilly across the Ruhr or the American Midwestern rustbelt seemed increasingly the stuff of lurid cinematic fantasy. As the sociologist Charles Kurzman keenly observed, increasingly the question being prompted by (non)events was why al Qaeda's investment in visually spectacular terrorism had failed to generate recruiting dividends.[7] Where, Kurzman asked, were the 'missing' martyrs Osama bin Laden had hoped to inspire? To be sure, few asked that question. Nevertheless, the terrifying uncertainty of an *unknown* unknown receded into a merely *known* unknown. Terrorism was on its way to becoming just another species of risk to be calibrated and managed.[8] As a result, it may well be that the perceived need for broad, prophylactic criteria of suspicion seemed to ebb somewhat – at least until the Islamic State (IS) arrived on the international scene in 2014.

Nevertheless, post-2001 contestation over religion as criterion and concept in counterterrorism law and policy never quite disappeared in either the United States or Europe. To the contrary, categorical denunciation of Muslims as security risks continued to play a role in political campaigns throughout this period and even re-emerged as a pivotal issue in 2016. At the policy level, no legal or policy resolution was reached on whether religious identity could be used as a proxy for terrorism risk. And as this chapter demonstrates, the range of ways in which Islamic concepts and criteria were deployed in counterterrorism law and policy only expanded through a process of accretion and incremental policy change.[9]

I see two larger dynamics at work behind the stubborn persistence of Islam's contested status in the counterterrorism sphere. First, violent Islamist groups have long mobilised a claim to shared religious identity, embedded in putative postcolonial heritages, as a ground of affiliation and connection with potential recruits in Europe and America. This is reflected in the geographic location of the

[6] Huq, 'The New Counterterrorism' (above n 2); and A Huq, 'The Signalling Function of Religious Speech in Counterterrorism' (2011) 89 *Texas Law Review* 833.

[7] C Kurzman, *The Missing Martyrs: Why There Are So Few Muslim Terrorists* (Oxford, Oxford University Press 2011).

[8] BC Ezell, SP Bennett SP, D Von Winterfeldt, J Sokolowski, and AJ Collins, 'Probabilistic Risk Analysis and Terrorism Risk' (2010) 30 *Risk Analysis* 575.

[9] In previous work, I have explored the use of religion as a proxy for terrorism risk in Huq, 'The New Counterterrorism' (above n 2); and the use of religion as evidence of violent intent in Huq, 'The Signalling Function of Religious Speech' (above n 6). Other scholars have examined efforts to establish an 'official' version of Islam. See SJ Rascoff, 'Establishing Official Islam: The Law and Strategy of Counter-Radicalization' (2012) 64 *Stanford Law Review* 125.

evolving threat. In the immediate wake of the 2001 attacks, al Qaeda was based around the Durand Line of 1893, separating Afghanistan from Pakistan and marking the farthest extent of nineteenth-century British colonial power. In al Qaeda's own accounts of its turn toward the 'far enemy' of America, anticolonial tropes in Islamist garb also play a considerable role.[10] Similarly, the rapid rise of IS has refocused attention onto a zone centring on the 1916 Skyes-Picot line and extending into Syria, Iraq, and Turkey.[11] The IS once celebrated its repudiation of that 1916 postcolonial dispensation, as a means of signalling a deliberately anticolonial Islamic political identity.

To encourage the flow of recruits from Europe and elsewhere, the IS has used an aggressive social media strategy that tries to forge affinities of identity among potential supporters and recruiters.[12] The idea of a *religious* identity, albeit one that trades on *anticolonial* motifs and resentments, threads through IS propaganda. Hence, a significant number of IS communications twin an agenda of doctrinal purity with the organisation's claim to be a successor of the caliphate abolished by the Kemelist regime on 3 March 1924.[13] It is not possible to demonstrate with precision whether or to what extent this claim to anticolonial religious affiliation has been successful. But there is some reason to think it has struck a chord that al Qaeda's propaganda operation never touched. One study estimates that roughly 30,000 foreign fighters entered Syria and Iraq to fight alongside IS between 2011 and 2015.[14] The extent and sophistication of IS propaganda has, at a minimum, engendered a perception that a new ideological front has opened in counterterrorism. In this new context, Islam operates as a shared basis of identity, grounded in historical anticolonial struggles, and it seems to have some appeal for disenfranchised minority communities in former colonial states.

A second dynamic has emerged over a longer timeframe as counterterrorism policy adapts to the strategic deployment of a historicised Islam as a

[10] FA Gerges, *The Far Enemy: Why Jihad Went Global* (New York, Cambridge University Press, 2009).

[11] P Cockburn, *The Rise of Islamic State: ISIS and the New Sunni Revolution* (New York, Verso Books, 2015).

[12] G Weimann, 'The Emerging Role of Social Media in the Recruitment of Foreign Fighters' in A de Guttry, F Capone, and C Paulussen (eds), *Foreign Fighters under International Law and Beyond* (The Hague, TMC Asser Press, 2016); HJ Ingram, 'The Strategic Logic of Islamic State Information Operations' (2015) 69 *Australian Journal of International Affairs* 729; and JP Farwell, 'The Media Strategy of ISIS' (2014) 56 *Survival* 49. In a single week in April 2015, the Islamic State put out 123 different media releases – an average of 18 per day. See AY Zelin, 'Picture or It Didn't Happen: A Snapshot of the Islamic State's Official Media Output' (2015) 9(4) *Perspectives on Terrorism*, available at http://www.terrorismanalysts.com/pt/index.php/pot/article/view/445.

[13] Zelin, 'Picture or It Didn't Happen' (ibid); and H Kennedy, *The Caliphate* (London, Pelican, 2016).

[14] E Bakker and M Singleton, 'Foreign Fighters in the Syria and Iraq Conflict: Statistics and Characteristics of a Rapidly Growing Phenomenon' in de Guttry, Capone, and Paulussen (eds) (above n 12). For a more contextual study of the flow of fighters from a single Danish city (Aarhus), see L Lindekilde, P Bertelsen, and M Stohl, 'Who Goes, Why, and with What Effects: The Problem of Foreign Fighters from Europe' (2016) 27 *Small Wars & Insurgencies* 858.

basis for mobilisation and recruitment. The September 2001 attacks precipitated dramatic institutional and legal shifts in the counterterrorism policy and practice of the United States, European states, the European Union, and the United Nations.[15] In this first post-2001 iteration, counterterrorism policy was rarely framed explicitly in terms of Islamic concepts and categories. Yet faith still operated *sub rosa* as a basis for investigation and coercion, though often not in explicit terms.[16] A central legal and normative question raised by new legal authorities of detention, surveillance, and restraint was therefore whether such powers were appropriately deployed predominantly against individuals perceived to be Muslim.[17]

A decade later, the incidence of Islamic concepts and the use of Islam as a criterion have proliferated far beyond their use in security profiling. To a large extent, this has been driven by concerns about the inefficacy of 'hard' state power against domestic recruitment by IS and al Qaeda. Starting with the Netherlands and the United Kingdom, a number of European states, the European Union, and the United States have adopted alternative 'soft' policies of 'counter-radicalisation'.[18]

Counter-radicalisation policies aim to influence the doxa and practice of Muslims.[19] This can take many forms, including selective support for certain religious groups; state regulation of religious practice and imams; and the suppression of sects perceived to be affiliated with terrorist groups. The heterogeneity of these strategies reflects persisting doubt as to whether there is a stable phenomenon of 'radicalisation',[20] as well as disagreement about how ideological persuasion is best countered.

Different countries have taken very different approaches to the mix of 'hard' and 'soft' counterterrorism tools. At one extreme, the Netherlands and the United Kingdom were early adopters of counter-radicalisation. Both experimented with a range of milder policies (or at least policies that fell short of the

[15] Many other countries also altered their security-related legal regimes after 2001, partially in response to United Nations Security Council resolutions seeking changes. KL Scheppele, 'Other People's Patriot Acts: Europe's Response to September 11' (2004) 50 *Loyola Law Review* 89.

[16] Huq, 'The New Counterterrorism' (above n 2).

[17] Harcourt (above n 4).

[18] E Bakker, 'EU Counter-Radicalization Policies: A Comprehensive and Consistent Approach?' (2015) 30 *Intelligence and National Security* 281 (for the European Union); C Heath-Kelly, 'Counter-Terrorism and the Counterfactual: Producing the "Radicalisation" Discourse and the UK PREVENT Strategy' (2013) 15 *British Journal of Politics and International Relations* 394 (for the United Kingdom); and AZ Huq, 'The Social Production of National Security' (2013) 98 *Cornell Law Review* 637 (for the United States and United Kingdom). For discussion of counter-radicalisation programmes in Germany, see the chapter in this volume by Andreas Armborst.

[19] For discussions of the way in which counterterrorism programmes can focus on altering religious practice in the United States and United Kingdom respectively, see Rascoff, 'Establishing Official Islam' (above n 8); and A Richards, 'The Problem with "Radicalization": The Remit of "Prevent" and the Need to Refocus on Terrorism in the UK' (2011) 87 *International Affairs* 143.

[20] For criticism of the term 'radicalisation', see PR Neumann, 'The Trouble with Radicalization' (2013) 89 *International Affairs* 873; and AZ Huq, 'Modeling Terrorist Radicalization' (2010) 2 *Duke Forum for Law and Social Change* 39.

coercion commonly associated with criminal and counterterrorism law). These include theological interventions, counter-messaging, and interventions by teachers, social workers, and child protective services.[21] In contrast, France did not have a national counter-radicalisation policy until April 2014.[22] Prior to that, a network of French counterterrorism institutions, spearheaded by powerful investigating judges working in close alliance with intelligence agencies, wielded hard power to generate security without much regard for a need to recognise and negotiate with divergent religious cultures. French notions of secularism (or *laïcité*) also preclude overt recognition of racial and religious heterogeneity, undermining the feasibility of many soft measures.[23] France's 2014 soft counter-radicalisation plan included an experimental programme for reintegration, a national 'Centre for Prevention, Integration, and Citizenship', a phone line, and a website. The centre, as well as an associated initiative focused on 'disengaging' convicted terrorists from their social networks, was derailed by local 'NIMBY' opposition.[24] A new national deradicalisation plan was announced in February 2018 by the Macron government. It comprises an eclectic blend of sixty different surveillance, detention, education, and research interventions.[25] It remains to be seen whether this compound takes coherent or effective shape.

Domestic political dynamics have also motivated the inclusion of notions of Islam in counterterrorism policy. In many European countries, right-of-centre populist organisations, such as the Dansk Folkeparti, the Bündnis Zukunft Österreich (Alliance for the Future of Austria), and the Dutch Partij voor de Vrijheid (Party for Freedom) have coalesced around restrictive immigration measures that aim to stanch Muslim migration, partly in the name of security.[26] Opposition to immigration is central to these parties' appeal.[27] In turn,

[21] L Lindekilde, 'Value for Money? Problems of Impact Assessment of Counter-Radicalisation Policies on End Target Groups: The Case of Denmark' (2012) 18 *European Journal on Criminal Policy and Research* 385; L Lindekilde, 'Introduction: Assessing the Effectiveness of Counter-radicalisation Policies in Northwestern Europe' (2012) 5 *Critical Studies on Terrorism* 335; and V Coppock and M McGovern, '"Dangerous Minds"? Deconstructing Counter-Terrorism Discourse, Radicalisation and the "Psychological Vulnerability" of Muslim Children and Young People in Britain' (2014) 28 *Children & Society* 242.

[22] D Hellmuth, 'Countering Jihadi Terrorists and Radicals the French Way' (2015) 38 *Studies in Conflict and Terrorism* 979.

[23] Hellmuth (ibid); F Foley, 'Reforming Counterterrorism: Institutions and Organizational Routines in Britain and France' (2009) 18 *Security Studies* 435; and S Gregory, 'France and the War on Terrorism' (2003) 15 *Terrorism and Political Violence* 124.

[24] Hellmuth (above n 22) 988. For the disengagement programme, see M Cowell, 'What Went Wrong with France's Deradicalization Program?' *Atlantic* (28 September 2017).

[25] J Chichizola, 'Déradicalisation: les principales mesures du plan gouvernemental', *Le Figaro* (23 February 2018).

[26] F Hafez, 'Shifting Borders: Islamophobia as Common Ground for Building Pan-European Right-Wing Unity' (2014) 48 *Patterns of Prejudice* 479, 485. See also the chapter in this volume by Victor Ramraj, as well as the chapter by David Irvine and Travers McCleod.

[27] E Ivarsflaten, 'What Unites Right-Wing Populists in Western Europe? Re-Examining Grievance Mobilization Models in Seven Successful Cases' (2008) 41 *Comparative Political Studies* 3. See also J Rydgren, 'Immigration Skeptics, Xenophobes or Racists? Radical Right-Wing Voting in Six West European Countries' (2008) 47 *European Journal of Political Research* 737.

concerns about terrorism motivate anti-immigrant sentiment.[28] The result is a 'securitisation' of immigration policy that both reflects and reinforces the political power of the populist right. This dynamic is summarised by the German writer Hans Monath's 2010 pronouncement that 'Islam is not part of Europe.'[29]

II. THE VARIED AND SUNDRY USES OF ISLAM

The forces described above have worked powerful changes in the ways security policy deploys concepts of Islam and the Muslim. I draw on both European and American illustrations to show how religious concepts and criteria can be put to work for security-related ends. The observed diversity of uses can be broken into three rough categories: Islam as a signal and proxy for risk, Islam as an object of reform, and Islam as an object of extirpation.

A. Islam as Signal and Proxy for Risk

Today, outward and visible signifiers of Islamic religiosity – skin pigmentation; use of Arabic or a language perceived as Middle Eastern or South Asian; beards for men; and veils for women – still serve as triggers for suspicion and official intervention in a range of contexts. These signifiers, of course, are imperfect proxies of Muslim identity. In the United States, for example, a majority of Arab-Americans are Christian. More generally, outward appearances such as skin colour and beard length are clearly imperfect proxies for any faith. More generally, it is a serious mistake to think that all those raised in Muslim households maintain the same religious beliefs, or even *any* religious beliefs at all, into adulthood. Profiling measures that employ a singular and narrow definition of the Muslim in many cases rather ironically end up paralleling the straitened accounts of what it is to be Muslim in doctrinaire Islamic texts, which have likewise narrow definitions of apostasy.[30]

The use of a religious proxy for security risk today, though, appears to result from the dispersed actions of street-level agents and the general public.[31] The counterterrorism investigations of the New York Police Department (NYPD) are an illustrative example. From 2002 onward, the NYPD Intelligence Division

[28] D Zucchino, 'I've Become a Racist: Migrant Wave Unleashes Danish Tensions Over Identity', *New York Times* (5 September 2016). For a review of the available empirical evidence, see A Huq, 'Terrorism and Democratic Recession' (2018) 85 *University of Chicago Law Review* 457.

[29] Quoted in JC Alexander, 'Struggling over the Mode of Incorporation: Backlash against Multiculturalism in Europe' (2013) 36 *Ethnic and Racial Studies* 531, 544.

[30] D Cook, 'Apostasy from Islam: A Historical Perspective' (2006) 31 *Jerusalem Studies in Arabic and Islam* 248. On the topic of parallels between secular and religious extremism, see also the chapter in this volume by Rumee Ahmed and Ayesha S Chaudhry.

[31] On the difficulty of regulating street-level bureaucrats, see P Hupe and M Hill, 'Street-Level Bureaucracy and Public Accountability' (2007) 85 *Public Administration* 279.

and NYPD Demographics Unit used Islamic identity as a criterion for long-term electronic and physical surveillance. Confidential informants and undercover agents targeted mosques, Muslim student associations, and social hubs in Muslim-majority neighbourhoods in New York City, New Jersey, Pennsylvania, and Connecticut.[32] Undercover officers targeted Muslim university students, trying to extract comments that could be used as basis for broad conspiracy charges.[33] Despite two legal challenges to these practices and a settlement in which the NYPD purported to repudiate religious criteria,[34] the Intelligence Division remains focused on Muslims: an August 2016 audit of the Division's activities found that more than ninety-five per cent of all files reviewed concerned Muslim suspects.[35]

In the United Kingdom, Section 44(1) and (2) and Section 45 of the Terrorism Act (2000) allow police to designate large geographic areas 'for the purpose of searching for articles of a kind which could be used in connection with terrorism'. These provisions derogate from the 1984 Police and Criminal Evidence Act by permitting street stops and searches even in the absence of 'due suspicion'.[36] In absolute numbers, Section 44 stops were employed during the late 1990s and early 2000s more frequently against non-minorities. Ethnic minorities, however, experienced higher *rates* of stops, and government ministers warned that such stops would be 'inevitably … disproportionately experienced' by British Muslims.[37] Ethnographic studies of British Pakistanis have indeed found broad resentment of counterterrorism powers, with particular umbrage incited by Section 44.[38]

In France, the deployment of emergency powers has been characterised by similar distributional asymmetries. These powers include warrantless home search and 'assigned residence' orders (barring a person from leaving a jurisdiction and requiring reports several times daily to a police station). After terrorist

[32] M Apuzzo and A Goldman, *Enemies Within: Inside the NYPD's Secret Spying Unit and Bin Laden's Final Plot against America* (New York, Touchstone, 2013); *Hassan v City of New York*, 804 F.3d 277 (3d Cir. 2015). Disclosure: I am counsel for the *Hassan* plaintiffs.

[33] J Theoharis, '"I Feel Like a Despised Insect": Coming of Age Under Surveillance in New York', *The Intercept* (18 February 2016), https://theintercept.com/2016/02/18/coming-of-age-under-surveillance-in-new-york/.

[34] M Apuzzo and A Baker, 'New York to Appoint Civilian to Monitor Police's Counterterrorism Activity', *New York Times* (7 January 2016), http://www.nytimes.com/2016/01/08/nyregion/new-york-to-appoint-monitor-to-review-polices-counterterrorism-activity.html.

[35] Office of the Inspector General for the NYPD, 'An Investigation of NYPD's Compliance with Rules Governing Investigations of Political Activity' (23 August 2016), https://www1.nyc.gov/assets/oignypd/downloads/pdf/oig_intel_report_823_final_for_release.pdf.

[36] S Hallsworth, 'Racial Targeting and Social Control: Looking behind the Police' (2006) 14 *Critical Criminology* 293, 296.

[37] C Pantazis and S Pemberton, 'From the "Old" to the "New" Suspect Community: Examining the Impacts of Recent UK Counter-Terrorist Legislation' (2009) 49 *British Journal of Criminology* 646, 656–58; and Hallsworth (ibid) 297–98.

[38] G Mythen, S Walklate, and F Khan, '"I'm a Muslim, but I'm Not a Terrorist": Victimization, Risky Identities and the Performance of Safety' (2009) 49 *British Journal of Criminology* 736.

attacks in Paris on 13 November 2015, French President François Hollande declared a three-month state of emergency, which was then extended five times, the last one only expiring in November 2017. A 2016 report by Amnesty International identified 3,242 searches between November 2015 and January 2016 and more than 350 assigned residence orders.[39] Almost all targeted French Muslims, despite the absence of any official religion criterion. The Amnesty report describes a pervasive pattern of violent and humiliating treatment during searches.[40] It found that in many cases, assigned residence orders appeared to be based on anonymous tips received though the counter-radicalisation hotline. The official justifications shared with those subjected to assigned residence orders were 'usually quite general', leaving the subjects of investigation no way to challenge their veracity.[41] Those searched noted that visible Islamic religiosity seemed to explain why they, and not their neighbours, were subject to emergency powers. Less than one percent of emergency action resulted in criminal investigation.[42]

These examples suggest that profiling can persist on the ground, even absent official policy, if there is a 'widespread tendency to associate Islamic behaviour and Muslims generally with terrorism'.[43] Disparate results emerge because widely shared negative beliefs about Muslims translate into higher rates of suspicion of that class. This background dynamic, moreover, is likely to be exacerbated by political mobilisations to remove signs of Islamic religiosity from public life. In Switzerland, for example, a 2009 referendum banned the construction of minarets.[44] In France, Belgium, Austria, and Denmark, as well as in some Swiss, Spanish, and Italian towns, there are now bans on religious facial coverings in public.[45] Prohibitions on visible and public manifestations of Muslim identity may suppress individual religious expression[46] while also reinforcing the belief that religious displays that do not conform to majority-held preferences

[39] Amnesty International, 'Upturned Lives: The Disproportionate Impact of France's State of Emergency', Index EUR 21/3364/2016 (4 February 2016), https://www.amnesty.org/en/documents/eur21/3364/2016/en/.

[40] Ibid.

[41] Ibid, 20–21.

[42] AJ Rubin, 'Muslims in France Say Emergency Powers Go Too Far', *New York Times* (17 February 2016), http://www.nytimes.com/2016/02/18/world/europe/frances-emergency-powers-spur-charges-of-overreach-from-muslims.html. On the state of emergency in France, see also the chapter in this volume by Marc-Antoine Granger.

[43] S Vertigans, 'British Muslims and the UK Government's "War on Terror" Within: Evidence of a Clash of Civilizations or Emergent De-Civilizing Processes?' (2010) 61 *British Journal of Sociology* 26, 33.

[44] N Göle, 'The Public Visibility of Islam and European Politics of Resentment: The Minarets-Mosques Debate' (2011) 37 *Philosophy & Social Criticism* 383, 385–86.

[45] R Michaels, 'Banning Burqas: The Perspective of Postsecular Comparative Law' (2018) 28(2) *Duke Journal of Comparatrive and International Law* 213. For Denmark, see S Samuel, 'Banning Muslims Veils Tend to Backfire – So Why Do Countries Keep Doing It?' *Atlantic* (3 August 2018).

[46] But in some cases, stigmatised symbols are adopted precisely because of the negative reaction they invoke. See N Göle, 'The Voluntary Adoption of Islamic Stigma Symbols' (2003) 70 *Social Research* 809.

are *ipso facto* repudiations of social norms unrelated to religious beliefs and practices.[47] As former French president Nicholas Sarkozy said of the Muslim veil, such manifestations are taken as 'rejection of our values'.[48] It is telling that the precise contents of those 'values' are not spelled out and neither is the referent for 'our'.

B. Islam as an Object for Reform

In addition to the outward signifiers and symbols of Islam becoming criteria for surveillance and coercion, Islam itself has become an object of security-related regulation in the hands of the state. This occurs most markedly in counter-radicalisation programmes. In this way, religious identity and practice shift from being a trigger of state coercion to being a mutable object of state regulation. A quintessential exercise in 'governmentality', counter-radicalisation treats Islam as a malleable object that is subject to state intervention, namely the 'cultivation of [individual] subjectivity in specific forms'.[49] The aim of counter-radicalisation is not to use Islam as a proxy for risk but rather to transform Islam. This new direction raises distinct concerns with respect to the scope of religious freedom and practice.

The British 'Prevent' programme provides a vivid example. This national programme avowedly seeks to 'challenge the ideologies that extremists believe can justify the use of violence, primarily by helping Muslims who wish to dispute these ideas to do so'.[50] A key measure of its success, explained the British government, would be 'demonstrable changes in attitudes among Muslims'.[51] It has pursued that change through religious 'roadshows', forums, advisory councils, a 'radicalisation' toolkit for secondary education professionals, and a referral programme named 'Channel' for early intervention.[52] Prevent also contains some mandates. Secondary-school teachers and university staff, for example, are required to report 'radical' behaviour by students.[53]

[47] See the chapter in this volume by Rumee Ahmed and Ayesha S Chaudhry.

[48] J Edmunds, 'The "New" Barbarians: Governmentality, Securitization and Islam in Western Europe' (2011) 6 *Contemporary Islam* 67.

[49] D Garland, '"Governmentality" and the Problem of Crime: Foucault, Criminology, Sociology' (1997) 1 *Theoretical Criminology* 173, 175.

[50] Quoted in Y Alam and C Husband, 'Islamophobia, Community Cohesion and Counter-Terrorism Policies in Britain' (2013) 47 *Patterns of Prejudice* 235, 247.

[51] T O'Toole et al, 'Governing through Prevent? Regulation and Contested Practice in State–Muslim Engagement' (2016) 50 *Sociology* 160, 162.

[52] Huq, 'The Social Production of National Security' (above n 18) 654–55; and R Briggs, 'Community Engagement for Counterterrorism: Lessons from the United Kingdom' (2010) 86 *International Affairs* 971, 971–72.

[53] D Gayle, 'Prevent Strategy "Could End up Promoting Extremism"', *Guardian* (21 April 2016), http://www.theguardian.com/politics/2016/apr/21/government-prevent-strategy-promoting-extremism-maina-kiai; and K Nabulsi, 'Don't Go to the Doctor', *London Review of Books* (18 May 2017).

In a single year (2008–09), £140 million was expended on Prevent with the explicit aim of altering the substantive content of Islamic beliefs in Britain.[54]

But Prevent has met considerable resistance from Muslim communities, service providers, and commentators. Teachers, for example, have voted to disobey the 'radical' reporting requirement, while many community organisations have protested or exited governmental programmes.[55] Prevent has also been dogged by criticisms that it is meant in fact to work as a covert surveillance programme.[56] Such hostility highlights a subtle paradox in the programme's logic. On the one hand, Prevent's avowed ambition is reformist. It is a substitute in that regard for 'hard' measures. On the other hand, Prevent treats Muslims as a 'security risk' and as a minority that is 'poorly integrated into British society'.[57] By quite literally classifying Muslims as a problematic minority, Prevent manifests a negative expressive effect that likely works at cross-purposes with its avowed reformist ambition.

Another unintended consequence of Prevent has been a securitisation of welfare and social services. Funding for the Prevent programme persisted though the 2008–09 financial crisis, during which direct welfare expenditures were otherwise plummeting in the United Kingdom. As a result, funding-starved social service providers have retooled their proposals to fit a counterterrorism agenda that appears more attractive to funding bodies. Welfare policy and the maintenance of a social safety net have thereby become increasingly entangled with and evaluated as security policy.[58] Paradoxically, even as the deployment of Section 44 stop-and-search powers imposed a new tax on manifest indicia of Muslim identity, the Prevent programme made the same identity status a quasi-prerequisite for access to certain benefits from the state, including monetary ones. As David Anderson, the UK Independent Reviewer of Terrorism Law, explained, Prevent became a 'significant source of grievance' among British Muslims, encouraging 'mistrust to spread and to fester'.[59]

One way to resolve these paradoxes is to use sticks alone rather than carrots. This has been the French way. Between 2001 and 2012, French authorities deported 166 people, including 31 imams, as 'Islamists'.[60] Selective deportations

[54] Briggs (above n 52) 971.

[55] O'Toole et al (above n 51) 172–74; and Gayle (above n 53).

[56] O'Toole et al (above n 51) 4; and Huq, 'The Social Production of National Security' (above n 18) 655–56.

[57] O'Toole et al (above n 51) 165.

[58] P Thomas, *Responding to the Threat of Violent Extremism: Failing to Prevent* (London, Bloomsbury, 2012).

[59] D Batty, 'Prevent Strategy "Sowing Mistrust and Fear in Muslim Communities"', *Guardian* (3 February 2016).

[60] F Ragazzi, 'Toward "Policed Multiculturalism"? Counter-Radicalization in France, the Netherlands and the United Kingdom', Centre d'Études et de Recherches Internationales (December 2014), http://www.sciencespo.fr/ceri/sites/sciencespo.fr.ceri/files/Etude_206_anglais.pdf. Few imams in France are native to the country; many arrive from North Africa as adults to take up these positions.

of this sort may curtail the growth and development of targeted mosques and factions, but the deterrent and expressive effects of such policies can lend them a very different meaning within Muslim communities more generally.

C. Islam as an Object of Extirpation

There is a third way in which Islam as a religion – a complex of beliefs, practices, dispositions, and religious tests – has increasingly come to be an object of regulation. This third category differs from the Prevent programme and other reformist measures because of its ends. The state's agenda here is thoroughly negative. Explicitly or not, Islam is construed as a problem to be eliminated as inconsistent with national or transcendental 'liberal' values. The ideological gist of such policies is crisply conveyed by Slovakian Prime Minister Robert Fico's claim that 'Islam has no place in Slovakia' and Hungarian Prime Minister Viktor Orbán's assertion that 'Islam was never part of Europe.'[61] No full-scale realisation of such sentiments has yet been observed (although the possibility cannot be ruled out). Nevertheless, the categorical negative force of such sentiments is echoed in both retail and wholesale security-related policies.

At a retail level, such security policies can have the practical effect of extinguishing religious communal life. Since November 2015, for example, French authorities have used emergency powers to shut down several mosques and Muslim community associations.[62] These efforts are not without precedent. In 2005, 22 regional units comprising representatives from police, tax, prefectures, and other regulatory offices were created to fight 'radical Islam'. These units closed mosques, Halal butchers, and small retail establishments.[63] In the United States at roughly the same time, several nationwide Islamic charities had assets frozen and officers prosecuted.[64] Asset-freezing orders, criminal investigations, and prosecutions (even when unsuccessful) effectively dismantled much of the nationwide civil society that American Muslims had constructed until then.

More subtly, these policies can be understood as evidence of a belief on the part of state actors that Muslims as a group are not or cannot become full citizens. Consider in this regard the revocation of citizenship measures either proposed or used in Europe. In France, President Hollande proposed a statutory mechanism for *déchéance de nationalité* (citizenship stripping)

[61] A Faiola and S Kirchner, 'Islam Is Europe's "New Fascism," and Other Things European Politicians Say about Muslims', *Washington Post* (7 June 2016).

[62] Amnesty International (above n 39) 24. In one case (in Lagny-sur-Marne), police publicly announced the seizure of inculpatory evidence, but Amnesty International found that police reports of the same raids recorded that no such evidence was found.

[63] Ragazzi (above n 60) 28.

[64] L Al-Marayati, 'American Muslim Charities: Easy Targets in the War on Terror' (2004) 25 *Pace Law Review* 321.

in December 2015, targeting dual nationals alone. The French Senate rejected the measure, but Hollande's proposal was widely understood as targeting French Muslims alone, a reflection of the general perception of their second-tier status as citizens whose loyalty is presumptively in question.[65]

At a more macro level, the extirpation of Islam has been advanced though immigration and citizenship policies. In the United States, several Republican presidential candidates have called for categorical bars on Muslim immigration, and while the travel ban ultimately implemented by President Donald Trump has been subject to extensive constitutional challenge, it has been upheld by the US Supreme Court.[66] In Europe, populist parties call for bans of a similar character. Some European nations have substantially reduced the permitted flow of lawful migrants under political pressure.

One means for both slowing migrant flows and altering the composition of migrant flows is the use of citizenship tests that screen based on culture or familiarity with local customs. These have been used in several European countries, including Austria, Germany, and the Netherlands, with the more or less explicit aim of ending Muslim immigration. The connection between security and migration is commonly rendered explicit on the face of such tests. In 2006, Heribert Rech, the interior minister of Baden-Württemberg, proposed thirty additional questions to be used on the citizenship test administered in that region. The questions expressly focused on terrorism as well as on cultural norms. So obvious was its bottom-line intent that Baden-Württemberg's test was quickly dubbed 'the Muslim test'.[67] In the Netherlands, the content of the citizenship test being used at the time of this writing focuses on values of sexual freedom, gender equality, freedom of speech, and individuality. It is fair to interpret the test's design as evidence that the responsible state actors assume that some of these values are inconsistent with some versions of Islam and hence comprise an effective screen against undesirable migrants.[68] The effect of such tests falls disproportionately on citizens invoking a right to family reunification, as opposed to high-skills migrants.[69] In Denmark, the citizenship test eschews such obvious generalisations, yet the Danish test has been recently reformed

[65] C Joppke, 'Terror and the Loss of Citizenship' (2016) 20 *Citizenship Studies* 728, 745.

[66] For a detailed history of calls for a Muslim ban, the actual Trump travel ban, and the associated litigation, see A Huq, 'Article II and Antidiscrimination Norms' (2019) *Michigan Law Review* (forthcoming).

[67] J Dempsey, 'Civic Test in Germany Draws Fire', *New York Times* (14 February 2006). Joppke has stated that the test was initially applied to only the Muslim applicants, although contemporaneous reporting does not reflect that. See C Joppke, 'Through the European Looking Glass: Citizenship Tests in the USA, Australia, and Canada' (2013) 17 *Citizenship Studies* 1, 10.

[68] M de Leeuw and S van Wichelen, 'Civilizing Migrants: Integration, Culture and Citizenship' (2012) 15 *European Journal of Cultural Studies* 195.

[69] For a discussion of the Dutch immigration test's effects in this regard, see SW Goodman, 'Controlling Immigration through Language and Country Knowledge Requirements' (2011) 34 *West European Politics* 235.

such that it is difficult even for native Danes. This led to 68.8 per cent failure rates for new immigrants.[70] Introduced at a moment at which migration flows were starting to be dominated by Muslims, the timing of this change seems to reflect a deeper belief: that it is *current* migrants that are the problem.

* * *

Islam and the Muslim are concepts with plural usages in the policy space of national security. Their use as criteria of suspicion is only part of the picture. In addition, Islam operates as a subject to be regulated and as an object of governmentality. The state can also aim at more categorical exclusions and prohibitions of Islam. The gap between liberal aspirations to equality and extensive personal liberty on the one hand and thoroughly illiberal forms of racial and religious discrimination on the other hand has proved all too easy to navigate in many different national jurisdictions and diverse political contexts.

III. THE (NEW) CRITIQUE OF COUNTERTERRORISM POLICY'S USES OF ISLAM

Concepts of Islam and the Muslim are exploited in many different ways across the regulatory apparatus of counterterrorism and related policies. The heterogeneity of Islam's uses suggests a need both to rethink old critiques and to develop new forms of criticism as means toward the vindication of the values of equality and non-discrimination.

A. The Limits of the Old Critiques

In the international human rights context, as well as within many domestic law frameworks, a central question is the rationality of official distinctions drawn in religious terms. As Daniel Moeckli has put it, the focus within international human rights law is commonly on 'the existence of an objective and reasonable justification for … differential treatment' and the 'existence of a reasonable relationship of proportionality between the difference in treatment and the legitimate aim sought to be realized'.[71]

An assessment of the rationality of discriminatory criteria remains necessary to a comprehensive normative critique of counterterrorism policy. But it is no longer sufficient. Consider as an example Harcourt's powerful argument against religious profiling set out in the first edition of this volume. Harcourt pointed out that the

[70] D Bilefsky, 'Denmark's Tougher Citizenship Test Stumps Even Its Natives', *New York Times* (7 July 2016).

[71] D Moeckli, *Human Rights and Non-Discrimination in the 'War on Terror'* (Oxford, Oxford University Press, 2008) 76–79.

value of faith as a signal of risk depended on the *relative* responses to such policing by *both* profiled and non-profiled classes. He pointed out (with rather more sophistication and clarity than I muster here) that if the profiled group reduces its activity, while the non-profiled group ramps it up, the profile no longer works.[72] Although powerful, Harcourt's critique does not necessarily illuminate contemporary profiling. The deployment of 'Muslim' or 'Islamic' as criteria for state coercion today no longer follows from a rational, centralised determination that such criteria are needful. Instead, they arise as an emergent quality of the individual preferences and beliefs of dispersed, unconnected officials (as well as members of the public). Such dispersed, 'street-level' actors are not making accurate or defensible cost–benefit judgements about the epistemic value of religious traits. Rather, they are acting on raw intuition, half-formed beliefs, and spontaneous emotional coloration. In the absence of centralised, comprehensive, and clearly articulated state policy, arguments for critique and reform should not focus on the internal *logic* of profiling (as Harcourt and other have done in an effort perhaps to stave off an inevitable emotional response). Rather, critics must directly address the stereotypes and fears that motivate discriminatory policing.

B. New Paths for Critical Inquiry

Viewed in the round, the concept of Islam in counterterrorism today performs a number of functions unrelated to the efficient allocation of security resources. Accounting for this broader array of uses of Islam in the service of counterterrorism should elicit new inquiries into the aggregate impact and political

[72] Harcourt (above n 4) 88. In my view, the assumption that Harcourt queried (the *relative* responsiveness of Muslims' and non-Muslims' behaviours to state scrutiny) is not critical to the debate on profiling. The more important question is whether behaviour is at all responsive to profiling. The question of relative elasticities in the behaviour of profiled and non-profiled groups, which was Harcourt's focus, arises from the so-called KPT model of racial profiling. (See J Knowles, N Persico, and P Todd, 'Racial Bias in Motor Vehicle Searches: Theory and Evidence' (2001) 109 *Journal of Political Economy* 203.) But the assumptions animating the KPT model have been powerfully challenged in part by pointing out that under most circumstances, members of racial groups that are diffused across the public lack sufficient evidence of police practice to respond dynamically to changes in policing in ways that produce the equilibria that the KPT model implies. (See RS Engel and R Tillyer, 'Searching for Equilibrium: The Tenuous Nature of the Outcome Test' (2008) 25 *Justice Quarterly* 54.) That is, the KPT model assumes that the public is fully informed of police behaviour and responds rationally by varying up or down their levels of criminality in response to that behaviour. I am sceptical that behavioural elasticity of the sort the KPT equilibrium assumes is likely to hold in the counterterrorism context. Instead, the *relative* offending rates of 'Muslim-seeming' and 'non-Muslim-seeming' groups are a function of variables exogenous to dynamic reactions to policing practices, such as experiences of economic disenfranchisement, changes in the levels of external propaganda, and personal disappointments and grievances. I therefore do not think the empirical question of comparative elasticities is as important in the national security context as Harcourt suggested. In other words, I have expressed scepticism about its relevance in the ordinary policing context. See A Huq, 'The Consequences of Disparate Policing: Evaluating Stop and Frisk as a Modality of Urban Policing' (2017) 101 *Minnesota Law Review* 2397.

economy of counterterrorism and related fields. I offer, in concluding, a sketch of some of these lines of critique.

First, an analysis of security policy is usefully situated in the larger context of public debates on Muslim migration and public symbols of Islam. These debates suggest that officials and members of the public juxtapose the moral legitimacy of the liberal state with the perceived normative bankruptcy of Islam.[73] Muslims are simultaneously figured as incapable of respecting basic norms of dress and civility and also as discarding basic rules of moral conduct. The claim that Islam 'has no place' in Europe is thus inextricable from concerns about culture and security. These parallel concerns are mutually reinforcing. Both imply that Muslims are incapable of coexisting peacefully with non-Muslim neighbours and co-residents. In this fashion, debates about national culture and national security may be mutually constitutive and mutually reinforcing.

One implication of this analysis may be that debates about highly visible symbols of Islam, such as the veil or the minaret, are counterproductive for advocates of non-discrimination and Muslim human rights. These debates condense the relationship of Muslim minorities to non-Muslim majorities into singular points of highly charged contestation that are resistant to compromise. Such debates obscure the fact that Muslim minority communities and their neighbours in fact engage routinely in negotiation and reach compromise over many issues. Indeed, such negotiated coexistence has been shown to be the dominant local experience in the Netherlands and the United Kingdom.[74] The tendency to highlight symbolic conflicts while ignoring local and pragmatic intercultural relations renders the putative tensions between Islam and liberalism as sharper and less amenable to compromise than they really are. As a result, they may push participants toward more extreme solutions in the security domain and elsewhere.

Second, my analysis of Islam's varied roles in security policy suggests a need to account for distributive effects, in particular how the costs of security are apportioned between marginal and mainstream groups across society. The profiling, reformist efforts, and prohibitory policies described above all have the likely effect of exacerbating existing forms of economic and social exclusion, which paradoxically but unsurprisingly may result in less security rather than more.

France provides a useful example of this dynamic. Recent research by Claire Adida, David Laitin, and Marie-Anne Valfort has used sophisticated causal inference methods to isolate the effect of Islamic or Muslim identities on the

[73] This theme is developed in JA Massad, *Islam in Liberalism* (Chicago, University of Chicago Press, 2016).

[74] For recent accounts of successful local practice, see AC Korteweg and T Triadafilopoulos, 'Is Multiculturalism Dead? Groups, Governments and the "Real Work of Integration"' (2015) 38 *Ethnic and Racial Studies* 663; and A Heath and N Demireva, 'Has Multiculturalism Failed in Britain?' (2014) 37 *Ethnic & Racial Studies* 161.

labour market and economic behaviour of French nationals. They provide robust evidence of substantial discrimination on the basis of perceived religious identity in the context of face-to-face interactions and arms-length economic transactions.[75] President Hollande's deployment of emergency powers has exacerbated the economic marginalisation and social isolation of French Muslims by validating the beliefs that animate such discrimination. The implicit expressive effect of profiling in Britain under Section 44 and the Prevent programme likely have the same consequence. Hence, the securitisation of Islam not only provides a substitute for discussion of the limits of practiced liberalism but also deepens the exclusionary elements of the liberal economic order.

Economic and social marginalisation further erodes security. Empirical studies in the United States and Britain show that policing perceived as biased against Muslims undermines the willingness of both Muslims and non-Muslims to cooperate with police.[76] At the same time, a growing body of robust evidence suggests that countries experiencing minority group economic discrimination are significantly more likely to experience domestic terrorism attacks.[77] If there is a strong correlation between minority economic exclusion and domestic terrorism, security policies that exacerbate such exclusion or retrench negative stereotypes of Muslims will have perverse and adverse effects on terrorism risk. Because politicians can profit from the cultivation of anti-Muslim sentiments, though, these negative spill-overs are unlikely to be accounted for in democratic policymaking.

Finally, the question of Islam and Muslims in the counterterrorism context is usefully viewed not merely as a matter of individual rights but also as an issue of distributive justice.[78] In the past decade and a half, the costs of the security state's expansion have not been allocated evenly across social groups. Rather, the costs of such policies fall in predictably asymmetrical and highly regressive patterns. To be sure, programmes such as Prevent may have the inadvertent and temporary effect of channelling state funds to Muslim-identified groups. By and large, though, the costs of security are borne by Muslims, in the forms of concentrated stigma, economic exclusion, fear of private violence, and barriers to familial reunification. This is not merely intrinsically unjust; it also

[75] CL Adida, DD Laitin, and M-A Valfort, *Why Muslim Integration Fails in Christian-Heritage Societies* (Cambridge, Harvard University Press, 2016).

[76] For a summary and extension of these studies, see AZ Huq, TR Tyler, and SJ Schulhofer, 'Mechanisms for Eliciting Cooperation in Counterterrorism Policing: Evidence from the United Kingdom' (2011) 8 *Journal of Empirical Legal Studies* 728.

[77] JA Piazza, 'Poverty, Minority Economic Discrimination, and Domestic Terrorism' (2011) 48 *Journal of Peace Research* 339, 347–49; JA Piazza, 'Types of Minority Discrimination and Terrorism' (2012) 29 *Conflict Management and Peace Science* 521, 536; and S Ghatak and A Gold, 'Development, Discrimination, and Domestic Terrorism: Looking beyond a Linear Relationship' (2015) *Conflict Management and Peace Science* 1.

[78] For a parallel argument in the philosophical literature, see J Waldron, 'Security and Liberty: The Image of Balance' (2003) 11 *Journal of Political Philosophy* 191.

amplifies existing economic stratification. In France, as well as in other European countries, Muslims tend toward the more impoverished end of income and wealth scales and are often less integrated into the labour market.[79]

Security against terrorism is a public good that all enjoy. It is unjust for the costs of its production to be concentrated on one minority group. This would be so even if there were good efficiency reasons for that concentration. But there are not. Profiling and selective coercion are measures of dubious worth. Extirpation is based on false and pernicious stereotyping of gaps between Islam and 'Western' culture. Reformist efforts raise the important question of how much the state can legitimately shape confessional practice. These questions must be considered in light of the fact that Muslim citizens have, if anything, a special contribution to make in terms of the kinds of arguments and social mobilisation they can (and do) bring to bear against propaganda from IS and al Qaeda.[80] How this contribution can be recognised and cultivated while ensuring that the burdens of security are equitably distributed – this is the central challenge of contemporary counterterrorism, a challenge that sounds as much in distributive justice terms as it does in the values captured by individual rights.

IV. CONCLUSION

The dynamics mapped out in this chapter will likely sharpen in the near term as right-of-centre populists in Europe and the United States exercise a greater measure of political influence. To date, judicial review and administrative mechanisms alike have failed to provide much traction against the rights-related and distributive inequities of security policy. Nevertheless, domestic Muslim civil-society organisations are increasingly vocal in their resistance to the myriad uses of Islam for security ends.[81] This chapter has described the challenge they face. Alas, it is a challenge that will not be surmounted quickly, and its greatest costs will be borne by European and American Muslims.

REFERENCES

Adida, CL, Laitin, DD, and Valfort, M-A, *Why Muslim Integration Fails in Christian-Heritage Societies* (Cambridge, MA, Harvard University Press, 2016).

Akkerman, T, 'Immigration Policy and Electoral Competition in Western Europe: A Fine-Grained Analysis of Party Positions over the Past Two Decades' (2015) 21 *Party Politics* 54.

[79] Open Society Institute, 'Muslims in Europe: A Report on 11 EU Cities' (December 2009), https://www.opensocietyfoundations.org/reports/muslims-europe-report-11-eu-cities.

[80] I have developed this argument at length in Huq, 'The Social Production of National Security' (above n 18).

[81] Edmunds (above n 48).

Alam, Y and Husband, C, 'Islamophobia, Community Cohesion and Counter-Terrorism Policies in Britain' (2013) 47 *Patterns of Prejudice* 235.
Alexander, JC, 'Struggling over the Mode of Incorporation: Backlash against Multiculturalism in Europe' (2013) 36 *Ethnic and Racial Studies* 531.
Al-Marayati, L, 'American Muslim Charities: Easy Targets in the War on Terror' (2004) 25 *Pace Law Review* 321.
Amnesty International, 'Upturned Lives: The Disproportionate Impact of France's State of Emergency', EUR 21/3364/2016 (4 February 2016), https://www.amnesty.org/en/documents/eur21/3364/2016/en/.
Apuzzo, M and Baker, A, 'New York to Appoint Civilian to Monitor Police's Counterterrorism Activity', *New York Times* (7 January 2016).
Apuzzo, M and Goldman, A, *Enemies Within: Inside the NYPD's Secret Spying Unit and Bin Laden's Final Plot Against America* (New York, Touchstone, 2013).
Bakker, E, 'EU Counter-Radicalization Policies: A Comprehensive and Consistent Approach?' (2015) 30 *Intelligence and National Security* 281.
Bakker, E and Singleton, M, 'Foreign Fighters in the Syria and Iraq Conflict: Statistics and Characteristics of a Rapidly Growing Phenomenon' in A de Guttry, F Capone, and C Paulussen (eds), *Foreign Fighters under International Law and Beyond* (The Hague, TMC Asser Press, 2016).
Batty, D, 'Prevent Strategy "Sowing Mistrust and Fear in Muslim Communities"', *Guardian* (3 February 2016).
Bigo, D, 'Security and Immigration: Toward a Critique of the Governmentality of Unease' (2002) 27 *Alternatives: Global, Local, Political* 63.
Bilefsky, D, 'Denmark's Tougher Citizenship Test Stumps Even Its Natives', *New York Times* (7 July 2016).
Briggs, R, 'Community Engagement for Counterterrorism: Lessons from the United Kingdom' (2010) 86 *International Affairs* 971.
Chichizola, J, 'Déradicalisation: les principales mesures du plan gouvernemental', *Le Figaro* (23 February 2018).
Cockburn, P, *The Rise of Islamic State: ISIS and the New Sunni Revolution* (New York, Verso Books, 2015).
Cook, D, 'Apostasy from Islam: A Historical Perspective' (2006) 31 *Jerusalem Studies in Arabic and Islam* 248.
Coppock, V and McGovern, M, '"Dangerous Minds"? Deconstructing Counter-Terrorism Discourse, Radicalisation and the "Psychological Vulnerability" of Muslim Children and Young People in Britain' (2014) 28 *Children & Society* 242.
Cowell, M, 'What Went Wrong with France's Deradicalization Program?' *Atlantic* (28 September 2017).
Dempsey, J, 'Civic Test in Germany Draws Fire', *New York Times* (14 February 2006).
Edmunds, J, 'The "New" Barbarians: Governmentality, Securitization and Islam in Western Europe' (2011) 6 *Contemporary Islam* 67.
Engel, RS and Tillyer, R, 'Searching for Equilibrium: The Tenuous Nature of the Outcome Test' (2008) 25 *Justice Quarterly* 54.
Faiola, A and Kirchner, S, 'Islam Is Europe's "new Fascism," and Other Things European Politicians Say about Muslims', *Washington Post* (7 June 2016).
Farwell, JP, 'The Media Strategy of ISIS' (2014) 56 *Survival* 49.
Foley, F, 'Reforming Counterterrorism: Institutions and Organizational Routines in Britain and France' (2009) 18 *Security Studies* 435.

Garland, D, '"Governmentality" and the Problem of Crime: Foucault, Criminology, Sociology' (1997) 1 *Theoretical Criminology* 173.

Gayle, D, 'Prevent Strategy "Could End up Promoting Extremism"', *Guardian* (21 April 2016).

Gerges, FA, *The Far Enemy: Why Jihad Went Global* (New York, Cambridge University Press, 2009).

Ghatak, S and Gold, A, 'Development, Discrimination, and Domestic Terrorism: Looking beyond a Linear Relationship' (2015) *Conflict Management and Peace Science* 1.

Göle, N, 'The Public Visibility of Islam and European Politics of Resentment: The Minarets-Mosques Debate' (2011) 37 *Philosophy & Social Criticism* 383.

—— 'The Voluntary Adoption of Islamic Stigma Symbols' (2003) 70 *Social Research* 809.

Goodman, SW, 'Controlling Immigration through Language and Country Knowledge Requirements' (2011) 34 *West European Politics* 235.

Goold, BJ and Lazarus, L (eds), *Security and Human Rights* (Oxford, Hart Publishing, 2007).

Gregory, S, 'France and the War on Terrorism' (2003) 15 *Terrorism and Political Violence* 124.

Hafez, F, 'Shifting Borders: Islamophobia as Common Ground for Building Pan-European Right-Wing Unity' (2014) 48 *Patterns of Prejudice* 479.

Hallsworth, S, 'Racial Targeting and Social Control: Looking behind the Police' (2006) 14 *Critical Criminology* 293.

Harcourt, B, 'Muslim Profiles Post 9/11: Is Racial Profiling an Effective Counter-terrorism Measure and Does It Violate the Right to be Free from Discrimination?' in BJ Goold and L Lazarus (eds), *Security and Human Rights* (Oxford, Hart Publishing, 2007).

Heath, A and Demireva, N, 'Has Multiculturalism Failed in Britain?' (2014) 37 *Ethnic & Racial Studies* 161.

Heath-Kelly, C, 'Counter-Terrorism and the Counterfactual: Producing the "Radicalisation" Discourse and the UK PREVENT Strategy' (2013) 15 *British Journal of Politics and International Relations* 394.

Hellmuth, D, 'Countering Jihadi Terrorists and Radicals the French Way' (2015) 38 *Studies in Conflict and Terrorism* 979.

Hupe, P and Hill, M, 'Street-Level Bureaucracy and Public Accountability' (2007) 85 *Public Administration* 279.

Huq, A, 'Article II and Antidiscrimination Norms' (2019) *Michigan Law Review* (forthcoming).

——, 'The Consequences of Disparate Policing: Evaluating Stop and Frisk as a Modality of Urban Policing' (2017) 101 *Minnesota Law Review* 2397.

——, 'Modeling Terrorist Radicalization' (2010) 2 *Duke Forum for Law and Social Change* 39.

——, 'Private Religious Discrimination, National Security, and the First Amendment' (2011) 5 *Harvard Law & Policy Review* 347.

——, 'The Signalling Function of Religious Speech in Counterterrorism' (2011) 89 *Texas Law Review* 833.

——, 'The Social Production of National Security' (2012) 98 *Cornell Law Review* 637.

——, 'Terrorism and Democratic Recession' (2018) 85 *University of Chicago Law Review* 457.

——, 'What is the Case against Muslims?' in M Nussbaum, Z Hasan, A Huq, and V Verma (eds), *'The Empire of Disgust': Prejudice, Stigma, and Discrimination in India and the US* (Delhi, Oxford University Press, 2018).

Huq, AZ, Tyler, TR, and Schulhofer, SJ, 'Mechanisms for Eliciting Cooperation in Counterterrorism Policing: Evidence from the United Kingdom' (2011) 8 *Journal of Empirical Legal Studies* 728.

Ingram, HJ, 'The Strategic Logic of Islamic State Information Operations' (2015) 69 *Australian Journal of International Affairs* 729.

Ivarsflaten, E, 'What Unites Right-Wing Populists in Western Europe? Re-Examining Grievance Mobilization Models in Seven Successful Cases' (2008) 41 *Comparative Political Studies* 3.

Joppke, C, 'Terror and the Loss of Citizenship' (2016) 20 *Citizenship Studies* 728.

——, 'Through the European Looking Glass: Citizenship Tests in the USA, Australia, and Canada' (2013) 17 *Citizenship Studies* 1.

Kennedy, H, *The Caliphate* (London, Pelican, 2016).

Knowles, J, Persico, N, and Todd, P, 'Racial Bias in Motor Vehicle Searches: Theory and Evidence' (2001) 109 *Journal of Political Economy* 203.

Korteweg, AC and Triadafilopoulos, T, 'Is Multiculturalism Dead? Groups, Governments and the "Real Work of Integration"' (2015) 38 *Ethnic and Racial Studies* 663.

Kurzman, C, *The Missing Martyrs: Why There Are So Few Muslim Terrorists* (Oxford, Oxford University Press, 2011).

de Leeuw, M and van Wichelen, S, 'Civilizing Migrants: Integration, Culture and Citizenship' (2012) 15 *European Journal of Cultural Studies* 195.

Lindekilde, L, 'Introduction: Assessing the Effectiveness of Counter-radicalisation Policies in Northwestern Europe' (2012) 5 *Critical Studies on Terrorism* 335.

——, 'Value for Money? Problems of Impact Assessment of Counter-Radicalization Policies on End Target Groups: The Case of Denmark' (2012) 18 *European Journal on Criminal Policy and Research* 385.

Lindekilde, L, Bertelsen, P, and Stohl, M, 'Who Goes, Why, and With What Effects: The Problem of Foreign Fighters from Europe' (2016) 27 *Small Wars & Insurgencies* 858.

Massad, JA, *Islam in Liberalism*, reprint edn (Chicago, University of Chicago Press, 2016).

Michaels, R, 'Banning Burqas: The Perspective of Postsecular Comparative Law' (2018) 28(2) *Duke Journal of Comparatrive and International Law* 213.

Moeckli, D, *Human Rights and Non-Discrimination in the 'War on Terror'* (Oxford, Oxford University Press, 2008).

Mythen, G, Walklate, S, and Khan, F, '"I'm a Muslim, but I'm Not a Terrorist": Victimization, Risky Identities and the Performance of Safety' (2009) 49 *British Journal of Criminology* 736.

Nabulsi, K, 'Don't Go to the Doctor', *London Review of Books* (18 May 2017).

Neumann, PR, 'The Trouble with Radicalization' (2013) 89 *International Affairs* 873.

O'Toole, T et al, 'Governing through Prevent? Regulation and Contested Practice in State–Muslim Engagement' (2016) 50 *Sociology* 160.

Office of the Inspector General for the NYPD, 'An Investigation of NYPD's Compliance with Rules Governing Investigations of Political Activity' (23 August 2016), http://www1.nyc.gov/site/oignypd/reports/reports.page.

Open Society Institute, 'Muslims in Europe: A Report on 11 EU Cities' (December 2009), https://www.opensocietyfoundations.org/reports/muslims-europe-report-11-eu-cities.

Pantazis, C and Pemberton, S, 'From the "Old" to the "New" Suspect Community Examining the Impacts of Recent UK Counter-Terrorist Legislation' (2009) 49 *British Journal of Criminology* 646.

Piazza, JA, 'Poverty, Minority Economic Discrimination, and Domestic Terrorism' (2011) 48 *Journal of Peace Research* 339.

——, 'Types of Minority Discrimination and Terrorism' (2012) 29 *Conflict Management and Peace Science* 521.

Ragazzi, F, 'Toward "Policed Multiculturalism"? Counter-Radicalization in France, the Netherlands and the United Kingdom', Centre d'Études et de Recherches Internationales (December 2014), http://www.sciencespo.fr/ceri/sites/sciencespo.fr.ceri/files/Etude_206_anglais.pdf.

Rubin AJ, 'Muslims in France Say Emergency Powers Go Too Far', *New York Times* (17 February 2016).

Rydgren, J, 'Immigration Skeptics, Xenophobes or Racists? Radical Right-Wing Voting in Six West European Countries' (2008) 47 *European Journal of Political Research* 737.

Samuel, S, 'Banning Muslims Veils Tend to Backfire – So Why Do Countries Keep Doing It?' *Atlantic* (3 August 2018).

Scheppele, KL, 'Other People's Patriot Acts: Europe's Response to September 11' (2004) 50 *Loyola Law Review* 89.

Theoharis, J, '"I Feel Like a Despised Insect": Coming of Age Under Surveillance in New York', *Intercept* (18 February 2016).

Thomas, P, *Responding to the Threat of Violent Extremism: Failing to Prevent* (London, Bloomsbury, 2012).

Vertigans, S, 'British Muslims and the UK Government's "War on Terror" Within: Evidence of a Clash of Civilizations or Emergent de-Civilizing Processes?' (2010) 61 *British Journal of Sociology* 26.

Weimann, G, 'The Emerging Role of Social Media in the Recruitment of Foreign Fighters' in A de Guttry, F Capone, and C Paulussen (eds), *Foreign Fighters under International Law and Beyond* (The Hague, TMC Asser Press, 2016).

Yılmaz, F, 'Right-Wing Hegemony and Immigration: How the Populist Far-Right Achieved Hegemony through the Immigration Debate in Europe' (2012) 60 *Current Sociology* 368.

Zelin, AY, 'Picture Or It Didn't Happen: A Snapshot of the Islamic State's Official Media Output' (2015) 9 *Perspectives on Terrorism*, http://www.terrorismanalysts.com/pt/index.php/pot/article/view/445.

Zucchino, D, '"I've Become a Racist': Migrant Wave Unleashes Danish Tensions Over Identity', *New York Times* (5 September 2016).

5

Curtailing Citizenship Rights as Counterterrorism

LUCIA ZEDNER*

I. INTRODUCTION

THE DECLARATION OF a 'War on Terror' following 9/11 led directly to the characterisation of terrorist suspects as 'enemy aliens' and made possible the introduction of exceptional measures such as indefinite administrative detention, extraordinary rendition, torture, and drone strikes. It also fostered resort to less procedurally demanding channels such as immigration law as central to national security strategy.[1] The fact that some followers of radical Islamic terror organisations openly reject Western liberal values and declare themselves hostile to the societies they attack has made possible their characterisation as enemy aliens.[2] Recourse to differential treatment of foreigners, asylum seekers, and those whose citizenship status is precarious as a mode of countering terrorism quickly became an established feature of UK national security policy, from the indefinite detention of foreign nationals[3] to the citizenship stripping of naturalised citizens.[4] But as David Cole observed

* The law discussed in this chapter is correct as of September 2018. It does not include, for example, changes brought about by the UK Counter-Terrorism and Border Security Act 2019, which received royal assent in February 2019. For more on that topic, see L Zedner, 'The Hostile Border: Crimmigration, Counterterrorism, or Crossing the Line on Rights?' (2019) 22(3) *New Criminal Law Review* (forthcoming).

[1] N Demleitner, 'Misguided Prevention: The War on Terrorism as a War on Immigrant Offenders and Immigration Violators' (2004) 40 *Criminal Law Bulletin* 550–75; and A Macklin, 'Borderline Security' in RJ Daniels, P Macklem, and K Roach (eds), *The Security of Freedom: Essays on Canada's Anti-Terrorism Bill* (Toronto, University of Toronto Press, 2001). See also Kent Roach's contribution to the first edition of this volume: K Roach, 'Sources and Trends in Post-9/11 Anti-Terrorism Laws' in BJ Goold and L Lazarus (eds), *Security and Human Rights* (Oxford, Hart Publishing, 2007).

[2] See the chapter in this volume by Aziz Z Huq.

[3] H Fenwick, 'Responding to 11 September: Detention without Trial under the Anti-Terrorism, Crime and Security Act 2001' in L Freedman (ed), *Superterrorism: Policy Responses* (Oxford, Blackwell Publishing, 2002).

[4] Under s 66 of the Immigration Act (2014). See L Zedner, 'Citizenship Deprivation, Security and Human Rights' (2016) 18 *European Journal of Migration and Law* 222–42.

in 2003, 'While the principal gambit in the trade-off between liberty and security has been to sacrifice the liberty of foreign nationals for the security of the citizenry, citizens have not been entirely spared.'[5] Counterterrorism laws and measures first introduced against foreign nationals have been extended to dual citizens, to naturalised citizens, and, in lesser degree, to all citizens.[6] The apparent readiness to label terrorists as enemy aliens has paved the way for security policies that radically restrict the rights of all those deemed to pose a terrorist threat.[7]

The rise of the so-called Islamic State (ISIS) in Syria and Iraq has since attracted worldwide attention and drawn support from citizens across Europe, the Middle East, and beyond.[8] Radicalisation creates the risk that those recruited will commit atrocities in the name of ISIS or travel to serve as foreign fighters, only to return home to execute terrorist attacks. Estimates about how many foreign terrorist fighters have travelled to Syria and Iraq since 2011 vary widely,[9] but by 2016 the official estimate was around 22,000, of whom about 5,000 were European.[10] Of the 850 or so from the United Kingdom,[11] just under half have since returned home, some to attempt or commit attacks.[12] In 2015 alone, 151 people were killed and over 360 injured in terrorist attacks across Europe.[13] Although the number of foreign fighters committing atrocities in Europe is

[5] D Cole, *Enemy Aliens: Double Standards and Constitutional Freedoms in the War on Terrorism* (New York, New Press, 2003) 72.

[6] Ibid, ch 5.

[7] See many of the contributions to the first edition of this volume: BJ Goold and L Lazarus (eds), *Security and Human Rights* (Oxford, Hart Publishing, 2007), including L Zedner, 'Seeking Security by Eroding Rights: The Side-stepping of Due Process'.

[8] B Boutin, G Chauzal, and J Dorsey et al, 'The Foreign Fighters Phenomenon in the European Union: Profiles, Threats, and Policies', International Centre for Counter-Terrorism (ICCT) Research Paper (April 2016), https://icct.nl/wp-content/uploads/2016/03/ICCT-Report_Foreign-Fighters-Phenomenon-in-the-EU_1-April-2016_including-AnnexesLinks.pdf; and E Bakker and M Singleton, 'Foreign Fighters in the Syria and Iraq Conflict' in A de Guttry, F Capone, and C Paulussen (eds), *Foreign Fighters under International Law and Beyond* (The Hague, Asser Press, 2016). See also the contribution by Aziz Z Huq in this volume.

[9] A Kirk, 'Iraq and Syria: How Many Foreign Fighters Are Fighting for Isil?' *Telegraph* (24 March 2016), http://www.telegraph.co.uk/news/2016/03/29/iraq-and-syria-how-many-foreign-fighters-are-fighting-for-isil/.

[10] C Walker, 'Foreign Terrorist Fighters and UK Counter Terrorism Laws', guest chapter (Annex 2) in D Anderson, 'The Terrorism Acts in 2015: Report of the Independent Reviewer' (December 2016), https://www.gov.uk/government/uploads/system/uploads/attachment_data/file/579233/THE_TERRORISM_ACTS_IN_2015__web_.pdf, 101.

[11] BBC, 'Who are Britain's Jihadists?', *BBC News* (12 October 2017), http://www.bbc.co.uk/news/uk-32026985 (accessed 8 February 2019).

[12] R Barrett, 'Beyond the Caliphate: Foreign Fighters and the Threat of Returnees', Soufan Centre Report (October 2017), http://thesoufancenter.org/wp-content/uploads/2017/11/Beyond-the-Caliphate-Foreign-Fighters-and-the-Threat-of-Returnees-TSC-Report-October-2017-v3.pdf.

[13] In total, six European countries faced 211 failed, foiled and completed terrorist attacks; and 1,077 individuals were arrested in the EU for terrorism-related offences. See Europol, '211 Terrorist Attacks Carried Out in EU Member States in 2015, New Europol Report Reveals', Press Release (20 July 2016), https://www.europol.europa.eu/newsroom/news/211-terrorist-attacks-carried-out-in-eu-member-states-in-2015-new-europol-report-reveals.

small, and fatalities from terrorism remain lower than in the 1970s,[14] each new incident increases pressure on national security services and police to tighten security.[15]

The relative ease with which citizens travel to Syria and Iraq as foreign fighters or cross borders within Europe to commit terrorist attacks[16] has led to the introduction of security laws and counterterrorism measures that limit mobility and curtail the citizenship rights of suspected terrorists.[17] The precept that suspected offenders are owed due process rights, however serious their crime, has long been challenged by the view that would-be terrorists stand outside civil society and are not owed the same legal protections as other citizens.[18] Chief among those targeted are prospective, serving, and returning Jihadi fighters. In the uncompromising words of former UK prime minister, David Cameron, 'It is not only the full force of the law that these people should face; they should also recognise that when they take up arms in this way in another country, they become *enemies of the state*.'[19]

This chapter explores the consequences of depicting citizens as 'enemies of the state' for recent security laws and measures in United Kingdom. It examines the grave threats posed by the rise of ISIS and its recruitment of European citizens as foreign fighters in Syria and Iraq and assesses resulting developments in counterterrorism and security laws. In particular, it explores security laws that target citizenship and mobility rights by introducing powers of temporary exclusion, travel restrictions, and forcible relocation. It considers how, in the name of national security, these laws threaten individual security by curtailing

[14] One study estimates that only one in 360 returnees perpetrated an attack on their return: T Hegghammer and P Nesser, 'Assessing the Islamic State's Commitment to Attacking the West' (2015) 9(4) *Perspectives on Terrorism*. See also T Stanley, 'West Europe Is Safer Now Than in the 1970s', *Telegraph* (25 March 2016), http://www.telegraph.co.uk/news/2016/03/25/west-europe-is-safer-now-than-in-the-1970s-and-safer-than-almost/.

[15] See, eg, M Evans, 'How the German Police and Security Service Blundered over the Berlin Terror Outrage', *Telegraph* (21 December 2016), http://www.telegraph.co.uk/news/2016/12/21/german-police-security-service-blundered-berlin-terror-outrage/; and J Delcker, 'Attack Exposes Missing Links in German Security', *Politico* (23 December 2016), http://www.politico.eu/article/attack-highlights-disconnect-in-german-security-berlin-attack/.

[16] See, eg, BBC, 'Paris Attacks: Who Were the Attackers?' *BBC News* (27 April 2016), http://www.bbc.co.uk/news/world-europe-34832512.

[17] S Macdonald, 'Prosecuting Suspected Terrorists: Precursor Crimes, Intercept Evidence and the Priority of Security' in L Jarvis and M Lister (eds), *Critical Perspectives on Counter-Terrorism* (Abingdon, Routledge, 2015); and C Gomez-Jara Diez, 'Enemy Combatants Versus Enemy Criminal Law' (2008) 11(4) *New Criminal Law Review* 529–62. See also the chapter in this volume by Victor Ramraj and the chapter by David Irvine and Travers McLeod.

[18] L Zedner, 'Seeking Security by Eroding Rights: The Side-Stepping of Due Process' in Goold and Lazarus (eds) (above n 1). Arguably, this trend towards the evasion of procedural safeguards has since intensified. See, eg, L Zedner, 'Criminal Justice in the Service of Security' in M Bosworth, C Hoyle, and L Zedner (eds), *The Changing Contours of Criminal Justice* (Oxford, Oxford University Press, 2016) 156ff.

[19] Speech quoted in B Farmer, 'David Cameron: Returning Jihadists Are "Enemies of the state"', *Telegraph* (17 November 2014), http://www.telegraph.co.uk/news/politics/david-cameron/11237012/David-Cameron-Returning-jihadists-are-enemies-of-the-state.html (emphasis added).

human rights. It concludes by considering the justice, as well as the efficacy, of these security measures.

The central questions addressed in my contribution to the first edition of *Security and Human Rights* (What is security for? Whose security do we pursue? And how should we pursue security?) are no less pertinent today. In considering these questions, the earlier chapter focused on the proliferation of civil and hybrid civil–criminal preventive orders that sidestep the protections of the criminal process and the fundamental right to a fair trial.[20] In the present chapter, these three questions continue to motivate the inquiry, but the substantive focus is the recent developments in counterterrorism law that challenge, even more profoundly, the complex relationship between security and human rights. If preventive orders evade the protections of the criminal process, the developments described in this chapter shift preventive policing very much further into the domain of immigration laws and mobility controls.

II. IMMIGRATION AND BORDER CONTROLS AS COUNTERTERRORISM

Laws that curtail mobility and citizenship rights as a tool of counterterrorism are by no means new. In the United Kingdom, during the thirty-year period of political violence in Northern Ireland, many such laws were enacted. For the purposes of preventing terrorism, individuals could be detained for up to twelve hours at ports between England and Northern Ireland,[21] and Exclusion Orders could be imposed on noncitizens to prohibit them from being in or entering the United Kingdom.[22] Breach of an order was an offence carrying a maximum sentence of five years' imprisonment. Despite the fact that the Prevention of Terrorism Act 1974 was intended as a temporary measure, it was repeatedly renewed as an emergency power, until it was made permanent by the Terrorism Act 2000. Significantly, that an 'emergency' was deemed to endure over several decades was never called into question.

Similarly in the United States since 9/11, immigration controls, detention, and deportation have been invoked as essential weapons of the War on Terror, even against those who have been long resident in the country.[23] UN Security Council Resolution 1373, issued after hurried consultation in September 2001, requires states to 'prevent the movement of terrorists or their groups by effective border controls' and to ensure asylum seekers have 'not planned, facilitated or participated in the commission of terrorist acts', 'refugee status was not abused

[20] Zedner, 'Seeking Security by Eroding Rights' (above n 18).

[21] S 3, Prevention of Terrorism (Temporary Provisions) Act 1974, passed in response to sustained terrorist attacks by the IRA on the UK mainland, including the Birmingham bombings that killed 21 and injured 184 that year.

[22] S 6, Prevention of Terrorism (Temporary Provisions) Act 1974 (ibid).

[23] Demleitner (above n 1).

by the perpetrators, organizers or facilitators of terrorist acts', and 'claims of political motivation are not recognized as grounds for refusing requests for the extradition of alleged terrorists.'[24] It is unclear why the UN Security Council singled out groups such as migrants, asylum seekers, and refugees as possible security threats, since none of the 9/11 bombers had entered the United States illegally or claimed refugee status.[25] Resolution 1373 further called on states not to grant refugee status to suspected terrorists, even if they otherwise qualified on grounds of political persecution. In so doing, it effectively condoned the deliberate breach of human rights.

Resolution 1373 was read by many states as a direct signal to resort to mobility restrictions and immigration laws as tools of counterterrorism. Immigration law was in any case attractive to legislators and policymakers because of its relaxed liability rules, lower burden of proof, and provision for increased or indefinite periods of investigative detention in immigration centres.[26] Border controls and immigration laws were seen as powerful tools that allowed states to avoid the usual strictures of due process and human rights protections required by the criminal process.[27]

It is unsurprising, therefore, that the United Kingdom moved quickly to single out foreign nationals as targets of counterterrorism policies. Shortly after 9/11, the Anti-Terrorism, Crime and Security Act 2001 Part IV provided that the Home Secretary could detain indefinitely any non-British citizens suspected of terrorist activity, either pending deportation or in cases where deportation was not possible for fear of torture.[28] Between 2001 and 2004, seventeen foreign national terrorist suspects were detained at Belmarsh Prison in London, dubbed by the media 'Britain's Guantanamo'.[29] Article 5(1)(f) of the European Convention on Human Rights (ECHR) permits detention of an individual 'to prevent his effecting an unauthorised entry into the country or of a person against whom action is being taken with a view to deportation or extradition', so the UK government was able to indefinitely detain foreign nationals without trial only by exercising the power to derogate from the ECHR under Article 15 in case of 'war or other public emergency threatening the life of the nation'.[30]

[24] UN Security Council, Resolution 1373 on Threats to International Peace and Security Caused by Terrorist Acts, 28 September 2001, S/RES/1373, para 2(g).

[25] K Roach, *The 9/11 Effect: Comparative Counter-Terrorism* (Cambridge, Cambridge University Press, 2011) 40.

[26] Ibid, 41.

[27] See the chapter by Kent Roach in the first edition of this volume: Roach, 'Sources and Trends in Post-9/11 Anti-Terrorism Laws' (above n 1).

[28] H Fenwick, 'The Anti-Terrorism, Crime and Security Act 2001: A Proportional Response to 11 September?' (2002) 65(5) *Modern Law Review* 724–62; and PA Thomas, 'Emergency and Anti-Terrorist Powers 9/11: USA and UK' (2003) 26(4) *Fordham International Law Journal* 1193–233.

[29] D Winterman, 'Belmarsh: Britain's Guantanamo Bay?', *BBC News* (6 October 2004), http://news.bbc.co.uk/1/hi/magazine/3714864.stm.

[30] The derogation permitted under Art 15 is not unlimited: measures taken must be 'strictly required by the exigencies of the situation'.

In the landmark judgment *A v the Home Secretary* (2004), indefinite detention of foreign nationals was finally ruled unlawful on the grounds that detention without trial on the basis of nationality or immigration status, though the threat of terrorism was not confined to noncitizens, was discriminatory.[31]

Nonetheless, the UK government continued to deploy immigration and citizenship laws as tools of counterterrorism. The Immigration, Asylum and Nationality Act 2006 provided for greater powers of deportation and removal, allowed for the denial of refugee status (section 54) on security grounds and for citizenship deprivation (section 56) if 'conducive to the public good'. Recourse to immigration law as a means of counterterrorism was firmly established as a central facet of the government's security policy in its 2007 policy report 'Security in a Global Hub', which insisted that 'border controls need to protect us against terrorism and crime'.[32] In the following years, a series of high-profile cases tested the conformity of UK border laws with Convention rights.[33] Leading cases addressed the rights implications of deportation on security grounds,[34] the scope of disclosure in Special Immigration Appeals Commission (SIAC) cases,[35] the exercise of Schedule 7 Terrorism Act 2000 powers of interrogation and search at the border,[36] and alleged UK complicity in practices of extraordinary rendition and torture overseas.[37]

One of the most significant recent trends is the shift from focus on foreign and dual nationals to counterterrorism measures that target the rights of membership and mobility of all citizens deemed to pose a threat to national security. Chief among present security threats are the hostilities in Syria and Iraq, recruitment of jihadi fighters, and the subsequent rise in ISIS-related terrorist attacks globally.[38] Responding to the gravity of the threat, the UN Security Council held a summit meeting in September 2014, presided over by then United States President Barack Obama, to consider the risks to national

[31] *A and Others v Secretary of State for the Home Department* [2004] UKHL 56.

[32] UK Cabinet Office, 'Security in a Global Hub: Establishing the UK's New Border Arrangements' (November 2007) 3.

[33] L Lazarus, 'Do Human Rights Impede Effective Counterterrorism?', UK Constitutional. Law Association Blog (15 June 2017), https://ukconstitutionallaw.org/2017/06/15/liora-lazarus-do-human-rights-impede-effective-counterterrorism/.

[34] *Othman v United Kingdom (2012) 55 EHRR 1*. The case of Abu Qatada, the Jordanian preacher Omar Othman whose deportation was achieved only after the ECtHR was satisfied that a Memorandum of Understanding (MoU) signed with Jordan would protect against violation of Art 3 (prohibition of torture, inhuman or degrading treatment).

[35] *ZZ v Secretary of State for the Home Department* [2013] EUECJ C-300/11.

[36] *Beghal v DPP* [2015] UKSC 49: appeal on the grounds that detention, questioning and search under Schedule 7 constituted an interference with Art 5 (right to liberty), Art 6 (privilege against self-incrimination), and Art 8 (right to private and family life) dismissed as the exercise of the power was found to be in accordance with the law, necessary and proportionate. *Miranda v SSHD* [2016] EWCA Civ 6: upheld the lawfulness of detention of David Miranda under Schedule 7, but ruled that stop powers under Schedule 7 lacked sufficient legal safeguards and were therefore incompatible with Art 10 (freedom of expression).

[37] *Belhaj and Another v Straw and Others* [2017] UKSC 3.

[38] See, eg, Boutin, Chauzal, Dorsey et al (above n 8).

and international security.[39] This was only the sixth time in seventy years that the Security Council had been convened at such a high level. The outcome, Security Council Resolution 2178, raised concerns about 'the establishment of international terrorist networks' and stated:

> [F]oreign terrorist fighters increase the intensity, duration and intractability of conflicts, and also may pose a serious threat to their States of origin, the States they transit and the States to which they travel, as well as States neighbouring zones of armed conflict in which foreign terrorist fighters are active.[40]

The Resolution stressed 'the particular and urgent need' to prevent the travel and support for foreign terrorist fighters[41] and called upon all states to 'prevent the movement of terrorists or terrorist groups by effective border controls and controls on issuance of identity papers and travel documents'.[42] Although Resolution 2178 also required states to develop strategies to prevent radicalisation and promote rehabilitation and reintegration for returning foreign fighters, its dominant focus was on disruption, prosecution, and punishment. It prevailed upon national governments to target would-be jihadis, those fighting overseas and returning foreign fighters by enacting new legal powers to monitor, disrupt, immobilise, and exclude.

III. CURTAILING CITIZENSHIP RIGHTS AND MOBILITY AS COUNTERTERRORISM

In line with global security policy, recent developments in Britain shift focus from the threat posed by foreigners to all those, including naturalised citizens, dual citizens, birth citizens and residents, whose intentions, conduct, or associations suggest they pose a threat. A feature of this development is the emphasis on curtailing citizenship rights and controlling mobility as means of achieving security. Just as 'crimes of mobility' have attracted increasing criminological attention,[43] so too managing mobility as a means of countering terrorism is now central to UK security policy. Limiting the movements of risky individuals

[39] UN Security Council, 'Security Council Unanimously Adopts Resolution Condemning Violent Extremism, Underscoring Need to Prevent Travel, Support for Foreign Terrorist Fighters', press release SC/115 (24 September 2014), http://www.un.org/press/en/2014/sc11580.doc.htm. For the text of UN Security Council Resolution 2178 (2014), see http://unscr.com/en/resolutions/doc/2178.

[40] Ibid.

[41] Ibid.

[42] Ibid. An earlier resolution, UNSCR 2170 (2014), had applied travel restrictions, asset freezing and encouraged Member States to take domestic measures against foreign fighters.

[43] S Pickering, M Bosworth, and KF Aas, 'The Criminology of Mobility' in S Pickering (ed), *Routledge Handbook on Crime and Migration* (London, Routledge, 2014); M Bosworth, 'Border Criminologies: How Migration Is Changing Criminal Justice' in Bosworth, Hoyle, and Zedner (eds) (above n 18); and B Bowling and L Weber, 'Valiant Beggars and Global Vagabonds: Select, Eject, Immobilize' (2008) 12(3) *Theoretical Criminology* 355–75.

was, as we saw above, a tactic deployed during the Troubles in Northern Ireland. Disruption was also the goal of preventive orders such Travel Restriction Orders,[44] Serious Crime Prevention Orders,[45] and Foreign Travel Restriction Orders.[46] Mobility-curtailing measures seek to prevent potential terrorists from associating with others, from traveling abroad, or from returning home unmonitored. The apparent ease with which even those already identified as terrorist risks flit under the radar of the security services continues to prompt demands for new tools with which to tighten security.[47] Prominent examples include Mohammed Emwazi (better known as 'Jihadi John'), who, although well known to the UK intelligence services, slipped through the net to travel to join IS.[48] Similarly, Anis Amri, despite being known to German security services, crossed European states to carry out the Berlin Christmas market attack in 2016 and then managed to travel as far as Italy before he was shot by police.[49]

Curtailing citizens' rights of freedom of movement has become a key aspect of UK security policy chiefly since the Counterterrorism and Security Act (CTSA) 2015, which introduced several powers aimed at disruption. Significantly, this legislation was introduced under expedited procedures that permitted little time for pre-legislative scrutiny or public consultation,[50] leading the Joint Committee on Human Rights (JCHR) to protest, 'We do not consider that the provision of an ECHR Memorandum at the time of the introduction of a fast-tracked Bill amounts to giving us a proper opportunity to scrutinise the legislation.'[51] The Act included draconian powers of immobilisation, temporary exclusion, and forcible relocation – itself a kind of internal banishment. The following sections examine some of the key measures introduced by this legislation and their implications for civil liberties and for the rights of citizenship.

[44] Criminal Justice and Police Act 2001, s 33.

[45] Serious Crime Act 2007, s 1.

[46] Counter-Terrorism Act 2008, Sched 5.

[47] M Townsend et al, 'The Race to Find the Manchester Terrorist Network', *Guardian* (28 May 2017), https://www.theguardian.com/uk-news/2017/may/28/race-to-find-manchester-terrorist-network; T Batchelor, 'Manchester Attack: Police Have Arrested "Large Part" of Terror Network Behind Salman Abedi', *Independent* (26 May 2017), http://www.independent.co.uk/news/uk/home-news/manchester-attack-police-terror-network-arrest-salman-abedi-suicide-bomber-arena-a7758056.html; and R Roig, 'Police Try to Unravel Terrorist Network Behind Attacks in Barcelona, Cambrils', *Globe and Mail* (20 August 2017), https://www.theglobeandmail.com/news/world/police-try-to-unravel-terrorist-network-behind-attacks-in-barcelona-cambrils/article36037758/.

[48] 'Isis Magazine Confirms Death of Mohammed Emwazi in "Eulogizing Profile"', *Guardian*, (20 January 2016), https://www.theguardian.com/uk-news/2016/jan/20/mohammed-emwazis-death-confirmed-in-isis-magazine.

[49] BBC, 'Berlin Truck Attacker Anis Amri Killed in Milan', *BBC News* (23 December 2016), http://www.bbc.co.uk/news/world-europe-38415287.

[50] F Webber, 'Farewell Magna Carta: The Counter-Terrorism and Security Bill', *Open Democracy UK* (19 January 2015), https://www.opendemocracy.net/ourkingdom/frances-webber/farewell-magna-carta-counterterrorism-and-security-bill.

[51] Joint Committee on Human Rights (JCHR), *Legislative Scrutiny: Counter-Terrorism and Security Bill, Fifth Report* (2014–15, HL 86, HC 859) 3–4.

A. Shutting In: Powers to Seize Travel Documents

Passport seizure enables a government to 'shut in' those seeking to travel abroad who are suspected of involvement in terrorist-related activity. Section 1 of CTSA 2015 extends existing powers to seize documents to disrupt travel in cases where there is a risk the individual plans to go to conflict zones or to engage in terrorist-related activity. The stated aim is to hinder travel to 'locations which facilitate terrorist networking, training, and experiences which provide individuals with enhanced capabilities on their return'.[52] Immediate disruption is said to buy 'operational time' for police and security services, while further consideration is given to 'whether long term disruptive measures are appropriate'.[53]

CTSA also extends existing powers of passport seizure and permits the police to stop, search for, seize, and retain 'travel documents where a person is suspected of intending to leave Great Britain … in connection with terrorism-related activity'.[54] Retention beyond seventy-two hours must be reviewed by a senior police officer.[55] Although the JCHR recommended that retention should be limited to seven days before judicial review, the legislation retains the longer fourteen-day period. Only if the police seek to retain the passport beyond fourteen days must they must issue a notice explaining the reason for seizure and retention 'as fully as possible without prejudicing national security' and seek judicial authority for renewal, which may be granted for up to thirty days from the day after the passport was first seized. The CTSA further created two new offences in relation to these seizure powers: an offence of failing to hand over travel documents without reasonable excuse, and an offence of intentionally obstructing or seeking to frustrate a search.[56] Both are summary offences with maximum penalties of six months' imprisonment.

These powers of passport seizure extend the existing prerogative power of the Home Secretary to refuse to issue or to cancel passports on public interest grounds. According to the government at the time of the Counterterrorism and Security Bill, since April 2013, the prerogative power had been used to cancel or refuse British passports to twenty-nine people on these grounds.[57] It was claimed that the existing power could not be exercised quickly enough to disrupt the travel plans of prospective jihadists effectively, nor could it be used other than on

[52] Home Office (UK), 'Counterterrorism and Security Bill – Temporary Passport Seizure: Impact Assessment' (18 November 2014), http://www.parliament.uk/documents/impact-assessments/IA14-22F.pdf, 8.

[53] Home Office (UK), 'Temporary Passport Seizure', Counter-Terrorism and Security Bill Factsheets (3 December 2014), https://assets.publishing.service.gov.uk/government/uploads/system/uploads/attachment_data/file/540542/CTS_Bill_-_Factsheet_2_-_Passport_Seizure.pdf.

[54] Section 1, Counter-Terrorism and Security Act (CTSA) 2015, http://www.legislation.gov.uk/ukpga/2015/6/part/1/enacted.

[55] Of the rank of chief superintendent or above.

[56] Under Sched 1, s 15, CTSA 2015 (above n 54).

[57] Home Office, 'Temporary Passport Seizure – Factsheet' (above n 53).

British passport holders, whereas the power to seize travel documents is a powerful means of immediate disruption.[58] Although the Home Office estimated that the power would be used only 'up to 50 times a year',[59] such powers risk being overused, as was the case with the Schedule 7, Terrorism Act 2000 power to stop, examine, and detain any traveller at a port or airport without ground for suspicion.[60] Unlike Schedule 7, the evidential standard upon which the CTSA power to seize travel documents may be excised is 'reasonable suspicion', which must be 'on an objective basis … based on the facts' and 'cannot be formed on the basis of assumptions about the attitudes, beliefs or behaviour of persons who belong to particular groups or categories of people'.[61] However, judging by the use of similar powers, there are serious grounds for concern that this power will likewise be prone to discriminatory application against individuals from particular minorities.[62]

Passport seizure powers have significant implications for the Article 8 ECHR right to private and family life.[63] However, the Home Office took the view that the interference with privacy was necessary in the interests of national security, struck an appropriate balance, and was therefore compliant with Article 8. This conclusion reflects the limited protection offered by the Convention, given that even on the face of Article 8, interference is permitted 'in the interests of national security, public safety' etc. In its exercise, passport seizure may also breach the Article 14 ECHR right not be discriminated against and may also interfere with rights to freedom of movement,[64] though restrictions are subject to proportionality requirements.[65]

While the need for a seizure power to prevent travel and permit further investigation if there were insufficient grounds for arrest was acknowledged by the JCHR in its pre-legislative scrutiny of CTSA, the Committee criticised the lack of sufficient procedural safeguards to ensure the measure would be exercised proportionately and consistent with the right to a fair hearing under Article 6 ECHR.[66] Although the Act provides for a judicial hearing, the court

[58] Home Office, 'Counterterrorism and Security Bill: Impact Assessment' (above n 52).

[59] Ibid, 6.

[60] For criticism of the overuse of Schedule 7, see A Ashworth and L Zedner, *Preventive Justice* (Oxford, Oxford University Press, 2014) 55.

[61] Home Office (UK), 'Code of Practice for Officers Exercising Functions under Schedule 1 of the Counter-Terrorism and Security Act 2015' (February 2015), https://www.gov.uk/government/uploads/system/uploads/attachment_data/file/403643/9781474115384.pdf, 8.

[62] A Parmar, 'Stop and Search in London: Counter-Terrorist or Counter-Productive?' (2011) 21(4) *Policing and Society* 369–82.

[63] Home Office (UK), 'Counter-Terrorism and Security Bill: European Convention on Human Rights', memorandum (2015), https://www.parliament.uk/documents/joint-committees/human-rights/ECHR_Memo_Counter_terrorism_Bill.pdf, 1–2.

[64] Article 12 of the International Covenant on Civil and Political Rights (ICCPR): 'Everyone shall be free to leave any country, including his own.' See discussion in JCHR, 'Legislative Scrutiny' (above n 51) 5.

[65] See *ZZ v Secretary of State for the Home Department* [2013] EUECJ C-300/11, http://eur-lex.europa.eu/legal-content/EN/TXT/HTML/?uri=CELEX:62011CJ0300&from=EN.

[66] Ibid, 8–9.

may exclude the individual and their legal representative on grounds of national security.[67] All or part of the hearing may be heard in closed material proceedings (CMPs) in order to shield security sensitive information from public scrutiny. CMPS make use of special advocates (security-cleared lawyers who cannot consult their clients once they have seen secret evidence against them).[68] Nonetheless, contrary to the recommendations of the JCHR, no provision for 'gisting' is made within Schedule 1 of the CTSA, so individuals may remain wholly ignorant of the charges against them, and it is difficult to see how this can be compliant with Article 6.[69]

The development of the 'proportionality principle' provides some protection in that it stipulates that restrictions on Convention rights must be proportionate and requires strong justification for interference in the relevant right. In *Pham*, a 2015 case on citizenship deprivation, proportionality was said to require that there be no 'less onerous means of achieving the same aim' and due regard be paid to factors such as the nature of the right involved, the seriousness of the interference with that right, and 'the nature of the justification for that interference'.[70] However, Member States enjoy a margin of appreciation: in the case of *XH and AI*, passport cancellation was deemed to be justified on the grounds that the executive had demonstrated the existence of 'a genuine, present and sufficiently serious threat to a vital national interest' to warrant the restriction on freedom of movement.[71] The risk therefore remains that a sufficiently serious threat to security will be allowed to trump rights protections.

B. Shutting Out: Temporary Exclusion and 'Managed Return'

If the first CTSA power is designed to 'shut in' potential terrorists, the second permits the UK government temporarily to 'shut out' those who seek to return home but are deemed to pose a security threat. Under section 2 of the CTSA, a Temporary Exclusion Order (TEO) can 'require an individual not to return' to the United Kingdom unless 'the return is in accordance with a permit to return issued by the Secretary of State'.[72] A TEO can be imposed when the Home Secretary is able to meet five specified conditions, of which the two most

[67] Ibid, 18.

[68] On the use of special advocates more generally, see A Kavanagh, 'Special Advocates, Control Orders, and the Right to a Fair Trial' (2010) 63(5) *Modern Law Review* 836–57.

[69] On the problems posed by closed proceedings more generally, see Justice (E Metcalfe, Director), 'Secret Evidence: A Justice Report' (10 June 2009), available at https://justice.org.uk/secret-evidence/, 29–32; and N Phillips, 'Closed Material' (2014) 366(8) *London Review of Books* 29–32.

[70] *Pham v SSHD* [2015] UKSC 19 s at §§40 and 117.

[71] *R (XH and AI) v SSHD* [2017] EWCA Civ 41 at §116. For comment, see AA Khan, 'Jihad and the Cancellation of British Passports', United Kingdom Immigration Law Blog (29 April 2017), https://asadakhan.wordpress.com/2017/04/29/jihad-and-the-cancellation-of-british-passports/.

[72] CTSA 2015 (above n 54). Or 'the return is the result of the individual's deportation to the United Kingdom.'

important are that the Secretary 'reasonably suspects that the individual is, or has been, involved in terrorism-related activity outside the United Kingdom' and 'reasonably considers that it is necessary, for purposes connected with protecting members of the public in the United Kingdom from a risk of terrorism'.[73] Such orders are not confined to British citizens but can be imposed on anyone who has a 'right of abode' in the United Kingdom. Unlike the passport seizure provisions, section 2 requires the Home Secretary to apply to the court for prior permission to impose a TEO. However, court authorisation is not required if the Home Secretary 'reasonably considers that the urgency of the case demands a temporary exclusion order to be imposed without obtaining such permission'.[74] Moreover, the court may consider the application in the absence of the individual, without notifying them of the application for a TEO, and, if an individual is aware, without providing any opportunity to challenge or rebut the evidence in court. For individuals subject to these orders, the implications for their right to return are significant: the immediate effect of a TEO is to render their passports invalid,[75] potentially leaving them in legal limbo. Their capacity to contest an order is likely to be seriously compromised by the fact that they may be left stranded overseas without ready access to legal representation.

Temporary Exclusion Orders are designed to protect the public by disrupting the unmonitored return to the Britain of those suspected of involvement in terrorist-related activity. The power, even temporarily, to exclude citizens is perhaps the most controversial provision of those under consideration. The government has acknowledged that despite the heavy operational costs of identifying possible subjects and enforcing exclusion orders, '[t]here can never be full assurance that those subject to TEOs will never get into the UK without being detected by the authorities.'[76] Given the international reach of terrorist networks, it is naive to think that exclusion will dim ambitions or effectively neutralise such threats.

Although formally 'temporary', a TEO may remain in force for two years and can be renewed into de facto permanency.[77] The repeated renewal of 'temporary' counterterrorism measures has many historic precedents, including the infamous renewal of powers to order 'suspicionless' stop and search under section 44 of the Terrorism Act 2000.[78] A vital restraint on the TEO is to be

[73] Ibid. Note that the standard of proof is 'reasonable suspicion'.

[74] Sche 2, s 2(7)(b) CTSA 2015 (above n 54).

[75] S 4(10) CTSA 2015 (above n 54).

[76] Home Office (UK), 'Counter-Terrorism and Security Bill – Temporary Exclusion Orders: Impact Assessment' (21 November 2014), http://www.parliament.uk/documents/impact-assessments/IA14-22E.pdf.

[77] S 4(8) CTSA 2015 (above n 54): 'The imposition of a temporary exclusion order does not prevent a further temporary exclusion order from being imposed on the excluded individual (including in a case where an order ceases to be in force at the expiry of its two-year duration).'

[78] Although the s 44 authorisation, pertaining to particular police force areas, was limited to twenty-eight days, the Metropolitan Police secured rolling renewal authorisations for the whole of London for several years. See Ashworth and Zedner (above 60) 55.

found in section 6(1) of CTSA, which provides that if 'an individual applies to the Secretary of State for a permit to return, the Secretary of State must issue a permit within a reasonable period after the application is made.' Yet permission to return is subject to stringent requirements of cooperation and conformity with the obligations imposed, and it may be revoked on breach, which is a criminal offence. The effect may be to discourage return, exacerbate alienation, and increase the threat that individuals pose while marooning them overseas. Even if this does not contravene the right to nationality under Article 15(1) of the Universal Declaration of Human Rights, it may engage the Article 8 ECHR right to private and family life and should be subject to the proportionality requirements discussed in the previous section.

Although citizenship is not expressly protected under the ECHR, decisions such as the imposition of an order to exclude clearly engage other protected rights. At the time of the Bill, the UK government attempted to assert that 'where an individual is not in the UK's jurisdiction for the purposes of the ECHR, that person's … rights will not be engaged'.[79] However, the issue of when rights protections are forfeited has been addressed in several leading cases, and the trend is 'towards a more expansive approach to extraterritorial jurisdiction'.[80] As Guy Goodwin-Gill has observed,

> It is certainly wishful legal thinking to suppose that a person's ECHR rights can be annihilated simply by depriving that person of citizenship while he or she is abroad. Even a little logic suffices to show that the act of deprivation only has meaning if it is directed at someone who is *within* the jurisdiction of the State. A citizen is manifestly someone subject to and within the jurisdiction of the State, and the purported act of deprivation is intended precisely to affect his or rights.[81]

TEOs have also been deemed to breach the right not to be arbitrarily deprived of the right to enter one's own country under Article 12(4) of the International

[79] Home Office (UK) 'Immigration Bill – European Convention on Human Rights: Supplementary Memorandum' (January 2014), https://assets.publishing.service.gov.uk/government/uploads/system/uploads/attachment_data/file/276660/Deprivation_ECHR_memo.pdf, para.13.

[80] Eg, *Al-Skeini and Others v United Kingdom*, App No 55721/07 (7 July 2011); *Al-Jedda v United Kingdom*, App No 27021/08 (7 July 2011); and *Jaloud v The Netherlands*, App No 47708/08 (20 Nov 2014). For discussion, see M Milanovic, '*Al-Skeini* and *Al-Jedda* in Strasbourg' (2012) 23 *European Journal of International Law* 121–35; and M Milanovic, 'The Bottom Line of Jaloud' (2014) *EJIL:Talk!* (European Journal of International Law Blog) (26 November 2014), https://www.ejiltalk.org/the-bottom-line-of-jaloud/; and JCHR, 'Legislative Scrutiny' (above n 51) 14, para 3.4.

[81] G Goodwin-Gill, 'Mr Al-Jedda, Deprivation of Citizenship, and International Law', Middlesex University (14 February 2014), https://www.parliament.uk/documents/joint-committees/human-rights/GSGG-DeprivationCitizenshipRevDft.pdf, 13. See also G Goodwin-Gill, '"Temporary Exclusion Orders" and Their Implications for the United Kingdom's International Legal Obligations, Part I', *EJIL:Talk!* (European Journal of International Law Blog) (8 December 2014), http://www.ejiltalk.org/temporary-exclusion-orders-and-their-implications-for-the-united-kingdoms-international-legal-obligations-part-i/. Goodwin-Gill's position is consistent with that taken by the Grand Chamber in *Al-Skeini and Others* (ibid). Although in this case and others, the Strasbourg Court has contemplated situations in which the exercise of state power entailing potential extraterritorial rights violations might fall outside the jurisdiction of the state.

Covenant on Civil and Political Rights, as well as the international law obligation to readmit its citizens owed by the United Kingdom to receiving countries.[82]

An individual subject to a TEO who, without reasonable excuse, returns to the United Kingdom in contravention of the restrictions imposed commits an offence liable to up to five years' imprisonment.[83] It is doubtful whether five years is a proportional punishment for breach or is justified by the gravity of the 'trigger', which may be relatively trivial pre-inchoate, preparatory, or associative conduct at the very fringes of terrorism-related activity.[84] There are thus significant risks of disproportionality in the application of TEOs. For those who do obtain a 'permit to return' under section 5 CTSA, the requirement to attend an interview with a police or immigration officer may contravene the Article 6(1) ECHR right against self-incrimination because there is no provision for legal advice, for a lawyer to be present, or for recording the interview to protect the suspect against self-incrimination.

Moreover, if used to bar an individual from returning home, a TEO would render impossible attempts to deradicalise and re-assimilate, and it would leave an individual who is deemed to be dangerous at large overseas; it would thereby contravene international law requirements to collaborate with other states to combat terrorism.[85] Notwithstanding the powerful rhetoric of exclusion that attended the introduction of TEOs,[86] it is likely they will be used less as means of 'shutting out' individuals than as a means to enable their managed return under the close surveillance of the security services.[87] Significantly, although the TEO provisions came into force in 2015, by December 2017 only nine orders had been imposed.[88] Although it is not widely used, it is possible the very existence of the TEO creates a disincentive to attempt return to the United Kingdom that runs counter to the aim of deradicalising foreign terrorist fighters.

[82] JCHR, 'Legislative Scrutiny' (above n 51) 15.

[83] S 10 CTSA 2015 (above n 54).

[84] Terrorism is very broadly defined in UK law, and 'terrorist-related activity' extends its reach further to conduct that poses only a very remote risk of harm. See Ashworth and Zedner (above 60) 98; and V Tadros and J Hodgson, 'How to Make a Terrorist Out of Nothing' (2009) 72(6) *Modern Law Review* 984–98.

[85] Eg, European Convention on the Suppression of Terrorism (1977); International Convention for the Suppression of Terrorist Bombings (1997); International Convention for the Suppression of the Financing of Terrorism (1999).

[86] Unhelpfully so, in the view of J Blackbourn and C Walker, 'Interdiction and Indoctrination: The Counter-Terrorism and Security Act 2015' (2016) 79(5) *Modern Law Review* 840–70, 852.

[87] Anderson, 'The Terrorism Acts in 2015: Report of the Independent Reviewer' (above n 10) 121; and Blackbourn and Walker (ibid) 850.

[88] Home Office, 'Transparency Report 2018: Disruptive and Investigatory Powers', Cm 9609 (July 2018), https://assets.publishing.service.gov.uk/government/uploads/system/uploads/attachment_data/file/728110/35962_R_APS_CCS207_CCS0418538240-1_Transparency_Report_2018_print.pdf, 26.

C. Internal Exile: Forced Relocation

In addition to 'shutting in' and 'shutting out', CTSA 2015 grants a third power to impose 'internal exile' by means of the forcible relocation of terrorist suspects. An earlier power of forcible relocation had been attached to Control Orders imposed upon those reasonably suspected of involvement in terrorist-related activity; it was introduced in 2005 but abolished on human rights grounds in 2011.[89] The abolition of forcible relocation was welcomed at the time by the JCHR on the grounds that 'internal exile imposed by executive order was an oppressive measure associated only with the most authoritarian regimes.'[90] Under the Terrorism Prevention and Investigation Measures Act 2011, TPIMs replaced the previous Control Order regime with less wide-ranging powers of restriction and surveillance of terrorist suspects that, significantly, did not include forcible relocation.[91] However, these more limited restrictions and the loss of the power to compel relocation led to criticism that TPIMs were ineffective, and in practice, they were little used. It was argued that repeal of the power to compel relocation had inhibited the ability of TPIMs to break up terrorist networks and that leaving suspects within their communities enabled them to radicalise others.[92] In response, section 16 of CTSA 2015 restored the power to forcibly relocate those subject to TPIMS up to 200 miles from home.[93]

The reintroduction of forced relocation was justified as a means to 'strengthen powers to disrupt people with a track record of involvement in terrorist related activity' and to 'increase TPIM subjects' opportunities to move away from terrorism related activity'.[94] Even if the case for forcible relocation has stronger empirical grounds than the two previous measures, whether compulsory relocation can reasonably be described as an 'opportunity' is dubious. Moreover, it should be recalled that in an earlier Control Order judgment, the Supreme Court held that forcible relocation, even if it did not amount to a breach under Article 8 ECHR (right to private and family life), could amount to deprivation of liberty sufficient to establish a breach of Article 5 ECHR (right to liberty

[89] The earlier power of forcible relocation was attached to Control Orders under the Prevention of Terrorism Act 2005, https://www.legislation.gov.uk/ukpga/2005/2/contents. It was abolished under the Terrorism Prevention and Investigation Measures Act 2011, http://www.legislation.gov.uk/ukpga/2011/23/contents/enacted.

[90] JCHR, 'Legislative Scrutiny' (above n 51) 18.

[91] See A Hunt, 'From Control Orders to TPIMs: Variations on a Number of Themes in British Legal Responses to Terrorism' (2014) 62(3) *Crime, Law and Social Change* 289–321.

[92] Anderson, D, 'Terrorism Prevention and Investigation Measures in 2013: Second Report of the Independent Reviewer on the Operation of the Terrorism Prevention and Investigation Measures Act 2011' (March 2013), https://assets.publishing.service.gov.uk/government/uploads/system/uploads/attachment_data/file/298487/Un_Act_Independent_Review_print_ready.pdf, 4 and 34–36.

[93] S 16 CTSA 2015 (above n 54).

[94] Home Office (UK), 'Counterterrorism and Security Bill – Terrorism Prevention and Investigation Measures: Impact Assessment' (18 November 2014), http://www.parliament.uk/documents/impact-assessments/IA14-22G.pdf, 1.

and security).[95] Although forcible relocation clearly interferes with Articles 8 and 11 (right to freedom of assembly and association), the Home Office again contended that because both are qualified rights, interference can be defended provided it is proportionate and justified in the interests of national security. By contrast, the JCHR reaffirmed its view that forcible relocation is disproportionate and 'too intrusive and potentially damaging to family life to be justifiable'[96] and questioned its compatibility with Article 8. Moreover, where TPIMs are imposed during closed material proceedings, limits on the ability of individuals to know the case against them and thus to refute the allegations against them raises issues of fair trial rights under Article 6 ECHR.[97]

A further intensification of the TPIM is to be found in the provisions for sentencing on breach. The maximum sentence for breach of a 'travel measure', by which the Home Secretary can impose restrictions on a person from leaving an area specified under a TPIM, has been increased from five to ten years.[98] Here again, it is doubtful whether ten years' imprisonment is proportional to what may be a trivial or technical breach of the conditions of the TPIM, such as mere movement beyond a prescribed zone or presence outdoors even in a back garden during curfew hours. This suggests a troubling distance between the demands of criminal justice on the one hand, which requires proportionate punishment following conviction by a criminal court following a fair trial, and a security model on the other hand, which condones coercive civil and executive measures justified consequentially without the benefit of trial. How far departures from proportionality are justified in the latter case merits further attention and debate. Though it should be observed that in practice, TPIMs, like TEOs, are relatively little used. Despite a number of terrorist attacks, by 2018 the number of those subject to TPIMs was just seven,[99] a statistic that raises questions about whether the intended force of these orders is more rhetorical than real.

IV. CONCLUDING THOUGHTS

The threat posed by international terrorism should not be underestimated: the radicalisation of citizens recruited as foreign terrorist fighters or homegrown

[95] *Secretary of State for the Home Department v AP* [2011] 3 WLR 53, paras 11–12 and 31. See also A Wagner, 'Control Order Breached Human Rights, Say Supreme Court', UK Human Rights Blog (16 June 2010), https://ukhumanrightsblog.com/2010/06/16/control-order-breached-human-rights-say-supreme-court/#more-2854.

[96] JCHR, 'Legislative Scrutiny' (above n 51) 19.

[97] See, eg, D Kelman, 'Closesd Trials and Secret Allegations: An Analysis of the "Gisting" Requirement' (2016) 80(4) *Journal of Criminal Law* 264–77. Presumably, these proceedings would now be subject to the requirement as to necessity and proportionality set out in *R (XH & AI) v SSHD* [2017] EWCA Civ 41.

[98] S 17 CTSA 2015 (above n 54).

[99] G Allen and N Dempsey, 'Terrorism in Great Britain: The Statistics', House of Commons Library Briefing Paper No VBP7613 (June 2018), available at https://researchbriefings.parliament.uk/ResearchBriefing/Summary/CBP-7613, 27.

terrorists has raised security threat levels across Europe.[100] As the power of ISIS wains, new risks arise as would-be foreign fighters are frustrated in their attempts to travel abroad[101] and increasing numbers of jihadis return.[102] While some are disillusioned by the crumbling of the caliphate, others are determined to carry out strikes at home.[103] Security services and police charged with the formidable task of averting the next attack seek to do so by 'defending further up the field',[104] and intercepting those who plan terrorist atrocities. There are good reasons to extend the operational space in which the authorities seek to counter terrorism. However, measures that curtail citizens' rights of membership and mobility, diminish procedural protections, and employ closed proceedings present another security threat – the threat to individual liberties posed by coercive state measures. Individual rights often stand in tension with the rights of others, and are prone to be restricted, especially in matters of national security and public safety.[105] The key issue is whether those restrictions are proportionate and fairly applied.

The radical techniques for curtailing citizenship rights and disrupting mobility discussed in this chapter have been promoted as essential to counterterrorism. In the United Kingdom, disruption has captured the political imagination and overshadowed earlier calls for the 'priority of prosecution' of terrorist suspects.[106] Time and again, politicians and policymakers are persuadable that, to the existing techniques of prevention and punishment, new means to disrupt, immobilise, and exclude must be added. Interdiction of plans to travel by passport removal and restriction, together with longer-term restraint through temporary exclusion, managed return, surveillance, and forced relocation are potentially seriously intrusive measures. Aside from brute expediency, the grounds on which these measures are justified are often less clear, particularly

[100] See the MI5 website regarding threat levels: https://www.mi5.gov.uk/threat-levels. See also O Smith, 'Mapped: The 48 Countries Where a Terrorist Attack Is Most Likely', *Telegraph* (26 May 2017), http://www.telegraph.co.uk/travel/maps-and-graphics/Mapped-Terror-threat-around-the-world/.

[101] DL Byman, 'Frustrated Foreign Fighters', *Order from Chaos* (Brookings Institute Blog) (13 July 2017), https://www.brookings.edu/blog/order-from-chaos/2017/07/13/frustrated-foreign-fighters/.

[102] M Chulov, J Grierson, and J Swaine, 'Isis Faces Exodus of Foreign Fighters as its "Caliphate" Crumbles', *Guardian* (26 April 2017), https://www.theguardian.com/world/2017/apr/26/isis-exodus-foreign-fighters-caliphate-crumbles; A Reed and J Pohl, 'Tackling the Surge of Returning Foreign Fighters', *NATO Review Magazine* (14 July 2017), http://www.nato.int/docu/review/2017/Also-in-2017/daesh-tackling-surge-returning-foreign-fighters-prevention-denmark-rehabilitation-programmes/EN/index.htm; and BBC, 'UK Terror Threat Increased by IS Losses, Security Minister Says' *BBC News* (19 August 2017), http://www.bbc.co.uk/news/uk-40985532.

[103] European Parliament, 'The Return of Foreign Fighters to EU Soil: Ex-post Evaluation', European Parliamentary Research Service (May 2018), http://www.europarl.europa.eu/RegData/etudes/STUD/2018/621811/EPRS_STU(2018)621811_EN.pdf, pt 3.

[104] D Anderson, 'Shielding the Compass: How to Fight Terrorism without Defeating the Law' (2013) 3 *European Human Rights Law Review* 233–46, 237.

[105] N McGarrity and J Blackbourn, 'Anti-terrorism Laws and Human Rights' in L Weber, E Fishwick, and M Marmo (eds), *The Routledge International Handbook of Criminology and Human Rights* (London, Routledge, 2016) 144.

[106] Macdonald (above n 17).

given the vague and expansive definition of terrorism and even wider scope of 'terrorism-related activity'.[107] Is it that those who seek to travel as jihadists to Syria or espouse extremist views so place themselves outside the obligations of citizenship that they are no longer deemed worthy of the full raft of legal protections?[108] If so, it is arguable that the status of citizenship is becoming ever more conditional upon conformity with defined standards of acceptable behaviour[109] or 'British values'.[110]

Yet arguably this raft of measures itself contravenes British values. As former Attorney-General Dominic Grieve observed in parliamentary debate on the CTS Bill, even temporary exclusion is a 'draconian and unusual power' that contravenes

> a fundamental principle of the common law in this country that an individual, unconvicted – the presumption of innocence applies – should be free to reside in his own land. The principle of exile, as a judicial or even an administrative tool, has not been tolerated in this country since the late 17th century. It is certainly no part of our criminal justice panoply, and certainly not part of administrative provisions or powers given to the state.[111]

These strong objections notwithstanding, police and security services continue to seek more tools to combat terrorism, even as they struggle to pursue terrorism cases successfully to prosecution.[112] It is significant that since 2001, of the 3,349 arrests on suspicion of terrorism-related activity in the United Kingdom, only 17.8 per cent have resulted in conviction.[113] Prosecution of terrorist suspects is often deemed inappropriate because the offences committed by foreign fighters against domestic criminal law are often comparatively minor and sentences low relative to threat.[114] Difficulties in securing convictions

[107] L Zedner, 'Terrorizing Criminal Law' (2014) 8(1) *Criminal Law and Philosophy* 99–121; and Ashworth and Zedner (above n 60) 179–81.

[108] For fascinating debate on questions of citizenship and exclusion, see A Macklin, 'Kickoff Contribution: The Return of Banishment' and the many responses thereto in A Macklin and R Bauböck (eds), 'The Return of Banishment: Do the New Denationalisation Policies Weaken Citizenship?' EUDO CITIZENSHIP Forum Debate (2015), EUI Working Paper RSCAS 2015/14, http://cadmus.eui.eu/bitstream/handle/1814/34617/RSCAS_2015_14.pdf.

[109] T Choudhury, 'The Radicalisation of Citizenship Deprivation' (2017) 37(2) *Critical Social Policy* 225–44, 226.

[110] The UK Government definition of extremism is 'vocal or active opposition to fundamental British values': J Dawson and S Godec, 'Counter-Extremism Policy: An Overview', House of Commons Briefing Paper 7238 (23 June 2017), available at https://researchbriefings.parliament.uk/ResearchBriefing/Summary/CBP-7238.

[111] HC Deb 2 December 2014, vol 589, col 228, https://publications.parliament.uk/pa/cm201415/cmhansrd/cm141202/debtext/141202-0003.htm.

[112] Note the comment by Home Secretary Amber Rudd in respect of Temporary Exclusion Orders: 'They're a tool which the law enforcement [agencies] wanted, we gave them that tool … The important thing is that government gives the security services the tools that are necessary to keep us safe.'

[113] V Dodd, 'Most Terrorism Arrests Lead to No Charge or Conviction, Figures Show', *Guardian* (15 December 2016), https://www.theguardian.com/uk-news/2016/dec/15/most-terrorism-arrests-lead-no-charge-conviction-figures-show.

[114] Reed and Pohl (above n 102).

include meeting the sufficiency of evidence test, as much intelligence is not admissible as evidence, and satisfying the standards of criminal procedure in open court in security-sensitive cases.[115] In consequence, faith in the priority of prosecution appears to be waning, rendering recourse to civil, administrative, and immigration measures more attractive. Laws that diminish and even strip citizenship,[116] which might once have been regarded as indefensible, are now endorsed as necessary and effective measures to be deployed against those who threaten national security. The evidence that many of those who travelled to join ISIS were young, naive, or vulnerable is disregarded.[117] As is the criticism that these rights-eroding measures seem 'calculated to entrench the treatment of British Muslims as non-citizens'.[118] The effect is to render citizenship and its attendant rights more precarious and more easily lost than was once the case.

Whatever motivates these reforms, two interdependent questions remain. First, the efficacy question: is it plausibly effective to tackle terrorism by practices of disruption, exclusion, and internal exile? Historically, UK security strategies have focused upon foreign nationals, dual and naturalised citizens. Yet there is little evidence to suggest that those whose citizenship status is precarious pose any greater threat than do those with full citizenship. We might ask why states have targeted foreign nationals and resorted so readily to immigration laws and measures as counterterrorism tools. Is it that aliens and marginalised communities are more readily pursued than the rest of the population and less likely to attract public sympathy and support?[119] Immigration law imposes less onerous procedural requirements, but the fact a measure operates under fewer constraints is no guarantee of efficacy. The Counterterrorism and Security Act 2015 extends these mobility disruptive measures to render full citizenship conditional on conduct in ways previously true only for dual and naturalised citizens.[120]

[115] Zedner 'Criminal Justice in the Service of Security' (above n 18) 159–61.

[116] Of thirty-three European states, fourteen have provisions for citizenship deprivation: GR de Groot, M Vink, I Honohan, 'Loss of Citizenship', EUDO Citizenship Policy Brief No 3 (2010), http://eudo-citizenship.eu/docs/policy_brief_loss.pdf. See also D Anderson (Independent Reviewer), 'Citizenship Resulting in Statelessness: First Report of the Independent Reviewer on the Operation of the Power to Remove Citizenship' (April 2016), https://www.gov.uk/government/uploads/system/uploads/attachment_data/file/518120/David_Anderson_QC_-_CITIZENSHIP_REMOVAL__web_.pdf.

[117] The Home Office acknowledged in 2016, 'The average age at time of travel of UK-linked individuals of national security concern engaging in the Syrian conflict has reduced significantly. Nearly half of those travelling aged 18 and under have departed since July 2014. We have also observed an increase in the number of women, families and minors engaging in the conflict, although they remain a small proportion of overall travellers.' Quoted in Walker (above n 10) 101.

[118] Webber (above n 50). See a number of the other chapters in this volume, including those by Rumee Ahmed and Ayesha S Chaudhry; Aziz Z Huq; Natasa Mavronicola; and Victor V Ramraj.

[119] L Zedner, 'Security, the State and the Citizen: The Changing Architecture of Crime Control' (2010) 13(2) *New Criminal Law Review* 379–403.

[120] Zedner, 'Citizenship Deprivation, Security and Human Rights' (above n 4).

One might have expected measures that target all citizens to provoke greater public resistance. Despite the fact that recent terrorist atrocities have been met by public calls for resilience, social solidarity, and a resolute return to normal life,[121] counterterrorism measures that erode due process and breach human rights attract relatively little public protest. Although in theory they are generally applicable, in practice these laws are applied mainly to minority and marginalised groups. To the extent that those targeted regard laws curtailing citizenship rights and restricting mobility as discriminatory or illegitimate, they risk provoking disaffection and hostility, feeding radicalisation and fostering recruitment to terrorist groups. It is a brave government that does not reactively reach to 'shut in' or 'shut out' those who threaten national security. Yet to label aspiring or actual foreign terrorist fighters as 'enemies of the state' is liable only to exacerbate their sense of alienation, to thwart opportunities to minimise the risks they pose, and to limit chances to mine the intelligence they hold.[122] Viable alternatives to repressive measures include intervention to thwart radicalisation, support for families of would-be jihadists, and programmes to encourage and enable the return of foreign terrorist fighters in order to deradicalise, rehabilitate, and reintegrate them into civil society.[123]

Finally and mostly importantly, the justice question remains: is it just to limit mobility so radically, to curtail citizenship rights, or to render someone stateless, whatever danger they are deemed to pose? Threats to individual liberties posed by current measures range from the infringement of rights to privacy and family life and freedom of movement for those whose passports are removed, to the loss of rights to liberty and security, freedom from torture or inhuman or degrading treatment for those who suffer citizenship deprivation, deportation, or exclusion. At the extreme, such measures may deny the right to life.[124] Damage is done to the rule of law when the basis for legal measures are uncertain or vague, when they are imposed in ways that appear arbitrary, discriminatory, or unfair, or in proceedings that do not allow for effective challenge and fair trial. Recent UK legislation, like the Immigration Act 2014[125] and the Counterterrorism and

[121] See, eg, H Pidd, '"I ♥ MCR": Thousands Gather at Manchester Attack Vigil', *Guardian* (23 May 2017), https://www.theguardian.com/uk-news/2017/may/23/i-heart-manchester-thousands-gather-at-attack-vigil.

[122] If this appears fanciful, see, eg, D Crouch and J Henley, 'A Way Home for Jihadis: Denmark's Radical Approach to Islamic Extremism', *Guardian* (23 February 2015), https://www.theguardian.com/world/2015/feb/23/home-jihadi-denmark-radical-islamic-extremism-aarhus-model-scandinavia.

[123] The European Commission Directorate-General (DG) Migration and Home Affairs Radicalisation Awareness Network (RAN) runs a Centre for Excellence to disseminate knowledge and support deradicalisation strategies: https://ec.europa.eu/home-affairs/what-we-do/networks/radicalisation_awareness_network_en. See also the proposals for hotlines, family support, encouraging return home, and rehabilitation programmes in R Briggs and T Silverman, 'Western Foreign Fighters: Innovations in Responding to the Threat', Institute for Strategic Dialogue (2014), https://www.isdglobal.org/wp-content/uploads/2016/02/ISDJ2784_Western_foreign_fighters_V7_WEB.pdf, 40–48.

[124] Walker (above n 10) 128.

[125] Which permits deprivation of naturalised citizens on security grounds. See Zedner, 'Citizenship Deprivation, Security and Human Rights' (above n 4).

Security Act 2015, greatly increases the power of the executive while diminishing the legal and procedural protections of individual citizens.[126] For those who find themselves in 'legal black holes'[127] marooned overseas, effective legal challenge or appeal may become impossible.

Ten years ago, my contribution to the first edition of *Security and Human Rights* tackled the erosions of rights effected by civil preventive measures that 'side-stepped' due process.[128] Those rights erosions, significant and worrying as they were, pale beside the attack on the fundamental rights of citizenship entailed by present security laws and measures. Precisely what the state owes to its citizens by way of security and what by way of loyalty citizens owe the state remain contested.[129] The irresolvable tension between the role of the state as the primary source of security and, at the very same time, as potential threat to citizens' rights lies at the heart of contemporary security debates.[130] Nowhere is this tension more acute than in respect of the state's treatment of citizens whose beliefs, ambitions, or conduct appear to threaten the existence of the state itself. Yet the inescapable conclusion is that, in consequence of the legal developments described in this chapter, the rights enjoyed by all citizens are today more precarious and their protection less secure than was previously the case.

REFERENCES

Allen, G and Dempsey, N, 'Terrorism in Great Britain: The Statistics', House of Commons Library Briefing Paper No VBP7613 (June 2018), available at https://researchbriefings.parliament.uk/ResearchBriefing/Summary/CBP-7613.

Anderson, D, 'Citizenship Resulting in Statelessness: First Report of the Independent Reviewer on the Operation of the Power to Remove Citizenship' (April 2016), https://www.gov.uk/government/uploads/system/uploads/attachment_data/file/518120/David_Anderson_QC_-_CITIZENSHIP_REMOVAL__web_.pdf.

——, 'Shielding the Compass: How to Fight Terrorism without Defeating the Law' (2013) 3 *European Human Rights Law Review* 233–46.

——, 'The Terrorism Acts in 2015: Report of the Independent Reviewer' (December 2016), https://www.gov.uk/government/uploads/system/uploads/attachment_data/file/579233/THE_TERRORISM_ACTS_IN_2015__web_.pdf.

[126] This shift in the balance of power is exacerbated by the slashing of the UK's legal aid budget, which impedes adequate legal representation, recourse to appeals procedures, and judicial review. See F Wilmot-Smith, 'Necessity or Ideology?' (2014) 36(21) *London Review of Books* 15–17.

[127] Zedner, 'Citizenship Deprivation, Security and Human Rights' (above n 4) 242.

[128] Zedner, 'Seeking Security by Eroding Rights' (above n 18).

[129] Choudhury suggests that the securitisation of citizenship involves a social sorting of citizens into 'good citizens', 'tolerated citizens', and 'bad citizens': Choudhury (above n 109) 240.

[130] See discussion in L Lazarus, 'The Right to Security' in R Cruft, M Liao, and M Renzo (eds), *Philosophical Foundations of Human Rights* (Oxford, Oxford University Press, 2015); and L Zedner, 'Security against Arbitrary Government in Criminal Justice' in A du Bois-Pedain M Ulväng, and P Asp (eds), *Criminal Law and the Authority of the State* (Oxford, Hart Publishing, 2017).

——, 'Terrorism Prevention and Investigation Measures in 2013: Second Report of the Independent Reviewer on the Operation of the Terrorism Prevention and Investigation Measures Act 2011' (March 2013), https://assets.publishing.service.gov.uk/government/uploads/system/uploads/attachment_data/file/298487/Un_Act_Independent_Review_print_ready.pdf.

Ashworth, A and Zedner, L, *Preventive Justice* (Oxford, Oxford University Press, 2014).

Bakker, E and Singleton, M, 'Foreign Fighters in the Syria and Iraq Conflict' in A de Guttry, F Capone, and C Paulussen (eds), *Foreign Fighters under International Law and Beyond* (The Hague, Asser Press, 2016).

R Barrett, 'Beyond the Caliphate: Foreign Fighters and the Threat of Returnees', Soufan Centre Report (October 2017), http://thesoufancenter.org/wp-content/uploads/2017/11/Beyond-the-Caliphate-Foreign-Fighters-and-the-Threat-of-Returnees-TSC-Report-October-2017-v3.pdf.

Batchelor, T, 'Manchester Attack: Police Have Arrested "Large Part" of Terror Network Behind Salman Abedi', *Independent* (26 May 2017), http://www.independent.co.uk/news/uk/home-news/manchester-attack-police-terror-network-arrest-salman-abedi-suicide-bomber-arena-a7758056.html.

BBC, 'Berlin Truck Attacker Anis Amri Killed in Milan', *BBC News* (23 December 2016), http://www.bbc.co.uk/news/world-europe-38415287.

——, 'Paris Attacks: Who Were the Attackers?' *BBC News* (27 April 2016), http://www.bbc.co.uk/news/world-europe-34832512.

——, 'UK Terror Threat Increased by IS Losses, Security Minister Says' *BBC News* (19 August 2017), http://www.bbc.co.uk/news/uk-40985532.

——, 'Who Are Britain's Jihadists?' *BBC News* (5 July 2017), http://www.bbc.co.uk/news/uk-32026985.

Blackbourn, J and Walker, C, 'Interdiction and Indoctrination: The Counter-Terrorism and Security Act 2015' (2016) 79(5) *Modern Law Review* 840–70.

Bosworth, M, 'Border Criminologies: How Migration Is Changing Criminal Justice' in M Bosworth, C Hoyle, and L Zedner (eds), *The Changing Contours of Criminal Justice* (Oxford, Oxford University Press, 2016).

Boutin, B, Chauzal, G, Dorsey, J et al, 'The Foreign Fighters Phenomenon in the European Union: Profiles, Threats, and Policies', International Centre for Counter-Terrorism (ICCT) Research Paper (April 2016), https://icct.nl/wp-content/uploads/2016/03/ICCT-Report_Foreign-Fighters-Phenomenon-in-the-EU_1-April-2016_including-AnnexesLinks.pdf.

Bowling, B and Weber, L, 'Valiant Beggars and Global Vagabonds: Select, Eject, Immobilize' (2008) 12(3) *Theoretical Criminology* 355–75.

Briggs, R and Silverman, T, 'Western Foreign Fighters: Innovations in Responding to the Threat', Institute for Strategic Dialogue (2014), https://www.isdglobal.org/wp-content/uploads/2016/02/ISDJ2784_Western_foreign_fighters_V7_WEB.pdf.

Byman, DL, 'Frustrated Foreign Fighters', *Order from Chaos* (Brookings Institute Blog) (13 July 2017), https://www.brookings.edu/blog/order-from-chaos/2017/07/13/frustrated-foreign-fighters/.

Cabinet Office (UK), 'Security in a Global Hub: Establishing the UK's New Border Arrangements' (November 2007).

Choudhury, T, 'The Radicalisation of Citizenship Deprivation' (2017) 37(2) *Critical Social Policy* 225–44.

Chulov, M, Grierson, J and Swaine, J, 'Isis Faces Exodus of Foreign Fighters as its "Caliphate" Crumbles', *Guardian* (26 April 2017), https://www.theguardian.com/world/2017/apr/26/isis-exodus-foreign-fighters-caliphate-crumbles.

Cole, D, *Enemy Aliens: Double Standards and Constitutional Freedoms in the War on Terrorism* (New York, New Press, 2003).

Crouch, D and Henley, J, 'A Way Home for Jihadis: Denmark's Radical Approach to Islamic Extremism', *Guardian* (23 February 2015), https://www.theguardian.com/world/2015/feb/23/home-jihadi-denmark-radical-islamic-extremism-aarhus-model-scandinavia.

Dawson, J and Godec, S, 'Counter-Extremism Policy: An Overview', House of Commons Briefing Paper 7238 (23 June 2017), available at https://researchbriefings.parliament.uk/ResearchBriefing/Summary/CBP-7238.

Delcker, J, 'Attack Exposes Missing Links in German Security', *Politico* (23 December 2016), http://www.politico.eu/article/attack-highlights-disconnect-in-german-security-berlin-attack/.

Demleitner, N, 'Misguided Prevention: The War on Terrorism as a War on Immigrant Offenders and Immigration Violators' (2004) 40 *Criminal Law Bulletin* 550–75.

European Parliament, 'The Return of Foreign Fighters to EU Soil: Ex-post Evaluation', European Parliamentary Research Service (May 2018), http://www.europarl.europa.eu/RegData/etudes/STUD/2018/621811/EPRS_STU(2018)621811_EN.pdf.

Europol, '211 Terrorist Attacks Carried Out in EU Member States in 2015, New Europol Report Reveals', Press Release (20 July 2016), https://www.europol.europa.eu/newsroom/news/211-terrorist-attacks-carried-out-in-eu-member-states-in-2015-new-europol-report-reveals.

Evans, M, 'How the German Police and Security Service Blundered over the Berlin Terror Outrage', *Telegraph* (21 December 2016), http://www.telegraph.co.uk/news/2016/12/21/german-police-security-service-blundered-berlin-terror-outrage/.

Farmer, B, 'David Cameron: Returning Jihadists Are "Enemies of the state"', *Telegraph* (17 November 20145), http://www.telegraph.co.uk/news/politics/david-cameron/11237012/David-Cameron-Returning-jihadists-are-enemies-of-the-state.html.

Fenwick, H, 'The Anti-Terrorism, Crime and Security Act 2001: A Proportional Response to 11 September?' (2002) 65(5) *Modern Law Review* 724–62.

——, 'Responding to 11 September: Detention without Trial under the Anti-Terrorism, Crime and Security Act 2001' in L Freedman (ed), *Superterrorism: Policy Responses* (Oxford, Blackwell Publishing, 2002).

Gomez-Jara Diez, C, 'Enemy Combatants Versus Enemy Criminal Law' (2008) 11(4) *New Criminal Law Review* 529–62.

Goodwin-Gill, G, 'Mr Al-Jedda, Deprivation of Citizenship, and International Law', Middlesex University (14 February 2014), https://www.parliament.uk/documents/joint-committees/human-rights/GSGG-DeprivationCitizenshipRevDft.pdf.

——, '"Temporary Exclusion Orders" and Their Implications for the United Kingdom's International Legal Obligations, Part I', *EJIL:Talk!* (European Journal of International Law Blog) (8 December 2014), http://www.ejiltalk.org/temporary-exclusion-orders-and-their-implications-for-the-united-kingdoms-international-legal-obligations-part-i/.

Goold, BJ and Lazarus, L (eds), *Security and Human Rights* (Oxford, Hart Publishing, 2007).

de Groot, GR, Vink, M, and Honohan, I, 'Loss of Citizenship', EUDO Citizenship Policy Brief No 3 (2010), http://eudo-citizenship.eu/docs/policy_brief_loss.pdf.

Guardian, 'Isis Magazine Confirms Death of Mohammed Emwazi in "Eulogizing Profile"', *Guardian*, (20 January 2016), https://www.theguardian.com/uk-news/2016/jan/20/mohammed-emwazis-death-confirmed-in-isis-magazine.

Hegghammer, T and Nesser, P, 'Assessing the Islamic State's Commitment to Attacking the West' (2015) 9(4) *Perspectives on Terrorism*.

Home Office (UK), 'Code of Practice for Officers Exercising Functions under Schedule 1 of the Counter-Terrorism and Security Act 2015' (February 2015), https://www.gov.uk/government/uploads/system/uploads/attachment_data/file/403643/9781474115384.pdf.

——, 'Counter-Terrorism and Security Bill: European Convention on Human Rights', memorandum (2015), https://www.parliament.uk/documents/joint-committees/human-rights/ECHR_Memo_Counter_terrorism_Bill.pdf.

——, 'Counter-Terrorism and Security Bill – Temporary Exclusion Orders: Impact Assessment' (21 November 2014), http://www.parliament.uk/documents/impact-assessments/IA14-22E.pdf.

——, 'Counter-Terrorism and Security Bill – Temporary Passport Seizure: Impact Assessment' (18 November 2014), http://www.parliament.uk/documents/impact-assessments/IA14-22F.pdf.

——, 'Counter-terrorism and Security Bill – Terrorism Prevention and Investigation Measures: Impact Assessment' (18 November 2014), http://www.parliament.uk/documents/impact-assessments/IA14-22G.pdf.

——, 'Immigration Bill – European Convention on Human Rights: Supplementary Memorandum' (January 2014), https://assets.publishing.service.gov.uk/government/uploads/system/uploads/attachment_data/file/276660/Deprivation_ECHR_memo.pdf.

——, 'Memorandum to the Home Affairs Committee: Post-Legislative Scrutiny of the Terrorism Prevention and Investigation Measures Act 2011' (October 2016), Cm 9348, https://www.gov.uk/government/uploads/system/uploads/attachment_data/file/562930/TPIMs_act_2011_Print.pdf.

——, 'Temporary Passport Seizure', Counter-Terrorism and Security Bill Factsheets (3 December 2014), https://assets.publishing.service.gov.uk/government/uploads/system/uploads/attachment_data/file/540542/CTS_Bill_-_Factsheet_2_-_Passport_Seizure.pdf.

——, 'Transparency Report 2018: Disruptive and Investigatory Powers', Cm 9609 (July 2018), https://assets.publishing.service.gov.uk/government/uploads/system/uploads/attachment_data/file/728110/35962_R_APS_CCS207_CCS0418538240-1_Transparency_Report_2018_print.pdf.

Hunt, A, 'From Control Orders to TPIMs: Variations on a Number of Themes in British Legal Responses to Terrorism' (2014) 62(3) *Crime, Law and Social Change* 289–321.

Joint Committee on Human Rights (JCHR), *Legislative Scrutiny: Counter-Terrorism and Security Bill, Fifth Report* (2014–15, HL 86, HC 859).

Justice (E Metcalfe, Director), 'Secret Evidence: A Justice Report' (10 June 2009), available at https://justice.org.uk/secret-evidence/.

Kavanagh, A, 'Special Advocates, Control Orders, and the Right to a Fair Trial' (2010) 63(5) *Modern Law Review* 836–57.

Kelman, D, 'Closesd Trials and Secret Allegations: An Analysis of the "Gisting" Requirement' (2016) 80(4) *Journal of Criminal Law* 264–77.

Khan, AA, 'Jihad and the Cancellation of British Passports', United Kingdom Immigration Law Blog (29 April 2017), https://asadakhan.wordpress.com/2017/04/29/jihad-and-the-cancellation-of-british-passports/.

Kirk, A, 'Iraq and Syria: How Many Foreign Fighters Are Fighting for Isil?' *Telegraph* (24 March 2016), http://www.telegraph.co.uk/news/2016/03/29/iraq-and-syria-how-many-foreign-fighters-are-fighting-for-isil/.

Lazarus, L, 'Do Human Rights Impede Effective Counterterrorism?', UK Constitutional. Law Association Blog (15 June 2017), https://ukconstitutionallaw.org/2017/06/15/liora-lazarus-do-human-rights-impede-effective-counterterrorism/.

——, 'The Right to Security' in R Cruft, M Liao, and M Renzo (eds), *Philosophical Foundations of Human Rights* (Oxford, Oxford University Press, 2015).

Macdonald, S, 'Prosecuting Suspected Terrorists: Precursor Crimes, Intercept Evidence and the Priority of Security' in L Jarvis and M Lister (eds), *Critical Perspectives on Counter-Terrorism* (Abingdon, Routledge, 2015).

Macklin, A, 'Borderline Security' in RJ Daniels, P Macklem, and K Roach (eds), *The Security of Freedom: Essays on Canada's Anti-Terrorism Bill* (Toronto, University of Toronto Press, 2001).

——, 'Kickoff Contribution: The Return of Banishment' in A Macklin and R Bauböck (eds), *The Return of Banishment: Do the New Denationalisation Policies Weaken Citizenship?* EUDO CITIZENSHIP Forum Debate (2015), EUI Working Paper RSCAS 2015/14.

Macklin, A and Bauböck, R (eds), *The Return of Banishment: Do the New Denationalisation Policies Weaken Citizenship?* EUDO Citizenship Forum Debate (2015), EUI Working Paper RSCAS 2015/14, http://cadmus.eui.eu/bitstream/handle/1814/34617/RSCAS_2015_14.pdf.

McGarrity, N and Blackbourn, J, 'Anti-terrorism Laws and Human Rights' in L Weber, E Fishwick, and M Marmo (eds), *The Routledge International Handbook of Criminology and Human Rights* (London, Routledge, 2016).

Milanovic, M, 'Al-Skeini and Al-Jedda in Strasbourg' (2012) 23 *European Journal of International Law* 121–35.

——, 'The Bottom Line of *Jaloud*' (2014) *EJIL:Talk!* (European Journal of International Law Blog) (26 November 2014), https://www.ejiltalk.org/the-bottom-line-of-jaloud/.

Parmar, A, 'Stop and Search in London: Counter-Terrorist or Counter-Productive?' (2011) 21(4) *Policing and Society* 369–82.

Phillips, N, 'Closed Material' (2014) 366(8) *London Review of Books* 29–32.

Pickering, S, Bosworth, M and Aas, KF, 'The Criminology of Mobility' in S Pickering (ed), *Routledge Handbook on Crime and Migration* (London, Routledge, 2014).

Pidd, H, '"I ♥ MCR": Thousands Gather at Manchester Attack Vigil', Guardian (23 May 2017), https://www.theguardian.com/uk-news/2017/may/23/i-heart-manchester-thousands-gather-at-attack-vigil.

Reed, A and Pohl, J, 'Tackling the Surge of Returning Foreign Fighters', *NATO Review Magazine* (14 July 2017), http://www.nato.int/docu/review/2017/Also-in-2017/daesh-tackling-surge-returning-foreign-fighters-prevention-denmark-rehabilitation-programmes/EN/index.htm.

Roach, K, *The 9/11 Effect: Comparative Counter-Terrorism* (Cambridge, Cambridge University Press, 2011).

——, 'Sources and Trends in Post-9/11 Anti-Terrorism Laws' in BJ Goold and L Lazarus (eds), *Security and Human Rights* (Oxford, Hart Publishing, 2007).

Roig, R, 'Police Try to Unravel Terrorist Network Behind Attacks in Barcelona, Cambrils', *Globe and Mail* (20 August 2017), https://www.theglobeandmail.com/news/world/police-try-to-unravel-terrorist-network-behind-attacks-in-barcelona-cambrils/article36037758/.

Smith, O, 'Mapped: The 48 Countries Where a Terrorist Attack Is Most Likely', *Telegraph* (26 May 2017), http://www.telegraph.co.uk/travel/maps-and-graphics/Mapped-Terror-threat-around-the-world/.

Stanley, T, 'West Europe Is Safer Now Than in the 1970s', *Telegraph* (25 March 2016), http://www.telegraph.co.uk/news/2016/03/25/west-europe-is-safer-now-than-in-the-1970s-and-safer-than-almost/.

Tadros, V and Hodgson, J, 'How to Make a Terrorist Out of Nothing' (2009) 72(6) *Modern Law Review* 984–98.

Thomas, PA, 'Emergency and Anti-Terrorist Powers 9/11: USA and UK' (2003) 26(4) *Fordham International Law Journal* 1193–233.

Townsend, M et al, 'The Race to Find the Manchester Terrorist Network', *Guardian* (28 May 2017), https://www.theguardian.com/uk-news/2017/may/28/race-to-find-manchester-terrorist-network.

UN Security Council, 'Security Council Unanimously Adopts Resolution Condemning Violent Extremism, Underscoring Need to Prevent Travel, Support for Foreign Terrorist Fighters', press release SC/115 (24 September 2014), http://www.un.org/press/en/2014/sc11580.doc.htm.

Wagner, A, 'Control Order Breached Human Rights, Say Supreme Court', UK Human Rights Blog (16 June 2010), https://ukhumanrightsblog.com/2010/06/16/control-order-breached-human-rights-say-supreme-court/#more-2854.

Walker, C, 'Foreign Terrorist Fighters and UK Counter Terrorism Laws', guest chapter (Annex 2) in D Anderson, 'The Terrorism Acts in 2015: Report of the Independent Reviewer' (December 2016).

Webber, F, 'Farewell Magna Carta: The Counter-Terrorism and Security Bill', Open Democracy UK (19 January 2015), https://www.opendemocracy.net/ourkingdom/frances-webber/farewell-magna-carta-counterterrorism-and-security-bill.

Wilmot-Smith, F, 'Necessity or Ideology?' (2014) 36(21) *London Review of Books* 15–17.

Winterman, D, 'Belmarsh: Britain's Guantanamo Bay?' *BBC News* (6 October 2004), http://news.bbc.co.uk/1/hi/magazine/3714864.stm.

Zedner, L, 'Citizenship Deprivation, Security and Human Rights' (2016) 18 *European Journal of Migration and Law* 222–42.

——, 'Criminal Justice in the Service of Security' in M Bosworth, C Hoyle, and L Zedner (eds), *The Changing Contours of Criminal Justice* (Oxford, Oxford University Press, 2016).

——, 'The Hostile Border: Crimmigration, Counterterrorism, or Crossing the Line on Rights?' (2019) 22(3) *New Criminal Law Review* (forthcoming).

——, 'Security against Arbitrary Government in Criminal Justice' in A du Bois-Pedain M Ulväng, and P Asp (eds), *Criminal Law and the Authority of the State* (Oxford, Hart Publishing, 2017).

——, 'Security, the State and the Citizen: The Changing Architecture of Crime Control' (2010) 13(2) *New Criminal Law Review* 379–403.

——, 'Seeking Security by Eroding Rights: The Side-stepping of Due Process' in BJ Goold and L Lazarus (eds), *Security and Human Rights* (Oxford, Hart Publishing, 2007).

——, 'Terrorizing Criminal Law' (2014) 8(1) *Criminal Law and Philosophy* 99–121.

6

Trusted Travellers and Trojan Horses: Security, Privacy, and Privilege at the Border

BENJAMIN J GOOLD*

MANY YEARS AGO, I travelled to the United Kingdom to begin work as a graduate student in law. Although I had been outside of my home country of Australia before, this was the first time that I had been to Europe or had travelled internationally as a student. My passport was still relatively new, and I had carefully arranged all of my documents to make sure that there would be no difficulty with my student visa on arrival at Heathrow Airport. I had an admission letter from my university confirming my enrolment and a letter from my funding body indicating that I had sufficient means of support to carry me through my degree. Despite being tired from the long flight and a little nervous, I wasn't worried about getting into Britain. Mostly, I just wanted to have a shower and get some much needed sleep.

On arrival at Heathrow, I was immediately reminded of the fact that I was not a UK or European citizen. As I approached immigration control, signs and airport staff directed me to the join the queue of 'Other Passport' holders, a queue far longer than that for UK and EU citizens. Unlike the UK/EU queue, my queue moved very slowly. There were fewer immigration officers assigned to us, and while the officers on the UK/EU queue only glanced at people's passports as they passed through to baggage claim, nearly everyone in front of me had their documents checked and were asked multiple questions. After about an hour of waiting, it was finally my turn. The officer flipped through the pages of my passport, examining the handful of entry and exit stamps before checking my visa and accompanying paperwork. I was asked what I was studying, where I would be living, and how long I expected to be in the United Kingdom. After some time, my passport was stamped, and I finally entered the country.

* I am grateful to Efrat Arbel, Lisa Y Gourd, and Liora Lazarus for their comments and suggestions on an earlier version of this chapter. Any remaining errors or omissions are my own.

In the years that followed, this was an experience that would be repeated over and over again. Every time I re-entered the United Kingdom during the course of my studies, I would be asked to confirm that I was still a student and still had the means to support myself. Sometimes there were more questions (What exactly do you study? When do you plan to finish?) and sometimes the immigration officer seemed especially interested in my answers. I learned fairly quickly to give shorter rather than longer answers (telling them I was studying criminology rather than writing a doctorate on police use of CCTV surveillance generally led to fewer questions) and to appear confident in my responses. I came to expect that the 'Other Passports' queue would be long, and if I arrived at Heathrow at the same time as a flight from a non-English-speaking country then I was in for a very long wait. Finally, I also got used to the fact that when standing in front of immigration officers, I had no choice but to answer their questions or provide whatever information they asked for.

Some years later, having completed my studies, I returned to the United Kingdom to take up a position as a university lecturer. Having swapped my student visa for a work visa, I still found myself in the 'Other Passports' queue, but the immigration officers now asked me fewer and less intrusive questions. Eventually, I became a permanent resident and then a naturalised British citizen. After many years of looking enviously at those in the UK/EU passport line, I was finally able to join the 'fast lane'. Even better, I was eligible to use my new UK passport at the e-Passport gates, which meant bypassing the immigration officers altogether. Suddenly, arriving at Heathrow was no longer a cause of apprehension about the possibility of a long wait and intrusive questions and instead inspired a sense of privilege and belonging. For a time, I also stopped thinking of the plight of those in the 'Other Passports' queue and chose to ignore the fact that every time I used the e-Passport gate, it was facial recognition software and a Home Office database – not a person in front of me – that was deciding whether I was entitled to enter the United Kingdom.

There is of course nothing especially unusual about my experiences of travelling in and out of the United Kingdom, either initially as a visa-holder or later as a citizen. Most countries impose different entry procedures on non-nationals and non-residents at their borders, subjecting them to greater scrutiny (and usually longer queues). Moreover, regardless of whether I was in the 'Other Passports' or UK/EU queue, I carried with me a range of privileges that effectively immunised me from some of the worst indignities and intrusions that are central to the experiences of many travellers who are not white, middle class, male law students or professors. As frustrating as it might have been for me to wait for hours in a queue after a long flight, or having to explain to a border officer why I was living in Britain, even as a student I knew that I was unlikely to be denied entry. The possibility even of being detained rarely entered my mind, and when it did, it was easily dismissed as so improbable as to hardly warrant a second thought.

Despite the commonplace nature of my UK border-crossings and the relative privilege I carried as an educated white male English-speaker, the sense of relief

I felt at eventually switching queues was palpable, and notably, it had something but not everything to do with convenience. While it is important not to draw too much from one's own experiences, my experiences at Heathrow are in part the product a shift that has been occurring at the border over the last twenty years. As borders have 'hardened' and 'thickened' through a combination of increasing restrictions on migration and the growing use of surveillance and security technologies,[1] the distinctions between different types of travellers – particularly with regard to the personal costs of travel – have become ever more acute. For those with the 'right' passport or the appropriate visa, border security is experienced mostly as a series of minor inconveniences, such as having to remove one's shoes before passing through airport security or explaining one's travel plans to a border officer. For those with the 'wrong' passport or without the necessary visa – or who are part of a group that has been designated as high-risk by border authorities – then travel can be an entirely different experience, characterised by intrusive surveillance, continuous suspicion, and insecurity. While almost every aspect of border surveillance and security has intensified in recent years, how much particular individuals are likely to be affected by this intensification (or even notice it) is largely determined by factors outside of their control, most notably citizenship and immigration status, but also by their race, ethnicity, socio-economic background, and the ever-changing landscape of national and international politics.

This chapter is not, however, about the continued securitisation of the border. Nor is it about the many ways in which changes in border governance have contributed to larger trends in the use of surveillance technologies and biometric identifiers. Thanks to the work of researchers such as Katja Franko Aas, Didier Bigo, Mary Bosworth, Benjamin Muller, and Mark Salter (to name but a few), there is now a rich theoretical and empirical literature about the changing nature of the border.[2] Instead, this chapter examines the ways in which certain travellers, namely those least likely to be labelled as 'high-risk', have

[1] On the idea of border 'thickening', see BJ Muller, 'Unsafe at Any Speed? Borders, Mobility and "Safe Citizenship"' (2010) 14(1) *Citizenship Studies* 75–88, 85. See also S Sassen, 'Bordering Capabilities *versus* Borders: Implications for National Borders' (2009) 30 *Michigan Journal of International Law* 567–597.

[2] See K Franko Aas, '"Crimmigrant" Bodies and Bona Fide Travelers: Surveillance, Citizenship and Global Governance' (2011) 15(3) *Theoretical Criminology* 331–46; K Franko Aas and H Gundhus, 'Policing Humanitarian Borderlands: Frontex, Human Rights and the Precariousness of Life' (2015) 55(1) *British Journal of Criminology* 1–18; D Bigo, 'Security, Exception, Ban and Surveillance' in D Lyon (ed), *Theorizing Surveillance: The Panopticon and Beyond* (Cullompton, Willan Publishing, 2006); D Bigo and E Guild (eds), *Controlling Frontiers: Free Movement into and within Europe* (Aldershot, Ashgate, 2005); M Bosworth, 'Border Control and the Limits of the Sovereign State' (2008) 17(2) *Social & Legal Studies* 199–215; BJ Muller, '(Dis)qualified Bodies: Securitization, Citizenship and "Identity Management"' (2004) 8(3) *Citizenship Studies* 279–94; Muller, 'Unsafe at Any Speed?' (ibid); MB Salter, 'Passports, Mobility, and Security: How Smart Can the Border Be?' (2004) 5 *International Studies Perspectives* 71–91; and MB Salter, 'At the Threshold of Security: A Theory of International Borders' in MB Salter and E Zureik (eds), *Global Policing and Surveillance: Borders, Security, Identity* (Cullompton, Willan Publishing, 2005).

become willing collaborators in processes of 'social sorting' at the border and enticed into surrendering their privacy in exchange for the promise of frictionless travel and membership of an emerging elite of 'trusted travellers'.[3] In particular, it focuses on the proliferation of 'safe' or 'trusted traveller' programmes such as the US Global Entry system and the UK Registered Traveller service and how they provide states with a new means of harvesting large quantities of personal data at the border. Like a modern-day Trojan Horse, trusted traveller programmes can be seen as a poisoned gift, promising freedom from tedious and time-consuming security procedures to those who surrender their privacy rights and consent to a level of state scrutiny that they would likely view as intolerable in other contexts.

In addition to considering some of the privacy implications of 'safe' and 'trusted' traveller programmes, this chapter asks whether the proliferation of such schemes has the potential to shift popular and political discourse around security, migration, and rights. Returning to my own experiences, as uncomfortable as it might be to admit, my early and immediate longing to join the UK/EU queue was never just about reducing the amount of time I spent passing through Customs and Immigration at Heathrow airport. It was also motivated by a desire to join the ranks of the 'safe', low-risk travellers who enjoyed a form of privilege that, for a time at least, was very visibly unavailable to me. If the desire to enrol in trusted traveller programmes is also motivated by a degree of status envy – or at least a desire to maintain one's privilege at the border – what does this mean for the relationship between security and rights at the border? Does allowing those with the necessary resources and social capital to 'jump the queue' at the border entrench existing inequalities based on privilege? This greater social stratification at the border goes well beyond distinctions between citizens and non-citizens and may be a harbinger of future changes in the relationship between security and human rights more generally. If some travellers are effectively able to buy frictionless passage through the border, with the result that they no longer have to share queues with or even see 'high-risk' travellers, what happens to the wider discourse about rights and security at the border? Do we risk exacerbating existing social and political divisions, and potentially hardening attitudes towards 'high-risk' travellers or supposedly 'irregular' entrants like refugees and asylum seekers?

[3] For discussion of the concept of social sorting and its relationship to contemporary forms of surveillance (both generally and at the border), see D Lyon, 'Surveillance as Social Sorting: Computer Codes and Mobile Bodies' in D Lyon (ed), *Surveillance as Social Sorting: Privacy, Risk and Digital Discrimination* (London, Routledge, 2003); D Lyon, 'National IDs in a Global World: Surveillance, Security, and Citizenship' (2010) 42(3) *Case Western Reserve Journal of International Law* 607–23; and P Adey, 'Surveillance at the Airport: Surveilling Mobility/Mobilising Surveillance' (2004) 36(8) *Environment and Planning A* 1365–80.

I. TRUSTED TRAVELLER SCHEMES AND THE THREAT TO PRIVACY

> Are you waiting in line at the airport watching others zip through security with less hassle? If you haven't signed up for a 'trusted traveler' program to cut your waiting time, this may be the year to do it.[4]

> The management of borders through technology is indeed very much about creating the means by which freedom of mobility can be enabled, smoothened and facilitated for the qualified elite; the belonging citizens, all the while allowing the allocation of more time and effort for additional security checks to be exercised on those who are considered as 'high-risk' categories.[5]

As long as there have been modern states, an individual's ability to enter or leave a country has largely been determined by questions of citizenship and immigration status. For much of the twentieth century at least, those charged with managing borders were required to distinguish between travellers with appropriate status and those without. In this context, passports and visas traditionally served as credentials, signalling to border agents and immigration officials that the individual in front of them had a right, or at least some form of lawful permission, to enter/exit. However, as concerns over cross-border crime, international terrorism, and unwanted migration have grown, borders have gradually emerged as key sites for surveillance, social sorting, and exclusion.[6] At the heart of this transformation has been a focus on what David Lyon has referred to as the 'securitisation of identity' and the coupling of ideas of citizenship with 'identity management'.[7] As border control has shifted to focus on risk and how to manage the transnational data flows that lie at the heart of national and international efforts to curb unwanted migration and cross-border crime, states have sought out new and more efficient ways of identifying and classifying those seeking to cross their borders. This has in turn meant that citizenship (or the lack of it) is now only one of a range of factors that need to be verified and assessed. Border agencies now deploy a wide array of biometric technologies (including iris scanning, electronic fingerprint readers, and facial recognition software) that allow them to identify individuals and immediately sort them into predetermined risk categories. These categories are then used to determine whether individuals should be subjected to additional security screening,

[4] M Higgins, 'Which "Trusted Traveler" Program Is Right for You?' *New York Times* (20 February 2017).

[5] B Ajana, 'Augmented Borders: Big Data and the Ethics of Immigration Control' (2015) 13(1) *Journal of Information, Communication and Ethics in Society* 58–78, 66.

[6] S Pickering and L Weber, *Borders, Mobility and Technologies of Control* (Dordrecht, Springer, 2006); and Bigo and Guild (eds) (above n 2).

[7] D Lyon, 'Filtering Flows, Friends and Foes: Global Surveillance' in MB Salter, P Adey, C Bennett, G and Fuller (eds), *Politics at the Airport* (Minneapolis, University of Minnesota Press, 2008) 36. As Lyon has acknowledged, the phrase 'securitisation of identity' has been used by Nikolas Rose to describe the relationship between 'freedom' and 'proof of legitimate identity' (36). See N Rose, *Powers of Freedom* (Cambridge, Cambridge University Press, 1999).

detained pending determination of their legal status (as in the case of refugees or asylum seekers), or immediately excluded from entry altogether. As Lyon has noted:

> In so-called control societies ... older means of determining who is 'innocent/guilty', 'approved/suspect', or 'legal/illegal' seem to be at a lower premium. In an analogous way to that in which the 'categorical suspicion' of today's policing renders everyone if not guilty at least dubious until proven innocent, so 'identity management' seems to be encroaching on older definitions of citizenship. The need for knowledge and visibility as management tools is clear here, which is why airports especially are dense surveillance sites.[8]

As surveillance has become more global in nature, the role of the border has shifted and broadened. No longer simply gateways between countries, borders now operate as sites of information-gathering, risk assessment, and the categorisation of citizens and non-citizens alike. When individuals now pass through borders, they do not simply have their documents checked; instead, their identities are evaluated against an array of national and international databases, and their physical selves are squared against data doubles that are largely constructed and controlled by states.[9] Although these processes are ostensibly in service of enhancing national security, combatting crime, and regulating migration, in many instances they also represent an expression of sovereignty, unbounded by the restraints imposed by the rule of law and the legal protections found within the regular boundaries of the state.[10]

While a great deal of the surveillance work that goes on at the border is directed at identifying and managing travellers who the state deems high-risk or undesirable, as many commentators have pointed out, it would be a mistake to see the securitisation of the border merely in terms of exclusion, or as a matter of insiders and outsiders. On one level, global surveillance is fundamentally concerned with distinguishing between 'tourists' and 'vagabonds', but as Franko Aas and others have argued, this is only part of the story.[11] Drawing on the

[8] Lyon, 'Filtering Flows' (ibid) 43.

[9] As Lyon has noted, these data doubles 'have far greater rates of mobility than their real-life counterparts; indeed, the travels of the one affect the travels of the other (especially if one is locally defined as an "other")'. Lyon, 'Filtering Flows' (above n 7) 30.

[10] There is now extensive literature on the question of whether borders should be seen as perpetual 'states of exception' (as understood from the work of Giorgio Agamben). For some examples of this claim, see MB Salter, 'When the Exception Becomes the Rule: Borders, Sovereignty, and Citizenship' (2008) 12(4) *Citizenship Studies* 365–80; C Boano and R Martén, 'Agamben's Urbanism of Exception: Jerusalem's Border Mechanics and Biopolitical Strongholds' (2013) 34 *Cities* 6–17; S Hanafi, 'Explaining Spacio-cide in the Palestinian Territory: Colonization, Separation, and States of Exception' (2013) 61(2) *Current Sociology* 190–205; and S Taylor, 'Sovereign Power at the Border' (2005) 16(1) *Public Law Review* 55–77.

[11] On the distinction between 'tourists' and 'vagabonds', see Z Bauman, 'From Pilgrim to Tourist – Or a Short History of Identity' in S Hall and P du Gay (eds), *Questions of Identity* (London, Sage, 1996) 18–36; Z Bauman *Postmodern Ethics* (London, Routledge, 1993); and Z Bauman, *Globalization: The Human Consequences* (Cambridge, Polity Press, 1998).

work of Muller, Mika Ojakangas, and Willem Schinkel, Franko Aas has noted that while 'markers of citizenship are the primary lines of distinction between gate closing and gate opening', at its core a great deal of contemporary border surveillance is biopolitical in nature, with the power of the state being directed at its own populace with a view to distinguishing between more and less deserving citizens:[12]

> [B]iopolitical surveillance internally differentiates the bios, and its forms of exclusion are primarily scientific and moral, rather than territorial exclusion from the polity as such. This process is exemplified by the heated debates about home grown terrorists, other types of 'crimmigrants' and integrating immigrant populations. This type of politics creates groups of subcitizens – or what might be termed 'outsiders inside' – who, although territorially included, find their citizenship status securitized and substantially depleted.[13]

It is against this backdrop of biopolitical surveillance that the emergence of 'safe' and 'trusted traveller' programmes in Europe, North America, and elsewhere must be understood.[14] Typically, these schemes enable citizens and permanent residents from the home state – and in some cases, travellers from a select list of favoured states – to gain access to streamlined immigration and security procedures at land borders and airports. Examples of such schemes include Germany's EasyPASS system,[15] the Singapore–USA Trusted Traveller Programme (TTP),[16] and the UK Registered Traveller service.[17] Perhaps the most extensive of these schemes is the US Trusted Traveller programme. Administered by the US Department of Homeland Security, it encompasses five distinct programmes: Global Entry, TSA Pre✓, SENTRI, NEXUS, and FAST (North or South).[18] Each Trusted Traveller programme is designed to serve different types

[12] Franko Aas (above n 2) 339. See also W Schinkel, 'From Zoepolitics to Biopolitics: Citizenship and the Construction of "Society"' (2010) 13(2) *European Journal of Social Theory* 155–72; Muller, '(Dis)qualified Bodies' (above n 2); Muller, 'Unsafe at Any Speed?' (above n 1); and M Ojakangas, 'Impossible Dialogue on Bio-Power: Agamben and Foucault' (2005) 2 *Foucault Studies* 5–28.

[13] Franko Aas (above n 2) 339.

[14] Here, the exercise of biopolitical power, which is directed inward against members of the polity, is to be distinguished from that of zoepolitical power, which is directed against 'outsiders'. See G Agamben, *Homo Sacer: Sovereignty and Bare Life*, D Heller-Roazen (trans) (Stanford, Stanford University Press, 1998); E Guild, *Security and Migration in the 21st Century* (Cambridge, Polity Press, 2009); and Franko Aas (above n 2) 339–40.

[15] See the EasyPASS website: https://www.easypass.de/EasyPass/EN/What_is_EasyPASS/home_node.html (accessed 4 March 2019).

[16] See the TTP website: https://eservices.ica.gov.sg/esvclandingpage/ttp (accessed 4 March 2019).

[17] See the UK Registered Traveller website: https://www.gov.uk/registered-traveller (accessed 4 March 2019).

[18] See the US Homeland Security webpage 'Trusted Traveler Programs': 'https://www.dhs.gov/trusted-traveler-programs (accessed 12 March 2019). Of these five programmes, the first four are specifically directed at individual travellers. In contrast, FAST (North or South) is for use by 'commercial truck drivers who are transporting low-risk shipments into the US from Canada and Mexico'.

of traveller, and in some cases, they overlap with other non-US trusted traveller programmes.[19]

Although procedures vary across schemes, eligible travellers are usually required to complete an application form, attend a screening interview, and pay a fee. In the case of the UK Registered Traveller service, for example, an applicant must be eighteen years or older and have an eligible passport.[20] In addition, the applicant must have a UK visa or entry clearance and have visited the United Kingdom 'at least four times in the last twenty-four months'. The applicant must then complete an online application, which includes questions about previous criminal convictions, whether the applicant has ever been refused entry to the United Kingdom, or 'ever had action or penalties taken against you for breaking customs laws or regulations'. Finally, once the application has been submitted and a fee of £70 has been paid, the applicant must then enter the United Kingdom through the 'Other Passports' lane, fill in a landing card, and have their details checked by an immigration officer. If the applicant meets all of the criteria, s/he is then admitted to the programme for a period of twelve months.

As onerous as this process may appear, for travellers used to entering Britain via the 'Other Passports' lane, the benefits are potentially very attractive. In July 2018, for example, immigration control wait-times for non-UK/EU nationals reached highs of two and a half hours at Heathrow Airport, prompting representatives of a number of major airlines to openly criticise UK Border Force.[21] Once a member of the Registered Traveller service, non-UK citizens are able to skip these queues altogether and enter via the UK/EU passport entry lanes – a process that I know from personal experience can take as little as a few minutes. In addition to the benefits of faster entry, Registered Travellers who also have e-passports can avoid dealing with border agents altogether by using automated e-gates,[22] reducing the likelihood of additional scrutiny or questioning.

[19] For example, such cooperation is at the heart of the Singapore–USA Trusted Traveller Programme (TTP), which enables approved US passport-holders (who are also members of the US Global Entry Programme) to use Singapore's Enhanced Immigration Automated Clearance System (eIACS), https://www.ica.gov.sg/enteranddeparting/border/enteranddeparting_border_travellers_eiacs.

[20] At the time of writing, passport holders from forty-one countries were eligible to enrol in the programme: Botswana, Namibia, Seychelles, Brunei, Hong Kong, Japan, Macao SAR, Malaysia, Maldives, Singapore, South Korea, Taiwan, Andorra, Monaco, Vatican City State, Israel, Bahamas, Canada, Mexico, Saint Vincent and the Grenadines, USA, Australia, Nauru, New Zealand, Papua New Guinea, Samoa, Tonga, Argentina, Belize, Brazil, Chile, Costa Rica, El Salvador, Guatemala, Honduras, Nicaragua, Panama, Paraguay, Trinidad and Tobago, Uruguay.

[21] P Greenfield, 'Border Queue Times at Heathrow Fail to Meet Targets', *Guardian* (13 August 2018), https://www.theguardian.com/business/2018/aug/13/heathrow-airport-border-force-queue-times-failing-targets.

[22] The term 'e-passport' is commonly used to refer to a passport that contains an embedded electronic chip that typically contains biometric data about the passport-holder and can be used by border officers and immigration officials for the purposes of identification. At the time of writing, well over one hundred countries issue e-passports. See the International Civil Aviation Organization webpage 'ePassport Basics', https://www.icao.int/Security/FAL/PKD/Pages/ePassportBasics.aspx (accessed 12 March 2019).

These benefits have not gone unnoticed by frequent travellers, as demonstrated by this post on a travel blog that recommends the Registered Traveller service:

> The 'All Passports' queue encompasses everyone outside the EU. Here you're relying on the organisation of others and the fact that their visit is legitimate. Foreign (non-EU) passports are more heavily scrutinised by officials and thus can take longer to process. You're also required to submit a Border Agency landing card. As a frequent visitor to the UK, these tedious pieces of paper will drive you to madness while you're counting how many months you have left on your visa. Should you happen to get it wrong you are likely to encounter further delays.[23]

In contrast to the UK Registered Traveller service, the US NEXUS programme is limited to US and Canadian nationals and permanent residents, and it can be used only when crossing the Canada–US border. While those wishing to join the NEXUS programme go through an application process similar to that of the Registered Traveller service, what distinguishes NEXUS is the fact that membership imposes a series of responsibilities. In addition to ensuring that their passport information is kept up to date at all times, members must report to a NEXUS Enrolment Centre to notify officials of any changes to citizenship documents, permanent resident cards, naturalisation certificates, work visas, and study permits. In addition, any change in employment, residential address, or driver's licence must be reported, along with any arrest, criminal charge, or conviction.[24] Failure to keep one's profile up to date or to inform NEXUS officials of a potential change in eligibility can result in permanent exclusion from the programme.

As with the UK Registered Traveller service, membership of the NEXUS programme can result in a significant reduction in the amount of time it takes to enter either Canada or the United States. Indeed, as Muller has observed, for those in the programme, the border may barely seem like an obstacle at all:

> Of relevance here is not only the way in which the process of enrollment into the NEXUS program renders one a 'safe citizen' from the perspective of state officials (and potentially jeopardizes one's safety in other ways, regarding privacy, identity theft, false internment, etc), but also the extent to which holders of this card enjoy enhanced rights and responsibilities as redesigned 'safe citizens'. The most obvious enhancement is the far less fettered experience of border crossing … Interestingly, the experience of the NEXUS cardholder also figures into the marketed and packaged experience of 'safe citizenship', as the border generally seems smooth, if not altogether absent. Indeed, at non-peak times, the pre-screening methods used for NEXUS often mean those in the NEXUS lane do not even come to a complete stop at the border, but instead simply slow down for a cordial greeting.[25]

[23] 'Why Expats in the UK Need to Understand the Registered Traveller Service', *Roaming Required* blog (10 August 2018), http://www.roamingrequired.com/registered-traveller-service/ (Accessed 27 February 2019).

[24] See the Canada Border Services Agency (CBSA) page 'NEXUS: Updates to Personal Information': https://www.cbsa-asfc.gc.ca/prog/nexus/contact-coordonnees-eng.html (accessed 5 March 2019).

[25] Muller, 'Unsafe at Any Speed?' (above n 1) 82.

From a privacy perspective, many of the trusted traveller schemes listed above raise a number of serious concerns. In the case of the NEXUS programme, for example, applicants are required to disclose not only information about their immigration status and any past criminal offences but also employment and address history for the last five years. Even more significant is the consent statement listed on the last page of the NEXUS application form, which encompasses the collection of various forms of personal information, including 'supporting documentation, background information, biometric data, and any other information obtained and collected for the purpose of the operation of the NEXUS program'. On the Canadian version of the form, moreover, an applicant must also consent to this information being shared with 'other government departments or agencies in Canada (including the Royal Canadian Mounted Police and the Canadian Security Intelligence Service), in accordance with the Privacy Act'.[26]

Since most NEXUS applicants will not be familiar with the provisions of the Canadian Privacy Act, they will likely be unaware that they are in effect authorising the Canadian Border Services Agency (CBSA) to share their personal information with broad swathes of the federal government. Although section 8(1) of the Privacy Act notes that personal information 'cannot be disclosed without the consent of the individual to whom it relates', section 8(2) provides for sharing without consent under a range of circumstances, including 'where, in the opinion of the head of the institution, the public interest in disclosure clearly outweighs any invasion of privacy that could result from the disclosure'.[27]

Requiring individuals to disclose and surrender control of large amounts of personal information in order to enrol in programmes like NEXUS clearly represents a serious threat to established privacy rights in countries like Canada, the United States, and the United Kingdom. While enrolment is voluntary, it would be naïve to assume that people understand what it is they are giving up in exchange for smoother travel across the border.[28] Most applicants will also be unaware that once this information is disclosed, in most cases it will continue to

[26] See the CBSA page 'NEXUS: Paper Application': https://www.cbsa-asfc.gc.ca/prog/nexus/paper-papier-eng.html (accessed 5 March 2019).

[27] Privacy Act (RSC 1985, c P-21), section 8(2)(m)(i). The information-sharing provisions of the Privacy Act have come under repeated criticism from the Office of the Privacy Commissioner of Canada. Appearing before a Parliamentary Standing Committee in November 2016, Privacy Commissioner Daniel Therrien raised concerns about 'excessive collection and sharing of personal information' by government. More specifically, the Office of the Privacy Commissioner has also drawn attention to the broad powers contained in paragraphs 8(2)(a) and (f) of the Privacy Act and has recommended that they be governed by written agreements. See Office of the Privacy Commissioner of Canada, 'Appearance before the Standing Committee on Access to Information, Privacy, and Ethics on the Study on Review of the Privacy Act' (1 November 2016), https://www.priv.gc.ca/en/opc-actions-and-decisions/advice-to-parliament/2016/parl_20161101/ (accessed 5 March 2019).

[28] In many cases, information disclosed as part of the application to become a member of a trusted traveller scheme or pre-clearance programme will be retained even if the application is rejected. See C Elliott, 'TSA's New Pre-check Programs Raises Major Privacy Concerns', *Washington Post* (3 October 2013).

be held (and presumably shared) by government even if the individual decides to leave the programme or has membership revoked. Finally, while information-sharing between different parts of government may be regulated (to varying degrees depending on national jurisprudence on the issue), the sharing of information *between* states remains a murky issue. Given that information-sharing between national security agencies is common, as well as opaque and difficult to regulate,[29] information disclosed as part of a trusted traveller application could very well be shared with a foreign power, especially when questions of national security or transnational crime are raised. Put simply, becoming a safe or trusted traveller is not without costs in terms of privacy.

As significant as these privacy concerns are, there are other reasons to be worried about the emergence of trusted traveller schemes like the UK Registered Traveller service and the NEXUS programme. As Muller has pointed out, by enrolling in such schemes, individuals necessarily expose themselves further to the state, with the result that they become more vulnerable to surveillance and categorisation:

> The irony [of trusted traveller schemes] is that not only do such schemes fail to guarantee that a citizen will be regarded as safe by the state; they also ignore the fact that citizens might well be compromising their safety by enabling the state to transform them into a digital identity – a netizen. Oddly, then, in order to satisfy the state's obsession with knowing unknowns and governing the ungovernable, citizens/netizens often choose to surrender themselves to the eyes/networks of the state and its intrusions so that they might avoid being categorized as deeply suspicious by the state and, ironically, protect themselves against future intrusions by the state.[30]

Going further, trusted traveller programmes pose a risk not only to the rights of the individuals who choose to enrol in them but also to those who do not or cannot join. As a growing body of research on the subject has demonstrated, institutional practices, public debate, and theoretical understandings of the border all sit within a nexus of axiological issues involving race, gender, religion, and globalisation, to name just a few. In the particular case of trusted traveller schemes, it is essential that we examine the role that they play in broader discourses that entrench existing divisions based not only on citizenship and immigration status, but also on race, gender, class, and socioeconomic status. In the context of the evolving debates over the meaning and function of the border, trusted traveller schemes can be seen as part of a fundamentally neoliberal discourse that invites those who already are privileged to actively participate in and openly enjoy the benefits of processes of sorting and othering.[31]

[29] See Privacy International, 'Secret Global Surveillance Networks: Intelligence Sharing between Governments and the Need for Safeguards' (April 2018), available at https://privacyinternational.org/report/1741/secret-global-surveillance-networks-intelligence-sharing-between-governments-and-need (accessed 18 March 2019).

[30] Muller, 'Unsafe at Any Speed?' (above n 1) 85.

[31] For further discussion of othering in the context of security and counterterrorism, see the chapters in this volume by Aziz Z Huq; Rumee Ahmed and Ayesha S Chaudhry; and Natasa Mavronicola.

II. PRIVILEGE AND SECURITY

> Enamored by the thought of being a pseudo-VIP at the airport, I decided to apply for Global Entry in late 2014 ... Global Entry has made traveling much quicker and more seamless for me. Landing from an international trip is a breeze now, with just a few moments on the fast-pass line at customs through the Global Entry kiosks. I also use the included TSA Precheck benefits frequently, usually when I'm traveling domestically. I really appreciate the time I save not having to wait in long security lines. Also, I don't have to fill up three bins with personal items, since I can keep my shoes, coat, and belt on and don't have to remove liquids and my laptop from my bag. In this age of unglamorous flying, it's nice to know $100 can get you something that can truly improve your air travel experience.[32]

> The concept of a line for elite travelers who can afford to pay a fee also strikes many observers as unfair, if not un-American. Critics say that, in the interests of safety, all travelers should be given the same careful screening whenever they fly.[33]

At the beginning of this chapter, I noted that part of my desire to join the UK/EU queue at Heathrow Airport years ago was driven by envy at seeing others breeze past me at UK Customs and Immigration. At the risk of engaging in what might be called 'anecdotal sociology', I have also examined various online travel advice forums and travel websites such as TripAdvisor and Fodor's, and it seems clear that many people join trusted traveller schemes for similar reasons: namely, to save time, avoid being questioned at the border, and claim (or reclaim) a privilege now more commonly associated with first-class and VIP travel. Uncoincidentally, these schemes began to emerge in the years immediately after 9/11,[34] when security and immigration checks at airports and land borders were undergoing major overhauls and becoming more extensive and stringent. As these processes have become more onerous, time-consuming, and costly, government agencies have understandably looked for ways to make entry and exit procedures more efficient and streamlined. At the same time, they have also sought to exploit the border – that is, to take advantage of the fact that some individuals may be willing to forgo certain rights and protections (and pay a fee) in order to reduce the time and stress involved with international travel.

At a time when debates about the future of migration have become increasingly heated, particularly regarding refugees and asylum seekers, it is important to ask how trusted traveller programmes like the UK Registered Traveller service, US Global Entry, and the NEXUS programme fit into public narratives about

[32] J Goldenberg Doner, 'I Got Global Entry and It Was One of the Best Travel Decisions I Ever Made', *Business Insider* (13 May 2018), https://www.businessinsider.com/global-entry-was-my-best-travel-decision-2018-5/?r=AU&IR=T/#1-visit-the-us-customs-and-border-protection-trusted-traveler-program-website-and-create-a-logingov-account-1.

[33] Elliott (above n 28).

[34] For example, according to the US Department of Homeland Security, NEXUS began operations in the summer of 2002.

borders, security, and immigration. More pointedly, is it possible that the existence and expansion of such programmes have helped to normalise (or at the very least, to render less visible) various forms of sorting and discrimination at the border? By making it possible for supposedly low-risk travellers to avoid the discomfort of having to rub shoulders with those the state (as well as large swathes of the public) regards as undesirable[35] – in much the same way first- and business-class travellers rarely have to concern themselves with those stuck back in economy – have trusted traveller programmes contributed to a shift in the politics of the border?

According to a number of commentators, the answer appears to be yes. As Tamara Vukov and Mimi Sheller have observed, 'New modes of surveillance, technologies for border control, and infrastructures to manage various flows across borders work together to reinforce social inequalities, re-make uneven spatialities, and re-create subjects with differential "network capital".'[36] More specifically, they have argued that a core function of the NEXUS programme is to define and identify through the use of biometric technologies the 'virtuous traveller'.[37] This traveller then provides the standard against which others are measured, and a tension is created:

> [The] dialectic between the expedited virtuous traveler and unwanted 'intruder' whose movements must be tracked and prevented through technological means (casting a wide net and reductive net over different forms of undocumented migration) is central to recently emergent projects of virtual borders.[38]

What is important here is that the 'virtuous traveller' maps on to pre-existing notions of status and privilege that play a role in people's lives well beyond the border.[39] In the case of NEXUS, for example, only those who are able to provide proof of continued employment and residence, as well as clean criminal

[35] The term 'undesirable' can be found in Canadian government reports on citizenship and immigration. For example, in the 2003 Report of the Auditor General to the House of Commons, it is noted that one of the aims on the Multiple Borders Strategy is 'to keep the Canada–US border open to legitimate travellers and goods, and to identify and intercept illegal and undesirable travellers as far away from North America as possible'. See 'Chapter 5: Citizenship and Immigration Canada – Control and Enforcement' in Office of the Auditor General of Canada, '2003 Report of the Auditor General of Canada to the House of Commons' (April 2003), 8.

[36] T Vukov and M Sheller, 'Border Work: Surveillant Assemblages, Virtual Fences, and Tactical Counter-media' (2013) 23(2) *Social Semiotics* 225–41, 230.

[37] According to Vukov and Sheller, 'On entering the virtual border space of the airport, one becomes not only a virtual passenger (shadowed by the 'data double', a kind of informational penumbra) but also a virtuous passenger (performing virtue and virtuosity). And through this labor of self-surveillance, the securitized air passenger contributes to the production of the other – the non-virtuous, devirtualized, and abject body of the unwanted entrant.' Vukov and Sheller (ibid) 229.

[38] Vukov and Sheller (above n 36) 233. See also G Popescu, 'Controlling Mobility' in G Popescu (ed), *Bordering and Ordering the Twenty-First Century: Understanding Borders* (Lanham, Rowman & Littlefield, 2011).

[39] For an excellent exploration of the notion of privilege at the border (focusing in particular on the US–Mexico border), see J Heyman, 'Trust, Privilege, and Discretion in the Governance of the US Borderlands with Mexico' (2009) 24(3) *Canadian Journal of Law and Society* 367–90.

records, are likely to be approved, with the result that many people who are already marginalised in society are ineligible to enrol. In addition, because applicants are asked to both disclose significant amounts of personal information and consent to that information being shared across government, they need to have considerable trust in the state. Although detailed demographic data on NEXUS enrolment is not publicly available, these barriers to entry suggest that most members are probably middle-class/wealthy citizens and permanent residents who enjoy a positive or at least neutral relationship with the American and Canadian governments. By the same logic, there are also good reasons to suspect that individuals from communities that have historically experienced over-policing and an antagonistic relationship with government agencies are underrepresented.

According to Muller, this re-creation and replication of privilege at the border is inherently neoliberal in its orientation. Noting that the 'voluntary nature of trusted traveler programs also fit well within Foucault's notion of "disciplinary society" and Gilles Deleuze's "societies of control"',[40] Muller has argued that such programmes do more than simply distinguish between the desirable and undesirable or the virtuous and non-virtuous. Instead, they contribute to the creation and commodification of different forms of citizenship:

> What emerges is a redesigned citizenship that is multi-speed: where access, convenience and/or hassle are the direct result of one's own (consumer) choices, with your passport allowing you into the slow lane, your enhanced driver's license into the somewhat faster lane and your trusted traveller program membership card allowing you into the most accelerated lane. And most importantly, your enrollment in these ever-accelerating border-crossing programs renders you a 'safe' citizen in the eyes of the state – as a citizen who has become readable, knowable data, and in some cases, disciplined.[41]

Writing in a similar vein, Matthew Sparke has argued that NEXUS is best understood as a 'context-contingent response to the contradictory imperatives of national securitization and economic facilitation'.[42] Consistent with the desire of states to ensure that the steady securitisation of the border does not interfere with the mobility of international-travellers-as-consumers, NEXUS enables a privileged class to avoid the indignities of the border and continue to travel in a largely borderless fantasy world, free to move and spend as part of a newly emergent elite global citizenry:

> NEXUS lane participants – the people who 'cross often' and want to 'make it simple', the people who are prepared to buy flexible citizenship because 'the fastlane is where

[40] BJ Muller, 'Travellers, Borders, Dangers: Locating the Political at the Biometric Border' in Salter, Adey, Bennett, and Fuller (eds) (above n 7) 137.

[41] Muller, 'Unsafe at Any Speed?' (above n 1) 80. For more on differentiated forms of citizenship, see also the chapter in this volume by Lucia Zedner.

[42] M Sparke, 'A Neoliberal Nexus: Economy, Security and the Biopolitics of Citizenship on the Border' (2006) 25 *Political Geography* 151–80, 152.

you want to be' – would seem to represent the paradigmatic neoliberal citizen-players on the transnational level playing field of free trade, neoliberal citizens for whom transnational mobility rights are part of the more general transnational business class privilege that continues to be expanded and entrenched globally through the 'new constitutionalism' of free trade and related laws.[43]

What is striking about Sparke's analysis of NEXUS and other trusted traveller programmes is his observation that the conferral of such privilege has come at the cost of a concomitant loss of status, privilege, and mobility for a group he refers to as the 'kinetic underclass'. Although Sparke has stopped short of suggesting that the distribution of privilege at the border is a zero-sum game, one is left wondering whether the emergence of this new class of trusted traveller has contributed to a politics that makes it even easier for governments to engage in processes of exclusion, detention, and deportation – to characterise 'undesirable' migrants such as refugees and asylum seekers as morally flawed and undeserving. If enrolment in programmes like the UK Registered Traveller Service, US Global Entry, and NEXUS serves to reconfirm a sense of privilege for particular elites, it is reasonable to assume that some of those same elites may also conclude that those unable to enjoy these privileges have only themselves to blame.

Building off Sparke's idea of the 'kinetic underclass' and returning to some of the themes I explored in the first edition of *Security and Human Rights*, we might also think about how the proliferation of trusted traveller programmes might be changing the ways in which borders contribute to the creation and entrenchment of certain forms of identity, particularly for the most vulnerable and insecure. In my earlier work, I noted that without stable, categorical identities, it is 'difficult for states to exercise any hold over those who live within their borders, or to ensure that they are able to protect against internal and external threats'.[44] As such, it is in the state's interest to identify individuals seeking to pass through the border and to ensure that their identity once determined is difficult to change. As has already been noted, programmes like NEXUS clearly manufacture new markers of identity, assigning the status of 'safe' or 'trusted' to those willing (and able) to join such schemes. Notably, however, these schemes require potential members to produce already stable identities in order to enrol: privilege from the point of view of the NEXUS programme means being able to document one's continued residence and employment and

[43] Sparke (ibid) 174. A similar point has also been made by Franko Aas, who has referred to Hyndman's concept of the 'supra-citizen' – a group that includes 'not only foreign business, diplomatic and cultural elites, frequent flyers (from visa white-listed and occasionally also from visa black-listed countries), but also those "humanitarian internationals", such as staff of international relief agencies, academics, consultants, lobbyists and international human rights workers'. See Franko Aas (above n 2) 340–41. See also J Hyndman, *Managing Displacement: Refugees and the Politics of Humanitarianism* (Minneapolis, University of Minnesota Press, 2000); and Guild (above n 14).

[44] B Goold 'Privacy, Identity and Security' in B Goold and L Lazarus (eds), *Security and Human Rights* (Oxford, Hart Publishing, 2007) 52.

to remain free of criminal convictions. Conversely, those unable or ineligible to join are affixed with an equally stable if unwanted identity: that of the 'unsafe' or 'untrustworthy'.

Schemes like NEXUS thus do three things: they replicate existing forms of privilege and enable socio-economic status to be transferred from inside the state to the liminal space of the border; they fix and entrench this form of privilege via scheme membership and the production of categories like 'safe' and 'trusted' traveller; and they simultaneously create a new class of travellers – those ineligible to join and enjoy various privileges at the border. Given that this new class of 'unsafe' or 'untrustworthy' traveller largely maps onto other classifications that lead to increased attention from the state (including detention and exclusion), it is easy to see how programmes like NEXUS and the UK Registered Traveller scheme not only contribute to processes of social sorting at the border, but also produce unwanted identities and entrench various forms of state-sanctioned discrimination and exclusion.[45]

Given all of the factors that affect the development of border policies and practices – not to mention the multivalent, complicated play of public attitudes to migration and national security – the claim that that creating layers of privilege at the border makes it easier for governments to disregard (or at least diminish) the rights and protections of 'irregular' travellers is hard to test empirically. Nonetheless, the proliferation of trusted traveller programmes over the last twenty years surely warrants more serious theoretical and empirical scrutiny. We should know more about not only why people join these schemes, but also if (and how) membership and its subsequent benefits change members' attitudes to travelling in general and to fellow travellers in particular. On the other side, how have the experiences changed for those who are not members of such schemes and who cross the border with yet another negative identity marker? Moreover, we need to know more about how trusted traveller programmes are understood by border agents and immigration officials. How do state agents understand 'trusted' or 'safe' in this context, and does the use of such language in relation to one group increase the likelihood that others are regarded as 'untrustworthy' or 'unsafe'? Are members of programmes like the UK Registered Traveller service, US Global Entry, and NEXUS treated differently when it comes to the exercise of official discretion at the border, especially as regards issues of security and immigration? Borders may be key sites for social sorting, but such processes are iterated and manifested daily through human interactions and individual decision-making and affected by institutional cultures as well as wider social attitudes. What happens at the border as a workplace when agents are provided with new labels and categories with which to identify the subjects of their discretion?

[45] I am particularly grateful to Efrat Arbel for her help in developing my thinking on the implications of assigning privilege at the border, and in particular the relationship between privilege and identity.

Thanks to the important work of researchers like Franko Aas, Muller, Sparke, and Josiah Heyman, we have nuanced accounts of how privilege is constructed at the border and a rich theoretical framework for understanding how such privilege fits into broader trends with respect to border surveillance and security. But we do not yet have a clear sociological picture of how various types of border privilege map onto other forms of socioeconomic advantage enjoyed by 'supra-citizens' (per Franko Aas and Hyndman) or 'safe citizens' (per Muller) in their home countries, or how those privileges move with 'global citizens' as they encounter different border regimes.[46] As has already been noted, this in part is because governments do not provide detailed demographic data on who joins their trusted traveller programmes. But perhaps more significantly. it is because we have only begun to see the border as a place where existing inequalities and divisions within the 'bios' are being deliberately recreated by state authorities, both in their pursuit of administrative efficiency and greater security, and in service of a neoliberal agenda aimed at ensuring that select 'citizens-as-consumers' are able to carry their status into otherwise liminal border spaces.

III. CONCLUSION

Borders have evolved significantly in the years since the first edition of this collection was published. They are no longer simply places where credentials are checked and various dichotomies between citizen and non-citizen, resident and non-resident are confirmed and reinforced. Instead, as many have observed, they have become spaces where complex social and political forces merge and are compressed into discourses on surveillance, security, and migration. They have become spaces where citizenship and other emergent forms of identity are reimagined and contested. It is perhaps not surprising then to find that states have through the development of trusted traveller schemes found a way to create new markers of privilege. What we now need to understand, however, is how the existence of these schemes changes the politics of the border. Does allowing people to pay to be in a different queue undermine the idea that citizenship is, at the border at least, a good that should be enjoyed equally by everyone who holds the same passport? Does it represent a step towards the eventual privatisation of the border, where economic status and the ability to pay will determine mobility?

In the first edition of this collection, many of the contributing authors reflected on the ways in which concerns about security in the aftermath of 9/11 had provided justification for an unprecedented expansion in the authority of the state. Faced with the prospect of other catastrophic attacks, many

[46] Heyman's examination of privilege at the US–Mexico border (above n 39) goes some way towards filling this gap.

democratic countries have seemed more than willing to surrender hard-won civil liberties and human rights in exchange for the promise of greater protection from terrorism. However, as prescient as many of the chapters in the first edition were, especially with regards to the relationship between security and the rule of law, it is fair to say that none of them fully anticipated the extent to which concerns about terrorism would merge with other narratives of fear and anxiety, most notably about threats to national identity and the supposed dangers of 'uncontrolled migration'.

In many respects, the border is something of a laboratory. It is a place where the state, freed from many of the restrictions imposed by domestic law and constitutionally protected human rights, is able to test the limits of its authority and exercise raw sovereign power. As a consequence, efforts on the part of states to create new, quasi-official forms of identity at the border and to establish new hierarchies of privilege based on neoliberal conceptions of 'safe' or 'trusted' travellers deserve our attention. This is not only because these moves have the potential to exacerbate and entrench existing inequalities at the border. Trusted traveller programmes also provide valuable insight into the complex relationship between security and rights, and the ways in which individuals are actively encouraged to participate in the securitisation of their identity and in the pervasive processes of surveillance and social sorting.

REFERENCES

Adey, P, 'Surveillance at the Airport: Surveilling Mobility/Mobilising Surveillance' (2004) 36(8) *Environment and Planning A* 1365–80.

Agamben, G, *Homo Sacer: Sovereignty and Bare Life*, D Heller-Roazen (trans) (Stanford, Stanford University Press, 1998).

Ajana, B, 'Augmented Borders: Big Data and the Ethics of Immigration Control' (2015) 13(1) *Journal of Information, Communication and Ethics in Society* 58–78.

Bauman, Z, *Globalization: The Human Consequences* (Cambridge, Polity Press, 1998).

——, 'From Pilgrim to Tourist – Or a Short History of Identity' in S Hall and P du Gay (eds), *Questions of Identity* (London, Sage, 1996).

——, *Postmodern Ethics* (London, Routledge, 1993).

Bigo, D, 'Security, Exception, Ban and Surveillance' in D Lyon (ed), *Theorizing Surveillance: The Panopticon and Beyond* (Cullompton, Willan Publishing, 2006).

Bigo, D and Guild, E (eds), *Controlling Frontiers: Free Movement into and within Europe* (Aldershot, Ashgate, 2005).

Boano, C and Martén, R, 'Agamben's Urbanism of Exception: Jerusalem's Border Mechanics and Biopolitical Strongholds' (2013) 34 *Cities* 6–17.

Bosworth, M, 'Border Control and the Limits of the Sovereign State' (2008) 17(2) *Social & Legal Studies* 199–215.

Elliott, C, 'TSA's New Pre-check Programs Raises Major Privacy Concerns', *Washington Post* (3 October 2013).

Franko Aas, K, '"Crimmigrant" Bodies and Bona Fide Travelers: Surveillance, Citizenship and Global Governance' (2011) 15(3) *Theoretical Criminology* 331–46.

Franko Aas, K and Gundhus, H, 'Policing Humanitarian Borderlands: Frontex, Human Rights and the Precariousness of Life' (2015) 55(1) *British Journal of Criminology* 1–18.

Goldenberg Doner, J, 'I Got Global Entry and It Was One of the Best Travel Decisions I Ever Made', *Business Insider* (13 May 2018).

Goold, B, 'Privacy, Identity and Security' in B Goold and L Lazarus (eds), *Security and Human Rights* (Oxford, Hart Publishing, 2007).

Greenfield, P, 'Border Queue Times at Heathrow Fail to Meet Targets', *Guardian* (13 August 2018).

Guild, E, *Security and Migration in the 21st Century* (Cambridge, Polity Press, 2009).

Hanafi, S, 'Explaining Spacio-cide in the Palestinian Territory: Colonization, Separation, and States of Exception' (2013) 61(2) *Current Sociology* 190–205.

Heyman, J, 'Trust, Privilege, and Discretion in the Governance of the US Borderlands with Mexico' (2009) 24(3) *Canadian Journal of Law and Society* 367–90.

Higgins, M, 'Which "Trusted Traveler" Program Is Right for You?' *New York Times* (20 February 2017).

Hyndman, J, *Managing Displacement: Refugees and the Politics of Humanitarianism* (Minneapolis, University of Minnesota Press, 2000).

Lyon, D, 'Filtering Flows, Friends and Foes: Global Surveillance' in MB Salter, P Adey, C Bennett, and G Fuller (eds), *Politics at the Airport* (Minneapolis, University of Minnesota Press, 2008).

——, 'National IDs in a Global World: Surveillance, Security, and Citizenship' (2010) 42(3) *Case Western Reserve Journal of International Law* 607–23.

——, 'Surveillance as Social Sorting: Computer Codes and Mobile Bodies' in D Lyon (ed), *Surveillance as Social Sorting: Privacy, Risk and Digital Discrimination* (London, Routledge, 2003).

Muller, BJ, '(Dis)qualified Bodies: Securitization, Citizenship and "Identity Management"' (2004) 8(3) *Citizenship Studies* 279–94.

——, 'Travellers, Borders, Dangers: Locating the Political at the Biometric Border' in MB Salter, P Adey, C Bennett, G and Fuller (eds), *Politics at the Airport* (Minneapolis, University of Minnesota Press, 2008).

——, 'Unsafe at Any Speed? Borders, Mobility and "Safe Citizenship"' (2010) 14(1) *Citizenship Studies* 75–88.

Office of the Auditor General of Canada, '2003 Report of the Auditor General of Canada to the House of Commons' (April 2003).

Ojakangas, M, 'Impossible Dialogue on Bio-Power: Agamben and Foucault' (2005) 2 *Foucault Studies* 5–28.

Pickering, S and Weber, L, *Borders, Mobility and Technologies of Control* (Dordrecht, Springer, 2006).

Popescu, G, 'Controlling Mobility' in G Popescu (ed), *Bordering and Ordering the Twenty-First Century: Understanding Borders* (Lanham, Rowman & Littlefield, 2011).

Privacy International, 'Secret Global Surveillance Networks: Intelligence Sharing between Governments and the Need for Safeguards' (April 2018), available at https://privacyinternational.org/report/1741/secret-global-surveillance-networks-intelligence-sharing-between-governments-and-need (accessed 18 March 2019).

Rose, N, *Powers of Freedom* (Cambridge, Cambridge University Press, 1999).

Salter, MB, 'Passports, Mobility, and Security: How Smart Can the Border Be?' (2004) 5 *International Studies Perspectives* 71–91.

——, 'At the Threshold of Security: A Theory of International Borders' in MB Salter and E Zureik (eds), *Global Policing and Surveillance: Borders, Security, Identity* (Cullompton, Willan Publishing, 2005).
——, 'When the Exception Becomes the Rule: Borders, Sovereignty, and Citizenship' (2008) 12(4) *Citizenship Studies* 365–80.
Sassen, S, 'Bordering Capabilities versus Borders: Implications for National Borders' (2009) 30 *Michigan Journal of International Law* 567–97.
Schinkel, W, 'From Zoepolitics to Biopolitics: Citizenship and the Construction of "Society"' (2010) 13(2) *European Journal of Social Theory* 155–72.
Sparke, M, 'A Neoliberal Nexus: Economy, Security and the Biopolitics of Citizenship on the Border' (2006) 25 *Political Geography* 151–80.
Taylor, S, 'Sovereign Power at the Border' (2005) 16(1) *Public Law Review* 55–77.
Vukov, T and Sheller, M, 'Border Work: Surveillant Assemblages, Virtual Fences, and Tactical Counter-media' (2013) 23(2) *Social Semiotics* 225–41.

Part II

Rights, Accountability, and the State

7

Secrecy as a Meta-paradigmatic Challenge

LIORA LAZARUS*

INSIDE AN IMPOSING office in Washington, DC, I conducted an interview with a senior legal official in the US government.[1] The official, previously an academic of high standing and well-informed, argued that most post-9/11 scholarship about security, human rights, and the rule of law was of little use to anyone outside of the academy. The official was adamant that the material scholars have been copiously producing was irrelevant to the issues at hand, that it was based on spurious assumptions about the basis of state security claims. When I retorted, 'That is not something we can change, as we don't have the relevant facts at hand,' the official replied, 'Well then, academics shouldn't say anything about things they know nothing about.'

Sparked by this methodological stand-off, this chapter reflects on the challenges that secrecy – legal secrets and secret law in particular – pose for scholarship and law.[2] It will argue that secrecy challenges academic scholarship in ways that mirror the conflict between secrecy and the rule of law. It seeks

* Very early versions of this chapter were presented to the 'Secrecy, Law, and Society' Workshop at the University of Sydney (6 and 7 February 2014) and to the 'Archive, History, and Law' Workshop at Harvard University (12 and 13 March 2015). I am grateful to participants for their comments during discussion. More recently, I must thank Benjamin Goold and Lisa Gourd for their critical interrogation of my arguments, as well as my BCL Criminal Justice, Security, and Human Rights class of 2019, who looked rather unimpressed with an earlier draft.

[1] This interview was conducted anonymously in Washington, DC on 13 October 2012.

[2] It is well known that legal processes protecting secret intelligence information ('secret facts') have proliferated since 9/11; it is also well known that secret legal processes can govern national security processes ('secret laws'). For a deeper exploration of these developments, see, *inter alia*, DS Rudesill, 'Coming to Terms with Secret Law' (2016) 7 *Harvard National Security Journal* 241–390; E Goitein, 'The New Era of Secret Law', research report for Brennan Center for Justice at New York University School of Law (2016); L Lazarus, C McCrudden, and N Bowles (eds), *Reasoning Rights* (Oxford, Hart Publishing, 2014) Part III; E Nanopoulos, 'European Human Rights Law and the Normalisation of the "Closed Material Procedure"' (2015) 78(6) *Modern Law Review* 913–44; M Scheinin, 'Protection of Human Rights and Fundamental Freedoms while Countering Terrorism: Report of the Special Rapporteur', UN Doc A/63/223 (6 August 2008); and D Barak-Erez

to open up debate about the way forward in this field and makes some general proposals about legal accountability for contemporary secret-keeping.

I. SECRECY AND SCHOLARSHIP

Academic scholarship is a site of profound and inherent contestation. Not only do academics disagree about the specific concepts they propose and the evidence they present; they also disagree at the foundational level about their capacity to make value-free 'knowledge claims'.[3] Notwithstanding these intractable disagreements, most academics at least agree that secrecy (state secrecy in particular) presents a significant impediment to scholarship. By blocking access to relevant and crucial information, state secrecy constrains the field of scholarly enquiry and undermines the capacity of academics to analyse and meaningfully engage with specific legal practices and the frameworks that govern important aspects of life and society.

However, as more than a practical hurdle for scholars, secrecy also constitutes a fundamental challenge for academic freedom more generally.[4] Writing at the early stages of the twentieth century, Max Weber argued that the notion of academic freedom (*Lernfreiheit*) rests on the assumption that academic enquiry is based on 'ethics and values that cannot be bought'.[5] Today, scholars argue that academic freedom is the 'cornerstone of academic identity',[6] 'highly prized by the vast majority of academics'.[7] In the United Kingdom, legislation protects the 'freedom within the law to question and test received wisdom, and to put forward new ideas and controversial or unpopular opinions',[8] while

and M Waxman (2009) 48(3) 'Secret Evidence and the Due Process of Terrorist Detentions' *Columbia Journal of Transnational Law* 4–60. For wider and fascinating accounts of the way in which secrecy has transformed US governance, see S Horton, *Lords of Secrecy: The National Security Elite and America's Stealth Warfare* (New York, Nation Books, 2015); and T Melley, *The Covert Sphere: Secrecy, Fiction, and the National Security State* (Ithaca, Cornell University Press, 2012).

[3] MP Lynch, 'Academic Freedom and the Politics of Truth' in J Lackey (ed), *Philosophy and Academic Freedom* (Oxford, Oxford University Press, 2018); T Dant, *Knowledge, Ideology & Discourse: A Sociological Perspective* (London, Routledge, 1991); M Whetherell, S Taylor, and S Yates, *Discourse Theory and Practice: A Reader* (London, Sage, 2001); P Ghosh, 'Beyond Methodology: Max Weber's Conception of *Wissenschaft*' (2014) 52(2) *Sociologia Internationalis* 157–218; B MacFarlane, *Intellectual Leadership in Higher Education* (London, Routledge, 2012) 83–84; A Bloom, *The Closing of the American Mind* (New York, Simon and Schuster, 1987); R Kimball, *Tenured Radicals* (New York, Harper & Row, 1990); and R Kimball, '"Tenured Radicals": A Postscript' (2019) 37(8) *New Criterion*.

[4] The modern articulated concept of academic freedom is traced by most scholars to the nineteenth-century Prussian education reforms of Wilhelm Von Humboldt, which enshrined the twin concepts of *Lehrfreiheit* (freedom to teach) and *Lernfreiheit* (freedom to learn). S Dea, 'A Brief History of Academic Freedom', *University Affairs* (9 October 2018).

[5] Ghosh (above n 3) 34. See also W Hennis, *Max Webers Wissenschaft vom Menschen* (Tübingen, Mohr Siebeck, 2003); and J Dewey, 'Academic Freedom' (1902) 23 *Educational Review* 1–14.

[6] MacFarlane (above n 3) 77.

[7] E Barendt, *Academic Freedom and the Law* (Oxford, Hart Publishing, 2010) 1.

[8] Education Reform Act 1988, s 202(2)(a); and Higher Education and Research Act 2017, s 36. See Barendt (ibid).

in the United States, the American Association of University Professors has expressed the value of academic freedom as 'the indispensable quality of institutions of higher education'.[9] At the international level too, UNESCO and the World University Service have endorsed academic freedom and the institutional autonomy of higher education institutions.[10]

Nevertheless, the meaning of academic freedom and its status relative to other values are highly contested. While there is significant concern about the policing of so-called 'radicalisation' on campus under government prevention programmes,[11] there is also considerable controversy about the use of academic freedom as a shield to protect the dissemination of objectionable arguments[12] and about the extent to which government should intervene in the 'no-platforming' of these voices.[13] It is also clear that academic freedom has been weaponised to silence marginalised voices seeking to transform or decolonise the canons of their disciplines.[14] This in turn can result in self-censorship

[9] American Association of University Professors (AAUP), '1940 Statement of Principles on Academic Freedom and Tenure', http://www.aaup.org/report/1940-statement-principles-academic-freedom-and-tenure (last accessed 18 February 2019).

[10] UNESCO, 'Recommendation Concerning the Status of Higher-Education Teaching Personnel' (11 November 1997), http://portal.unesco.org/en/ev.php-URL_ID=13144&URL_DO=DO_TOPIC&URL_SECTION=201.html; World University Service, 'Lima Declaration on Academic Freedom and Autonomy of Institutions of Higher Education' (6–10 September 1988).

[11] L Zedner, 'Counterterrorism on Campus' (2018) 68(4) *University of Toronto Law Journal* 545–87; Joint Parliamentary Committee on Human Rights, 'Freedom of Speech in Universities' (HC 589, HL 111) (27 March 2018); Equality and Human Rights Commission, 'Freedom of Expression: A Guide for Higher Education Providers and Student Unions in England and Wales' (2 February 2019), https://www.equalityhumanrights.com/en/publication-download/freedom-expression-guide-higher-education-providers-and-students-unions-england (last accessed 25 March 2019). See also the chapters in this volume by Aziz Z Huq and Andreas Armborst.

[12] Certainly, the enjoyment of academic freedom by legal academics such as John Yoo and John Finnis, whose arguments breach clear anti-torture norms of international law and LGBT rights, have come under serious attack. See R O'Neill, 'Academic Freedom: New Challenges in the United States' (2009) 57 *International Higher Education* 3–5; and A Benn and D Taylor, 'We Don't Think John Finnis Should Teach at Oxford University. Here's Why', *Guardian* (11 January 2019).

[13] In the United Kingdom, Government guidance on no-platforming has been issued by the Equality and Human Rights Commission (above n 11). See also K Rawlinson, 'Trigger Warmings OK, but No-Platforming May Be Illegal, Universities Warned', *Guardian* (2 February 2019).

[14] It is beyond the scope of this chapter to discuss the contemporary battle surrounding renditions of Empire, brought to the fore most recently by the Rhodes Must Fall movement in South Africa and the United Kingdom. See G Bhambra, D Gebrial, and K Nisancioulu (eds), *Decolonising the University* (London, Pluto Press, 2018); S Chigudu, 'Rhodes Must Fall and the Politics of Historical Consciousness', presentation at the Centre of African Studies, University of Edinburgh (2016), https://www.academia.edu/24732358/Rhodes_Must_Fall_and_the_Politics_of_Historical_Consciousness (last accessed 25 March 2019); T Garton Ash, 'Rhodes Hasn't Fallen but the Protesters Are Making Me Rethink Britain's Past', *Guardian* (4 March 2016); J McDougall et al, 'Ethics and Empire: An Open Letter from Oxford Scholars', *Conversation* (19 December 2017; P Gopal et al, 'A Collective Statement on Ethics and Empire', *Scholars of Empire* (21 December 2017), https://medium.com/oxfordempireletter/a-collective-statement-on-ethics-and-empire-19c2477871a0 (last accessed 18 February 2019). It is worth noting that the recent European Parliament Resolution of 26 March 2019 on fundamental rights of people of African descent in Europe (2018/2899 RSP)

of the very groups whose voices need most urgently to be heard.[15] In short, the meaning and status of academic freedom are rightly contested. As Edward Carvalho and David Downing have noted, while academic freedom is 'so foundational to higher education … that even today, no one will argue against it …, everyone will argue about it.'[16]

While academic freedom and university autonomy are contested and contestable, these values continue to be viewed as hallmarks of democratic and liberal societies.[17] Conversely, the decline of academic freedom is commonly associated with the rise of illiberalism and populism. The political threats to academic freedom range in intensity. In the runup to the UK Brexit referendum, Michael Gove's famous assertion that 'Britain has had enough of experts' was a sign of the longstanding antipathy between populist rhetoric and specialised knowledge.[18] In Hungary, the conservative Christian regime of Viktor Orban launched a sustained attack on the freedom of the Central European University, leading to the CEU's recent move to Vienna.[19] In Turkey, thousands of academics have been dismissed, arrested, and put on trial, resulting in what Human Rights Watch has referred to as a 'hollowing out' of academic freedom there.[20] But Hungary and Turkey are only the latest examples of historical recurrences that include the obliteration of university autonomy in Nazi Germany and the suspension of academic freedom in the McCarthy-era United States.[21] Such is the concern regarding occurrences like these that in November 2018, the European Parliament adopted a formal recommendation in defence of academic freedom.[22] This instrument acknowledges that there is a 'general need … to raise awareness of the importance of

'encourages Member States to make the history of people of African descent part of their curricula and to present a comprehensive perspective on colonialism and slavery which recognises their historical and contemporary adverse effects on people of African descent, and to ensure that teachers are adequately trained for this task and properly equipped to address diversity in the classroom' (s 20).

[15] See more generally S Ahmed, *On Being Included: Racism and Diversity in Institutional Life* (Durham, Duke University Press, 2012).

[16] EJ Carvalho and DB Downing, *Academic Freedom in the Post-9/11 Era* (New York, Palgrave MacMillan, 2010) 1. For recent discussion on the broad range of controversies affecting academic freedom, see J Lackey (ed), *Academic Freedom* (Oxford, Oxford University Press, 2018).

[17] European Parliament Committee on Foreign Affairs, 'Report on European Parliament Recommendation on Defence of *Academic Freedom* in the EU's External Action', A8-0403/2018 (27 November 2018), http://www.europarl.europa.eu/doceo/document/A-8-2018-0403_EN.pdf; M Ignatieff, 'Academic Freedom and the Future of Europe', Centre for Global Higher Education Working Paper No 40 (July 2018), https://www.researchcghe.org/perch/resources/publications/wp40.pdf, 6.

[18] H Mance, 'Britain Has Had Enough of Experts, Says Gove', *Financial Times* (3 June 2016).

[19] Ignatieff (above n 17).

[20] Human Rights Watch, 'Turkey Government Targeting Academics: Dismissals, Prosecutions Create Campus Climate of Fear', *Human Rights Watch* (14 May 2018); Eurasia Review, 'Turkey: Academic Freedom Under Threat', *Eurasia Review* (7 August 2018), https://www.eurasiareview.com/07082018-turkey-academic-freedom-under-threat/ (last accessed 26 March 2019).

[21] Dea (above n 4).

[22] European Parliament Recommendation (above n 17). See point L of the Preamble concerning Hungary directly: 'Foreign education institutions within the European Union are facing attacks from national governments and encountering violations of their academic freedom.'

academic freedom as a tool to promote democracy, respect for the rule of law and accountability'.[23]

Academic freedom might thus be conceptualised as a realm of political accountability, as an independent space from which to speak truth to power. Instead of being cast as a 'privilege of professors', academic freedom might be recognised as the sixth estate within a constitutional order, as the critical reflective domain in which social knowledge is rigorously scrutinised and contested. As the EU Parliament Recommendation puts it,

> Academic freedom – including its constituent freedoms of thought, opinion, expression, association, travel, and instruction – contributes to creating the space in which any open and stable pluralistic society is free to think, question, share ideas and produce, consume and disseminate knowledge.[24]

Simply put, academics ought at the very least to be protected from pressure to make claims in the pursuit of a specific government, corporate, or political agenda. We ought to receive some protection as the guardians of independent knowledge, the seekers and speakers of what Weber prized as 'inconvenient facts'.[25] Our independence and activity sit at the core of the democratic exchange of truth and ideas. As Michael Ignatieff, President and Rector of the Central European University, has argued, 'Academic freedom is one element of a counter-majoritarian fabric that is integral to the health of a democratic society.'[26]

From this perspective, it is easy to see how state secrecy fundamentally undermines academic freedom. Scholars depend on information. The state's control over material that we need in order to draw well-reasoned conclusions constitutes a silent but powerful form of intellectual influence. I hardly need to point to the Foucauldian nexus of knowledge and power to make the case that the state's monopoly on knowledge is maintained by the management of the information it keeps to itself and, through this, by the erosion of critical academic scrutiny.

For any scholar, this lack of access to relevant data is problematic. However, for legal academics (and by this I mean anyone who has an academic interest in the law), the fundamental challenge presented by state secrecy has particularly direct and wide-reaching consequences. As part of the wider legal system, or to use Dworkinian language, as part of the interpretive community that criticises and examines law from the inside,[27] legal scholars are a key component of the law writ large. While we cannot determine the law authoritatively in the sense of law-making, we are part of a dialogic audience to which the law speaks. In this

[23] Ibid, Preamble, point P.
[24] Ibid, Preamble, Point E.
[25] M Weber, 'Science as Vocation' in HH Gerth and CW Mills (eds), *From Max Weber: Essays in Sociology* (Oxford, Oxford University Press, 1946).
[26] Ignatieff (above n 17) 6.
[27] I am borrowing liberally here from the general ideas of Ronald Dworkin. See R Dworkin, *Law's Empire* (Cambridge, MA, Harvard University Press, 1988).

broader exchange, legal academics and commentators bring the essential quality of expertise and knowledge.

The part played by legal academics within a legal system is nevertheless culturally manifested, as the extent of academic influence will depend on where we sit as legal authority within a particular jurisdiction's rule of recognition.[28] In a civil law system, a legal academic is explicitly a part of the legal interpretive community and forms part of the codification system as a whole.[29] But in the Anglo-American model, legal scholars are less formally acknowledged within the material of the law. Notwithstanding this difference, legal academics are a service to law; our normative evaluations and our legal analyses form part of a process that shapes and sustains the rule of law.

If, as argued above, academics more generally have a counter-majoritarian role in holding knowledge accountable, then legal academics have a more specific role of critiquing, shaping, interpreting, guarding, and refining the rule of law, as well as the paradigm of law itself. As Jeremy Waldron has argued, law is an 'intellectual formation', an 'articulate, self-conscious intellectual discipline'.[30] Historically, the norms common to all – the norms of *ius gentium* (the 'law of nations') – have transcended courts of particular jurisdictions and have been identified by the 'learned doctors of jurisprudence'.[31] Legal academia is thus an interpretive and normative legacy distinct from other academic disciplines in its situated place within the formation of law and legal principles.

If this is right, then legal academics have a double obligation: to scholarship and to the rule of law. If we are part of law too, our job is to evaluate all relevant normative considerations when evaluating the normative standing of law and the extent to which it guides social and state behaviour. The quality of the arguments produced, their factual basis, and their intellectual rigour are essential parts of legal accountability. Thus, both our role as scholars and our role within the legal community require the same conditions in order to be adequately fulfilled. Legal academics need the relevant evidence that courts (acting properly) also require. We need all the facts relevant to the normative considerations at play within the legal process. Legal academics are challenged in both positions – as legal actors and as legal scholars – by the existence of secret information, since this information forms the tacit background to the legal processes we study. Without material that is held secret, how can we fulfil our function or proceed at all?

[28] HLA Hart, *The Concept of Law*, 3rd edn (Oxford, Oxford University Press, 2012) 100.

[29] See R van Caenegem, *Judges, Legislators and Professors: Chapters in European Legal History* (Cambridge, Cambridge University Press, 1987).

[30] J Waldron, *'Partly Laws Common to All Mankind': Foreign Law in American Courts* (New Haven, Yale University Press, 2012) 205–6.

[31] Ibid, 206.

II. THE ANATOMY OF LEGAL SECRETS

Drawing on Kim Lane Scheppele and others,[32] David Pozen has distinguished between deep and shallow secrets.[33] For Pozen, a state secret is deep if:

> … a small group of similarly situated officials conceals its existence from the public and from other officials, such that the outsiders' ignorance precludes them from learning about, checking, or influencing the keepers' use of the information.[34]

Such a deep state secret is distinguished from a 'shallow secret', when 'ordinary citizens understand they are being denied relevant information and have some ability to estimate its content'.[35]

The distinction for Pozen is between what we *know* we don't know, and what we *don't know* we don't know – a simplification of Donald Rumsfeld's argument, upon which Pozen draws. Rumsfeld's aphorism has more methodological importance than we might realise. Academics may be able to draw limited conclusions about partial information but not about information that is invisible to them. As Pozen has explained further about deep secrets:

> Because no one outside of a small, cohesive circle is aware of their existence, deep secrets relieve their keepers of the burden of reason giving. There can be no public defense of deep secrets, no case made to the parties who may be affected, because if any such case could be made, then the secret should not be deep in the first place. Paradoxically, the best justification for keeping deep secrets is that they cannot be justified to others.[36]

So deep secrets are problematic not only because it is impossible to know of their existence but also because, as outsiders, observers cannot be privy to the logic or rationales that might play a role in determining a normative appreciation of them. Deep secrets create a divide and a power imbalance between those who know and those who don't know they don't know, not only in terms of factual knowledge but also in our understanding of the reasoning around those facts.

On the other hand, Pozen has argued:

> Shallow secrets at least put members of the public on notice of the gaps that exist in their knowledge. They can learn the general contours of the material that is being withheld and can frame the decision problems that face them. The world is not entirely knowable, but it is not entirely mysterious either.[37]

Shallow secrets at least leave the public – and scholars – with the potential for some partial analysis. By being explicit about the existence of a secret, shallow secrecy allows some recourse to scrutiny, albeit incomplete.

[32] See KL Scheppele, *Legal Secrets: Equality and Efficiency in the Common Law* (Chicago, University of Chicago Press, 1988); and MJ Rozell, *Executive Privilege: Presidential Power, Secrecy and Accountability*, 3rd edn (Lawrence, University Press of Kansas, 2010).

[33] D Pozen, 'Deep Secrecy' (2011) 62(2) *Stanford Law Review* 257–339.

[34] Ibid, 274.

[35] Ibid.

[36] Ibid, 289.

[37] Ibid.

To a large degree, the legal material that many academics are concerned with (closed material proceedings, for example) involve shallow secrets:

> In many information-access disputes, the government has restricted public access to something: a trial, a hearing, a prison, a foreign visa. These are important domains of secrecy, but they are not likely to involve very deep secrecy.[38]

Nevertheless, deep secrets are more likely to become the object of scholarly study if they are closely connected to the redacted material contained in legal proceedings: 'Deep secrecy might still be lurking, as information might emerge from the courtroom deposition, the administrative hearing, the prison interview, or the foreign country that was not anticipated.'[39] Moreover, key elements of the evaluative background for the rationale of shallow secrecy may be deeply secret. The line between what is lawful and unlawful in the 'war on terror' is often blurred, and scholars of the subject need to be just as concerned with unlawful processes that may operate out of sight as we are with lawful processes. Extraordinary rendition is one example, targeted killing another (although both have arguably moved along the spectrum towards shallower secrets), and certainly meta-data surveillance and the system of 'secret law' that applied to it is another.[40] At any time, when examining a counterterrorist policy, there are deep secrets lurking in the background. Deep secrecy 'is generally more likely to occur in backrooms and back channels, in government discussions and decisions that take place outside of any formal, regularized, quasi-public structure'.[41]

A. The Moral Ambiguity of Secrecy

Just as secrets may vary in depth, their moral status may be complex and ambiguous. The holding of secrets is not always and automatically wholly illegitimate. For example, most agree that protecting the anonymity of an endangered witness during a legal process is justified.[42] In his seminal work on secrecy, Georg Simmel emphasised this key distinction between the existence of a secret and its moral status:

> We must not allow ourselves to be deceived by the manifold ethical negativeness of secrecy. Secrecy is a universal sociological form, which, as such, has, nothing to do with the moral valuations of its contents.[43]

[38] Ibid, 305.

[39] Ibid, 306.

[40] For more on the topic of targeted killing, see the chapter in this volume by Shiri Krebs; on surveillance and data, see the chapter in this volume by Arianna Vedaschi; on revelations about US and other counterterrorist policies, see the chapter in this volume by Kent Roach. On secret law, see Goitein (above n 2); and Rudesill (above n 2).

[41] Pozen (above n 33) 305.

[42] For further discussion of witness and other types of anonymity during trial, see the chapter in this volume by Juan-Pablo Pérez-León-Acevedo.

[43] G Simmel, 'The Sociology of Secrecy and of Secret Societies' (1906) 4 *American Journal of Sociology* 441–98. See also C Birchall, 'Six Answers to the Question "What is Secrecy Studies" (2016) 1(1) *Secrecy and* Society 2–13.

The difficulty for scholars engaging with most national security secrets is that we do not know the reasons for keeping shallow secrets or the surrounding facts behind these reasons; nor do we know about the existence of deep secrets. Without that knowledge and knowledge of the secret itself, we cannot evaluate the legitimacy or illegitimacy of secret-keeping. Equally, we may be overly attracted towards transparency despite lack of knowledge for the secret-keeping in the first place. David Cole has argued that transparency may be overrated, while secrecy may be underrated:

> Some advocates of transparency seem to treat any exposure of secrets as an unmitigated good; this appears to be the philosophy behind Assange's WikiLeaks. But that position is morally untenable; there are undoubtedly good reasons for secrecy in many aspects of government, especially foreign relations, and particularly during wartime. And there are many legitimate bases for condemning disclosures, particularly when they reveal the identities of sources and methods of foreign intelligence.
>
> Security hawks consider any unauthorized disclosure of classified information unacceptable, stressing that cleared employees take an oath not to disclose such information, and that no government can operate without some secret deliberations and covert actions. But this, too, is an untenably extreme position. History demonstrates that secrecy is used not only for legitimate purposes of national security but too often to shield illegal or embarrassing activity from public scrutiny. Even the most ardent security proponent must concede that the benefits from revealing illegal abuses of authority will sometimes outweigh the costs of disclosing those secrets.[44]

Consequently, scholars need to keep the moral ambiguity of secrecy in the balance when we approach secrecy and law. There is a tendency to deny that there may be good reasons for secrets and a strong temptation to leap to critical suspicion. But it is possible that with greater information, the basis of such suspicion could be viewed as an assumption. It may in such circumstances be necessary to limit our conclusions when we simply do not know.

B. Shallow Secrecy, Partial Information, and Academic Inquiry

Partial information is information we know that we don't know – material we can only glean from the existence of a shallow secret. An example of partial information is the kind of material available during the open part of a closed material procedure. This is information shown in a legal document or government file that is redacted for legal or policy reasons. It might also consist of leaked information that indicates the existence of a broader set of shallow secrets. Whatever the content, we know that data is missing. We are without the information required to draw firm scholarly conclusions.

[44] D Cole, 'The Three Leakers and What to Do about Them', *New York Review of Books* (6 February 2014).

What are academics to do with partial information? How are we to avoid it skewing our perspective? How should we weigh partial information? Empirical social scientists have mechanisms for dealing with partial information and controlling for variables that cannot be empirically substantiated.[45] But for interpretive legal scholars and normative critics, it is less clear how to utilise such partial information. Can we draw normative conclusions without all relevant normative material? What can we define as normatively relevant material? Are we entitled to make suppositions in place of facts when weighing up the normative considerations in play?

In actuality, partial information provides clues to deeper inquiry, and partial information is rarely static, with secrets becoming increasingly shallow as inquiry progresses or leaks gaining a critical mass in response to a particular policy flashpoint. In such cases, a scholar's best approach is to wait until the secrets unfold to a sufficient tipping point at which commentary is possible. But in this process, scholars must also be conscious of their access to partial information and of their approach to its sources. Was the information leaked by a rebellious, heroic individual or a determined journalist? Or is it part of a state-sanctioned leaking programme aimed at tacit acknowledgment of policies such as targeted killing? There may be ways in which scholars respond to different kinds of partial information that colour their approach to this material. Are we drawn towards believing one source over another? Are we inclined towards suspicion of state sources? Does our view of a policy change in light of how it was exposed? How neutral are we in the assessment of these sources? What methodology do we choose to approach this material? These are all questions which must be considered, for example, when unravelling the national security context of a rights-limiting policy.

C. Deep Secrecy as a Deep Scholarly Challenge

Deep secrets present different challenges to shallow secrets, as academics are simply without knowledge of their existence.[46] Because of this, deep secrets

[45] HJ Adèr, 'Missing Data' in HJ Adèr and GJ Mellenbergh (eds), *Advising on Research Methods: A Consultant's Companion* (Huizen, Johannes van Kessel Publishing, 2008) 305–32; and SF Messner, 'Exploring the Consequences of Erratic Data Reporting for Cross-National Research on Homicide' (1992) 8(2) *Journal of Quantitative Criminology* 155–73.

[46] Examples of deep secrets that have come to light are the surveillance order procedures under the US Foreign Intelligence Surveillance Courts (see Goitein (above n 2) and Rudesill (above n 2) for overviews); and the programme of extraordinary rendition operated by the CIA and facilitated by US allies in the early years post 9/11. The latter has been exposed in a range of reports and cases. See, *inter alia*, Commission of Inquiry into the Actions of Canadian Officials in Relation to Maher Arar ('Arar Commission'), 'Report of the Events Relating to Maher Arar' (2006), available at http://publications.gc.ca/site/eng/9.688875/publication.html (last accessed 26 March 2019); the chapter in this volume by Kent Roach; D Marty (Special Rapporteur), 'Secret Detentions and Illegal Transfers of Detainees Involving Council of Europe Member States: Second Report', Council of Europe Parlia-

appear at first glance not to raise the sort of methodological dilemmas brought on by shallow secrets as discussed above. After all, we may well ask: what is lost by not knowing what we don't know?

These are precisely the epistemological questions around which serious legal academic inquiry pivots. How should academics manage deep secrets? Do we in fact need to know what we don't know before we can complete any normative critique or empirical analysis? Do we need to acknowledge the constraints on our ability to draw conclusions, as background deep secrets may play a role in the normative landscape of those who seek to protect shallow secrets? Scholars must face the methodological conflict between our own scholarly ideals on the one hand and deep secrets on the other, as the very essence of a deep secret is that it avoids scrutiny and evaluation: 'Deep secrets block out all sunlight from the decisional process beyond the small circle of secret-keepers. No public reasons need be given, no adversarial testing need occur.'[47]

Pozen's work on deep secrecy is primarily aimed at the policy, normative, and constitutional implications of its existence. He has been less focused on the implications that deep secrecy has for scholarship. Nevertheless, his work emphasises the serious challenge raised by the impossibility of knowing something:

> When members of the public and their representatives are unaware that information is being concealed from them, their ability to provide input, oversight, and criticism relating to that information is not simply inhibited but nullified.[48]

He has recognised in a footnote how this nullification process challenges scholarly assessment:

> It would be quite a challenge to test empirically the relationship between the depth of state secrets and the quality of policy outcomes. The researcher would have to devise not only quantitative measures of depth and quality but also a reliable way to monitor state secrets, to assess their impact, and to predict how outcomes would have differed had alternative types or amounts of secrecy been used. The study of particular deep secrets would perforce be conducted retrospectively, after the relevant

mentary Assembly report (7 June 2007), http://assembly.coe.int/CommitteeDocs/2007/EMarty_20070608_NoEmbargo.pdf; B Emmerson, 'Framework Principles for Securing the Accountability of Public Officials for Gross or Systematic Human Rights Violations Committed in the Context of State Counter-Terrorism Initiatives', UN Doc A/67/396 (1 March 2013); Intelligence and Security Committee of Parliament (UK), 'Detainee Mistreatment and Rendition: 2001–2010' (28 June 2018, HC 1113); *Mohamed v Jeppesen Dataplan* [2010] 614 F 3d 1070; *Khaled El-Masri v United States*, Inter-Am CHR (Admissibility) Case 419.08, Report No 21/16 (15 April 2016); *El-Masri v Tenet*, 437 F Supp 2d 530, 539; *El-Masri v United States*, 479 F.3d 296, 300 (4th Cir 2007) cert denied, 552 US 947 (2007); *El-Masri v the Former Yugoslav Republic of Macedonia* (2013) 57 EHRR 25; *Al Nashiri and Husayn v Poland* (2015) 60 EHRR 16; *Nasr and Ghali v Italy* (2016) ECHR 210; *Abu Zubaydah v Lithuania* (2018) (App No 46454/11) (31 May 2018); and *Belhaj v Straw and Rahmatullah v Ministry of Defence* [2017] UKSC 3.

[47] Pozen (above n 33) 280.

[48] Ibid, 279.

> information has emerged, and even then, one could never be sure how those secrets compare to others that may remain entirely unknown.[49]

This particular focus of Pozen's – the question of whether deep secrecy lends itself to better policymaking – is of course one way in which we might wish to engage with a deep secret, and we will return to others below. But Pozen's brief reflection here on scholarly methodology highlights the difficulty of critique or analysis of deep secrets in real time.

There is a particular and subtle sense in which deep secrets may conceptually be more urgently challenging to legal scholarship in ways that other fields do not encounter. It is the relationship between deep secrecy and the likelihood that such actions are taken outside, or at the edges, of law. As Pozen has argued, 'Illegal programs will tend to be deeper secrets than legal ones, all else equal, given the assumption that laws are followed.'[50] If the reason for maintaining deep secrecy of a particular set of policy actions and decisions is because that set is without legal authority, then the issue becomes more pressing for legal scholars, who, as argued earlier, constitute a crucial dialogic audience within law itself.[51] Officially sanctioned choices to pursue a policy without legal authority in an otherwise legal state may have implications for our understanding of the nature and boundaries of legality and for our evaluation of the effectiveness of what we know to be legal. Our lack of knowledge of such covert unlawful activity in real time undermines our insight into the law as a whole, making our understanding necessarily partial; we cannot subject the law to comprehensive analysis.

When deep secrets relating to unlawful behaviour become shallow or even transparent, they often lead to re-evaluation of the law or even changes to it. This can happen in a range of complex ways. Frequently, legal officials seek to rationalise their actions *ex post facto*, proposing arguments of legality to cover their previously secret unlawful activity. This is evident in the fallout from the leaks regarding the US National Security Agency surveillance programme.[52] In such a case, unlawful activity held as a deep secret can over time become the source of a challenge to the legal *status quo* and start to test the boundaries of the legal.

Legal scholars can also view the existence of a deep secret masking an unlawful policy as a signal that there is something wrong with existing legal arrangements. They are often drawn to reconsider the boundaries of legality in order to pre-empt official recourse to deep secrecy or a sidestepping of law. Alan Dershowitz's proposal for torture warrants was in many ways an attempt to bring otherwise unlawful behaviour into the light.[53] His was clearly a wrong

[49] Ibid, fn 62.

[50] Ibid, 274.

[51] See above section I.

[52] Such arguments were indeed successful in *ACLU v Clapper*, 959 F Supp 2d 724 (SDNY 2013).

[53] AM Dershowitz, *Why Terrorism Works: Understanding the Threat, Responding to the Challenge* (New Haven, Yale University Press, 2002); AM Dershowitz, *Shouting Fire: Civil Liberties in a*

turn and has been roundly rejected,[54] but it highlights one conceptual challenge that deep secrecy may raise for legal scholars in particular: once deep secrets touching on the boundaries of legality come to light, how are legal scholars to respond? Is the pre-emptive response always off the table? Should legal scholars think more closely about the conditions of *ex post facto* accountability? Should we be thinking more about how law and regulatory structures prompt deep secrets?

D. Secrecy as a Meta-paradigmatic Challenge

Secrecy in law challenges the basic premises of the rule of law, the commitment to open justice, to fair proceedings, to transparency and foreseeability.[55] Secrecy as a whole is hard to reconcile *prima facie* with the rule of law. But secrecy does more than that. It not only tests the premises of legal proceedings or the premises of their benchmark – the rule of law – against which the normative integrity of these proceedings is normally evaluated. It also undermines the capacity of legal scholars to evaluate these proceedings, thus preventing them from fulfilling one of their core functions as dialogic participants in the creation of law. In this way, state secrecy serves to impoverish the legal project.

In the context of security and rights, secrecy (deep and shallow) hampers the ability of legal academics to evaluate the normative reasoning behind supposed trade-offs between security and the rule of law, between security and human rights. If we don't know any or all of the facts at the time that secrecy is invoked (even though we may well know them later), then we can only surmise what these facts are – and this isn't a sufficient basis upon which to draw firm normative conclusions. Legal scholars are thus left falling back on a general rule-of-law critique: we can make statements about the rule of law but are unable to reflect on the validity of the specific security claims being made. Even when faced with shallow secrets, we are in no stronger position in a

Turbulent Age (Boston, Little, Brown and Company, 2002); AM Dershowitz, 'Want to Torture? Get a Warrant', *San Francisco Chronicle* (22 January 2002); AM Dershowitz, 'Legal Torture', interview, *60 Minutes* (17 January 2002).

[54] See, *inter alia*, J Waldron, 'Torture and Positive Law: Jurisprudence for the White House' (2005) 105(6) *Columbia Law Review* 1681–750; RA Posner, 'Torture, Terrorism, and Interrogation' in S Levinson, *Torture: A Collection* (Oxford, Oxford University Press, 2004) 291; E Scarry, 'Five Errors in the Reasoning of Alan Dershowitz' in S Levinson (ed), *Torture: A Collection* (Oxford, Oxford University Press, 2004) 281; RS Brown, 'Torture, Terrorism, and the Ticking Bomb: A Principled Response' (2007) 4 *Journal of International Law and Policy* 1–33; RD Covey, 'Interrogation Warrants' (2005) 26(5) *Cardozo Law Review* 1867–946; J Kleinig, 'Ticking Bombs and Torture Warrants (2005) 10(2) *Deakin Law Review* 614–27.

[55] For an articulate judicial outline of the incompatibility of closed material procedures and *in camera* proceedings with the rule of law, see *Guardian News & Media Ltd v Incedal* [2016] HLRL 9 (also discussed further below). On the wrong of secret law, see also Goitein (above n 2) 16–20; and Rudesill (above n 2) 313–25.

secret proceeding than is the defendant. We can respond only to a set of partial statements, unable to ascertain the full foundation of the claims in question, unable to know whether the secret information itself would affect or undermine security operations or intelligence, or how the information fits into a web of otherwise secret information.

If the rule-of-law critique of secrecy is persuasive, then it follows that the position of scholars is also weakened. In normal circumstances, failing to expose all relevant information to all relevant parties and to subject this information to the proper process of legal contestation is considered not to satisfy the conditions of the rule of law. The same may be said for the standards of rigorous academic scholarship. How, then, are scholars able to move beyond mere assertions that secrecy conflicts with the rule of law or human rights? How do we confidently move to a deeper assessment of the balance between counterposing security claims and rule-of-law considerations? We are left locked in the claim that there is a challenge to the rule of law or to human rights, without the relevant information against which to test the balance. We do not have the information we need to draw comprehensive independent conclusions about how the balance has been struck and whether it was necessary and legitimate. The force of academic critique, from a rule-of-law perspective, must apply equally to our own capacity to draw specific conclusions, and this in turn undermines our capacity to draw larger conclusions.

This is a challenge that legal scholars must confront. While history certainly gives academics ample reasons to approach secrecy claims with critical suspicion,[56] our capacity to deliver coherent real-time analysis is constrained. The danger also exists that a lopsided assessment of secret material may thus be made at the expense of material hiding in plain sight. As Baroness Manningham-Buller, former Director General of MI5, has commented, 'sometimes secrets take on more power … than open facts'.[57]

III. CONTEMPORARY SECRECY AND RETROSPECTIVE ACCOUNTABILITY

> Deep secrets [cause] corruption and abuse, ideological amplification, bias, and groupthink will be more likely to flourish.… More speculatively, deep secrets may also exacerbate the social trust, perverse consequences, and budgetary arguments

[56] See the references listed above at nn 2 and 46, as well as D Gibbs, 'Sigmund Freud as a Theorist of Government Secrecy' in S Maret (ed), *Government Secrecy* (Bingley, Emerald Group Publishing, 2011); S Bok, *Secrets: On the Ethics of Concealment and Revelation* (Oxford, Oxford University Press, 1984); and C Elkins, *Imperial Reckoning: The Untold Story of Britain's Gulag in Kenya* (New York, Henry Holt, 2005).

[57] E Manningham-Buller, 'From Bugs to Bugs', Lecture, Oxford Martin School (15 February 2016); see also KS Olmstead, 'Government Secrecy and Conspiracy Theories' in S Maret (ed), *Government Secrecy* (Bingley, Emerald Group Publishing, 2011) 91.

> against government secrecy.... Deep secrets are the stuff of conspiracy theories. A government that uses them cannot help but engender skepticism.[58]

Let us return to the warning of the US official I interviewed: that academics shouldn't say anything about things they know nothing about. Evidently this warning poses a dilemma. Some may argue that the challenge to the rule of law and human rights is so great that it is necessary to assume that all information held secret is done so illegitimately. For them, the onus of justification must rest on the state, and if secret information remains unexposed, then this onus remains unfulfilled. Others argue that some matters are more complex, and if there is secret or missing material, then scholarly rigour requires us to heed the official's warning and remain silent because we will not have the information necessary in that case to evaluate the balance between security, human rights, and the rule of law. Between these opposing positions, however, a potential resolution may be found in the timing of scholarly analysis. A framework for considering the temporality of scrutiny might make it possible for scholars and legal commentators to move beyond abstract scepticism and denunciation and into true academic critique that is based on genuine expertise.

While always demanding adequate scrutiny of the justifications for secrecy claims in real time and insisting that secret mechanisms violate the rule of law and human rights, academics and other critics may nonetheless need to delay their full conclusions for a later date. To achieve this, we will need to fight consistently for the prospect of future scrutiny of contemporary secrecy claims. We need to think of the prospect of retrospective accountability (in law) and evaluation (in scholarship) once we can gain access to full information. This notion of 'retrospective accountability and evaluation' ought to feature more in the law itself. The more secrecy claims arise and the stronger the claim that secrecy is a necessary handmaiden to security in contemporary contexts, the more we will need to demand structures of retrospective accountability within law. The state should know that the secrets it holds now will be fully scrutinised later, once the justification for such secrecy has diminished or elapsed. So too within legal scholarship: while some limitations to contemporaneous analysis might be accepted, the conditions in which rigorous scholarly conclusions can be made about a particular policy or legal outcome may be scheduled to materialise later.[59]

[58] Pozen (above n 33) 280. On the tendency of government secrecy to encourage conspiracy theory, see Olmsted (ibid).

[59] In light of this self-limitation, it is striking that Pozen has felt confident to draw conclusions about the consequentialist arguments for and against state secrecy while in his argument using historical cases both for and against it. In so many respects, Pozen's work is insightful and exemplary, but his keenness to draw generalised conclusions about the utilitarian value of deep secrecy may be one step too far. If Pozen is right about all the other aspects of what he describes, then I would have expected a more tentative conclusion on this question. If deep secrecy nullifies all evaluation, then how is it possible to conclude confidently that 'although it would be wrong to maintain that deep state secrecy categorically produces inferior outcomes, the rule-utilitarian case in its favor

A. Case Law

Case law relating to historical truth provides us with lessons about how to ensure current decisions are subject to future scrutiny. *Mutua v The Foreign and Commonwealth Office* was heard in 2011,[60] after the exposure of colonial torture of Mau Mau fighters in Kenya between 1954 and 1959 in two historical studies based on painstaking archival research.[61] The detailed evidence contained in these studies became the central part of an action in tort by five surviving claimants against the Foreign and Commonwealth Office of the UK Government for remedies related to their 'physical mistreatment of the most serious kind, including torture, rape, castration, and severe beating'.[62] The preliminary hearings in the case centred on whether it was possible to hold a 'fair trial' so long after these events had taken place. The case was settled after two preliminary judgments from Justice Richard McCombe forced the disclosure of further archival evidence and revealed that document destruction was ordered by colonial authorities during the period in question. Justice McCombe concluded that there was ample historical evidence to launch a fair trial, despite the absence of live witnesses. An otherwise sober and conservative judge, he was evidently concerned with the ways in which the UK government had sought to bury the relevant material:

> I consider that there is good evidence of attempts by both governments, throughout the emergency, to limit enquiries and investigations into abuses committed in the camps. This I think is conduct that has some relevance to the exercise of my discretion under the section in favour of the claimants, although obviously it can only be a 'make weight' over and above my view that I have reached that a fair trial of these issues on cogent evidence is still possible. It also detracts to some little degree from the intrinsic merit of the defendant's submission that those at senior levels who could give an account on behalf of the defendant are no longer alive to explain what happened and what is recorded in the documents.[63]

Once the legal action was allowed to move forward and had forced disclosure of further archival materials at Hanslope Park, the Government knew it had no option but to settle the claim in order to avoid more damaging revelations if the case were to be heard in full. *Mutua* is thus a lesson in the power of deep scholarly archival research to trigger retrospective accountability.

In contrast, just a few years later in *Keyu v Secretary of State*, the attempt to force an inquiry into establishing the historical truth of the Batang Kali massacre

appears as precarious and narrow as the case against appears clear and robust'? See Pozen (above n 33) 285.

[60] *Mutua and Others v The Foreign and Commonwealth Office* [2011] EWHC 1913 (QB), [2012] EWHC 2678 (QB).

[61] Elkins (above n 56); and D Anderson, *Histories of the Hanged: Britain's Dirty War in Kenya and the End of Empire* (London, Weidenfeld and Nicolson, 2005).

[62] *Mutua* (above n 60) para 1.

[63] Ibid, para 40.

failed,[64] despite new historical research contesting the official narrative.[65] While acknowledging the 'desire to discover "historical truth"', the majority of the UK Supreme Court were swayed by the 'justifiable concern that the truth may not be ascertainable'.[66] This view was taken despite the general concession that the official account of the killings 'may well not be correct' and constituted a 'cover up',[67] that the 'killings may well have been unlawful',[68] and that the case involved 'investigating whether a serious wrong, indeed a war crime, may have been committed'.[69]

In her dissent, Lady Hale took issue with the way in which the majority had 'set the bar so high as to establishing the truth' by focusing on the criminal responsibility of the actors, such that it obscured the wider 'beneficial purposes' served by the 'value of recognising the truth'. Instead of seeking to establish facts that could lead to criminal liability,

> [The majority] did not seriously consider the 'bigger picture': the public interest in properly inquiring into an event of this magnitude; the private interests of the relatives and survivors in knowing the truth and seeing the reputations of their deceased relatives vindicated; the importance of setting the record straight – as counsel put it, balancing *the prospect of the truth* against *the value of the truth*.[70]

Mutua and *Keyu* dealt with historical evidence, but in both, the arguments and outcomes were shaped by questions of evidential reliability for the purposes of meeting civil or criminal standards of proof. In *Mutua*, that standard was met, but in *Keyu*, it was not. Nevertheless, Lady Hale's dissent in *Keyu* points to wider interests, both public and private, served by an inquiry into the past. This wider public interest is expressed increasingly in the concept of the right to truth, which, unlike the narrow focus on establishing individual culpability or compensation for secret wrong-doing, provides a potential platform for a general principle of retrospective accountability and protects the possibility of future academic scrutiny.

B. The Right to Truth and the Duty of Archival Integrity

The right to truth emerged in the late 1940s in international humanitarian law, was subsequently cast by the International Red Cross as part of international customary law,[71] and came to prominence during the 1970s in Latin America

[64] *Keyu v Secretary of State for Foreign and Commonwealth Affairs* [2015] UKSC 69.
[65] I Ward and N Miraflor, *Slaughter and Deception at Batang Kali* (Singapore, Media Masters, 2009).
[66] *Keyu* (above n 64) para 136.
[67] Ibid, paras 137 and 138.
[68] Ibid, para 137.
[69] Ibid, para 136.
[70] Ibid, paras 312 and 313, emphasis added.
[71] Art 32 of the Additional Protocol to the Geneva Conventions relating to the Protection of Victims of International Armed Conflicts (entry into force 7 December 1978); Rule 117 in J-M Henckaerts and L Doswald-Beck, *Customary International Humanitarian Law (International Committee of*

in response to the practice of enforced disappearances.[72] More recently, the right to truth has been 'explicitly recognised' by an extensive range of international instruments,[73] intergovernmental mechanisms, peace agreements, international and regional soft law materials, as well as forming the basis of several truth commissions within domestic jurisdictions.[74] The right to truth in the context of gross violations of the right to life has received legal affirmation from, *inter alia*, the UN Human Rights Committee,[75] the Inter-American Court and Inter-American Commission on Human Rights;[76] the European Court of Human Rights (ECtHR);[77] the Constitutional Courts of Colombia and Peru;[78] the federal criminal courts of Argentina;[79] and the Human Rights Chambers of Bosnia and Herzegovina.[80]

the Red Cross): Volume I, Rules (Cambridge, Cambridge Press University, 2005) 421. See in general UN Commission on Human Rights, 'Study on the Right to the Truth: Report of the Office of the United Nations High Commissioner for Human Rights', E/CN.4/2006/91 (8 February 2006) paras 5–7.

[72] See in general Y Naqvi, 'The Right to the Truth in International Law: Fact or Fiction' (2006) 88(862) *International Review of the Red Cross* 245–73; D Groom, 'The Right to Truth in the Fight Against Impunity' (2011) 29(1) *Berkeley Journal of International Law* 175–99; S Szoke-Burke, 'Searching for the Right to Truth: The Impact of International Human Rights Law on National Transitional Justice Policies' (2015) 33(2) *Berkeley Journal of International Law* 526–78.

[73] For example, UN Commission on Human Rights, 'Updated Set of Principles for the Protection and Promotion of Human Rights through Action to Combat Impunity', E/CN.4/2005/102/Add.1 (8 February 2005), https://documents-dds-ny.un.org/doc/UNDOC/GEN/G05/109/00/PDF/G0510900.pdf?OpenElement:

> **Principle 2 (The Inalienable Right to the Truth):** Every people has the inalienable right to know the truth about past events concerning the perpetration of heinous crimes and about the circumstances and reasons that led, through massive or systematic violations, to the perpetration of those crimes. Full and effective exercise of the right to the truth provides a vital safeguard against the recurrence of violations.

See also UN General Assembly, 'Basic Principles and Guidelines on the Right to a Remedy and Reparation for Victims of Gross Violations of International Human Rights Law and Serious Violations of International Humanitarian Law', Commission Resolution 2005/35 and General Assembly Resolution 60/147, Principles 11, 22(b), and 24.

[74] UNCHR, 'Study on the Right to the Truth (above n 71) paras 9–22.

[75] *Quinteros v Uruguay*, UN Human Rights Committee, Communication 107/198, decision of 21 July 1983.

[76] *Trujillo-Oroza v Bolivia*, Inter-Am CtHR No 92 (27 February 2002) para 112–15; *Gomes Lund and Others v Brazil*, Inter-Am CtHR No 219 (24 November 2010) paras 200–2 and verdict; *Massacres of El Mozote and Nearby Places v El Salvador*, Inter-Am CtHR No 252 (25 October 2012) paras 297–98 and 354–65; *Gudiel Álvarez et al ('Diario Militar') v Guatemala*, Inter-Am CtHR (Ser C) No 253 (20 November 2012); *Heliodoro Portugal v Panama*, preliminary objections, merits, reparations and costs, judgment of 12 August 2008, Series C No 186); and *Ellacuria and Others v El Salvador*, Inter-Am CtHR Case 10.488, Report No 136/99 (12 December 1999).

[77] *Janowiec v Russia* (2014) 58 EHRR 30, paras 142–44; *Association '21 December 1989' v Romania* (2015) 60 EHRR 25, para 106; *Varnava v Turkey* (2009) nos 16064/90–16073/90, ECHR 2009; and *Brecknell v the United Kingdom*, no 32457/04 (27 November 2007).

[78] Constitutional Court of Colombia, Judgments of 20 January 2003, Case T-249/03 and C-228 of 3 April 2002; and Constitutional Tribunal of Peru, Judgment of 18 March 2004, Case 2488-2002-HC/TC.

[79] See Agreement of 1 September 2003 of the National Chamber for Federal Criminal and Correctional Matters, Case *Suárez Mason*, Rol 450 and Case *Escuela Mecánica de la Armada*, Rol 761.

[80] *Palic v Republika Srpska*, Case No CH/99/3196, Decision of 11 January 2001; '*Srebrenica Cases*', Cases Nos CH/01/8365 et al, Decision of 7 March 2003, para 220 (4).

Most recently, the ECtHR examined the question of whether the right to truth as a stand-alone right applied to victims of torture and arbitrary detention in the context of extraordinary rendition activities.[81] In *El-Masri*, the concurring opinion of Judges Françoise Tulkens, Dean Spielmann, Linos Sicilianos, and Helen Keller called for an explicit recognition of the right to truth of applicants who have suffered serious rights violations. This call and its reasoning were subsequently confirmed by the ECtHR in two later cases dealing with extraordinary rendition: *Al Nashiri v Poland* and *Abu Zubaydah v Lithuania*.[82] The reasoning in *El-Masri* highlighted a number of key elements to the right to truth that are important for our purpose of framing a general principle of retrospective state accountability and ensuring future scrutiny.

First, the judgment was clear that the right to truth served both the individual victims of human rights violations as well as the broader public: 'For society in general, the desire to ascertain the truth plays a part in strengthening confidence in public institutions and hence the rule of law.'[83] Second, the judgment framed the value in obtaining the truth beyond the narrow question of culpability or compensation:

> For those concerned – the victims' families and close friends – establishing the true facts and securing an acknowledgment of serious breaches of human-rights and humanitarian law constitute forms of redress that are just as important as compensation, and sometimes even more so.[84]

Third, the judgment twice cast the right to truth as an antidote to the harm of secrecy. Early on it referred to the 'right to the truth' as a 'particularly compelling norm in view of the secrecy surrounding the victims' fate';[85] later it noted that 'ultimately, the wall of silence and the cloak of secrecy prevent these people from making any sense of what they have experienced and are the greatest obstacles to their recovery'.[86] Fourth and finally, the concurring judgment linked the right to truth to access to detailed and comprehensive information:

> The applicant was denied the 'right to the truth': that is, the right to an accurate account of the suffering endured and the role of those responsible for that ordeal.

[81] See *El-Masri v the Former Yugoslav Republic of Macedonia* (2013) 57 EHRR 25; *Al Nashiri v Poland* (above n 46); *Nasr and Ghali v Italy* (2016) ECHR 210; and *Abu Zubaydah v Lithuania* (above n 46).

[82] *Al Nashiri v Poland* (above n 46); and *Abu Zubaydah v Lithuania* (above n 46).

[83] *El-Masri* (above n 81) Joint Concurring Opinion of Judges Tulkens, Spielmann, Sicilianos and Keller, para 6. This collective or public aspect has been confirmed in *Al Nashiri v Poland* (above n 46) para 495 and *Abu Zubaydah v Lithuania* (above n 46) para 610. In *Al Nashiri*, however, the Court joined the majority in *El-Masri* in rejecting the argument that the collective right to truth might be grounded in the right to receive information under Art 10 of the European Convention on Human Rights. On this point, the justices in *Al Nashiri* were not persuaded by the submission of the UN Special Rapporteur on the promotion of truth, justice, reparation and guarantees of nonrecurrence.

[84] Ibid.

[85] Ibid, para 1.

[86] Ibid, para 6.

> Obviously, this does not mean 'truth' in the philosophical or metaphysical sense of the term but the right to ascertain and establish the true facts.[87]

The reasoning in the concurring judgment in *El-Masri* thus presents a general justification for a broad principle of retrospective accountability, as well as a practical requirement of the preservation of information required for future scrutiny. This latter aspect is echoed in a number of sources. The report of the United Nations High Commissioner for Human Rights on the Right to Truth makes it plain that 'access to information, to official archives, is crucial to the exercise of the right to truth'.[88] Similarly, detailed guarantees relating to archival information are set out in the 'Updated Principles for the Protection and Promotion of Human Rights through Action to Combat Impunity'.[89] Importantly, Basic Principle 3 (The Duty to Preserve Memory) connects the right to truth with archival protection:

> A people's knowledge of the history of its oppression is part of its heritage and, as such, must be ensured by appropriate measures in fulfilment of the state's duty to preserve archives and other evidence concerning violations of human rights and humanitarian law and to facilitate knowledge of those violations. Such measures shall be aimed at preserving the collective memory from extinction and, in particular, at guarding against the development of revisionist and negationist arguments.

This connection is reiterated in Section C of the Updated Principles on the 'Preservation of and Access to Archives Bearing Witness to Violations', which lays out a range of detailed guarantees relating to archive preservation.[90] Chief amongst these is Principle 14:

> The right to know implies that archives must be preserved. Technical measures and penalties should be applied to prevent any removal, destruction, concealment or falsification of archives, especially for the purpose of ensuring the impunity of perpetrators of violations of human rights and/or humanitarian law.

Indeed, the connection between archival integrity and human rights more generally was expressed in 2016 by the International Council on Archives in the 'Basic Principles on the Role of Archivists and Records Managers in Support of Human Rights'[91] and in 2011 by UNESCO's Universal Declaration on Archives.[92]

[87] Ibid, para 1.

[88] UN Commission on Human Rights, 'Study on the Right to the Truth (above n 71) para 52.

[89] UN Commission on Human Rights, 'Updated Set of Principles' (above n 73).

[90] Section C of the Updated Principles (above n 73) includes Principles 14 (Measures for the Preservation of Archives); Principle 15 (Measures for Facilitating Access to Archives); Principle 16 (Cooperation between Archive Departments and the Courts and Non-judicial Commissions of Inquiry); Principle 17 (Specific Measures Relating to Archives Containing Names); and Principle 18 (Specific Measures Related to the Restoration of or Transition to Democracy and/or Peace).

[91] International Council on Archives Human Rights Working Group, 'Basic Principles on the Role of Archivists and Record Managers in Support of Human Rights' (September 2016), https://www.ica.org/sites/default/files/ICA%20HRWG%20Basic%20Principles_endorsed%20by%20PCOM_2016_Sept_English.pdf.

[92] UNESCO, 'Universal Declaration on Archives', adopted by the 36th Session of the General Conference of UNESCO (2011), https://www.ica.org/sites/default/files/UDA_June%202012_press_EN.pdf.

Just as the right to truth is premised on the protection of archives, so too is the requirement of future scrutiny, which is incapable of realisation without adequate state records. The case law on historical accountability plainly bears this out. The *Mutua* case was a success because of rigorous and extensive scholarship into deep secrets, which came to light retrospectively. But the achievements of the researchers would have been impossible without the archival material they uncovered.

The duty to sustain archival integrity, which flows from the right to truth, may thus also be viewed as essential to maintaining historical and future accountability.[93] As Elizabeth Denham, UK Information Commissioner, has argued,

> Effective record-keeping and the proper maintenance of government information is an essential public service and is a prerequisite to good governance. The responsible management of these records ensures the maintenance of institutional memory, that appropriate information is available to decision-makers, that evidence of a public body's activities is retained, and that legal requirements are met.[94]

Presently, however, there are a number of battles relating to the preservation of historical records. On 26 December 2017, it was revealed that the UK Foreign Office had been withdrawing thousands of historical documents from the National Archives and 'losing' them.[95] The 'loss' of this archival material has elicited significant concern from historians and human rights organisations alike. Human rights groups are concerned that the prospect of achieving accountability for historical wrongs committed under colonial rule is under threat.[96] Historians, critical of the liberal accounts of colonialism, are rightly suspicious that the 'loss' of this material will play directly into the hands of those seeking to maintain a particular rendition of Empire.[97] Both the larger

[93] In the United Kingdom, any 'records in central government departments and agencies, the courts and the National Health Service' are subject to the Public Records Act 1958, which stipulates a range of duties on record keepers. For example, s 3(1) reads, 'It shall be the duty of every person responsible for public records of any description which are not in the Public Record Office or a place of deposit appointed by the Secretary of State under this Act to make arrangements for the selection of those records which ought to be permanently preserved and for their safe-keeping.' In the United States, a similar framework is developed under the Federal Records Act 1950, which regulates federal agencies overseen by the National Archives and Records Administration. The Act is supplemented by a range of additional provisions. See National Archives and Records Administration (USA), 'Basic Laws and Authorities of the National Archives and Records Administration' (2016 edition), https://www.archives.gov/files/about/laws/basic-laws-book-2016.pdf (last accessed 26 March 2019).

[94] E Denham, 'Keynote Speech at the Archive and Records Association (ARA) Conference' (31 August 2017), available at https://ico.org.uk/about-the-ico/news-and-events/news-and-blogs/2017/08/archives-and-records-association-annual-conference/ (last accessed 26 March 2019).

[95] I Cobain, 'Government Admits "Losing" Thousands of Papers from National Archives', *Guardian* (26 December 2017); and S Fenton, 'Why Do Archive Files on Britain's Colonial Past Keep Going Missing', *Guardian* (27 December 2017).

[96] M Busby, 'Theresa May Must Search for Missing Archive Papers, Say Human Rights Groups', *Guardian* (26 December 2017).

[97] See the discussion above at n 14. A recent victory in this respect has been won in the European Parliament Resolution of 26 March 2019 on fundamental rights of people of African descent in Europe (2018/2899 RSP). This instrument 'encourages the EU institutions and the Member States to

project of historical erasure and the destruction of evidence of human rights violations work hand in hand here to undermine legal and democratic accountability. As historian Richard Drayton has argued,

> Public archives are instruments through which democracies recognise their citizens ownership of and responsibility for government. The practice of full release [of state documents] acts as a break on abuses of power. The hand of the present is kept honest by the gaze of the future.[98]

A similar controversy taken place in the United States over the records of the torture programme of the Central Intelligence Agency (CIA) in the years following 9/11.[99] There appeared to be early progress from the US Senate Select Committee on Intelligence. The 480-page executive summary, including twenty findings and conclusions of the five-year study on the CIA Detention and Interrogation Program were declassified in 2014.[100] This opened the way for detailed analysis by legal scholars and other commentators. The remaining 6200-page report of the Committee remains classified, however. Just before President Barack Obama stepped down, there were urgent calls for him to declassify the report entirely.[101] Carl Levin, previously Chair of the Senate Armed Services Committee, and Jay Rockefeller, previously Chair of the Senate Select Committee, made a public and urgent entreaty:

> Drawing on our decades of work in the Senate and our chairmanships of the Armed Services and Intelligence Committees, we are calling on President Obama to preserve the full torture report as a matter of profound public interest. We … are asking him to protect it as an important piece of history.[102]

After Obama stepped down, the American Civil Liberties Union (ACLU) failed in its attempt to sue for its release,[103] and the Trump Administration handed

officially acknowledge and mark the histories of people of African descent in Europe, including of past and ongoing injustices and crimes against humanity, such as slavery and the transatlantic slave trade, or those committed under European colonialism (s 5) and 'calls on Member States to declassify their colonial archives' (s 9).

[98] R Drayton, 'The Foreign Office Secretly Hoarded 1.2 Million Files: It's Historical Narcissism', *Guardian* (27 October 2017), https://www.theguardian.com/commentisfree/2013/oct/27/uk-foreign-office-secret-files.

[99] As of March 2019, a further potential controversy is brewing in the United States. At the time of writing, it is unclear whether the Mueller Report on President Donald Trump's possible collusion with Russia will be released in full to Congress or to the wider public for further evaluation. See Reuters, 'Democrats Want Full Mueller Report Released to Congress by April 2, While Republicans Resist', *CNBC* (26 March 2019), https://www.cnbc.com/2019/03/26/democrats-want-full-mueller-report-released-to-congress-by-april-2-while-republicans-resist.html.

[100] Office of US Senator Dianne Feinstein, 'Intelligence Committee Votes to Declassify Portions of CIA Study' (3 April 2014), http://www.feinstein.senate.gov/public/index.cfm/2014/4/senate-intelligence-committee-votes-to-declassify-portions-of-cia-detention-interrogation-study (last accessed 18 February 2018).

[101] C Levin and J Rockfeller, 'The Torture Report Must Be Saved', *New York Times* (9 December 2016), http://www.nytimes.com/2016/12/09/opinion/the-torture-report-must-be-saved.html?_r=0.

[102] Ibid.

[103] See the ACLU website, https://www.aclu.org/cases/senate-torture-report-foia (24 April 2017) (last accessed 18 February 2019).

the unopened Report back to Congress, which is not subject to freedom of information obligations. Many therefore fear that the Report could be buried for good.[104] If so, not only will public officials be held unaccountable for their actions under US law, but the chance for victims to vindicate their rights or for scholars to draw fine-grained, evidence-based conclusions about this period in history will be significantly undermined. The opportunity to enhance legal safeguards will thus be lost.

The idea of a duty of archival integrity and access could thus not be more prescient. As the declassification of the Pentagon Papers in 2011 demonstrated, archival declassification can bring about crucial insights into state action.[105] An expectation of such future declassification, preferably within a shorter time frame than current legal arrangements,[106] should be embedded in contemporary state action when secrecy is invoked. Certainly, the destruction of archival documents can be viewed as a violation of the right to truth.

C. Open Justice: *Incedal* and the Library of Closed Judgments

Alongside the right to truth, the rule of law principle of open justice offers a complimentary foundation for the principle of retrospective accountability and the preservation of national security material for future scrutiny. In *Guardian News v Incedal*,[107] the UK Court of Appeal dealt with a challenge to the *in camera* trial of Erol Incedal, who was charged with terrorist crimes. The case dealt predominantly with the question of when and under what circumstances a departure from the rule-of-law principle of open justice might be permitted on the grounds of national security. The argument of the press was that while it accepted the 'necessity' for the trial to be held *in camera* two years earlier, there was 'no longer any proper justification for departing from the principles of open justice'.[108] The Court of Appeal dismissed the appeal, holding that the evidence (included in a closed annex to the judgment) 'continued to necessitate a departure from the principle of open justice after the conclusion of the trial and at the present time'.[109]

[104] This stands in contrast to the decision of the UK Parliamentary Intelligence and Security Committee of Parliament to publish its 2018 report 'Detainee Mistreatment and Rendition: 2001–2010'. See Intelligence and Security Committee of Parliament (above n 46).

[105] M Cooper and S Roberts, 'After 40 Years, the Complete Pentagon Papers', *New York Times* (7 June 2011), https://www.nytimes.com/2011/06/08/us/08pentagon.html.

[106] Rudesill (above n 2) and Goitein (above n 2) suggest a four-year period for declassification of secret laws. I suggest this timeframe could apply also to secret facts included in closed material procedures and *in camera* proceedings.

[107] *Guardian v Incedal* (above n 55) para 40.

[108] Ibid.

[109] Ibid, para 74. In coming to this conclusion, the Court of Appeal noted that public accountability could still be served by the scrutiny of the Parliamentary Intelligence and Security Committee.

However, in three short paragraphs, the Court of Appeal made a crucial set of 'observations'.[110] Noting that courts were likely for 'some time' to have to deal with applications for *in camera* proceedings on the grounds of national security, Lord Thomas stated:

> Whilst the judgments given in open court are a matter of public record and can be referred to, the closed judgments which contain the detailed reasons why the court has decided that the evidence should be heard *in camera* are not retained within the court files or, as far as we have been able to ascertain, in any specified place within the court.[111]

This was in Lord Thomas's view an unsatisfactory state of affairs, as it prevented courts from being able to take advantage of the 'experience to be derived from the way in which the issues were approached'.[112] He then went on to provide a secondary reason of significant importance:

> Furthermore, for the reasons we have explained, it must always be a possibility that at a future date, disclosure will be sought at a time when it is said that there could no longer be any reason to keep the information from the public, including this Court's reasons for upholding the decision of the trial judge.[113]

Consequently, Lord Thomas announced that they had asked that the 'Registrar of this Court to form a working party from those interested in these matters to advise the Court of Appeal, Criminal Division on the course of action it should adopt'.[114]

The outcome of these working party deliberations was produced on 18 January 2019 in the form of a one-page, six-paragraph Practice Direction entitled 'Closed Judgments'.[115] This simple document requires:

> A single printed copy and an electronic copy of each closed judgment and any related open judgment must be lodged with the RCJ Senior Information Officer within 14 days of being delivered or handed down, for consideration for inclusion in the library of closed judgments now established in the Royal Courts of Justice.[116]

The creation of a 'closed judgment library' has been welcomed in principle by observers. Lawrence McNamara, for example, has taken the view that 'it adds considerable certainty to the closed judgments regime and will ensure that judgments can be considered in subsequent cases'.[117]

[110] Ibid, paras 77–80.

[111] Ibid, para 78.

[112] Ibid, para 79.

[113] Ibid.

[114] Ibid, para 80.

[115] Courts and Tribunals Judiciary (UK), 'Practice Direction: Closed Judgments' (14 January 2019), available at https://www.judiciary.uk/announcements/practice-direction-closed-judgments/ (last accessed 26 March 2019).

[116] Ibid, para 2.

[117] L McNamara, 'Closed Judgments: Security, Accountability and Court Processes', *UK Human Rights Blog* (25 January 2019), https://ukhumanrightsblog.com/2019/01/25/closed-judgments-security-accountability-and-court-processes/.

However, the Practice Direction also contains a number of problems, not least that it refers to a document entitled 'Closed Judgments Library: Security Guidance of 2017', which is itself marked as officially sensitive and not available to the public.[118] But the most glaring difficulty with the Practice Direction is that it explicitly provides for the destruction of some judgments:

> If it is decided to retain the judgment in the library, the relevant judge(s) or tribunal judge(s) will be informed. If the judgment is not to be retained, it will be disposed of securely.[119]

The risks to future accountability in this respect are considerable, and it is no surprise that McNamara has called for no judgments to be destroyed, arguing strongly that closed material procedures are 'concerned with the actions of the state in matters of liberty and rights':[120]

> There are massively important public interests at stake. It is of course hugely challenging for the government and the courts to manage information it needs rightly to keep secret for good reasons, but it is important that the management of closed judgments works to enhance not only security but also transparency and accountability.[121]

Allowing the destruction of documents is moreover inconsistent with the direction of the Court of Appeal in *Incedal*, where it was stated clearly that there is always a possibility that disclosure will be sought in the future.[122]

There is no question therefore that the prospect of future accountability is both enhanced by the closed judgment library and also undermined by its allowing for the destruction of documents, especially as there is little principled guidance as to which judgments might be selected. Further guidance on this issue may indeed be available in the 'Security Guidance of 2017', but in a twist of irony, we cannot establish this for certain.

IV. CONCLUSION: FUTURE SCRUTINY

Contemporary state secrecy inhibits rigorous academic scrutiny and limits academic freedom. When relevant information is missing, scholars cannot move beyond generalised critique and suspicion of secrecy claims to engage in normative evaluation of the particularities of any individual case in which secrecy is applied. This asymmetry places scholars at an immediate informational disadvantage and allows state actors to discredit the general critique of

[118] Ibid.

[119] Courts and Tribunals Judiciary, 'Practice Direction: Closed Judgments' (above n 115) para 3.

[120] McNamara (above n 117). McNamara is currently doing a research project entitled 'Opening Up Closed Judgments: Balancing Secrecy, Security and Accountability' and funded by the Joseph Rowntree Charitable Trust Foundation.

[121] McNamara (above n 117).

[122] *Guardian v Incedal* (above n 55) para 79.

secrecy's metastasisation within law. Secrecy thus has profound implications for the status or standing of academic critics of law and security. More fundamentally, by constraining our ability to critique, interpret, guard, and refine the rule of law, secrecy prevents scholars from fulfilling their role in the interpretive community of law.

There is therefore an urgent need for legal scholars and commentators to acknowledge the limits of academic scrutiny and to reconcile the fundamental challenges that secrecy presents. Legal academics must fight to gain access to material, if not immediately then certainly in the future. If we are successful, we will be serving not only the demands of academic rigour but the rule of law. For a structure of future accountability ought to be embedded too in contemporary procedures when secrecy is invoked against those whose rights are at stake. We must all, in short, think more carefully about bolstering future accountability. We should interrogate the temporal frameworks of national security secrets and insist that they are subject to future review close enough in time to ensure the capacity for real accountability and the right to truth.

While it is beyond the scope of this chapter to develop a comprehensive proposal for ensuring state accountability when secrecy is invoked, there are nonetheless a number of key guarantees that should feature in any such system. First, accountability measures must be grounded in the collective and individual right to truth and the principle of open justice. It must be clear, as a consequence, that it is a violation of the rule of law and of human rights to cover up material in bad faith or use national security-based secrecy as a veil to cover up unlawful state action. As an extension of the right to truth, this wrong must have clear grounds, and there must be a human rights remedy. Second, we need to strengthen the human rights dimension of the duty to maintain the integrity of public records and archives, in particular in light of the prospect of subsequent review. Tampering with archival material and destroying closed judgments must be clearly conceptualised as human rights wrongs. This can also be framed as a violation of the principle of open justice.

Third, when rights are restricted through secrecy claims, there should be an established future judicial check on these claims, with temporal and substantive dimensions. A time limit must be established for when judicial review of an initial decision to maintain a closed material procedure is permissible. These time limits cannot be too far apart and must have a proportionate justification. While a rebuttal on national security grounds against a challenge to open up the secret file in a further closed material procedure may be possible, that second procedure should be subject to subsequent review. In short, there should be an escalation of timed checks. Each review can assess all previous reviews, until such time that the presumption falls against the national security exception. Moreover, a substantive standard of review will need to be established under which the initial decision to hold a closed material procedure will be assessed. Proportionality would serve here as an initial starting point, and we would need to establish the way in which this test would apply when the judge reviews the second, third time, and last time. Questions would include whether the initial material was adequately reviewed in closed material proceedings. Was the first instance judge sufficiently rigorous in testing the closed material? Was there bad faith in deploying a closed material proceeding?

Fourth, in the case of deep secrets coming to light, we need to think hard about the nature of evidence required to trigger a broader review of materials. Is it to be left to scholars, documentary makers, authors, whistleblowers, or leakers to create a weight of evidence that can convince a government minister or court that there are sufficient grounds to investigate further? What benchmark is appropriate in light of the general right to truth held by those who are subject to illegalities covered by deep secrets?

In sum, as secrecy metastasises in law and as the dignity and fair trial rights of those subject to secret processes are undermined, academic scrutiny and freedom are also implicated. The right to truth (both individual and collective) and the principle of open justice serve as a platform for two valuable ends: the prospect of retrospective accountability in law and the realisation of future scrutiny for scholarship. In supporting these ideals, academic scholarship on security and human rights may find an answer to the challenge posed by the government official at the beginning of this chapter. By engaging in this way with the temporal dimension of scrutiny and accountability, we can also send a message to officials more generally: that the actions they take now will be subject to judicial and scholarly scrutiny in the future. In this way, 'the hand of the present' might be 'kept honest by the gaze of the future'.[123]

REFERENCES

Adèr, HJ, 'Missing Data' in HJ Adèr and GJ Mellenbergh (eds), *Advising on Research Methods: A Consultant's Companion* (Huizen, Johannes van Kessel Publishing, 2008).

Ahmed, S, *On Being Included: Racism and Diversity in Institutional Life* (Durham, Duke University Press, 2012).

Alexander, L, 'Academic Freedom', University of San Diego Legal Studies Paper No 07-38 (March 2006).

American Association of University Professors (AAUP), '1940 Statement of Principles on Academic Freedom and Tenure', http://www.aaup.org/report/1940-statement-principles-academic-freedom-and-tenure.

American Civil Liberties Union (ACLU), 'Senate Torture Report and the FOIA' (updated 24 April 2017), https://www.aclu.org/cases/senate-torture-report-foia.

Anderson, D, *Histories of the Hanged: Britain's Dirty War in Kenya and the End of Empire* (London, Weidenfeld and Nicolson, 2005).

Barak-Erez, D and Waxman, M, 'Secret Evidence and the Due Process of Terrorist Detentions' (2009) 48(3) *Columbia Journal of Transnational Law* 4–60.

Barendt, E, *Academic Freedom and the Law* (Oxford, Hart Publishing, 2010).

[123] Drayton (above n 98).

Benn, A and Taylor, D, 'We Don't Think John Finnis Should Teach at Oxford University. Here's Why', *Guardian* (11 January 2019).

Bhambra, G, Gebrial, D, and Nisancioulu, K (eds), *Decolonising the University* (London, Pluto Press, 2018).

Birchall, C, 'Six Answers to the Question "What is Secrecy Studies"' (2016) 1(1) *Secrecy and Society* 2–13.

Bloom, A, *The Closing of the American Mind* (New York, Simon and Schuster, 1987).

Bok, S, *Secrets: On the Ethics of Concealment and Revelation* (Oxford, Oxford University Press, 1984).

Brown, RS, 'Torture, Terrorism, and the Ticking Bomb: A Principled Response' (2007) 4 *Journal of International Law and Policy* 1–33.

Busby, M, 'Theresa May Must Search for Missing Archive Papers, Say Human Rights Groups', *Guardian* (26 December 2017).

Carvalho, E J and Downing, DB, *Academic Freedom in the Post-9/11 Era* (New York, Palgrave MacMillan, 2010).

Chigudu, S, 'Rhodes Must Fall and the Politics of Historical Consciousness', presentation at the Centre of African Studies, University of Edinburgh (2016), https://www.academia.edu/24732358/Rhodes_Must_Fall_and_the_Politics_of_Historical_Consciousness.

Cobain, I, 'Government Admits "Losing" Thousands of Papers from National Archives', *Guardian* (26 December 2017).

Cole, D, 'The Three Leakers and What to Do about Them', *New York Review of Books* (6 February 2014).

Commission of Inquiry into the Actions of Canadian Officials in Relation to Maher Arar ('Arar Commission'), 'Report of the Events Relating to Maher Arar' (2006), available at http://publications.gc.ca/site/eng/9.688875/publication.html.

Cooper, M and Roberts, S, 'After 40 Years, the Complete Pentagon Papers', *New York Times* (7 June 2011).

Courts and Tribunals Judiciary (UK), 'Practice Direction: Closed Judgments' (14 January 2019), available at https://www.judiciary.uk/announcements/practice-direction-closed-judgments.

Covey, RD, 'Interrogation Warrants' (2005) 26(5) *Cardozo Law Review* 1867–946.

Dant, T, *Knowledge, Ideology & Discourse: A Sociological Perspective* (London, Routledge, 1991).

Dea, S, 'A Brief History of Academic Freedom', *University Affairs* (9 October 2018).

Denham, E, 'Keynote Speech at the Archive and Records Association (ARA) Conference' (31 August 2017), available at https://ico.org.uk/about-the-ico/news-and-events/news-and-blogs/2017/08/archives-and-records-association-annual-conference.

Dershowitz, AM, 'Legal Torture', interview, *60 Minutes* (17 January 2002).

——, *Shouting Fire: Civil Liberties in a Turbulent Age* (Boston, Little, Brown and Company 2002).

——, 'Want to Torture? Get a Warrant', *San Fransisco Chronicle* (22 January 2002).

——, *Why Terrorism Works: Understanding the Threat, Responding to the Challenge* (New Haven, Yale University Press, 2002).

Dewey, J, 'Academic Freedom' (1902) 23 *Educational Review* 1–14.

Drayton, R, 'The Foreign Office Secretly Hoarded 1.2 Million Files: It's Historical Narcissism', *Guardian* (27 October 2017).

Dworkin, R, *Law's Empire* (Cambridge, MA, Harvard University Press, 1988).

Elkins, C, *Imperial Reckoning: The Untold Story of Britain's Gulag in Kenya* (New York, Henry Holt, 2005).

Emmerson, B, 'Framework Principles for Securing the Accountability of Public Officials for Gross or Systematic Human Rights Violations Committed in the Context of State Counter-Terrorism Initiatives', UN Doc A/67/396 (1 March 2013).

Equality and Human Rights Commission, 'Freedom of Expression: A Guide for Higher Education Providers and Student Unions in England and Wales' (2 February 2019), https://www.equalityhumanrights.com/en/publication-download/freedom-expression-guide-higher-education-providers-and-students-unions-england.

Eurasia Review, 'Turkey: Academic Freedom Under Threat', *Eurasia Review* (7 August 2018).

European Parliament Committee on Foreign Affairs, 'Report on European Parliament Recommendation on Defence of Academic Freedom in the EU's External Action', A8-0403/2018 (27 November 2018), http://www.europarl.europa.eu/doceo/document/A-8-2018-0403_EN.pdf.

Feinstein, D (Office of US Senator), 'Intelligence Committee Votes to Declassify Portions of CIA Study' (3 April 2014), http://www.feinstein.senate.gov/public/index.cfm/2014/4/senate-intelligence-committee-votes-to-declassify-portions-of-cia-detention-interrogation-study.

Fenton, S, 'Why Do Archive Files on Britain's Colonial Past Keep Going Missing', *Guardian* (27 December 2017).

Garton Ash, T, 'Rhodes Hasn't Fallen but the Protesters Are Making Me Rethink Britain's Past', *Guardian* (4 March 2016).

Ghosh, P, 'Beyond Methodology: Max Weber's Conception of *Wissenschaft*' (2014) 52(2) *Sociologia Internationalis* 157–218.

Gibbs, D, 'Sigmund Freud as a Theorist of Government Secrecy' in S Maret (ed), *Government Secrecy* (Bingley, Emerald Group Publishing, 2011).

Goitein, E, 'The New Era of Secret Law', research report for Brennan Center for Justice at New York University School of Law (2016).

Gopal, P, et al, 'A Collective Statement on Ethics and Empire', *Scholars of Empire* (21 December 2017), https://medium.com/oxfordempireletter/a-collective-statement-on-ethics-and-empire-19c2477871a0.

Groom, D, 'The Right to Truth in the Fight Against Impunity' (2011) 29(1) *Berkeley Journal of International Law* 175–99.

Hart, HLA, *The Concept of Law*, 3rd edn (Oxford, Oxford University Press, 2012).

Henckaerts, J-M and Doswald-Beck, L, *Customary International Humanitarian Law (International Committee of the Red Cross): Volume I, Rules* (Cambridge, Cambridge Press University, 2005).

Hennis, W, *Max Webers Wissenschaft vom Menschen* (Tübingen, Mohr Siebeck, 2003).

Horton, S, *Lords of Secrecy: The National Security Elite and America's Stealth Warfare* (New York, Nation Books, 2015).

Hudson, C and Williams, J (eds), *Why Academic Freedom Matters: A Response to Current Challenges* (London, Civitas, 2016).

Human Rights Watch, 'Turkey Government Targeting Academics: Dismissals, Prosecutions Create Campus Climate of Fear', *Human Rights Watch* (14 May 2018).

Ignatieff, M, 'Academic Freedom and the Future of Europe', Centre for Global Higher Education Working Paper No 40 (July 2018), https://www.researchcghe.org/perch/resources/publications/wp40.pdf.

Intelligence and Security Committee of Parliament (UK), 'Detainee Mistreatment and Rendition: 2001–2010' (28 June 2018, HC 1113).

International Council on Archives Human Rights Working Group, 'Basic Principles on the Role of Archivists and Record Managers in Support of Human Rights' (September 2016), https://www.ica.org/sites/default/files/ICA%20HRWG%20Basic%20Principles_endorsed%20by%20PCOM_2016_Sept_English.pdf.

Joint Parliamentary Committee on Human Rights (UK), 'Freedom of Speech in Universities' (HC 589, HL 111) (27 March 2018).

Kimball, R, *Tenured Radicals* (New York, Harper & Row, 1990).

——, '"Tenured Radicals": A Postscript' (2019) 37(8) *New Criterion*.

Kleinig, J, 'Ticking Bombs and Torture Warrants (2005) 10(2) *Deakin Law Review* 614–27.

Lackey, J (ed), *Academic Freedom* (Oxford, Oxford University Press, 2018).

Lazarus, L, McCrudden, C and Bowles, N (eds), *Reasoning Rights* (Oxford, Hart Publishing, 2014).

Levin, C and Rockfeller, J, 'The Torture Report Must Be Saved', *New York Times* (9 December 2016).

Lynch, MP, 'Academic Freedom and the Politics of Truth' in J Lackey (ed), *Philosophy and Academic Freedom* (Oxford, Oxford University Press, 2018).

MacFarlane, B, *Intellectual Leadership in Higher Education* (London, Routledge, 2012).

Mance, H, 'Britain Has Had Enough of Experts, Says Gove', *Financial Times* (3 June 2016).

Manningham-Buller, E, 'From Bugs to Bugs', lecture, Oxford Martin School (15 February 2016).

Marty, D (Special Rapporteur), 'Secret Detentions and Illegal Transfers of Detainees Involving Council of Europe Member States: Second Report', Council of Europe Parliamentary Assembly report (7 June 2007), http://assembly.coe.int/CommitteeDocs/2007/EMarty_20070608_NoEmbargo.pdf.

McDougall, J, et al, 'Ethics and Empire: An Open Letter from Oxford Scholars', *Conversation* (19 December 2017), http://theconversation.com/ethics-and-empire-an-open-letter-from-oxford-scholars-89333.

McNamara, L, 'Closed Judgments: Security, Accountability and Court Processes', *UK Human Rights Blog* (25 January 2019).

Melley, T, *The Covert Sphere: Secrecy, Fiction, and the National Security State* (Ithaca, Cornell University Press, 2012).

Messner, SF, 'Exploring the Consequences of Erratic Data Reporting for Cross-National Research on Homicide' (1992) 8(2) *Journal of Quantitative Criminology* 155–73.

Nanopoulos, E, 'European Human Rights Law and the Normalisation of the "Closed Material Procedure"' (2015) 78(6) *Modern Law Review* 913–44.

Naqvi, Y, 'The Right to the Truth in International Law: Fact or Fiction' (2006) 88(862) *International Review of the Red Cross* 245–73.

National Archives and Records Administration (USA), 'Basic Laws and Authorities of the National Archives and Records Administration' (2016 edn), https://www.archives.gov/files/about/laws/basic-laws-book-2016.pdf.

Olmstead, KS, 'Government Secrecy and Conspiracy Theories' in S Maret (ed), *Government Secrecy* (Bingley, Emerald Group Publishing, 2011).

O'Neill, R, 'Academic Freedom: New Challenges in the United States' (2009) 57 *International Higher Education* 3–5.

Posner, RA, 'Torture, Terrorism, and Interrogation' in S Levinson (ed), *Torture: A Collection* (Oxford, Oxford University Press, 2004).

Pozen, D, 'Deep Secrecy' (2011) 62(2) *Stanford Law Review* 257–339.

Rawlinson, K, 'Trigger Warmings OK, but No-Platforming May Be Illegal, Universities Warned', *Guardian* (2 February 2019).

Reuters, 'Democrats Want Full Mueller Report Released to Congress by April 2, While Republicans Resist', *CNBC* (26 March 2019).

Richardson, L, 'Secrecy and Status: The Social Construction of Forbidden Relationships' (1988) 53(2) *American Sociological Review* 209–19.

Rozell, MJ, *Executive Privilege: Presidential Power, Secrecy and Accountability*, 3rd edn (Lawrence, University Press of Kansas, 2010).

Rudesill, DS, 'Coming to Terms with Secret Law' (2016) 7 *Harvard National Security Journal* 241–390.

Scarry, E, 'Five Errors in the Reasoning of Alan Dershowitz' in S Levinson (ed), *Torture: A Collection* (Oxford, Oxford University Press, 2004).

Scheinin, M, 'Protection of Human Rights and Fundamental Freedoms while Countering Terrorism: Report of the Special Rapporteur' on Counter-terrorism and Human Rights: Fair Trial Guarantees While Countering Terrorism, UN Doc A/63/223 (6 August 2008).

Scheppele, KL, *Legal Secrets: Equality and Efficiency in the Common Law* (Chicago, University of Chicago Press, 1988).

Simmel, G, 'The Sociology of Secrecy and of Secret Societies' (1906) 4 *American Journal of Sociology* 441–98.

Szoke-Burke, S, 'Searching for the Right to Truth: The Impact of International Human Rights Law on National Transitional Justice Policies' (2015) 33(2) *Berkeley Journal of International Law* 526–78.

UN Commission on Human Rights, 'Updated Set of Principles for the Protection and Promotion of Human Rights through Action to Combat Impunity', E/CN.4/2005/102/Add.1 (8 February 2005), https://documents-dds-ny.un.org/doc/UNDOC/GEN/G05/109/00/PDF/G0510900.pdf.

——, 'Study on the Right to the Truth: Report of the Office of the United Nations High Commissioner for Human Rights', E/CN.4/2006/91 (8 February 2006).

UNESCO, 'Recommendation Concerning the Status of Higher-Education Teaching Personnel' (11 November 1997), http://portal.unesco.org/en/ev.php-URL_ID=13144&URL_DO=DO_TOPIC&URL_SECTION=201.html.

——, 'Universal Declaration on Archives', adopted by the 36th Session of the General Conference of UNESCO (2011), https://www.ica.org/sites/default/files/UDA_June%202012_press_EN.pdf.

van Caenegem, R, *Judges, Legislators and Professors: Chapters in European Legal History* (Cambridge, Cambridge University Press, 1987).

Waldron, J, *'Partly Laws Common to All Mankind': Foreign Law in American Courts* (New Haven, Yale University Press, 2012).

——, 'Torture and Positive Law: Jurisprudence for the White House' (2005) 105(6) *Columbia Law Review* 1681–750.

Ward, I and Miraflor, N, *Slaughter and Deception at Batang Kali* (Singapore, Media Masters, 2009).

Weber, M, 'Science as Vocation' in HH Gerth and CW Mills (eds), *From Max Weber: Essays in Sociology* (Oxford, Oxford University Press, 1946).

Whetherell, M, Taylor, S and Yates, S, *Discourse Theory and Practice: A Reader* (London, Sage, 2001).

World University Service, 'Lima Declaration on Academic Freedom and Autonomy of Institutions of Higher Education' (6–10 September 1988).

Zedner, L, 'Counterterrorism on Campus' (2018) 68(4) *University of Toronto Law Journal* 545–87.

8

Accountability Mechanisms for Transnational Counterterrorism

KENT ROACH*

THE SNOWDEN REVELATIONS, as well as earlier revelations about the US's post-9/11 use of rendition and secret prisons, have highlighted the prominence of transnational counterterrorism activities that involve a number of states and, increasingly, the private sector. There are many reasons to be pessimistic about the ability of states and society to achieve accountability for transnational counterterrorism. Even domestic accountability mechanisms have lagged behind the increased intensity and coordination of government counterterrorism activities.[1] If the international community cannot achieve accountability for the activities of domestic security networks of multiple agencies, then surely we will be unable to impose accountability on security networks that involve different sovereign states and quasi-sovereign corporations? In this chapter, I will argue that this pessimistic thesis about accountability for transnational counterterrorism is overstated. As in many things in life, transnational accountability can be seen as a glass that is half empty or half full. Much depends on how we define and understand accountability. If accountability is seen as something that happens only when state agencies control or sanction abuses, then the accountability glass is less than half full. Indeed, if accountability equals the ability to control and sanction, transnational accountability may often be impossible. If, however, accountability is understood more broadly to include informed criticism from both state and non-state actors that places pressures on security agencies to explain and justify their actions, then the accountability glass can be seen as half full.

In this chapter I will argue that accountability should be understood as an ongoing process of exposure, criticism, and demands for justification and not

* I thank the Pierre E Trudeau Foundation and the Centre for Transnational Legal Studies for their support of my work; and the editors for challenging comments on an earlier draft.

[1] See, for example, Commission of Inquiry into the Activities of Canadian Officials in Relation to Maher Arar (DR O'Connor, Commissioner), 'A New Review Mechanism for the RCMP's National Security Activities' (December 2006), http://www.sirc-csars.gc.ca/pdfs/cm_arar_rcmpgrc-eng.pdf.

limited to the power to control and sanction. Drawing on examples such as rendition and surveillance, I will suggest that such a broad form of accountability has already occurred in the post-9/11 era. Such accountability will continue to occur if the relevant state and civil society actors remain attentive and vigilant.

The first part of this chapter will explore the critical threshold issue of how accountability should be defined and understood. I will argue that it is a mistake to equate accountability with state-based command and control and sanctions or even to limit it to something that is achieved exclusively by state institutions such as courts, legislative committees, or executive bodies dedicated to review and accountability. Rather, I will argue that accountability can be achieved by a broad range of state and non-state mechanisms that can place pressures on those who exercise security powers to explain and attempt to justify their actions. My point is not that sanctions for official misconduct and redress for victims of state abuse are not important: it is simply that accountability is not limited to such outcomes. Moreover, accountability should be understood as a complex and iterative process involving a broad range of state and non-state actors, including national and transnational courts, executive watchdogs, legislative committees, leakers, the media, corporations, academe, and transnational civil society advocacy groups.

The second part of this chapter will provide a taxonomy of accountability measures that can apply to transnational counterterrorism activities. This taxonomy will include the role that courts, the executive (including executive watchdogs), and the legislature can play at both the national and supranational levels. At the same time, it will also include a variety of non-state actors, such as leakers (including whistleblowers who follow state procedures for leaking) and transnational civil society groups and corporations. My purpose in presenting this taxonomy is to build on the broad definition of accountability offered in the first part of the chapter.

The remaining sections will examine these different accountability measures in greater depth, with examples taken from well-known counterterrorism measures such as rendition and mass surveillance. It will be argued that a decent amount of accountability has already been achieved in democracies for some of the most extreme post-9/11 abuses of rights. In some cases, accountability has been achieved by domestic states in the form of courts, legislative committees, and executive watchdogs reviewing not only the activities of their own domestic agencies but also indirectly the activities of other states.

Some but by all means not all of my examples will involve Canada. As a relatively less powerful state with fairly robust accountability measures, Canada has frequently been required to examine the conduct of more powerful security partners. I will also examine the role of the transnational state, with special attention to how various institutions of the United Nations, the European Union, and the European Community have responded to counterterrorism abuses.

Finally, I will examine the role of a range of non-state actors in publicising various counterterrorism abuses in a manner that has placed pressure on security agencies to explain and even change their conduct. The examples discussed in this chapter are obviously not an exhaustive catalogue of accountability measures. They are simply some illustrative examples. My primary purpose is to encourage policymakers and scholars to think about accountability more broadly and creatively.

Those who equate accountability with sanctions, measurable control of state actions, and redress will likely not be satisfied with the broad approach to accountability that is taken in this chapter. I can only say that I agree with such critics that control, sanction, and redress for blatant misconduct is important and often missing. My hope, however, is that critics of my broad and somewhat soft approach to accountability will recognise that the broad array of processes and mechanisms discussed in this chapter have played a significant role in raising awareness about transnational security abuses such as renditions and that such awareness is a precondition to control, sanction, and redress.[2]

I. WHAT IS ACCOUNTABILITY?

An important but often neglected threshold issue in much work in the security field is the meaning of accountability. There is a large literature on accountability in different contexts, but it often takes the meaning of accountability as assumed.[3] Critical questions of definition and who are the appropriate agents of accountability are often bypassed.

A. Accountability as the Requiring of Explanations and Justifications

In what follows, I will argue for a broad understanding of accountability as any activity that requires security actors to explain and justify their conduct. This is a broad process that is dependent on information and persuasion and

[2] For my own criticism of the American approach to misconduct that allows impunity because of claims of state secrets and political questions, see K Roach, *The 9/11 Effect: Comparative Counter-Terrorism* (Cambridge, Cambridge University Press, 2011) ch 4. Although Canada is far from perfect, I would suggest it has done better than the US at least with respect to redress, with significant compensation packages for victims of transnational counterterrorism abuses that involved Canadian and American conduct. For example, Maher Arar, a Canadian victim of US rendition to torture, and Omar Khadr, a Canadian victim of US torture and detention at Guantanamo Bay, both received CAD$10 million compensation packages and apologies from the Canadian government for the role they played in the abuse. See A Emmons, 'The Country Paying Omar Khadr $10 million Is Not the Country that Tortured Him', *The Intercept* (6 July 2017), https://theintercept.com/2017/07/06/canada-guantanamo-torture-omar-khadr-pay-10-million-us/. Both of these significant acts of redress built on some of the indirect and softer accountability measures such as inquiry reports and court decisions that indirectly reviewed and criticised post-9/11 Canadian/American counterterrorism practices.

[3] For an exception, see P Stenning (ed), *Accountability for Criminal Justice* (Toronto, University of Toronto Press, 1995).

does not necessarily encompass the power to control or sanction the activities being reviewed. The above definition makes non-state actors such as the media key agents of accountability. It also includes state actors that engage in *ex post* review and criticism of security activities as agents of accountability even though they often lack the power to control or sanction the activities that they review. Indeed, there are concerns that those who have the power to control may for that reason become implicated in the activities being reviewed and thus lack critical distance from them.[4] Similarly, those with the power to sanction security actors may also pull their punches because of a reluctance to sanction even errant security officials for 'doing their jobs'. In other words, the broad definition of accountability used in this chapter is designed to include the work of a range of state and non-state actors who evaluate and criticise transnational counterterrorism activity even though they lack the power to actually control or sanction that activity.

I concede that those with the power to engage in oversight or to punish security misconduct may be in the strongest position to demand accountability. The minister who fires a security official for an abuse or a court that awards damages for similar abuses obviously act as agents of accountability. But those who control and sanction security officials are not the exclusive agents of accountability. In other words, an agency can be made accountable without those demanding an account having the power to sanction past conduct or control behaviour going forward. For example, an informed legislative committee report, executive watchdog review, or even a good piece of investigative journalism can be a powerful instrument of accountability. Similarly, leakers of secret information about abuses,[5] also serve as a mechanism of accountability, even though they have no power to control security agencies.

I will suggest that a broad definition of accountability that is focused on publicity and explanation as opposed to one that limits the notion to control and censure is particularly appropriate to transnational counterterrorism. First, however, it is important to examine a common approach to accountability that I will argue is *not* appropriate, especially in the context of transnational counterterrorism.

B. Accountability as Command, Coercion, and Sanction

Accountability is commonly equated with the ability to control and sanction those involved in misconduct. Thus it is often stated that there has been no accountability for human rights abuses if there have been no prosecutions or other coercive forms of redress for the harms caused. One who accepts

[4] Commission of Inquiry, 'A New Review Mechanism for the RCMP' (above n 1) 456–64.
[5] See the chapter in this volume by Liora Lazarus.

this definition of accountability will have plenty of reasons to conclude that post-9/11 accountability has been a failure. For example, American officials who are responsible for renditions and torture have not been 'held to account' by prosecutions or even successful civil lawsuits and damage awards.[6]

The idea that accountability requires control and sanctions and that there is no accountability in the absence of coercive remedies can be related to legal positivism, which sees law as a series of enforceable commands. It is most famously demonstrated by Oliver Wendell Holmes's arguments that law is simply a prediction of the consequences that a bad man will experience for his actions.[7] As many critics have noted, however, Holmes' approach is based on a narrow version of positivism.[8]

Those who reject such positivism and instead see law as an ongoing attempt at persuasion will be less worried about criticisms that do not result in sanctions or other coercive remedies. Their understanding of law is based more on persuasion than on command. It can be seen in the theory of legal theorists such as Lon Fuller and Ronald Dworkin, who view law not simply as binary commands.[9] It is also implicit in John Braithwaite's theory of responsive regulation, which warns that sanctions and incapacitation should be used only when attempts at education and persuasion fail.[10]

The broader approach to accountability used in this chapter is not without its faults. Accountability that depends on persuasion and criticism from multiple actors is more difficult to measure than accountability that results in sanctions or explicit mechanisms of control. It can be criticised as amorphous and even aspirational. That said, the fact that accountability is not easily seen or measured does not mean that it does not occur.

C. Accountability for Transnational Counterterrorism: Requiring Explanations and Justifications

In addition to the other arguments referenced above that have been raised against equating accountability with control and sanctions, there are some independent reasons to reject such a limited view of accountability in the context of transnational counterterrorism.

[6] J Pfander, *Constitutional Torts and the War on Terror* (New York, Oxford University Press, 2017).

[7] OW Holmes, 'The Path of the Law' (1897) 10 *Harvard Law Review* 457.

[8] W Twining, 'Other People's Power: The Bad Man and English Positivism, 1897–1997' (1997) 63(1) *Brooklyn Law Review* 189, 192.

[9] L Fuller, *The Morality of Law* (New Haven, Yale University Press, 1969); and R Dworkin, *Taking Rights Seriously* (Cambridge, MA, Harvard University Press, 1977).

[10] J Braithwaite, *Restorative Justice and Responsive Regulation* (Oxford, Oxford University Press, 2002).

One reason is that security agencies often act in secret, and public exposure of their actions is often an important prerequisite to public criticism of their activities. In short, public exposure of security activities is no small accomplishment. Such exposure is often a necessary prelude to any subsequent control and sanction of misconduct by security actors that may take place. The approach to accountability taken in this chapter is not dismissive of attempts to control and sanction the misconduct of security actors: rather, it argues that accountability as exposure and critique of national security activities in a manner that demands explanations and justifications from security actors is often a vital pre-condition for controls and sanctions, as well as for public deliberation about security powers.

A second reason is that one of the prime concerns with respect to accountability for counterterrorism is human rights. One of the distinguishing features of the post-9/11 era is that (with some exceptions, especially in the United States) courts are more willing to review security activities. For example, the House of Lords invalidated a key plank of the UK response to 9/11 in the Belmarsh case,[11] and the United States Supreme Court extended habeas corpus to Guantanamo Bay.[12] As I have argued elsewhere, one reason why courts have left behind pre-9/11 deference towards national security is the increased judicial use of theories of proportionality, which allow courts to accept the importance of the state's national security objectives but to question whether certain means that violate human rights are truly necessary to achieve those goals.[13] The questions that are central to proportionality analysis are not the binary or black-and-white questions of legality or illegality that may result in sanction and redress. Rather, proportionality analysis focuses on more multi-valiant issues and greyish questions of alternatives that lend themselves to a dialogic process of questioning state activity and asking state actors to explain and justify their conduct.

A third reason is that even when courts or indeed other domestic state actors such as legislative committees and executive watchdogs criticise transnational counterterrorism activities, they often lack powers to impose coercive remedies on all aspects of the conduct that they criticise. For example, a number of supranational and national courts have criticised on due process grounds the listing of terrorists for the purposes of asset freezes and travel bans.[14] Similarly, a number of non-American courts have indirectly opined on American counterterrorism activities, but none have sought to extend the remedies they ordered beyond their own jurisdiction to apply to American actors.[15] In short, courts have struggled to provide full and effective remedies for counterterrorism activities with

[11] *A v Secretary of State* [2004] UKHL 56.

[12] *Boumediene v Bush* 553 US 723 (2008).

[13] K Roach, 'Judicial Review of the State's Anti-Terrorism Activities' (2009) 3 *Indian Journal of Constitutional Law* 138.

[14] For a survey of these cases, see C Forcese and K Roach, 'Limping into the Future: The UN 1267 Committee at the Crossroads' (2010) 42 *George Washington International Law Review* 217.

[15] For a survey of these cases, see K Roach, 'Substitute Justice? Challenges to American Counter-Terrorism Activities in Non-American Courts' (2013) 84 *Mississippi Law Journal* 901.

transnational elements. This suggests that an understanding of accountability that insists on control and sanction will be inappropriate and generally unattainable in the context of transnational counterterrorism.

A final reason to reject the idea that accountability is limited to control and sanction is that transnational counterterrorism activities engages various forms of supranational law that, even more than domestic law, operate by way of persuasion and criticism as opposed to command. As my colleagues Jutta Brunnée and Stephen Toope have argued, international norms, including even basic norms such as prohibitions on torture, require continual and multiple reinforcement from a range of supranational institutions and non-state actors, including civil society. My understanding of the multiple actors and iterative processes that are necessary to achieve transnational accountability is quite similar to Brunnée and Toope's interactionalist approach to international law, which similarly stresses the role of multiple state and non-state actors, including civil society.[16]

D. Summary

One's views about the prospects for accountability can depend on how one defines accountability and whether it is equated, on the one hand, with control, sanction, and redress or, on the other hand, with publicity, critique, and persuasion. If accountability is about controlling and sanctioning misconduct, it may be a lost cause, especially with respect to transnational counterterrorism. If, however, accountability is primarily achieved through publicity, critique, and persuasion, then the prospects for transnational accountability are considerably brighter. Courts can contribute to this latter process even when they struggle to order effective remedies. Similarly, supranational and non-state institutions, including the media and civil society advocacy groups, can contribute to accountability even though they lack the power to control or punish security officials who engage in transnational counterterrorism abuses.

II. A TAXONOMY OF THE MULTIPLE MECHANISMS AND PROCESSES OF ACCOUNTABILITY

In assessing accountability mechanisms for transnational counterterrorism, it is helpful to break the activities into three main categories: 1) domestic state-based mechanisms; 2) supranational state-based mechanisms; and 3) various non-state mechanisms. It is also helpful to break both domestic and supranational mechanisms into 1) judicial, 2) legislative, and 3) executive mechanisms, with sub-categories in the executive measures between a) permanent review bodies

[16] J Brunnée and S Toope, *Legitimacy and Legality in International Law* (Cambridge, Cambridge University Press, 2010).

and b) discretionary bodies that are often appointed in response to particular concerns and scandals.

Non-state mechanisms of accountability are the most novel and may well constitute an open-ended category. At present, I divide them into: 1) the media and academe; 2) leakers and whistleblowers; 3) civil society groups; and 4) corporations. Undoubtedly, others could be added to this list. The result of these interlocking and self-reinforcing mechanisms of accountability can be represented in the form of the following chart:

State (Domestic) Mechanisms	State (Supranational) Mechanisms	Non-state Mechanisms
• **Courts** (including direct review of domestic activities and indirect review of foreign activities) • **Legislature** (including formal inquiries and resolutions) • **Executive** (both permanent review bodies and *ad hoc* inquiries)	• **Courts** (especially the European Court of Justice and the European Court of Human Rights) • **Legislature** (including the European Parliament and investigations by its institutions) • **Executive** (eg, the 1267 Ombudsperson)	• **Media and academe** (eg, regarding rendition) • **Leakers and whistleblowers** • **Civil society** (eg, Amnesty International, Human Rights Watch) • **Corporate security partners** (eg, Twitter)

These ten categories of accountability mechanisms do not operate in isolation. They feed off and reinforce each other. For example, the media and civil society often depend on leakers. Developments at the supranational level, such the creation of an UN Ombudsperson for the 1267 listing process,[17] in turn depend on concerns raised by domestic courts. The cumulative nature of the accountability process means that the sum is often greater than the individual parts. That said, because of their cumulative and iterative nature, such forms of accountability are not easily measured. They can perhaps best be understood by historical modes of analysis rather than social science methods that look for measurable effects.

III. DOMESTIC STATE MECHANISMS OF ACCOUNTABILITY

A. Courts

In theory, the judiciary should be the least capable branch when it comes to reviewing domestic, let alone transnational, national security activities.

[17] UN Security Council Resolution 1267 (1999), S/RES/1267 (15 October 1999).

Canada's Arar Commission noted the reactive nature of the judiciary and the secret nature of most national security activities, cautioning against reliance on courts as a means to ensure accountability for domestic national security activities.[18] That said, even in the comparatively small jurisdiction of Canada, courts have engaged productively with a range of transnational counterterrorism activities in the years since the 2006 Arar Report.

Canadian courts, like courts in many other countries, have been prepared indirectly to review transnational listing cases. In the course of determining that the Canadian government had violated a citizen's right to return to Canada, a judge examined the 1267 listing process and criticised it as Kafkaesque.[19] The domestic court could not of course order that the person be delisted. Nevertheless, the person was eventually delisted by the 1267 committee, and the UN Security Council has in subsequent cases taken care to indicate that travel bans do not apply in cases in which a listed person returns to his or her country of citizenship. Thus, although domestic judicial review may not apply directly to transnational processes, it can reveal some of their effects and implications and influence change.

Canadian courts have also indirectly reviewed American detention practices at Guantanamo Bay. The Supreme Court of Canada has twice held that Canadian officials violated both the Canadian Charter and international law when they interviewed Omar Khadr, a Canadian teenager who was detained at a time when habeas corpus and other forms of legal relief were not available for Guantanamo detainees.[20] This litigation demonstrates how domestic courts can both directly hold domestic officials to account for their role in transnational counterterrorism activities, and indirectly review the activities of other nations. In these cases, the Canadian courts held that the Canadian Charter of Rights and Freedoms would not apply abroad unless the activities in question also violated international law. This allowed the Court to opine on whether American practices of military detention violated international law. To be sure, the Canadian Supreme Court was diplomatic in relying on a 2006 decision of the US Supreme Court as authority for concluding that detention at Guantanamo Bay in 2003 violated international law, but it is clear that the Canadian Court did lend its weight to those who criticised Guantanamo Bay as a 'legal black hole'. Indeed, the origins of that phrase can be found in a 2002 UK court decision that found that British citizens detained at Guantanamo Bay had reasonable expectations that the UK government would consider their requests that diplomatic representations be made with the United States on their behalf.[21] It is interesting to note that in both the Canadian and earlier British Guantanamo cases, the

[18] Commission of Inquiry, 'A New Review Mechanism for the RCMP' (above n 1) 491.

[19] *Abdelrazik v Canada* [2009] FC 580.

[20] *Canada (Attorney General) v Khadr* [2008] 2 SCR 125; and *Canada (Prime Minister) v Khadr* [2010] 1 SCR 44.

[21] *Abbasi v Secretary of State* [2002] EWCA 1598, para 64.

courts declined to order their domestic government to make diplomatic representations to the United States.[22] This underlines how judicial contributions to accountability may not fit into a positivistic command-and-control model and may not even provide effective remedies for those harmed by transnational counterterrorism.

The Supreme Court of Canada's decisions did not result in Omar Khadr's release, but they added to the growing chorus of international criticism of the Guantanamo Bay detention camp. They also were part of a complex process that eventually led to Khadr's return to Canada. The Canadian government relied on the Supreme Court's rulings when in June 2017 it settled Khadr's lawsuit for CAD$10 million.[23] The controversial settlement underlines how the earlier court decisions were able to raise awareness of Khadr's situation without engaging in the fraught process of formulating redress for Khadr.

Canadian courts have stopped attempts by the United States to extradite one of Omar Khadr's brothers, Abdullah Khadr, to face terrorism charges in the United States as a remedy consequent on its findings that the United States was complicit in misconduct by Pakistan's Inter-Services Intelligence Directorate when they initially detained Abdullah Khadr in Pakistan without access to courts or consular services.[24] This case demonstrates how domestic courts can use transnational proceedings such as extradition proceedings or requests for legal assistance both to raise awareness about transnational counterterrorism abuses and to impose some tangible remedy that can be seen as a form of sanction and redress.

To be sure, the tangible remedy in the Abdullah Khadr case is exceptional. In many cases involving transnational counterterrorism activities, domestic courts will not be able to impose tangible remedies. One interesting case in this regard is litigation brought on behalf of Yunus Rahmatullah, a Pakistani national who was captured by British forces in Iraq in 2004 but was subsequently transferred to US custody and moved from Iraq to the Bagram airbase in Afghanistan.[25] I have elsewhere characterised this and similar litigation as 'substitute justice' litigation because it seeks indirectly to review American counterterrorism activities after US courts refuse to do so.[26] This case can, however, also be seen as a means of publicising and providing some accountability for joint UK and US counterterrorism operations in Iraq. In 2012, the UK Supreme Court affirmed that habeas corpus was correctly issued but concluded that the United Kingdom had discharged its obligations by asking for the United States to produce Rahmatullah.[27] The United States refused to produce Rahmatullah, and a

[22] Ibid.

[23] Emmons, 'The Country Paying Omar Khadr $10 Million' (above n 2).

[24] *Khadr v United States of America* (2011) Can LII 358.

[25] *Al Maqaleh v Gates* 605 F 3d 84 (DC Cir 2010).

[26] Roach, 'Substitute Justice?' (above n 15).

[27] *Secretary of State v Rahmatullah* (2012) UKSC 48, para 74, per Lord Kerr; and para 113, per Lord Reed.

request was all that could reasonably be demanded of the United Kingdom. In subsequent litigation involving Rahmatullah and others claiming to be victims of UK complicity in American renditions, the UK Supreme Court rejected the notion that it should refrain from implicit criticism of the conduct of the United States or other foreign states and rejected state claims of immunity based on the acts of foreign states.[28] From the perspective of control and redress, the litigation was a failure, but it still raised awareness both about Rahmatullah's plight and about American conduct. In this sense, it contributed to an ongoing accountability process in which first the UK courts and subsequently the UK executive demanded that the US government explain and attempt to justify its controversial conduct towards prisoners of war who they suspected of involvement in terrorism.

The Rahmatullah case illustrates how each country that joins counterterrorism efforts provides a potential for litigation in that country as well as for other forms of accountability measures. In other words, transnational counterterrorism produces a transnational accountability trail. It also suggests that domestic judicial review is an accountability mechanism that can make clear some of the harsher implications of transnational counterterrorism. Such court decisions are often not an endpoint. Rather, in the cases of both Omar Khadr and Yunis Rahmatullah, they were part of continued diplomatic and civil society campaigns that eventually led to each man being released from American military custody. Courts may rarely be able to order effective remedies for transnational counterterrorism, but they can be part of a larger and multifaceted accountability process that may eventually result in remedies.

B. Legislatures

A number of legislative committees have been active in the United Kingdom, investigating UK involvement in renditions. The Intelligence and Security Committee has had access to secret information when investigating such matters, but other committees such as the Joint Committee on Human Rights have not. The issue of secrecy poses perhaps the greatest challenge for accountability.[29] In both the United Kingdom and United States, legislative committees may be 'briefed in' on problematic counterterrorism activities but may be unable publicly to reveal or to object to them. This can lead to claims that legislators approved a particular contested security activity. This is an important reason not to conflate the oversight process, which can imply approval, and the retrospective review function of legislative bodies.

[28] *Belhaj and Ramatullah v Secretary of State* [2017] UKSC 3, 11, per Lord Mance; 134, per Lord Neuberger; and para 241, per Lord Sumption.

[29] See also the chapter in this volume by Liora Lazarus.

The UK Intelligence and Security Committee in its 2007 report on rendition was quite sympathetic to the Security Services. Its conclusions and recommendations started with the following statement:

> Our intelligence-sharing relationships, particularly with the United States, are critical to providing the breadth and depth of intelligence coverage required to counter the threat to the UK posed by global terrorism. These relationships have saved lives and must continue.[30]

It also stressed that the Security Services had expected that most renditions would be 'to justice' rather 'to detention' and that it had assumed that the United States would obtain appropriate assurances against mistreatment. It concluded that it would be 'unreasonable and impractical' for authorities to determine that every flight that landed in the United Kingdom was not involved in a rendition operation.[31] In contrast, the Joint Committee on Human Rights took a different approach. It concluded in 2009 that the refusal of the Home Secretary and the Minister of Foreign Affairs to testify before it about UK involvement in renditions was a manifestation of a larger accountability gap problem.[32] One of the Joint Committee's conclusions was that the Intelligence and Security Committee had failed to ensure proper ministerial accountability and that an inquiry should be appointed.

The differing conclusions drawn by the Intelligence and Security Committee and the Joint Committee on Human Rights regarding the UK role in renditions suggest that an important subject of accountability measures is the adequacy of accountability itself. The flexible and non-positivistic definition of accountability used in this chapter facilitates the turning of the tools and instruments of accountability – exposure and critique – onto agencies that exercise accountability functions. This can serve to critique and improve accountability processes over time. By engaging multiple actors, including multiple legislative committees, in the processes of accountability, there is less danger of drawing erroneous conclusions about the appropriate conduct of security agencies.

Another check in the context of legislative review of the UK role in rendition has been an *ad hoc* all-party group that examines extraordinary renditions over time. In 2011, this group even published its own book on renditions entitled *Account Rendered: Extraordinary Renditions and Britain's Role*.[33] This demonstrates how legislative accountability mechanisms can inform and even drift into non-state mechanisms, especially in the media. Because of its open and political

[30] Intelligence and Security Committee (UK), 'Rendition', Cm 7171 (July 2007), available at https://www.gov.uk/government/publications/rendition-report-by-the-intelligence-and-security-committee, 64, para A.

[31] Ibid, 68, para HH.

[32] Joint Committee on Human Rights (UK), '23rd Report: Allegations of UK Complicity in Torture' (2008–09, HL Paper 152, HC 230).

[33] A Tyrie, R Gough, and S McCracken, *Account Rendered: Extraordinary Rendition and Britain's Role* (London, Biteback Publishing, 2011). On the work of this group, see http://www.extraordinaryrendition.org.

nature, legislative accountability may foster and promote civil society forms of accountability. Those who define accountability as requiring control and sanctions may dismiss this accountability as 'just talk', but as suggested in the first part of this chapter, such an approach discounts how awareness and criticism of secret state activities are necessary preconditions for any subsequent sanction. The broader form of accountability has its own value in encouraging democratic deliberation and debate about security policies.

C. Executives

Useful distinctions can be drawn between permanent executive review and watchdog agencies on the one hand and, on the other hand, *ad hoc* ones that are appointed by governments in response to particular scandals. The Arar Commission that was appointed by the Canadian government in 2004 to examine the role of Canadian officials in the US rendition of Maher Arar to Syria was an example of the latter. Such inquiries can be effective, especially if they are given jurisdiction to examine all relevant questions and materials and if they have unfettered access to secret information. This was true of the Arar Commission, but even it had no jurisdiction over foreign officials who were involved in Arar's initial immigration detention in the United States, his rendition to Syria, and his subsequent torture in that country. The Commission did, however, extend invitations to both the American and Syrian governments to participate in the inquiry process. Both governments declined, and the US government maintained Arar on a terrorist watch list even after he had been exonerated in a three-volume report by the Canadian inquiry headed by a respected judge.[34]

Although the Arar Commission was unable to compel the governments of the United States and Syria to participate and had no ability to require governments to follow its recommendations, the Canadian government accepted its recommendations shortly after the release of its first report and paid Arar over CAD$10 million in compensation.[35] The success of the Canadian inquiry can be contrasted with an aborted *ad hoc* inquiry in the United Kingdom into possible complicity with torture. The UK inquiry was dogged from the start with concerns about its independence from Government, in terms of both its composition and its access to secret information.[36]

[34] Commission of Inquiry into the Actions of Canadian Officials in Relation to Maher Arar ('Arar Commission'), 'Report of the Events Relating to Maher Arar' (2006), available at http://publications.gc.ca/site/eng/9.688875/publication.html (last accessed 26 March 2019). See also K Roach, 'Uneasy Neighbors: Comparative American and Canadian Counter-Terrorism' (2012) 38 *William Mitchell Law Review* 1701.

[35] Canadian Broadcasting Corporation, 'Ottawa Reaches $10 Million Settlement with Arar', *CBC News*, (25 January 2007).

[36] See generally K Roach, 'Public Inquiries as an Attempt to Fill Accountability Gaps Left by Judicial and Legislative Review' in F Davies and F De Londras (eds), *Critical Debates on Counter-Terrorism Judicial Review* (Cambridge, Cambridge University Press, 2014).

One problem with many permanent executive review bodies is that they are tied to the jurisdiction of particular security agencies. As governments increasingly take a whole-of-government (and transnational) approach to security matters, the result can be an 'accountability gap'. For example, there are separate dedicated review bodies in Canada that can examine the Royal Canadian Mounted Police and the Canadian Security Intelligence Service (CSIS), who were both key players in the Canadian end of Maher Arar's rendition. Those bodies, the Civilian Review and Complaints body (for the RCMP) and the Security Intelligence Review Commission (for CSIS) cannot share classified information with each other, and they have no jurisdiction to examine the conduct of border security and foreign affairs officials, who were also important Canadian actors in the Arar affair. The actions of such officials likely would not have been examined by any official state reviewer had the Canadian government not exercised its discretion to appoint a multiyear and multimillion-dollar inquiry into the Arar case. As recommended by the Arar Commission, however, pending legislation in Canada will create a new and permanent review body with government-wide jurisdiction to review intelligence and security matters.[37] This is a necessary form of catch-up to whole-of-government security approaches. Nevertheless, even such a state-of-the-art, whole-of-government permanent domestic review agency will not have jurisdiction to compel cooperation from foreign allies, even when, as in the Arar rendition, the foreign agencies played the dominant role in the counterterrorism activity being reviewed.

From a purely domestic perspective, accountability by executive bodies may be the most important form of accountability because executive watchdogs are more likely than courts or legislatures to have access to secret information and to be able to discover wrongful conduct by security agencies. With respect to transnational counterterrorism activities, however, judicial and legislative forms of accountability may be more important because they often have higher profiles and visibility than executive watchdog agencies such as American Inspectors General and the UK Independent Reviewer of Terrorism Legislation, who issue annual and topical reports that are often detailed but also subject to redaction. At the same time, however, executive watchdog reviews can provide detailed foundations for more accessible criticisms of security activity in courts and legislatures.

A final consideration with respect to the role that domestic executive bodies can play in transnational accountability is their ability to reveal previously secret information. Executive review bodies may often be given access to classified information. This allows them to ask security agencies informed questions, but it also places limits on what can be made public. The same dilemma also

[37] See National Security Act (2017) introduced as Bill C-59: 'An Act Respecting National Security Matters' HC Bill C-59 (2015–16–17) First Reading (17 June 2017), http://www.parl.ca/DocumentViewer/en/42-1/bill/C-59/first-reading.

confronts legislative committees that have access to secret information. More thought should be given to allowing both legislative and executive watchdogs to challenge governmental claims to secrecy, especially those based on harms to foreign relations that could exist by exposing any information about the role of foreign agencies in transnational counterterrorism. In Canada, the Arar Commission went to court to challenge the Canadian government's claims of secrecy;[38] and the Commission used this power with some success to place more information about the American role in Arar's rendition into the public domain.

IV. SUPRANATIONAL STATE MECHANISMS OF ACCOUNTABILITY

A. Courts

Like domestic courts, supranational courts have played an increased role in accountability since 9/11 with respect to counterterrorism. A number of rendition victims have commenced litigation before the European Court of Human Rights (ECtHR), alleging that Member States were complicit in American-led rendition, detention, and torture at various secret prisons. Such litigation, including the cases described below, has provided rendition victims with a venue where, with the assistance of various civil society groups, they have been able to advance and publicise their claims.

Khaled El-Masri made a successful claim for damages in the ECtHR against Macedonia for its complicity in a 23-day detention in that country as well as his subsequent detention for four months in a secret CIA detention facility in Afghanistan.[39] A striking aspect of this case was the wide range of evidence that the applicants were able to place before the Court. The Court relied upon investigative reports prepared by Senator Dick Marty for the European Parliament as well as works of investigative journalism and reports by Human Rights Watch and Amnesty International. In the end, the Court only awarded El-Masri €60,000 in just satisfaction (though he had claimed €300,000). Nonetheless, from an accountability as opposed to a redress perspective, the litigation represented the pinnacle or confirmation of other accountability measures taken by state and non-state actors.

Somewhat more generous damage awards of €100,000 each were made by the ECtHR in two subsequent cases brought by Abd al-Rahim al-Nashiri and Abu Zubaydah. In these cases, the damage awards were largely symbolic because both applicants remained in American custody in Guantanamo, and any payment to them was prohibited under the UN 1267 listing process.[40] Nevertheless, the

[38] *Canada (Commission of Inquiry) v Canada (Attorney General)* (2007) FC 766.

[39] *El-Masri v The Former Yugoslav Republic of Macedonia*, Application 39630/09 (13 December 2012) (Grand Chamber).

[40] See UNSC Resolution 1267 (above n 17).

ECtHR again served as an instrument of accountability, helping to combat Polish denial about the role of that country in hosting a CIA black site.[41] In this case, the Court again relied upon reports prepared by legislatures and civil society groups but strengthened its fact-finding legitimacy by allowing the authors of some of the reports to be cross-examined.

The ECtHR also found that Italy violated the rights of Abu Omar (Hassan Mustafa Osama Nasr) for its role in his capture in Milan and subsequent rendition by the United States to Egypt.[42] The case demonstrates how national and supranational accountability measures can reinforce each other. Italian prosecutors investigated both Italian and American officials for their role in the abduction and convicted many of them. The American executive, however, refused to extradite their officials, and the Italian executive has pardoned some of the convicted American officials, including one who was extradited to Italy when she visited Portugal.[43] Thus, American officials have typically escaped punishment. Nevertheless, they have faced the exposure and criticism that comes with accountability. For some, this will not be enough, but it also illustrates the difficulty of imposing controls and sanctions for transnational counterterrorism abuses.

The ECtHR in the Abu Omar case again made effective use of the principles of free evidence in the face of Italy's denial that its agents had anything to do with Abu Omar's abduction in Milan. In the end, it remains highly unlikely that any American official will be extradited or punished for egregious counterterrorism abuse. This may look like a failure of accountability for those who associate accountability with control and punishment. Again, however, this understanding of accountability is both too pessimistic and positivistic. It discounts the continued and indeed unprecedented exposure and criticism of US use of rendition and torture in the aftermath of 9/11.

B. Legislatures

Both the European Parliament and the Parliamentary Assembly of the Council of Europe have played prominent roles with respect to transnational counterterrorism accountability. These two European legislatures have passed a number of resolutions exposing and denouncing the role of various member states in renditions and CIA black sites.

[41] *Al Nashiri v Poland* (No 28761/11) decided 24 July 2014.

[42] *Nasr and Ghali v Italy* (No 44883/09) decided 23 February 2016.

[43] R Hersher, 'Ex-CIA Officer in Rendition Case Is Released after Italy Grants Partial Clemency', *National Public Radio* (1 March 2017), http://www.npr.org/sections/thetwo-way/2017/03/01/517916196/italy-grants-partial-clemency-to-ex-cia-officer-over-extraordinary-rendition.

A 2007 Resolution of the European Parliament on this subject contained 234 paragraphs.[44] The Resolution referred to leaked information about renditions and called on judicial, legislative, and executive authorities in EU Member States to continue investigations into such matters. The Resolution also endorsed the type of non-control-based understanding of accountability used in this chapter when it stated that the European Parliament:

> Believes that the serious lack of concrete answers to the questions raised by victims, non-governmental organisations (NGOs), the media and parliamentarians has only served to strengthen the validity of already well-documented allegations.[45]

In other words, the Resolution effectively called on states to respond to allegations of misconduct made by both state and non-state institutions including the media and civil society. Another feature of this 2007 Resolution is that it 'called out' various countries and condemned specific actions, including Italian involvement in the abduction and rendition of Abu Omar, as well as documented stopovers of CIA flights in the United Kingdom.

A less elaborate 2006 Resolution by the Parliamentary Assembly of the Council of Europe criticised both American and European involvement with renditions in part by noting:

> [A]cross the world, the United States has progressively woven a clandestine 'spiderweb' of disappearances, secret detentions and unlawful inter-state transfers, often encompassing countries notorious for their use of torture. Hundreds of persons have become entrapped in this web, in some cases merely suspected of sympathising with a presumed terrorist organisation.
>
> The spiderweb has been spun out with the collaboration or tolerance of many countries, including several Council of Europe member states. This co-operation, which took place in secret and without any democratic legitimacy, has allowed the development of a system that is utterly incompatible with the fundamental principles of the Council of Europe.[46]

These supranational legislative resolutions, like the decisions of the ECtHR examined above, rely heavily on the work of non-state actors such as the investigative media and civil society groups. The cumulative result of these overlapping forms of accountability may place more pressure on security agencies to explain and perhaps adjust their behaviour.

Both the European Parliament and the Parliamentary Assembly of the Council of Europe have also commissioned investigators to assist the work of

[44] European Parliament Resolution on Transportation and Illegal Detention of Prisoners, P6-TA(2007)0032, http://www.europarl.europa.eu/sides/getDoc.do?pubRef=-//EP//NONSGML+TA+P6-TA-2007-0032+0+DOC+PDF+V0//EN.

[45] Ibid, para 14.

[46] Parliamentary Assembly of the Council of Europe, 'Alleged Secret Detentions and Unlawful Inter-State Transfers of Detainees Involving Council of Europe Member States', Resolution 1507 (2006), http://assembly.coe.int/nw/xml/XRef/Xref-XML2HTML-en.asp?fileid=17454&lang=en, paras 5–6.

the legislatures. In this regard, the reports of Senator Dick Marty played an important role in exposing and popularising knowledge about extraordinary rendition.[47] One advantage of legislatures is that if properly motivated, they can be more proactive than courts with respect to accountability.

The first report by Dick Marty to the Parliamentary Assembly of the Council of Europe in June 2006 admitted that there was an absence of 'hard evidence, at least according to the strict meaning of the term'.[48] At the same time, drawing on a wide range of public sources, Marty concluded that there were patterns of conduct in relation to the renditions, CIA black sites, and the complicity of various European states in such activities.

The European Parliament in turn appointed Giovanni Fava to investigate CIA prisons. This inquiry held 130 meetings and sent delegations to many countries.[49] Although it did not receive complete cooperation from all states, the Committee was able to identify over 1,200 CIA flights in European airspace from the end of 2001 to the end of 2005. This evidence in turn has been used by the ECtHR.[50]

The lack of cooperation of some states in the above transnational accountability efforts is an intractable problem. In my view, it underlines that it is unrealistic to expect complete international cooperation with respect to security matters and especially with respect to accountability for abuse of security powers. This supports the approach taken in this chapter to define accountability not as control and sanction, but as demands for explanations and justifications. Such an approach allows transnational actors such as the European Parliament and the ECtHR to draw adverse conclusions about even a noncooperating state's conduct in the absence of persuasive explanations and justifications of the state's impugned conduct.

The gradual discovery of European involvement in US programs of rendition and secret prisons suggests that accountability for transnational counterterrorism is likely to be an incremental and iterative process that is achieved by a variety of state and non-states institutions working on the same subject over time. The results of such accountability efforts may not always be dramatic or always consistent, but it is difficult to deny that over the last decade there has been much previously secret information about transnational counterterrorism abuses placed into the public domain. The result may even have played some role in subsequent American restrictions on the use of rendition and secret prisons.

[47] See, for example, D Marty, 'Alleged Secret Transfers and Unlawful Inter-State Transfers Involving Council of Europe Member States', Council of Europe Doc 10957 (12 June 2006), available at http://assembly.coe.int/nw/xml/XRef/Xref-DocDetails-EN.asp?fileid=11527.

[48] Ibid, para 287.

[49] European Parliament, 'CIA Activities in Europe: European Parliament Adopts Final Report Deploring Passivity from Some Member States', press release (14 February 2007), http://www.europarl.europa.eu/sides/getDoc.do?language=EN&type=IM-PRESS&reference=20070209IPR02947.

[50] *Al Nashiri v Poland* (above n 41) paras 266–67.

C. Executives

Both the Council of Europe and the European Union have several executive bodies that can investigate transnational counterterrorism activities. In the Council of Europe, these bodies include the Commissioner for Human Rights, who writes reports on privacy,[51] and a Committee for the Prevention of Torture, which issues reports on various countries. The European Union has both an Ombudsperson and a Data Protection Supervisor, who could in appropriate cases also examine matters involving transnational counterterrorism, though the EU bodies in particular seem to be directed at activities at the EU level.[52]

Supranational executive bodies, like supranational courts and legislatures, often have to rely on public information, such as information on the CIA's secret prisons in Europe. This underlines how the accountability that they exercise is often dependent on domestic demands for explanations and publicity of security activity, including the actions of leakers. Just as it is difficult to draw bright-line distinctions between domestic and transnational security activities, so too is it difficult to draw such distinctions between such accountability mechanisms.

Supranational executive bodies seem to have had less impact in publicising and criticising transnational counterterrorism activities than either supranational legislatures or courts. Although executive bodies in theory have superior ability to investigate and closely supervise transnational counterterrorism activities, the post-9/11 story has largely involved the politicisation of successive security scandals from rendition to the mass surveillance revealed by the Snowden leaks. With respect to these matters, the more visible processes used by courts and legislatures may be more important than the detailed and often less newsworthy processes employed by executive bodies. This underlines how state-based accountability mechanisms need to interact with non-state actors, most notably the media, in order to achieve maximum exposure and demands on security agencies to explain and justify their conduct.

One supranational executive institution that has emerged in the post-9/11 era is the UN Security Council Ombudsperson for the 1267 sanctions committee. The creation of this office in 2010 can be seen as a direct response to growing concerns about the fairness of the listing process, including successful judicial challenges to listing in both national and supranational courts and related criticisms of the listing process by civil society groups and academics.[53] Since the creation of the position, the Ombudsperson has completed investigation of 74 cases, with 52 individuals and 28 entities being delisted and 17 delisting requests refused.[54]

[51] Council of Europe Commissioner for Human Rights, 'The Rule of Law on the Internet and in the Wider Digital World' (2014).

[52] For the work of the European Union Ombudsperson, see https://www.ombudsman.europa.eu/. For the work of the European Union Data Protection Supervisor see https://edps.europa.eu/.

[53] For this background, see Forcese and Roach (above n 14).

[54] UN Office of the Ombudsperson website, https://www.un.org/sc/suborg/en/sc/ombudsperson/status-of-cases (last accessed 2 September 2018).

Although the Ombudsperson does not have guaranteed access to secret information, she requests information and if need be attends at relevant capitals to receive information from states about terrorist listings. The Ombudsperson has entered into arrangements with 17 states to provide access to classified information, including most recently the United States and Canada.[55] At the same time, this access to classified information comes with a price: petitioners do not have access to the final reports that the Ombudsperson issues to the 1267 Committee. A former Ombudsperson noted in 2015 that the process is 'unnecessarily shrouded in mystery. Regrettably, this means that, while detailed documents exist to demonstrate the reasoned nature of the process, they are not made available.'[56]

The Ombudsperson has also raised concerns about the lack of guarantees of institutional independence, concluding that the terms of the consultancy contract are 'fundamentally inconsistent with the independent role and functions of the Ombudsperson'.[57] These are real concerns, and the effectiveness of an accountability mechanism can be undermined by real or perceived lack of independence. The example of the 1267 Ombudsperson also underlines how executive watchdogs who attempt to control security activities and provide redress (in this case by requests for delisting) may be limited by their focus on individual cases and by their access to secret information. Their ability to criticise security conduct may therefore be more constrained than other actors such as UN special rapporteurs, civil society groups, and domestic courts, who have at various times been very critical of the 1267 listing process.

V. NON-STATE MECHANISMS OF ACCOUNTABILITY

Most analyses of accountability focus on state institutions at the national and sometimes supranational levels. State-centric understandings of accountability ignore the increasingly important role played by non-state actors such as private policing. The private sector has assumed an expanding role with respect to counterterrorism. Financial institutions are the frontline enforcers of terrorism financing regulation; internet companies similarly are in a position to censor or remove much terrorist propaganda.

A focus on the state also ignores the critical role that the media, civil society, and whistleblowers have played with respect to accountability. An examination of non-state actors paints a fuller picture of accountability, but it also reveals accountability to be contingent and fragile: the media and civil society groups are

[55] UN Office of the Ombudsperson website, 'Access to Classified Information', https://www.un.org/sc/suborg/en/ombudsperson/classified_information (last accessed 2 September 2018).

[56] UN Security Council, 'Report of the Office of the Ombudsperson Pursuant to Security Council Resolution 2161 (2014)', S/2015/533 (14 July 2015), http://www.un.org/ga/search/view_doc.asp?symbol=S/2015/533, para 40.

[57] Ibid, para 61.

subject to economic pressures, and whistleblowers are subject to prosecutions. Nonetheless, the role of non-state actors is virtually limitlessness, and what follows is simply a partial illustration of the important but often neglected role that they play in accountability processes.

A. The Media and Academe

A number of investigative journalists have written important stories about the CIA rendition programme and European complicity in it. For example, Stephen Grey, a British investigative journalist, broke a story about rendition in a 2004 article in the *New Statesman* entitled 'America's Gulag'.[58] The article won the Amnesty International UK media award, illustrating how the work of investigative journalists can be reinforced and often amplified through the work of civil society advocacy groups such as Human Rights Watch and Amnesty International, which have issued reports on renditions.[59] Grey followed up in 2006 with an important book, *Ghost Plane: The True Story of the CIA Rendition Program*,[60] which won an award for investigative reporting on human rights from the Overseas Press Club of America. Its award citation explains that the book was:

> … the consummation of years of investigation, not only by the author, but, as he acknowledges, [by] the informal global network of journalists with whom he collaborated to reveal the murky world of rendition, extraordinary rendition and proxy torture. By tracing the landings and takeoffs of clumsily concealed CIA flights, his work not only demonstrates concerned investigative journalism in action, it lifts the lid on a global gulag of prisons and torture chambers, assembled by US officials in defiance of domestic and international human rights law.[61]

In 2005, Jane Mayer, an American investigative journalist, also published an important article in the *New Yorker* on the CIA rendition programme.[62] She followed up in 2007 with another *New Yorker* article, this one on CIA black sites,[63] and in 2008 published an award-winning book, *The Dark Side*.[64]

The work of these and other journalists has been critical in exposing the US rendition programme, and this sort of exposure can in turn feed into other

[58] S Grey, 'America's Gulag', *New Statesman* (17 May 2004).

[59] Human Rights Watch, 'Double Jeopardy: CIA Renditions to Jordan' (April 2008), https://www.hrw.org/sites/default/files/reports/jordan0408_1.pdf; and Amnesty International, *State of Denial: Europe's Role in Rendition and Secret Detention* (London, Amnesty International, 2008).

[60] S Grey, *Ghost Plane: The True Story of the CIA Rendition Program* (London, St Martin's Press, 2007).

[61] Ibid (back cover).

[62] J Mayer, 'Outsourcing Torture: The Secret History of America's "Extraordinary Rendition" Program', *New Yorker* (14 February 2005).

[63] J Mayer, 'The CIA's Black Sites', *New Yorker* (13 August 2007).

[64] J Mayer, *The Dark Side: The Inside Story of How the War on Terror Turned into a War on American Ideals* (New York, Anchor Press, 2008).

accountability measures in legislatures, courts, and civil society. Despite its fragile economics, the investigative media has successfully forced security agencies to explain their conduct in a few instances. For example, the *New York Times* played a critical role in 2005 in exposing surveillance of Americans by the National Security Agency. The public exposure subsequently led to civil society mobilisation, lawsuits, and legislative reforms.[65]

Such successes notwithstanding, it would be manifestly unsafe to rely on the media playing a similar role in the future. The media is faced with an obsolete and quickly declining market model. To be sure, non-traditional (and unpaid) media may fill the gaps, but a blog on the internet is much less likely to feed legislative, executive, or judicial processes of accountability than established and credible news sources such as the *New York Times*, *Der Spiegel*, and *The Guardian* which have played a key role in exposing many post-9/11 abuses. In other words, the elite and traditional media has an accountability advantage over new media. The media is also heavily reliant on security officials being willing to talk to them. This may change given the increasing post-Snowden crack down on state officials who have or ever had access to secret information on discussing matters in the media.

Like the media, the academy also plays a role with respect to accountability in the form of demanding access to information about security activities and demanding explanations and justifications. Academics who gain expertise and experience about security powers may be in a good position to question security agencies about the way they exercise their counterterrorism powers. Like journalists, many academics who specialise in national security make use of access to information laws to obtain detailed information about otherwise secret security activities by states and corporations. In the United States and elsewhere, academics have influenced policy on national security activities, often by using unconventional means of publicity such as blogs, 'instant books', and op-ed commentary in the traditional media.[66] Again, this illustrates the interactive and iterative nature of accountability that focuses on transparency and justifiable explanations for security conduct.

B. Leakers and Whistleblowers

The role of the media with respect to accountability for national security activities critically depends on its ability to speak to present and former security officials. The traditional media, like the security services themselves, take great

[65] See E Lichtblau, *Bush's Law: The Remaking of American Justice* (New York, Anchor, 2008).

[66] In the United States, blogs such as *Just Security* and *Lawfare* play an important role and often interact with the traditional media. For further reflections on the role of academics, see K Roach, 'Criminal Justice and National Security Reform in a Time of Populism' (2017) 64 *Criminal Law Quarterly* 286.

pains to protect their sources, but expanding surveillance capabilities make it more difficult for reporters to guarantee their sources' anonymity.

In the United States, a number of security officials have been prosecuted for leaking information to reporters. For example, an ex-CIA official, John Kiriakou, who spoke to the media about matters involving detention and torture, was prosecuted under the Espionage Act and eventually pled guilty and received a 2.5-year prison sentence.[67] The Obama Administration conducted at least eight other prosecutions for leaks – more than under all previous Presidents combined.[68] The United States has differed from many other democracies in not accepting prior restraint on freedom of expression,[69] but this robust First Amendment tradition has been challenged by the Trump Administration, which has vowed to prosecute all known leakers (but has yet to mount any high-profile prosecutions such as those by the Obama Administration).[70] In any event, many other democracies can rely on their version of an Official Secrets Act to prosecute leakers.

Whistleblowers are distinct from leakers because they use state-authorised procedures to reveal their concerns about misconduct.[71] State-authorised whistleblowing can be an attractive form of accountability that mitigates the real dangers that those who leak information to the press or civil society might inadvertently jeopardise ongoing investigations and the safety of sources. Nevertheless, such options depend on the viability of official review bodies and their ability to ensure that only legitimate secrets are protected from disclosure. Again, the picture that emerges is of accountability processes that require multiple and often mutually dependent institutions. The limited success of whistleblowing illustrates how accountability is a contingent and fragile process that changes in response to new attempts to prevent and punish those who leak security information.

C. Civil Society Groups

Effective review depends on the ability of the reviewer to 'follow the trail' and mirror the activities that are being reviewed.[72] This fundamental principle helps

[67] J Jouvena, 'Former CIA Official Sentenced to 30 Months in Prison', *Washington Post* (25 January 2013).

[68] C Savage and E Sullivan, 'Leak Investigations Triple under Trump, Sessions Says', *New York Times* (4 August 2017); and M Sullivan, 'The Dangers of Suppressing the Leaks', *New York Times* (9 March 2013).

[69] *New York Times v United States*, 403 US 713 (1971).

[70] Savage and Sullivan (above n 68).

[71] See, for example, the Canadian Security of Information Act (1985), RSC 1985 c O-5, s 15 (limited public interest defence to leaking offences requiring prior disclosure to designated officials).

[72] For a justification of this principle, see Commission of Inquiry, 'A New Review Mechanism for the RCMP' (above n 1) 477–82.

explain the general pessimism about the ability to impose accountability for transnational terrorism. As discussed above, transnational institutions generally have weak, nascent, or nonexistent accountability mechanisms, and even the most robust of national mechanisms have limited ability to reach out and review activities that involve foreign states.

As David Cole has argued there is a need to pay attention to the role of civil society groups in providing accountability. Indeed, Cole has shown that such groups effectively enforce standards such as those found in the American Constitution.[73] What Cole observes in the American domestic context may be even more true in the transnational context, where civil society groups have played a key role in publicising violations of international law. For example, Amnesty International released a detailed forty-six-page report called *Partners in Crime: Europe's Role in US Renditions* in June 2006 that identified seven European countries as complicit in the rendition of named prisoners.[74] This was followed up in 2008 with a 76-page report entitled *State of Denial: Europe's Role in Rendition and Secret Detention*, which urged European states to investigate, provide reparations, and bring perpetrators such as those involved in the kidnapping of Abu Omar to justice.[75] Human Rights Watch similarly engaged with the issue of rendition with a series of reports, starting with one in 2004 called *Empty Promises* that detailed the failure of diplomatic assurances to prevent mistreatment in countries such as Egypt and Syria.[76] The next year it issued two reports, one focused on Maher Arar's rendition, which was used by the Canadian inquiry into the rendition, and another called *Black Hole*, which focused on the fate of those rendered to Egypt.[77] Human Rights Watch also published a 2007 report, *Ghost Prisoner*, on CIA detention sites;[78] and in December 2015, it issued a 170-page report that drew on details from a US Senate Select Committee on Intelligence investigation and called for the reopening of criminal investigations into a number of named US officials, including former President George W Bush and former Vice President Dick Cheney.[79]

[73] D Cole, 'Where Liberty Lies: Civil Society and Individual Rights after 9/11' (2012) 57 *Wayne Law Review* 1203, 1260; and D Cole, *Engines of Liberty* (New York, New Press, 2016).

[74] Amnesty International, 'Partners in Crime: Europe's Role in US Renditions', EUR 01/008/2006 (June 2006), https://www.amnesty.org/download/Documents/76000/eur010082006en.pdf.

[75] Amnesty International, *State of Denial* (above n 59).

[76] Human Rights Watch, 'Empty Promises: Diplomatic Assurances No Safeguard against Torture' (14 April 2004), https://www.hrw.org/report/2004/04/14/empty-promises/diplomatic-assurances-no-safeguard-against-torture.

[77] Human Rights Watch, 'Report to the Canadian Commission of Inquiry into the Actions of Canadian Officials in Relation to Maher Arar' (7 June 2005), https://www.hrw.org/legacy/backgrounder/eca/canada/arar/arar_testimony.pdf; and Human Rights Watch, 'Black Hole: The Fate of Islamists Rendered to Egypt' (May 2005), https://www.hrw.org/sites/default/files/reports/egypt0505.pdf.

[78] Human Rights Watch, 'Ghost Prisoner: Two Years in Secret CIA Detention' (February 2007), https://www.hrw.org/reports/2007/us0207/us0207webwcover.pdf.

[79] Human Rights Watch, 'No More Excuses: A Roadmap to Justice for CIA Torture' (December 2015), https://www.hrw.org/sites/default/files/report_pdf/us1215web.pdf.

These series of reports follow patterns that demonstrate the iterative and cumulative processes of accountability. An open question in the next decade, however, will be whether such mechanisms, which were relatively effective with respect to torture (regarding which international law prohibitions are absolute), will be as effective with respect to surveillance, speech, and targeted killing, regarding which international law is less clear.

D. Corporations

The Snowden revelations have made clear how a variety of corporations are involved in mass surveillance. The publicity of these revelations since 2013 has placed new pressures on these corporations. This opens up possibilities that the corporations themselves may become agents of accountability by exposing and criticising attempts by governments to have them cooperate in counterterrorism activities; they may be influenced by consumer concerns about their participation in such activities.

As with many forms of accountability, corporate accountability may be connected with other forms of accountability, such as those involving civil society groups. For example, even before the Snowden revelations, the civil society group Reprieve had a campaign designed to question various corporations about alleged involvement in renditions and black site operations.[80] Issues of corporate accountability will become only more important as states outsource counterterrorism work in part to avoid and minimise accountability.

Apple refused to help decrypt a cellular phone in relation to the investigations of the Islamic-State-inspired San Bernardino shootings, even in the face of a court order.[81] Apple responded to the demand with a letter to its customers explaining that while it had cooperated with the FBI on other matters and would comply with 'valid subpoenas and search warrants', it would not place the privacy and data security of its customer at risk by creating a 'backdoor' to the iPhone.[82]

That said, corporate power can cut both ways. Twitter, Facebook, and other social media companies are playing an important role as frontline censors of accounts associated with the Islamic State, often without state policies or even basic transparency.[83] The 'Twitter Rules' prohibit among other matters 'certain types of content that glorifies violence or the perpetrator of a violent act',

[80] See the Reprieve website, http://www.reprieve.org.uk/renditions-inc/ (last accessed 12 December 2018).

[81] S Dredge and D Yadron, 'Apple Challenges "Chilling" Demand to Decrypt San Bernardino Shooter's iPhone', *Guardian* (17 February 2016).

[82] T Cook (Apple Inc), 'A Message to our Customers' (16 February 2016), http://www.apple.com/customer-letter/.

[83] A Tugend, 'Barred from Facebook and Wondering Why', *New York Times* (19 September 2014).

including 'celebrating any violent act in a manner that may inspire others to replicate it'[84] – a standard that, if adopted, would be opposed in many democracies as a vague and unreasonable limit on freedom of expression. Financial institutions, which play a key role in terrorism financing regulation, may engage in ethnic and racial profiling. As has been argued by Natasha Tusikov, such 'private transactional regimes' often lack transparency.[85] Although they can be responsive to consumer demands and media criticism, they may not always act in a manner consistent with public values such as freedom of expression and equality, and they may also exercise state-like powers.

To the extent that corporations exercise counterterrorism powers, they need to be subject to the range of accountability measures that have been discussed in this chapter. This suggests that customers of such corporations have an important role to play in demanding explanations and justifications for the increasing role that corporations play in counterterrorism, including the regulation of terrorism financing and the censoring of terrorist-related speech on the internet.

VI. CONCLUSION

The prospects for accountability for transnational counterterrorism are bleak, if accountability requires control, punishment, and redress. National institutions struggle with the challenges presented by a whole-of-government approach to terrorism, and these challenges are much greater when domestic security agencies interact, as they frequently do, with foreign agencies. In addition, there are relatively few state institutions dedicated to transnational accountability. Moreover, those that exist, such as the UN 1267 Ombudsperson, often lack complete access to secret information or intelligence that is possessed at the domestic level.

Such a pessimistic conclusion about the lack of accountability for transnational counterterrorism is, however, based on a flawed and limited understanding of accountability. As argued in the first part of this chapter, accountability can be achieved whenever those in power are forced to explain and justify their actions. In other words, accountability should not be limited to oversight mechanisms that imply some measure of control over the activities. This broader understanding of accountability means it can be promoted by a broad range of non-state actors, particularly the media and civil society groups.

To be sure, those who equate accountability with control, sanction, and redress will not accept the above definition of accountability. But even such critics must acknowledge that publicity, questioning, and critique around post-9/11

[84] Twitter Inc, 'The Twitter Rules', https://about.twitter.com/en_us/safety/enforcing-our-rules.html (last accessed 4 February 2019).

[85] N Tusikov, *Chokepoints: Global Private Regulation on the Internet* (Oakland, University of California Press, 2016) 25.

abuses of human rights (including those related to transnational terrorist listing processes, rendition, and CIA black sites) are generally a necessary prelude to control, sanction, and redress.

The accountability that has been achieved with respect to transnational counterterrorism abuses has been contingent and fragile. It has depended in no small part on the work of investigative journalists and the willingness of various security officials to speak to these reporters and to leak secret information. If conditions change – for example, if potential leakers are deterred or if resources available for the investigative media or civil society advocacy dramatically decrease – it is entirely possible that the transnational abuses will no longer be revealed and criticised. Indeed, it is possible that abuses may increase in the coming years as countries such as Egypt, Russia, China, and the United States become even more aggressive in counterterrorism. These states may be better able to maintain secrecy over future counterterrorism abuses than the abuses committed in the decade after 9/11.

One normative contribution of this chapter has been to argue that it is a mistake to equate accountability with state-based attempts to control and sanction the activities of security agencies. To be sure, control, sanction, and redress as responses to human rights abuses are desirable, but such coercive processes depend on prior processes whereby such abuses are publicised, and security agencies are given opportunity to explain and justify their actions. Although it is true that American officials have not been punished or otherwise had to pay for participating in renditions that resulted in torture and secret detention, it is no small accomplishment that such abuses are now widely known and in the public domain.

This chapter has also provided a taxonomy of accountability measures that can be applied to transnational counterterrorism measures. This taxonomy has emphasised the importance of both state actors and non-state actors such as the media, civil society, and corporations. It has also highlighted the distinct but overlapping roles played by legislatures, the executive, and the judiciary in promoting accountability. With respect to both national and supranational levels of governance, it is useful to break down accountability measures on a traditional separation of powers basis. Adjudicative bodies have demonstrated a surprising willingness to review transnational counterterrorism activities. For example, the European Court of Human Rights has indirectly reviewed American counterterrorism activities involving rendition and secret detention. The European Parliament has also conducted multiple investigations of rendition. Some may disparage such investigations as journalistic, but this reveals a limited understanding of accountability that does not include publicity and also neglects how state processes can reinforce and legitimate the role of the investigative media. Even though in theory, executive watchdogs are in the best position to discover security wrongdoing, legislatures and courts have played a more public and important role with respect to matters such as rendition and mass surveillance. The fact that there are so few supranational executive watchdogs may help to explain why the executive role in accountability has been overshadowed by better publicised forms of judicial and legislative accountability.

A complete account of transnational accountability should not be limited to official state institutions of accountability but should include non-state institutions, including the media, and the corporate and civil society sectors. Indeed, these institutions have multinational structures that more closely mirror the multinational activities that are being reviewed. They also have a tendency to focus on international standards and to point out shortcomings and gaps in official state accountability processes.

Non-state forms of accountability are important, but they lack the coercive powers of the state. They depend on the willingness of those with knowledge of secret counterterrorism activities to reveal that knowledge and, in the case of corporations, an ability to reveal the demands that the state has made on them. This makes such forms of accountability especially vulnerable to attempts to deter and prosecute the revealing of information that the government has classified as secret. Although this chapter has suggested that the transnational accountability glass can be seen as half full, such a conclusion should not be equated with complacency. The accountability for post-9/11 abuses that has been achieved has been contingent and fragile. The increased emphasis on secrecy by the Trump Administration, paired with increased US aggressiveness, presents a grave danger to even the limited forms of accountability that have been achieved since 9/11.

Non-state forms of accountability are also dependent on economic factors. Corporations are unlikely to expose and resist demands by governments for counterterrorism cooperation in the absence of market demands for privacy. Market demands for privacy may be greater and have more of an impact on corporations than demands that corporations not be complicit in other forms of abuse, including torture. In other words, we may get only the accountability from corporations that we effectively demand.

The role of the investigative media remains extremely precarious and will only become more fragile if sources dry up or if the media themselves are threatened with prosecution or other sanctions for their work. The United States has been exceptional with respect to its rejection of prior restraint and the willingness of security officials to leak secret information. Civil society advocacy groups have played an important role, but they remain dependent on charitable giving, and countries such as China, Egypt, and Russia are making it difficult for such groups to conduct the international investigations required to understand and critique transnational counterterrorism. The use of war and targeted killing as methods of counterterrorism also poses formidable challenges for accountability because of a lack of detailed and accurate information about what is being done in the name of counterterrorism.[86]

[86] For discussion of targeted killing, see the chapter in this volume by Shiri Krebs.

This chapter has suggested that one's evaluation of accountability in the post-9/11 era will depend on one's definition of accountability. If accountability is reduced to control, sanction, and redress, then one's evaluation will be bleak. If, however, one accepts the argument in this chapter that accountability can be achieved by publicity and critique even in the absence of control and sanction, then there are reasons to conclude that the accountability glass is half full even while recognising that accountability will face severe challenges in the future.

The examples used in this chapter have suggested that there has been a surprising amount of exposure and critique of abuses such as renditions, listings, and mass surveillance in the decade after 9/11. It has also suggested that the sum of accountability instruments is much greater than their individual parts, and accountability activities by non-state actors such as the media and civil society have nourished accountability instruments by both domestic and supranational state bodies, including courts, legislatures, and executive watchdogs.

Accountability is often iterative, overlapping, and cumulative. The synergies obtained through multiple and even repetitious forms of accountability by supranational, state, and non-state actors should not be discounted even if they are not easily measured by traditional social science methods. Although there has been a surprising amount of information and questioning about post-9/11 transnational counterterrorism abuses, there is no guarantee that this accountability will continue in the future. Much accountability depends on the leaking of secret information and the economic viability and independence of non-state actors, including the investigative media and various civil society advocacy groups. We must all work to sustain even the limited forms of accountability that we have achieved in the past.

REFERENCES

Amnesty International, 'Partners in Crime: Europe's Role in US Renditions', EUR 01/008/2006 (June 2006), https://www.amnesty.org/download/Documents/76000/eur010082006en.pdf.

——, *State of Denial: Europe's Role in Rendition and Secret Detention* (London, Amnesty International, 2008).

Braithwaite, J, *Restorative Justice and Responsive Regulation* (Oxford, Oxford University Press, 2002).

Brunnée, J and Toope, S, *Legitimacy and Legality in International Law* (Cambridge, Cambridge University Press, 2010).

Canadian Broadcasting Corporation, 'Ottawa Reaches $10 Million Settlement with Arar', *CBC News* (25 January 2007).

Cole, D, *Engines of Liberty* (New York, New Press, 2016).

——, 'Where Liberty Lies: Civil Society and Individual Rights after 9/11' (2012) 57 *Wayne Law Review* 1203.

Commission of Inquiry into the Activities of Canadian Officials in Relation to Maher Arar, 'A New Review Mechanism for the RCMP's National Security Activities' (December 2006), http://www.sirc-csars.gc.ca/pdfs/cm_arar_rcmpgrc-eng.pdf.

——, 'Report of the Events Relating to Maher Arar' (2006), available at http://publications.gc.ca/site/eng/9.688875/publication.html (last accessed 26 March 2019).

Cook, T (Apple Inc), 'A Message to our Customers' (16 February 2016), http://www.apple.com/customer-letter/.

Council of Europe Commissioner for Human Rights, 'The Rule of Law on the Internet and in the Wider Digital World' (2014).

Dredge, S and Yadron, D, 'Apple Challenges "Chilling" Demand to Decrypt San Bernardino Shooter's iPhone', *Guardian* (17 February 2016).

Dworkin, R, *Taking Rights Seriously* (Cambridge, MA, Harvard University Press, 1977).

Emmons, A, 'The Country Paying Omar Khadr $10 million Is Not the Country that Tortured Him', *Intercept* (6 July 2017).

Forcese, C and Roach, K, 'Limping into the Future: The UN 1267 Committee at the Crossroads' (2010) 42 *George Washington International Law Review* 217.

Fuller, L, *The Morality of Law* (New Haven, Yale University Press, 1969).

Grey, S, 'America's Gulag', *New Statesman* (17 May 2004).

——, *Ghost Plane: The True Story of the CIA Rendition Program* (London, St Martin's Press, 2007).

Hersher, R, 'Ex-CIA Officer in Rendition Case Is Released after Italy Grants Partial Clemency', *National Public Radio* (1 March 2017), http://www.npr.org/sections/thetwo-way/2017/03/01/517916196/italy-grants-partial-clemency-to-ex-cia-officer-over-extraordinary-rendition.

Holmes, OW, 'The Path of the Law' (1897) 10 *Harvard Law Review* 457.

Human Rights Watch, 'Black Hole: The Fate of Islamists Rendered to Egypt' (May 2005), https://www.hrw.org/sites/default/files/reports/egypt0505.pdf.

——, 'Double Jeopardy: CIA Renditions to Jordan' (April 2008), https://www.hrw.org/sites/default/files/reports/jordan0408_1.pdf.

——, 'Empty Promises: Diplomatic Assurances No Safeguard against Torture' (14 April 2004),https://www.hrw.org/report/2004/04/14/empty-promises/diplomatic-assurances-no-safeguard-against-torture.

——, 'Ghost Prisoner: Two Years in Secret CIA Detention' (February 2007), https://www.hrw.org/reports/2007/us0207/us0207webwcover.pdf.

——, 'No More Excuses: A Roadmap to Justice for CIA Torture' (December 2015), https://www.hrw.org/sites/default/files/report_pdf/us1215web.pdf.

——, 'Report to the Canadian Commission of Inquiry into the Actions of Canadian Officials in Relation to Maher Arar' (7 June 2005), https://www.hrw.org/legacy/backgrounder/eca/canada/arar/arar_testimony.pdf.

Intelligence and Security Committee (UK), 'Rendition', Cm 7171 (July 2007), available at https://www.gov.uk/government/publications/rendition-report-by-the-intelligence-and-security-committee.

Joint Committee on Human Rights (UK) Committee, '23rd Report: Allegations of UK Complicity in Torture' (2008–09, HL Paper 152, HC 230).

Jouvena, J, 'Former CIA Official Sentenced to 30 Months in Prison', *Washington Post* (25 January 2013).

Lichtblau, E, *Bush's Law: The Remaking of American Justice* (New York, Anchor, 2008).

Mayer, J, 'The CIA's Black Sites', *New Yorker* (13 August 2007).

——, *The Dark Side: The Inside Story of How the War on Terror Turned into a War on American Ideals* (New York, Anchor Press, 2008).

——, 'Outsourcing Torture: The Secret History of America's "Extraordinary Rendition" Program', *New Yorker* (14 February 2005).

Parliamentary Assembly of the Council of Europe, 'Alleged Secret Detentions and Unlawful Inter-State Transfers of Detainees Involving Council of Europe Member States', Resolution 1507 (2006), http://assembly.coe.int/nw/xml/XRef/Xref-XML2HTML-en.asp?fileid=17454&lang=en.

Pfander, J, *Constitutional Torts and the War on Terror* (New York, Oxford University Press, 2017).

Roach, K, *The 9/11 Effect: Comparative Counter-Terrorism* (Cambridge, Cambridge University Press, 2011).

——, 'Criminal Justice and National Security Reform in a Time of Populism' (2017) 64 *Criminal Law Quarterly* 286.

——, 'Judicial Review of the State's Anti-Terrorism Activities' (2009) 3 *Indian Journal of Constitutional Law* 138.

——, 'Public Inquiries as an Attempt to Fill Accountability Gaps Left by Judicial and Legislative Review' in F Davies and F de Londras (eds), *Critical Debates on Counter-Terrorism Judicial Review* (Cambridge, Cambridge University Press, 2014).

——, 'Substitute Justice? Challenges to American Counter-Terrorism Activities in Non-American Courts' (2013) 84 *Mississippi Law Journal* 901.

——, 'Uneasy Neighbors: Comparative American and Canadian Counter-Terrorism' (2012) 38 *William Mitchell Law Review* 1701.

Savage, C and Sullivan, E, 'Leak Investigations Triple under Trump, Sessions Says', *New York Times* (4 August 2017).

Sullivan, M, 'The Dangers of Suppressing the Leaks', *New York Times* (9 March 2013).

Tugend, A, 'Barred from Facebook and Wondering Why', *New York Times* (19 September 2014).

Tusikov, N, *Chokepoints: Global Private Regulation on the Internet* (Oakland, University of California Press, 2016).

Twining, W, 'Other People's Power: The Bad Man and English Positivism, 1897–1997' (1997) 63(1) *Brooklyn Law Review* 189.

Tyrie, A, Gough, R, and McCracken, S, *Account Rendered: Extraordinary Rendition and Britain's Role* (London, Biteback Publishing, 2011).

UN Security Council, 'Report of the Office of the Ombudsperson Pursuant to Security Council Resolution 2161 (2014)', S/2015/533 (14 July 2015), http://www.un.org/ga/search/view_doc.asp?symbol=S/2015/533.

9

Security and Human Rights after the Nationalist Backlash

VICTOR V RAMRAJ

IN THE PREVIOUS edition of this book, the editors noted a tension between security and human rights in liberal democratic regimes. Terrorism seemed to require that human rights be tempered in response to security considerations; immigration law was deployed in service of security, and borders were hardened. At the same time, however, many facets of globalisation remained more or less intact: capital, goods, ideas continued to flow across borders. And human rights norms, however contested, could still be seen as part of a cosmopolitan legal order. Despite the threats a post-9/11 national security agenda posed for human rights, the United States continued to work through international institutions, including the United Nations Security Council, in its counterterrorism efforts.

However, geopolitical developments in 2016 suggest a challenge of a different order for those who seek to restrain state power through law, including human rights: a return to a kind of nationalism and xenophobia (Brexit, US protectionism, anti-immigration backlash) that is at odds with the human rights values and international institutions that emerged initially in the post-war era and were entrenched in the closing decades of the twentieth century. While post-9/11 tensions have continued to pose a serious threat to human rights, a retreat from internationalism, when coupled with the rise of nationalism and xenophobia, gives rise to another fundamental threat. Not only do these developments weaken human rights relative to security concerns, they also threaten to undermine the institutions that have embedded those rights in decision-making procedurals, creating the culture of justification that David Dyzenhaus and others appealed to in the previous edition of this book.[1]

[1] D Dyzenhaus, 'Deference, Security, and Human Rights' in BJ Goold and L Lazarus (eds), *Security and Human Rights* (Oxford, Hart Publishing, 2007) 137ff.

This chapter considers the potential threat to human rights posed by rising nationalism and its rejection of formal international institutions. It asks whether and how human rights and internationalism could withstand a rising nationalist tide. Specifically, assuming that economic globalisation is in retreat in at least some parts of the world and that some form of legal-political-economic consolidation is taking place within modern states, what are the implications of this shift for security and human rights? This chapter proposes that although international institutions remain under threat, human rights norms have been and continue to be embedded in a variety of transnational regulatory bodies, including non-state bodies, and need not wither in the face of nationalism and xenophobia. Moreover, examples from outside the liberal democracies that have long defended human rights show that human rights can moderate political and economic power even in contexts in which states are resistant to formal international institutions: the operation of the Equator Principles and the Accord on Fire and Safety in Bangladesh, as we shall see, offer helpful examples. Non-state mechanisms for resisting public and private concentrations of power can, in some contexts, be fragile. However, globalisation opens the door to the embedding of human rights norms into the fabric of a vast network and variety of institutions beyond and within the state that can collectively help to resist state overreach.

My argument takes the following path. In the first section of this chapter, I situate human rights and security at the turn of the last century, positioning the last decade of the twentieth century as a highwater mark in the history of human rights and internationalism, on the eve of the 9/11 attacks in 2001. I argue that although the responses to 9/11 could be seen in some respects as pushback against globalisation, they nevertheless continued to engage post-war international institutions in a direct and deliberate way. The second section considers the rising nationalism that was marked in 2016 by the Brexit vote in the United Kingdom; by the election of a President in the United States who promised a withdrawal from international institutions and the implementation of expressly protectionist and xenophobic trade and foreign policies; and by a rising anti-immigration backlash, particularly in but not limited to Europe. The third section considers the steady rise in the last decade of the twentieth century of transnational law and the embedding of legal norms, including human rights norms, in a variety of non-state institutions. It will show how these institutions can be used to resist state oppression, while acknowledging the challenges they face.

What will become clear in this chapter is that a consolidation of state institutions can only ever be partial, that threats to human rights and the means of defending them can come from both state and non-state actors, and that when state human rights institutions fails us, non-state institutions can provide, even temporarily, a shelter for human rights norms and resistance.

I. HUMAN RIGHTS, SECURITY, AND GLOBALISATION

Historians of human rights are divided as to their modern origins – and as to when precisely human rights history began. For some such as Laura Hunt, our modern conception of human rights can be understood only by looking beyond political history – including the American and French revolutions in the eighteenth century – to the social and psychological changes that allowed rights claims 'to make … sense in societies where they had not previously done so'.[2] For Hunt, it was the 'ability to empathize in new ways across class, race, sex and national boundaries' that had to be learned, and 'this learning emerged in the eighteenth century from a concatenation of new cultural practices that ranged from the increasing differentiation of domestic space to reading epistolary novels.'[3] These cultural practices allowed ordinary people to develop 'a new sensitivity to the interiority of selves and to the similarity of other selves (servants, slaves, criminals, for example) to their own'.[4]

Other historians, while acknowledging the significance of Hunt's deeper history of human rights, have sought to locate a revolutionary change in human rights history much more recently – either in the 1970s (for Samuel Moyn[5]) or the 1990s (for Stefan-Ludwig Hoffmann[6]). For Hoffmann, 'we can first speak of individual human rights as a basic concept (*Grundbegriff*), that is, a contested, irreplaceable and consequential concept of global politics, only in the 1990s, after the end of the Cold War', and it was 'only after the end of the Cold War that "human rights" emerged as an explanatory framework for understanding what had just happened'.[7] It was after the events of 1989–91, which marked the 'collapse of the old and emergence of a new international order'[8] that human rights could 'acquire historical meaning', and 'a particular version of human rights, pre-state and individual' would emerge.[9] Moyn, on the other hand, has stressed the 'lines of continuity between the 1970s and the 1990s', arguing that 'the full set of factors that led to the human rights revolution of our time deserves attention',[10] with the nongovernment organisation (NGO) movement of the 1970s and the invocation of the language of human rights having a 'catalytic effect' on the end of the Cold War and post-1989 developments.[11]

[2] L Hunt, 'The Long and the Short of the History of Human Rights' (2016) 233 *Past and Present* 323–31, 329.

[3] Ibid.

[4] Ibid.

[5] S Moyn, 'The End of Human Rights History' (2016) 233 *Past and Present* 307–32.

[6] SL Hoffmann, 'Human Rights and History' (2016) 232 *Past and Present* 279–310.

[7] Ibid, 282.

[8] Ibid, 290.

[9] Ibid, 291.

[10] Moyn (above n 5) 309.

[11] Ibid, 312.

Even as historians debate the origins of the idea of individual human rights as a regulatory idea in the 1990s, the terrorist attacks on New York and Washington on 11 September 2001 were watershed events that would challenge the late-twentieth-century liberal-democratic commitment to human rights – suggesting that the 1990s might be regarded as the highwater mark of human rights history instead of the dawn of a new era. As the editors of the first edition of this book observed in 2006, the 2001 attacks were transformative: while 'constitutional and international human rights once claimed a privileged moral status' with their 'limitation always requiring justification', in the post-9/11 climate in which they were writing, 'claims to security now appear to receive less scrutiny than the assertion of rights that may restrict measures in its pursuit.'[12]

But was 9/11 really a watershed event for human rights? Certainly, as the political case for more restrictive security measures became stronger, new measures restrictive of constitutional and human rights were introduced and litigated.[13] And in many liberal democracies, measures were tolerated and even normalised that might not have passed judicial muster in the immediately preceding earlier era – although precedents from previous eras of terrorism or wartime abound.[14] But all that said, what was remarkable about the post-9/11 period was the extent to which both the security apparatus and the human rights push-back took on both an international and a transnational character. Within days of the attacks, the United States went to the UN Security Council to obtain its approval for what would become the framework of an enhanced international sanctions regime.[15] Counterterrorism laws that had stagnated in the legislative or policy toolkit were dusted off and activated, with many 'model' laws proliferating quickly around the globe.[16] The emerging security regime itself was seen as requiring intergovernmental or international coordination, often within a framework of multilateral institutions.[17]

The *Kadi* case and its aftermath provide a striking example of the tension between the human rights and security regimes – in particular, how both regimes have transcended the state. In *Kadi*, the European Court of Justice was confronted with a situation in which two individuals and a foundation had been blacklisted by the Sanctions Committee of the United Nations Security Council

[12] L Lazarus and BJ Goold, 'Introduction: Security and Human Rights – The Search for a Language of Reconciliation' in Goold and Lazarus (eds) (above n 1) 3–4.

[13] K Roach, *The 9/11 Effect: Comparative Counter-Terrorism Law* (Cambridge, Cambridge University Press, 2011).

[14] Ibid.

[15] CH Powell, 'The United Nations Security Council, Terrorism, and the Rule of Law' in VV Ramraj, M Hor, K Roach, and G Williams (eds), *Global Anti-terrorism Law and Policy*, 2nd edn (Cambridge, Cambridge University Press, 2012) 19–43.

[16] K Roach, 'The Post-9/11 Migration of Britain's Terrorism Act 2000' in S Chowdhry (ed), *The Migration of Constitutional Ideas* (Cambridge, Cambridge University Press, 2006); and LK Donohue, 'Transplantation' in Ramraj et al (eds) (ibid).

[17] K Jayasuriya, 'Struggle over Legality in the Midnight Hour: Governing the International State of Emergency' in VV Ramraj (ed), *Emergencies and the Limits of Legality* (Cambridge, Cambridge University Press, 2008).

under Security Council Resolution 1267.[18] The blacklist had been prepared by the Committee without notice to the affected individuals, but the European Union was nevertheless obligated to implement the sanctions, which were mandatory for all states to carry out under Chapter VII of the UN Charter. The European Union had therefore taken steps to freeze the corresponding assets, but the affected individuals claimed that these actions contravened their fundamental rights under EU law. The European Court of Justice held in this case that although the UN Security Council's sanctions regime was legally primary, the implementing measures were inconsistent with fundamental rights to the extent that they were 'adopted without any guarantee being given as to the communication of the inculpatory evidence against [the appellants] or as to their being heard in that connection', and as a result, 'the regulation was adopted according to a procedure in which the appellants' rights of defence were not observed, which has had the further consequence that the principle of effective judicial protection has been infringed.'[19]

The European Court of Justice found a creative but controversial solution to the tension between the UN security regime (specifically, sanctions) and European human rights law[20] – but what is particularly revealing in this case is that both the security regime and the human rights regime were supranational. Despite US President George W Bush's with-us-or-with-the-terrorists rhetoric[21] – and in contrast with today's 'America First' agenda – international institutions remained the terrain on which counterterrorism policy evolved. Recent developments, however, suggest a marked shift away from international cooperation on security matters with the potentially moderating influence of international human rights law, and toward a more nationalised approach – one that puts the 'national' squarely back into 'national security'.

II. RISING NATIONALISM AND NATIONAL SECURITY

Without the benefit of hindsight yet, it is difficult to gauge the impact that political events of 2016 – such as the Brexit vote in the United Kingdom and the election in the United States of a President with an overtly nationalist and protectionist agenda – will have on security and human rights. We also need more distance to fully understand the root causes of these political upheavals, although the rising income inequality within countries is sometimes cited as

[18] *Kadi and Al-Barakaat v Council of the European Union* (3 September 2008), C-402/05 P & 415/15 P.

[19] Ibid, para 352.

[20] See, for example, G de Burca, 'The European Court of Justice and the International Legal Order After *Kadi*' (2010) 51 *Harvard International Law Journal* 1–49.

[21] See, for example, his public speech to a joint session of Congress (20 September 2001), available at https://www.theguardian.com/world/2001/sep/21/september11.usa13.

an important factor,[22] and the forced displacement of millions of refugees, from Syria in particular, into Europe has also contributed both to a far-right, anti-immigrant backlash and to a hardening of national borders in Europe,[23] mirroring rising ethno-religious nationalist trends in Asia.[24] Nevertheless, there are several nascent trends that suggest a trend away from a broadly internationalist approach to security – specifically, a retreat from multilateral institutions and a hardening of national borders – both of which suggest a shift away from the moderating influence of international human rights norms.

The decision by voters in the United Kingdom to leave the European Union is an obvious high-profile example of a retreat from multilateral institutions, as is the decision of the United States of America to withdraw from the 2015 Paris Agreement on climate change. Although it is important not to overstate the impact of these developments – for there are some currents pulling in the opposite direction – the nationalist politics that inspired these decisions is very much alive in other parts of the world, from Egypt to Russia to India.[25] How these developments affect security policy and cooperation remains to be seen. For example, the leaking of sensitive intelligence information by the White House to Russia in the nationalist era may well have consequences for the Five Eyes intelligence grouping (Australia, Britain, New Zealand, Canada, and the United States) as intelligence agencies reconsider their sharing protocols with the United States.[26] And the political hostility of the Trump Administration to the United Nations may well make cooperation on security issues more difficult.[27] However, the most serious casualty of the nationalist era may well be an even greater hardening of national borders in the name of national security.

Immigration and national security policy have long been closely linked,[28] often against evidence,[29] both in terms of restricting or prohibiting entry to suspected terrorists and in terms of deporting those already in the country. For example, in the aftermath of 9/11, the United States and Canada took steps

[22] H Gusterson, 'From Brexit to Trump: Anthropology and the Rise of Nationalist Populism' (2017) 44 *American Ethnologist* 209–14.

[23] See, for example, JM Dostal, 'The German Federal Election of 2017: How the Wedge Issue of Refugees and Migration Took the Shine off Chancellor Merkel and Transformed the Party System' (2017) 88 *Political Quarterly* 589–602; and C Thorleifsson, 'Disposable Strangers: Far-Right Securitisation of Forced Migration in Hungary' (2017) 25 *Social Anthropology* 318–34.

[24] G Robinson and S Roughneen, 'The Price of Extremism', *Nikkei Asian Reivew* (18–24 December 2017) 11–16.

[25] *Economist*, 'League of Nationalists,' *Economist* (19 November 2016).

[26] See H Overton, 'The Five Eyes in the Trump Era: Dominant or Diminished?' *Foreign Brief* (7 July 2017), http://www.foreignbrief.com/united-states/five-eyes-trump-era-dominant-diminished.

[27] BW Jentleson, 'Global Governance, the United Nations, and the Challenge of Trumping Trump' (2017) 23 *Global Governance* 143–49.

[28] D Cole, *Enemy Aliens: Double Standards and Constitutional Freedoms in the War on Terrorism* (New York, New Press, 2003).

[29] K Roach, *September 11: Consequences for Canada* (Montreal, McGill-Queens University Press, 2003) 145.

to integrate their immigration regimes,[30] and in the United Kingdom, the use of immigration detention as the counterterrorism tool of choice became the subject of extensive human rights litigation.[31] However, the rhetorical link (with policy consequences) between refugees, religion, and national security, which has permeated nationalist politics from the United States to Myanmar,[32] is perhaps the most serious development from a human rights perspective.

Donald Trump's Executive Order on 27 January 2017 banning entry into the United States of citizens from seven Muslim-majority countries (Iran, Iraq, Libya, Syria, Somalia, Sudan, and Yemen),[33] ostensibly on the basis that the countries in question posed heightened terrorism risks, is one of the most striking examples of this phenomenon. After a successful challenge in the lower courts, a revised order was issued on 6 March 2017 suspending entry into the United States of nationals of six of the seven countries designated in the first Executive Order: Iran, Libya, Somalia, Sudan, Syria, and Yemen. It also suspended entry into the United States of refugees for 120 days. The legal challenge to the Executive Order was based on the claim that it was motivated not by national security concerns but by Islamophobia.[34] Two lower courts granted injunctions suspending the Executive Order; however, the order was restored in part by the Supreme Court in June 2017,[35] pending a final ruling that was expected in October.

The Supreme Court reasoned that in balancing the equities of the case to fashion interim relief, the injunctions went too far in as much as they barred the enforcement of the ban on entry of foreign nationals 'who have no connection to the United States at all'.[36] It therefore decided that the second Executive Order could not be enforced against 'foreign nationals who have a credible claim of a bona fide relationship with a person or entity in the United States' but that all other foreign nationals were subject to its provisions.[37] It also lifted the injunction entirely in relation to its 120-day ban on refugees on the ground that in respect of 'refugees who lack any such connection to the United States … the balance tips in favor of the Government's compelling need to provide for the Nation's security'.[38]

[30] Ibid, 136–47.

[31] C Harvey, 'Our Responsibility to Respect the Rights of Others: Legality and Humanity' in Ramraj et al (eds) (above n 15).

[32] G Robinson, 'Metamorphosis of a Crisis', *Nikkei Asian Review* (13–19 February 2017) 10–13.

[33] White House, 'Executive Order No 13780, Protecting the Nation from Foreign Terrorist Entry into the United States', 82 Fed Reg 8977 (EO–1) (27 January 2017), available at https://www.whitehouse.gov/presidential-actions/executive-order-protecting-nation-foreign-terrorist-entry-united-states/ (accessed 30 November 2018).

[34] *Donald J Trump v International Refugee Assistance Project*, 582 US __ (2017), 4.

[35] Ibid.

[36] Ibid, 10.

[37] Ibid, 12.

[38] Ibid, 13.

By the time the second Executive Order reached the Supreme Court, it had expired, and a third version was issued on 24 September 2017 – adding North Korea and some Venezuelan officials to the list, with some refinement and exemptions for citizens of other countries on the list. That Proclamation, which was temporarily blocked and declared unconstitutional by lower courts, was allowed by the Supreme Court to take effect temporarily while the case was being litigated.[39]

The majority of the Supreme Court upheld the Proclamation, finding it to be facially neutral and justified by national security considerations, refusing to look beyond the wording of the Executive Order to statements by the President and his Administration indicating that the Proclamation was motivated by anti-Muslim animus.[40] The dissenting judges, in contrast, argued that there was sufficient evidence to suggest that the policy was not being implemented in accordance with its wording (eg, that exemptions were not being granted), which warranted further factual inquiry before the lower courts;[41] and evidence of anti-Muslim animus made by the executive during the drafting of the Proclamation and subsequently in defence of it demonstrated a violation of the First Amendment's commitment to religious neutrality and tolerance.[42]

With this decision, the Supreme Court has allowed the US government's assertion of national security considerations (even if motivated by animus toward a particular religion) to eclipse human rights and humanitarian considerations. In this context, the rights of individuals are increasingly viewed as arising not by virtue of their humanity[43] but because of their citizenship[44] or religious affiliation, and the courts seem unable to resist this shift. The earlier idea in *Kadi* that a cosmopolitan, supranational human rights regime might provide a safeguard against decisions taken on the basis of international security considerations stands in sharp contrast with the nationalistic understanding of immigration and security that is emerging in the United States. This is of course but one high-profile example from one jurisdiction, but corresponding nationalist-populist developments have been documented in Europe.[45]

The next section of this chapter considers the future of human rights in an era potentially marked by a deeply nationalistic understanding of national security and a parochial understanding of rights that is subordinated to national security considerations.

[39] *Trump v Hawaii*, 138 SCt 542 (2017); and *Trump v IRAP*, 138 SCt 542 (2017).

[40] *Trump v Hawaii*, 585 US __, 138 SCt 2392 (2018), per Roberts CJ.

[41] Ibid, per Breyer J.

[42] Ibid, per Sotomayor J.

[43] J Carens, *The Ethics of Immigration* (New York, Oxford University Press, 2013).

[44] M Bosworth, I Hasselberg, and S Turnball, 'Punishment, Citizenship and Identity: An Introduction' (2016) 16 *Criminology and Criminal Justice* 257–66.

[45] B Burgoon, T Oliver, and P Trubowitz, 'Globalization, Domestic Politics, and Transatlantic Relations' (2017) 54 *International Politics* 420–33. See also M Bosworth, 'Penal Humanitarianism? Sovereign Power in an Era of Mass Migration' (2017) 20 *New Criminal Law Review* 39–65, 44.

III. EMBEDDING HUMAN RIGHTS NORMS BEYOND THE STATE

The narrative in the previous section suggests a shift toward a more nationalist legal order and away from the cosmopolitan understanding of human rights that emerged in the post-World War II, decolonisation period. It hints at a broader return to an era of nationalist politics, a hardening of borders, and an increasing securitisation of the state against the menacing Other. How these developments will play out in the years ahead is hard to predict, and there are clearly countervailing developments that suggest that the twentieth-century struggle to establish a cosmopolitan human rights order is not entirely lost. This section of the chapter considers how human rights proponents might respond to a national backlash of uncertain intensity, duration, and scope. Specifically, it considers how an international human rights regime might shift away from its dependence on the institutions of the nation-state, embedding itself in a variety of non-state or sub-state institutions – from transnational non-state regulators that operate across national borders to sanctuary cities. These non-state institutions operate not simply as sites of resistance against oppressive state policies but as sanctuaries for human rights norms themselves. The goal of this section is not to provide an exhaustive survey of possibilities but to illustrate, using a few concrete examples, the range of possibilities that open to us when our imagination is untethered from the institutions of the nation-state.

A preliminary example concerns the protection of social and environmental rights through a transnational private regulatory body – the Equator Principles – in the context of a military regime in Thailand.[46] The Equator Principles (now in their third iteration and referred to in short as the EP III) is a self-regulatory mechanism developed by a group of international financial institutions to govern their lending practices in relation to infrastructure mega-projects such as hydroelectric dams that can have significant social and environmental consequences.[47] The EP III regime draws on standards developed by the International Finance Corporation (IFC) and the World Bank, and it directs member institutions (known as Equator Banks) to ensure compliance with the relevant environmental and social standards. By way of example, for a project 'with potential significant adverse environmental and social risks and/or impacts that are diverse, irreversible or unprecedented', Equator Banks must ensure that the project complies with the relevant IFC and World Bank standards[48] and develops or maintains an Environmental and Social Management System (ESMS).[49]

[46] This discussion draws extensively on VV Ramraj and T Tengaumnuay, 'Privatization of Constitutional Law: Thailand' in DS Law (ed), *Constitutionalism in Context* (Cambridge, Cambridge University Press, forthcoming).

[47] Equator Principles, 'Equator Principles III' (June 2013), available at http://www.equator-principles.com/.

[48] Ibid, Principle 3.

[49] Ibid, Principle 4.

The Equator Principles distinguish between jurisdictions that have 'robust environmental and social governance legislation systems and institutional capacity designed to protect their people and the natural environment' and those that do not.[50] In the latter case, environmental and social assessments conducted under the EP III framework will 'evaluate compliance with the then applicable IFC Performance Standards on Environmental and Social Sustainability … and the World Bank Group Environmental, Health and Safety Guidelines' rather than with relevant host country's regulations, thus holding Equator Banks to higher environmental and social standards than under national laws. In the context of Thailand, which has been ruled by a military government since 2014, Equator Banks operating there are held to the higher IFC–World Bank standards. This is particularly important since recent amendments to the Thai Constitution, including the current version, have removed environmental and community rights that were guaranteed in the 1997 Constitution, and the military government has exempted a range of mega-projects from national environmental regulations, including the requirement to conduct environmental impact assessments.[51] The Equator Principles appear to be taken seriously by Equator Banks and their legal advisors;[52] are subject to ongoing critical scrutiny by NGO watchdogs such as BankTrack;[53] and operate in a legal space unmediated by state institutions.

The Equator Principles – in the context of Thailand, in particular – show that the challenge is not simply, as some sceptics of transnational regulation imply, a matter of choosing between state and private regulation[54] but rather a matter of determining the form or forms of regulation appropriate to distinct local and global configurations of political and economic power. The Equator Principles is a stark example because it involves a form of private regulation. Another example, the Accord on Fire and Building Safety in Bangladesh[55] shows how a different kind of non-state regulation – a multi-stakeholder regime – can work in conjunction with the state to regulate when the state lacks the capacity or the will to do so.

The Accord was developed by a coalition of NGOs, unions, and international brands, with the support of the International Labour Organization (ILO),

[50] Ibid, 'Designated Countries', Glossary of Terms, 15.

[51] Ramraj and Tengaumnuay (above n 46).

[52] See, for example, the 'Practice Note' by John Mackay in Ramraj and Tengaumnuay (above n 46) (explaining how the Equator Principles are used in practice in the context of infrastructure project finance); and the practice guides on the Equator Principles produced by global law firms such as Norton Rose Fulbright: Norton Rose Fulbright, 'Equator Principles III: An Introduction and Practical Guide' (January 2014), http://www.nortonrosefulbright.com/files/equator-principles-iii-pdf-17mb-111048.pdf.

[53] See the BankTrack website: http://www.banktrack.org.

[54] J Bakan, 'The Invisible Hand of Law: Private Regulation and the Rule of Law' (2015) 48 *Cornell Journal of International Law* 279–300.

[55] 'Accord on Fire and Building Safety in Bangladesh' (21 June 2017), http://bangladeshaccord.org/wp-content/uploads/2018-Accord-full-text.pdf.

in response to the Rana Plaza factory collapse in Bangladesh in April 2013, in which 1,134 workers were killed. The Accord set up a regulatory regime that includes provisions for credible inspections, remediation of defects, training for workers, managers, and security staff, a complaints process, and a dispute resolution mechanism, including mediation and arbitration.[56] The effectiveness of the Accord is a matter of some controversy. According to one study, the Accord has created a 'safer, better equipped, and more comfortable working environment', although some compliance initiatives 'destroy[ed] existing social value … [leading] to the impairment of certain social, cultural, and economic rights'.[57] Another has noted that the Accord has enabled unions to 'increase their own belief in themselves and to participate in public discourse'[58] while inviting criticism that the Accord was not a legitimate actor, with 'domestic elites increasingly blam[ing] the Accord for problems in the garment industry'.[59] The often unstated question in these studies is whether effectiveness should be measured in absolute terms (on a stand set of criteria for workplace safety) or relative to the pre-existing state regime. If the question is whether the Accord has been better able to secure workplace safety in the factories within its ambit than did the formal regulatory regime in place before the Rana Plaza disaster, the evidence appears to support an affirmative answer.

The Equator Principles and the Accord offer two examples of non-state regulatory regimes, representing respectively, industry-driven and multi-stakeholder regimes in distinct sectors (infrastructure project finance and workplace safety). But they are examples that form part of an expanding transnational regulatory space in which legal norms are created, enforced, or adjudicated (and sometimes all three) largely by non-state actors.[60] To these examples, we could add others purporting to regulate a range of activities from forestry practices (the Forest Stewardship Council) to labour standards (Fair Labor Association) to palm oil production (Roundtable on Sustainable Palm Oil). And if we add hybrid, public–private initiatives (eg, the Better Factories Cambodia program, which also governs factory safety, and the Extractive Industries Transparency Initiative, which seeks to reduce corruption) and meta-regulators such as the International Social and Environmental Accreditation and Labelling (ISEAL) Alliance, the numbers of such bodies multiply further. The literature abounds with attempts to provide a typology of these transnational regulatory or global

[56] Ibid, paras 5–13.

[57] N Sinkovics, S Ferdous Hoque, and RR Sinkovics, 'Rana Plaza Collapse Aftermath: Are CSR Compliance and Auditing Pressures Effective?' (2016) 29 *Accounting, Auditing & Accountability Journal* 617–49, 627.

[58] S Zajak, 'International Allies, Institutional Layering and Power in the Making of Labour in Bangladesh' (2017) 48 *Development and Change* 1007–30, 1024.

[59] Ibid, 1025.

[60] C Scott, F Cafaggi, and L Senden, 'The Conceptual and Constitutional Challenge of Transnational Private Regulation' (2011) 38 *Journal of Law and Society* 1–19.

governance institutions,[61] to establish criteria for assessing their legitimacy,[62] to assess their efficacy in securing compliance,[63] to uncover their supposedly neoliberal provenance,[64] to examine their relationship to other legal orders,[65] or to define their legal status and the challenge they pose to statist understandings of law and jurisprudence.[66]

The formal status of transnational legal norms is controversial in part because of an abiding scepticism regarding their ability to serve as a vehicle for securing human rights. This controversy arises, for instance, in the context of debates over the need for a formal business and human rights treaty – with proponents seeking to advance the case for a formal legal instrument,[67] and detractors defending less conventional documents such as the UN Guiding Principles on Business and Human Rights[68] as a practical solution that, while informal, has the potential to command the broad support of states and companies while having a significant impact on business practices.[69] The practical effect of the business and human rights (and corporate social responsibility) movement and its ability to protect human rights is contested, but even sceptics acknowledge that multinational corporations are changing, at least in their public rhetoric and some of the steps they have taken to address human rights concerns. For example, Joel Bakan has recognised the emergence of a

> … new corporate ethos manifest in new approaches to CSR, whereby corporations appear as advocates for social and environmental values rather than threats to them, leaders in the search for solutions to global problems rather than contributors to them, and partners with governments rather than subordinates to them.[70]

[61] See, for example, J Braithwaite and P Drahos, *Global Business Regulation* (Cambridge, Cambridge University Press, 2000); B Kingsbury, N Krisch, and RB Stewart, 'The Emergence of Global Administrative Law' (2004–05) 68(3) *Law and Contemporary Problems* 15–61; and T Hale and D Held (eds), *Handbook of Transnational Governance: Institutions and Innovations* (Cambridge, Polity Press, 2011).

[62] See, for example, S Bernstein, 'When Is Non-state Global Governance Really Governance?' (2010) *Utah Law Review* 91–114; and Scott, Cafaggi, and Senden (above n 60).

[63] See, for example, F Cafaggi (ed), *Enforcement of Transnational Regulation: Ensuring Compliance in a Global World* (Cheltenham, Edward Elgar, 2012).

[64] Bakan (above n 54).

[65] N Roughan, *Authorities* (Oxford, Oxford University Press, 2013); and VV Ramraj, 'Transnational Non-state Regulation and Domestic Administrative Law' in S Rose-Ackerman, PL Lindseth, and B Emerson (eds), *Comparative Administrative Law*, 2nd edn (Cheltenham, Edward Elgar, 2017).

[66] N Roughan and A Halpin (eds), *In Pursuit of Pluralist Jurisprudence* (Cambridge, Cambridge University Press, 2017).

[67] L McConnell, 'Assessing the Feasibility of a Business and Human Rights Treaty' (2017) 66 *International and Comparative Law Quarterly* 143–80.

[68] United Nations, 'Guiding Principles on Business and Human Rights: Implementing the United Nations "Protect, Respect and Remedy" Framework' (2011), https://www.ohchr.org/Documents/Publications/GuidingPrinciplesBusinessHR_EN.pdf.

[69] JG Ruggie, *Just Business: Multinational Corporations and Human Rights* (New York, Norton, 2003) Introduction.

[70] Bakin (above n 54) 293.

At the same time, however, he remains sceptical that corporations would be willing to 'sacrifice share value [to] social and environmental concerns'.[71]

Undergirding this controversy are deeper disputes about the nature of law and its relationship to social practice. What does it tell us about the direction of global politics when the leaders of some of the world's largest multinational companies speak out against racist and climate change-sceptical policies of one of the world's most powerful states?[72] And what are the long-term implications for corporate culture of changing attitudes about the role of corporations in society, when coupled with the rise of state capitalism as a model that sees corporations as instruments of the public good?[73] Those who stress the importance of formal law tend to focus less on these societal forces and more on formal law's potential to bring about social change; those who hold a more expansive or pluralistic view of the definition of law stress that informal norms have an even more powerful hold (for better or worse) over practice precisely because they are able to command widespread social acceptance without the use of coercion.[74] It is therefore conceivable that non-state regulatory regimes can have a real impact on the behaviour of project developers even in the absence of formal state support.

Even if we allow, provisionally, that non-state legal regimes can have a real impact in the realm of business and human rights in circumstances in which states refuse to regulate, such as environmental and social regulation, critics might question whether they could play an effective or constructive role when the state is exercising coercive national security powers – eg, its powers to exclude, arrest, detain, interrogate, deport, and even torture. One response would be to stress the role that NGOs have historically played in relation to human rights issues. International human rights organisations such as Amnesty International, Human Rights Watch, and the International Commission of Jurists, have for decades played a critical role in monitoring, raising awareness of, and indirectly enforcing human rights norms in the face of state abuses of power or intransigence. Although the role of these organisations is distinct from transnational private regulators in the motivations of their constituencies and the manner in which they seek to enforce human rights norms, they nevertheless play a similar function in using non-state-based mechanisms (respectively withholding finance; awareness-raising, public shaming, and advocacy) at the supra-state level to secure compliance.

[71] Ibid.

[72] J McGregor, 'Trump's Business Councils Disband as CEOs Repudiate President over Charlottesville', *Washington Post* (16 August 2017); and H Shaban, 'Facebook, Apple, Google and Amazon Are Joining a Campaign to Support the Paris Climate Accord', *Washington Post* (5 June 2017).

[73] For one example of how such a model has worked, see CH Tan, DW Puchniak, and U Varottil, 'State-Owned Enterprises in Singapore: Historical Insights into a Potential Model for Reform' (2015) 28(2) Columbia Journal of Asian Law 61–97.

[74] R Cotterrell, 'Transnational Communities and the Concept of Law' (2008) 21 *Ratio Juris* 1–18, 13.

For example, in the context of the US government's post-9/11 detention of 'enemy combatants' in off-shore facilities at the military base in Guantánamo Bay, Cuba, David Cole has argued that the formal legal victories in the US Supreme Court and significant changes in policy, including the Bush Administration's release of more than 500 of the 779 detainees, can be explained in large measure by the activities of civil society organisations,[75] including 'international human rights groups, such as Human Rights Watch, Human Rights First, and Amnesty International'.[76] Cole has argued generally that the story of how constitutional law changes requires taking into account the role that 'citizen activists' and civil society groups play in their 'sustained advocacy … over many years … in a wide variety of venues'[77] outside the courtroom. In the specific context of post-9/11 US national security policy, he shows how civil society groups used, among others, 'public shaming tactics that human rights groups often use where more formal avenues of redress are unavailing'.[78] This included turning 'to foreign audiences and governments, exhorting them to bring pressure to bear on the United States to conform its actions to basic human rights'.[79] And in this respect, the Internet offered an important tool, allowing 'coordination across borders' and with the 'language and law of international human rights in the post-World War II period … [giving] foreign audiences … a ready moral and legal compass by which to assess and criticize US practices that ran roughshod over such rights'.[80] Cole's explanation of the power of civil society activism shows how foreign and domestic groups worked together to protect human rights in the post-9/11 era and recalls Roger Cotterrell's idea of 'transnational communities' that are starting to develop 'a sense of legal authority and validity as given or refused, in some way, by networks of community that are not restricted to homogeneous nation-state populations'.[81]

But not all non-state invocations of law occur at the supra-state level, and in an era of nationalist resurgence, a variety of subnational bodies have sought to enforce human rights without the support of central or federal governments – and often in opposition to them. For example, again in the United States, the role of sub-federal immigration regulation has increased steadily in recent years, with more state and local authorities adopting their own immigration regulations,[82] transforming and 'redefining the nature and scope of constitutional

[75] D Cole, *Engines of Liberty: The Power of Citizen Activists to Make Constitutional Law* (New York, Basic Books, 2016) 151–220.

[76] Ibid, 191.

[77] Ibid, 9.

[78] Ibid, 154.

[79] Ibid, 153.

[80] Ibid, 187.

[81] Cotterrell (above n 74) 13.

[82] At the local government level, see X Huang and CY Liu, 'Welcoming Cities: Immigration Policy at the Local Government Level' (2018) 54 *Urban Affairs Review* 3–32. The state of California has, for example, passed legislation effectively declaring the entire state a 'sanctuary' for the undocumented migrants living there: 'In California, a Direct if Costly Resistance to President Trump's Washington',

immigration power'.[83] This shift to local immigration regulation is nevertheless governmental (and not necessarily aimed at securing immigrants' rights), transferring the level at which immigration regulation is formulated and enforced. When coupled with the rise of sanctuary cities[84] and, more recently, sanctuary campuses[85] that refuse (in different ways and to different extents) to cooperate with government officials in the deportation of undocumented immigrants (which is the kind of civil society activism described by Cole), it would appear that the enforcement of human rights norms can shift in a sub-national direction as well as in a supranational direction.

Another concern is that relocating human rights in non-state institutions concedes too much: it detracts from efforts to build strong, effective nation-state and international institutions. For example, in a joint statement with three other NGOs[86] in the context of business and human rights, the International Commission of Jurists observed that although 'existing mechanisms could be useful', they are 'not sufficient and … a new binding instrument at the global level is needed'.[87] The push by the Commission and other groups for a binding business and human rights treaty signals a faith in formal international law and its institutions, as well as a scepticism about soft law instruments such as the UN Guiding Principles on Business and Human Rights.[88] A similar scepticism might arise in the national security context. Even in the face of state intransigence and weak judicial controls of executive powers, formal international institutions might be considered preferable to non-state human rights institutions. However, we have already seen that outside the national security context, private regulators draw on international human rights norms when designing their regulatory regime. So in terms of the *substance* of the normative regime, non-state mechanisms would not be ceding standard-setting power to non-state bodies.

Washington Post (18 October 2017). See California Senate Bill No 54 (Chapter 495), 5 October 2017, https://leginfo.legislature.ca.gov/faces/billNavClient.xhtml?bill_id=201720180SB54.

[83] See B Figueroa-Santana, 'Immigration Reform through Subfederal Regulation' (2015) 115 *Columbia Law Review* 2219–64, 2256, arguing that by 'entrenching policies at the local level, integrationists and immigrants' rights advocates can demand deference to local policy and dig in against future restrictionist pre-emption, thereby redefining the nature and scope of constitutional immigration power' (2256).

[84] H Bauder, 'Sanctuary Cities: Policies and Practices in International Perspective' (2017) 55 *International Migration* 174–87; and CN Lasch, RL Chan, IV Eagly, et al, 'Understanding "Sanctuary Cities"' (2018) 59(5) *Boston College Law Review* 1703.

[85] See B Bronson, 'Campus Politics in the Age of Trump', *New York Times* (11 February 2017), https://www.nytimes.com/2017/02/10/opinion/campus-politics-in-the-age-of-trump.html. In some US states, the sanctuary campus movement has provoked state legislatures to push back, threatening to withhold public funding from public universities that declare themselves to be sanctuary campuses: P Schmidt, 'State Lawmakers Seek to Ban "Sanctuary" Campuses', *Chronicle of Higher Education* (24 March 2017).

[86] Franciscans International, the Colombian Commission of Jurists, and the International Federation of Human Rights Leagues (FIDH).

[87] The statement (9 March 2017) is available at https://www.icj.org/wp-content/uploads/2017/03/HRC34-Joint-Statement-IGWG-Transnational-Corporations-Advocacy-2017.pdf.

[88] See McConnell (above n 67).

The question, then, is whether international institutions are necessarily better at championing and securing compliance with human rights norms than non-state institutions in the face of state intransigence.

The answer to this question depends in large measure on our understanding of the nature of law and, in particular, our conception of public law and its operation. Legal scholars in the sociolegal tradition remind us that the presence of formal legal institutions is not itself a guarantee of law's efficacy: law in the books is distinct from law in action.[89] And the same may be said for public international law, where the efficacy of a legal norm or legal regime can be considered independently from its formal legal status.[90] In the context of the US government's efforts to insulate the detention practices at Guantánamo Bay from judicial review by US courts, Mark Tushnet has argued that the most effective procedural protections for detainees might be found not in the courts but rather in military lawyers' sense of honour 'and a concern for reciprocity, deeply imbued in their training, that push in the "rule-of-law" direction.'[91] A similar argument could be made in relation to the role of supra-state and other non-state human rights institutions in relation to national security powers.

Scholars working on transnational regulation have emphasised the important point (noted earlier) that transnational private regulators exercise a number of functions that are often associated with the state, from standard-setting to monitoring, compliance, and enforcement. At the very least, human rights watchdogs can play a critical monitoring role in relation to intransigent states and can use the public international law technique of naming and shaming as an indirect means of encouraging compliance with human rights norms.[92]

The understanding of law articulated in this chapter is associated with legal pluralism – in particular, the notions that formal state law represents only one way 'to organize and control behavior through the use of explicit rules'[93] and that non-state norms are particularly significant means of regulating all

[89] R Pound, 'Law in Books and Law in Action' (1910) 44 *American Law Review* 12–36.

[90] J Pauwelyn, 'Is It International Law or Not, and Does It Even Matter?' in J Pauwelyn, RA Wessel, and J Wouters (eds), *Informal International Lawmaking* (Oxford, Oxford University Press, 2012).

[91] M Tushnet, 'The Political Constitution of Emergency Powers: Some Conceptual Issues' in Ramraj (ed) (above n 17) 155.

[92] These strategies can be seen not only in the national security context described by Cole, *Engines of Liberty* (above n 75) but also in the business and human rights work of organisations such as the Business and Human Rights Resource Centre, which seek to monitor abuses by companies, pushing for an immediate response, following up systematically, and strengthening accountability by seeking responses from companies – while giving 'companies a real opportunity to respond in full to allegations of abuse before we post them'. See the website of the Centre: https://business-humanrights.org/en/about-us. The organisation's description of its successful interventions (not verified by the author) can be found at https://business-humanrights.org/sites/default/files/documents/Examples-of-impact-full-Jan-2015.pdf.

[93] M Krygier, 'Legal Pluralism and the Value of the Rule of Law' in Roughan and Halpin (eds) (above n 66) 307, citing S Falk Moore, *Law as Process: An Anthropological Approach*, 2nd edn (London, James Currey, 2001) 2–3.

kinds of societies in complex relationships with state law.[94] Although the legal pluralist literature is often associated with legal-anthropological research on legal ordering that exists apart from the formal legal institutions of the modern state,[95] it is equally relevant to a discussion of public law as a means of constraining public power. Public law scholars working on transnational law have argued that public law principles and associated ideas such as the rule of law should be understood as norms aimed at moderating[96] or tempering[97] power, whatever its source. So Martin Krygier has argued that the rule of law, as an ideal concerned with arbitrary exercises of power, is relevant even when 'non-state power is arbitrarily exercised by oligarchs, Mafiosi, warlords, tribal elders, Al Qaeda, NGOs, business executives, currency speculators, international rating agencies, financial institutions, or indeed university administrators.'[98] But he has also argued, as I do in this chapter, that 'barriers to arbitrary power might come from non-state sources as well',[99] and when 'extra-state institutions, practices, and so on, contribute to diminishing the opportunities for arbitrary exercise of power, they serve the *ideal* of the rule of law, perhaps more than can the law itself.'[100]

Similar arguments have been made by Jutta Brunnée and Stephen Toope in the context of international law.[101] In advancing their theory of interactional international law, they have highlighted the role that social actors play in the creation and implementation of international legal norms. Social actors in this context include states, 'but the interactional framework acknowledges the importance of robust participation by intergovernmental organizations, civil society organizations, civil society organizations, other collective entities, and individuals'.[102] These actors are important, they have argued, because they generate a fidelity to law by grounding norms in 'shared understandings [that] adhere to the conditions of legality',[103] which in turn provide 'stronger safeguards against political domination and power than a purely formal account of international law'.[104] As with Krygier and the legal pluralist tradition he draws on, Brunnée and Toope acknowledge the power of non-state actors to co-constitute and enforce legal norms. And both accounts reinforce the particular importance of non-state actors when formal institutions are unable on their own to prevent arbitrary exercises of power by the state.

[94] Krygier (ibid) 307.
[95] Much of this work is inspired by S Falk Moore (above n 93) 54–81.
[96] VV Ramraj, 'Constitutional Interpretation in an Age of Globalisation: Challenges and Prospects' in J Neo (ed), *Constitutional Interpretation in Singapore: Theory and Practice* (London, Routledge, 2017).
[97] Krygier (above n 93).
[98] Ibid, 318.
[99] Ibid, 319.
[100] Ibid, 320 (original emphasis).
[101] J Brunneé and S Toope, 'Interactional International Law: An Introduction' (2011) 3 *International Theory* 307–18.
[102] Ibid, 309.
[103] Ibid, 315.
[104] Ibid, 316.

All that said, it is important to acknowledge the objection that an overreliance on non-state actors has the potential to undermine power-moderating state institutions or to subvert human rights capacity-building. But this concern loses its force when the state exercises national security powers in a manner that undermines institutions designed to prevent the abuse of state power. In an ideal liberal-democratic world, state powers over national security and their triggering conditions would be authorised *ex ante* by the constitution and be time-limited, with minimal interference with constitutional rights, and all exercises of emergency powers would be subject to *ex post* judicial review by judges who are fully independent from the executive. Where national security considerations require that steps to be taken to protect sources or sensitive security intelligence information, careful institutional design would ensure that the procedural rights of suspects are minimally compromised. But this ideal world is not the world many (or any) of us live in – and its universality and neutrality as a means of organising political power institutionally can reasonably be contested.

Perhaps the most anyone could agree on is that state power over matters of national security should not be abused – with the institutional means of achieving that broad goal (whether legal, political, or some creative combination of the two) subject to reasonable disagreement and difference.[105] In these real-world circumstances, reliance on non-state institutions as sites from which human rights norms could be used obliquely to moderate abuses of state power may well be a necessary and pragmatic response. As Amartya Sen has argued in his critique of John Rawls, a theory of justice that

> … can serve as the basis of practical reason must include ways of judging how to reduce injustice and advance justice, rather than aiming only at the characterization of perfectly just societies – an exercise that is such a dominant feature of many theories of justice in political philosophy today.[106]

Non-state institutions are not a panacea, but in a less-than-perfect world, they might, to different degrees in different contexts, provide an institutional means of moderating abuses of state power, sometimes complementing state mechanisms, sometimes serving as surrogates when state institutions are unable to operate adequately or at all.

IV. CONCLUSION

It may be that the view of non-state legality advanced in this chapter is itself too optimistic about the ability of non-state actors to resist determined governments that are set on pushing their national security powers to the fullest while

[105] See VV Ramraj, 'Between Idealism and Pragmatism: Legal and Political Constraints on State Power in Times of Crisis' in Goold and Lazarus (eds) (above n 1).

[106] A Sen, *The Idea of Justice* (London, Allen Lane, 2009) ix.

trampling on formal institutions designed to curtail those powers. And the recent rise of nationalist parties with xenophobic national security agendas may well give optimists pause. But the argument in this chapter is that even in the face of rising nationalism and the rejection of cosmopolitan ideas of human rights, the consolidation and insulation of state institutions can only ever be partial.[107] Just as threats to security emanate from both state and non-state actors, so too can the sustenance and protection of human rights: the Equator Principles can prevent access to project finance when states are prepared to waive social and environmental regulations for unscrupulous developers; the Bangladesh Accord can provide a measure of protection and capacity-building on factory safety when the state lacks the capacity to enforce state laws; and campuses, cities, and civil society organisations can help to moderate – if not resist – the implementation of unjust immigration policies.

These institutions serve different functions. On the one hand, they serve as alternative sources of political and legal authority, providing evidence of legal pluralism and raising questions about their relationship to state law. On the other hand, they also demonstrate that legality – including the protection of human rights – thrives in institutions beyond the courts[108] and that the interaction between state and non-state institutions – the dynamic social dimensions of law – cannot be ignored in an account of human rights. This observation is particularly salient in an age of rising nationalist politics. When state institutions fail us, non-state institutions beyond and within the state can provide a sanctuary, temporary or permanent, from which human rights regimes can rebuild, regroup, and reimagine ways of resisting abuses of powers invoked by the state in the name of national security.

REFERENCES

Bakan, J, 'The Invisible Hand of Law: Private Regulation and the Rule of Law' (2015) 48 *Cornell Journal of International Law* 279–300.

Bauder, H, 'Sanctuary Cities: Policies and Practices in International Perspective' (2017) 55 *International Migration* 174–87.

Bernstein, S, 'When Is Non-state Global Governance Really Governance?' (2010) *Utah Law Review* 91–114.

Bosworth, M, 'Penal Humanitarianism? Sovereign Power in an Era of Mass Migration' (2017) 20 *New Criminal Law Review* 39–65.

[107] As Sally Falk Moore argued in her classic study (above n 93), since 'the law of sovereign states is hierarchical in form, no social field within a modern polity could be absolutely autonomous from a legal point of view. Absolute domination is also difficult to conceive, for even in armies and prisons and other rule-run institutions, there is usually an underlife with some autonomy' (78).

[108] M Tushnet, *Taking the Constitution Away from the Courts* (Princeton, Princeton University Press, 1999).

Bosworth, M, Hasselberg, I and Turnball, S, 'Punishment, Citizenship and Identity: An Introduction' (2016) 16 *Criminology and Criminal Justice* 257–66.

Braithwaite, J and Drahos, P, *Global Business Regulation* (Cambridge, Cambridge University Press, 2000).

Bronson, B, 'Campus Politics in the Age of Trump', *New York Times* (11 February 2017), https://www.nytimes.com/2017/02/10/opinion/campus-politics-in-the-age-of-trump.html.

Brunneé, J and Toope, S, 'Interactional International Law: An Introduction' (2011) 3 *International Theory* 307–18.

Burgoon, B, Oliver, T and Trubowitz, P, 'Globalization, Domestic Politics, and Transatlantic Relations' (2017) 54 *International Politics* 420–33.

Cafaggi, F (ed), *Enforcement of Transnational Regulation: Ensuring Compliance in a Global World* (Cheltenham, Edward Elgar, 2012).

Carens, J, *The Ethics of Immigration* (New York, Oxford University Press, 2013).

Cole, D, *Enemy Aliens: Double Standards and Constitutional Freedoms in the War on Terrorism* (New York, New Press, 2003).

——, *Engines of Liberty: The Power of Citizen Activists to Make Constitutional Law* (New York, Basic Books, 2016).

Cotterrell, R, 'Transnational Communities and the Concept of Law' (2008) 21 *Ratio Juris* 1–18.

de Burca, G, 'The European Court of Justice and the International Legal Order After Kadi' (2010) 51 *Harvard International Law Journal* 1–49.

Donohue, LK, 'Transplantation' in VV Ramraj, M Hor, K Roach, and G Williams (eds), *Global Anti-terrorism Law and Policy*, 2nd edn (Cambridge, Cambridge University Press, 2012).

Dostal, JM, 'The German Federal Election of 2017: How the Wedge Issue of Refugees and Migration Took the Shine off Chancellor Merkel and Transformed the Party System' (2017) 88 *Political Quarterly* 589–602.

Dyzenhaus, D, 'Deference, Security, and Human Rights' in BJ Goold and L Lazarus (eds), *Security and Human Rights* (Oxford, Hart Publishing, 2007).

Economist, 'League of Nationalists,' *Economist* (19 November 2016).

Falk Moore, S, *Law as Process: An Anthropological Approach*, 2nd edn (London, James Currey, 2001).

Figueroa-Santana, B, 'Immigration Reform through Subfederal Regulation' (2015) 115 *Columbia Law Review* 2219–64.

Gusterson, H, 'From Brexit to Trump: Anthropology and the Rise of Nationalist Populism' (2017) 44 *American Ethnologist* 209–14.

Hale, T and Held, D (eds), *Handbook of Transnational Governance: Institutions and Innovations* (Cambridge, Polity Press, 2011).

Harvey, C, 'Our Responsibility to Respect the Rights of Others: Legality and Humanity' in VV Ramraj, M Hor, K Roach, and G Williams (eds), *Global Anti-terrorism Law and Policy*, 2nd edn (Cambridge, Cambridge University Press, 2012).

Huang, X and Liu, CY, 'Welcoming Cities: Immigration Policy at the Local Government Level' (2018) 54 *Urban Affairs Review* 3–32.

Hunt, L, 'The Long and the Short of the History of Human Rights' (2016) 233 *Past and Present* 323–31.

Jayasuriya, K, 'Struggle over Legality in the Midnight Hour: Governing the International State of Emergency' in VV Ramraj (ed), *Emergencies and the Limits of Legality* (Cambridge, Cambridge University Press, 2008).

Jentleson, BW, 'Global Governance, the United Nations, and the Challenge of Trumping Trump' (2017) 23 *Global Governance* 143–49.

Kingsbury, B, Krisch, N, and Stewart, RB, 'The Emergence of Global Administrative Law' (2004–05) 68(3) *Law and Contemporary Problems* 15–61.

Krygier, M, 'Legal Pluralism and the Value of the Rule of Law' in N Roughan and A Halpin (eds), *In Pursuit of Pluralist Jurisprudence* (Cambridge, Cambridge University Press, 2017).

Lasch, CN, Chan, RL, Eagly, IV et al, 'Understanding "Sanctuary Cities"' (2018) 59(5)8 *Boston College Law Review* 1703.

Lazarus, L and Goold, BJ, 'Introduction: Security and Human Rights – The Search for a Language of Reconciliation' in BJ Goold and L Lazarus (eds), *Security and Human Rights* (Oxford, Hart Publishing, 2007).

McConnell, L, 'Assessing the Feasibility of a Business and Human Rights Treaty' (2017) 66 *International and Comparative Law Quarterly* 143–80.

McGregor, J, 'Trump's Business Councils Disband as CEOs Repudiate President over Charlottesville', *Washington Post* (16 August 2017).

Moyn, S, 'The End of Human Rights History' (2016) 233 *Past and Present* 307–32.

Norton Rose Fulbright, 'Equator Principles III: An Introduction and Practical Guide' (January 2014), http://www.nortonrosefulbright.com/files/equator-principles-iii-pdf-17mb-111048.pdf.

Overton, H, 'The Five Eyes in the Trump Era: Dominant or Diminished?' *Foreign Brief* (7 July 2017), http://www.foreignbrief.com/united-states/five-eyes-trump-era-dominant-diminished.

Pauwelyn, J, 'Is It International Law or Not, and Does It Even Matter?' in J Pauwelyn, RA Wessel, and J Wouters (eds), *Informal International Lawmaking* (Oxford, Oxford University Press, 2012).

Pound, R, 'Law in Books and Law in Action' (1910) 44 *American Law Review* 12–36.

Powell, CH, 'The United Nations Security Council, Terrorism, and the Rule of Law' in VV Ramraj, M Hor, K Roach, and G Williams (eds), *Global Anti-terrorism Law and Policy*, 2nd edn (Cambridge, Cambridge University Press, 2012).

Ramraj, VV, 'Between Idealism and Pragmatism: Legal and Political Constraints on State Power in Times of Crisis' in BJ Goold and L Lazarus (eds), *Security and Human Rights* (Oxford, Hart Publishing, 2007).

——, 'Constitutional Interpretation in an Age of Globalisation: Challenges and Prospects' in J Neo (ed), *Constitutional Interpretation in Singapore: Theory and Practice* (London, Routledge, 2017).

——, 'Transnational Non-state Regulation and Domestic Administrative Law' in S Rose-Ackerman, PL Lindseth, and B Emerson (eds), *Comparative Administrative Law*, 2nd edn (Cheltenham, Edward Elgar, 2017).

Ramraj, VV and Tengaumnuay, T, 'Privatization of Constitutional Law: Thailand' in DS Law (ed), *Constitutionalism in Context* (Cambridge, Cambridge University Press (forthcoming)).

Roach, K, *The 9/11 Effect: Comparative Counter-Terrorism Law* (Cambridge, Cambridge University Press, 2011).

——, 'The Post-9/11 Migration of Britain's Terrorism Act 2000' in S Chowdhry (ed), *The Migration of Constitutional Ideas* (Cambridge, Cambridge University Press, 2006).

——, *September 11: Consequences for Canada* (Montreal, McGill-Queens University Press, 2003).

Robinson, G, 'Metamorphosis of a Crisis', *Nikkei Asian Review* (13–19 February 2017) 10–13.

Robinson, G and Roughneen, S, 'The Price of Extremism', *Nikkei Asian Reivew* (18–24 December 2017) 11–16.

Roughan, N, *Authorities* (Oxford, Oxford University Press, 2013).

Roughan, N and Halpin, A (eds), *In Pursuit of Pluralist Jurisprudence* (Cambridge, Cambridge University Press, 2017).

Ruggie, JG, *Just Business: Multinational Corporations and Human Rights* (New York, Norton, 2003).

Schmidt, P, 'State Lawmakers Seek to Ban "Sanctuary" Campuses', *Chronicle of Higher Education* (24 March 2017).

Scott, C, Cafaggi, F, and Senden, L, 'The Conceptual and Constitutional Challenge of Transnational Private Regulation' (2011) 38 *Journal of Law and Society* 1–19.

Sen, A, *The Idea of Justice* (London, Allen Lane, 2009).

Shaban, H, 'Facebook, Apple, Google and Amazon Are Joining a Campaign to Support the Paris Climate Accord', *Washington Post* (5 June 2017).

Sinkovics, N, Ferdous Hoque, S, and Sinkovics, RR, 'Rana Plaza Collapse Aftermath: Are CSR Compliance and Auditing Pressures Effective?' (2016) 29 *Accounting, Auditing & Accountability Journal* 617–49.

Tan, CH, Puchniak, DW, and Varottil, U, 'State-Owned Enterprises in Singapore: Historical Insights into a Potential Model for Reform' (2015) 28(2) *Columbia Journal of Asian Law* 61–97.

Thorleifsson, C, 'Disposable Strangers: Far-Right Securitisation of Forced Migration in Hungary' (2017) 25 *Social Anthropology* 318–34.

Tushnet, M, *Taking the Constitution Away from the Courts* (Princeton, Princeton University Press, 1999).

United Nations, 'Guiding Principles on Business and Human Rights: Implementing the United Nations "Protect, Respect and Remedy" Framework' (2011), https://www.ohchr.org/Documents/Publications/GuidingPrinciplesBusinessHR_EN.pdf.

Washington Post, 'In California, a Direct if Costly Resistance to President Trump's Washington', Washington Post (18 October 2017).

Zajak, S, 'International Allies, Institutional Layering and Power in the Making of Labour in Bangladesh' (2017) 48 *Development and Change* 1007–30.

10

The Demise of Rights as Trumps

ROBERT DIAB

I. INTRODUCTION

THE DAMAGE DONE to human rights in the period since 2001 as a consequence of various measures in the 'war on terror' is well known. What is perhaps new in recent years is an emerging sense of the extent of the damage, an awareness that a corner has been turned and that human rights may be entering a long-term eclipse, even where rights are at the centre of a nation's political self-conception. To identify this sense is not to deny the important work of courts and legislatures in resisting these trends. The point is to make sense of the fact that much of the apparatus of the war on terror remains intact, with no sign of change on the horizon. Scores of detainees at Guantanamo approach two decades in custody without charge.[1] The United States continues its targeted killing programme free of judicial due process;[2] terrorist suspects are still frequently subjected to rendition;[3] and extensive technologies of state surveillance are pervasive across the globe.[4] Citizens in modern democracies are, to a large degree, acquiescent.

The sense that we may be entering a longer-term decline in the currency of rights is further shaped by responses to more recent terror unfolding across the West. In the wake of what were by any measure small-scale events (3 soldiers killed), Canada passed a law in 2015 allowing courts to issue warrants to

[1] 'The Guantánamo Docket', *New York Times* (updated 2 May 2018), https://www.nytimes.com/interactive/projects/guantanamo.

[2] M Hussain, 'US Has Only Acknowledged a Fifth of Its Lethal Strikes, New Study Finds', *The Intercept* (13 June 2017): '[T]he drone program is intensifying. Since President Donald Trump took office earlier this year, the rate of drone strikes per month has increased by almost four times Obama's average.' See also Human Rights Watch, 'United States' in *World Report 2017* (New York, Human Rights Watch, 2017). For more on targeted killing, see also the chapter in this volume by Shiri Krebs.

[3] International Commission of Jurists, *Transnational Injustices: National Security Transfers and International Law* (Geneva, International Commission of Jurists, 2017).

[4] See contributions to the special issue of *Surveillance and Society* entitled 'Surveillance and the Global Turn to Authoritarianism' edited by David Murakami Wood, (2017) 15(3/4) *Surveillance and Society*.

intelligence agents to carry out not only searches and arrests but acts that would violate *any* of the rights guaranteed under the nation's constitutional bill of rights.[5] After two larger-scale attacks in 2015, France remained in a state of emergency until the fall of 2017, when it passed legislation making many of the emergency powers permanent.[6] And further attacks in Berlin, Barcelona, and London have only added to a climate of fear in which governments in Britain, Australia, and other nations have embraced deportation to torture, citizenship-revocation for terrorist suspects, and other infringements.[7]

In light of both this second wave of terrorism and the responses to it, earlier debates about rights and security in the years after 2001 have now taken on a different valence. Much of the scholarship of the post-9/11 period – including many contributions to the first edition of this volume – was premised on the view that rights and security were not incompatible.[8] A hope widely shared in these early debates was that much of the overstated fear would eventually subside, and rights would make something of a comeback.[9] Many commentators were therefore sceptical that terrorism posed a greater threat to national security after 2001.[10] But some prominent voices – Bruce Ackerman, Michael Ignatieff, Ronald Dworkin, eg – took seriously the claim that 9/11 had somehow changed the equation or at least called for a fundamental reassessment.[11]

[5] The Anti-terrorism Act 2015, SC 2015, c 20, affecting the Canadian Charter of Rights and Freedoms, Part I of the Constitution Act 1982, being Schedule B to the Canada Act 1982 (UK), 1982, c II [hereafter, 'Canadian Charter']. For an extensive overview and critique of the bill, see C Forcese and K Roach, *False Security: The Radicalization of Canadian Anti-Terrorism* (Toronto, Irwin Law, 2015).

[6] Library of Congress, 'France: State of Emergency Officially Ends as New Security Measures Come into Force', *Global Legal Monitor* (29 November 2017), http://www.loc.gov/law/foreign-news/article/france-state-of-emergency-officially-ends-as-new-security-measures-come-into-force/. The article notes the bill's powers for establishing 'protection perimeters' around vulnerable sites (concerts, sporting events) at which searches may be conducted and entry denied; powers to close places of worship where violence or terror are promoted; and powers for the monitoring of suspects without charge. Law No 2017-1510 of 30 October 2017 Reinforcing Domestic Security and the Fight Against Terrorism. For discussion on the state of emergency in France, see the chapter in this volume by Marc-Antoine Granger.

[7] BBC, 'Theresa May: Tories to Consider Leaving European Convention on Human Rights', *BBC News* (9 March 2013), citing May: 'When Strasbourg constantly moves the goalposts and prevents the deportation of dangerous men like Abu Qatada, we have to ask ourselves, to what end are we signatories to the convention?'; and S Medhora, 'Law to Strip Dual Nationals of Australian Citizenship Set to Pass Parliament', *Guardian* (10 November 2015). For discussion on the curtailment of citizenship rights as a response to terrorism, see the chapter in this volume by Lucia Zedner.

[8] L Lazarus and BJ Goold, 'Security and Human Rights: The Search for a Language of Reconciliation' in BJ Goold and L Lazarus (eds), *Security and Human Rights* (Oxford, Hart Publishing, 2007) 2.

[9] See, eg, D Cole and J Lobel, *Less Safe, Less Free: Why America is Losing the War on Terror* (New York, New Press, 2007); and International Commission of Jurists, *Addressing Damage, Urging Action: Report of the Eminent Jurists Panel on Terrorism, Counter-Terrorism and Human Rights* (Geneva, International Commission of Jurists, 2009).

[10] See both sources cited ibid for examples of scepticism to this effect.

[11] B Ackerman, *Before the Next Attack: Preserving Civil Liberties in an Age of Terrorism* (New Haven, Yale University Press, 2006); M Ignatieff, *The Lesser Evil: Political Ethics in an Age of Terror* (Princeton, Princeton University Press, 2004); and R Dworkin, 'The Threat to Patriotism',

At the heart of the debate about rights and security, then, was a question about the nature of the threat of terrorism and its implications. In what follows, I show how and why this issue continues to be central to the debate and to the diminished currency of rights.

More specifically, I advance the claim that to better understand why security has continued to prevail over rights in much of present political discourse, we need to return to a recent high-watermark of rights consciousness and revisit some of its axiomatic assumptions. In ways to be explored, beliefs about terrorism have continued to evolve in recent years, but they still complicate assumptions that were fundamental to the defence of rights in the mid- to late twentieth century.

I refer, in this regard, to the period from roughly the mid-1950s to the 1970s, primarily in the United States but also in eastern Europe and many parts of the world in the process of decolonising, when civil and human rights had come to the fore of political thinking, with rights emerging as a 'last utopia'.[12] It was in this very different context that Dworkin first advanced his theory of 'rights as trumps'[13] – a theory that crystallised much of the discourse around rights in the period. A key aspect about rights for Dworkin was the contrast they entailed to utilitarian or communitarian approaches to politics. To 'take rights seriously', Dworkin began to argue around 1970, did not involve balancing them with collective interests; it involved giving them priority. This followed from the value we place on the Kantian sense of the inherent dignity and equality of each individual and the view that to protect these interests, we had to be prepared – in at least some cases – to place rights before and above the majority's interests.[14]

Dworkin happened to articulate this theory at roughly the point in time when concerns about security were becoming prominent in Anglo-American politics.[15] Across much of the United States and Britain, anxiety was rising

New York Review of Books (28 February 2002) 44; R Dworkin, 'Terror and the Attack on Civil Liberties', *New York Review of Books* (6 November 2003) 37; and R Dworkin, *Is Democracy Possible Here? Principles for a New Political Debate* (Princeton, Princeton University Press, 2006) ch 2.

[12] S Moyn, *The Last Utopia: Human Rights in History* (Cambridge, Harvard University Press, 2012).

[13] R Dworkin, *Taking Rights Seriously* (Cambridge, Harvard University Press, 1977). The chapter in which Dworkin set out the theory first appeared as the essay R Dworkin, 'A Special Supplement: Taking Rights Seriously', *New York Review of Books* (17 December 1970).

[14] Dworkin, *Taking Rights Seriously* (ibid) 198. See also Dworkin's later essays (cited above n 11). Dworkin was neither new nor unique in making this claim; congenial formulations of rights were at least implied in L Fuller, *The Morality of Law* (New Haven, Yale University Press, 1963). Rights as trumps also resonated with the importance of equality in the work of John Rawls in the period. See, eg, J Rawls, 'The Sense of Justice' (1963) 72 *Philosophical Review* 281. But Dworkin's foregrounding and articulation of the contrast between the instrumental thinking implied in utilitarian conceptions of liberalism and rights as political trumps were unique and influential.

[15] D Garland, *The Culture of Control: Crime and Social Order in Contemporary Society* (Chicago, University of Chicago Press, 2001); L Zedner, 'Seeking Security by Eroding Rights: The Side-Stepping of Due Process' in Goold and Lazarus (eds) (above n 8); and J Simon, *Governing*

along with crime rates and racial and class tensions.[16] Electoral politics became increasingly focused on security and punishment.[17] Yet despite this, Dworkin's theory of rights still held a measure of currency as a normative account, resonating with much of the jurisprudence of the period – notably, the first decade or so of Canada's Supreme Court under the new Charter of Rights and Freedoms and many decisions of the European Court of Human Rights.[18]

The events of 9/11, however, would come to pose a much greater challenge. From the outset, ideas about rights were in tension with evolving beliefs about the nature of terrorism and the degree of harm it was capable of posing. In earlier work, I have explored these beliefs in terms of what can be called the harbinger theory.[19] This was a view, discernible in a wide range of political discourse and popular culture, that 9/11 marked the emergence of terrorism on a new scale. Rather than being an anomaly in the history of terrorism (which earlier had involved casualties in the tens or low hundreds), 9/11 was seen as a harbinger of further attacks likely resulting in a similar or greater degree of carnage as that of 9/11, possibly involving weapons of mass destruction.

For at least a decade after 9/11, when the harbinger theory was most pervasive, terrorism became a kind of privileged exception to rights as trumps, or at least the focal point of tension. Dworkin grappled with it repeatedly. Our perceptions of terrorism have since continued to evolve. But we persist in seeing terrorism as a significant and possibly unique threat, and this belief still poses complications for the theory of rights as trumps. Exploring why this is so lends insight into the challenge we face in reconciling ideas about right and security, and in reviving the currency of rights in the present.

II. THE LAST UTOPIA, OR RIGHTS AS TRUMPS IN CONTEXT

Before turning to the theory of rights as trumps, it may be helpful to briefly address the context in which Dworkin initially formulated it. I do so not to suggest that it remains a product of its time or that it reflects a set of values we no longer recognise. Rather, the context here is vital to understanding the power and force with which concepts at the heart of the theory resonated in the period – namely, dignity and equality – and thus the nature of their displacement in the present. The point of this brief excursion will be to demonstrate

Through Crime: How the War on Crime Transformed American Democracy and Created a Culture of Fear (Oxford, Oxford University Press, 2007).

[16] Garland (ibid) Introduction.

[17] Garland (above n 15). See also Simon (above n 15) ch 2.

[18] *R v Oakes* [1986] 1 SCR 103; *Hunter v Southam Inc* [1984] 2 SCR 145; *Reference Re BC Motor Vehicle Act* [1985] 2 SCR 486; *Ireland v United Kingdom* (5310/71) [1978] ECHR 1; and *Dudgeon v United Kingdom* (7525/76) [1981] ECHR 5.

[19] R Diab, *The Harbinger Theory: How the Post-9/11 Emergency Became Permanent and the Case for Reform* (New York, Oxford University Press, 2015).

the link between the central concepts in Dworkin's theory and a specific historical and political juncture. This in turn will be relevant to the discussion in the second half of this chapter regarding the challenge of restoring the currency of rights as trumps in the current climate.

Looking back at Dworkin's first extended formulation of the theory in 1970, we risk overlooking the fact that he was writing at the culmination of a global rights revolution that had been unfolding from roughly the 1950s onward.[20] The story of how human rights emerged as a prominent theme nationally and globally in this period has lately become a matter of some contention, yet certain broad features seem beyond debate.[21] In the two decades following the UN's Universal Declaration of Human Rights (1948),[22] the language of the Declaration became a significant political motif in a range of contexts, including the civil rights movement in America and decolonisation movements across Africa and Asia.[23] As Samuel Moyn has noted, while the emphasis in human rights discourse in the early years after the Declaration was primarily on the liberation of peoples, or with group rather than individual rights, over the course of the 1960s, human rights assumed a different character.[24] They became a focal point, or as Moyn has put it, a 'last utopia', after the demise or discrediting of so many of the century's large-scale political programmes, from communism and fascism to post-colonialism.[25] Forsaking the often violent search for perfect social ordering in favour of the valorisation of humanity itself, the central theme of much of this discourse was the inherent dignity and worth of the individual, or an underlying universal humanity, which came to be widely embraced in the period as a transcendent political value in its own right.[26] We glean some indication of this by noting Amnesty International's receipt of the Nobel Prize in 1977; President Carter's frequent invocations of human rights in his foreign policy statements, along with those of other world leaders; and the embrace of human rights by Charter 77 and a host of other Eastern European dissident groups presaging the end of the Soviet order.[27]

An essential element of this constellation of events but of more immediate relevance to Dworkin was the jurisprudential revolution unfolding in the United States Supreme Court of the 1950s and 1960s. As the focus of constitutional litigation shifted from issues of state and federal power to questions of individual liberty,[28] the Warren Court decided a series of now canonical cases that effected

[20] A Iriye, P Goedde, and W Hitchcock (eds), *The Human Rights Revolution: An International History* (Oxford, Oxford University Press, 2012).

[21] Moyn, *The Last Utopia* (above n 12) taking issue with L Hunt, *Inventing Human Rights* (New York, Norton, 2007) and launching a wider debate. See also Iriye et al (ibid).

[22] UN General Assembly, *Universal Declaration of Human Rights* (10 December 1948), 217 A (III).

[23] S Moyn, *Human Rights and the Uses of History* (London, Verso, 2014) 80.

[24] Ibid.

[25] Ibid, 83.

[26] Ibid, 81.

[27] Ibid.

[28] M Glendon, *Rights Talk: The Impoverishment of Political Discourse* (New York, Free Press, 1991) 4.

a sea-change in social relations and often employed a form of reasoning overtly germane to rights as trumps. Among the most important of these cases were those dealing with segregation (*Brown v Board of Education* in 1954), free speech (*New York Times v Sullivan* in 1964), and the right to privacy (*Griswold v Connecticut* in 1965; *Katz v United States* in 1967; and *Roe v Wade* in 1973).[29] No less crucial were those cases effecting a shift of emphasis in US criminal law from a 'crime control' model valorising victims' rights, factual findings of guilt, and police powers to one favouring due process and findings of legal rather than factual guilt (*Mapp* in 1961; *Gideon* in 1963; and *Miranda* in 1966).[30]

A central motif in these cases, either explicitly or implicitly, was dignity. In *Brown v Board of Education*, school segregation was contrary to the constitutional protection of equality because it engendered among blacks 'a feeling of inferiority as to their status in the community that may affect their hearts and minds in a way unlikely ever to be undone'.[31] In *Miranda*, Chief Justice Warren sought to anchor the rationale for protecting the accused against coerced confessions by highlighting the often 'menacing police interrogation procedures' in which they were obtained and their effect on suspects presumed innocent.[32] As Justice Warren wrote,

> It is obvious that such an interrogation environment is created for no purpose other than to subjugate the individual to the will of his examiner. [...] To be sure, this is not physical intimidation, but it is equally destructive of human dignity.[33]

Approaching Dworkin's theory in this wider context suggests that his motivation in advancing it was at least in part to address concerns (or dispel confusion) as to why courts had gone to such lengths to protect rights to a point that appeared detrimental to collective interests, or to certain perceptions of it. On Dworkin's view, the Supreme Court's work could best be understood as an effort not to expand liberty so much as to advance a broader humanist project through the protection of individual dignity and equality. His reading aimed to frame the Court's work in the period as part of a wider and insurgent progressive movement. The Court portrayed here was not only more favourably constituted, from a liberal perspective, than the divided bench of the period after 2001; it was also less preoccupied than later courts would be with external threats, collective security, and justified limits on rights.

[29] *Brown v Board of Education of Topeka, Kansas*, 347 US 483 (1954); *New York Times Co v Sullivan*, 376 US 254 (1964); *Griswold v Connecticut*, 381 US 479 (1965); *Katz v United States*, 389 US 347 (1967); and *Roe v Wade*, 410 US 113 (1973).

[30] H Packer, *The Limits of the Criminal Sanction* (Stanford, Stanford University Press, 1968); *Mapp v Ohio*, 367 US 643 (1961); *Gideon v Wainwright*, 372 US 335 (1963); and *Miranda v Arizona*, 384 US 436 (1966).

[31] *Brown v Board of Education of Topeka, KS* (above n 29) 494.

[32] *Miranda v Arizona* (above n 30) 457.

[33] Ibid.

III. DWORKIN'S THEORY OF THE RIGHTS REVOLUTION

Dworkin's argument for rights as trumps was first elaborated in an essay published in the *New York Review of Books* in 1970[34] and later included as a chapter in his seminal 1978 book *Taking Rights Seriously*.[35] The book situated Dworkin's theory of rights within a broader challenge to dominant ideas in jurisprudence at that time, namely positivism and utilitarianism. The former entails a denial of the validity of rights or law not codified or inscribed in positive law, while the latter view assesses a law's validity primarily in terms of whether it serves the general welfare. In contrast, Dworkin began to stake a position for what might be described as the most prominent form of natural law theory in the closing decades of the twentieth century, one that distinguishes between law and morality, with law's validity and authority deriving from its consistency with underlying moral principles. He thus described the US Constitution as containing legal rights that protect conceptually prior political rights (eg, free speech in the First Amendment protecting a political freedom to open debate). A key question for Dworkin here and in later work is how governments and courts should define the legal rights of citizens to best protect their underlying moral rights.

In clear-cut cases, the task is easy – we ought to be free to express unpopular opinions. But what about advocating violence to secure racial equality? What happens when rights impose serious burdens on the majority's interests? We tend, in Dworkin's view, to take one of two approaches, the first of which is often invoked in law and politics and is superficially appealing but fatally flawed.[36] This involves striking a balance between individual and collective interests, trying to avoid infringing a right unduly by defining its limits too narrowly, or inflating a right excessively by defining its limits too broadly.[37] On the balance model, incursions in either direction are equally bad – either for or against the majority. But for Dworkin, the assumption of equivalence is 'false' and prevents us from understanding what it means to take rights seriously – and the balance metaphor is the root of the problem.[38]

Dworkin instead favoured a second model: the idea of rights as a political trump card; and his argument made clear that this idea has deep roots in our legal imagination. In many cases where governments or courts seek to protect an important right, they do so not by striking a balance but by imposing a

[34] Dworkin, 'A Special Supplement' (above n 13).

[35] Dworkin, *Taking Rights Seriously* (above n 13) ch 7 (citations to the essay in what follows are to its reprint in this edition).

[36] Ibid, 197–98.

[37] The balance model is not to be confused with proportionality theory. See J Weinrib, 'When Trumps Clash: Dworkin and the Doctrine of Proportionality' (2017) 30 *Ratio Juris* 341, arguing that despite Dworkin's criticisms of proportionality theory, his theory of rights as trumps is a notable instance of it.

[38] Dworkin, *Taking Rights Seriously* (above n 13) 198.

significant cost to the collective interest, drawing an imbalance in favour of the individual. Our reasoning in these instances is grounded in our commitment to 'the vague but powerful idea of human dignity'.[39] Identifying this idea with Kant, Dworkin asserted that it is premised on the view that 'there are ways of treating a man that are inconsistent with recognizing him as a full member of the human community, and holds that such treatment is profoundly unjust.'[40] Violating a core right is a 'serious matter' because it entails 'treating a man as less than a man, or as less worthy of concern than other men'. We recognise and protect rights as an expression of our conviction that unequal or undignified treatment does 'a grave injustice', one for which we deem it worthwhile to pay an 'incremental cost in social policy or efficiency' to avoid.[41]

If the point of protecting rights is to protect underlying values of dignity and equality, it is more serious to violate an important right than it is to inflate it.[42] We may need to strike a balance when competing rights come into conflict, but not when asking whether the law should recognise a dignity-related right or when defining its limits against the collective.[43] As Dworkin noted, in the one area where 'the stakes for the individual are the highest', the criminal law, 'We say that it is better that a great many guilty men go free than that one innocent man be punished, and that homily rests on the choice of the second model for government.'[44]

If rights sometimes function as trumps, as they appear to in criminal law, when can they be justifiably infringed? In Dworkin's view, in only three instances. The first is where the government shows that values protected by the right (ultimately, dignity and equality) are not at stake in a given case, or only 'in some attenuated form'.[45] Second, the government may show that if a right is defined in a certain way, it will entail a conflict with an equally important right. And third, the government may show that defining a right would entail a 'cost to society [that] would not be simply incremental, but would be of a degree far beyond the cost paid to grant the original right involved, a degree great enough to justify whatever assault on dignity or equality might be involved'.[46]

The second and third of these limits are clearly relevant to contemporary debates about security and are often central points of contention in ways to be explored later in this chapter. First, let us consider the unspoken assumptions that render the theory of rights as trumps plausible within these limits. We can discern these assumptions in Dworkin's own application of the theory to

[39] Ibid.
[40] Ibid.
[41] Ibid.
[42] Ibid.
[43] Ibid.
[44] Ibid, 200.
[45] Ibid.
[46] Ibid.

particular examples. These assumptions are key to what makes the theory less plausible in the present.

A crucial example he considered concerns free speech. Amidst the unrest that surrounded the 1968 Democratic Convention in Chicago, Abbie Hoffman, Jerry Rubin, and other protesters were charged and convicted of crossing state lines with the intent of inciting a riot.[47] Dworkin queried the constitutionality of the provisions and took this as a paradigm case of the challenge of defining the limits of free speech as a political and moral right. He conceded that, if challenged, on the logic of balancing collective and individual interests, the law might plausibly have been defended. But on the trump model, a law criminalising 'emotional speeches which argue that violence is justified in order to secure political equality' is invalid because it fails to fall within any of his three justified limits to core rights.[48] Protecting free speech, even provocative speech, clearly engages dignity and equal respect. He then considered the other two justified limits together – the competing right of other individuals to be safe from personal attacks in the course of a riot, or the 'grave threat to society' itself to which a riot would give rise through looting, vandalism, and general lawlessness.[49] The law fails both of these tests for the crucial reason that the state was not in a position to know 'with any confidence how much and what sort of violence the anti-riot law might be expected to prevent'.[50] It was not clear whether the protesters' expressions were necessary or sufficient conditions for the unrest that followed or whether police actions were a significant contributing cause. Curtailing speech in order to prevent the possibility of a riot entailed 'speculation' in 'conditions of high uncertainty' when the very 'institution of rights, taken seriously, limits [the state's] freedom to experiment under such conditions'.[51] The infringement of free speech here would lead to a 'certain and profound insult' to dignity while yielding only a 'speculative benefit'; but 'if rights mean anything, then the Government cannot simply assume answers that justify its conduct.'[52]

What, then, of the competing rights of others to be free from the violence to which a riot – however speculative – might give rise? Should this potential harm not be considered despite the uncertainty surrounding cause and effect? As Dworkin put it:

> Shall we say that some rights to protection are so important that the Government is justified in doing all it can to maintain them? Shall we therefore say that the Government may abridge the rights of others to act when their acts might simply increase the risk by however slight or speculative a margin, that some person's right to life or property will be violated?[53]

[47] Ibid, 197. The convictions were overturned on appeal on procedural grounds: *United States of America v David Dellinger*, et al, 472 F.2d 340 (1972).
[48] Dworkin, *Taking Rights Seriously* (above n 13) 197.
[49] Ibid, 202.
[50] Ibid.
[51] Ibid.
[52] Ibid.
[53] Ibid, 203.

This, for Dworkin, encapsulated the thrust of the opposition to much of the due process jurisprudence of the 1960s; but it was wrong-headed because significant infringements to dignity or equality cannot be justified on the basis that 'other men's risk of loss may be marginally reduced'.[54]

It is on this point that Dworkin drew a crucial contrast:

> When lawyers say that rights may be limited to protect other rights, or to prevent catastrophe, they have in mind cases in which cause and effect are relatively clear, like the familiar example of a man falsely crying 'Fire!' in a crowded theatre.[55]

The theatre case is one in which there is a 'clear and substantial risk that [a person's] speech will do great damage to the person or property of others and no other means of preventing this are at hand'.[56]

On closer inspection, the riot and theatre cases reveal core unspoken assumptions underlying Dworkin's theory. The anti-riot law is an unjustified limit on free speech because it involves a clear and substantial infringement of dignity without it being clear how much harm it avoids. By contrast, the prohibition on yelling 'fire' in a theatre entails a slight infringement of dignity and almost certainly avoids a significant degree of harm. The theory of rights as trumps therefore works best where a proposed limit:

a. is intended to prevent something amounting to a clear and substantial risk to the collective;
b. bears a direct or close causal link to preventing or significantly minimising the risk; and
c. does not entail a radical infringement of a core right.

It bears emphasising that the theory of rights as trumps is plausible in this text in large measure because Dworkin's paradigm case of a right trumping a freedom in the area of public safety entails a close connection between infringement and harm avoided, and the infringement is minor. The theory is further supported by the fact that his two main examples of unjustified limits – the anti-riot law and the idea that we generally prefer several acquittals of guilty persons to a single wrongful conviction – are cases in which protecting the right at issue entails a risk, but one that is vague and speculative – one that we have difficulty *imagining*.

Conditions that arose after 2001 – giving rise to the harbinger theory but also to fears of lesser forms of terror – have complicated this picture fundamentally. The prospect of mass terrorism presents Dworkin with an example that blurs the distinction between riot and theatre, giving rise to plausible arguments about a threat of enormous gravity, a causal connection between infringement and security that may not be direct but is more than speculative, and the need to

[54] Ibid.
[55] Ibid, 204.
[56] Ibid.

violate rights to a significant degree in light of a belief in the catastrophic cost of doing otherwise.

IV. FROM CARTER TO BUSH

It is important to distinguish why conditions after 2001 presented Dworkin's theory with a challenge it had not faced before. As noted earlier, just as Dworkin was articulating the larger philosophical rationale informing the rights revolution approaching its peak in the 1970s, signs of a profound shift away from the discourse of rights and toward a culture of security and control began to gain pace throughout the Anglo-American world. As many scholars have made clear, the late 1960s to roughly the early 1980s may in some quarters have been a triumphal period for rights, but they were also a time of rising crime rates, growing racial tensions in decaying urban centres, and election cycles increasingly marked by the rhetoric of law and order.[57] As David Garland and others have argued, much of the law and policy of the United States and Britain during this time moved further away from a sympathetic view of the accused to a framing of crime as a problem involving 'unruly youth, dangerous predators, and incorrigible career criminals'.[58] Separating and 'warehousing' poor, racialised, and dangerous populations made up much of the criminal law mandate in the period.[59] Looking at the United States in particular, Jonathan Simon has suggested that by the early 1980s, the crime victim had become the 'dominant model of the citizen',[60] with victims' interests central not only to the criminal law but to the very 'mission of representative government'. What, then, remained of the currency of rights as trumps?

In other quarters, a fair amount remained. The 1980s were still a period in which important milestones in the development of human rights were claimed, including and perhaps most notably the UN Convention Against Torture.[61] Adopted in 1984 and ratified by some 160 countries, Article 2 of the Convention notoriously held the right against torture to be absolute or non-derogable – asserting that 'No exceptional circumstances whatsoever, whether a state of war or a threat of war … or any other public emergency, may be invoked as a justification of torture'. That the United States ratified the Convention with significant qualifications should not detract from the basic symbolic import of the document as a collective affirmation of a belief that in principle

[57] See, eg, Simon (above n 15).

[58] Garland (above n 15) 10. See also Simon (above n 15); and Zedner (above n 15).

[59] L Wacquant, *Punishing the Poor: The Neoliberal Government of Social Insecurity* (Durham, Duke University Press, 2007); M Alexander, *The New Jim Crow: Mass Incarceration in the Age of Colorblindness* (New York, New Press, 2010).

[60] Simon (above n 15) Kindle edition, location 629.

[61] UN General Assembly, *Convention Against Torture and Other Cruel, Inhuman or Degrading Treatment or Punishment* (10 December 1984), UN Treaty Series, vol 1465, 85.

at least some individual rights ought to function as absolute trumps.[62] Despite the practical shortcomings of the Convention as a tool of torture prevention, it is clearly a formulation of rights sympathetic to Dworkin's theory. Further examples consistent with rights as trumps can also be found in the list of non-derogable rights under Article 15 of the European Convention on Human Rights (1950)[63] and the Canadian Supreme Court's application of its new Charter of Rights and Freedoms from 1982.[64] In an early and crucial Charter decision, known as the '*Motor Vehicle* reference,'[65] the Court held that violations of the core right to 'life, liberty, and security of the person' would 'rarely' if ever be justified for reasons of mere 'administrative expediency' and should be permitted only 'in cases arising out of exceptional conditions, such as natural disasters, the outbreak of war, epidemics, and the like'.[66]

But if Dworkin's theory maintained a certain currency in Anglo-American jurisprudence as a normative or aspirational principle, this is not to say that in practical terms human and political rights maintained the broad cultural prominence they had gained by the mid-1970s. On the contrary, the retrenchment was clear. Garland, writing in the months prior to September 11, captured the thrust of the demise in the status of rights by noting:

> The call for protection *from* the state has been increasingly displaced by the demand for protection *by* the state. Procedural safeguards (such as the exclusionary rule in the USA and the defendant's right of silence in the UK) have been part-repealed, surveillance cameras have come to be a routine presence on city streets, and decisions about bail, parole or release from custody now come under intense scrutiny.[67]

Yet as lamentable as this 'displacement' of rights was by 2001, this passage is notable for a certain absence – the absence of the extraordinary. The measures that Garland catalogued are relatively moderate: more scrutiny of procedural

[62] The Reagan administration was reluctant to recognise the 'competence' of the UN Committee Against Torture to assess reports of torture involving US interests: Ronald Reagan, 'Message to the Senate Transmitting the Convention Against Torture and Inhuman Treatment or Punishment' (20 May 1988), available at G Peters and JT Woolley, *The American Presidency Project*, http://www.presidency.ucsb.edu/ws/?pid=35858.

[63] Council of Europe, *European Convention for the Protection of Human Rights and Fundamental Freedoms*, as amended by Protocols Nos 11 and 14 (4 November 1950), ETS 5. Article 15 precludes derogation in any circumstances from Articles 2 (the right not to be deprived of life, except pursuant to a lawful sentence or pursuant to a lawful act of war), 3 (torture), 4(1) (slavery), and 7 (arbitrary punishment).

[64] *Canadian Charter* (above n 5).

[65] *Re BC Motor Vehicle Act* [1985] 2 SCR 486.

[66] Ibid, para 85.

[67] Garland (above n 15) 12. But see also L Lazarus, 'Positive Obligations and Criminal Justice: Duties to Protect or Coerce?' in L Lazarus and JV Roberts (eds), *Principles and Values in Criminal Law and Criminal Justice: Essays in Honour of Andrew Ashworth* (Oxford, Oxford University Press, 2012), suggesting that the trends Garland has described here capture only part of the currency of rights in the period. Lazarus has noted that the call for protection from the state was reflected in an emerging jurisprudence of protective duties, or a discourse of positive rights (to life, liberty, security), that compel the state to prevent and criminalise harmful acts.

protections, more frequent use of custody and surveillance. But there was still a commitment – at least in theory – to *basic* due process protections. Certain lines had not been crossed. Torture, indefinite detention without charge, and targeted killing of one's own citizens would all have seemed excessive if not unthinkable, even for the most cautious advocates of security. In this sense, the change in the landscape that September 11 ushered in did not merely mark a movement toward further securitisation – more of what we saw from the 1970s onward – but rather a dramatic shift in kind. Suddenly, the unspeakable was openly debated. And while we may look back on debates about torture or other radical measures in the early years after 9/11 with growing scepticism or even disbelief, we cannot deny the significance of the fact that we *had* such debates. What, then, was it about the events of 9/11 and the reaction they provoked that brought this about?

V. THE HARBINGER THEORY

The events of 9/11 provoked rights advocates and security theorists alike to re-evaluate assumptions about the danger that individuals are capable of posing to public safety and, consequently, about the extent to which governments should prioritise rights. This re-evaluation was reflected in a set of new assumptions that can be called the harbinger theory, a claim that became pervasive in a wide range of political and cultural discourse in roughly the first decade after 2001. This is the belief that 9/11 marked the harbinger of a new order of terror, one in which further attacks could be expected at some point soon in a large urban centre on a similar or greater scale as 9/11, possibly involving weapons of mass destruction (WMD). Rather than being perceived as anomalous and unlikely to be repeated, 9/11 was believed to presage a qualitative shift in the nature of terrorism: later events would likely entail carnage on a much greater scale than attacks preceding 9/11 precisely on the basis that those events had demonstrated what a small group of non-state actors using relatively crude tools could accomplish: casualties several orders of magnitude greater than earlier acts of terrorism, which had remained in the tens and low hundreds. (The largest terrorist attack in the world prior to 9/11 was the Air India bombing of 1985, which claimed 331 lives.[68]) In the wake of an act of terrorism involving a small group of men causing close to 3,000 deaths, it became more plausible to contemplate the prospect of attacks involving several thousand casualties or possibly even millions. Within this new paradigm, the notion that certain rights

[68] Global Terrorism Database, maintained by the US National Consortium for the Study of Terrorism and Responses to Terrorism, cited in J Mueller and M Stewart, *Terror, Security, Money: Balancing the Risks, Benefits, and Costs of Homeland Security* (Oxford, Oxford University Press, 2011) Kindle location 844.

should be non-derogable or protected in some absolute way – to function as ultimate trumps against collective interests – became problematic and, for some, altogether implausible.[69]

It is beyond the scope of this chapter to examine in detail the various ways in which the harbinger theory became a central part of security policy in North America in the post-9/11 period; I refer the reader to an earlier work on point and offer instead a brief sketch.[70] The theory can be traced to the earliest days after 9/11 and the Bush administration, as the President and other officials frequently invoked the prospect of large-scale terrorist attacks, possibly involving WMD; these invocations were often in defence of the USA PATRIOT Act (2001), the Guantanamo Bay detention camp, and the National Security Agency (NSA) surveillance programme (which was secret prior to 2005).[71] The theory also gained broad cultural resonance in various works of popular culture, often featuring an impending nuclear or mass terrorist attack narrowly averted through the use of torture or other acts of cruelty. The trope could be found in television series such as *24* and *Homeland*, and in countless books and films of the early years after 9/11.[72]

The harbinger theory also gained credence through the work of authorities in the fields of nuclear, biological, and radiological weaponry. Graham Allison, Director of Harvard's Belfer Center for Science and International Affairs, asserted in 2004, without qualification, that a 'nuclear terrorist attack on America in the decade ahead is more likely than not'[73] – forgetting that in 1995 he had claimed that an act of nuclear terrorism against the US would occur 'before the decade is out.'[74] Many nuclear experts agreed with such dire warnings, citing

[69] See, eg, Ignatieff (above n 11); and Ackerman (above n 11). Works that were at a further extreme, contrary to prevailing scholarly opinion about rights and security in the period but still influential, include: A Dershowitz, *Preemption: A Knife That Cuts Both Ways* (New York, Norton, 2006); R Posner, *Not a Suicide Pact: The Constitution in a Time of National Emergency* (Oxford, Oxford University Press, 2006); and J Yoo, *War by Other Means: An Insider's Account of the War on Terror* (New York, Atlantic Monthly Press, 2006). See the discussion in chs 4 and 5 of Diab (above n 19) on the role that fears of terror involving WMD played in defences of extraordinary measures in the work of each of the authors cited here.

[70] Diab (above n 19) chs 3 and 4.

[71] See, eg, The White House, 'Text of President Bush's 2002 State of the Union Address', *Washington Post* (29 January 2002); The White House, 'The National Security Strategy of the United States of America' (17 September 2002), https://www.state.gov/documents/organization/63562.pdf; the White House, 'We Strive To Be A Compassionate, Decent, Hopeful, Society' (text of the President's 2006 State of the Union Address), *New York Times* (31 January 2006); the White House, 'The National Security Strategy of the United States of America' (March 2006), https://www.state.gov/documents/organization/64884.pdf. For further examples, see Diab (above n 19) ch 3.

[72] A list and discussion of these can be found in Diab (above n 19) 112–13. See also I Lustick, *Trapped in the War on Terror* (Philadelphia, University of Pennsylvania Press, 2006) 25; and K Dodds, 'Screening Terror: Hollywood, the United States and the Construction of Danger' (2008) 1(2) *Critical Studies on Terrorism* 227.

[73] G Allison, *Nuclear Terror: The Ultimate Preventable Catastrophe* (New York, Henry Holt, 2005) 15.

[74] G Allison, 'Must We Wait for the Nuclear Morning After?' *Washington Post* (30 April 1995).

as reasons the poor security around nuclear installations in the countries of the former Soviet Union, open access to bomb-building methods, and the fact that al Qaida and other groups were known to harbour nuclear ambitions.[75] A similar claim was often made in relation to bioterrorism. Numerous authorities noted that some of the most lethal toxins known to science can be cultivated from natural sources and readily produced in large quantities using knowledge and techniques readily accessible on the internet.[76] Radiological terrorism seemed even more likely, given the ready availability of highly radioactive material in unguarded industrial and institutional sites such as hospitals, universities, and factories.[77]

The harbinger theory also played a role in the rhetoric of the Obama administration, in defence of targeted killing and other extreme measures.[78] A notable example arose with Edward Snowden's revelations in June of 2013 of the NSA's secret bulk collection of phone metadata of all Americans, along with the content of internet communications of large numbers of foreigners visiting US websites.[79] In a press release issued within days of the first revelations, James Clapper, Director of National Intelligence, claimed that the surveillance programmes had helped to 'impede the proliferation of weapons of mass destruction'.[80] In a speech of January 2014, the President justified the continued use of mass surveillance by making several references to the prospect of large-scale terror, including the claim that '[t]he men and women at the NSA know if another 9/11 or massive cyberattack occurs, they will be asked by Congress and the media why they failed to connect the dots'.[81]

[75] C Ferguson and W Potter, *The Four Faces of Nuclear Terrorism* (London, Routledge, 2005); M Bunn, 'Securing the Bomb 2010: Securing All Nuclear Materials in Four Years', Project on Managing the Atom, Belfer Center for Science and International Affairs, Harvard Kennedy School and Nuclear Threat Initiative (April 2010).

[76] On biological terror, see B Kellman, *Bioviolence: Preventing Biological Terror and Crime* (Cambridge, Cambridge University Press, 2007); J Davis, 'A Biological Warfare Wake-Up Call: Prevalent Myths and Likely Scenarios' in J Davis and B Schneider (eds), *The Gathering Biological Warfare Storm* (Westport, Praeger, 2004); and F Barnaby, *How to Build a Nuclear Bomb and Other Weapons of Mass Destruction* (London, Granta Books, 2004).

[77] M Levi and H Kelly, 'Weapons of Mass Disruption', *Scientific American* (November 2002) 77. See also Diab (above n 19), exploring a tendency on the part of authorities on terror involving WMD to infer the likelihood of such events on the basis of their theoretical simplicity. The book also demonstrates a common failure among such authors to acknowledge a host of challenges that terrorists are likely to confront in practice. It surveys a body of skeptical literature to outline these practical impediments and call into question the near-term probability of terror involving WMD.

[78] See, eg, the White House, 'National Security Strategy' (May 2010), http://nssarchive.us/NSSR/2010.pdf; the White House, 'National Strategy for Counterterrorism' (June 2011), https://obamawhitehouse.archives.gov/sites/default/files/counterterrorism_strategy.pdf.

[79] G Greenwald, *No Place Left to Hide: Edward Snowden, the NSA, and the US Surveillance State* (New York, Metropolitan Books, 2014) 92–118.

[80] J Clapper, 'Facts on the Collection of Intelligence Pursuant to Section 702 of the Foreign Intelligence Surveillance Act', Office of the Director of National Intelligence, Washington, DC (8 June 2013) 3.

[81] B Obama, 'Remarks by the President on Review of Signals Intelligence', Department of Justice (17 January 2014).

To be clear, while the harbinger theory played an important role in debates about terror and security in roughly the first decade after 9/11, perceptions of terrorism have continued to evolve. Nonetheless, terrorism continues to be associated with large-scale casualties. More recent attacks in Europe – 130 killed in Paris in 2015, 84 in Nice in 2016, 23 in Manchester in 2017 – garnered wide media coverage and engaged broader national and international interest.[82] This suggests an ongoing tendency to view terrorism as a kind of super-crime or a special kind of threat. Rights advocates, including Dworkin, have sought to contest this view, and the reason flows directly from terrorism's problematic implications for rights.

VI. REASSESSING RIGHTS AS TRUMPS AFTER 9/11

Soon after 2001, as Dworkin began to weigh in on debates about rights, he was seized by the harbinger theory and the prospect of mass terror and grappled with them repeatedly. That rights as trumps would need to be qualified or revised precisely in light of this new catastrophic imagination was clear from the dramatic way he opened one of his first essays on national security in the period:

> Two years after the September 11 catastrophe Americans remain in great danger … Well-financed terrorists, who live and undergo training in various foreign countries, are determined to kill Americans and are willing to die in order to do so. If they gain access to nuclear weapons, they would be able to inflict even more terrible harm.[83]

The prevailing assumption driving the adoption of the various extraordinary measures – mass preventive detention of Arabs and Muslims, 'contempt for the Geneva Conventions,' etc – was that in light of the possibly unprecedented gravity of the threat to security, we could no longer offer the same protections to suspected terrorists as those we offer to persons accused of lesser crimes:

> [I]t may be right, in more normal times, to allow a hundred guilty defendants to go free rather than convict one innocent one, but we must reconsider that arithmetic when one of the guilty may blow up the rest of Manhattan.[84]

Consistent with the third of Dworkin's justified limits on rights in 1970, the cost of protecting rights in this context was not simply incrementally different but qualitatively different or altogether prohibitive.

But if this was the rationale for embracing extraordinary measures, Dworkin argued, we should have been clear about it. We should have avoided falling in to the trap of assuming the nature of terrorism calls for a different balancing

[82] See en.wikipedia.org: 'November 2015 Paris Attacks'; '2016 Nice Attack'; 'Manchester Arena Bombing', as well as a host of contemporary articles and news stories from major national and international news outlets.

[83] Dworkin, 'Terror and the Attack on Civil Liberties' (above n 11) 37.

[84] Dworkin, 'The Threat to Patriotism' (above n 11) 47, paraphrasing Laurence Tribe.

between rights and security. This only encouraged the error of thinking the 'requirements of fairness are fully satisfied' when we apply 'laxer standards of criminal justice' in dealing with terrorist suspects despite the greater risk of wrongful convictions.[85] Once again, for Dworkin the balance metaphor was 'deeply misleading' because it suggested 'a false description of the decision the nation must make'.[86] The leadership, or electorate as a whole, was not being asked to decide how much security or freedom 'we' want but rather how much freedom to accord to a small few. The question for Dworkin once again was 'not where our interest lies on balance, but what justice requires'.[87]

Instead, Dworkin sought to salvage the theory of rights as trumps from the threat of obsolescence in light of fears of mass terrorism by showing that, with certain qualifications, it could be reconciled with them. On this view, we should speak more plainly and admit that 'laxer standards would be unfair' but agree that 'we must nevertheless adopt them to protect ourselves from disaster'.[88] In this case, however, rather than feeling justified in lowering our standards, we should be more 'discriminating' and 'insist that government show that unfair treatment is necessary, not for some widely defined category of persons, but, so far as this is practicable, for individual suspects or detainees, one by one'.[89] Rights may thus be justifiably infringed in this case, and to a radical degree perhaps, but something of the logic of rights as trumps should be preserved: a sense that any serious violation of dignity and equality is profoundly undesirable wherever it occurs and for whatever reason.

The more crucial question for Dworkin, however, was whether the United States did in fact 'face such extreme danger from terrorism that we must act unjustly'.[90] This appeared to him at the time 'a difficult question' given that it was impossible to 'accurately gauge the actual power' of the various groups believed to harbour the desire to carry out further attacks.[91] Dworkin then made the following crucial concession:

> al-Qaeda killed, by latest reckoning, approximately 3,000 people in minutes on September 11, which is a quarter of the number of murders in the entire country in 1999. If they or some other terrorist organization has or gains access to nuclear, chemical, or biological weapons and the means to use them, then the threat to us would be truly enormous. It would justify unusual and, in themselves, unfair measures if the government thought that these would substantially reduce the risk of catastrophe.[92]

[85] Ibid.
[86] Ibid, 48.
[87] Ibid.
[88] Ibid, 47.
[89] Ibid.
[90] Ibid, 49.
[91] Regarding the issue of secrecy in the context of evaluating security claims, see the chapter in this volume by Liora Lazarus.
[92] Dworkin, 'The Threat to Patriotism' (above n 11) 49.

Yet even so, Dworkin concluded that 'it would be imperative to permit only the smallest curtailment of traditional rights that could reasonably be thought necessary', and in various ways, the new policies 'fail that test'.[93]

This passage gives us the crux of the conundrum that rights as trumps has faced after 9/11 and the impasse at which the larger debate about rights and security has been stalled for over a decade. As Dworkin readily conceded, when one version of the harbinger theory or another is granted, security must trump rights. But what prevented Dworkin from a full or unqualified surrender to this logic was the question of the *likelihood* of mass terrorism on that scale. Were we in such a situation? Not being in a position to say either way, he was unable to do more than emphasise that short of proof of the imminence of mass terrorism, the earlier rationale for upholding rights – for insisting on the smallest necessary curtailments – remains valid. With the passage of time, however, Dworkin became more confident in his assessment of the threat of terrorism and offered a new defence for rights as trumps.

VII. SECURITY AS TRUMP?

Dworkin's last extended treatment of rights as trumps was set out in a chapter titled 'Terrorism and Human Rights' in his 2006 book *Is Democracy Possible Here?*[94] Once again, his analysis was framed from the outset in terms of the harbinger theory, suggesting that he continued to see the possibility of mass terrorism as the crucial test of his conception of rights. The chapter opened with another bracing set of images:

> Thousands of fanatics around the world would be glad to die if they could kill Westerners – particularly Americans. They created an unbelievable catastrophe in September 2001, and they may already have weapons of apocalyptic murder that could dwarf the horror of that destruction.[95]

Dworkin then considered a host of Bush administration measures in a discussion similar to those found in the essays of 1970 and 2003. Bush supporters invoked the need for a rebalancing of freedom and security, but a proper assessment of rights – in this case human rights – called for a greater emphasis on Kantian notions of dignity and equality for reasons similar to those canvased earlier. Drawing upon this reasoning, some measures were clearly unjustified, including coercive interrogation amounting to torture, which had recently come to light.[96] But other infringements, such as indefinite detention without charge and the use of military tribunals involving secret evidence, presented a greater challenge.

[93] Ibid.
[94] Dworkin, *Is Democracy Possible Here?* (above n 11) ch 2.
[95] Ibid, 24.
[96] Ibid, 40.

One common view held that while some detainees may be innocent, others may be quite dangerous, and in the current climate, a system guaranteeing a fairer trial would be too risky, given that 'such trials sometimes allow dangerous people to go free.'[97] But for Dworkin, applying different standards for terrorist suspects (eg, through military tribunals) showed that 'we do not regard [the latter] as fully human.'[98] Just as we reject the prospect of mistakenly incarcerating 'ordinary citizens' who are accused of more ordinary crimes because 'we think people have a right not to be injured in that very serious way' for some 'marginal' improvement in our safety, so too should we reject imposing lesser standards against certain foreigners for marginal improvement in national security.[99] Or at least, this was the analogy that Dworkin sought to draw. The crucial question was whether the menace of domestic crime and the threat of terrorism on a large scale were analogous in 2006 – a question that remains relevant still.

Dworkin's chapter culminates in an assessment of precisely this point. Dworkin's response – and thus his final defence of rights as trumps – involved an effort to make the gap appear smaller between the risk posed by conventional crime and that posed by mass terrorism. With the events of 9/11 receding into the past, Dworkin sought to shrink the gap by emphasising the abstract character of many of our more extreme fears – suggesting they were now to be relegated to the realm of the hypothetical. In a passage worth examining closely, he wrote:

> [E]ven human rights are not absolute.... [I]n a sufficiently grave emergency, a government is justified in violating even the most basic and fundamental human rights after these have been precisely stated. There is a stock example whose familiarity may have deadened its force. Suppose we have a captured terrorist who we know has planted a nuclear bomb timed to explode in two hours somewhere in Manhattan. It would be absurd, people say, not to torture him if we thought torture would force him to tell us where the bomb is in time to diffuse it. Let us now accept, if only for the sake of this discussion, that it is morally permissible to violate human rights in a sufficiently grave emergency like this one. Then our question becomes: how grave must the emergency be?[100]

Thus, the force of the concern about mass terrorism lies not in questions around its likelihood or practical import but in its effect as a theoretical abstraction. But, as Dworkin argued, as soon as we begin to interrogate the theory with practical considerations, it loses force. Unless we have clear proof that we find ourselves in a similarly extreme situation, we have no reason to conclude that serious violations are justified:

> We must take care not to define 'emergency' as simply 'great danger' or to suppose that any act that improves our own security, no matter how marginally, is for that

[97] Ibid.
[98] Ibid, 45.
[99] Ibid.
[100] Ibid, 49–50.

> reason justified. We must hold to a very different virtue: the old-fashioned virtue of courage.... We show courage in our domestic criminal law and practice: we increase the statistical risk that each of us will suffer from violent crime when we forbid preventive detention and insist on fair trials for everyone accused of crime. We must show parallel courage when the danger comes from abroad because our dignity is at stake in the same way.[101]

Put otherwise, short of clear proof that the threat we face in relation to terrorism is qualitatively greater than that posed by domestic crime – both in terms of the likelihood of a large-scale attack occurring and the extent of the damage if one is attempted – serious rights violations are unjust. Fears of mass terrorism are, for the most part, too speculative to serve as the basis for law or policy for similar reasons that applied in the case of the anti-riot laws in 1968:

> Now notice the crucial dimensions of the stock example about the ticking nuclear bomb hidden in Manhattan. The danger is both horrific and certain; we know that our victim is responsible for that danger, and we assume that if we torture him and he yields, we can remove the danger. None of that is true about our policy of imprisonment without charge or trial in Guantanamo and our other bases around the world. We are in danger of another devastating attack, to be sure. But there is no reason yet to think that the danger approaches certainty or that our violations of human rights are well calculated to end or even significantly to reduce that danger.[102]

The key, then, to Dworkin's treatment of the harbinger theory (or the prospect of large-scale terrorism) is knowledge. Without certainty or a reasonable sense of the risk at issue, we cannot and should not draw a *qualitative* distinction between the threat posed by mass terrorism and conventional crime. Rights should therefore still serve as trumps.

On one reading, Dworkin was persuasive. He plausibly defended the currency of rights as trumps with the qualification that at a certain hypothetical extreme, torture or other extraordinary measures *might* be justified. But in this case, as Dworkin implied by offering a similar analysis to the one in the anti-riot law case, the prospect of mass terrorism does not present us with anything new. It is simply a more striking version of Dworkin's third justified limit on rights, a case where a core right may be curtailed to avoid an unusually grave danger to society.

But on another reading, the harbinger theory or even fears of lesser forms of terrorism – attacks where scores of people are killed but fewer than, say, a hundred, as has become increasingly common throughout Europe – pose a greater challenge. On this reading, we note that a consistent feature of Dworkin's defence of rights as trumps over the years is that it is premised on the notion that all threats conform to one of only two possible models. A threat may be like a speech that gives rise to a riot, and in this case, since we do not know the likelihood of a riot occurring or the harm it may entail, no significant curtailment

[101] Ibid, 50.
[102] Ibid.

of rights (speech) is justified. Or a threat is like the act of falsely yelling 'fire!' in a crowded theatre, which will almost certainly give rise to a stampede, which in turn will certainly cause serious injury to several people – and therefore a minimal impairment of rights (a prohibition on that speech) is clearly justified. Dworkin's defence of rights as trumps after 2001 is premised upon the assumption that our fear of mass terrorism and our approach to terrorist suspects are variations on the riot case. We do not know whether any detention, interrogation, or surveillance we carry out will prevent an act of terrorism because we cannot know how likely it is that terrorist suspects will attempt acts of large-scale terrorism or what harm they will in fact cause if they attempt it.

But reading Dworkin against the grain, we can readily see that the mass terrorism example does not map onto the riot case so neatly. In fact, it straddles both the riot and the theatre examples, blurring the distinction between them and undermining Dworkin's narrow set of instances in which rights can be violated. Like the riot example, in which the harm that might flow from an incendiary speech is difficult to predict, we often cannot quantify the probability that a terrorist suspect will act and thus what harm he or she might cause. But unlike the riot case, in which the consequences of a speech are uncertain, when a terrorist succeeds in setting off a bomb or carrying out some other large-scale attack, serious harm is very likely. And while the harm that would follow from yelling 'fire!' in a crowded theatre or from setting off a bomb in a crowded theatre is likely to be serious in either case, the measures that may be necessary to prevent these acts are not the same: they are far less invasive in the one case (a prohibition on yelling 'fire!') than in the other (detention, surveillance, etc).

To make clear how and why this reading poses a significant challenge to the theory of rights as trumps, it may help to step back from a close analysis of Dworkin's examples and from his narrow set of justified limits, to offer some broader observations about the perception of rights in the present climate.

One might approach current debates about security with a healthy dose of scepticism about claims made in relation to the threat of terrorism. But certain facts cannot be ignored. While the harbinger theory may have proven to be illusory in the sense that an attack on the scale of 9/11 (some three thousand lives) now seems to us more an anomaly than a harbinger, what can still be described as mass or large-scale terrorist attacks (roughly ten to one hundred lives) have been occurring in the past few years with distressing frequency across the Europe and the United States. This fact alone lends a certain plausibility to official claims that significant incursions on rights are necessary – emergency rule in France, for example – on the basis that in at least some cases, persons of interest to authorities present a more than hypothetical prospect of mass carnage. While we can certainly agree with Dworkin that taking rights seriously calls for a clearer causal connection between the threats that are said to justify serious limits on rights on the one hand and the harm we may prevent in the course of dealing with a given suspect on the other hand, when the potential threat is as serious as a mass casualty attack, reasonable people may take a different view.

They might plausibly assert that they are justified in accepting that a reasonable possibility of averting a large-scale attack is a sufficient basis to warrant limits on rights, even significant limits, in at least some cases. We may certainly disagree with this and implore our adversaries to muster greater 'courage' as Dworkin suggested, but we cannot dismiss the logic in question as altogether implausible or misguided.

To be clear, the argument in this chapter is not that mass terrorism invalidates the theory of rights as trumps. The argument is that fears of mass terrorism fundamentally affect its *currency*. The prospect of mass terrorism has come to complicate the theoretical simplicity of Dworkin's ideal of rights as trumps, and this, together with other geopolitical realities, hinders the ideal from resonating in our time as it did in the 1970s.[103] The claims that it makes on voters, let alone on politicians, must vie daily with images of carnage that unsettle older cultural or political assumptions about when and where terrorism occurs. It has become so common and proximate a possibility to Western populations that it recalls the scene in Terry Gilliam's 1985 film *Brazil* in which a bomb explodes in the middle of a department store and the customers, so inured to such violence, dust themselves off and carry on shopping in seeming indifference. While we have not yet and may never reach that point emotionally, we do not seem far off in terms of the sheer frequency and unpredictability of events. Acts of terrorism still have the power to dominate our news cycle and shape our politics, hence the dissonance many feel when invited to think of rights as trumps. The impasse at which we find ourselves in broader debates about human rights and security is thus at root an effect of our inability to reconcile the theory with this new reality.

REFERENCES

Ackerman, B, *Before the Next Attack: Preserving Civil Liberties in an Age of Terrorism* (New Haven, Yale University Press, 2006).

Alexander, M, *The New Jim Crow: Mass Incarceration in the Age of Colorblindness* (New York, New Press, 2010).

Allison, G, *Nuclear Terror: The Ultimate Preventable Catastrophe* (New York, Henry Holt, 2005).

[103] This is not to say that the theory of rights as trumps has not maintained a significant measure of currency, at least impliedly, in important legal and political contexts in the post-9/11 period, including among jurists, law scholars, and right advocates. Notable examples include D Luban, 'Liberalism, Torture, and the Ticking Bomb' (2005) 91 *Virginia Law Review* 1425; and J Mayerfeld, 'In Defence of the Absolute Prohibition of Torture' (2008) 22(2) *Public Affairs Quarterly* 109. See also *Saadi v Italy*, App No 37201/06, European Court of Human Rights (28 February 2008), affirming the absolute prohibition on torture in the context of deportation giving rise to the risk of torture; and *Bundesverfassungsgericht* [BVerfG] (15 February 2006), 1 BvR 357/05, a decision of the German Federal Constitutional Court finding unconstitutional the prospect of the military shooting down a plane hijacked by terrorists and destined for a particular target.

Barnaby, F, *How to Build a Nuclear Bomb and Other Weapons of Mass Destruction* (London, Granta Books, 2004).
BBC, 'Theresa May: Tories to Consider Leaving European Convention on Human Rights', *BBC News* (9 March 2013).
Bunn, M, 'Securing the Bomb 2010: Securing All Nuclear Materials in Four Years', Project on Managing the Atom, Belfer Center for Science and International Affairs, Harvard Kennedy School and Nuclear Threat Initiative (April 2010).
Clapper, J, 'Facts on the Collection of Intelligence Pursuant to Section 702 of the Foreign Intelligence Surveillance Act', Office of the Director of National Intelligence, Washington, DC (8 June 2013).
Cole, D and Lobel, J, *Less Safe, Less Free: Why America is Losing the War on Terror* (New York, New Press, 2007).
Council of Europe, *European Convention for the Protection of Human Rights and Fundamental Freedoms*, as amended by Protocols Nos 11 and 14 (4 November 1950), ETS 5.
Davis, J, 'A Biological Warfare Wake-Up Call: Prevalent Myths and Likely Scenarios' in J Davis and B Schneider (eds), *The Gathering Biological Warfare Storm* (Westport, Praeger, 2004).
Dershowitz, A, *Preemption: A Knife That Cuts Both Ways* (New York, Norton, 2006).
Diab, R, *The Harbinger Theory: How the Post-9/11 Emergency Became Permanent and the Case for Reform* (New York, Oxford University Press, 2015).
Dodds, K, 'Screening Terror: Hollywood, the United States and the Construction of Danger' (2008) 1(2) *Critical Studies on Terrorism* 227.
Dworkin, R, *Is Democracy Possible Here? Principles for a New Political Debate* (Princeton, Princeton University Press, 2006).
——, 'A Special Supplement: Taking Rights Seriously', *New York Review of Books* (17 December 1970).
——, *Taking Rights Seriously* (Cambridge, Harvard University Press, 1977).
——, 'Terror and the Attack on Civil Liberties', *New York Review of Books* (6 November 2003).
——, 'The Threat to Patriotism', *New York Review of Books* (28 February 2002).
Ferguson, C and Potter, W, *The Four Faces of Nuclear Terrorism* (London, Routledge, 2005).
Forcese, C and Roach, K, *False Security: The Radicalization of Canadian Anti-Terrorism* (Toronto, Irwin Law, 2015).
Fuller, L, *The Morality of Law* (New Haven, Yale University Press, 1963).
Garland, D, *The Culture of Control: Crime and Social Order in Contemporary Society* (Chicago, University of Chicago Press, 2001).
Glendon, M, *Rights Talk: The Impoverishment of Political Discourse* (New York, Free Press, 1991).
Greenwald, G, *No Place Left to Hide: Edward Snowden, the NSA, and the US Surveillance State* (New York, Metropolitan Books, 2014).
Human Rights Watch, 'United States' in *World Report 2017* (New York, Human Rights Watch, 2017).
Hunt, L, *Inventing Human Rights* (New York, Norton, 2007).
Hussain, M, 'US Has Only Acknowledged a Fifth of Its Lethal Strikes, New Study Finds', *The Intercept* (13 June 2017).

Ignatieff, M, *The Lesser Evil: Political Ethics in an Age of Terror* (Princeton, Princeton University Press, 2004).

International Commission of Jurists, *Addressing Damage, Urging Action: Report of the Eminent Jurists Panel on Terrorism, Counter-Terrorism and Human Rights* (Geneva, International Commission of Jurists, 2009).

——, *Transnational Injustices: National Security Transfers and International Law* (Geneva, International Commission of Jurists, 2017).

Iriye, A, Goedde, P and Hitchcock, W (eds), *The Human Rights Revolution: An International History* (Oxford, Oxford University Press, 2012).

Kellman, B, *Bioviolence: Preventing Biological Terror and Crime* (Cambridge, Cambridge University Press, 2007).

Lazarus, L, 'Positive Obligations and Criminal Justice: Duties to Protect or Coerce?' in L Lazarus and JV Roberts (eds), *Principles and Values in Criminal Law and Criminal Justice: Essays in Honour of Andrew Ashworth* (Oxford, Oxford University Press, 2012).

Lazarus, L and Goold, BJ, 'Security and Human Rights: The Search for a Language of Reconciliation' in BJ Goold and L Lazarus (eds), *Security and Human Rights* (Oxford, Hart Publishing, 2007).

Levi, M and Kelly, H, 'Weapons of Mass Disruption', *Scientific American* (November 2002).

Library of Congress, 'France: State of Emergency Officially Ends as New Security Measures Come into Force', *Global Legal Monitor* (29 November 2017), http://www.loc.gov/law/foreign-news/article/france-state-of-emergency-officially-ends-as-new-security-measures-come-into-force/.

Luban, D, 'Liberalism, Torture, and the Ticking Bomb' (2005) 91 *Virginia Law Review* 1425.

Lustick, I, *Trapped in the War on Terror* (Philadelphia, University of Pennsylvania Press, 2006).

Mayerfeld, J, 'In Defence of the Absolute Prohibition of Torture' (2008) 22(2) *Public Affairs Quarterly* 109.

Medhora, S, 'Law to Strip Dual Nationals of Australian Citizenship Set to Pass Parliament', *Guardian* (10 November 2015).

Moyn, S, *Human Rights and the Uses of History* (London, Verso, 2014).

——, *The Last Utopia: Human Rights in History* (Cambridge, Harvard University Press, 2012).

Mueller, J and Stewart, M, *Terror, Security, Money: Balancing the Risks, Benefits, and Costs of Homeland Security* (Oxford, Oxford University Press, 2011).

New York Times, 'The Guantánamo Docket', *New York Times* (updated 2 May 2018), https://www.nytimes.com/interactive/projects/guantanamo.

Obama, B, 'Remarks by the President on Review of Signals Intelligence', Department of Justice (17 January 2014).

Packer, H, *The Limits of the Criminal Sanction* (Stanford, Stanford University Press, 1968).

Posner, R, *Not a Suicide Pact: The Constitution in a Time of National Emergency* (Oxford, Oxford University Press, 2006).

Rawls, J, 'The Sense of Justice' (1963) 72 *Philosophical Review* 281.

Reagan, R, 'Message to the Senate Transmitting the Convention Against Torture and Inhuman Treatment or Punishment' (20 May 1988).

Simon, J, *Governing Through Crime: How the War on Crime Transformed American Democracy and Created a Culture of Fear* (Oxford, Oxford University Press, 2007).

UN General Assembly, *Convention Against Torture and Other Cruel, Inhuman or Degrading Treatment or Punishment* (10 December 1984), UN Treaty Series, vol 1465.

——, *Universal Declaration of Human Rights* (10 December 1948), 217 A (III).

Wacquant, L, *Punishing the Poor: The Neoliberal Government of Social Insecurity* (Durham, Duke University Press, 2007).

Weinrib, J, 'When Trumps Clash: Dworkin and the Doctrine of Proportionality' (2017) 30 *Ratio Juris* 341.

White House, 'The National Security Strategy of the United States of America' (17 September 2002), https://www.state.gov/documents/organization/63562.pdf.

——, 'The National Security Strategy of the United States of America' (March 2006), https://www.state.gov/documents/organization/64884.pdf.

——, 'National Security Strategy' (May 2010), http://nssarchive.us/NSSR/2010.pdf.

——, 'National Strategy for Counterterrorism' (June 2011), https://obamawhitehouse.archives.gov/sites/default/files/counterterrorism_strategy.pdf.

——, 'Text of President Bush's 2002 State of the Union Address', *Washington Post* (29 January 2002).

——, 'We Strive To Be A Compassionate, Decent, Hopeful, Society' (text of the President's 2006 State of the Union Address), *New York Times* (31 January 2006).

Yoo, J, *War by Other Means: An Insider's Account of the War on Terror* (New York, Atlantic Monthly Press, 2006).

Zedner, L, 'Seeking Security by Eroding Rights: The Side-Stepping of Due Process' in BJ Goold and L Lazarus (eds), *Security and Human Rights* (Oxford, Hart Publishing, 2007).

11

Violence, Human Rights, and Security

CHETAN BHATT

I. INTRODUCTION

THE OPPOSITION BETWEEN human rights and security has become the key binary for thinking about the most compelling political issues today. Indeed, questions of security and rights seem to structure the entire field of political discourse in several Western and non-Western liberal democracies. The 2016 US presidential election victory of Donald Trump, for example, rested on the appeal among major sections of the white, evangelical Protestant, often lower-middle class electorate for authoritarian actions in the name of what they understood to be – and what Trump articulated to them as – their or America's 'security'. Similarly, the severe curtailment of rights he proposed, such as his ban on Muslims travelling from six countries, relied on a zero-sum calculus: 'their' constitutional rights diminished 'our' security.[1] It is additionally significant that Trump's political discourse identified national 'glory' with enlarged 'security': 'Make America Great Again / Make America Safe Again'.

As extreme and fearsome as is the Trump assault on the ground of human rights – and it arises from a political theology that is different in kind and not just in tone to liberal, hawkish predecessors – it is important to consider a deeper series of questions. Why are issues about human rights and issues about security so readily associable such that the opposition of rights to security is now virtually naturalised in both popular and academic discourse? Why is a 'balance' between rights and security (one which Trump tilted overwhelmingly in illiberal directions) a key theme in this relation?[2]

[1] C Mortimer, 'Donald Trump Rejects Intelligence Report on Travel Ban Because It Doesn't Say What He Wants It To', *Independent* (25 February 2017), http://www.independent.co.uk/news/world/americas/us-politics/donald-trump-muslim-ban-travel-ban-intelligence-homeland-security-terrorism-threat-us-iran-somalia-a7599126.html.

[2] J Waldron, 'Security and Liberty: The Image of Balance' (2003) *Journal of Political Philosophy* 191–210. See also Ian Loader's chapter in the first edition of this volume: I Loader, 'The Cultural

While it is common to think of human rights and security in a linear, oppositional relation to each other, this is only one of the ways that human rights and security are related. For example, another Trump retort hovers around the social stability and group rights for whites that have been lost in favour of the human rights claimed by minorities.[3] In the name of social security, communal group rights can be marshalled against universal human rights. Indeed, much right-wing and far-right discourse often contrasts desirable liberties, which nestle within a nostalgic vision of social security, with detested international human rights, which are claimed to undermine that same security.[4] Another key theme among Trump supporters is the loss of rights due to the political and economic neglect of (some) white populations by the federal state.[5] Here, somehow, the alleged loss of rights is woven by Trump and his supporters into a political discourse that proposes a security remedy to re-establish those rights: tougher immigration control, a border wall with Mexico, and the like. The language of greater security is imagined together with a gain in group rights for some white populations and a consequent loss of the rights of others. If this is another zero-sum fiction, the key point here is that greater security is alleged to result in greater liberties, a familiar rhetorical trope in several populist-right movements.

Leaving aside the many deceptions here, this last point alerts us to other relations between human rights and security that are not based on their opposition to each other. The fields of social life articulated under the rubric of 'security' have expanded so enormously in recent decades that they controvert a simple understanding of the 'balance' between international human rights and national security. Security is an ill-defined and malleable concept. Yet it has informed vast areas of public, national, and international policy, often in contradictory or incoherent ways. While we may be alive to the sharp divergence of ideas about national/state as against human/individual security, there are a 'multiplicity of interlinked yet discordant security discourses'.[6] These cover various scales (national, international, collective) and many substantive areas, including development, the environment, food, health, and so on.

The proliferation of security discourse is related to the post-9/11 political and policy environment. But it is also associated with a range of other independent developments, including the burgeoning field of human security that evolved rapidly after the mid-1990s, especially in the aftermath of the 1994

Lives of Security and Rights' in BJ Goold and L Lazarus (eds), *Security and Human Rights* (Oxford, Hart Publishing, 2007).

[3] R Griffin and R Teixeira, 'The Story of Trump's Appeal: A Portrait of Trump Voters', Democracy Fund Voter Study Group (June 2017), https://www.voterstudygroup.org/reports/2016-elections/story-of-trumps-appeal.

[4] C Bhatt, 'The New Xenologies of Europe: Civil Tensions and Mythic Pasts' (2012) 8(3) *Journal of Civil Society* 307–26.

[5] Griffin and Teixeira (above n 3).

[6] R Luckham, 'The Discordant Voices of Security' (2007) 17(4/5) *Development in Practice* 685–89.

United Nations Human Development Report.[7] Human security was defined in this report as having an embedded relation to human rights. Indeed, for some, human rights flow from an attention to human and individual security.[8] Additionally, questions of human, social, and national security often become intertwined in complex ways, such that human security and the security of the state can be articulated together as part of a common policy discourse. Indeed, the association between individual, social, and national security is an older one, often linked to social democratic welfare and citizenship rights, and thus civil and human rights.[9] In this sense, the emergence of a discourse of human security associated with human rights can be seen as part of an older tradition that linked rather than opposed rights and security.

Human security and human rights have also become integrated directly with belligerent areas of national security, including counterterrorism and counterinsurgency. Perhaps counterintuitively, through the vehicle of human security, human rights have been articulated in explicit national security terms and within a firmly militarised discourse. The argument here is not simply that human rights discourse has been used illegitimately to justify illegal wars and invasions[10] but that deeper policy relations have emerged between human security, human rights, and militarisation. For example, official US counterinsurgency (COIN) policy describes how a military approach can integrate human security *and therefore* human rights within a comprehensive COIN strategy.[11] Human security and national security have been associated in other political and policy areas. For example, strategies to prevent violent extremism in the United Kingdom emphasise the 'safeguarding' of children and young people who may otherwise commit atrocities that kill and maim others.[12] Here, we see the articulation of a double concern for the safety, rights, and security of children, and the security of those they might kill were they to become beholden to salafi-jihadi ideologies.[13]

The proliferation of security discourses – human, social, national, and other – should not surprise us. Security, whether conceived of in human or state

[7] UNDP, 'Human Development Report 1994: New Dimensions of Human Security' (1994), http://hdr.undp.org/en/content/human-development-report-1994.

[8] FO Hampson with J Daudelin, JB Hay, T Martin, and H Reid, *Madness in the Multitude: Human Security and World Disorder* (Don Mills, ON, Oxford University Press, 2002).

[9] TH Marshall, *Citizenship and Social Class and Other Essays* (Cambridge, Cambridge University Press, 1950).

[10] A Bartholomew, 'Empire's Law and the Contradictory Politics of Human Rights' in A Bartholomew (ed), *Empire's Law: The American Imperial Project and the 'War to Remake the World'* (London, Pluto Press, 2006).

[11] US Government, 'Counterinsurgency Guide', US Bureau of Political-Military Affairs (January 2009), https://www.state.gov/documents/organization/119629.pdf, emphasis added.

[12] UK Department of Education, 'Protecting Children from Radicalisation: The Prevent Duty' (July 2015), https://www.gov.uk/government/publications/protecting-children-from-radicalisation-the-prevent-duty.

[13] See also the chapter by Liora Lazarus in the first edition of this volume: L Lazarus, 'Mapping the Right to Security' in BJ Goold and L Lazarus (eds), *Security and Human Rights* (Oxford, Hart Publishing, 2007).

terms, is a fundamental element of the management and governance of populations and territories by states.[14] It is therefore not easy to separate contemporary national security concerns and their relation to (or often diminishing of) human rights and civil liberties from wider apprehensions around security in many contemporary liberal democracies. In this article, and in the manner of a think-piece, I want to explore the associations between security and human rights by considering some deeper issues in liberal political philosophy regarding the relation between security, rights, violence, and law. Central to both older and contemporary discussions of rights and security is a series of tensions around key themes that are important to liberalism: rights/security; politics/violence; civility/barbarism; the rule of law/anarchy.

Debates about human rights and security metonymically represent a more fundamental discussion about the relationship between politics and violence. In liberal democratic thinking, the desire for an absolute separation between politics and violence, as in the work of Hannah Arendt,[15] cannot account for how modern questions of security necessarily imbricate other forms of institutional violence, as seen with Michel Foucault's discussion of security. Similarly, the way the relation between politics and violence is understood in much liberal political theory structures the field of understanding of human rights and national or social security. Our ideas about human rights and security are deeply entangled with our ideas about politics and its relation to legitimate and illegitimate violence. If the relation between human rights and security reflects a deeper relationship between politics and violence, I want first to consider this relation and to develop the argument from there to a discussion of law, rights, and security.

II. VIOLENCE AND RIGHTS

One of the ways in which political liberalism after Locke can be characterised is that it seeks to delimit, sometimes severely, the powers of the state so as to enable the expansion of certain economic liberties and political rights, while at the same time liberalism seeks to expand significantly the powers of the state to enforce ('promote, respect, fulfil'[16]) its obligations towards human rights. This seeming paradox is the essence of international human rights and exemplifies a dual orientation that acknowledges the coercive powers of the state in both restricting and enforcing human rights. At some remove, this orientation is a recognition of the potential violence of the modern state.

[14] M Foucault, *Society Must Be Defended: Lectures at the College de France, 1975–76* (New York, Picador, 2003).

[15] H Arendt, 'Reflections on Violence', *New York Review of Books* (27 February 1969), http://www.nybooks.com/articles/archives/1969/feb/27/a-special-supplement-reflections-on-violence/.

[16] International Covenant on Economic, Social and Cultural Rights (ICESCR), adopted by UN General Assembly Resolution 2200A (XXI) (16 December 1966, entered into force 3 January 1976).

Writing in 1915, Sigmund Freud described the horrors of the war in Europe, which had been declared the previous year: the war was 'at least as cruel, as embittered, as implacable as any that has preceded it'.[17] Freud said:

> [The war] disregards all the restrictions known as International Law, which in peace-time the states had bound themselves to observe; it ignores the prerogatives of the wounded and the medical service, the distinction between civil and military sections of the population, the claims of private property. It tramples in blind fury on all that comes in its way, as though there were to be no future and no peace among men after it is over.[18]

The people in Europe to whom Freud addressed his thoughts were educated to cultivate morality and refinement, relinquish aggression, reason rather than fight. Their states instilled in them the highest standards of peaceful morality as citizens of a civilised world. These citizens, who had dutifully followed state guidance and patient education, now watched in horror as states indulged every kind of atrocity, conceit, and murder that they had taught their people to iron out of their characters, sensibilities, and civilisation. As Freud put it, 'A belligerent state permits itself every such misdeed, every such act of violence, as would disgrace the individual.'[19] Moreover, he argued, the state demands from its citizens the greatest possible sacrifice, their voluntary death in wars for the nation, and yet it infantilises them. It absolves itself from the guarantees and treaties by which it was bound to other states and confesses shamelessly to its own rapacity and lust for power, which citizens must then sanction in the name of patriotism.

If, for many citizens (and for a while, Freud was one of them), credulous patriotism takes over, then this patriotism is the performance of 'love' for an entity that has betrayed them in the deepest sense, since it has assumed responsibility for creating who they are as modern, civilised, rights-bearing individuals. This is because the modern liberal state has roles in education, the protection of family life, public health and welfare, the enabling of spheres for political deliberation, the promotion of standards of public and private behaviour, manners and tastes, the upholding of rituals and symbols of peace that assist in smoothing our coarse edges, expunging our primordial instincts.[20] On the other hand, the state wilfully engages in the most bestial behaviour that it has forbidden in the name of the same cultured, civilised morality that it now destroys. As this despicable behaviour of the state becomes evident, Freud said a profound disillusionment falls upon people – a breaking of illusions.

[17] S Freud, 'Thoughts for the Times on War and Death, Part I: The Disillusionment of the War' (1915), https://www.panarchy.org/freud/war.1915.html, 4.

[18] Freud, 'Thoughts for the Times on War and Death' (ibid).

[19] Ibid.

[20] N Elias, *The Civilizing Process, Volume 1: The History of Manners* (Oxford, Blackwell, 1969); and N Elias, *The Civilizing Process, Volume 2: State Formation and Civilization* (Oxford, Blackwell, 1982).

In his thoughts on the First World War, Freud elaborated an important series of themes regarding the association between peaceful politics and violence, between civilisation, the rule of law, the spheres of liberal rights, and the barbarism that seemingly resides outside law. The horrors of the First World War continued to magnify after Freud wrote his reflections, and both the patriotism and the disillusionment can be seen as comprising an enduring orientation towards the modern state – during and after the Second World War and the Judeocide in Europe, after the Korean and Vietnam Wars, after 9/11 and the 2003 invasion of Iraq. Of course, for Freud, these contrary orientations towards the same object would not have been unusual; indeed, they were necessary for each other. We cheerfully celebrate the human rights gifted to us by the same state that we know is the main violator of our human rights, often in the name of our security. Argued differently, two objects in which we might have vastly different investments could also be the same empirical object.

If the discussion above seems to convey a troubling understanding of the relation between politics and violence, civilised liberty and belligerence, it also draws attention to the persistence of the form of thinking that sees – and fears – violence in the ordinary, peaceful, routine functioning of politics and society, a hidden element of the social contract, an essential if bitter infusion in political water. Consider Max Weber's account of military discipline as the protean form of discipline to which owe all the other forms of social order and bureaucratic organisation.[21] Or Zygmunt Bauman's view of the potential for extraordinarily ferocious violence in the logic as well as the normally peaceful apparatuses of liberal modernity.[22] Or indeed Foucault's view of 'war as the grid of intelligibility' that structures political relations and the government of security once a homogenised society of 'the people' becomes established in history.[23] Or his discussion about war:

> [W]ar continues to rage within the mechanisms of power, or at least to constitute the secret motor of institutions, laws, and order. Beneath the omissions, the illusions, and the lies of those who would have us believe in the necessities of nature or the functional requirements of order, we have to rediscover war: war is the cipher of peace.[24]

Indeed, in Foucault's conceptions of discipline, security, and, later, governmentality, the metaphor of war can be seen as structuring the apparatuses and techniques by which human populations are subject to governance by the state. If human rights are methods for the governance and management of populations, and require enforcement and thus the use of force, then they are also imbricated in apparatuses of security.

[21] M Weber, 'The Meaning of Discipline' in HH Gerth and CW Mills (eds), *From Max Weber: Essays in Sociology* (Oxford, Routledge, 2009) 261.

[22] Z Bauman, *Modernity and the Holocaust* (Cambridge, Polity, 1991).

[23] J Spieker, 'Foucault and Hobbes on Politics, Security, and War' (2011) 36(3) *Alternatives: Global, Local, Political* 187.

[24] Foucault (above n 14) 268.

Violence thus seems to be 'sticky' for politics, and this has consequences for how a public sphere in which rights and freedoms are exercised relates to the conditions that enable that sphere to exist in the first place. The argument is not that violence is an attribute of politics or vice versa, nor can we speak of violence as the essence of politics, even in (for example) belligerent interpretations of Carl von Clausewitz's trinity that generate a linear relation between politics (policy) and war.[25] Contemporary reductionist accounts of Clausewitz's trinity do often present a continuum between politics (seen as the peaceful exercise of rights) and violence – in the most extreme military examples, as a horizontal axis that represents free political elections at one end and, at the other, thermonuclear war.[26]

III. PEACEFUL POLITICS

Despite these various complexities in their relation, politics and violence are predominantly seen to inhabit entirely different spheres. This separation of peaceful politics from illegitimate violence is reflective of a duality in much Western philosophy in which politics is the domain of thought and speech, whereas violence is about the body and action. Hannah Arendt provided one of the clearest modern statements in which politics and violence are opposed to each other. Politics, no matter how fiercely adversarial, is in the sphere of nonviolence, public communication, deliberation, and the free exercise of rights.[27] Arendt asked us to distinguish between violence and other distinct phenomena, such as power, strength, force, might, and authority; these are not synonymous. The political is irreducibly about power. Power, Arendt stated, 'is inherent in the very existence of political communities' and is 'the essence of all government, but violence is not'.[28] She warned us not to 'disastrously' reduce 'public affairs to the business of domination':

> Power and violence are opposites; where the one rules absolutely, the other is absent. Violence appears where power is in jeopardy, but left to its own course its end is the disappearance of power. This implies that it is not correct to say that the opposite of violence is nonviolence: to speak of nonviolent power is actually redundant. Violence can destroy power; it is utterly incapable of creating it.[29]

For Arendt, violence is therefore the negation and the destruction of the sphere of politics. Unlike peace, violence is always a means, never an end. It is an instrumental tactic, which also means that, strictly speaking, violence has no necessary relation to any political end.

[25] C von Clausewitz, *On War* (Oxford, Oxford University Press, 2008).
[26] WH Darley, 'Clausewitz's Theory of War and Information Operations' (2006) 40 *Joint Force Quarterly* 73–79.
[27] Arendt (above n 15).
[28] Ibid.
[29] Ibid.

Arendt's opposition between power (politics and government) and violence has been critically analysed from several perspectives.[30] Is not much political violence an exercise of power, or concerned with gaining power to effect changes in laws, policies, governments, states? It is difficult to conceive of a theory of power circumscribed solely within democratic forms of power-making and power-taking without also remaining alive to the possibility of political violence arising from the application of power itself. Similarly, the outright separation of means from ends can impoverish our understanding of phenomena that are not captured easily within one or other of those terms. Moreover, several overburdened third terms undertake a great deal of theoretical labour to maintain the conceptual separation of politics from violence ('power' in Arendt's case) or sanction some kind of transition between the two ('power' or 'security' in Foucault's case).

Political violence (or the perceived threat of it) is characterised in minute detail within law and public policy, and then expelled by law so that it resides hopefully outside of what is legally sanctioned within the liberal democratic polity. However, its detail is already inscribed inside the polity. The liberal democratic state can be and often is violent externally. But also, political violence by the liberal democratic state manifests within the polity against some of its citizens through a range of sociological processes. Indeed, Arendt made an important point about the dangers of increasingly bureaucratised societies in which it is impossible to find someone to argue with, a person with clear and direct responsibility, and this risks political violence: 'the greater the bureaucratization of public life, the greater will be the attraction of violence.'[31] Hence, despite the separation of the modern liberal democratic polity from political violence, the threads of political violence are seemingly woven into its bureaucratic fabric.

There are also other social processes that complicate the relationship further. For example, the 2014 events in Ferguson, Missouri highlighted (though they did not create) a breakdown in the liberal consensus that had developed over the 1990s about the limits of lethal state violence enacted against mainly African-American citizens. What has been called the 'civilianisation of military functions' has its complement: the progressive militarisation of key aspects of civic life.[32] There is not necessarily an easy division between internally peaceful and externally violent spheres. This is especially so when certain policy areas allow a mirroring within the liberal democratic polity of violent acts by the state that the state has otherwise expelled in law as criminal or illegal acts conducted by its enemies. Torture, extrajudicial assassinations, extraordinary renditions

[30] E Frazer and K Hutchings, 'On Politics and Violence: Arendt *contra* Fanon' (2008) 7 *Contemporary Political Theory* 90–108; and DE Howes, 'Terror In and Out of Power' (2011) 11(1) *European Journal of Political Theory* 25–58.

[31] Arendt (above n 15).

[32] C Bhatt, 'Human Rights and the Transformations of War' (2012) 46(5) *Sociology* 813–28.

and the legal mobilisation of *hostis humani generis* during the so-called 'global war on terror' are recent examples where certain figures are cast outside 'normal' law or ordinary humanity.

IV. FEAR

The dense relations between politics and violence, security and human rights, governance and law discussed above owe to a formative tradition of liberal philosophy, one that crosses from Hobbes into Locke, Kant, and Hegel, and which delimits the field of possible thinking about human rights and security. This is because rights and security, violence and law, peace and the birth of society were intimately related to each other at the moment of their inception in liberal thinking in ways that are now intractable. Many of the boundaries of liberal political vision were established when ideas about natural rights, the idea of the social, positive law, political authority, and a foundational idea of security emerged conjointly. In an important sense, Thomas Hobbes, perhaps like no other major Western thinker, including Machiavelli, Carl Schmitt, and Leo Strauss, told the 'truth' about the boundaries and limits of liberal political philosophy. Critically, the origin of law, human rights, and secure society are intimately related to the transfer of violence, or the fear of violence, from the mass of individuals to an artificial sovereign. We remain burdened with Hobbes' anthropology in the way we often think about politics and violence, security and rights. If we are creatures ('bearers') of his idea of natural rights, it is also his conception of security – individual, social, political – that forms and informs our discussions today.

For Hobbes, natural rights – the progenitors for our modern secular human rights – are coextensive with the unbounded liberty to use one's power to preserve one's life.[33] Thus, human rights in their originary form are enmeshed with and inseparable from individual security and from the fear of a violent death.[34] This natural right of self-preservation leads to a secular law of nature whereby one is forbidden to do anything that might lead to the destruction of one's life.[35] Individual security – the 'instinct' of self-preservation – is thus the essence of the law of nature. It is deeply significant that the first modern conception of secular human rights and natural law emerged as a mode of security. Critically also, *social* security is considered to emerge at the point at which we voluntarily transfer almost all our natural rights to the sovereign. In other words, the social (a voluntary agreement) emerges concurrently with voluntary subjection to an

[33] T Hobbes, *Leviathan* (Cambridge, Cambridge University Press, 1996).

[34] JFM Arends, 'From Homer to Hobbes and Beyond: Aspects of "Security" in the European Tradition' in HG Brauch, UO Spring, C Mesjasz, et al (eds), *Globalization and Environmental Challenges: Reconceptualizing Security in the 21st Century*, vol 3 (Heidelberg, Springer, 2008) 273.

[35] Hobbes (above n 33).

absolute authority.[36] The social compact – and therefore stable, secure sociality itself – is a consequence of the collective mutual transfer of human rights. In Hobbes' philosophical anthropology, secure society, political authority, and law arise from the logic of natural (human) rights. The causal chain moves from the social compact to the birth of the state and origin of political authority and law, to security, the exercise of natural law, and finally peace.[37]

Within this framework, the imagined state of nature is followed by the happy resolution of this terrible state by the hypothetical social compact and its apparatus of law, and then by the potential authoritarianism of the sovereign. Both the state of nature and the absolute sovereign are like conceptual sentinels around liberal political visions of rights and freedoms. Hannah Arendt was of course deeply alive to the violence and terror that a totalitarian sovereign could inflict. But equally, she sought to preserve a modern *ekklesia* governed by reason and rights in which anarchy, lawlessness, and violence were hopefully banished. The Athenian-Kantian ideal can be seen as the desirable political island surrounded, as it were, by the fear of violence from the state and from uncivil unsociety. The modern liberal political subject can be seen as an entity that lives peacefully in liberty under the rule of law, in fear of the violence against its life from either the totalitarian state or social disintegration.

Many writers have described the economy of fear that energises Hobbes' political theory.[38] The fear of the annihilation of one's life in the state of nature generates a bargain with others and an exchange of one's rights for collective peace and the establishment of sovereignty and law as a common power over all. Terror, in other words, is the hypothetical condition that originates simultaneously both law and political power. But this in turn leads to the fear of the absolute sovereign that has been collectively instituted and to whom all relevant power has been gifted. Indeed, the sovereign for Hobbes must also be a figure of terror –, the rule of law must be terrifying if the laws of nature are to be observed.[39] Fear of death generates the sovereign who cannot be rebelled against (unless one's life is threatened), since rebellion risks society falling back into the fearful state of nature.

In the dominant liberal Enlightenment political tradition (with Rousseau and some Romantic thinkers being the exceptions), the terror of the state of nature is a fundamental absolute such that another terror – of the sovereign and the rule of law – has to be instituted permanently for the secure social field to exist. Furthermore, the state of nature is seemingly always less desirable than any possible tyranny. For Hobbes and for much liberal political thought that

[36] Arends (above n 34) 274.

[37] Ibid.

[38] Hobbes (above n 33) 90; PJ Ahrensdorf, 'The Fear of Death and the Longing for Immortality: Hobbes and Thucydides on Human Nature and the Problem of Anarchy' (2000) 94(3) *American Political Science Review* 579–93; and JH Blits, 'Hobbesian Fear' (1989) 17(3) *Political Theory* 417–31.

[39] Howes (above n 30) 35.

followed him, positing a state of nature leaves only one remedy – an unlimited, undifferentiated, absolute authority, and all the consequences and contradictions which follow regarding rights and security, politics and violence. One important factor in the Hobbesian vision is that the distinction between terror and the rule of law cannot be absolute.[40] Moreover, the Hobbesian vision allows political authority to be exercised only by an absolute sovereign: there cannot be divided, multiple, or factionalised sovereignty. But from the field of political possibilities available to us, we cannot conceive of our rights, security, or civil society under other forms of political order or organisation, since the original conception of state, civil society, security, and rights given to us has been so narrow.[41]

There is another important aspect of Hobbes' philosophy that relates to how the sovereign rises out of the maelstrom of the state of nature. While Hobbes described several forms of the Commonwealth,[42] it can be argued that there is no higher truth that gives rise to the *particular* entity to whose subjection the citizens consent and from which arises the social order.[43] There is no superior truth that one entity possesses that makes it, rather than another, the focus of the citizens' allegiance.[44] Indeed, in the context of the English civil wars about which Hobbes wrote, claims to moral or epistemic certitude were the sources of violence. Seemingly any ideological claim to sovereignty is legitimate if it is able (hypothetically) to drag law, the social contract, security, and social peace out of the state of nature. It seems contingent might or power is the primary factor, rather than the truth or morality of any particular conviction. This implies a radical political contingency regarding the substantive content of the system of appropriate sovereignty. Similarly, the law that materialises from the quantum foam of the state of nature must also be originally arbitrary since there is not a higher truth that it can reflect. (Thus, only positive law can arise.) Political order is the victory of any arbitrary system of 'reason' against chaotic passions.[45] Expressed in different terms, any regime of truth and power can claim to have found a secure social order if it convincingly generates a state of nature as its absolute other.

For Hobbes and indeed for Kant, once a system of lawful power is established, violent resistance or conspiracy to rebel against the sovereign is forbidden (unless, for Hobbes, the law of nature is threatened and one's self-preservation is in jeopardy). For Kant,

> not only does one lack a legally enforceable right to rebel but also … one lacks the *moral freedom* to rebel, no matter how tyrannical, oppressive, and murderous the lawful regime may be.[46]

[40] Ibid.
[41] GS Kavka, 'Hobbes's War of All Against All' (1983) 93(2) *Ethics* 297.
[42] Hobbes (above n 33) 129–45.
[43] Ibid, 117–21 and ch 14.
[44] Spieker (above n 23).
[45] Ibid, 193–94.
[46] TE Hill, 'A Kantian Perspective on Political Violence' (1997) 1(2) *Journal of Ethics* 111.

As Hill says, the key reason for why Kant made this argument is related to escaping the state of nature and the moral obligation 'to join … with others to enter a civil order',[47] this order representing the authority of the 'general will'. As with Hobbes, the united will of the people cannot be divided among multiple sovereigns. But most importantly, we cannot have a 'legally enforceable right to destroy the only available mechanisms for legally enforcing anything'.[48] One can also see Hobbes' economy of fear at work here: the fear of sliding into chaos, the terrifying vision of the primordial horde at the gates of the derived political order. The precondition for rationally judging that something can be rebelled against is the thing being rebelled against, namely the precondition, the possibility of that judgement about rebellion itself. This possibility is given by (a form of) the categorical imperative and ultimately reason. But why should the categorical imperative be the origin of law and not something else?[49] And why should we accept the system of law it generates as the most desirable, if we also know that it is arbitrary and contingent?

V. CONCLUSION

The Hobbesian concept of security dominates modern conceptions of security, just as Hobbes' natural rights are a key foundation for modern secular human rights. If Hobbes' security emerged with the 'intention to prevent civil war',[50] it has travelled extremely far and wide. However, while Hobbes' philosophy creates hard boundaries around possible liberal visions for politics, security, peace, and rights, it arguably also betrays an important 'truth' about many modern political philosophies and their relation to violence, law, and liberty.

It is deeply significant in this context that the key imperative articulated by Al Qaeda and Islamic State is that of managing the state of nature and bringing people into law under an absolute political authority.[51] It is this imperative that will ultimately bring internal order, 'peace', and the 'liberty' that is alleged to arise from adhering to the 'shari'a' of Islamic State. It is indeed striking that a dominant theme in salafi-jihadi ideology is the governance of global law across the entire planet in opposition to what salafi-jihadi militia like Al Qaeda and Islamic State perceive as illegitimate law, including international human rights and humanitarianism. In parallel, they conceive their shari'a as granting a

[47] Ibid, 114.

[48] Ibid, 115.

[49] Kant answers this question, but the 'Hobbesian' point remains: Kant's faculty of reason may be a claim to a higher truth that 'we' now live by, but it can only have 'first' arisen in a contingent way.

[50] Arends (above n 34) 263.

[51] AB Naji, 'The Management of Savagery: The Most Critical Stage through which the Umma Will Pass', W McCants (trans), John M Olin Institute for Strategic Studies, Harvard University (23 May 2006), https://azelin.files.wordpress.com/2010/08/abu-bakr-naji-the-management-of-savagery-the-most-critical-stage-through-which-the-umma-will-pass.pdf.

genuine 'security' that is for them inconceivable under existing international law (which is viewed by them as criminal defilement.) What salafi-jihadi ideology has sought to present is indeed a system of law that creates 'the state of nature' as its absolute other.

Drawing attention to this extreme example helps us highlight the philosophical anthropological foundation of 'the state of nature' underlying many political philosophies. This foundation and its potentially violent consequences remain, even after the scope of liberty and rights has been expanded and even after the boundaries of the state's power and authority have been delimited in philosophically important ways, such as by Locke and his followers. Those violent consequences are the ones we see of the liberal democratic state that can torture or invade. The bureaucratic power that such a state can marshal in unpredictably coercive ways generates multiple relations between the sphere of politics and the fields of violence, between the practices of security that align with human rights and those that snatch these rights away.

REFERENCES

Ahrensdorf, PJ, 'The Fear of Death and the Longing for Immortality: Hobbes and Thucydides on Human Nature and the Problem of Anarchy' (2000) 94(3) *American Political Science Review* 579–93.

Arends, JFM, 'From Homer to Hobbes and Beyond: Aspects of "Security" in the European Tradition' in HG Brauch, UO Spring, C Mesjasz, et al (eds), *Globalization and Environmental Challenges: Reconceptualizing Security in the 21st Century*, vol 3 (Heidelberg, Springer, 2008).

Arendt, H, 'Reflections on Violence', *New York Review of Books* (27 February 1969), http://www.nybooks.com/articles/archives/1969/feb/27/a-special-supplement-reflections-on-violence/.

Bartholomew, A, 'Empire's Law and the Contradictory Politics of Human Rights' in A Bartholomew (ed), *Empire's Law: The American Imperial Project and the 'War to Remake the World'* (London, Pluto Press, 2006).

Bauman, Z, *Modernity and the Holocaust* (Cambridge, Polity Press, 1991).

Bhatt, C, 'Human Rights and the Transformations of War' (2012) 46(5) *Sociology* 813–28.

——, 'The New Xenologies of Europe: Civil Tensions and Mythic Pasts' (2012) 8(3) *Journal of Civil Society* 307–26.

Blits, JH, 'Hobbesian Fear' (1989) 17(3) *Political Theory* 417–31.

Darley, WH, 'Clausewitz's Theory of War and Information Operations', (2006) 40 *Joint Force Quarterly* 73–79.

Elias, N, *The Civilizing Process, Volume 1: The History of Manners* (Oxford, Blackwell, 1969).

——, *The Civilizing Process, Volume 2: State Formation and Civilization* (Oxford, Blackwell, 1982).

Foucault, M, *Society Must Be Defended: Lectures at the College de France, 1975–76* (New York, Picador, 2003).

Frazer, E, and Hutchings, K, 'On Politics and Violence: Arendt *contra* Fanon' (2008) 7 *Contemporary Political Theory* 90–108.

Freud, S, *Thoughts for the Times on War and Death Part I: The disillusionment of the war* (1915), https://www.panarchy.org/freud/war.1915.html.

Griffin, R and Teixeira, R, 'The Story of Trump's Appeal: A Portrait of Trump Voters', Democracy Fund Voter Study Group (June 2017), https://www.voterstudygroup.org/reports/2016-elections/story-of-trumps-appeal.

Hampson, FO with Daudelin, J, Hay, JB, Martin, T and Reid, H, *Madness in the Multitude: Human Security and World Disorder* (Don Mills, ON, Oxford University Press, 2002).

Hill, TE, 'A Kantian Perspective on Political Violence' (1997) 1(2) *Journal of Ethics* 111.

Hobbes, T, *Leviathan* (Cambridge, Cambridge University Press, 1996).

Howes, DE, 'Terror In and Out of Power' (2011) 11(1) *European Journal of Political Theory* 25–58.

Kavka, GS, 'Hobbes's War of All against All' (1983) 93(2) *Ethics* 297.

Lazarus, L, 'Mapping the Right to Security' in BJ Goold and L Lazarus (eds), *Security and Human Rights* (Oxford, Hart Publishing, 2007).

Luckham, R, 'The Discordant Voices of Security' (2007) 17(4/5) *Development in Practice* 685–89.

Marshall, TH, *Citizenship and Social Class and Other Essays* (Cambridge, Cambridge University Press, 1950).

Mortimer, C, 'Donald Trump Rejects Intelligence Report on Travel Ban Because It Doesn't Say What He Wants It To', *Independent* (25 February 2017), http://www.independent.co.uk/news/world/americas/us-politics/donald-trump-muslim-ban-travel-ban-intelligence-homeland-security-terrorism-threat-us-iran-somalia-a7599126.html.

Naji, AB, 'The Management of Savagery: The Most Critical Stage through which the Umma Will Pass', W McCants (trans), John M Olin Institute for Strategic Studies, Harvard University (23 May 2006), https://azelin.files.wordpress.com/2010/08/abu-bakr-naji-the-management-of-savagery-the-most-critical-stage-through-which-the-umma-will-pass.pdf.

Spieker, J, 'Foucault and Hobbes on Politics, Security, and War' (2011) 36(3) *Alternatives: Global, Local, Political* 187.

UK Department of Education, 'Protecting Children from Radicalisation: The Prevent Duty' (July 2015), https://www.gov.uk/government/publications/protecting-children-from-radicalisation-the-prevent-duty.

UNDP, 'Human Development Report 1994: New Dimensions of Human Security' (1994), http://hdr.undp.org/en/content/human-development-report-1994.

US Government, 'Counterinsurgency Guide', US Bureau of Political–Military Affairs (January 2009), https://www.state.gov/documents/organization/119629.pdf.

von Clausewitz, C, *On War* (Oxford, Oxford University Press, 2008).

Waldron, J, 'Security and Liberty: The Image of Balance' (2003) *Journal of Political Philosophy* 191–210.

Weber, M, 'The Meaning of Discipline' in HH Gerth and CW Mills (eds), *From Max Weber: Essays in Sociology* (Oxford, Routledge, 2009).

Part III

Privacy, Anonymity, and Dissent

12

Privacy versus Security: Regulating Data Collection and Retention in Europe

ARIANNA VEDASCHI

THIS CHAPTER ADDRESSES the challenging relationship between privacy and national security within the European Union during the post-9/11 era, with a focus on the legislative and jurisdictional interactions between the EU and Member States. Since the earliest stages of the 'war on terror' privacy has been one of the rights that is most targeted by securitarian counterterrorism policies.[1] In recent years, there has been a clear shift in Europe from a data protection perspective to a data retention one, both at the domestic level and within European political institutions. This shift is one of the main features of the European fight against terrorism, especially jihadist terrorism. The collection, storage, processing, and exchange of significant amounts of personal data is now considered crucial for the prevention of attacks, or at least for the reduction of risk. In the face of international terrorism, security is now pursued mainly through a system of mass surveillance, and this approach has significant impacts on privacy and on other rights related to it, including freedom of expression.[2]

Unlike other fundamental rights that admit no derogation, such as the right not to be tortured, the right to privacy can be legitimately restricted under specific conditions. This chapter considers whether restrictions placed on this right by counterterrorism legislation within the EU meet these conditions and whether a balance can be found between the two seemingly conflicting needs of privacy and security. Section I focuses on the Court of Justice of the European Union (CJEU), and specifically on the approach the Court took in

[1] For a comprehensive overview of the 'war on terror', see V Ramraj, M Hor, K Roach, and G Williams (eds), *Global Anti-terrorism Law and Policy* (Cambridge, Cambridge University Press, 2012). See also G Lennon and C Walker (eds), *Routledge Handbook of Law and Terrorism* (New York, Routledge, 2015).

[2] For a discussion of privacy immediately after 9/11, see BJ Goold, 'Privacy, Identity and Security' in BJ Goold and L Lazarus (eds), *Security and Human Rights* (Oxford, Hart Publishing, 2007).

two cases: *Digital Rights Ireland* (2014) and *Schrems* (2015).[3] On the one hand, the Court has stood firm in its commitment to protect privacy-related rights; on the other hand, it has recognised a certain degree of legitimacy to surveillance techniques and the need for security. Section II analyses the effect of these two landmark judgments at the domestic level, from both legislative and judicial perspectives. The concluding section reflects on these developments and considers in particular the role of the CJEU and national courts in developing a principled framework for balancing rights with security in Europe.

I. THE COURT OF JUSTICE OF THE EUROPEAN UNION AND THE RIGHT TO PRIVACY

A. The Invalidation of the Data Retention Directive (DRD)

In the wake of bombings in Madrid in 2004 and London in 2005, the European Parliament and Council issued what became known as the Data Retention Directive (DRD).[4] Based on the widespread belief that more surveillance would result in increased security,[5] the Directive aimed to harmonise the domestic legislation of Member States around the issue of electronic data collection and data retention. It imposed an obligation on telephone and Internet service providers to collect and retain metadata relating to the source, recipient, type, date, time, duration, and location of electronic communications (but not the content), in order to 'ensure that data are available for the purpose of the investigation, detection, and prosecution' of terrorist acts and other serious crimes.[6]

The Directive made no distinction between ordinary citizens and criminal suspects: as long as communications took place on EU territory, metadata could be collected. It also did not require the data to be stored within EU territory. The time that such data should be retained was between six and twenty-four months, but the Directive did not specify any criteria for how Member States should choose a retention timespan within these limits. Moreover, the period of retention could be extended by national authorities on unspecified grounds.

[3] Joined cases C-293/12 and C-594/12, *Digital Rights Ireland v Minister for Communications, Marine and Natural Resources et al and Kärtner Landesregierung et al* [2014] ECR I-238; and Case C-362/14, *Schrems v Data Protection Commissioner* [2016] 2 CMLR 2.

[4] European Parliament and Council Directive 2006/24/EC (15 March 2006) on the retention of data generated or processed in connection with the provision of publicly available electronic communications services or of public communications networks and amending Directive 2002/58/EC, [2006] OJ2006 L105/54.

[5] Commission of the European Communities, 'Proposal for a Directive of the European Parliament and of the Council on the retention of data processed in connection with the provision of public electronic communication services and amending Directive 2002/58/EC', COM(2005) 438 final.

[6] Directive 2006/24/EC (above n 4) recital 21. See C Coq and F Galli, 'Comparative Paper on Data Retention Regulation in a Sample of EU Member States', EUI Seventh Framework Programme, Surveille deliverable 4.3 (30 April 2013).

Crucially, data collected under the DRD had to be directly available to public authorities, with no interference from the providers. Member States could designate which of their national authorities had access, and several Member States included intelligence agencies on their lists of 'competent authorities'.[7]

The regime imposed by the DRD suffered from several flaws. First, it was vague in how it defined 'serious crime', 'competent authorities', and other important terms; additionally, the procedures for access to data and the retention period were likewise unclear. Second, there were few specific safeguards in relation to data security, and while data had to be destroyed at the end of the retention period, the fate of data accessed and preserved was unclear. Third, the lack of geographical limits to data retention meant that data could be stored in countries where there were poor data protection standards. Huge databases and increased ease of cross-referencing also bring an increased chance of profiling, with attendant consequences in terms of discrimination towards some categories of people.[8] Last but not least, the Directive placed the entire European population on a massive pre-emptive surveillance programme since the metadata of ordinary people and that of terrorist suspects and other criminals were collected and retained without any distinction. This clearly violated basic standards related to the presumption of innocence.

On 8 April 2014, the Grand Chamber of the CJEU ruled in *Digital Rights Ireland* that the DRD was entirely invalid.[9] The Luxembourg judges held the Directive to be incompatible with the right to privacy and the right to data protection, enshrined respectively in Articles 7 and 8 of the Charter of Fundamental Rights of the European Union, read in conjunction with the principle of proportionality, which is guaranteed by Article 52 of the Charter.[10] The Court engaged in careful proportionality scrutiny, and while it recognised that fighting terrorism and serious crime was a legitimate pursuit in the interest of the public, it found that the measures of the Directive constituted disproportionate interference with the right to privacy. Moreover, the indiscriminate collection and retention of metadata were declared to be inconsistent with Articles 7 and 8 of the Charter, read in the light of Article 52.

In its reasoning, the Court pointed out that when metadata such as that collected under the DRD is cross-referenced, it can reveal much about people's private lives, including intimate personal information about habits, movements,

[7] See FE Bignami, 'Privacy and Law Enforcement in the European Union: The Data Retention Directive' (2007) 8(1) *Chicago Journal of International Law* 233–55.

[8] And potentially breaching Arts 20 and 21 of the Charter of Fundamental Rights of the European Union. Regarding the risks of profiling, see H Duffy, *The 'War on Terror' and the Framework of International Law* (Cambridge, Cambridge University Press, 2015) 637.

[9] *Digital Rights Ireland* (above n 3) Opinion of AG Cruz Villalón. See F Fabbrini, 'Human Rights in the Digital Age: The European Court of Justice Ruling in the Data Retention Case and Its Lessons for Privacy and Surveillance in the United States' (2015) 28 *Harvard Human Rights Journal* 65–95, 77.

[10] The Directive had also been challenged on Art 11 grounds (freedom of expression), but the Court did not deem it necessary to rule on this point after ruling on other violations.

activities, and so on.[11] Furthermore, the subjective scope of application of the data retention regime did not meet Article 8 standards, according to which data must be processed 'for specified purposes' and on the basis of, if not consent, then legislative provision, which must in turn conform to requirements of clarity and specificity.[12] The Court also took issue with the fact that national authorities could access data owned by private companies without limits or conditions other than having generic 'law enforcement' objectives in relation to undefined 'serious crimes'. Additionally, access to the metadata was not subject to judicial warrant, administrative authorisation, judicial review, or independent administrative oversight.[13] The range of allowed retention time (between six months and two years) was found to be overly broad, without specific criteria by which to differentiate between ordinary citizens and criminal suspects,[14] and it was possible to extend retention at the discretion of Member States. Because metadata was not required by the Directive to be retained within European territory, EU standards relating to privacy and data protection could potentially be violated.[15] And lastly, the provisions of the DRD derogated from the metadata confidentiality regime set up by the e-Privacy Directive and the Data Protection Directive.[16]

To summarise, the Court of Justice found that data retention may be a legitimate instrument in the fight against international terrorism and, more generally, against serious crimes. Nevertheless, strict guarantees must be established to safeguard fundamental rights and personal freedoms. Collection and retention of metadata can be neither generalised nor indiscriminate; on the contrary, it is necessary to circumscribe carefully their subjective scope. The access and subsequent use of metadata by national authorities should be explicitly laid out and must be strictly regulated by national laws. Consequently, any framework that allows access and use without the need to provide substantial grounds relating to suspicion of specific crimes and without the possibility of judicial (or at least independent) oversight is not lawful in the European Union. Data retention must

[11] *Digital Rights Ireland* (above n 3) paras 27–28. See G Gonzáles Fuster and A Scherrer, 'Big Data and Smart Devices and Their Impact on Privacy', study for the LIBE Committee (September 2015).

[12] *Digital Rights Ireland* (above n 3) para 51.

[13] Ibid, paras 58–62.

[14] Ibid, para 63.

[15] Ibid, para 68.

[16] Ibid, para 32. The DRD modified Art 15 of Directive 2002/58/EC, restricting its guarantees. See European Parliament and Council Directive 2002/58/EC (12 July 2002) concerning the processing of personal data and the protection of privacy in the electronic communication sector ('e-Privacy Directive') [2002] OJ L 201; and European Parliament and Council Directive 95/46/EC (24 October 1995) on the protection of individuals with regard to the processing of personal data and on the free movement of such data ('Data Protection Directive') [1995] OJ L 281. See also F Fabbrini, 'The EU Charter of Fundamental Rights and the Rights to Data Privacy: The EU Court of Justice as a Human Rights Court' in S de Vries, U Bernitz, and S Weatherill (eds), *The EU Charter of Fundamental Rights as a Binding Instrument: Five Years Old and Growing* (Oxford, Hart Publishing, 2015) 261; and A Vedaschi and V Lubello, 'Data Retention and Its Implications for the Fundamental Right to Privacy' (2015) 20(1) *Tilburg Law Review* 14–34, 21.

be temporary, and its duration must be precisely defined through clear selective criteria. Lastly, data must be retained within the EU territory in order to ensure independent and effective enforcement of privacy and data protection rights.

The *Digital Rights Ireland* decision has been praised by many scholars as an important step towards better enforcement of privacy and data protection rights in the EU context.[17] Yet it also has its critics,[18] according to whom the CJEU focused too closely on procedural issues and thereby largely legitimised in a more general sense the massive intrusion into individuals' private lives brought about by the DRD and other similar measures. However, it is undeniable that the judgment in *Digital Rights Ireland* set out pivotal guidelines and crucial principles as to the relationship between privacy and national security, and it continues to have significant influence on EU national legal frameworks.

Notably, the Charter of Fundamental Rights was (and indeed still is) used by the Court as a parameter *per se*, strengthening its role as the European 'bill of rights'. This approach has been affirmed in relation to privacy rights in subsequent decisions, including the *Tele2 Sverige* case (2016), in which the Court found incompatibility between the EU data protection framework and UK and Swedish legislation,[19] and Opinion 1/15 (2017), in which the CJEU held the draft agreement between the EU and Canada on the exchange of PNR data incompatible with the Charter.[20]

Despite the CJEU case law, the principles it has articulated with regard to privacy and data retention have not been implemented by all Member States. While some changes have been made after *Digital Rights Ireland*, the following sections show that there remains in some European countries the pervasive belief that the risk of terrorism is significant enough to warrant even extreme surveillance, to the extent that security demands should prevail over rights.

B. The Invalidation of the US Safe Harbour Agreement

A second landmark decision by the CJEU confirmed the need for independent review mechanisms when the rights to privacy and data protection are at stake. *Schrems v Data Protection Commissioner* involved an Irish Facebook subscriber

[17] See V Mitsilegas, 'Surveillance and Digital Privacy in the Transatlantic "War on Terror": The Case for a Global Privacy Regime' (2016) 47(3) *Columbia Human Rights Law Review* 1–77; Vedaschi and Lubello (above n 16); and A Roberts, 'Privacy, Data Retention and Domination: *Digital Rights Ireland Ltd v Minister for Communication*' (2015) 78(3) *Modern Law Review* 535–48.

[18] FJ Zuiderveen Borgesius and A Arnbak, 'New Data Security Requirements and the Proceduralization of Mass Surveillance Law after the European Data Retention Case', Amsterdam Law School Research Paper No 2015-41 (October 2015).

[19] Joint cases C-203/15 and C-698/15, *Tele2 Sverige AB v Post-och Telestyrelsen and Secretary of State for the Home Department v Tom Watson and Others* [2016] All ER (D) 107.

[20] CJEU, Opinion 1/15 (26 July 2017). See A Vedaschi, 'The European Court of Justice on the EU–Canada Passenger Name Record Agreement, ECJ, 26 July 2017, Opinion 1/15' (2018) 14(2) *European Constitutional Law Review* 410–29.

who claimed that his personal data, while collected in Ireland, was not being adequately protected because it could be transferred and subsequently stored within the social network's servers, which were located in the United States.[21] Mr Schrems was concerned in particular that US legislation did not meet EU standards and might allow his data to be accessed, processed, and further transferred without his consent.

The flow of personal data to third countries was regulated within the European Union by Article 25 of the Data Protection Directive (1995), which allowed data transfer when the country of destination ensures an 'adequate level of protection'.[22] The Directive empowered both the European Commission and national data protection authorities to assess the level of protection guaranteed by third countries for the purposes of Article 25. At the time of *Schrems*, EU–US data flows were grounded on an adequacy decision taken by the Commission in 2000.[23] The Safe Harbour scheme, as it became known, came about through negotiations between the European Union and the United States, based on principles of good practice issued by the US Department of Commerce. It allowed US operators (mainly in the private sector) to self-certify that they would comply with such principles and ensure an 'adequate level of protection' in order to be the addressees of data transfers from EU countries.

Mr Schrems's complaint before Irish authorities alleged that the US data protection system did not comply with the principles that US companies had self-certified. However, the Irish Data Protection Authority denied its competence to evaluate the validity of the adequacy decision taken by the Commission or to autonomously assess the level of protection offered by the United States with regard to personal data. It therefore rejected the claim.[24] The Irish High Court, before which Mr Schrems filed an appeal, cast doubts on the compliance of US data protection rules with Articles 7 and 8 of the Charter of Fundamental Rights in light of the strict interpretation provided by the CJEU in *Digital Rights Ireland*.[25] The matter was hence referred to the Luxembourg Court for a preliminary ruling.

The Irish judges asked the CJEU to clarify whether, pursuant to Article 25 of the Data Protection Directive, national data protection authorities are absolutely

[21] *Schrems* (above n 3).

[22] Art 25, Data Protection Directive (above n 16). The Data Protection Directive has been replaced by Regulation (EU) 2016/679 of the European Parliament and of the Council of 27 April 2016 on the protection of natural persons with regard to the processing of personal data and on the free movement of such data, and repealing Directive 95/46/EC OJ L 111, 1–88. Art 45 of Regulation 2016/679 provides for the exchange of data on the basis of an adequacy decision and takes into account several principles enshrined in *Schrems*.

[23] Commission Decision 2000/520/EC of 26 July 2000 pursuant to Directive 95/46/EC of the European Parliament and of the Council on the adequacy of the protection provided by the Safe Harbour privacy principles and related frequently asked questions issued by the US Department of Commerce OJ L 215 25/08/2000, 7–47.

[24] Data Protection Commissioner (Ireland), Letter of 26 July 2013 to M Schrems, available at http://www.europe-v-facebook.org/DPC_PRISM_all.pdf.

[25] *Schrems v Data Protection Commissioner* [2014] IEHC 310 (18 June 2014).

and completely bound by a decision of the Commission declaring the adequacy of the data protection standards offered by a third country. Alternatively, do they have leeway to reassess the adequacy of data protection in third countries? The Grand Chamber of the CJEU answered these questions unequivocally by according wide powers to national authorities, but it also took the chance to set forth a number of relevant principles on the issue.

The Court held that when an EU citizen lodges a complaint on a specific issue, EU national authorities (ie, independent data protection bodies) can never refrain from scrutinising the adequacy of privacy guarantees of third parties *vis-à-vis* EU data protection rules, irrespective of previous adequacy decisions issued by the Commission. Instead, data protection bodies should always ensure thorough investigation and, if a complaint is found to be well grounded, take concrete action in order to forbid further transfer of data towards the state in question, by means of the wide powers they are granted by the Data Protection Directive and by domestic law. Moreover, national data protection authorities can bring proceedings before national courts and ask them to refer the matter to the CJEU.[26] Therefore, according to the CJEU, the Irish Data Protection Authority should not have dismissed the case but should have engaged in an analysis of the merits of the US data protection system, eventually suspending the transfer of data.

The CJEU went further and declared the Commission adequacy decision on the US data protection system invalid, pursuant to EU Treaties and fundamental principles of EU law. This was because the decision lacked any specific indication on how to avoid excessive impairment of privacy-related rights since it only generically referred to the 'adequate protection' standard. Moreover, no effective remedy was provided in case of violations of citizens' rights. In addition, the CJEU pointed out that US courts interpret the right to privacy and data protection in restrictive ways, often prioritising other competing interests such as public order and national security. The Commission, in its decision, had not taken this tendency into account and so failed to consider that departures from the Safe Harbour principles may be deemed appropriate and justified under the US legal framework. Furthermore (and once again), the Court pointed out an imbalance between the right to data protection and other interests – in this case, the commercial considerations that were the focus of the Safe Harbour scheme. The Court of Justice thus reaffirmed the importance of more weighted appraisal of privacy-sensitive policies.

In conclusion, the CJEU stance in *Schrems* not only emphasised the need for substantial oversight by independent authorities when privacy and data protection are involved, but also declared invalid an act of a European institution on the basis of Articles 7 and 8 of the Charter.[27]

[26] *Schrems* (above n 3) para 64.

[27] Since the invalidation of the Safe Harbour scheme, the exchange of data between the European Union and the United States has been regulated by the EU–US Privacy Shield, which entered into

II. PRIVACY AND DATA PROTECTION IN EUROPE AFTER THE CJEU RULINGS

Even before the CJEU ruling in *Digital Rights Ireland*, some domestic constitutional and supreme courts in the European Union had already declared that some national legislation transposing the DRD contravened the presumption of innocence and violated the right to privacy and related rights.[28] In particular, the mass collection, storage, and retention of metadata that formed the basis of the DRD were criticised, irrespective of the real processing and actual use. After the *Digital Rights Ireland* judgment in 2014, domestic courts struck down national legislation implementing the annulled directive,[29] while in some jurisdictions, such provisions were repealed directly by lawmakers.[30]

Nonetheless, the invalidation of the Data Retention Directive did not in all cases result in national legislation that is more protective of privacy. In the United Kingdom and France, for example, surveillance policies in fact expanded. While the Brexit referendum triggered a procedure for the United Kingdom to leave the European Union, and even if UK policies will no longer technically be governed by EU law in the future, the transfer of data and surveillance cooperation with the European Union will continue to be subject to EU law, including notably those regarding third-party countries. It therefore seems likely that UK laws will continue to apply EU standards in this area.

Notwithstanding the continuing application of CJEU case law (and in Britain the ongoing debate over how best to leave the European Union), both the United Kingdom and France have adopted laws and policies that directly affect

force in July 2016. See Commission Implementing Decision (EU) 1250/16 (12 July 2016) pursuant to Directive 95/46/EC of the European Parliament and of the Council on the adequacy of the protection provided by the EU–US Privacy Shield (notified under document C(2016) 4176) [2016] OJ L 207). Indeed, the CJEU rulings triggered a whole revision of EU privacy and data protection law, which resulted in the approval of European Parliament and Council Regulation (EU) 2016/679 (27 April 2016) on the protection of natural persons with regard to the processing of personal data and on the free movement of such data, and repealing Directive 95/46/EC (General Data Protection Regulation) [2016] OJ L 119/1 and of Directive (EU) 2016/680 of the European Parliament and of the Council of 27 April 2016 on the protection of natural persons with regard to the processing of personal data by competent authorities for the purposes of the prevention, investigation, detection or prosecution of criminal offences or the execution of criminal penalties, and on the free movement of such data, and repealing Council Framework Decision 2008/977/JHA [2016] OJ L 119/89, reframing EU data protection system.

[28] Bulgarian Supreme Administrative Court, judgment No 13627/2008 (11 December 2008); Romanian Constitutional Court, judgment No 1258 (8 October 2009); German Constitutional Court, judgment No 11/2010 (2 March 2010) 1 BvR 256/08; Cypriot Supreme Court, Apps No 65/2009, 78/2009, 82/2009 and 15/2010-22/2010 (1 February 2011); and Czech Constitutional Court, PI US 24/10 (22 March 2011).

[29] Austrian Federal Constitutional Court, Decision G 47/2012 (27 June 2014); Slovenian Constitutional Court, Decision U-I-65/13-19 (3 July 2014); District Court of the Hague, Netherlands, Case No C/09/480009/KG ZA 14/1575, Decision of 11 March 2015; Slovak Constitutional Court, Decision PL US 10/2014 (29 April 2015); Belgian Constitutional Court, Decision 84/2015 (11 June 2015); and Romanian Constitutional Court, Decision No 440 (8 July 2015).

[30] See below s II-A.

and often impinge the protection of data and privacy. The role of the judiciary with regard to this shift towards increased surveillance in the two countries varies, however, and it will be examined more closely in the following sections.

A. The UK Data Retention and Investigatory Powers Act (DRIPA) 2014

In the United Kingdom, the Data Retention and Investigatory Powers Act (DRIPA) entered into force in July 2014, repealing previous data retention rules, including the Data Retention Regulations 2009, which implemented the old DRD. The DRIPA empowered the Secretary of State by way of a notice to oblige telecommunication providers to retain a wide range of data generated or processed in providing their services. The Secretary of State was entitled to use this power when deemed necessary in order to pursue a number of legitimate purposes, including both 'the interest of national security' and 'preventing or detecting crime or […] preventing disorder'.[31] The type of data that could be retained overlapped with the categories set out by the 2009 Regulation. The maximum period of retention was twelve months (which under the 2009 Regulation was the minimum). Additionally, governmental bodies and agencies could perform surveillance activity even outside the United Kingdom and with the assistance, if needed, of third-party persons or companies. Furthermore, there was no need to have retention notices preventively authorised by judicial or independent bodies. Therefore, the discretion left to the government and to public authorities was very wide.[32] In other words, though the DRIPA nominally repealed the 2009 Regulations (which had been designed to implement the now nullified DRD), it reiterated the previous data retention obligations.

For these reasons, the DRIPA faced legal challenges that ended up with a preliminary reference to the CJEU. The proceedings were triggered by an action brought before the English High Court by two members of the House of Commons seeking an order of disapplication of section 1 of the DRIPA. The High Court ruled in 2015, finding that section 1 of the Act was inconsistent with EU law, in particular Articles 7 and 8 of the EU Charter of Fundamental Rights.[33] Firstly, the High Court criticised the lack of specific or clear rules in relation to the access and use of retained data. Detailed rules were necessary, it felt, in order to ensure that such data is accessed and used only for the purpose of preventing and detecting a list of precisely defined serious crimes. Secondly, the Court pointed to the lack of prior oversight by a judicial authority or at least

[31] Listed by s 22(2) of the Regulation of Investigatory Powers Act (RIPA) 2000.

[32] For an overview of the DRIPA and its features, see D Anderson (UK Independent Reviewer of Terrorism Legislation), 'A Question of Trust: Report of the Investigatory Powers Review' (June 2015).

[33] *David Davis and Others v Secretary of State for the Home Department* [2015] EWHC 2092 (Admin).

by an independent administrative body. Such review would be essential to avoid data being used for purposes beyond what is strictly necessary in light of the pursued objectives. In reaching these conclusions, the High Court relied on the principles set out by the CJEU in *Digital Rights Ireland* and on the case law of the European Court of Human Rights.[34]

During proceedings, a request for a preliminary ruling was presented, but the High Court rejected it on the grounds of it not being a court of last resort (hence not obliged to refer matters to the CJEU). Moreover, due to its sunset clause, the DRIPA was due to expire on 31 December 2016, and according to the High Court, it was unlikely that the CJEU would rule before that date. However, within the UK jurisdiction, the claim was successful, and section 1 DRIPA was declared unlawful. The government appealed the decision of the High Court to the Court of Appeal, which delivered its ruling in November 2015.[35] This time, the judges of second instance reconsidered the request for a preliminary ruling and referred the matter to the CJEU.

The CJEU delivered its ruling on the matter on 21 December 2016 (ten days before the expiry of the Act).[36] In its judgment, the Court joined the UK request for preliminary ruling with one from the Administrative Court of Stockholm that was based on similar grounds to those alleged by the UK court, with the difference that the Swedish legislation in question had not been approved after the invalidation of the DRD. The UK Court of Appeal asked the CJEU whether the *Digital Rights Ireland* judgment intended to set mandatory requirements to be respected by the domestic law of each Member State.[37] Similarly, the Swedish Court asked the CJEU to clarify the impact of the *Digital Rights Ireland*

[34] *Zakharov v Russia,* App No 47143/06, judgment of 4 December 2015; and *Szabó and Vissy v Hungary*, App No 37138/14, judgment of 12 January 2016. On the interrelations between the ECtHR and the CJEU on the topic of privacy and data protection, see C Gearty, 'State Surveillance in an Age of Security' in F Davis, N McGarrity, and G Williams (eds), *Surveillance, Counterterrorism and Comparative Constitutionalism* (New York, Routledge, 2013); and MD Cole and A Vandendriessche, 'From *Digital Rights Ireland* in Luxembourg to *Zakharov* and *Szabò/Vissy* in Strasbourg: What the ECtHR Made of the Deep Pass by the CJEU in the Recent Cases on Mass Surveillance' (2016) 2(1) *European Data Protection Law Review* 121–29.

[35] *Secretary of State for the Home Department v David Davis and Others* [2015] EWCA Civ 1185.

[36] *Tele2 Sverige* (above n 19).

[37] It also questioned whether the CJEU intended to expand the scope of Arts 7 and 8 CFREU beyond the effects of Art 8 ECHR, as interpreted by the ECtHR. Art 8 ECHR constitutes a sort of constitutional parameter for the right to privacy in the United Kingdom, per the Human Rights Act 1998. The UK approach towards privacy is influenced by the ECtHR, so courts grant quite broad protection rather than embracing the restrictive approach that is typical of US case law. For UK case law related to privacy, see AW Bradley, KD Ewing, and CJS Knight, *Constitutional and Administrative Law*, 16th edn (Harlow, Pearson, 2015). Although recognising Art 8 CFREU as more specific than Art 8 ECHR, the UK Court was not sure that the CJEU, by means of the Digital Rights decision, intended to impose stricter privacy and data protection standards than those enshrined in Art 8 ECHR. Indeed, Art 52(3) CFREU provides that when the CFREU guarantees rights that correspond to those enshrined in the ECHR, these rights should be given the same meaning they are given under the ECHR according to the jurisprudence of the ECtHR. In this case, while the Court accepted that Art 7 CFREU corresponds to Art 8 ECHR, the Art 8 CFREU guarantees are more specific than the Art 8 ECHR ones. For a comparison between the ECHR, US and European

judgment on national regimes and the extent of the obligations arising from Articles 7 and 8 of the EU Charter. In particular, the Swedish judge cast doubts on the compatibility of Swedish legislation with Article 15 of the Privacy and Electronic Communication Directive (e-Privacy Directive),[38] read in light of Articles 7, 8, and 52 of the Charter.

In its judgment, after affirming that both retention of data and access to it fall within the scope of the e-Privacy Directive,[39] the CJEU underlined that, even when allowed, derogation from the maximum protection of privacy rights shall be strictly interpreted.[40] This means that any exceptions adopted by Member States must comply with relevant standards set by the Charter of Fundamental Rights.

Drawing from its own stance in *Digital Rights Ireland*, the Court stressed that, even if retained data does not reveal the content of communications, this does not make surveillance less intrusive, since public authorities would still be able to identify detailed information about individuals' private lives. The Court noted that both the UK and Swedish frameworks did not provide for 'differentiation, limitation or exception according to the objective pursued'.[41] In light of the principles set out in *Digital Rights Ireland*, the Court concluded that measures in force in the United Kingdom and Sweden at the time were not acceptable. The main points that were criticised were the lack of prior review by an independent body and the questionable effectiveness of existing remedies. In addition, the Court remarked that collected data should be retained within the European Union.[42] In brief, the CJEU judgment confirmed the position taken in *Digital Rights Ireland*.

In spite of the ongoing legal challenge on the DRIPA, in November 2016 the UK legislature passed the Investigatory Powers Act (IPA), which largely replicated some of the most criticised features of the DRIPA, such that it has been referred to by Amnesty International as one of the most sweeping surveillance regimes in the world.[43] The IPA was challenged before the High Court, on grounds that it allowed for the collection and retention of data without safeguards.[44]

standards, see D Cole, 'Preserving Privacy in a Digital Age: Lessons of Comparative Constitutionalism' in Davis, McGarrity, and Williams (eds) (above n 34).

[38] Directive 2002/58/EC (above n 16). Art 15 regulates derogations from the principle of confidentiality of data established by Art 5(1) of the Directive itself. Exceptions to confidentiality can be provided by Member States on the basis of public interest, including fighting crime and terrorism.

[39] *Tele2 Sverige* (above n 19) para 76.

[40] Ibid, para 89.

[41] Ibid, para 105.

[42] Ibid, para 125.

[43] Amnesty International, 'Dangerously Disproportionate: The Ever-Expanding National Security State in Europe', Report EUR 01/5342/2017 (17 January 2017), 35.

[44] LIBERTY, 'LIBERTY Begins Legal Proceedings in *People vs Snoopers' Charter* Challenge' (28 February 2017), https://www.liberty-human-rights.org.uk/news/press-releases-and-statements/liberty-begins-legal-proceedings-people-vs-snoopers%E2%80%99-charter.

In April 2018, the High Court ruled the Act incompatible with EU law and gave the UK government a term of six months to redraft it.[45]

B. *Loi sur le Renseignement* (2015): The 'French Patriot Act'

Although the CJEU delivered its milestone judgment in *Digital Rights Ireland* in 2014, two pieces of French legislation were introduced in 2014 and in 2015 that show very little if any influence from that decision. As a matter of fact, the so-called *loi sur le renseignement* ('Law on intelligence services')[46] and *décret sur l'accès administratif aux données de connexion* ('Decree on administrative access to communications data')[47] are paradigmatic examples of a controversial trend towards mass surveillance and an attendant diminution in privacy and data protection guarantees. The Decree endowed public authorities with broad powers to access data relating to Internet activity, without any kind of judicial review, and several French associations for the protection of data[48] have challenged it before the *Conseil d'État*, the highest administrative court. However, the *Conseil* has refused to repeal the Decree and has declined to refer it to the CJEU.[49]

Even before its enactment, the *loi sur le renseignement* was highly criticised. In particular, the *Commission Nationale de l'Informatique et des Libertés* (CNIL) (the French Data Protection Authority) pointed out that, according to this law, mere authorisation from the Executive (with no judicial oversight) is enough to allow the collection of data.[50] The CNIL argued that data collection should be reserved for '*uniquement une personne identifiée comme devant faire l'object d'une surveillance particulière*' – in other words, allowed only when dealing with persons requiring special surveillance; it should not be uniformly adopted with regard to '*personnes tout à fait étrangères à la mission de renseignement*'

[45] *R (National Council for Civil Liberties (Liberty)) v Secretary of State for the Home Department* [2018] EWHC 975 (Admin).

[46] *Loi* n° 2015-912 of 24 July 2015 on surveillance. The changes brought by this law are codified in the French Internal Security Code. This law was enacted through a fast-track procedure that prevented a second reading in the French legislative Assembly. See P-A Chardel, R Harvey, and H Volat, 'The French Intelligence Act: Resonances with the USA PATRIOT Act', *Technology Science* (15 March 2016), http://techscience.org/a/2016031501/.

[47] Decree n° 2014-1576 of 24 December 2014 on administrative access to connection data. This decree is an application of the French Military Programming Law (*Loi* n° 2013-1168 of 18 December 2013 on military programming for 2014–2019).

[48] *FDN*, *FDN Fédération* and *La Quadrature du Net*. The same association filed another action against the refusal of the French Government to abrogate other provisions about indiscriminate data retention, in particular, decree 2011-219 of 25 February 2011 and Article R 10-13 of the Postal and Electronic Communications Code. This application is still pending.

[49] *Conseil d'État* decisions n° 388134 and 388255 (12 February 2016).

[50] See the opinion of the French Data Protection Authority (*Commission Nationale de l'Informatique et des Libertés* (CNIL)), issued on 5 March 2015, according to which the bill provided for overly broad and intrusive measures compared to the previous legal framework.

(persons who are wholly unrelated to the intelligence mission).[51] Nevertheless, this standard is not reflected in the final version of the law.

On the contrary, in March 2015, the *Conseil d'État* deemed the bill compatible with fundamental rights, pointing to the '*liste unique de finalités*' ('list of purposes') for intelligence as adequate provision.[52] Four months later, the *Conseil Constitutionnel* also validated the law, striking down only part of it.[53] Among these: the provisions allowing surveillance on foreign communications (because of the lack of detailed conditions under which data would be used, retained, and deleted); the ambiguous description of the role of the *Commission Nationale de Contrôle des Techinques de Renseignement* (CNCTR);[54] and the lack of clear jurisdictional mechanisms through which people could seek redress. The *Conseil* also invalidated some marginal provisions related to individual recourse, deeming them too restrictive of rights.

The *loi sur le renseignement*, which has been dubbed the 'French Patriot Act',[55] entered into force the day after the *Conseil* ruling. It allows intelligence agencies to collect electronic communications, information, and documents held by electronic operators, but only in relation to the fight against terrorism and with authorisation from the Prime Minister, who may consult the CNCTR but may forgo such consultation in situations of 'absolute emergency'.[56] The law also sets some time limits for data retention: data about individuals who are linked to a person who is himself or herself subject to authorisation or wiretapping data should be destroyed after thirty days;[57] metadata is subject to a maximum retention period of four years; and for encrypted data, the period of allowable retention is calculated from the day of decryption but cannot exceed six years from the date of collection.[58] With regards to complaint and appeal procedures, there is a first (non-jurisdictional) step before the CNCTR, whose decisions can be challenged before the *Conseil d'État*. The CNCTR, which has a broad oversight over the abovementioned measures, can order the interruption of intelligence surveillance and the destruction of data.

[51] See B Dambrine, 'The State of French Surveillance Law', Future of Privacy Forum White Paper (22 December 2015), emphasising how this advice was not taken into account by the French legislator.

[52] *Conseil d'État* opinion n° 389.754 (12 March 2015).

[53] *Conseil Constitutionnel* decision n° 2015-713 DC (23 July 2015). The *Conseil* weighed in on the law through the mechanism of the *saisine*, which allows for a parliamentary minority to challenge the constitutionality of a law before its entry into force.

[54] An independent administrative authority comprising magistrates, members of the legislature, and technical experts.

[55] See É Quillatre, 'The New Bill on Intelligence: Toward a French *Patriot Act* (Act II)?' (2015) 1(2) *European Data Protection Law Review* 140–43; Chardel, Harvey, and Volat (above n 46); and W Mastor, 'The French Intelligence Act: The French Surveillance State?' (2017) 23(4) *European Public Law* 707–722.

[56] According to Art L 811-3 of the French Internal Security Code: prevention of terrorism; the safeguard of national integrity and territory; and prevention of immediate threat.

[57] Art 2, *Loi* n° 2015-912 (above n 46).

[58] Art L 822-2 of the French Internal Security Code, as modified by Art 2, *Loi* n° 2015-912 (above n 46). According to it, there is also another term of 120 days for private spaces and vehicle wiretapping and certain categories of log data.

Almost exactly four months after the enactment of the *loi sur le renseignement*, Paris suffered a series of high-profile terrorist attacks, and in the immediate aftermath, a formal state of emergency (*état d'urgence*) was declared,[59] and Law 2015-1556 was passed,[60] further strengthening national surveillance measures. The *Conseil Constitutionnel* again found the law compatible with constitutional guarantees related to the right to privacy.[61] Law 2016-987 was then passed in July 2016, extending the state of emergency and amending Article L 851-2 of the French Internal Security Code as well.[62] Notably, it authorises the collection of data not only of people who are suspected of constituting a national security threat but also of those suspected of '*être en lien avec une menace*' ('being linked to a threat'). Although Law 2017-1510 ended the state of emergency in France in October 2017,[63] it turned many related measures, including some involving surveillance, into ordinary law – thus instituting a 'normalisation' of emergency powers.[64]

The *Conseil Constitutionnel* had another chance to address surveillance and its related issues in October 2016 in a case relating to Article L 811-5 of the French Internal Security Code, which enabled the surveillance of radio communications without any procedural or substantive conditions or specific guarantees. The *Conseil Constitutionnel* struck down the provision[65] but delayed the effects of its ruling until December 2017 in order to allow Parliament to remedy the unconstitutionality of the provision. However, no changes have been made yet, despite the deadline set by the *Conseil*.

This series of events, which all occurred after the CJEU ruling in *Digital Rights Ireland*, make clear the French legal system's disregard for the principles affirmed by the CJEU. Unlike in the United Kingdom, the French trend towards harsh securitisation appears to have swept up not only lawmakers but constitutional judges as well. While security is understandably a significant concern at legislative and executive levels, courts have traditionally been a bulwark of rights and acted to stem such drifts. This trend is therefore worrying.

C. Legislative Trends in Other European Countries

Other EU countries beside the United Kingdom and France have enacted harsh surveillance measures too, even in the wake of the CJEU efforts to shift the

[59] Decree n° 2015-1475 (14 November 2015) applying *Loi* n° 55-385 (3 April 1955).

[60] *Loi* n° 2015-1556 (30 November 2015) on surveillance of international electronic communications.

[61] *Conseil Constitutionnel* decision 2015-722 (26 November 2015).

[62] *Loi* n° 2016-987 (21 July 2016) extending the application of *Loi* n° 55-385 (3 April 1955) on the state of emergency and reinforcing measures to fight against terrorism. For discussion of the state of emergency in France, see the chapter in this volume by Marc-Antoine Granger.

[63] *Loi* n° 2017-1510 (30 October 2017).

[64] See further A Vedaschi, *À la guerre comme à la guerre? La disciplina della guerra nel diritto costituzionale comparato* (Turin, Giappichelli, 2007) 75.

[65] *Conseil Constitutionnel* decision n° 2016-590 QPC (21 October 2016).

balance between rights and national security towards the former. This section will briefly outline some key changes, with a focus on the ways that domestic courts have either endorsed the securitarian approach of the legislative and executive branches or revealed some 'muscularity' in resisting the encroachment upon privacy and related rights.

In Italy, the Data Retention Directive had been implemented by Article 132 of the Personal Data Protection Code[66] and, despite the invalidation of the DRD by the CJEU, it has not been repealed. In February 2015, as part of new counterterrorist policies, the Italian government issued Decree Law 7/2015, which made an exception to Article 132 of the Code, introducing even longer retention periods than those provided for in the previous data retention framework.[67] Specifically, Article 4*bis* of the Decree extended the retention of electronic telecommunication and missed calls metadata until 31 December 2016; and this deadline was subsequently extended again until 30 June 2017.[68] In November 2017, Parliament passed an even more restrictive law by extending the retention period to six years.[69]

Notably, immediately after the entry into force of Decree 7/2015, the Italian Data Protection Authority released a statement in which they pointed out that the Decree does not comply with the standards set out in *Digital Rights Ireland*.[70] As yet, the Italian Constitutional Court has not ruled on the issue, but given the Court's record on national security-related issues,[71] it seems likely that it would take a rights-restrictive approach in order to accommodate supposed counterterrorism priorities.

Also in 2015, the German Parliament (*Bundestag*) passed a new law that entered into force in January 2016 and amended section 113 of the German Telecommunication Act and some provisions of the Criminal Code and the Code of Criminal Procedure.[72] This law raises some concerns as it provides for wide data retention powers and, in some cases, allows the retention of the contents of communications too.[73] In April 2016, the German Constitutional

[66] Legislative Decree 196 of 30 June 2003. Many provisions of this Decree have been repealed or modified by Legislative Decree 101 (10 August 2018), updating the Italian data protection framework to Regulation (UE) 2016/679.

[67] Decree Law 7 of 18 February 2015.

[68] Decree Law 210 of 30 December 2015.

[69] Law 167 of 20 November 2017.

[70] Data Protection Authority (Italy), 'Declaration on the Amendment to the Antiterrorism Decree' (24 March 2015), http://www.garanteprivacy.it/web/guest/home/docweb/-/docweb-display/docweb/3807700.

[71] For example, regarding the issue of state secrecy, it endorsed the notion of national security as priority government policy. See A Vedaschi, 'The Dark Side of Counter-terrorism: *Arcana Imperii* and *Salus Rei Publicae*' (2018) 66(4) *American Journal of Comparative Law* 877–926.

[72] *Endgültiges Ergebnis der Namentlichen Abstimmung Nr 1, Deutscher Bundestag*, 2015-10-16. For more on counterterrorism policies in Germany, see the chapter in this volume by Andreas Armborst.

[73] Retention of content is allowed when technical reasons make it unfeasible to retain metadata without stripping the content.

Court heard a case involving surveillance by the federal police, who had relied on provisions in the Federal Criminal Police Act.[74] The Court ruled that the provisions were overly vague, which had allowed the police to interpret them in an excessively broad manner and to resort too readily to extreme measures. Nonetheless, in October 2016, the *Bundestag* passed another law, this one authorising surveillance on foreign-to-foreign communications – that is, communications between individuals who are not German citizens.[75] There are no clauses providing for independent oversight, and indeed judicial authorities are not involved at any stage of the procedures, not even to authorise interception. Additionally, foreseeability is impaired by the lack of clear and strict interception and retention conditions. These and other criticisms were raised by many institutional actors while the law was still at a draft stage, including three different UN special rapporteurs, who wrote to the German government to express their concerns.[76] Despite these objections from international and domestic stakeholders, as well as recent attempts by the Constitutional Court to stem the legislative drift towards state-sanctioned surveillance, the law was passed anyway. In June 2017, the reach of law enforcement agencies was again expanded, allowing them to conduct online searches and surveillance, even through the use of malware.[77]

In Austria, a new state security law was passed in 2016.[78] The *Polizeiliches Staatschutzgesetz* (PStSG) is a comprehensive reform of secret services, with many provisions that reshape surveillance and data retention obligations.[79] Its most troubling features include broad surveillance powers that are not counterbalanced by appropriate authorisation and oversight procedures, as well as a very weak standard of suspicion. Only 'an estimated possibility of an attack endangering the Constitution' is required to apply the measures.[80] Last but not least, the scope of the measures is not restricted to

[74] German Federal Constitutional Court, 1 BvR 966/09, 1 BvR 1140/09 (20 April 2016).

[75] *Gesetz zur Ausland-Ausland-Fernmeldeaufklärung des Bundesnachrichtendienstes*, amending *Gesetz über den Bundesnachrichtendienst*.

[76] See Letter to Ambassador Hans Joachim-Daerr, Permanent Mission of the Federal Republic of Germany to the United Nations (Geneva), from the UN Special Rapporteur on the right to promotion and protection of the right to freedom of opinion and expression; UN Special Rapporteur on the situation of human rights defenders; and UN Special Rapporteur on the independence of judges and lawyers (29 August 2016), https://www.reporter-ohne-grenzen.de/fileadmin/Redaktion/Presse/Downloads/Berichte_und_Dokumente/2016/20160902_Kritik_UN_am_BND-Gesetzesentwurf.pdf. For an overview of this law that focuses on its drawbacks in terms on human rights, see also Amnesty International (above n 43).

[77] Gesetz zur effektiveren und praxistauglicheren Ausgestaltung des Strafverahrens, BGBI I 3203 (17 August 2017).

[78] *Polizeiliches Staatsschutzgesetz* (26 February 2016). For a detailed analysis of this law, see G Heissl, 'Polizeiliches Staatsschutzgesetz: Überblick und Besprechung ausgewählter Aspekte' (2016) 16 *Österreichische Juristen Zeitung* 719–26.

[79] The authority under the Police State Security Act (Federal Authority on constitutional protection and terror prevention) is competent for information within Austria. There is also a second law concerning the military information service. The military information service is competent for information from outside of Austria but concerning Austria.

[80] PStSG, s 1, para 6.

the prevention of terrorism but extends to whistle-blowers, protesters, and political extremists since 'attacks endangering the Constitution' can be interpreted very broadly. The constitutionality of the law has unsurprisingly been challenged by two major opposition parties, the Freedom Party of Austria (FPÖ) and the Green Party.[81] The Austrian Constitutional Court will adjudicate the case within the next months. It will be interesting to see whether this judgment will collocate the Austrian Court among courts taking a firm stance towards privacy in spite of national security concerns, or the other way around. Indeed, it was this court, together with the Irish High Court, that asked the CJEU for a preliminary ruling in *Digital Rights Ireland*, thus showing, at least an earlier strong commitment to privacy rights.

Nonetheless, in January 2017, the Austrian government proposed a new 'surveillance package', the key features of which are very much akin to the surveillance laws approved in other European countries and discussed above. There is, for example, a complete lack of differentiation between criminal suspects and ordinary citizens within the scope of the measures. Due to the campaigns of various NGOs and public interest groups, the most worrying measures were dropped.[82] The law was enacted in April 2018, and its provisions are progressively entering into force.[83]

In Belgium, a new law on data retention also entered into force in July 2016.[84] It differentiates retention periods according to the seriousness of the crime under investigation. For minor crimes the maximum period of retention is six months; for severe crimes it is nine months; and a maximum of twelve months is possible in relation to the most serious crimes. At the same time, a database for the exchange and cross-checking of data relating to foreign terrorist fighters was established as part of a broader framework of measures addressing violent extremism.[85] These measures are explicitly exempted from general privacy and data protection safeguards. The 2016 law came about following a ruling by the Belgian Constitutional Court that earlier legislation on data retention was unconstitutional.[86] However, it is unclear whether the Court was merely deferring to the CJEU judgment in *Digital Rights Ireland* or whether it was demonstrating a genuine commitment to data protection and privacy rights. Its stance on the 2016 law will be illustrative.

[81] There had already been a pending challenge launched in the province of Carinthia.

[82] Epicenter.works, 'Success Story: A Win on Austrian Surveillance Legislation', *European Digital Rights (EDRi)* (18 October 2017), https://edri.org/success-story-austrian-surveillance-legislation/.

[83] Sicherheitspaket. PK-Nr 469/2018. The package includes: Strafprozessrechtsänderungsgesetz (amendments to Austrian Criminal Procedure Law), entered into force June 2018; a new law on judicial cooperation in criminal law (entered into force July 2018); and an Amendment to the Austrian Telecommunication Act (entered into force January 2019).

[84] *Loi* n° 2016-9288 (29 May 2016) on the collection and conservation of data of electronic communications.

[85] Royal Decree of 22 September 2016 on common databases on Foreign Terrorist Fighters and giving execution to provisions of section 1-bis '*de la gestion des informations*' of chapter IV of the law on the functioning of the police.

[86] Belgian Constitutional Court, Decision 84/2015 (11 June 2015).

Lastly, in the Netherlands, a law reforming the security services entered into force in May 2018,[87] despite a consultative referendum rejecting its content.[88] Its features strongly resemble some of the most worrying elements of the Austrian measures described above.[89]

The developments in law and policies in the context of surveillance, data collection, and data retention that have been briefly outlined in this section reveal a common trend across Europe. Reforms enacted in the United Kingdom and in France appear to have propelled other European legislators in a similar direction. While some national constitutional courts seem reluctant to jump on the security bandwagon, others have clearly done so by offering little to no resistance to rights-restrictive legislation. Ultimately, it may remain true that the *Digital Rights Ireland* ruling was a watershed moment for privacy rights and data protection in Europe, but the lesson offered by the CJEU has – at least for the moment – gone largely unheeded.

III. CONCLUSION

Recent terrorist events have triggered a preventive security-based approach by European national governments. Pre-emptive surveillance appears to be a popular counterterrorism tool, and EU citizens frequently seem ready to accept considerable restrictions on their personal freedoms and fundamental rights in the name of security. In other words, efforts to feel 'safer' during the post-9/11 era often lead to limitations on the right to privacy and the connected guarantee of data protection, as well as to a devaluing of longstanding democratic principles such as the presumption of innocence and the importance of procedural rights.

This approach assumes that greater amounts of collected and retained data will lead to greater safety, against terrorist threats in particular.[90] However, there is some research to suggest that secret services and law enforcement agencies may be equally or even more inefficient when they have at their disposal large amounts of undifferentiated data. An impact assessment by the European Commission, for example, has shown that when financial surveillance data is

[87] Intelligence and Security Services Act 2017 (Wet op de Inlichtingen- en veiligheidsdiensten, Wiv).

[88] A Deutsch, 'Netherlands to Hold Referendum on New Surveillance Law', *Reuters* (1 November 2017), https://www.reuters.com/article/us-netherlands-referendum-intelligence/netherlands-to-hold-referendum-on-new-surveillance-law-idUSKBN1D145Y.

[89] For an overview on this law while still at the draft stage, see Amnesty International (above n 43) 33.

[90] On the use of surveillance according to a 'utilitarian logic', see C Murphy, *EU Counter-terrorism Law* (Oxford, Hart Publishing, 2016) 146 and 149. Against securitarianism, with specific regard to the use of data for prevention purposes, see A Vedaschi, 'L'Accordo internazionale sui dati dei passeggeri aviotrasportati (PNR) alla luce delle indicazioni della Corte di giustizia dell'Unione europea' (2017) *Giurisprudenza costituzionale* 1913–40.

selectively collected only from people who have at least allegedly some link with terrorism, the marginal benefit is higher in terms of reducing terrorist attacks, improving the public perception of security, and minimising negative impact.[91] This is not an absolute claim against surveillance. On the contrary, as the CJEU has clearly stated,[92] collection, retention and access to data are essential in the fight against international terrorism, as long as applied to those who are reasonably suspected to be involved with terrorism.[93]

The CJEU has recently taken action to prevent the popular and legislative drift towards securitarianism by invalidating the Data Retention Directive and then the Safe Harbour agreement on grounds of incompatibility with the Charter of Fundamental Rights of the European Union. While the US approach to the Safe Harbour scheme demonstrates a belief that privacy is something that must accommodate other competing interests, the CJEU has enshrined it as a key component of the rule of law. As such, the Court is acting as a proper constitutional court and identifying itself as an effective forum for the enforcement of fundamental rights and personal freedoms.[94] The CJEU defence of the rights to privacy and to data protection in the face of disproportionate and unnecessary interference could be a rallying cry for other likeminded constitutional courts, as well as for rights-oriented legislators and policymakers, especially during challenging times when the threat of international terrorism is very real.

However, this position has not always been embraced at the national level. As this chapter has shown, domestic lawmakers have often tipped the balance in favour of security, regarding surveillance as a priority in their counterterrorism strategies. In some jurisdictions, legislation that was designed to implement the now defunct DRD is still in force; in others, it has been substituted with new laws that are nothing if not a strengthening of surveillance networks. The United Kingdom and France are paramount examples of this worrying legislative trend, displaying increasing indifference towards the guarantees that are foundational to democracy. And while long retention periods, extraterritoriality, and the treatment of ordinary citizens as criminal suspects are issues that seem ripe for judicial intervention, some domestic European courts prove reticent, leaving regimes of mass indiscriminate surveillance uncontested and unconstrained

[91] European Commission, 'Impact Assessment: Communication from the European Commission to the European Parliament and the Council on a European Terrorist Financing Tracking System (TFTS)', Commission Staff Working Document, SWD(2013) 488 final (27 November 2013), https://ec.europa.eu/home-affairs/sites/homeaffairs/files/what-is-new/news/news/docs/20131127_tfts_ia_en.pdf.

[92] See the cases discussed in this chapter: *Digital Rights Ireland* (above n 3); *Schrems* (above n 3); *Tele2 Sverige* (above n 19); and Opinion 1/15 (above n 20).

[93] See W Wensink, B Warmenhoven, R Haasnoot, et al, 'The European Union's Policies on Counter-terrorism: Relevance, Coherence, and Effectiveness', European Parliament Directorate General for Internal Policies, PE 583.124 (January 2017), http://www.europarl.europa.eu/RegData/etudes/STUD/2017/583124/IPOL_STU(2017)583124_EN.pdf.

[94] Vedaschi and Lubello (above n 16) 17.

by limitations of necessity and proportionality.[95] French courts, for example, have so far appeared deferential to popular and political will with regard to wide-reaching counterterrorism powers. UK courts, on the other hand, have been more closely aligned with the CJEU regarding human rights and personal freedoms, the recent High Court ruling on the Investigatory Powers Act being a case in point.[96]

It remains to be seen whether other EU national courts will likewise follow suit. In this regard, the CJEU stance in *Digital Rights Ireland*, *Schrems*, and *Tele2 Sverige* could and should serve as a balanced, even-handed model: respectful of rights but mindful of security. The executive, legislative, and judicial branches of Member States could fortify the important role of the CJEU in this regard, both by taking direct heed of specific judgments and repealing rights-restrictive legislation and by taking seriously the principles enshrined in these decisions when drafting new laws and regulations. Although perfect security that has no cost for personal freedoms may be a utopian ideal, advanced democracies, even in stressful times, should not automatically resort to pre-emptive, intrusive securitarian regimes that threaten to undermine the very essence of democracy. In other words, state surveillance should not treat everyone as a terrorist suspect. The emerging CJEU framework provides hope that it is possible to maintain fundamental rights and still attend to the very real needs of national security.

REFERENCES

Amnesty International, 'Dangerously Disproportionate: The Ever-Expanding National Security State in Europe', Report EUR 01/5342/2017 (17 January 2017).

Anderson, D (UK Independent Reviewer of Terrorism Legislation), 'A Question of Trust: Report of the Investigatory Powers Review' (June 2015).

Bignami, FE, 'Privacy and Law Enforcement in the European Union: The Data Retention Directive' (2007) 8(1) *Chicago Journal of International Law* 233–55.

Bradley, AW, Ewing, KD and Knight, CJS, *Constitutional and Administrative Law*, 16th edn (Harlow, Pearson, 2015).

Chardel, PA, Harvey, R and Volat, H, 'The French Intelligence Act: Resonances with the USA PATRIOT Act', *Technology Science* (15 March 2016), http://techscience.org/a/2016031501/.

Cole, D, 'Preserving Privacy in a Digital Age: Lessons of Comparative Constitutionalism' in F Davis, N McGarrity, and G Williams (eds), *Surveillance, Counterterrorism and Comparative Constitutionalism* (New York, Routledge, 2013).

[95] For further critical discussion, see M Tzanou, *The Fundamental Right to Data Protection* (Oxford, Hart Publishing, 2017); and ZK Goldman and SJ Rascoff, *Global Intelligence Oversight: Governing Security in the Twenty-First Century* (Oxford, Oxford University Press, 2016). On the principle of proportionality in particular, see K Moller, 'Constructing the Proportionality Test: An Emerging Global Conversation' in L Lazarus, C McCrudden, and N Bowles (eds), *Reasoning Rights: Comparative Judicial Reasoning* (Oxford, Hart Publishing, 2014).

[96] *Liberty v Home Department* (above n 45).

Cole, MD and Vandendriessche, A, 'From *Digital Rights Ireland* in Luxembourg to *Zakharov and Szabò/Vissy* in Strasbourg: What the ECtHR Made of the Deep Pass by the CJEU in the Recent Cases on Mass Surveillance' (2016) 2(1) *European Data Protection Law Review* 121–29.

Coq, C and Galli, F, 'Comparative Paper on Data Retention Regulation in a Sample of EU Member States', EUI Seventh Framework Programme, Surveille deliverable 4.3 (30 April 2013).

Dambrine, B, 'The State of French Surveillance Law', Future of Privacy Forum White Paper (22 December 2015).

A Deutsch, 'Netherlands to Hold Referendum on New Surveillance Law', *Reuters* (1 November 2017), https://www.reuters.com/article/us-netherlands-referendum-intelligence/netherlands-to-hold-referendum-on-new-surveillance-law-idUSKBN1D145Y.

Duffy, H, *The 'War on Terror' and the Framework of International Law* (Cambridge, Cambridge University Press, 2015).

European Commission, 'Impact Assessment: Communication from the European Commission to the European Parliament and the Council on a European Terrorist Financing Tracking System (TFTS)', Commission Staff Working Document, SWD (2013) 488 final (27 November 2013), https://ec.europa.eu/home-affairs/sites/homeaffairs/files/what-is-new/news/news/ docs/20131127_tfts_ia_en.pdf.

Fabbrini, F, 'The EU Charter of Fundamental Rights and the Rights to Data Privacy: The EU Court of Justice as a Human Rights Court' in S de Vries, U Bernitz, and S Weatherill (eds), *The EU Charter of Fundamental Rights as a Binding Instrument: Five Years Old and Growing* (Oxford, Hart Publishing, 2015).

——, 'Human Rights in the Digital Age: The European Court of Justice Ruling in the Data Retention Case and Its Lessons for Privacy and Surveillance in the United States' (2015) 28 *Harvard Human Rights Journal* 65–95.

Gearty, C, 'State Surveillance in an Age of Security' in F Davis, N McGarrity, and G Williams (eds), *Surveillance, Counterterrorism and Comparative Constitutionalism* (New York, Routledge, 2013).

Goldman, ZK and Rascoff, SJ, *Global Intelligence Oversight: Governing Security in the Twenty-First Century* (Oxford, Oxford University Press, 2016).

Gonzáles Fuster, G and Scherrer, A, 'Big Data and Smart Devices and Their Impact on Privacy', study for the LIBE Committee (September 2015).

Goold, BJ, 'Privacy, Identity and Security' in BJ Goold and L Lazarus (eds), *Security and Human Rights* (Oxford, Hart Publishing, 2007).

Heissl, G, 'Polizeiliches Staatsschutzgesetz: Überblick und Besprechung ausgewählter Aspekte' (2016) 16 *Österreichische Juristen Zeitung* 719–26.

Lennon, G and Walker, C (eds), *Routledge Handbook of Law and Terrorism* (New York, Routledge, 2015).

Mastor, W, 'The French Intelligence Act: The French Surveillance State?' (2017) 23(4) *European Public Law* 707–722.

Mitsilegas, V, 'Surveillance and Digital Privacy in the Transatlantic "War on Terror": The Case for a Global Privacy Regime' (2016) 47(3) *Columbia Human Rights Law Review* 1–77.

Moller, K, 'Constructing the Proportionality Test: An Emerging Global Conversation' in L Lazarus, C McCrudden, and N Bowles (eds), *Reasoning Rights: Comparative Judicial Reasoning* (Oxford, Hart Publishing, 2014).

Murphy, C, *EU Counter-terrorism Law* (Oxford, Hart Publishing, 2016).

Quillatre, É, 'The New Bill on Intelligence: Towards a French Patriot Act (Act II)?' (2015) 1(2) *European Data Protection Law Review* 140–43.

Ramraj, V, Hor, M, Roach, K, and Williams, G (eds), *Global Anti-terrorism Law and Policy* (Cambridge, Cambridge University Press, 2012).

Roberts, A, 'Privacy, Data Retention and Domination: *Digital Rights Ireland Ltd v Minister for Communication*' (2015) 78(3) *Modern Law Review* 535–48.

Tzanou, M, *The Fundamental Right to Data Protection* (Oxford, Hart Publishing, 2017).

Vedaschi, A, 'L'Accordo internazionale sui dati dei passeggeri aviotrasportati (PNR) alla luce delle indicazioni della Corte di giustizia dell'Unione europea' (2017) *Giurisprudenza costituzionale* 1913–40.

——, 'The Dark Side of Counter-terrorism: Arcana Imperii and Salus Rei Publicae' (2018) 66(4) *American Journal of Comparative Law* 877–926.

——, 'The European Court of Justice on the EU–Canada Passenger Name Record Agreement, ECJ, 26 July 2017, Opinion 1/15' (2018) 14(2) *European Constitutional Law Review* 410–29.

——, *À la guerre comme à la guerre? La disciplina della guerra nel diritto costituzionale comparato* (Turin, Giappichelli, 2007).

Vedaschi, A and Lubello, V, 'Data Retention and Its Implications for the Fundamental Right to Privacy' (2015) 20(1) *Tilburg Law Review* 14–34.

Wensink, W, Warmenhoven, B, Haasnoot, R, et al, 'The European Union's Policies on Counter-terrorism: Relevance, Coherence, and Effectiveness', European Parliament Directorate General for Internal Policies, PE 583.124 (January 2017), http://www.europarl.europa.eu/RegData/etudes/STUD/2017/583124/IPOL_STU(2017)583124_EN.pdf.

Zuiderveen Borgesius, FJ and Arnbak, A, 'New Data Security Requirements and the Proceduralization of Mass Surveillance Law after the European Data Retention Case', Amsterdam Law School Research Paper No 2015-41 (October 2015).

13

Anonymity for Victims at the Special Tribunal for Lebanon: Security and Human Rights at Work in International Criminal Justice

JUAN-PABLO PÉREZ-LEÓN-ACEVEDO*

On 30 May 2007, United Nations Security Council Resolution 1757 brought into force the provisions of the Agreement between the UN and Lebanon to establish a Special Tribunal for Lebanon (STL) to try those suspected of the assassination of former Lebanese Prime Minister Rafiq Hariri, who was among 22 total killed and 226 injured by a car bomb in Lebanon on 14 February 2005.[1] The Security Council qualified this and related attacks as terrorist and 'a threat to international peace and security'. Under Article 1 of the STL Statute (STLS),[2] the Special Tribunal has jurisdiction over the February 2005 attack, connected attacks in Lebanon (from October 2004 through December 2005), and later related attacks. *Ayyash et al* has been the only STL trial so far, and the four co-accused are Hezbollah senior members.[3] Trial hearings for *Ayyash et al* concluded on 21 September 2018, but as of 1 November 2018, judgment had not yet been rendered.[4] Unlike other

* Funding for this chapter was gratefully received from the Research Council of Norway (Project Number 223274).

1 SC Resolution 1757 (2007), UN Doc S/RES/1757 (30 May 2007), https://www.securitycouncilreport.org/atf/cf/%7B65BFCF9B-6D27-4E9C-8CD3-CF6E4FF96FF9%7D/Chap%20VII%20SRES%201757.pdf, Annex, para 1(a).

2 Statute of the Special Tribunal for Lebanon (STLS), UN Doc S/Res/1757 (10 June 2007), Annex, https://www.stl-tsl.org/en/documents/statute-of-the-tribunal/223-statute-of-the-special-tribunal-for-lebanon.

3 *Prosecutor v Ayyash et al* (STL-11-01). The STL Prosecutor submitted the original indictment to the pretrial judge on 17 January 2011. The indictment was amended four times between 2011 and 2016, with the trial opening on 16 January 2014. For further information, see the STL webpage (https://www.stl-tsl.org), especially regarding *Ayyash et al*: https://www.stl-tsl.org/en/the-cases/stl-11-01.

4 See Special Tribunal for Lebanon, 'Conclusion of the Closing Arguments in the *Ayyash et al Case*' (21 September 2018), https://www.stl-tsl.org/en/media/press-releases/6290-conclusion-of-the-closing-arguments-in-the-ayyash-et-al-case.

international and hybrid criminal tribunals (ICTs), the Special Tribunal for Lebanon has jurisdiction over terrorist acts.[5] Concerning terrorism, the STLS refers to the Lebanese Criminal Code. This exemplifies the hybrid character of the Special Tribunal.

The STL Appeals Chamber found that Lebanese provisions on terrorism must be interpreted in light of international law and, for the first time at the international level, concluded that international terrorism constitutes an autonomous customary international law crime in peace times, the elements of which are: a criminal act or threat thereof; intent to spread fear among the population or to coerce authorities (not) to act; and a transnational character.[6] Some have partially criticised these elements.[7] Moreover, there is no accepted definition of international terrorism. However, certain international terrorist acts may arguably constitute a core international crime if they meet a gravity threshold, namely, transnational actions with some state involvement that concern the whole international community and threaten peace.[8] Terrorism as the preponderant STL-jurisdiction crime requires the STL to pay attention to security concerns in accordance with international human rights law (IHRL).

Accordingly, anonymity for victims as an exceptional protective measure at the Special Tribunal for Lebanon is examined here as a means to discuss how security and human rights interact in international criminal justice concerning terrorism. Whereas anonymity is nondisclosure of the identity of victim participants and witnesses to the defence, other protective measures concern this nondisclosure to only the public and media.[9] The first section of this chapter analyses how security and human rights work at the Special Tribunal for Lebanon. The second and third sections examine, respectively, anonymity during STL pretrial and trial. Finally, reconciliation of competing rights and security concerns related to anonymity at the Special Tribunal for Lebanon is discussed.

I. SECURITY AND HUMAN RIGHTS AT THE SPECIAL TRIBUNAL FOR LEBANON

Within the liberal tradition, security and rights have frequently had a fraught relationship, and the pursuit of one must be reconciled with preservation of

[5] STLS (above n 2) Art 2(a).

[6] *Prosecutor v Ayyash et al* (STL-11-01/PT/T26), Interlocutory Decision on the Applicable Law, AC (16 February 2011) paras 83–85.

[7] M Gillet and M Schuster, 'Fast-Track Justice: The Special Tribunal for Lebanon Defines Terrorism' (2011) 9 *Journal for International Criminal Justice* 989, 1008–14.

[8] A Cassese, *International Criminal Law* (Oxford, Oxford University Press, 2003) 129.

[9] Y Alvarez-Reyes, 'The Protection of Victims Participating in International Criminal Justice' in K Tibori-Szabó and M Hirst (eds), *Victim Participation in International Criminal Justice* (The Hague, Asser/Springer, 2017) 187.

the other.[10] In international law, security must be complemented by respect for rights, which are ultimately safeguarded by the judiciary.[11] Since the Special Tribunal for Lebanon is part of the international legal order, the rule of law applies to it.[12] This section examines how security and human rights operate at the Special Tribunal for Lebanon, mainly by focusing on defendants and victims.

In accordance with the Lebanese request to establish a tribunal of international character, the legal foundation of the STL was originally a UN – Lebanon agreement.[13] However, Hezbollah's political opposition prevented parliamentary ratification, so the Security Council brought the STL Agreement provisions into force under Chapter VII of the UN Charter. SC Resolution 1757 qualified the above-mentioned terrorist attacks as 'a threat to international peace and security'. The enforcement of the STL Agreement via SC Resolution 1757 arguably reshaped the legal foundation of the Special Tribunal for Lebanon, changing it from an agreement-based tribunal to one imposed by the Security Council under its Chapter VII mandate.[14] Despite its creation by the Security Council, however, the STL is not a UN tribunal.[15] In a decision that was upheld by the Appeals Chamber,[16] the STL Trial Chamber declined to review the legality of its own creation.[17] The Trial Chamber nonetheless exercised some limited power of review in terms of the consistency of its instruments with international human rights law.[18] Importantly, the Trial Chamber found that: i) the UN Charter authorises the Security Council to create such a tribunal, and as such, when someone is accused before the tribunal, his/her right to be tried by a court established by the law is not breached; and ii) the STL legal instruments respect the rights of those accused.[19] Under Article 8(1) of the STL Agreement, the Tribunal was established outside Lebanon, and the Hague was selected as a location due to considerations of fairness, security, victim rights, and access to witnesses.

[10] L Lazarus and B Goold, 'Introduction: Security and Human Rights – The Search for a Language of Reconciliation' in BJ Goold and L Lazarus (eds), *Security and Human Rights* (Oxford, Hart Publishing, 2007) 1–2.

[11] CH Powell, 'The Legal Authority of the United Nations Security Council' in Goold and Lazarus (eds) (ibid) 175.

[12] Ibid, 181.

[13] Included as Annex to SC Resolution 1757 (see above n 1).

[14] B Fassbender, 'Reflections on the International Legality of the Special Tribunal for Lebanon' (2007) 5 *Journal of International Criminal Justice* 1091, 1098.

[15] *Prosecutor v Ayyash et al* (STL-11/01/PT/AC/AR90.1), Decision on the Defence Appeals Against the Trial Chamber's Decision on the Defence Challenges to the Jurisdiction and Legality of the Tribunal, AC (24 October 2012) para 39.

[16] Ibid, paras 11–54.

[17] *Prosecutor v Ayyash et al* (STL-11/01/PT/TC), Decision on the Defence Challenges to the Jurisdiction and Legality of the Tribunal, TC (27 July 2012) para 55.

[18] D Fransen, 'The Special Tribunal for Lebanon and the Rule of Law' in G De-Baere and J Wouters (eds), *The Contribution of International and Supranational Courts to the Rule of Law* (Cheltenham, Edward Elgar, 2015) 340.

[19] *Ayyash et al*, Appeal Decision on Jurisdiction and Legality of the Tribunal (above n 15) paras 62–88.

Lebanon must adopt measures connected to security of the STL and related persons.[20]

STL instruments include human rights clauses on rights of defendants and victims. Article 16 of the Statute contains a catalogue of rights that were adapted from a variety of human rights treaties. These include rights to: a fair and public hearing (Article 16(2)), adequate time and facilities for defence preparation (Article 16(4)(b)), a trial without undue delay (Article 16(4)(d)), and examination of witnesses and evidence against the accused (Article 16(4)(e)–(f)). The right to examine witnesses is part of equality of arms and relates to adequate defence preparation.[21] Additionally, the STLS (Articles 5, 9, and 16(3) respectively) recognises inter alia the prohibition of double jeopardy, the right to be tried by an independent and impartial tribunal, and the presumption of innocence. The STL Rules of Procedure and Evidence detail these rights.[22] The wide scope of these fair trial rights means that STL judges may form their own notions of fairness and infer procedural rights that are not explicitly listed in the STL instruments but are procedurally necessary.[23]

To meet IHRL standards on defence rights, the Special Tribunal for Lebanon has some important institutional and procedural features. An independent Defence Office (the first among international and hybrid criminal tribunals) seeks to strengthen equality of arms.[24] For their part, prosecutors are required to provide assistance in truth determination and victim/witness protection and to respect defence rights.[25] The Trial Chamber may exclude evidence gathered in violation of defence rights or when a fair trial must be ensured.[26] Amendments to the Rules cannot prejudice defence rights in pending cases.[27]

One of the procedural issues for which the Special Tribunal has received criticism involves trials *in absentia*.[28] *Ayyash et al* was held in *absentia* because the co-accused absconded and did not wish to participate. Unlike common law jurisdictions, civil law jurisdictions (Lebanon included) allow for trials *in absentia*, as the STL President has pointed out.[29] Furthermore, international human rights law admits trials *in absentia* subject to safeguards for the accused,[30] which the STLS contains in Article 22(2).

[20] STL Agreement (above n 1), Art 14.

[21] J Jones and M Zgonec-Rožej 'Rights of Suspects and Accused' in A Alamuddin et al (eds), *The Special Tribunal for Lebanon-Law and Practice* (Oxford, Oxford University Press, 2014).

[22] Updated information on the STL Rules of Procedure and Evidence (hereafter 'STL Rules') is available at https://www.stl-tsl.org/en/documents/rules-of-procedure-and-evidence.

[23] N Croquet, 'The Special Tribunal for Lebanon's Innovative Human Rights Framework' (2016) 47(2) *Georgetown Journal of International Law* 351–95, 359–60.

[24] STL President, 'Rules of Procedure and Evidence-Explanatory Memorandum' (12 April 2012) para 22.

[25] STL Rules (above n 22) Rule 55(C).

[26] Ibid, Rule 149(D).

[27] Ibid, Rule 5(H).

[28] W Jordash and T Parker, 'Trials *in Absentia* at the Special Tribunal for Lebanon' (2010) 8 *Journal of International Criminal Justice* 487–509.

[29] STL President (12 April 2012) (above n 24) paras 3 and 38.

[30] *Krombach v France*, App no 29731/96 [2001] II ECHR 35, paras 85–89.

As part of international and hybrid criminal tribunals, witnesses are crucial. Testifying may moreover have therapeutic effects on victims, who may benefit from healing as part of a truth-telling process.[31] At the Special Tribunal for Lebanon, victim witnesses have testified about events that they personally know and provide evidence to prove crimes.[32] Their testimony may be connected to other evidence, including documentary and forensic evidence.[33]

In 2007, the UN International Independent Investigation Commission, which was set up to investigate the attack against Hariri, identified challenges to the physical security of witnesses.[34] STLS Article 12(4) outlines the Tribunal's obligation via its Victims and Witnesses Unit to protect the physical security of victims and witnesses.[35] The pretrial judge (PTJ) and Trial Chamber may order protective measures if they are consistent with the accused's rights.[36] To grant protective measures, there must be a real fear for the physical security of the witness/victim participant (a matter of neccesity), and the measures should be minimally restrictive of defence rights (a matter of proportionality).[37]

Numerous requests for additional protective measures prompted the introduction of amendments to the Rules in order to safeguard defence rights.[38] For example, amended Rule 133 provides for streamlined request procedures: defence and prosecution can present their views as regards a requested variation without first receiving consent from the witness concerned, and in turn, the identity of a protected witness can be preserved.[39] Additionally, Rule 140 makes seeking reconsideration of a decision more straightforward; and Rules 167, 177, and 187 simplify appeal proceedings. In making STL proceedings more expeditious, predictable, and consistent, these changes aimed to balance defence and victim/witness rights.[40]

Since jurisdiction over terrorism is challenging,[41] written testimony statements (including anonymous witness testimony) are allowed if the accused's rights are protected. Evidentiary principles included in the Rules guide how to protect defence rights. If the need to guarantee a fair trial outweighs the probative value of certain evidence, the Tribunal may exclude it, particularly

[31] J O'Connell, 'Gambling with the Psyche: Does Prosecuting Human Rights Violators Console their Victims?' (2005) 46 *Harvard International Law Journal* 295, 330.

[32] W Schabas, *The UN International Criminal Tribunals* (Cambridge, Cambridge University Press, 2006) 471.

[33] C Bassiouni, *Introduction to International Criminal Law* (Ardsley, Transnational Publishers, 2003) 633.

[34] UN International Independent Investigation Commission, 'Eighth Report', S/2007/424 (12 July 2007) para 58.

[35] STL Rules (above n 22) Rule 50.

[36] Ibid, Rules 97 and 133(A).

[37] *Prosecutor v Ayyash et al* (STL-11-01/PT/PTJ), Decision on the Legal Representative of Victims' First, Second and Third Motions for Protective Measures for Victims Participating in the Proceedings, PTJ (19 December 2012) para 19.

[38] Special Tribunal for Lebanon, 'Eighth Annual Report (2016–2017)' (23 March 2017) 14.

[39] STL Plenary of Judges, 'Summary of Approved Rule Amendment Proposals' (March 2016) 2.

[40] Special Tribunal for Lebanon, 'Eighth Annual Report' (above n 38) 14.

[41] STL President (12 April 2012) (above n 24) para 35.

if evidence was gathered in violation of defence rights.[42] Concerning admissibility of evidence, the mode and order of questioning and cross-examination, the Tribunal is guided by determination of truth priorities as well as by principles of efficiency and effectiveness.[43]

As proceedings relating to terrorism may require the protection of confidential information, nondisclosure of information in the prosecution's possession is permitted if disclosure would seriously threaten the physical security of a witness or his/her family. However, the Trial Chamber may order counterbalancing/rectifying measures such as the identification of similar information, provision of information in summarised/redacted form, or disclosure of relevant facts.[44] If these measures are determined to be insufficient to protect defence rights, the Trial Chamber may order amendment or withdrawal of charges.[45] This is consistent with IHRL jurisprudence on counterterrorism practices, particularly the jurisprudence of the European Court of Human Rights (ECtHR) in cases involving terrorism and national security.[46] The ECtHR has found that although discussion of confidential material may be unavoidable, government officials and agencies are subject to judicial control in this regard.[47] The ECtHR has also crucially determined that authorities with legitimate security concerns must still 'accord the individual a substantial measure of procedural justice'.[48]

The right of victims to participate at the Special Tribunal for Lebanon is outlined in Article 17 of the STLS, which is largely based on Article 68(3) of the International Criminal Court (ICC) Statute. Article 17 is the legal basis for victim participation in the STL and reads as follows:

> Where the personal interests of the victims are affected, the Special Tribunal shall permit their views and concerns to be presented and considered at stages of the proceedings determined to be appropriate by the Pretrial Judge or the Chamber and in a manner that is not prejudicial to or inconsistent with the rights of the accused and a fair and impartial trial.

Victim participation at the STL is important to realise victims' right to justice.[49] Victim participation pursues three goals: judicial (namely, assistance to the Tribunal to determine the truth); reparative; and symbolic (namely, in helping victims to feel connected to the Tribunal).[50] However, the need to ensure defence

[42] STL Rules (above n 22) Rule 149.
[43] See ibid, Rule 150.
[44] Ibid, Rule 116(B).
[45] Ibid, Rule 116(C).
[46] See, eg, *Öcalan v Turkey* (2005) 41 EHRR 985; and *Chahal v United Kingdom* (1996) 23 EHHR 413.
[47] *Chahal v UK* (ibid), para 131.
[48] Ibid.
[49] M Wierda et al, 'Early Reflections on Local Perceptions, Legitimacy and Legacy of the Special Tribunal for Lebanon' (2007) 5 *Journal of International Criminal Justice* 1065, 1072–73.
[50] J De-Hemptinne, 'Challenges Raised by Victims' Participation in the Proceedings of the Special Tribunal for Lebanon' (2010) 8 *Journal of International Criminal Justice* 165, 167–68.

rights has sometimes limited the attainment of these goals at the STL.[51] The challenge of balancing defendant rights and victim participant rights (and more generally, the challenge of balancing security and rights) has been addressed by the Tribunal through the judicially drafted/amended Rules and through STL case law, both of which will be examined more closely below.

First, the victim participant status has been narrowly defined to avoid excessive numbers of victim participants, which would risk compromising the defence–prosecution balance.[52] When deciding whether to grant victim participant status, the pretrial judge shall consider whether: the applicant is *prima facie* a Rule 2(A) victim (ie, suffered harm as a direct result of an STL-jurisdiction attack); the applicant's personal interests are affected; the applicant intends to express his/her views and concerns; and participation would affect the accused's rights.[53] Whether victim participation would affect the security of the proceedings or of any person involved may also be considered.[54] 'Physical harm' for victim participation has been narrowly construed by STL case law;[55] and victim participation 'cannot be to undermine the integrity or the fair and efficient conduct of the proceedings'.[56] Moreover, victim participant status granted during pretrial can be judicially re-examined during trial in order to guarantee defence rights.[57] Some of these checks and restrictions have the potential to limit the restorative effects of victim participation, but they have been implemented with regard to the rights of the accused and are largely consistent with other legal sources, including other international and hybrid criminal tribunals.[58]

Second, to avoid delays in proceedings, the STL Rules exclude victim participation from the investigation process.[59] Victim participation thus begins after confirmation of the indictment.[60] While this means that victims' interests are sidelined in determination of the truth during investigation, it arguably better guarantees defence rights to expeditious proceedings and equality of arms. To deal with this issue, the ICC allows victim participation during investigation but only within judicial proceedings.[61]

Third, the scope and exercise of procedural rights of victim participants are subject to judicial discretion during the proceedings at the STL. Victim participant

[51] H Morrison and E Pountney, 'Victim Participation at the Special Tribunal for Lebanon' in Alamuddin et al (eds) (above n 21).

[52] STL President (12 April 2012) (above n 24) paras 18–19.

[53] STL Rules (above n 22) Rule 86(B)(i)–(iv).

[54] Ibid, Rule 86(B)(ix).

[55] *Prosecutor v Ayyash et al* (STL-11-01/PT/PTJ), Decision on Victims' Participation in the Proceedings, PTJ (8 May 2012) para 65.

[56] Ibid, para 96.

[57] Ibid, paras 100–1.

[58] See Morrison and Pountney (above n 51) 163–66.

[59] STL President (12 April 2012) (above n 24) para 20.

[60] STL Rules (above n 22) Rule 86(A).

[61] *Situation in the DRC* (ICC-01/04-593), Decision on Victims' Participation in Proceedings Relating to the Situation in the Democratic Republic of Congo, Pre-Trial Chamber-I (PTC-I) (11 April 2011) para. 9.

rights may involve: calling witnesses, tendering evidence, examining/cross-examining witnesses, and filing motions and briefs.[62] Since victims are not parties, exercise of these rights is subject to judicial authorisation, and in principle can only be done through legal representatives.[63] At the STL, groups of victims have been represented by the same lawyer(s), who is/are court-appointed.

There have been some concerns that the benefits of victim participation are curtailed by STL restrictions.[64] However, due consideration has been given to the matter, and the Tribunal has determined that victim participation should aim at efficient, expeditious, and objective proceedings.[65] In *Ayyash et al*, for example, the pretrial judge attempted to balance fairness for the accused with the interests of victims by allowing the lawyers of victim participants to access documents and filings but excluding access to *ex parte* materials.[66] The pretrial judge also established security measures and other conditions with regard to confidential material (eg, victim lawyers could not share some of the accessed information with their clients).[67] The Trial Chamber likewise pointed out that victim participants are not themselves parties to STL proceedings and referred to the trial practices of other international tribunals.[68] It concluded that the exercise of victim rights as participants or witnesses must respect defendant rights.[69]

Fourth, the issue of dual-status victim participants/witnesses has been thoroughly debated. The original version of STL Rule 150(D) stipulated that a victim participant 'shall not be permitted to give evidence unless a Chamber decides that the interests of justice so require'. However, the Rule was amended in 2012, so now victim participants can serve as witnesses more generally. Unlike the original Rule, the current Rule 150(D) flexibly allows for dual-status victim participants/witnesses, which aligns with ICC case law.[70] Furthermore, STL judges can in any procedural stage review victim participation and/or witness intervention.

There are crucial differences between victim participants and witnesses.[71] Victim participation is voluntary; victim participants may express their interests

[62] STL Rules (above n 22) Rule 87(B).

[63] See Rule 86(C)–(D).

[64] See Morrison and Pountney (above n 51) 173.

[65] *Ayyash et al*, Decision on Victims' Participation (above n 55) para 102(iii).

[66] *Prosecutor v Ayyash et al* (STL-11-01/PT/PTJ), Decision on the VPU's Access to Materials and the Modalities of Victims' Participation in Proceedings before the Pre-Trial Judge, PTJ (18 May 2012) paras 32–62.

[67] Ibid.

[68] *Prosecutor v Ayyash et al* (STL-11-01/T/TC), Directions on the Conduct of the Proceedings, TC (16 January 2014) paras 1–2.

[69] See ibid, paras 1–19.

[70] Eg, *Prosecutor v Lubanga* (ICC-01/04-01/06-1119), Decision on victims' participation, TC-I (18 January 2008) paras 132–34.

[71] *Prosecutor v Ayyash et al* (STL-11-01/PT/AC/AR126.3), Decision on Appeal by Legal Representative of Victims Against Pre-trial Judge's Decision on Protective Measures, AC (10 April 2013) para 36; and Morrison and Pountney (above n 51) 157.

and concerns; and parties cannot question them. Victim participant statements, moreover, are not evidence. On the other hand, witnesses can be called by the defence, prosecution, other victim participants, or the Tribunal; they provide evidence by testifying and answering related questions; and they assist the Tribunal and calling party. As determined in *Ayyash et al*, when dual-status victim participants/witnesses intervene, tailored judicial protective measures may be required and 'must be managed carefully … to safeguard the rights of the accused'.[72] When deciding to grant victim participant status, the pretrial judge may consider whether the applicant is 'likely to be a witness'.[73] As a result of these differences, anonymous witnesses and anonymous victim participants will be discussed separately below in sections II and III. In any event, protective measures are applicable to victims as witnesses and/or as participants.

Overall, STL judges have aimed to reach a balance between defence and victim participant rights (and generally between security and rights). During the *Ayyash et al* trial, there were 307 witnesses, whose participation included live testimony, video-link testimony, and written statements. There were 72 victim participants, including six dual-status victim participants/witnesses.[74] The inclusion of terrorism victims as witnesses or participants intervening at international and hybrid criminal tribunals was a legal first.

IHRL sources also constitute applicable external and/or guiding sources at the STL. Article 28(2) STLS states that judges 'shall be guided by … the highest standards of international criminal procedure, with a view to ensuring a fair and expeditious trial'. This involves examining the practices of other international and hybrid criminal tribunals,[75] which have in turn relied on international human rights law. While Article 28(2) constitutes an important advance for international and hybrid criminal tribunals,[76] Article 21(3) of the ICC Statute demonstrates a more explicit commitment to human rights: 'application and interpretation of law [ICC law] must be consistent with internationally recognized human rights'. Notwithstanding the weaker statement in Article 28(2), Rules 3(A) and 3(B) of the STL Rules stipulate that '[the Rules] shall be interpreted in a manner consonant with … international standards on human rights', and in case of ambiguity, 'the most favourable' interpretation for defence rights shall prevail. Moreover, evidence obtained in violation of international human rights law will be excluded,[77] and the right of an accused to self-representation is exercised in accordance with international human rights law and international criminal law.[78]

[72] *Ayyash et al*, Decision on Access to Materials and the Modalities of Victim Participation (above n 66) para 61.

[73] STL Rules (above n 22) Rule 86(B)(v).

[74] See Special Tribunal for Lebanon, 'Closing Arguments' (above n 4).

[75] STL President (12 April 2012) (above n 24) para 1.

[76] Croquet (above n 23) 357–58.

[77] STL Rules (above n 22) Rule 162(B).

[78] Ibid, Rule 59(F).

II. ANONYMITY PRIOR TO TRIAL

Unlike at other international and hybrid criminal tribunals, anonymous witness evidence is explicitly admissible at the Special Tribunal for Lebanon. STL Rule 93(A) lays down proceedings to question anonymous witnesses. This corresponds to the need to protect witnesses within the specificities of large-scale terrorism under the STL jurisdiction. However, limitations to defence rights must be minimal.[79] Under Rule 93(A), the pretrial judge may conduct anonymous witness questioning 'at any stage of the proceedings'; and the prosecution, defence, and lawyers of victim participants may request it. The pretrial judge shall question the witness in the absence of the parties or victim participants' lawyer if there is a 'serious risk that imperative national security might be jeopardized should the witness's identity or affiliation be revealed', or

> [if] a serious risk that a witness or a person close to the witness would lose his life or suffer grave physical or mental harm as a result of his identity being revealed, and measures for the protection of witnesses as provided for in Rule 133 would be insufficient to prevent such danger.

Anonymous testimony hence constitutes an exceptional measure to be adopted only when other protective measures provide insufficient protection and in cases of serious risks to the life or integrity of the witness if his/her identity is disclosed to the defence. Under Rule 93(B), the prosecution, defence, and/or lawyers of victim participants can 'convey questions to the witness without revealing [his/her] identity', and the pretrial judge will transmit these questions to the witness. The judge may *proprio motu* question the witness.

The pretrial judge shall give the prosecution, defence and victim participants' lawyers 'a provisional transcript of the witness's answers', 'the opportunity to submit additional questions to the Pretrial Judge for transmittal to the witness',[80] a copy of 'the final transcript', and 'a declaration stating his opinion as to the veracity of the witness's statement, as well as the potential for any serious risk resulting from the witness's identity or affiliation being revealed'.[81]

The Tribunal has applied the STL Rules on anonymous witnesses in a manner that generally strikes a fine balance between the right of witnesses to protection of their physical security and defendant rights. Anonymous testimonies have been admissible during pretrial, including for *Ayyash et al*.[82] However, admissibility has been exceptional, interim (only during pretrial), and subject to the above-detailed procedures. The Tribunal proceedings regarding anonymous

[79] Fransen (above n 18) 343.

[80] STL Rules (above n 22) Rule 93(C).

[81] Ibid, Rule 93(D).

[82] *Prosecutor v Ayyash et al* (STL-11-01/PT/PTJ), Decision on the Motion by the Ayyash Defence to Compel the Disclosure of the Identities of 29 Proposed Prosecution Witnesses, PTJ (4 September 2013).

witnesses have therefore so far been consistent with practices of other international and hybrid criminal tribunals.[83]

Unlike witness anonymity, the issue of anonymous victim participation is not covered specifically by the STLS and Rules. Regarding those who applied for victim participation in *Ayyash et al*, the pretrial judge determined that withholding their identities and applications was justified to protect their interests during pretrial.[84] This decision was consistent with the general provision in Rule 115(A) for the anonymity of victims and witnesses during pretrial. While the pretrial judge granted that, subject to a Chamber's authorisation, the parties may be provided with some or all of the identities of victim participants or their applications at a later stage in the proceedings, 'withholding the identity of the applicants and their applications does not prejudice the rights of the accused' during pretrial.[85]

Anonymous victim participation is sound during pretrial because determination of the accused's guilt or innocence is not yet at stake. Thus, protection of the accused from anonymous accusations is less likely to be adversely and irreversibly affected in pretrial than in trial. Indeed, the Trial Chamber can apply corrective measures during trial, even when the pretrial judge has respected the prosecution's duty of protection of 'interests of the victims and witnesses'.[86] STL proceedings have again been consistent with ICC case law in this regard.[87] In *Ayyash et al*, the pretrial judge added this further safeguard: if those granted victim participation 'wish to remain anonymous or seek other protective measures, a request to that end should be submitted to the Pre-Trial Judge ... pursuant to Rule 133(A)'.[88]

As upheld by the Appeals Chamber,[89] the pretrial judge allowed anonymous victim participation during *Ayyash et al* pretrial but subjected their anonymity to some stringent limitations in order to protect the accused's rights.[90] The pretrial judge determined that the duration of this (interim) anonymity would depend on how anonymous victim participation takes place. Whereas 'active' victim participants who inter alia tender evidence shall disclose their identities to the parties sufficiently prior to such participation, 'passive' victim participants can remain anonymous during pretrial.[91] Victim participation is

[83] G Acquaviva and M Heikkilä, 'Protective and Special Measures for Witnesses' in G Sluiter et al (eds), *International Criminal Procedure: Principles and Rules* (Oxford, Oxford University Press, 2013) 835–47.

[84] *Ayyash et al*, Decision on Victims' Participation (above n 55) para 130.

[85] Ibid.

[86] STL Rules (above n 22) Rule 55(C).

[87] Eg, *Katanga and Ngudjolo-Chui* (ICC-01/04-01/07-474), Decision on the Set of Procedural Rights Attached to Procedural Status of Victim at the Pre-trial Stage of the Case, PTC-I (13 May 2008) para 184.

[88] *Ayyash et al*, Decision on Victims' Participation (above n 55) para 131.

[89] *Ayyash et al*, Appeal Decision on Protective Measures (above n 71) para. 39.

[90] *Ayyash et al*, Decision on Motions for Protective Measures (above n 37) paras 28–31.

[91] Ibid, paras 30–31.

generally conducted not directly but through common legal representative(s), which ensures that anonymous victim participants are not better off than their non-anonymous peers.[92] Compared to non-anonymous victim participation, however, there are important limitations on the modalities of anonymous victim participation, and these largely entail procedural rights.[93] For example, judges may allow only non-anonymous victim participants to access confidential parts of the case record and to attend closed session hearings.[94] Limiting the scope of anonymous victim participation while granting them protective measures aims to reach a fine balance between victim and defendant rights. Thus, in *Ayyash et al*, all victim participants (both anonymous and non-anonymous) were allowed to participate during pretrial only through common lawyers, in other words, as part of a group with common legal representation.[95]

Concerning applicants who were denied victim participation, the pretrial judge in *Ayyash et al* concluded that (temporary) anonymity was required to ensure that their personal information was protected and not disclosed to the parties, as those applicants cannot participate, and the Tribunal cannot protect their physical security.[96] However, out of consideration for the rights of the accused, the nondisclosure was limited to determination of victim participant status in pretrial. In other words, the judge did not bar parties *ad infinitum* from accessing such information and did not wish to prejudice any future determination on whether and how the parties should access that information.[97] Decisions by the Trial Chamber and Appeals Chamber regarding victim participation modalities can therefore be made independently of the pretrial judge's decisions.[98]

As with other international and hybrid criminal tribunals, anonymity has normally been granted at the Special Tribunal for Lebanon during pretrial rather than during trial because the accused's innocence or guilt is determined in trial. Two features of the Tribunal aim to further mitigate the impact of anonymity on defence rights during pretrial. First, the pretrial judge has broad powers over pretrial matters and ensures preparation for a fair and expeditious trial.[99] As mentioned above, the pretrial judge may question anonymous witnesses.

[92] *Ayyash et al*, Decision on Access to Materials and Victim Participation (above n 66) para 80.

[93] Ibid, fn 77.

[94] Ibid (invoking *Katanga and Ngudjolo-Chui*, Decision on Procedural Rights at the Pre-trial Stage (above n 87)).

[95] *Ayyash et al*, Decision on Access to Materials and Victim Participation (above n 66), paras 20 and 80.

[96] *Prosecutor v Ayyash et al* (STL-11-01/PT/PTJ), Decision on Defence Motion of 17 February 2012 for an Order to the Victims' Participation Unit to Refile its Submission *Inter Partes* and Inviting Submissions on Legal Issues Related to Applications for the Status of Victim Participating in the Proceedings, PTJ, 5 April 2012, para 44.

[97] Ibid, para 53.

[98] *Ayyash et al*, Decision on Access to Materials and Victim Participation (above n 66) para 4.

[99] Fransen (above n 18) 335.

Additionally, the pretrial judge may support a party request for Lebanese cooperation based on Rule 20. This provision has played out to the benefit of the defence in *Ayyash et al*,[100] since Lebanon has at times been uncooperative with the defence.[101] Such cooperation with both the prosecution and the defence is necessary for both sides to have adequate time and facilities for preparation and equality of arms. In *Ayyash et al*, such cooperation has been especially necessary for the defence because the proceedings have taken place with the accused *in absentia*.

Second, whereas ICC victim participation may start during investigation, STL victim participation is possible only late in pretrial, after confirmation of the indictment.[102] Victims have legitimate interests in participating during investigation and early pretrial proceedings; but considerations related to efficiency, defence rights, and prosecutorial discretion prevail.[103] These considerations are related mainly to investigation goals, namely, the prosecutorial gathering of information/evidence to indict suspects in a timely manner. Despite the importance of victim interests, the exclusion of victim participation (including anonymous participation and participation by dual-status victim participants/witnesses) from investigation arguably better safeguards defence rights. The right to timely proceedings, for example, could otherwise be adversely affected, as would equality of arms regarding potential suspects who are yet to be singled out and hence lack legal counsels before the indictment process.

III. ANONYMITY DURING TRIAL

STL Rule 115(C) states that 'the identity of the victim or witness shall be disclosed in sufficient time prior to the trial to allow adequate time for preparation of the defence.' However, the Rules exceptionally provide for anonymous witnesses during trial, unlike instruments of other international and hybrid criminal tribunals, which remain silent on this issue. Rule 93(A) allows anonymous witnesses 'at any stage of the proceedings'. Nevertheless, under Rule 159(B), 'conviction may not be based solely, or to a decisive extent' on an anonymous witness statement. This constitutes a fundamental safeguard for the rights of the accused.[104] According to the STL Chambers Guide on Procedural Law:

> Given the specific nature of terrorist cases, the [Rules] allow exceptionally for a witness (be it, for example, an intelligence officer or an individual whose life, or that of his close family, is in danger) to give evidence, at any stage …, anonymously,

[100] *Prosecutor v Ayyash et al* (STL-11-01/PT/PTJ), Decision on the Defence Request Seeking to Obtain the Cooperation of Lebanon, PTJ (11 February 2013).

[101] Jones and Zgonec-Rožej (above n 21) 199–200.

[102] STL Rules (above n 22) Rule 86(A).

[103] De-Hemptinne (above n 50) 172–74.

[104] STL President (12 April 2012) (above n 24) para 36.

> ie, without his identity being revealed to the Parties or even to the Trial Chamber. His deposition is then recorded by the Pretrial Judge, who is the only person to have knowledge of his identity and who can ask him any questions he considers necessary, including those sent to him in writing by the Parties or the legal representatives of the victims. He should then send a record of the witness's deposition (if appropriate, in redacted form so as not to reveal the identity of the witness), giving an assessment as to the credibility of the deposition. The Trial Judges cannot, under any circumstances, convict solely on the basis of the evidence of an anonymous witness.[105]

Rule 93(A) is under Part 5 ('Confirmation of Charges and Pretrial Proceedings') of the Rules. However, under Rule 149(F), which is in Part 6 ('Proceedings before the Trial Chamber') of the Rules, the Trial Chamber 'may receive the evidence of a witness orally or, pursuant to Rules 93 [anonymous witness statements] … in written or other form'. Rule 93(A) mentions 'any stage of proceedings', which contrasts with 'during pretrial phase' or 'proceedings' used elsewhere in Part 5. Former STL President Antonio Cassese has said that 'concerning anonymous witnesses … who may be crucial in trials of terrorism … Rule 93 provides for a procedure'.[106] In *Ayyash et al*, the pretrial judge and Appeals Chamber both referred to applicability of witness anonymity during trial subject to requirements under the Rules.[107]

Against the context of large-scale terrorism cases like those handled by the Special Tribunal for Lebanon, this systematic analysis reaffirms the appropriateness of admitting anonymous witnesses during trial but as an exceptional protective measure. This helps to balance defendant and witness rights. Compared to instruments of other international and hybrid criminal tribunals, the STL Rules explicitly and in detail regulate matters on anonymous testimonies and thereby promote legal certainty/predictability and consistent judicial practice. As former STL President Cassese has noted, the Rules 'create a careful distinction between various categories of written probative value'.[108] In other words, the admissibility of anonymous testimony notwithstanding, it remains more susceptible to critique than other testimony. Such differences in evidentiary weight encourage non-anonymous testimony during trial and thus better protect the accused from anonymous accusations and help to guarantee the defence right to adequate preparation and full and proper witness examination. There has been a particular need to attend to these rights in *Ayyash et al* because the proceedings have occurred while the accused are *in abstentia*. While anonymous witness written statements are admissible during trial, it is only if the previously detailed requirements (Rules 93 and 159(B)) are met. Such requirements aim to avoid irreversible breaches of defence rights while considering the interests of witnesses.

[105] STL Chambers, 'The Procedure of the Special Tribunal for Lebanon' (2010) para 101.
[106] STL President, 'Rules of Procedure and Evidence-Explanatory Memorandum' (25 November 2010) para 36.
[107] *Ayyash et al*, Decision on Motions for Protective Measures (above n 37) para 26; and *Ayyash et al*, Appeal Decision on Protective Measures (above n 71) para 36.
[108] STL President (25 November 2010) (above n 106) para 35.

The nature of large-scale terrorism under STL jurisdiction may exceptionally require granting anonymity to witnesses if there are high concerns of risk against their life and limb. As Cassese has explained:

> concerning anonymous witnesses ... who may be crucial in trials of terrorism (either because they are persons who fear for their lives or those of persons close to them or because they are intelligence officials not prepared, or allowed, to disclose their identities), Rule 93 provides for a procedure whereby the anonymous witness testifies *in camera* before the Pretrial Judge alone, so that only that judge is in a position to know his identity.[109]

Under Rule 159(A), anonymous witness statements made under Rule 93 and before the pretrial judge shall be subject to Rule 149(D), which further protects defence rights:

> A Chamber may exclude evidence if its probative value is substantially outweighed by the need to ensure a fair trial. In particular, the Chamber may exclude evidence gathered in violation of the rights of the suspect or the accused as set out in the Statute and the Rules.

The Appeals Chamber *in abstracto* has remarked that witnesses 'receive this protection [of anonymity] only because of risks related to their giving of evidence, which may be involuntary'.[110] Additionally, the prosecution shall disclose all statements of witnesses called to testify at trial. However, redaction of information that threatens witness safety may be allowed if the prosecution adopts rectifying measures, as actually happened in *Ayyash et al*.[111] There were no anonymous witnesses during trial in *Ayyash et al*, as the prosecutor disclosed witness identities to the defence before trial or, in some instances, withdrew witnesses.[112]

Concerning anonymous victim participants, the Appeals Chamber of the Tribunal upheld a decision by the pretrial judge,[113] effectively excluding anonymous victim participation from trial in *Ayyash et al* because:

> [A]nonymous participation by victims is inherently prejudicial to the accused, regardless of how active or passive their desired method of participation and even for victims who do not seek to give or tender evidence.
>
> ... If VPPs [victim participants] are not required to disclose their identity at all, this would amount to an anonymous accusation against the accused, in breach of fair trial guarantees under Article 16 of the Statute.

[109] Ibid, para 36.
[110] *Ayyash et al*, Appeal Decision on Protective Measures (above n 71) para 36.
[111] STL Rules (above n 22) Rules 110(A)(ii), 116(A)(ii)–(iii). See *Prosecutor v Ayyash et al* (STL-11-01/PT/PTJ), Public Redacted Version of 'Decision on the Prosecution Application for Non-Disclosure of Certain Statements of Witnesses Pursuant to Rule 116' Dated 20 December 2012, PTJ (28 May 2013) paras 16–17 and 21–22.
[112] *Ayyash et al*, Decision on Disclosure of Witness Identities (above n 82) para 11.
[113] *Ayyash et al*, Decision on Motions for Protective Measures (above n 37) paras 22–27 and 38–39.

> … [A]nonymity is so prejudicial to the rights of the accused and the fair conduct of the trial that this exceptional measure should not be available in these proceedings, especially in consideration of the fact that extensive protective measures are otherwise available.[114]

The Appeals Chamber concluded that:

> [A]nonymous participation of VPPs [victim participants] in the proceedings is generally prejudicial to and inconsistent with the rights of the accused and the fairness of the trial and is not a valid form of victim participation within the meaning of Article 17 of the Statute. This includes 'passive' or 'silent observer' VPPs.… [A]nonymous participation by victims is inherently prejudicial in the present proceedings, and … the identities of VPPs should be disclosed sufficiently in advance to give the Defence adequate time to prepare.[115]

This absolute prohibition of anonymous victim participation during trial is problematic. Neither the STL Statute nor the STL Rules prohibits anonymous victim participation during trial. If a victim can under the Rules be exceptionally authorised to testify anonymously during trial, *a fortiori* anonymous victim participation should likewise be exceptionally allowed during trial, especially taking into account the differences between victim witnesses and victim participants. The Appeals Chamber correctly stated that, unlike victim participants (whose participation is voluntary), witnesses may be compelled to testify.[116] However, compared to victim participation, victim witness testimonies are more clearly oriented to affect the accused. Whereas victim witnesses give testimony (evidence), victim participants state their views and concerns (not evidence). Judge Sir David Baragwanath, in his concurring opinion to the Appeals Chamber decision, acknowledged that witness status is 'more obviously calculated to prejudice an accused than a mere second-stage victim, whose identification may or may not allow the Defence to embark on a process of enquiry whether that is to go'.[117]

Nonetheless, both the pretrial judge and the Appeals Chamber have regarded the prejudice to the accused's rights brought by anonymous victim participation during trial as an absolute or conclusive presumption rather than an admissibility issue to be decided on a case-by-case basis. While this prohibitive approach may be appropriate with regard to victim participants who are interested in actively and directly presenting their views and concerns before the Trial Chamber, those who wish to be 'passive' or 'silent' victim participants are in a different position.

While the right of the accused to a fair trial should in case of conflict prevail over certain modalities of victim rights to participate in trial,[118] the absolute

[114] *Ayyash et al*, Appeal Decision on Protective Measures (above n 71) paras 27–28 and 31.

[115] Ibid, para 39.

[116] Ibid, para 36.

[117] *Ayyash et al* (STL-11-01/PT/AC/AR126.3), Concurring Opinion of Judge Baragwanath (10 April 2013) para 23.

[118] Ibid, para 38.

ban on anonymous victim participation during trial at the Special Tribunal is excessive and moreover breaks with ICC law and practice. Despite the fact that the legal framework of victim participation at the Tribunal was modelled on that of the ICC, the STL Appeals Chamber found the ICC reasons for allowing anonymous victim participation during trial to be unpersuasive and concluded that such practice does not fully consider the potential prejudice against the accused.[119] The more reconciliatory approach of the ICC allows for anonymous victim participation in trial while prohibiting certain 'active' forms of victim participation, such as anonymous testimony by dual-status victim participants/witnesses, in order to protect the accused's rights.[120] In any event, the STL Appeals Chamber reasoned that anonymity may be granted exceptionally, subject to stringent Rule 93 requirements, but only to the few dual-status victim participants/witnesses who will provide testimony (evidence). In other words, anonymity will not be granted to victims who are participants only.[121] However, the Appeals Chamber's general reference to exceptional admissibility of anonymous testimony is merely hypothetical at this point because no anonymous witness has played a role during the *Ayyash et al* trial.

IV. CRITERIA FOR RECONCILING COMPETING RIGHTS AND SECURITY AT THE SPECIAL TRIBUNAL

This section discusses how the Special Tribunal for Lebanon has dealt with victim anonymity as a method to reconcile the fair trial rights of the accused with the right of victims to their own physical safety. In addressing this (potential) conflict, a structured consideration of rights and security rather than a balancing approach is adopted due to the limitations and dangers of the latter, including the attainment of security at the expense of rights in criminal justice systems.[122] Four criteria are used based *mutatis mutandis* on standards from international case law and legal literature.[123] As witness anonymity during trial is particularly controversial, the analysis herein pays special but not exclusive attention to it.

The first criterion is consideration of both contextual and particular personal circumstances, and both have been considered in *Ayyash et al.*[124] Like other international and hybrid criminal tribunals, the Special Tribunal for Lebanon deals with complex scenarios. When considering anonymity in the specific

[119] *Ayyash et al*, Appeal Decision on Protective Measures (above n 71) para 26.

[120] *Prosecutor v Katanga and Ngudjolo-Chui* (ICC-1/04-01/07-1788), Decision on Modalities of Victim Participation at Trial, TC-II (22 January 2010) para 92.

[121] *Ayyash et al*, Appeal Decision on Protective Measures (above n 71) para 36.

[122] For a discussion of these dangers, see Lazarus and Goold (above n 10) 16–17.

[123] Acquaviva and Heikkilä (above n 83) 850–57.

[124] *Prosecutor v Ayyash et al* (STL-11-01/T/TC), Consolidated Decision on the Prosecution Motions for Protective Measures Regarding Ten Witnesses, TC (2 July 2014) paras 10–12.

context of the Special Tribunal, relevant factors include the nature, circumstances, and perpetrators of the acts that are under STL jurisdiction;[125] risks to the physical security of all actors and proceedings; and the volatile Lebanese context.[126] Recent and current circumstances in Lebanon suggest that anonymity measures may now be less necessary at the Special Tribunal than before. While Hezbollah has perpetrated many terrorist bombings and assassinations in Lebanon since 2004, these have substantially decreased during the *Ayyash et al* trial period (2014–18).[127] Moreover, Saad Hariri (Rafic Hariri's son) has remained Lebanon's Prime Minister, even in the face of alleged security threats related to his withdrawn resignation.[128] Undoubtedly, judges consider such contextual aspects when deciding on questions of anonymity. For example, a variety of contextual circumstances prompted the International Criminal Tribunal for the Former Yugoslavia (ICTY) in *Tadić* to allow anonymous witnesses during trial – the only time this has happened at any international or hybrid criminal tribunal.[129] The ICTY decision in this regard was in response to the insecurity caused by armed conflict in the Balkans and the fact that those on trial had close ties to groups that still controlled entire regions.

However, generalised security concerns alone are insufficient to grant protective measures for witnesses.[130] Anonymity at an international or hybrid criminal tribunal may prevent re-victimisation of those who have already been casualties of terrorism and other violence,[131] but a case-by-case risk assessment is required in order to determine: an objective fear for the physical security of a victim/witness; the level of importance of specific testimony; *prima facie* trustworthiness; strict necessity; and the absence of alternative protective measures.[132]

The second criterion is human rights standards as expressed by international human rights law. Under Article 16(2) of the STL Statute, the accused is 'entitled to a fair and public hearing, subject to measures … for the protection of victims and witnesses'. However, under Article 16(4)(b), (e), and (f), the accused has the right to: have adequate time and facilities for defence preparation, as well as to examine or have examined witnesses and evidence against him/her.

[125] C Aptel, 'Some Innovations in the Statute of the Special Tribunal for Lebanon' (2007) 5 *Journal of International Criminal Justice* 1107, 1109 and 1116; and Acquaviva and Heikkilä (above n 83) 857.

[126] Special Tribunal for Lebanon, 'Eighth Annual Report' (above n 38) 38; and *Ayyash et al*, Consolidated Decision on Motions for Protective Measures (above n 124) para 10.

[127] See the US Department of State 'Country Reports on Human Rights Practices: Lebanon' for the past several years, available at https://www.state.gov/j/drl/rls/hrrpt/index.htm (last accessed 17 December 2018).

[128] See 'Lebanon's PM Saad Hariri Withdraws Resignation', *SkyNews* (2 May 2018), https://news.sky.com/story/lebanons-pm-saad-hariri-withdraws-resignation-11169116.

[129] *Prosecutor v Tadić* (IT-94-1), Decision on the Prosecutor's Motion Requesting Protective Measures for Victims and Witnesses, TC (10 August 1995) para 61.

[130] *Ayyash et al*, Consolidated Decision on Motions for Protective Measures (above n 124) para 10.

[131] C Chinkin, 'Due Process and Witness Anonymity' (1997) 91(1) *American Journal of International Law* 75–79, 78.

[132] *Tadić*, Decision on Protective Measures (above n 129) paras 62–66.

Article 17 conditions the exercise of victims' rights to 'a manner that is not prejudicial to or inconsistent with the rights of the accused'. Furthermore, protective measures must be 'consistent with the rights of the accused'.[133]

The ECtHR has determined that judicial safeguards can 'counterbalance' the disadvantages that an accused faces when addressing anonymous testimonies.[134] The accused's right to disclosure of evidence is not absolute: there may be competing interests such as witness protection.[135] The ECtHR has not completely banned anonymous testimony but subjected it to conditions. Strict necessity is required, and relevance of evidence is considered.[136] Anonymous testimony should not form the sole or decisive basis for conviction:[137]

> Even when 'counterbalancing' procedures are found to compensate sufficiently the handicaps under which the defence labours, a conviction should not be based either solely or to a decisive extent on anonymous statements.[138]

The Special Tribunal for Lebanon has invoked ECtHR case law to interpret the equivalent Rule 159(B).[139] Sufficient safeguards are always required, not only when an anonymous witness alone contributes to the judge's conviction.[140] As examined, the STL Rules include most of these conditions *mutatis mutandis*, and in some instances, they are even more demanding than usual IHRL standards.[141] When granting anonymity in *Tadić*, the ICTY also invoked international human rights law.[142]

Unlike the rights of the accused, protective rights of victims/witnesses are not explicitly outlined by international human rights treaties. Instead, they are indirectly regulated via, for example, the rights to life and privacy.[143] Protective rights are also listed in human rights declarations[144] and recognised by binding instruments like the UN Convention against Transnational Organized Crime (2000) and EU Directive 2012/29 Establishing Minimum Standards on the Rights, Support and Protection of Victims of Crime.

Sometimes, fair trials would simply not be possible and justice may be denied, unless crucial witnesses are allowed to testify anonymously.[145] Nevertheless, when

[133] STL Rules (above n 22) Rule 133(A).

[134] *Kostovski v The Netherlands* (1989) 12 EHHR 434, paras 37–45.

[135] *Dowsett v United Kingdom* (2003) 38 EHHR 41, para 42.

[136] Ibid.

[137] *Kostovski* (above n 134) para 44.

[138] *Doorson v The Netherlands* (1996) 22 EHRR 330, para 76.

[139] *Prosecutor v Ayyash et al* (STL-11-01/T/TC), Decision on Trial Management and Reasons for Decision on Joinder, TC (25 February 2014) para 93 (invoking *Al-Khawaja & Tahery v United Kingdom*, App Nos 26766/05 and 22228/06 judgment [GC] (15 December 2011) para 119).

[140] *Delta v France* (1990) 16 EHHR 574, para 36.

[141] Croquet (above n 23) 382–84.

[142] *Tadić*, Decision on Protective Measures (above n 129) para 70.

[143] *Doorson* (above n 138) paras 70–83.

[144] UN General Assembly, Declaration of Basic Principles of Justice for Victims of Crime and Abuse of Power, UN Doc A/Res/40/34/Annex (1985).

[145] Women's Caucus for Gender Justice, 'Recommendations and Commentary for the ICC Rules of Procedure and Evidence-Part I' (26 July–13 August 1999) 28–30.

anonymity threatens fair trial rights, the ICTY concluded, 'the right of the accused to an equitable trial must take precedence' and 'the veil of anonymity [must in that case] be lifted'.[146]

The matter of anonymity at international and hybrid criminal tribunals, especially witness anonymity during trial, continues to be widely debated by scholars and commentators[147] and is generally the protective measure that is considered most problematic for the rights of the accused.[148] As the ECtHR has stated, 'in principle, all evidence must be produced in the presence of the accused at a public hearing with a view to adversarial argument'.[149] The ECtHR has further pointed out that should the accused be unaware of the witness's identity

> ... it may be deprived of the very particulars enabling it to demonstrate that he or she is prejudiced, hostile or unreliable. Testimony or other declarations inculpating an accused may well be designedly untruthful or simply erroneous.[150]

In its decision to allow exceptional anonymity in *Tadić*, the ICTY made reference to ECtHR case law.[151] For its part, Article 16 of the STL Statute, which details the 'Rights of the Accused', was based largely on Article 21 of the ICTY Statute, which was based in turn on Article 6 of the European Convention on Human Rights (ECHR) and Article 14 of the International Covenant on Civil and Political Rights.

Witness anonymity during trial might compromise or even violate the accused's right to question witnesses due to the fact that the defence can conduct effective cross-examination only if the accused knows the witness's identity.[152] Since *Ayyash et al* is proceeding *in absentia*, anonymous witnesses and/or extensive anonymous victim participation would further complicate matters. In any event, as Andrew Ashworth has pointed out, ECtHR case law on anonymity 'insists on maximal protection of the respective rights of defendants and of witnesses and plainly does not regard this as a "zero-sum game"'.[153]

[146] *Prosecutor v Blaškić* (IT-95-14-T), Decision on the Application of the Prosecutor Dated 17 October 1996 Requesting Protective Measures for Victims and Witnesses, TC (5 November 1996) para 24.

[147] For opposition, see M Leigh, 'Witnesses Anonymity is Inconsistent with Due Process' (1997) 91 *American Journal of International Law* 80; and M Kurth, 'Anonymous Witnesses before the International Criminal Court' in C Stahn and G Sluiter (eds), *The Emerging Practice of the International Criminal Court* (Leiden, Martinus Nijhoff, 2009). For support of anonymity, see Chinkin (above n 131) 78.

[148] Acquaviva and Heikkilä (above n 83) 852–55; and Alvarez-Reyes (above n 9) 187–88.

[149] *Kostovski* (above n 134) para 41.

[150] Ibid, para 42.

[151] *Tadić*, Decision on Protective Measures (above n 129) para 54.

[152] *Prosecutor v Tadić* (IT-94-1), Separate Opinion of Judge Stephen on the Prosecutor's Motion Requesting Protective Measures for Victims and Witnesses (10 August 1995).

[153] A Ashworth, 'Security, Terrorism and the Value of Human Rights' in Goold and Lazarus (eds) (above n 10) 221.

The third criterion for reconciling victim rights with the rights of the accused is national and international criminal law standards. Certain national jurisdictions permit anonymous testimony and/or hearsay evidence.[154] This usually pertains to cases of terrorism and/or grave domestic crimes where victims and witnesses have experienced serious threats to their physical security.[155] Given the events that gave rise to the Special Tribunal for Lebanon and the circumstances surrounding it, there is an *a fortiori* case for anonymity as a protective measure, notwithstanding the stance usually taken in some national judicial systems. As for other international criminal justice institutions, the ICC has not ruled out evidence from anonymous statements, provided they are subject to safeguards.[156]

However, some domestic practices that allow anonymity are not entirely consistent with international human rights standards on due process and other rights of the accused.[157] State responsibility for ECHR violations (Article 6) has been found when a conviction was based only on an anonymous testimony.[158] Apart from the STL Rules and the Specialist Kosovar Chambers Rules (adopted in 2017), international and hybrid criminal tribunal instruments have not contained explicit provision for anonymous witnesses, and other than in *Tadić*, anonymous witnesses have not been allowed during ICTs trials. Even when the ICC or tribunals such as the ICTY have dealt with ongoing, high-intensity armed conflicts, security concerns have been found to be insufficient to allow anonymous witnesses during trials.

The consistent inadmissibility of anonymous witnesses during ICTs trials contrasts with more varied criteria in national jurisdictions. The Special Tribunal for Lebanon, as an international body, has aimed to align its practices with international criminal justice standards, and this largely holds true regarding the inadmissibility of anonymous witnesses during trial. On the other hand, the blanket ban on anonymous *victim participation* during trial that has been employed in STL case law is inconsistent with more reconciliatory approaches under international criminal justice. For example, as mentioned earlier, the ICC has allowed for anonymous victim participants but stipulated that they cannot testify anonymously during trial.[159]

The fourth criterion consists in practical considerations such as implementation and alternative protective measures. Appropriately implemented anonymity

[154] Eg, England and Wales, the Netherlands, New Zealand, Poland, and Germany. See K Roach (ed), *Comparative Counter-Terrorism Law* (Cambridge, Cambridge University Press, 2015).

[155] Roach (ibid); and L Karsai, 'You Can't Give my Name-Rethinking Witness Anonymity in Light of the United States and British Experience' (2011) 79(1) *Tennessee Law Review* 29–94.

[156] *Prosecutor v Katanga* (ICC-01/04-01/07-3436-tENG), Judgment Pursuant to Article 74 of the Statute, TC-II (7 March 2014) para. 90.

[157] J Doak and R Huxley-Binns, 'Anonymous Witnesses in England and Wales: Charting a Course from Strasbourg' (2009) 73(6) *Journal of Criminal Law* 508–29.

[158] *Rachdad v France*, Application no 71846/01 (13 November 2003) paras 24–25.

[159] *Katanga and Ngudjolo-Chui*, Decision on Victim Participation at Trial (above n 120) paras 92–93.

may be admissible. For example, in *Tadić*, the admissibility of anonymous witnesses was subject to stringent requirements and guidelines.[160] As a possible course of action, the Special Tribunal for Lebanon may first grant anonymity but subject its implementation to later decisions on whether anonymous witnesses or victim participants can actually play their respective roles. Moreover, anonymity may not be as onerous to implement as is often thought. For instance, in *Tadić*, only two out of the four persons who were granted anonymity were eventually called to testify, and one of them decided to testify in public; the defence counsel was permitted to see the other witness, and the accused could hear this witness's undistorted testimony.

On the other hand, international practice has shown that anonymity for witnesses and victim participants carries risks. The single anonymous witness in the *Tadić* trial was discovered to have lied.[161] At the ICC, three victim participants who provided non-anonymous testimony in the *Lubanga* trial lost their participation rights, and their testimonies were dismissed because of internal inconsistencies and the likelihood that they had stolen identities.[162] Had they testified anonymously, the consequences would have been significant. Rule 93 of the Special Tribunal for Lebanon, which outlines the interactions of the pretrial judge with otherwise anonymous witnesses, is thus an attempt to mitigate the risks of anonymity. Due judicial consideration to the impact of anonymity on the weight of anonymous testimony is also an advisable safeguard.[163]

There are other measures at the Special Tribunal that aim to protect witnesses and victims but have less impact on the rights of the accused than the nondisclosure of the identities of witnesses to the accused. These include public nondisclosure of names or other identifying information or the removal thereof from STL public records, the use of image/voice-altering devices, testimony via closed circuit television or video-conference link, and the use of pseudonyms.[164] Moreover, the right to a public trial notwithstanding,[165] a closed session may be ordered in response to serious security reasons as an alternative to anonymity measures.[166] In *Ayyash et al*, several of these strategies have been utilised.[167] Importantly, they can be rescinded, varied, or augmented.[168]

Whereas the ICTY initially lacked a witness and victim protection programme – a factor in the decision to allow anonymous testimony in *Tadić*[169] – Rule 166 of the Special Tribunal for Lebanon provides for a protection programme

[160] *Tadić*, Decision on Protective Measures (above n 129) paras 53–86.
[161] O Swaak-Goldman, 'The ICTY and the Right to Fair Trial' (1997) 10(2) *Leiden Journal of International Law* 215–21, 221.
[162] *Prosecutor v Lubanga* (ICC-01/04-01/06-2842), Judgment Pursuant to Article 74 of the Statute, TC-I (14 March 2012) paras 499–501.
[163] Swaak-Goldman (above n 161) 220–21.
[164] STL Rules (above n 22) Rule 133(C)(i).
[165] *Blaškić* (above n 146) para 24.
[166] STL Rules (above n 22) Rule 133(C)(ii).
[167] Special Tribunal for Lebanon, 'Eighth Annual Report' (above n 38) 21.
[168] Rule 133(G)–(K).
[169] *Tadić*, Decision on Protective Measures (above n 129) para 65.

within the Victims and Witnesses Unit, including victim/witness relocation. This Unit which maintains a Beirut-based office for victim participation and witness support, has arguably developed good practices on assessing security risks.[170] Lebanese authorities have generally cooperated with the Tribunal with regard to protections for victims and witnesses,[171] but since relocation programmes involve national implementation, the Unit has continuously sought related state cooperation agreements.[172] This is necessary because neither Security Council Resolution 1757 nor the STL Statute explicitly obligates states other than Lebanon to cooperate with the Special Tribunal.

The criteria discussed above suggest that anonymity as an exceptional protective measure can be generally reconciled with defence rights at the Special Tribunal for Lebanon. Due to security concerns that affect victims and witnesses, anonymity may be possible, but it is conditional on defence rights. In particular, witness anonymity during trial is subject to strict scrutiny and controls, while anonymous victim participation during trial and witness anonymity at pretrial are arguably easier to reconcile with due process and other rights of the accused.

V. CONCLUSION

Security challenges and the need to protect the physical safety of victims and witnesses of terrorism have given rise to anonymity as a possible protective measure in court cases around the world, including at the Special Tribunal for Lebanon. Despite a legal framework that makes room for it, the Special Tribunal has not employed anonymity measures during trial, although it has done so for the pretrial phase. This chapter has questioned the complete and pre-emptive exclusion of anonymous victim participants (in distinction from anonymous witnesses) from all STL trial proceedings. Such blanket exclusion undermines the protective measures that support the international criminal justice goals of determining the truth and establishing historical record.[173] The inadmissibility of anonymous witnesses at STL trials, on the other hand, is a legitimate strategy for protecting the fair trial rights of the accused; otherwise, anonymous accusations and witnesses who cannot be fully cross-examined at the trial stage may lead to potentially irreversible breaches of defence rights.

However, there are additional and alternative methods for managing the security challenges that may affect victims and witnesses and hence affect the Special Tribunal. Rolling or delayed disclosure of anonymous witness identities be used more often than at other international and hybrid criminal tribunals. Withholding the victim/witness identity from the accused but not from

[170] Alvarez-Reyes (above n 9) 176–77.
[171] Special Tribunal for Lebanon, 'Eighth Annual Report' (above n 38) 23.
[172] Ibid, 38.
[173] Acquaviva and Heikkilä (above n 83) 855.

his/her counsel may also be an option (except in cases of self-representation). These methods for partially anonymising vulnerable people and sensitive information can sometimes effectively address both security concerns and issues of professional ethics,[174] while ultimately helping to ensure a fair trial.

In any event, anonymity as a protective measure at the Special Tribunal for Lebanon must be aligned with respect for defence rights. This chapter has reviewed the ways that international human rights law and international criminal justice standards have dealt with the issue, with the conclusion being that anonymity should be granted on a case-by-case basis and only exceptionally. As stated by the UN Special Rapporteur on the Protection of Human Rights while Countering Terrorism, specifically concerning evidentiary issues, 'terrorism must be combated within the framework of the law', and 'judicial organs need to remain vigilant'.[175] This applies not only to national criminal courts but also to international criminal justice institutions such as the Special Tribunal for Lebanon. By reconciling security concerns with the rights guaranteed by international criminal law, the Special Tribunal can meaningfully contribute to the rule of law in the face of international terrorism and the complex court cases that result from it. The Special Tribunal for Lebanon may even prove to be a source for national courts when handling terrorism-related cases in which the challenges of reconciling security with rights are very real indeed.

REFERENCES

Acquaviva, G and Heikkilä, M, 'Protective and Special Measures for Witnesses' in G Sluiter et al (eds), *International Criminal Procedure: Principles and Rules* (Oxford, Oxford University Press, 2013).

Alvarez-Reyes, Y, 'The Protection of Victims Participating in International Criminal Justice' in K Tibori-Szabó and M Hirst (eds), *Victim Participation in International Criminal Justice* (The Hague, Asser/Springer, 2017).

Aptel, C, 'Some Innovations in the Statute of the Special Tribunal for Lebanon' (2007) 5 *Journal of International Criminal Justice* 1107.

Ashworth, A, 'Security, Terrorism and the Value of Human Rights' in BJ Goold and L Lazarus (eds), *Security and Human Rights* (Oxford, Hart Publishing, 2007).

Bassiouni, C, *Introduction to International Criminal Law* (Ardsley, Transnational Publishers, 2003).

Cassese, C, *International Criminal Law* (Oxford, Oxford University Press, 2003).

Chinkin, C, 'Due Process and Witness Anonymity' (1997) 91(1) *American Journal of International Law* 75–79.

[174] See, eg, International Criminal Court, 'Code of Professional Conduct for Counsel' (2011), https://www.icc-cpi.int/resource-library/Documents/COPCEng.pdf, Art 16(1).

[175] M Scheinin (UN Special Rapporteur), 'Report of the Special Rapporteur on the Promotion and Protection of Human Rights and Fundamental Freedoms while Countering Terrorism', A/63/223 (6 August 2008) para 34.

Croquet, N, 'The Special Tribunal for Lebanon's Innovative Human Rights Framework' (2016) 47(2) *Georgetown Journal of International Law* 351–95.

De-Hemptinne, J, 'Challenges Raised by Victims' Participation in the Proceedings of the Special Tribunal for Lebanon' (2010) 8 *Journal of International Criminal Justice* 165.

Doak, J and Huxley-Binns, R, 'Anonymous Witnesses in England and Wales: Charting a Course from Strasbourg' (2009) 73(6) *Journal of Criminal Law* 508–29.

Fassbender, B, 'Reflections on the International Legality of the Special Tribunal for Lebanon' (2007) 5 *Journal of International Criminal Justice* 1091.

Fransen, D, 'The Special Tribunal for Lebanon and the Rule of Law' in G De-Baere and J Wouters (eds), *The Contribution of International and Supranational Courts to the Rule of Law* (Cheltenham, Edward Elgar, 2015).

Gillet, M and Schuster, M, 'Fast-Track Justice: The Special Tribunal for Lebanon Defines Terrorism' (2011) 9 *Journal of International Criminal Justice* 989.

International Criminal Court (ICC), 'Code of Professional Conduct for Counsel' (2011), https://www.icc-cpi.int/resource-library/Documents/COPCEng.pdf.

Jones, J and Zgonec-Rožej, M, 'Rights of Suspects and Accused' in A Alamuddin et al (eds), *The Special Tribunal for Lebanon: Law and Practice* (Oxford, Oxford University Press, 2014).

Jordash, W and Parker, T, 'Trials *in Absentia* at the Special Tribunal for Lebanon' (2010) 8 *Journal of International Criminal Justice* 487.

Karsai, L, 'You Can't Give my Name: Rethinking Witness Anonymity in Light of the United States and British Experience' (2011) 79 *Tennessee Law Review* 29.

Kurth, M, 'Anonymous Witnesses before the International Criminal Court' in C Stahn and G Sluiter (eds), *The Emerging Practice of the International Criminal Court* (Leiden, Martinus Nijhoff, 2009).

Lazarus, L and Goold, BJ, 'Introduction: Security and Human Rights – The Search for a Language of Reconciliation' in BJ Goold and L Lazarus (eds), *Security and Human Rights* (Oxford, Hart Publishing, 2007).

Leigh, M, 'Witnesses Anonymity is Inconsistent with Due Process' (1997) 91 *American Journal of International Law* 80.

Morrison, H and Pountney, E, 'Victim Participation at the Special Tribunal for Lebanon' in A Alamuddin et al (eds), *The Special Tribunal for Lebanon: Law and Practice* (Oxford, Oxford University Press, 2014).

O'Connell, J, 'Gambling with the Psyche: Does Prosecuting Human Rights Violators Console Their Victims?' (2005) 46 *Harvard International Law Journal* 295.

Powell, CH, 'The Legal Authority of the United Nations Security Council' in BJ Goold and L Lazarus (eds), *Security and Human Rights* (Oxford, Hart Publishing, 2007).

Roach, K (ed), *Comparative Counter-Terrorism Law* (Cambridge, Cambridge University Press, 2015).

Swaak-Goldman, O, 'The ICTY and the Right to Fair Trial' (1997) 10(2) *Leiden Journal of International Law* 215–21.

Schabas, W, *The UN International Criminal Tribunals* (Cambridge, Cambridge University Press, 2006).

UN International Independent Investigation Commission, 'Eighth Report', S/2007/424 (12 July 2007).

Wierda, M et al, 'Early Reflections on Local Perceptions, Legitimacy and Legacy of the Special Tribunal for Lebanon' (2007) 5 *Journal of International Criminal Justice* 1065.

14

The Legal Death of Rebellion: Counterterrorism Laws and the Shrinking Legal Freedom of Violent Political Resistance

BEN SAUL

I. INTRODUCTION

THIS CHAPTER ARGUES that certain influential democracies have increasingly cooperated in the repression of legitimate and non-terroristic political resistance, under the guise of universally countering terrorism within the United Nations legal framework. The argument begins in the history of violent 'political offenders' under national extradition law. Transnational criminal cooperation against terrorism sprang out of interstate tensions over the non-extradition of political offenders in nineteenth-century Europe and Britain. National extradition laws often required the refusal of requests to extradite political offenders, so as not to interfere in foreign internal affairs and to guarantee political asylum for fugitives.

From the second half of the nineteenth century, beginning in Europe and spreading elsewhere, national legislation and courts, as well as bilateral, regional, and multilateral treaties, gradually confined the scope of the political offence exception by excluding certain types of atrocious violence, even if politically motivated. Impunity for genuine atrocities justified in the name of politics could thus be addressed, while other safeguards developed to preserve perpetrators' rights to fair trial and non-discrimination. European and British law and practice gradually influenced extradition laws worldwide, including through the colonial transplantation of civil and common law traditions to other continents.

Violent political resistance thus had to play by certain rules, but the rules still left space to oppose authoritarian regimes without routinely returning people to face summary justice or retaliation in their own states. In addition, after the adoption of the Geneva Conventions in 1949, when resistance violence crossed the threshold of non-international armed conflict, international humanitarian law (IHL) governed the hostilities, without itself criminalising resistance violence or non-state armed groups. IHL has gained near universal adherence by states since 1949.

The rapid and haphazard development of national counterterrorism laws after 9/11 – spurred on by the counterterrorism obligations imposed by the United Nations Security Council in its quasi-legislative Resolution 1373 (2001)[1] – has increasingly eroded this careful albeit imperfect balancing of competing interests that evolved in extradition law and IHL over the preceding century and a half. Now some influential national terrorism laws criminalise all violence (even nonviolent resistance) against all governments, regardless of the means or methods used, even if IHL applies, and irrespective of the legitimacy of a rebellion or the illegitimacy of a repressive government. Domestic political violence, hitherto largely the concern of the affected state, has been reclassified and elevated to an international security concern that demands transnational criminal repression. The political offence exception to extradition is being eroded to a vanishing point.

In addition, armed resistance in armed conflict is frequently criminalised, intruding on the previously cautious regulation of violence by IHL, which reflects a delicate balancing of competing interests. Some terrorism laws include exceptions designed to accommodate other legitimate interests, such as a 'democratic protest' clause or partial exclusions for certain conduct or actors under IHL. Such exceptions are, however, rare and frequently too narrow.

As a result, some states have increasingly cooperated in the repression of legitimate and non-terroristic resistance under the imprimatur of universally countering terrorism. Repressive states have been empowered, and human rights have been relegated in priority beneath global security. The blanket outlawing of resistance forces may also have the paradoxical effect of stimulating more – not less – terrorism. Actors who no longer enjoy any legal privileges, regardless of how they behave, have little incentive to accept IHL restraints or to 'buy in' to a legal regime that simply condemns them as terrorists. Criminal law responses to terrorism can certainly promise to constrain the resort to more militant or excessive reactions to terrorism.[2] There is, however, a different danger in stretching the criminal law too far in ways that undermine other legal regimes and the principles that they seek to uphold, including the human freedom to violently resist political or other oppression.

[1] UN Security Council Resolution 1373 on Threats to International Peace and Security Caused by Terrorist Acts (28 September 2001).

[2] B Saul, 'Criminality and Terrorism' in AM Salinas de Friás, KLH Samuel, and ND White (eds), *Counter-Terrorism: International Law and Practice* (Oxford, Oxford University Press, 2012) 139–41.

II. 'TERRORIST' VIOLENCE AND THE POLITICAL OFFENCE EXCEPTION TO EXTRADITION BEFORE 2001

By the mid-nineteenth century, modern international law had evolved to take a laissez-faire approach to domestic political and civil violence if it remained contained within the territory of a single state. The many species of exceptional political violence that occasionally arose – unrest, civil disorder, coups, rebellion, revolution, civil war, and so on – were treated as ostensibly internal matters not to be interfered with by foreign states, being within the domestic jurisdiction of the affected sovereign state.[3] This approach departed from earlier common practice amongst European sovereigns of surrendering one another's political offenders.[4] Paradoxically, not extraditing such offenders could equally be seen as a form of intervention, since it implicitly takes the side of the foreign government's opponents.[5]

Even high intensity violence, such as civil war, fell largely outside of international law, not becoming directly regulated until 1949 with the adoption of common Article 3 of the four Geneva Conventions regulating armed conflict.[6] The duty of non-intervention in civil wars was originally grounded in respect for the domestic jurisdiction and sovereignty of the affected state.[7] After the adoption of the United Nations Charter in 1945, that duty acquired an additional justification in the international human and people's right of self-determination. The right entitles peoples to freely determine their own political status,[8] which may manifest in violent internal struggles within a 'people' for political supremacy over governance, institutions, or territory.

When violent political fugitives fled to another country to escape punishment or retaliation, international law remained largely indifferent. Extradition was a matter left to national law, facilitated by ad hoc bilateral treaties.[9] There was accordingly no 'international extradition law' as such, and international law did not intercede to standardise or harmonise national rules, at least until the growth of certain multilateral criminal cooperation treaties in the second half of the twentieth century (discussed in the next section). Thus, in nineteenth-century

[3] C Van den Wijngaert, *The Political Offence Exception to Extradition* (Boston, Kluwer, 1980) 204.

[4] Ibid, 9.

[5] Ibid, 204.

[6] Geneva Convention (I) for the Amelioration of the Condition of the Wounded and Sick in Armed Forces in the Field (1949), Art 3; Geneva Convention (II) for the Amelioration of the Condition of Wounded, Sick and Shipwrecked Members of Armed Forces at Sea (1949), Art 3; Geneva Convention (III) Relative to the Treatment of Prisoners of War (1949), Art 3; and Geneva Convention (IV) Relative to the Protection of Civilian Persons in Time of War (1940), Art 3.

[7] G Draper, 'Wars of National Liberation and War Criminality' in M Howard (ed), *Restraints on War* (Oxford, Oxford University Press, 1979) 141.

[8] International Covenant on Civil and Political Rights (ICCPR) 1966, Art 1(1); International Covenant on Economic, Social and Cultural Rights (ICESCR) 1966, Art 1(1).

[9] Van den Wijngaert (above n 3) 21.

Europe, violence was variously used by political rebels against monarchical or authoritarian regimes, by ethnic separatists against imperial powers, and by socialist revolutionaries or anarchists. Some acts were narrowly targeted at state agents while others deliberately or indiscriminately harmed civilians. Perpetrators often fled across national borders to escape retribution or justice, triggering demands from the victim state for their surrender and producing interstate tension. Courts and governments then developed legal criteria to decide whether a suspect should be surrendered or their extradition refused.

Starting with Belgium in 1833,[10] closely followed by France, the United States, and England, it became common for Western states to refuse extradition for 'political offences' against another state.[11] However, national laws differed significantly on what offences were considered 'political'.[12] There was most commonality on 'pure' or 'absolute' political offences (particularly in common law countries), which involve no underlying common crime (such as violence) but are acts directed against the government or state institutions (such as treason, sedition, subversion, conspiracy, espionage, and collaboration with the enemy).[13] More problematic were 'relative' or 'connected' political offences (more common in continental legal systems),[14] which additionally involve an underlying common crime (typically violence, including death, injury, or property damage), such as sabotage, rebellion, assassination, and the like. Here courts took different approaches, for example, focusing variously on whether the act was incidental to a political disturbance; was directed against the state's political organisation; had a predominantly political motive or purpose; or was sufficiently proximate or proportionate.[15]

One rationale for the political offence exception was that the state of refuge should not interfere in domestic political struggles in a foreign state by assisting the foreign government to repress its political adversaries. As Hersch Lauterpacht wrote in 1954,

> [The] international community was no longer a society for the mutual protection of governments. A revolution might be a crime against the established state, but it was no longer a crime against the international community. So long as international society

[10] Belgian Extradition Act 1833. See Van den Wijngaert (above n 3) 12.

[11] See G Gilbert, *Transnational Fugitive Offenders in International Law: Extradition and Other Mechanisms* (Dordrecht, Martinus Nijhoff, 1998); Van den Wijngaert (above n 3); MC Bassiouni, *International Extradition and World Public Order* (Leiden, AW Sijthoff, 1974) 370–428; and A Sofaer, 'The Political Offence Exception and Terrorism' (1986) 15 *Denver Journal of International Law and Policy* 125.

[12] Van den Wijngaert (above n 3) 191; and I Stanbrook and C Stanbrook, *Extradition Law and Practice*, 2nd edn (Oxford, Oxford University Press, 2000) 68.

[13] Van den Wijngaert (above n 3) 106–8; and Stanbrook and Stanbrook (ibid) 69.

[14] Van den Wijngaert (above n 3) 108–11; and Stanbrook and Stanbrook (above n 12) 66.

[15] See the key cases discussed in Van den Wijngaert (above n 3) 120–32 and Stanbrook and Stanbrook (above n 12) 70–78.

> did not effectively guarantee the rights of men against arbitrariness and oppression by governments, it could not oblige states to treat subversive activities … as a crime.[16]

Such rationale may seem especially attractive where the foreign government is authoritarian or repressive, and less attractive where the foreign state is democratic and rights-respecting. Most states and their courts, however, avoid declaring foreign states to be authoritarian or otherwise. The principle of non-intervention avoids these hard choices and abstains from taking sides in political struggles in any other state, thus shielding political offenders against democracies and authoritarian regimes alike.[17] It enables foreign states to remain neutral, which also has the benefit of ensuring those states can establish friendly diplomatic relations with a violent political movement that succeeds in becoming the new government.[18]

Another rationale for the political offence exception was that individuals should be protected from return to political persecution in their home countries,[19] which typically manifests in unfair trial or summary punishment. Refusal of extradition was thus closely bound up with the evolution of political asylum in Western European democracies and the view that it would be 'unthinkable' to return those who resist political oppression to oppressive regimes.[20] The grant of asylum implicitly passes adverse judgment on the political conditions in the foreign state in question, but the institution of asylum aims to serve humanitarian purposes and in theory is not supposed to be seen as a diplomatically unfriendly act[21] (even if it may be viewed as such in practice by persecutor states).

The political offence exception created a risk, however, of impunity for atrocities. Criminal jurisdiction is foremost territorial under international law. Few states in the nineteenth century consequently extended extraterritorial criminal jurisdiction over violence committed by foreign nationals abroad, so that prosecution of such violence in the state of refuge was seldom possible. There was accordingly a risk that assassins, anarchists, nihilists, or 'terrorists' would walk free in a country of refuge. Some states and courts responded by narrowing the political offence exception, not only by tightening the definition of 'political offences' but by introducing explicit exceptions to the exception – even if acts were politically motivated – for particularly unacceptable violence.

Thus, the influential Belgian *attentat* clause of 1856 rendered extraditable the attempted killing of heads of state or government and their families, in large

[16] Quoted in United Nations, *Yearbook of the International Law Commission 1954, Volume I*, summary records of the sixth session (3 June–28 July 1954) 141.

[17] The political offence exception commonly applies to any political offenders, regardless of the justifiability of their cause. See, eg, *Schtraks v Israel* [1964] AC 556, 583 (Lord Reid); and *Quinn v Robinson* 783 F.2d 776 (9th Cir, 1986). See also Van den Wijngaert (above n 3) 18–19.

[18] Stanbrook and Stanbrook (above n 12) 67.

[19] Van den Wijngaert (above n 3) 9–12.

[20] Stanbrook and Stanbrook (above n 12) 66. See also Van den Wijngaert (above n 3) 9 and 11.

[21] United Nations General Assembly, 'Declaration on Territorial Asylum', A/RES/2312(XXII) (14 December 1967) preamble.

part because such killings were thought to destabilise international relations.[22] Subsequently, other types of violence came to be treated by the courts or in bilateral extradition treaties as non-political and thus extraditable. These included acts that were regarded as indiscriminate or atrocious[23] (such as those that target innocent civilians); or as too remote from or disproportionate (or excessive relative) to a political end.[24] Courts later applied similar factors in interpreting the meaning of serious 'non-political' offenders from modern refugee protection.[25]

The notion of 'terrorism' was, however, rarely used as a legal concept in the extradition context, courts preferring to focus on the nature of the physical acts of violence rather than more elaborate or pejorative descriptions of them. More recently, however, some courts since the 1990s have favoured using the term 'terrorism' to depoliticise offences on the basis that it can be more precise than the more subjective above-mentioned tests.[26] Although the political offence exception is common in bilateral extradition treaties and national laws, there remains wide variation in its scope,[27] particularly its application to putative 'terrorists'.[28]

In addition to these developments in national law and bilateral treaties, from the 1890s efforts were made to stimulate wider multilateral cooperation. Indeed, transnational efforts to confront 'terrorism' grew precisely out of perceived inadequacies in and the lack of harmonisation between national extradition laws, which facilitated impunity for serious offenders. Thus, between 1934 and 1937, the League of Nations drafted a convention to suppress terrorism, largely in response to an Italian court having applied the political offence exception to the Croatian assassins of King Alexander of Yugoslavia, who had been killed while visiting France.[29] But that convention never entered into force.[30]

[22] Van den Wijngaert (above n 3) 14–16 and 135–38.

[23] See, eg, *Ellis v O'Dea*, Record No 441 SS/1990 (30 July 1990), transcript, 36; *Della Savia*, Swiss Federal Tribunal (26 November 1969) 95 ATF I, 469; *Morlacci*, Swiss Federal Tribunal (12 December 1975), 101 ATF Ia, 605; and *Re Atta (Mahmoud Abed)* (1989) 706 F Supp 1032, approved (1990) 910 F.2d 1063.

[24] See, eg, *McGlinchey v Wren* [1983] Irish L Rep Monthly 169; *Shannon v Fanning* [1984] IR 548; and *Folkerts v Public Prosecutor* (1978) 74 ILR 498. See also Van den Wijngaert (above n 3) 16–17.

[25] Under Art 1F(b) of the Convention relating to the Status of Refugees (Refugee Convention 1951), adopted 28 July 1951, 189 UNTS 150, entered into force 22 April 1954. See, eg, *T v Home Secretary* [1996] 2 All ER 865; *McMullen v INS* (1986) 788 F 2d 591; *Minister for Immigration v Singh* [2002] HCA 7; and *Zrig v Canada (Minister of Citizenship and Immigration)* (CA) [2003] 3 FC 761.

[26] See *T v Home Secretary* [1996] 2 All ER 865 (Lord Mustill).

[27] T Stein, 'Extradition' in *Max Planck Encyclopedia of Public International Law* (Oxford University Press online database, article updated February 2011).

[28] Stanbrook and Stanbrook (above n 12) 67.

[29] *Pavelic, Kwaternic, Artucovic* Case, Court of Appeal of Torino, 23 November 1934, (1933–34) 7 Ann Dig 372.

[30] League of Nations Convention for the Prevention and Punishment of Terrorism (adopted 16 November 1937, never entered into force) (1938) *League of Nations Official Journal* 19. See B Saul, 'The Legal Response of the League of Nations to Terrorism' (2006) 4 *Journal of International Criminal Justice* 78.

The depoliticisation of some political violence over time, however, accentuated the risk that offenders could thereby be returned to political persecution or unfair trial. Even if offenders had committed egregious violence, humanitarian concerns remained about the treatment even of 'terrorists'. As a result, two further developments occurred. First, separate, more targeted safeguards arose in some extradition laws and treaties[31] (as well as under contemporary human rights treaties[32]) to protect suspects from being returned to a jurisdiction where they face harms such as discrimination, unfair trial, torture/ill treatment, or the death penalty. Second, where extradition was not possible for the aforementioned reasons, it increasingly became possible to prosecute offenders in a state of refugee where the latter had established extraterritorial criminal jurisdiction. Such extended criminal jurisdiction was often enabled by multilateral criminal cooperation treaties, based on the 'extradite or prosecute' principle (discussed below) – which thus prevented impunity while avoiding political persecution.[33]

III. TRANSNATIONAL COUNTERTERRORISM CONVENTIONS SINCE THE 1960S

Particular impetus was given to the harmonisation of extradition laws by the rise of transnational 'terrorism' from the 1960s, typically connected with national liberation movements struggling for independence from European colonial powers. Because of intractable disagreements over defining terrorism,[34] the international community responded incrementally by adopting numerous 'sectoral' treaties addressing common methods of 'terrorist' violence (such as hijacking, hostage-taking, endangering maritime facilities, and so on).[35]

None of the treaties establishes a general crime of terrorism, although the Terrorist Financing Convention 1999 comes closest in providing a general

[31] See, eg, UN Model Treaty on Extradition, UN General Assembly resolution 45/116 (14 December 1990), Art 3 (mandatory grounds for refusal include discriminatory trial or punishment, unfair trial, or torture or cruel, inhuman or degrading treatment or punishment) and Art 4 (optional grounds for refusal include the death penalty and humanitarian considerations); Extradition Act 2003 (UK), s 87 (no extradition unless compatible with human rights) and s 94 (no extradition to the death penalty).

[32] Refugee Convention 1951 (above n 25), Art 33(1) (no return to persecution); Convention against Torture 1984, Art 3 (no return to torture); ICCPR (above n 8), Art 6 (no return to arbitrary deprivations of life, including to the death penalty where the requested state has itself abolished the death penalty) and Art 7 (no return to torture or cruel, inhuman, or degrading treatment); European Convention on Human Rights 1950, no return in certain circumstances involving violations to Art 2 (right to life), Art 3 (torture and inhuman treatment), Art 5 (liberty and security), Art 6 (fair trial), and Art 8 (respect for private and family life).

[33] Van den Wijngaert (above n 3) 161.

[34] See B Saul, *Defining Terrorism in International Law* (Oxford, Oxford University Press, 2016).

[35] Most of the treaties avoid referring to 'terrorism', with the exception of the three most recent treaties (since 1997) on terrorist financing, terrorist bombings, and nuclear terrorism.

definition for the limited purpose of criminalising terrorist financing.[36] The treaties typically require states to criminalise certain dangerous conduct, establish extraterritorial jurisdiction, and cooperate by prosecuting or extraditing suspects (the *aut dedere aut judicare* principle). Many of the treaties deem the specified offences to provide a basis for extradition under any extradition treaty between the state parties.[37] However, only a few of the most recent treaties require their offences not to be regarded as 'political offences' in national extradition law[38] – namely those concerning civilian aviation, nuclear material, terrorist bombings of civilians, and terrorist financing. Most of the treaties do not have this requirement, thus leaving the question to national law. Some treaties expressly preserve the political offence exception in national law[39] and/or preserve asylum[40] (of necessity, even for political offenders), and many provide other safeguards against persecution.[41] Otherwise, extradition may be refused in accordance with a particular state's own law.[42]

As they evolved over a century and a half to 2001, extradition laws often struck a delicate balance between state security interests; prevention of impunity

[36] International Convention for the Suppression of the Financing of Terrorism 1999 (Terrorist Financing Convention 1999).

[37] Convention for the Suppression of Unlawful Seizure of Aircraft 1970 (Hague Convention 1970), Art 8; Hague Convention 1970 as amended by the Protocol Supplementary to the Convention for the Suppression of Unlawful Seizure of Aircraft 2010 (Beijing Protocol 2010), Art 8; Convention for the Suppression of Unlawful Acts against the Safety of Civil Aviation 1971 (Montreal Convention 1971), Art 8; Convention on the Prevention and Punishment of Crimes against Internationally Protected Persons, including Diplomatic Agents 1973 (Protected Persons Convention 1973), Art 8; Convention for the Suppression of Unlawful Acts against the Safety of Maritime Navigation 1988 (Rome Convention 1988), Art 11; International Convention against the Taking of Hostages, UN General Assembly, No 21931 (17 November 1979) (Hostages Convention 1979), Art 10; Convention on the Physical Protection of Nuclear Material 1980, Art 11; International Convention for the Suppression of Acts of Nuclear Terrorism 2005 (Nuclear Terrorism Convention 2005), Art 13; International Convention for the Suppression of Terrorist Bombings 1997 (Terrorist Bombings Convention 1997), Art 9; and Terrorist Financing Convention 1999 (ibid), Art 11.

[38] Hague Convention 1970 as amended by the Beijing Protocol 2010 (ibid), Art 8 *bis*; Nuclear Terrorism Convention 2005 (ibid), Art 15; Terrorist Bombings Convention 1997 (ibid), Art 11; Terrorist Financing Convention 1999 (above n 36), Art 14; Protocol 2005 to the Rome Convention 1988, inserting Art 11 *bis*; Amendment 2005 to the Convention on the Physical Protection of Nuclear Material 1980, inserting Art 11A.

[39] As under the Convention on Offences and Certain Other Acts Committed on Board Aircraft 1963 (Tokyo Convention 1963) Art 2.

[40] Protected Persons Convention 1973 (above n 37), Art 12; and Hostages Convention 1979 (above n 37), Art 15.

[41] Some of the treaties explicitly require extradition or cooperation to be refused where it is for the purpose of punishment or prosecution on account of a person's race, religion, nationality, ethnicity, or political opinion: Hague Convention 1970 as amended by the Beijing Protocol 2010, Art 8 *ter*; Hostages Convention 1979, Art 9(1); Nuclear Terrorism Convention 2005 (above n 37), Art 16; Terrorist Bombings Convention 1997 (above n 37), Art 12; and Terrorist Financing Convention 1999 (above n 36), Art 15. See similarly the Tokyo Convention 1963 (above n 39), Art 2.

[42] These commonly include, for instance, that the state does not extradite its nationals; that principles of 'dual criminality' (the conduct must be an offence in both states) or 'specialty' (the suspect must only be prosecuted for the requested offence) are not satisfied; or if a person would be returned to the death penalty or unfair trial.

for atrocities; non-intervention in foreign political contests; internal struggles over the exercise of sovereignty and self-determination; and the protection of political asylum. Assassinations of heads of government and atrocities against civilians were generally extraditable (subject to protections against persecution). Extradition law did not, however, ordinarily oblige states to surrender foreign fugitives who committed other kinds of politically motivated violence against their own governments. The main exceptions are the egregious crimes covered by the recent terrorism treaties (mentioned in the previous paragraph), as well as international crimes such as genocide, war crimes, and crimes against humanity.[43] National extradition laws and bilateral extradition treaties were consequently shaped by overriding obligations under international criminal law treaties.[44]

As a result, there was left a considerable zone for violent political resistance in relation to which foreign governments had the freedom not to (and generally did not) cooperate with the victim state's attempts to suppress it. For instance, targeted, discriminate, proportionate attacks on state military, police or security personnel or property, avoiding excessive civilian casualties, and not involving prohibited methods (such as nuclear terrorism) was protected from extradition by the political offence exception. More problematically, attacks on government institutions, premises and personnel, as representatives of the opposed regime, also potentially benefited from the exception, depending on the particular national extradition laws.

At the same time, international law has not recognised any 'right to rebel' which would positively authorise political resistance to authoritarian regimes. (The separate question of self-determination violence is considered further below.) This is despite Hannah Arendt's observation that many modern political communities were founded on violence and thus originated in crime.[45] At best there is a preambular reference in the Universal Declaration of Human Rights 1948, which states:

> Whereas it is essential, if man is not to be compelled to have recourse, as a last resource, to rebellion against tyranny and oppression, that human rights should be protected by the rule of law ...[46]

A drafting proposal to refer to a 'right' of resistance was not accepted in the Declaration,[47] and only peaceful rights of political participation are mentioned in the International Covenant on Civil and Political Rights (ICCPR) 1966.[48] Further, there are no duties on affected states not to suppress or criminalise

[43] Van den Wijngaert (above n 3) 140–46.

[44] See Van den Wijngaert (above n 3) 140–45.

[45] H Arendt, *On Revolution* (Penguin, London, 1990) 20.

[46] Universal Declaration of Human Rights 1948, preamble.

[47] ECOSOC Official Records (6th Session), Supplement No. 1, Report of the UN Commission on Human Rights (17 December 1947) 19.

[48] Eg, ICCPR (above n 8), Arts 18–19, 21–22, and 25.

legitimate rebellions[49] or duties on other states to assist legitimate rebellions.[50] Nor does international law require states to shield rebels from extradition for political crimes (as opposed to protect them from persecution);[51] at most, there are certain common traditions in national extradition law as described above. Equally, international law does not require transnational cooperation to repress political resistance, other than in the limited categories of violence defined in criminal cooperation treaties.

IV. THE PROLIFERATION OF COUNTERTERRORISM LAWS CRIMINALISING POLITICAL RESISTANCE

The proliferation of international and national counterterrorism laws after the terrorist attacks on the United States of 11 September 2001 has, in significant ways, shrunk the space for political resistance. The UN Security Council required all states to criminalise 'terrorist acts' in paragraph 2(e) of Resolution 1373 (2001), adopted under Chapter VII of the UN Charter.[52] In doing so, the Security Council circumvented the protracted international debates about defining terrorism, as well the contemporaneous deadlock in the General Assembly over the drafting of a comprehensive counterterrorism convention. It was able to do so in part because it refrained from dictating to states any common definition of terrorism. Instead, it permitted states discretion in implementation. States could thus enact their own unilateral criminal definitions and offences of terrorism.

The decentralised criminalisation of terrorism shifted the hitherto widespread attitude of states that it was sufficient to prosecute terrorism as ordinary crime rather than as a special offence. It signalled a new preparedness by the international community to explicitly demarcate 'terrorism' as a form of universal deviance to be condemned and stigmatised in the strongest way by domestic criminal laws. The absence of a universal definition of terrorism, however,[53]

[49] J Crawford, 'The Right of Self-Determination in International Law: Its Development and Future' in P Alston (ed), *Peoples' Rights* (Oxford, Oxford University Press, 2001) 48–49 (states are entitled to forcibly suppress rebellions); and C Gray, *International Law and the Use of Force* (Oxford, Oxford University Press, 2000) 57 (states may request foreign assistance in suppressing rebellions). When a rebellion reaches the level of a civil war, other states arguably may no longer assist the government: Crawford (above) 41; Gray (above) 57; and W Werner, 'Self-Determination and Civil War' (2001) 6(2) *Journal of Conflict and Security Law* 171–90, 190.

[50] *Nicaragua* case (1986) ICJ Reports 14, 108–9, paras 206–9 (no right of third states to intervene in aid of the moral or political values of a rebellion). See also Geneva Conventions Additional Protocol II 1977, Art 3(2).

[51] Van den Wijngaert (above n 3) 133. The political offence exception to extradition is a question of national (and bilateral treaty) law rather than international law: Stanbrook and Stanbrook (above n 12) 4 and 65. Cf I Shearer, *Extradition in International Law* (Manchester, Manchester University Press, 1971) 22.

[52] UNSC Resolution 1373 (above n 1) para 2(e).

[53] In Resolution 1566 (2004) the UN Security Council provided a working definition of terrorism, but it is non-binding and has not perceptibly influenced national laws.

produced a wide range of disparate definitions in national legal systems. This is problematic for at least five reasons.

First, many national laws have defined terrorist offences in ways that are inconsistent with international human rights law, including by criminalising nonviolent protest, as the UN High Commissioner for Human Rights has pointed out:

> [M]any States have adopted national legislation with vague, unclear or overbroad definitions of terrorism. These ambiguous definitions have led to inappropriate restrictions on the legitimate exercise of fundamental liberties, such as association, expression and peaceful political and social opposition … Some States have included nonviolent activities in their national definitions of terrorism. This has increased the risk and the practice that individuals are prosecuted for legitimate, nonviolent exercise of rights enshrined in international law, or that criminal conduct that does not constitute 'terrorism' may be criminalized as such … There are several examples of hastily adopted counter-terrorism laws which introduced definitions that lacked in precision and appeared to contravene the principle of legality …
>
> Particular care must be taken … in defining offences relating to the support that can be offered to terrorist organizations or offences purporting to prevent the financing of terrorist activities in order to ensure that various nonviolent conducts are not inadvertently criminalized by vague formulations of the offences in question ….[54]

The UN Human Rights Committee has also criticised the vagueness of terrorism laws.[55] The Security Council's own monitoring mechanism, the Counter-Terrorism Committee (CTC), which was set up under Resolution 1373, also drew criticism[56] for explicitly declaring that human rights were outside its security mandate.[57] It was only in 2004 that a human rights expert was appointed to the CTC and human rights concerns began to be systematically addressed.

Secondly, most national laws (aside from Australia, Canada, and New Zealand) do not provide a 'democratic protest' exception to terrorism offences. Such exception is for acts of advocacy, protest, dissent, or industrial action that are not intended to cause death, serious bodily harm, or serious risk to public

[54] UN High Commissioner for Human Rights, 'Report on the Protection of Human Rights and Fundamental Freedoms while Countering Terrorism', A/HRC/8/13 (2 June 2008), https://digitallibrary.un.org/record/628535/files/A_HRC_8_13-EN.pdf, paras 20–23.

[55] See UN Human Rights Committee (HRC), 'Consideration of Reports Submitted by State Parties: Concluding Observations – USA', CCPR/C/USA/CO/3 (15 September 2006) para 11; UN HRC, 'Concluding Observations: Algeria', CCPR/C/79/Add.95 (18 August 1998) para 11; UN HRC, 'Concluding Observations: Egypt', CCPR/C/79/Add.23 (9 August 1993) para 8; UN HRC, 'Concluding Observations: Democratic Peoples' Republic of Korea', CCPR/CO/72/PRK (27 August 2001) para 14; UN HRC, 'Concluding Observations: Portugal (Macao)', CCPR/C/79/Add.115 (4 November 1999) para 12; and UN HRC, 'Concluding Observations: Peru', CCPR /C/79/Add.67 (25 July 1996) para 12.

[56] Human Rights Watch, 'UN Counterterrorism Body Neglects Human Rights' (10 August 2004), www.hrw.org/news/2004/08/10/un-counterterrorism-body-neglects-human-rights.

[57] UN Security Council Counter-Terrorism Committee, 'Protecting Human Rights While Countering Terrorism', http://www.un.org/en/sc/ctc/rights.html (last accessed 20 January 2006).

health or safety.[58] While property damage may exceed the limits of freedom of expression and amount to public order offences, they should not be additionally stigmatised as terrorism. The exception prevents criminalising as 'terrorism' minor harms (property damage) in the course of the traditions of direct democratic action.

In Britain, some of these issues have been ventilated in a debate about whether prosecutorial discretion is sufficient to address the public interest in not prosecuting cases of 'just' violence against oppressive regimes, or to prevent overreach (for example through the criminal prosecution of military acts of fighters already covered by international humanitarian law). Whereas a UK Independent Reviewer of Terrorism Legislation thought prosecutorial discretion was a sufficient safeguard,[59] the UK Supreme Court opined that reliance on prosecutorial discretion was 'intrinsically unattractive' because it would abdicate Parliament's legislative function to an unelected prosecutor, render legal liability uncertain, and detract from the rule of law.[60] A narrower definition of terrorism that targets violence that Parliament considers truly wrongful is preferable to allowing wide discretion for prosecutors to apply an over-broad definition.

Thirdly, many laws exert extraterritorial jurisdiction over foreign or international terrorism and are not limited to domestic terrorism occurring within the state's own territory. Terrorism is frequently defined to include violence against governments, regardless of whether they are democratic or authoritarian. UK courts, for instance, rejected an argument that the definition of terrorism should be restrictively interpreted so as not to protect authoritarian governments.[61] Before 9/11, a state targeted by political violence was always entitled to protect itself by resorting to the criminal law, and as mentioned, there was no right to rebel. A new development after 9/11, however, is that foreign terrorism laws also now seek to repress violence against even authoritarian states that themselves coercively repress democratic freedoms and human rights.

The fourth development is related to the point above. In paragraph 3(g) of Resolution 1373, the Security Council called on all states to '[e]nsure, in conformity with international law ... that claims of political motivation are not recognized as grounds for refusing requests for the extradition of alleged terrorists'. The paragraph is only recommendatory but nonetheless exerts considerable normative influence on state practice, endorsing the removal of the political offence exception for terrorism offences as unilaterally defined by states. Other actors have supported this approach. For example, the UN Office on Drugs and Crime has encouraged states to remove the political offence

[58] Canadian Criminal Code, s 83.01(1)(E); Australian Criminal Code, s 100.1(3); and Terrorism Suppression Act 2002 (New Zealand), s 5(5).

[59] Lord Carlile of Berriew, 'The Definition of Terrorism: A Report by the Independent Reviewer of Terrorism Legislation', Cm 7052 (March 2007), paras 60–64.

[60] *R v Gul (Appellant)* [2013] UKSC 64, para 36.

[61] *R v F* [2007] EWCA Crim 243.

exception for all sectoral treaty offences, even though most of the treaties do not require this.

The effect of this development is that foreign states may increasingly cooperate with victim states in surrendering 'terrorist' fugitives who earlier would have been protected as political offenders. This would not be problematic if there were a common definition of terrorism limited to serious violence against innocent civilians. However, the Security Council's devolution to individual states of the definition of terrorism has had the dangerous consequence of potentially green-lighting cooperative repression of all political violence.

At the same time, decentralisation also has the contrary potential to constrain transnational cooperation. Some states may be unable to extradite suspects or cooperate in foreign terrorism investigations when the underlying crimes are defined differently (due to the double criminality rule in extradition). In addition, excessive or abusive foreign terrorist laws may prevent a requested state from cooperating because of the protections imposed by the latter state's human rights or constitutional laws, or by their regional or international human rights treaty obligations. However, these protections themselves have come under strain after 9/11 within even model liberal democracies, such as Sweden, when cooperating in the return of suspected to terrorists to torture in foreign states.[62]

V. TERRORISM IN ARMED CONFLICT UNDER INTERNATIONAL HUMANITARIAN LAW

The fifth and final reason why the Security Council's endorsement of unilateral national terrorism definitions undermines the space for political resistance concerns the regulation of armed conflict. On the one hand, the Council has recognised that state counterterrorism measures must conform to state obligations under IHL.[63] On the other hand, while the CTC monitoring of human rights impacts improved after 2004, the same cannot be said for IHL impacts. No IHL expert has ever been appointed to the CTC, despite the fact that, as discussed below, the International Committee of the Red Cross (ICRC) has criticised the excessive intrusion of counterterrorism laws on IHL. Examination of the monitoring practice of the CTC reveals that it has not objected to national laws that adversely intrude on matters already regulated by IHL, nor has it required states to defer to IHL as the *lex specialis* governing armed conflict.

[62] *Agiza v Sweden*, UN Human Rights Committee Communication No 233/2003 (20 May 2005) (expulsion to Egypt involved a real risk of torture or ill treatment).

[63] See, eg, UN Security Council Resolution 1456 (20 January 2003).

Sectoral counterterrorism treaties have generally taken a cautious approach to regulating acts in armed conflict that are covered by IHL. The treaties cover only transnational offences and thus exclude purely domestic civil wars.[64] The Hostages Convention 1979 does not apply at all to the war crime of hostage-taking under IHL.[65] Other treaties exclude attacks on certain military targets (such as military aircraft or ships[66] or combatants[67]), thus applying only to attacks on civilians or civilian targets during armed conflict (thereby dually regulating such acts alongside existing IHL prohibitions on war crimes). Some treaties exclude acts committed by armed forces,[68] again deferring to IHL as the *lex specialis*.

However, national counterterrorism laws after 9/11 have often intruded more deeply into the domain of IHL by criminalising various acts that are not criminal under IHL. For example, individuals and entities listed under Security Council sanctions resolutions as associated with Al Qaeda or the Taliban are subject to restrictive financial measures,[69] even if they are also members of non-state armed groups that are parties to non-international armed conflict. The implications of such designation for compliance with IHL are considered below.

Moreover, some national laws (such as those in the United Kingdom and Australia) have criminalised violence in armed conflict without any exception or qualification to accommodate armed conflict and IHL.[70] Such laws criminalise acts that are not prohibited or criminalised by IHL, such as proportionate attacks on state military forces or military objectives by non-state armed groups; or direct participation in hostilities by civilians. Such laws provide a basis for transnational criminal cooperation with other states in order to suppress terrorism.

[64] Specifically, the treaties typically do not apply when an offence is committed in a single state, the offender and victims are nationals of that state, the offender is found in the state's territory, and no other state has jurisdiction under those treaties: Tokyo Convention 1963 (above n 39), Art 5(1); Hague Convention 1970, Art 3(3)–(4); Hague Convention 1970, Art 3(5) as amended by the Beijing Protocol 2010; Montreal Convention 1971 (above n 37), Art 4(2)–(5); Rome Convention 1988 (above n 37), Art 4(1)–(2); Protocol for the Suppression of Unlawful Acts against the Safety of Fixed Platforms Located on the Continental Shelf 1988, Art 1(2); Hostages Convention 1979 (above n 37), Art 13; Convention on the Physical Protection of Nuclear Material ('Vienna Convention') 1980, Art 14; Nuclear Terrorism Convention 2005 (above n 37), Art 3; Terrorist Bombings Convention 1997 (above n 37), Art 3; and Terrorist Financing Convention 1999 (above n 36), Art 3.

[65] Hostages Convention 1979 (above n 37).

[66] Tokyo Convention 1963 (above n 39), Art 1(4); Hague Convention 1970 (above n 37), Art 3(2); Montreal Convention 1971 (above n 37), Art 4; and Rome Convention 1988 (above n 37), Art 2. See also Protocol on the Suppression of Unlawful Acts of Violence at Airports Serving International Civil Aviation ('Montreal Protocol') 1988, Art II (military air bases).

[67] Terrorist Financing Convention 1999 (above n 36), Art 2(1)(b).

[68] Nuclear Terrorism Convention 2005 (above n 37), Art 4(2); Terrorist Bombings Convention 1997 (above n 37), Art 19(2); Terrorist Financing Convention 1999 (above n 36), Art 2(1)(b); Vienna Convention 1980 (as amended by the Amendment 2005), Art 2(4)(b); Hague Convention 1970 (as amended by the Beijing Protocol 2010), Art 3 *bis*; Rome Convention 1988 (as amended by the Protocol 2005), Art 2 *bis* (2); and Plastic Explosives Convention 1991, Arts 3–4.

[69] UN Security Council Resolution 1267 (1999) and subsequent related resolutions. See https://www.un.org/sc/suborg/en/sanctions/1267/resolutions.

[70] UK Terrorism Act 2000, s 1; and Australian Criminal Code 1995, s 100(1).

In *R v Gul* (2013),[71] the UK Supreme Court found that international law does not prohibit the national criminalisation as terrorism of hostile acts in non-international armed conflicts (NIACs), even those confined to targeting military objectives. It found that international counterterrorism instruments and national laws were inconsistent in regard to the existence and scope of exclusionary provisions and did not establish a general exclusionary rule applying to national terrorism offences.[72] It further noted that no combatant immunity exists in NIACs.[73] The Court concluded that while international law may not prohibit such hostilities, it does not positively authorise them.

The consequence of this approach is that all armed resistance to state forces, as well as fighting between non-state armed groups, becomes 'terrorism', regardless of how the fighting occurs or whether those involved respect IHL. It makes armed resistance to authoritarian regimes *ipso facto* illegal, regardless of means. While dually criminalising attacks on civilians as both war crimes and 'terrorism' may be relatively unobjectionable, criminalising IHL-compliant fighting raises significant legal, policy, and practical difficulties.

A potentially serious adverse policy impact of this approach is the undermining of IHL and its humanitarian objectives. The ICRC has warned against criminalising acts that are not unlawful under IHL,[74] including, for example, attacks on military objectives.[75] There is ample evidence that many non-state armed groups are prepared to respect IHL under the right conditions,[76] but criminalising fighting by such groups as terrorism undermines their incentive to comply with IHL,[77] if there is no longer any difference in legal consequence between proportionately attacking the military or indiscriminately targeting civilians.

Admittedly, in the context of NIACs, states have long been entitled to criminalise violence by members of armed groups for domestic offences,[78] whether they are common crimes, labelled as terrorist acts, or considered to threaten national security. This includes violence that is directed solely and proportionately against military objectives and otherwise complies with IHL. There is no combatant immunity in NIACs, as the UK Court noted, and at most, IHL encourages states to grant the widest possible amnesty at the end of a conflict

[71] *R v Gul (Appellant)* [2013] UKSC 64 (affirming *R v Gul* [2012] EWCA Crim 280).

[72] Ibid, paras 48 and 50.

[73] Ibid, para 51.

[74] ICRC, 'Terrorism and International Law: Challenges and Responses – The Complementary Nature of Human Rights Law, International Humanitarian Law and Refugee Law', Report from events hosted by the International Institute of Humanitarian Law conferences in San Remo (2002).

[75] J Pejic, 'Armed Conflict and Terrorism' in AM Salinas de Frias, K Samuel, and N White (eds), *Counter-Terrorism: International Law and Practice* (Oxford, Oxford University Press, 2012) 177.

[76] See B Saul, 'Enhancing Civilian Protection by Engaging Non-state Armed Groups under International Humanitarian Law' (2017) 22(1) *Journal of Conflict and Security Law* 39–66.

[77] Pejic (above n 75) 203.

[78] H Lauterpacht (ed), *Oppenheim's International Law: Volume II*, 8th edn (London, Longmans, Green and Co, 1955) 210–12.

for hostile acts that did not violate IHL.[79] The incentives for armed groups to comply with IHL have thus always been limited, largely in order to protect the sovereign right of states to restore order within their own territories.

However, the additional criminalisation of non-state hostilities as terrorism exacerbates the existing disincentives for armed groups to comply with IHL.[80] First, such measures are intended to enable transnational criminal cooperation on terrorism, whereas hostile acts in NIAC (which are not war crimes) were hitherto typically treated as non-extraditable, quintessentially 'political' offences. Foreign states are thereby encouraged to cooperate in the universal repression of domestic political rebellion, even if civilians are not targeted and there is no violation of IHL. Admittedly there are still the human rights-based safeguards in the extradition laws of some states. However, many states in the business of countering terrorism are not well functioning democracies based on the rule of law, judicial independence, respect for rights and due process, or adherence to strong regional institutions such as those found in Europe. There is ample scope for things to go badly wrong.

Secondly, national laws now carry the imprimatur of UN Security Council counterterrorism obligations. This arguably accords them an additional layer of legal authority and political legitimacy, as well as an expectation of foreign legal recognition and cooperation that is greater than for ordinary domestic offences. The Security Council has rarely utilised its binding powers to intrude on national legal sovereignty by compelling states to adopt domestic legislation to address security threats. Its counterterrorism resolutions impose an exceptional kind of national law-making obligation on states that integrates all states in a common global enterprise to suppress terrorism. The Security Council's special licensing of states to so legislate helps to elevate this network of counterterrorism laws to a comparable plane as IHL and to validate potentially problematic national legal choices.

In addition, terrorism carries a special stigma, and the labelling of all hostilities as such may widen political and social divisions between the relevant parties and therefore dampen the prospects for peace and reconciliation.[81] Finally, as evidence from Afghanistan, Somalia, and elsewhere suggests, the criminalisation of terrorists may prompt armed groups to further distrust the international

[79] Additional Protocol II 1977 (above n 50), Art 6(5). Further, if belligerents do not commit war crimes, 'it is in the spirit of the [Geneva] Convention that trials and executions for treason should be reduced to an indispensable minimum required by the necessities of the situation': Lauterpacht (ibid) 211. Although prosecution is permitted, it is often impractical or unwise: J Brierly, *The Outlook for International Law* (Oxford, Clarendon, 1944) 52. In practice, some states have conferred de facto recognition on non-state groups which generally comply with IHL, and third states commonly do not regard insurgents as criminals: N Ronzitti, 'The Law of the Sea and the Use of Force against Terrorist Activities' in N Ronzitti (ed), *Maritime Terrorism and International Law* (Dordrecht, Martinus Nijhoff, 1990) 3.

[80] Pejic (above n 75) 185.

[81] Ibid, 196–98.

community and discourage them from allowing humanitarian assistance to reach civilians.[82]

VI. CONCLUSION

The above trends in counterterrorism laws after 9/11 have substantially diminished the unregulated space for political resistance (violent and nonviolent), whether the governments being resisted are authoritarian or democratic. Some national laws have increasingly overclassified violence by criminalising all violence against all governments as terrorism, regardless of the means, methods, or targets involved (in addition often to criminalising even nonviolent protest). Many such national laws have furthermore been extended extraterritorially to enable the repression of violence against foreign governments, regardless of their political stripes or human rights records. National laws have further reduced or eliminated the political offence exception to extradition, even for discriminate, proportionate force against state actors that was previously exempt from extradition. Some national laws have moreover criminalised all violence by non-state forces in armed conflict, even if certain activities are not unlawful or criminal under IHL (such as discriminately and proportionately targeting military objects while avoiding civilian casualties, as well as the use of prohibited weapons, methods, or means).

Certainly many jurisdictions apply and respect (to varying degrees) other human rights safeguards against extradition, even where the political offence exception has been removed (including unjustifiably in the name of tough counterterrorism). However, the extraterritorial criminalisation of such violence now means that even where extradition is refused on human rights grounds, the foreign violence in question can still be prosecuted as terrorism under the law of the state of refuge which refused extradition; archetypal political rebels can thereby be prosecuted for conduct that previously attracted the benefit of the political offence exception. Criminal justice safeguards may apply, but a fair trial is little comfort if the underlying substantive criminal liability is excessive and infringes political freedom. The upshot of these developments is a tilting of the odds in favour of the mutual transnational consolidation of state authority.

Counterterrorism laws can entrench a state's power at the expense of its own people, even when the latter have legitimate grievances about authoritarian, rights-disrespecting governance or even mass atrocities. Domestic political resistance is increasingly criminalised and stigmatised as terrorism, and outside governments have adopted the legal tools to cooperate in its repression. There has been a rapid rebalancing of the delicately-tuned equilibrium of competing

[82] Ibid, 198–201. See also A Jackson and E Davey, 'From the Spanish Civil War to Afghanistan: Historical and Contemporary Reflections on Humanitarian Engagement with Non-state Armed Groups', HPG Working Paper, Overseas Development Institute (May 2014) 1–2.

interests that had incrementally evolved in extradition law through practice and experience since the mid-nineteenth century.

At the same time, there has been radical selectivity in the application of counterterrorism laws. Many states still politically pick sides in various armed conflicts: 'our' rebels are not terrorists; only those of the enemy are. In certain conflicts, including notably in Syria, foreign states even arm and fund rebel groups fighting against the government. Such selective application of counterterrorism laws further delegitimises this already highly politicised area of law, and the unequal treatment of like groups further undermines the procedural dimension of the rule of law, compounding the injustices inherent in the substantive domestic laws themselves.

This criminalisation of self-help comes at a time when collectively managed intervention to protect populations from grave rights violations is at a low ebb. As the Syrian conflict since 2012 suggests, collective action is often paralysed even when faced with the use of chemical weapons, genocidal attacks on minorities, enslavement of girls and women, systematic state torture, summary executions, and the deliberate targeting of civilians. The 'responsibility to protect' doctrine appears dead in the water, or at least in danger of drowning.[83] Great-power geopolitics looks bleak, with the human rights attitudes of the permanent members of the Security Council being variously disinterested or hostile (China), violative (Russia), confusingly belligerent, dismissive, or isolationist (the United States under President Donald Trump), or in retreat (the United Kingdom post-Brexit). All of this – the legal death of rebellion, the criminalisation of democratic protest, and the cooperative repression of resistance – means that the light of political freedom continues to fade.

A number of concrete steps could be immediately taken to help restore (and improve) the old balance of interests while ensuring justice for terrorist crimes. First, legal definitions should be more carefully circumscribed to ensure that they do not automatically sweep up all types of violence against government as terrorism, regardless of its severity or purpose. Secondly, laws that extraterritorially criminalise terrorism should not automatically apply to protect all foreign governments from violence, regardless of their conduct and the nature of the violence targeted against them. Thirdly, the political offence exception should not be eliminated for ostensible terrorism offences but maintained and resurrected, albeit in a more calibrated fashion, to preserve the classical space for discriminate political resistance, particularly against authoritarian regimes. Finally, there should be a clearer demarcation between the ambit of terrorism offences and international humanitarian law in order to ensure that only

[83] For discussion of the 'responsibility to protect', see the chapters by Jennifer Welsh and Neil MacFarlane in the first edition of this volume: J Welsh, 'The Responsibility to Protect: Securing the Individual in International Society' in BJ Goold and L Lazarus (eds), *Security and Human Rights* (Oxford, Hart Publishing, 2007); and SN MacFarlane, 'Human Security and the Law of States' in BJ Goold and L Lazarus (eds) (above).

violence against civilians is dually criminalised while IHL-compliant fighting is not made *ipso facto* illegal, thereby undermining humanitarian incentives.

Practically speaking, the horse may have already bolted: widereaching terrorism laws have been extensively adopted since 2001.[84] Moreover, the political and populist rhetoric of counterterrorism is typically far more powerful than liberal pleas for moderation, calibration, and the preservation of seemingly archaic legal traditions such as the political offence exception. Nonetheless, excessive terrorism measures have a habit of aggravating rather than curing terrorism, so at the very least there is a prudential argument in favour of treating different kinds of violence differently, and not crushing everything – violent resistance to threats against human rights as well as the violence of true terror – under the same rock of counterterrorism.

REFERENCES

Arendt, H, *On Revolution* (Penguin, London, 1990).

Bassiouni, MC, *International Extradition and World Public Order* (Leiden, AW Sijthoff, 1974).

Brierly, J, *The Outlook for International Law* (Oxford, Clarendon, 1944).

Crawford, J, 'The Right of Self-Determination in International Law: Its Development and Future' in P Alston (ed), *Peoples' Rights* (Oxford, Oxford University Press, 2001).

Draper, G, 'Wars of National Liberation and War Criminality' in M Howard (ed), *Restraints on War* (Oxford, Oxford University Press, 1979).

Gilbert, G, *Transnational Fugitive Offenders in International Law: Extradition and Other Mechanisms* (Dordrecht, Martinus Nijhoff, 1998).

Gray, C, *International Law and the Use of Force* (Oxford, Oxford University Press, 2000).

Human Rights Watch, 'UN Counterterrorism Body Neglects Human Rights' (10 August 2004), www.hrw.org/news/2004/08/10/un-counterterrorism-body-neglects-human-rights.

Jackson, A and Davey, E, 'From the Spanish Civil War to Afghanistan: Historical and Contemporary Reflections on Humanitarian Engagement with Non-state Armed Groups', HPG Working Paper, Overseas Development Institute (May 2014).

Lauterpacht, H (ed), *Oppenheim's International Law: Volume II*, 8th edn (London, Longmans, Green and Co, 1955).

Lord Carlile of Berriew, 'The Definition of Terrorism: A Report by the Independent Reviewer of Terrorism Legislation', Cm 7052 (March 2007).

Pejic, J, 'Armed Conflict and Terrorism' in AM Salinas de Frias, K Samuel, and N White (eds), *Counter-Terrorism: International Law and Practice* (Oxford, Oxford University Press, 2012).

Ronzitti, N, 'The Law of the Sea and the Use of Force against Terrorist Activities' in N Ronzitti (ed), *Maritime Terrorism and International Law* (Dordrecht, Martinus Nijhoff, 1990).

[84] See the summary of national laws in Saul, *Defining Terrorism in International Law* (above n 34) 262–69.

Saul, B, 'Criminality and Terrorism' in AM Salinas de Friás, KLH Samuel, and ND White (eds), *Counter-Terrorism: International Law and Practice* (Oxford, Oxford University Press, 2012).

——, *Defining Terrorism in International Law* (Oxford, Oxford University Press, 2016).

——, 'Enhancing Civilian Protection by Engaging Non-state Armed Groups under International Humanitarian Law' (2017) 22(1) *Journal of Conflict and Security Law* 39–66.

——, 'The Legal Response of the League of Nations to Terrorism' (2006) 4 *Journal of International Criminal Justice* 78.

Shearer, I, *Extradition in International Law* (Manchester, Manchester University Press, 1971).

Sofaer, A, 'The Political Offence Exception and Terrorism' (1986) 15 *Denver Journal of International Law and Policy* 125.

Stanbrook, I and Stanbrook, C, *Extradition Law and Practice*, 2nd edn (Oxford, Oxford University Press, 2000).

Stein, T, 'Extradition' in *Max Planck Encyclopedia of Public International Law* (Oxford University Press online database, article updated February 2011).

United Nations, *Yearbook of the International Law Commission 1954, Volume I*, summary records of the sixth session (3 June–28 July 1954).

United Nations High Commissioner for Human Rights, 'Report on the Protection of Human Rights and Fundamental Freedoms while Countering Terrorism', A/HRC/8/13 (2 June 2008), https://digitallibrary.un.org/record/628535/files/A_HRC_8_13-EN.pdf.

United Nations Human Rights Committee, 'Consideration of Reports Submitted by State Parties: Concluding Observations – USA', CCPR/C/USA/CO/3 (15 September 2006).

Van den Wijngaert, C, *The Political Offence Exception to Extradition* (Boston, Kluwer, 1980).

Werner, W, 'Self-Determination and Civil War' (2001) 6(2) *Journal of Conflict and Security Law* 171–90.

15

Indirectly Inciting Terrorism? Crimes of Expression and the Limits of the Law

HELEN DUFFY AND KATE PITCHER*

I. INTRODUCTION

In March 2018, two Spanish musicians were independently convicted for rapping 'praise for terrorism'.[1] A year earlier, twenty-one-year-old Cassandra Vera was convicted and sentenced to a year in prison for posting jokes on Twitter about the 1973 assassination of 'a senior figure in the Franco dictatorship', which, despite their historic nature, were found to glorify terrorism and humiliate victims – conduct that would subsequently be deemed a 'bad taste joke but not subject to criminal law' by Spain's highest court, the *Tribunal Supremo*.[2] The month after Vera was convicted, Mohamed Ramadan, an Egyptian former human rights lawyer, was convicted *in absentia* for inciting terrorism under Egypt's new counterterrorism legislation and sentenced to ten years' imprisonment for posts on social media that insulted the incumbent Egyptian President.[3] A few months before that, a French teenager was found

* Kate Pitcher is a former research associate who contributed to this chapter between August 2016 and 26 February 2017.

[1] Valtonyc and Pablo Hasel were sentenced respectively to three and two years in prison. See Tribunal Supremo, Sala de lo Penal Sentencia 79/2018 (15 February 2018); and Audiencia Nacional, Sala de lo Penal, Penal Sentencia 3/2018 (2 March 2018).

[2] Case no STS 493/2018, ECLI: ES:TS:2018:493, Decision of the Spanish Supreme Court (26 February 2018); and A France-Presse, 'Spanish Woman Given Jail Term for Tweeting Jokes about Franco-Era Assassination', *Guardian* (30 March 2017), https://www.theguardian.com/world/2017/mar/30/spanish-woman-given-jail-term-for-tweeting-jokes-about-franco-era-assassination.

[3] Ramadan formerly worked for the Arabic Network for Human Rights Information. For responses to his case, see Amnesty International, 'Egypt: 10-Year Prison Term for Insulting President an Outrageous Assault on Freedom of Expression', *Amnesty International* (13 April 2017), https://www.amnesty.org/en/latest/news/2017/04/egypt-10-year-prison-term-for-insulting-president-an-outrageous-assault-on-freedom-of-expression; and Front Line Defenders, 'Mohamed Ramadan Sentenced under Counter-Terrorism Law', *Front Line Defenders* (13 April 2017), https://www.frontlinedefenders.org/en/case/mohamed-ramadan-sentenced-under-counter-terrorism-law.

guilty and given a three-month suspended sentence under parallel provisions on glorifying terrorism by naming his WiFi network 'Daesh 21'.[4] Meanwhile, in Turkey, in the same period, hundreds of journalists, academics, lawyers, and other human rights defenders were arrested for 'propagandising' for terrorism.[5]

It is tempting to dismiss these as extreme cases that make their way into headlines precisely because they are exceptional, but developments in the counterterrorism field suggest otherwise. There is a global trend with international, regional, and national offshoots that sees the criminalisation and prosecution of the expression of ideas. This trend upends the balance enshrined in the law between the appropriate preventive role of criminal law and the protection of freedom of expression. At its core, freedom of expression, often described as one of the essential foundations of democracy, embraces the freedom to express ideas and opinions that 'offend, shock, or disturb'.[6] As the European Court of Human Rights (ECtHR) has reminded us, 'Such are the demands of … pluralism, tolerance and broadmindedness without which there is no "democratic society".'[7]

While freedom of expression is not absolute, restrictions on it are correspondingly exceptional and must be strictly construed.[8] Incitement to violence has long and consistently been recognised as one of those exceptions, providing a legitimate basis to restrict free expression and in certain circumstances a basis for individual criminal responsibility. However, emerging examples of 'crimes of expression' across very different political and legal systems transform the international legal landscape and call for urgent consideration of the limits on permissible interferences with freedom of expression, specifically the acceptable reach of criminal law.

Around the globe, legislation has proliferated, enshrining ever more expansive offences based on sharing or making available ideas and opinions deemed

[4] Le Parisien, 'Dijon: il nomme son Wifi, "Daesh 21", et est condamné à de la prison avec sursis', *Le Parisien* (4 November 2016), http://www.leparisien.fr/faits-divers/dijon-il-nomme-son-wifi-daesh-21-et-est-condamne-a-de-la-prison-avec-sursis-04-11-2016-6289875.php; and R McGuinness, 'French Teen Guilty of "Defending Terrorism" after Naming Wi-Fi Network "Daesh 21"', *Sunday Express* (7 November 2016), http://www.express.co.uk/news/world/729742/French-teen-Wi-Fi-network-Daesh-21-guilty-defending-terrorism-Dijon-France.

[5] See N Muižnieks (Council of Europe Commissioner for Human Rights), 'Memorandum on Freedom of Expression and Media Freedom in Turkey', Doc CommDH(2017)5 (15 February 2017).

[6] *Handyside v the United Kingdom*, ECtHR Judgment (Application 5493/72) (7 December 1976) para 49; see also *The Observer Ltd & Others and Guardian Newspapers Ltd & Others v the United Kingdom*, ECtHR, Report of the Commission (Application13585/88) (12 July 1990) para 75; *Ürper & Others v Turkey*, ECtHR Judgment (Applications 14526/07, 14747/07, 15022/07, 15737/07, 36137/07, 47245/07, 50371/07, 50372/07 and 54637/07) (20 October 2009) para 35; *Case of Döner & Others v Turkey*, ECtHR Judgment (Application 29994/02) (7 March 2017) para 98; *Ekin v France*, ECtHR Judgment (Application 39288/98) (17 July 2001) para 56; *Ceylan v Turkey*, ECtHR Judgment (Application 23556/94) (8 July 1999) para 32; and *Zana v Turkey*, ECtHR Judgment (Application 69/1996/688/880) (25 November 1997) para 51.

[7] *Handyside v UK* (ibid) para 49.

[8] *Ceylan v Turkey* (above n 6) para 32; and *Zana v Turkey* (above n 6) para 51.

'dangerous' to society in an era of terrorism. These crimes of expression include the offences of direct incitement, instigation, and inducement to commit violent acts, the criminalisation of which is well established in some form in domestic systems and reflected in international criminal law and practice.[9] Of particular note is the tendency to criminalise and punish (often with gradually more onerous penalties) *indirect* incitement of terrorism; this includes speech that does not contribute or even necessarily aim to contribute to acts of violence but which encourages, praises, or justifies an ever broader range of activity deemed to constitute terrorism or extremism.

The mounting criminalisation and prosecution of crimes of expression have not transpired in a vacuum. First, the trend has emerged in the face of realities surrounding terrorist attacks, travel, and recruitment, in particular the extensive use of social media and the Internet by Islamic State (IS) and its perceived impact on 'lone actor' attacks, recruitment, and 'foreign fighter' mobilisation.[10] Second, international and regional legal measures, notably UN Security Council Resolution 1624, have 'called on' states to criminalise certain forms of speech associated loosely with the dissemination of 'terrorist ideology'.[11] These developments form part of what has been described as increased emphasis by the Security Council on coercive responses and an expanded role for the Council in 'directing national legislative practice' in the criminal sphere.[12] Third, these developments in turn form part of a broader incremental shift towards a more proactive and preventive approach to criminal law, particularly in the counter-terrorism context.[13] The understandable desire to prevent acts of terrorism has

[9] See below s II; and other examples in Annex I of B van Ginkel, 'Incitement to Terrorism: A Matter of Prevention or Repression?' International Centre for Counter-Terrorism (ICCT) Research Paper (August 2011), https://www.icct.nl/download/file/ICCT-Van-Ginkel-Incitement-To-Terrorism-August-2011.pdf.

[10] The extent of this impact may not be thoroughly understood, and factors are multiple. See R Frenett and T Silverman, 'Foreign Fighters: Motivations for Travel to Foreign Conflicts' in A de Guttry, F Capone, and C Paulussen (eds), *Foreign Fighters under International Law and Beyond* (The Hague, Springer, 2016); P Gurski, *Western Foreign Fighters: The Threat to Homeland and International Security* (Lanham, Rowman and Littlefield, 2017); UN Office of Counter-Terrorism, *Enhancing the Understanding of the Foreign Terrorist Fighters Phenomenon in Syria* (July 2017), https://www.un.org/en/counterterrorism/assets/img/Report_Final_20170727.pdf, 5; JM Berger, 'Promoting Disengagement from Violent Extremism', ICCT Policy Brief (August 2016), https://icct.nl/wp-content/uploads/2016/08/CVE-Policy-Brief-FINAL.pdf; and K Gilsinan, 'Is ISIS's Social-Media Power Exaggerated?' *Atlantic* (23 February 2015).

[11] See UN Security Council Resolution 1624, S/RES/1624 (14 September 2005), http://unscr.com/en/resolutions/doc/1624. See further section II below regarding the plethora of international instruments that have ricocheted around the globe during the last decade.

[12] F Ní Aoláin, 'The UN Security Council, Global Watch Lists, Biometrics, and the Threat to the Rule of Law', *Just Security* (17 January 2018), https://www.justsecurity.org/51075/security-council-global-watch-lists-biometrics/.

[13] H Duffy, *The War on Terror and the Framework of International Law*, 2nd edn (Cambridge, Cambridge University Press, 2015) ch 4; and more broadly, L Zedner, 'Pre-Crime and Post-Criminology' (2007) 11(2) *Theoretical Criminology* 261–81. For Security Council resolutions embracing a preventive criminal law approach in the context of foreign terrorist fighters, see in particular UNSC Resolution 2178 (2014), S/RES/2178 (24 September 2014); and UNSC Resolution 2396 (2017), S/$ES/2396 (21 December 2017).

led to efforts to defend 'further up the field'.[14] Further 'operational' challenges in obtaining and using admissible evidence to prosecute terrorist activity itself[15] also feed an impetus towards broader criminalisation of associated offences based on, for example, what people say rather than what they do.[16]

On one view, the shift towards increased engagement of criminal law may in certain circumstances mark a positive change. Criminal investigation and prosecution, as well as countering impunity for serious crimes, may be seen as dimensions of a rule-of-law response to terrorism, reflecting positive state obligations under international human rights law (IHRL).[17] Likewise, the principle of legality and its attendant safeguards may well be better served through the use of criminal law than the alternatives that have characterised much of the dark side of counterterrorism practice in recent years, such as arbitrary detention, detainee torture and abuse, targeted killings, deportation, and executive measures.

Nevertheless, the appropriateness, legitimacy, and effectiveness of criminal law responses cannot be assumed. Resort to criminal law can serve these ends only so far as it is justified by and unfolds in a manner consistent with basic principles of criminal law and international human rights law. Just as human rights law may require resort to criminal law as a legal obligation in certain circumstances, it also constrains overly expansive and coercive responses.[18] This framework maintains the exceptional nature – and power – of criminal law and acknowledges that its implementation must occur in a context that respects the range of human rights at stake. Difficult questions therefore arise as to the extent to which criminal law can or should reach back to the 'pre-crime' phase, or out to environments that seem to nourish or sustain criminality.[19] How far can criminal law stretch in the name of terrorism prevention?

The challenges are real, and the question of limits is complex. There is certainly no simple blueprint for when prosecution is a permissible and

[14] D Anderson (UK Independent Reviewer of Terrorism Legislation), 'Shielding the Compass: How to Fight Terrorism without Defeating the Law' (2013), https://terrorismlegislationreviewer.independent.gov.uk/wp-content/uploads/2013/04/SHIELDING-THE-COMPASS1.pdf.

[15] This may be due to investigative challenges and, commonly in this field, intelligence restrictions or indeed unlawfulness in the way that evidence was obtained. See Duffy (above n 13) ch 4.

[16] Anderson (above n 14) 6.

[17] States are obliged to investigate and, where appropriate, prosecute serious violations of human rights, within the framework of human rights law and consistently with the right of the accused. Note, however, that the 'seriousness' of the crimes in question in the terrorism context varies starkly. Moreover, as noted below, these positive obligations must be consistent with the human rights and criminal law discussed in this chapter. For a critical reflection on positive obligations and the relationship with criminal law, see L Lazarus, 'Positive Obligations and Criminal Justice: Duties to Protect or Coerce?' in L Zedner and JV Roberts (eds), *Principles and Values in Criminal Law and Criminal Justice: Essays in Honour of Andrew Ashworth* (Oxford, Oxford University Press, 2012).

[18] See, eg, below s III on the principles of criminal law restraint, as well as the need for the law to be implemented in ways that are consistent with the rights of the accused. See also Lazarus (ibid).

[19] Duffy (above n 13); and Zedner (above n 13), who has referred to an 'emerging pre-crime society'.

appropriate restriction on free speech. However, as this chapter explores, there is a flexible legal framework that constrains a rule-of-law approach to the punishment of crimes of expression in the era of modern terrorism. This must be brought to bear in the analysis of the many examples of emerging national and international practice, as illustrated in the section below.

II. PRACTICE

In recent years, legal frameworks around the globe have changed to embrace a range of new 'preventive' terrorism-related offences, such as acts preparatory to terrorism, possession, association with or support for terrorist entities, as well as the crimes of expression that are the focus of this chapter. A key impetus for this flurry of legislative activity around the globe was a series of international and regional developments calling for states to adopt invigorated and progressively more expansive responses to certain forms of expression.

A. International Legal Measures against 'Incitement': The UN, Council of Europe, and EU

Promoted by the United Kingdom in the aftermath of the '7/7' London bombings, UN Security Council Resolution 1624 (2005) called on states 'to take all measures as may be necessary and appropriate and in accordance with their obligations under international law to counter incitement of terrorist acts'.[20] States were called upon specifically to 'prohibit by law' incitement to terrorism.[21] However, neither 'terrorist acts' nor 'incitement' were defined. In this way, the Resolution was reminiscent of post-9/11 resolutions, including SC Resolution 1373, which imposed wide-reaching terrorism-related obligations without defining terrorism and was criticised *inter alia* for 'opening the hunting season on terrorism without defining the target'.[22] UNSC Resolution 1624 expanded the hunt by including undefined 'incitement' to terrorism.[23] The Resolution's preamble cast the net further by 'repudiating' what it refers to as 'attempts at the justification or glorification (*apologie*) of terrorist acts'.

The role of Resolution 1624 in authorising broad-reaching crimes of expression should not be overstated. It is a nonbinding resolution that does not specifically deal with *criminal* law responses at all. With regard to the reference

[20] Resolution 1624 (above n 11) para 3.

[21] Ibid, paras 1 and 3.

[22] Statement of Jean-François Gayraud, Chief Commissioner of the French National Police, and of French judge David Sénat, as reported in F Andreau-Guzmán, 'Terrorism and Human Rights No 2', International Commission of Jurists Occasional Paper (March 2003) 26.

[23] It failed to refer to the SC's own 'guidance' on a possible definition drawn up some years before in response to criticism – UNSC Res 1566, UN Doc S/RES/1566 (8 October 2004).

to 'glorification' (unlike incitement), it does not call on states to prohibit it by law. It therefore falls to states to consider carefully the appropriateness of criminalisation and prosecution, consistent with law, including the human rights constraints explicitly recognised in the Resolution. In practice, however, such distinctions may have been lost in translation through domestic implementation processes, and the Resolution has been cited in support of legislative and prosecutorial action against the full range of forms of speech referred to in the Resolution.[24]

An important subsequent development was the UN Secretary-General's Report on Resolution 1624, which went some way in trying to rein in the impact of the Resolution. First, it defined incitement quite strictly as:

> a direct call to engage in terrorism … with the intention that this will promote terrorism, and in a context in which the call is directly causally responsible for increasing the actual likelihood of a terrorist act occurring.[25]

Second, the Report drew a bright line between direct incitement on the one hand and glorification or *apologie* on the other, stating unequivocally that while 'the first may be legally prohibited, the second may not'.[26] It noted that *apologie* may offend, but it should not be prohibited on the basis that it 'applauds past acts' but only where it meets the definition of incitement set out above.

Around the same time as UNSC Resolution 1624, incitement to terrorism was also included in the Council of Europe (CoE) Convention on the Prevention of Terrorism,[27] which in several ways reaches further than UNSC Resolution 1624. State parties are specifically required to establish as *criminal* offences:

> the distribution, or otherwise making available, of a message to the public, with the intent to incite the commission of a terrorist offence, where such conduct, whether or not directly advocating terrorist offences, causes a danger that one or more such offences may be committed.[28]

The Convention's Explanatory Memorandum states, with considerable ambiguity, that 'public provocation' may be done directly or indirectly, and the provisions allow 'a certain amount of discretion' for states parties.[29] Consistent with the focus on criminalisation, however, the incitement it covers is qualified by two important elements: first, the alleged offender must have the 'intent to incite the

[24] See Reports by Member States pursuant to Security Council Resolution 1624, https://www.un.org/sc/ctc/resources/assessments/. Note in particular the French statement linking 'extending [the law] to include the offence of incitement to commit terrorist acts', which, as noted above, it subsequently did. Implementation of United Nations Security Council Resolution 1624: Report of France in response to the questions of the Counter-Terrorism Committee (S/2006/547) 4.

[25] UN General Assembly, 'The Protection of Human Rights and Fundamental Freedoms while Countering Terrorism: Report of the Secretary General', UN Doc A/63/337 (28 August 2008) para 61.

[26] Ibid.

[27] Council of Europe Convention on the Prevention of Terrorism, CETS No 196 adopted in May 2005, in force from 1 June 2007.

[28] Ibid, Art 5: Public Provocation to Commit a Terrorist Offence.

[29] Explanatory Report to the Council of Europe Convention on the Prevention of Terrorism (16 May 2005) paras 95–98.

commission of a terrorist offence'; and second, there must be a 'danger' of an offence being committed as a result.[30]

At the same time, the Convention is extremely broad-reaching and vague in the range of speech captured, the nature of any impact (causing a 'danger'), and the individual's intent (to commit a terrorist *offence*). Concerns as to the breadth of speech are borne out by the Explanatory Memorandum, which specifically lists 'presenting a terrorist offence as necessary and justified' and 'the dissemination of messages praising the perpetrator of an attack, the denigration of victims [and] calls for funding for terrorist organisations or other similar behaviour' as examples of the conduct covered.[31] This has provided a basis for the criminalisation of glorification or *apologie*, even though the Convention does not specifically use these terms. The scope is plainly far broader than the 'direct public incitement' in the UN Secretary-General's Report on Resolution 1624.[32]

A third important successive development was the Directive on Combating Terrorism, adopted by the EU Parliament and Council on 15 March 2017, requiring the criminalisation of public provocation to commit a terrorist offence.[33] Article 5 states:

> Member States shall take the necessary measures to ensure that the distribution, or otherwise making available *by any means, whether online or offline*, of a message to the public, with the intent to incite the commission of one of the offences listed in points (a) to (i) of Article 3(*1*), where such conduct, *directly or indirectly, such as by the glorification of terrorist acts, advocates the commission of* terrorist offences, *thereby causing* a danger that one or more such offences may be committed, is punishable as a criminal offence when committed intentionally.[34]

While stricter in some respects than its predecessors, the Directive is strikingly broad in others. It delineates more clearly what might constitute a terrorist 'offence'[35] and includes some level of criminal intent and the existence of a 'credible danger'.[36] It seeks to exclude 'the expression of radical, polemic, or controversial views in the public debate'.[37]

[30] Ibid, paras 99–100.

[31] Ibid, para 98.

[32] For expressions of concern, see, eg, International Commission of Jurists (ICJ), 'Response to the European Commission Consultation on Inciting, Aiding or Abetting Terrorist Offences' (16 February 2007), available at https://www.icj.org/response-to-the-european-commission-consultation-on-inciting-aiding-or-abetting-terrorist-offences/ (accessed 5 March 2019), 1–2.

[33] Council and Parliament Directive 2017/541 of 15 March 2017 on combating terrorism and replacing Council Framework Decision 2002/475/JHA and amending Council Decision 2005/671/JHA [2017] OJ L88/6.

[34] Ibid, Title III, Art 5, emphasis added.

[35] Unlike earlier efforts, 'terrorist offences' are defined in the Directive by reference to a list of acts found within Article 3(1), which includes kidnapping, attacks upon a person's life, the release of dangerous substances, and threatening to commit any of the listed acts, provided they are committed with one of four aims. See the EU Directive (above n 33) Title II, Art 3.

[36] Ibid, para 10.

[37] Ibid, para 40.

However, the Directive is wide-reaching in its approach to incitement and provocation, stating that they comprise '*inter alia*, the glorification and justification of terrorism or the dissemination of messages or images … including those related to the victims of terrorism as a way to gather support for terrorist causes or seriously intimidating the population'.[38] The crime can be committed not only by the individual who authored the message but also by others that 'make it available' in any way, such as by reposting online content, lending a book, or distributing an image – without the need for any proven impact on the public.

The Directive's ambiguous offences of advocating or making available 'dangerous messages' are a further step beyond the indirect incitement offences of the CoE Convention and considerable strides away from both the notion of direct incitement of violent acts of terrorism in the UN Secretary-General's Report on Resolution 1624 and international criminal law and practice.[39] The pattern that emerges is of a gradual expansion of criminal offences from the international level to the European level. Most significant in practice is how these then translate on the national level.

B. National Practice

Certain crimes of expression have long been features of national legal systems, as reflected in international criminal law. Incitement or provocation are generally treated domestically as 'a particular form of criminal participation' or as 'a form of complicity'.[40] As noted during the International Criminal Tribunal for Rwanda (ICTR), common and civil law systems embrace crimes of incitement and usually require that the incitement be done publicly and directly.[41] Directness requires 'more than mere vague or indirect suggestion', and the incitement must be directed towards a particular offence.[42]

By contrast, what are sometimes referred to as offences of 'indirect incitement' contain no such qualifications of being 'public' and/or 'direct'. There may or may not be any required link between the accused's conduct – in this context consisting often only of speech, publication, blog, or tweet – and any subsequent harm or influence on other persons. There may or may not be the obligation to prove that an accused person *intended* to incite any crime at all. Some such laws encompass speech that justifies or legitimises past acts or dishonours victims of terrorism – disconnected in any tangible way from

[38] Ibid, para 10.

[39] See below s III-A regarding the limited modes of liability under international criminal law.

[40] *Prosecutor v Jean-Paul Akayesu (Trial Judgement)*, ICTR-96-4-T, International Criminal Tribunal for Rwanda (ICTR) (2 September 1998), paras 552 and 555 et seq.

[41] Ibid.

[42] Ibid, paras 555–57.

the risk of or intent to contribute to future crime and blurring the line between incitement as a contribution to crime and perhaps morally dubious or offensive expressions of opinion.

This section will illustrate a selection of recent examples of laws and practice criminalising and prosecuting terror-related crimes of expression. Practice is emerging rapidly, and this chapter does not attempt to provide a full survey of all relevant developments. But a range of practice indicates that some states have relied upon pre-existing crimes, sometimes dusting off rarely used criminal provisions, while others have subjected existing laws to expansive interpretations,[43] and yet more have introduced new legislation (sometimes hastily) to cover broader forms of 'indirect' incitement to or support for terrorism.[44] The result is a broad spectrum of offences criminalising 'dangerous' expression, such as provocation or encouragement,[45] glorification,[46] justification,[47] apology,[48] possession,[49] dissemination or making available prohibited information or materials,[50] or professing to be a member of or associated with prohibited organisations.[51]

[43] Examples include Germany and Costa Rica. See van Ginkel (above n 9) Annex I, 20–21 and 42–43.

[44] Examples include Tunisia, the United Kingdom, France, Spain, and Turkey. See van Ginkel (above n 9) Annex I, 38–42, 87–88, 95, and 97–99; B Saul, 'Australia and International Counter-Terrorism Law and Practice' in D Rothwell and E Crawford (eds), *International Law in Australia*, 3rd edn (Sydney, Thomson Reuters, 2016); and Duffy (above n 13) ch 2.

[45] See, eg, 'encouragement of terrorism' in the UK Terrorism Act 2006, https://www.legislation.gov.uk/ukpga/2006/11/contents.

[46] Ibid. For criticism of UK laws, see Muižnieks (above n 5); and UNHRC, 'Concluding Observations in Consideration of Reports Submitted by States Parties', CCPR/C/GBR/CO/6 (30 July 2008), https://www.refworld.org/docid/48a9411a2.html. For criticism of Canadian Bill C-51, which proposed amending the Canadian Security Intelligence Act to include similar new crimes of 'promoting' or 'advocating' terrorism offences, see UNHRC, 'Concluding Observations on the Sixth Periodic Report of Canada', CCPR/C/CAN/CO/6 (13 August 2015). For criticism of Spanish 'glorification and justification' laws, see UNHRC, 'Report of the Special Rapporteur Martin Scheinin: Addendum – Mission to Spain', A/HRC/10/3/Add.2 (16 December 2008), para 11.

[47] Eg, Russian Federal Law No 35-Fz (6 March 2006) on Counteracting Terrorism criminalises 'justification of terrorism' and 'popularisation of terrorist ideas'.

[48] See, eg, the French *Code pénal*, Art 421(2)5 (created by Loi N° 2014-1353 du 13 novembre 2014), reflected in Spanish law or recent additions in Peru and Honduras. See also the joint press release by the Inter-American Commission on Human Rights and the Office of the UNHCHR (23 February 2017) on changes to the Honduran penal code, http://www.oas.org/en/iachr/expression/showarticle.asp?artID=1054&lID=1 (accessed 5 March 2019).

[49] See, eg, the Australian Criminal Code Act (1995), Sched, ss 101.4–101.5, which refers to 'possessing things connected with terrorist acts' and 'collecting or making documents likely to facilitate terrorist acts'.

[50] See, eg, Wetboek van Strafrecht (Criminal Code, Netherlands), Art 132 (as translated in *Prosecutor v Imane B et al*, Judgment of 10 December 2015 [the 'Context case'], Case Nos 09/842489-14, 09/767038-14, 09/767313-14, 09/767174-13, 09/765004-15, 09/767146-14, 09/767256-14, 09/767238-14, 09/827053-15, 09/767237-14, 09/765002-15, and 09/767077-14, http://uitspraken.rechtspraak.nl/inziendocument?id=ECLI:NL:RBDHA:2015:16102, para 11.12. For further discussion of this case, see below s II-B-iii.

[51] See, eg, Strafgesetzbuch (German Criminal Code), ss 129 and 129a.

i. Encouragement Offences in the United Kingdom

The United Kingdom was one of the driving forces behind UNSC Resolution 1624[52] and unsurprisingly moved quickly to implement it. The Terrorism Act 2006 provided for new terrorist offences, including encouragement of terrorism and dissemination of terrorist material,[53] 'complementing' the pre-existing common law offence of incitement.[54] Statements that are likely to be *understood* as a direct or indirect encouragement to commit terrorist acts are covered, including those that glorify terrorism in a way that that others might infer that a terrorist act should be copied.[55] Whether an individual *is* actually incited to commit an offence and whether the person making the statement so intended are 'irrelevant'.[56] The new provisions have been criticised, including by the UN Human Rights Committee, due to their breadth, their susceptibility to abuse, and their disproportionate impact upon freedom of expression.[57]

Numerous convictions have followed, many of them relating to manifestations of support for IS through social media. Some involve statements directly referring to 'tak[ing] to arms and not the keyboard', albeit in quite a general undirected way, as in Tareena Shakil's tweets and posting of IS iconography,[58] which ultimately led to a sentence of two years' imprisonment for the encouragement of terrorism.[59] Often what constitutes 'encouragement' in these cases is broader though. Troublingly, it could embrace opinions and debate on the causes of terrorism. In the Mohammed Moshin Ameen case, for example, the accused was described by the court as expressing support for IS and risking 'the emulation of terrorist actions' through opinions which 'establish[ed] religious and social grounds for terrorist action'.[60]

[52] UN Security Council, 5261st Meeting, UN Doc S/PV.5261 (14 September 2005).

[53] See, eg, the Explanatory Notes to s 1–2 of the UK Terrorism Act 2006.

[54] Ibid.

[55] UK Terrorism Act 2006 (above n 45) ss 1(1)–(3).

[56] Ibid, s 1(5).

[57] See UN Human Rights Committee, 'Consideration of Reports Submitted by States Parties under Article 40 of the Covenant: Concluding observations of the Human Rights Committee on the United Kingdom of Great Britain and Northern Ireland', UN Doc CCPR/C/GBR/CO/6 (30 July 2008), para 26.

[58] See BBC News, 'Tareena Shakil Jailed for Six Years for Joining IS', *BBC News* (1 February 2016), http://www.bbc.com/news/uk-england-35460697; and the 2016 summary of *R v Tareena Shakil* by the Crown Prosecution Service on the CPS webpage 'The Counter-terrorism Division of the Crown Prosecution Service (CPS): Successful Prosecutions since the end of 2006' (10 February 2017), https://www.cps.gov.uk/counter-terrorism-division-crown-prosecution-service-cps-successful-prosecutions-end-2006 (accessed 6 March 2019).

[59] Crown Prosecution Service, 'The Counter-terrorism Division of the Crown Prosecution Service: Successful Prosecutions' (ibid). See also the summary in M Hill (UK Independent Reviewer of Terrorism Legislation), 'The Terrorism Acts in 2016: Report on the Operation of the Terrorism Acts 2000 and 2006' (January 2018), https://terrorismlegislationreviewer.independent.gov.uk/wp-content/uploads/2018/01/Terrorism-Acts-in-2016.pdf.

[60] See Press Association, 'Security Guard Jailed for Five Years over Tweets Glorifying Isis', *Guardian* (29 April 2016), https://www.theguardian.com/uk-news/2016/apr/28/security-guard-mohammed-moshin-ameen-jailed-for-five-years-over-tweets-glorifying-isis; and the 2016 summary of *R v Mohammed Moshin Ameen* by the Crown Prosecution Service on the CPS webpage 'The Counter-terrorism Division of the Crown Prosecution Service (CPS): Successful Prosecutions since the End of 2006' (ibid). After pleading guilty, Ameen was sentenced to five years' imprisonment due

In turn, Anjem Choudary and Mohammed Rahman were convicted for the related offence of 'inviting support for a proscribed organisation' by signing an oath of allegiance and for two lectures broadcast on the Internet, which were considered to endorse the legitimacy of an Islamic caliphate.[61] The accused argued that their support was for *an* Islamic state, rather than specifically IS, but this was not given weight by the court. They had not called for violent acts, and no evidence was presented to suggest anyone had been incited to commit a crime, but the judge found that they were 'inviting support for ISIS' and had 'indirectly encouraged violent terrorist activity'.[62] The judgment noted they had 'said nothing to limit' the way their statements were understood, and 'said nothing to condemn any aspect of what [IS] was doing'.[63] They were convicted and sentenced to five and a half years' imprisonment for what they had said – and what they had not.

ii. 'Apology' and 'Justification' Laws in France, Spain, and Beyond

A swathe of domestic laws criminalise conduct that 'justifies', 'glorifies', expresses 'sympathy' for acts of terrorism or terrorists, or provides apology (*apologie*) for terrorism, defined as the 'public expression of praise, support or justification of terrorists and/or terrorist acts'.[64] Within Europe, states such as Denmark, Spain, France, the United Kingdom, and Turkey[65] have related criminal offences, while others have been proposed in Germany, Belgium, and the Netherlands.[66] Outside Europe, Canada,[67] Peru,[68] Russia,[69] Bahrain,[70] and

to the 'explicit and intentional nature of the encouragement and by the persistence with which it was pursued'. He had sent 'approximately 8,000 tweets using 16 different Twitter accounts in 42 different names' between March and November 2015.

[61] *R v Anjem Choudary and Mohammed Rahman*, Sentencing Remarks of Holroyde J (Central Criminal Court, 6 September 2016), https://www.judiciary.gov.uk/wp-content/uploads/2016/09/r-v-choudary-sentencing.pdf.

[62] Ibid.

[63] Ibid. See further the International Crimes Database, '*R v Anjem Choudary and Mohammed Rahman*' (UK Central Criminal Court, 6 September 2016), http://www.internationalcrimesdatabase.org/Case/3273.

[64] O Ribbelink, '"Apologie du terrorisme" and "incitement to terrorism": Analytical Report', Council of Europe Committee of Experts on Terrorism (24 June 2004) 5, cited in C Forcese and K Roach, 'Terrorist Babble and the Limits of the Law: Assessing a Prospective Canadian Terrorism Glorification Offense', TSAS Working Paper Series No 15-02 (2015), https://papers.ssrn.com/sol3/papers.cfm?abstract_id=2546555, 28. See further examples below.

[65] Ribbelink (ibid); and Turkish Counter-terrorism Law 2006, Art 7 of Law 3713.

[66] See, eg. the proposals in Amnesty International, 'Amnesty International Report 2016/17: The State of the World's Human Rights' (2017), https://www.amnesty.org.au/wp-content/uploads/2017/02/air201617-english_2016-17.pdf, 43.

[67] National Post, 'Don't Criminalize the Glorification of Terrorism, Law Professors Urge Government', *National Post* (22 January 2015), http://nationalpost.com/news/canada/dont-criminalize-the-glorification-of-terrorism-law-professors-urge-government-citing-uncertain-constitutional-terrain.

[68] See Legislative Decree 1233 (26 September 2015). See also US Department of State, 'Country Reports: Western Hemisphere Overview', Country Reports on Terrorism 2015, available at https://www.state.gov/j/ct/rls/crt/2015/257519.htm (accessed 6 March 2019).

[69] See Russian Federal Law No 35-Fz (6 March 2006) on Counteraction against Terrorism.

[70] In 2015 Bahrain's legislature approved a law increasing sentences for those who 'promote or glorify' terrorist acts to ten years. See US Department of State, 'Country Reports: Middle East and

Israel[71] are among the many states globally to adopt or propose wide-reaching offences that relate, in different formulations, to the justification or glorification of terrorism.[72]

France has been particularly active in its resort to domestic laws covering *provocation* and '*apologie du terrorisme*' in the wake of attacks on its territory. While previously enshrined in the 'Press Law' (*Loi sur la liberté de la presse*) of 29 July 1881,[73] the offences were shifted into the French Criminal Code (*Code pénal*) in November 2014 in order to, *inter alia*, apply different procedural rules to expedite the criminal justice process.[74] The offence of provocation to terrorism was amended so that it need no longer be carried out publicly, though it must still be direct.[75] In contrast, *apologie* retains the 'public' element, which may include commission online through a message distributed to an undetermined number of people,[76] and is broadly framed as presenting or favourably commenting upon a terrorist attack that has already been committed.[77] There need be no link to any future criminal act.

Since their enactment, the new crimes have been frequently prosecuted in France,[78] presenting a 'litmus test' for freedom of expression.[79] This practice

North Africa Overview', Country Reports on Terrorism 2015, available at https://www.state.gov/j/ct/rls/crt/2015/257517.htm (accessed 6 March 2019).

[71] See s 24 of Israel's Counter Terrorism Law 5775-2015, which, in addition to an offence of incitement to terrorism, includes demonstrating solidarity with a terrorist organisation or an act of terrorism, which may be by public praise or support, display of flags or symbols, utterance of slogans and anthems. See also E Chachko, 'Israel's New Counter-Terrorism Law', *Lawfare* (13 July 2016), https://www.lawfareblog.com/israels-new-counterterrorism-law.

[72] Others, including Argentina, have long had such laws on the books but rarely invoked them in practice until recent years. Charges were brought and dropped against journalist Pablo Suarez, and recently indigenous Maipuche campaigners in the south have been threatened with prosecution under the anti-terrorism laws. Regarding the first, see Reporters without Borders, 'Newspaper Editor Facing 12 Years in Prison under Anti-terrorism Law', *Reporters without Borders: For Freedom of Information* (14 May 2014), https://rsf.org/en/news/newspaper-editor-facing-12-years-prison-under-anti-terrorism-law; and regarding prosecution in Argentina and Chile, see S Weinstein, 'Are we all Terrorists?', *New Internationalist* (1 December 2017), https://newint.org/features/2017/12/01/are-we-all-terrorists.

[73] *Loi sur la liberté de la presse* focused on freedom of the press but also included this offence. See D Barak-Erez and D Sharia, 'Freedom of Speech, Support for Terrorism, and the Challenge of Global Constitutional Law' (2011) 2(1) *Harvard National Security Journal* 1–30, 9.

[74] *Code pénal* (France), Art 421-2-5, which includes '*provocation ou apologie du terrorisme*'. It refers to the crimes of direct provocation and public apology for terrorism (*provoquer directement à des actes de terrorisme ou de faire publiquement l'apologie de ces actes*). For additional discussion of counterterrorism in France, see the chapter in this volume by Marc-Antoine Granger.

[75] The offender must have foreseen the material facts, such as the identification of particular person or a place: Ministère de la Justice, 'Circulaire du 5 décembre 2014 de présentation de la loi n°2014-1353', Bulletin Officiel du Ministère de la Justice, NOR : JUSD1429083C (5 December 2014), http://www.textes.justice.gouv.fr/art_pix/JUSD1429083C.pdf, 5; and Gouvernement Français, 'Apologie du terrorisme – Provocation au terrorisme', *Service-Public.fr* (28 February 2017), https://www.service-public.fr/particuliers/vosdroits/F32512.

[76] Ministère de la Justice, 'Circulaire du 5 décembre 2014' (ibid). The 'public' element includes comments made on social networks.

[77] Gouvernement Français, 'Apologie du terrorisme – Provocation au terrorisme' (above n 75).

[78] Le Monde avec AFP, '1847 délits d'apologie et de provocation au terrorisme enregistrés en 2016', *Le Monde* (19 January 2017), http://mobile.lemonde.fr/police-justice/article/2017/01/19/1-847-delits-d-apologie-et-de-provocation-au-terrorisme-enregistres-en-2016_5064989_1653578.html.

[79] Amnesty International, 'France Faces "Litmus Test" for Freedom of Expression as Dozens Arrested in Wake of Attacks', *Amnesty International* (16 January 2015), https://www.amnesty.org/

reflects a January 2015 circular by then-Minister for Justice Christiane Taubira calling for prosecutors to use '*la plus grande vigueur*'[80] in investigating and prosecuting, *inter alia*, *apologie* offences.[81] In the week following the Charlie Hebdo attack, which took place on 7 January 2015, at least 69 arrests took place for comments made in relation to the attack,[82] while government statistics indicate thousands of incidents and hundreds of convictions for *apologie* during 2015 and 2016 – a significant leap from only ten in 2014.[83] A broad array of expression has led to charges and convictions under these provisions: comedian Dieudonné M'Bala M'Bala, who posted the message '*Je me sens Charlie Coulibaly*' on Facebook;[84] an inebriated thirty-four-year-old who made comments supportive of the Charlie Hebdo shooters following a car accident; a twenty-one-year-old who made similar drunken comments when discovered using public transport without a valid ticket; and a twenty-seven-year-old man who published photos of jihadists described as the 'brothers in Marseille' on Facebook.[85]

Like France, Spain also criminalises both provocation and apology (*apologia*) of terrorism,[86] originally to limit expressions of support for the Basque separatist group Euskadi Ta Azkatasuna (ETA).[87] Since 2000, a broad range of speech that may lead to the 'glorification or justification (*el enaltecimiento o la justificación*) of terrorist offences, or their perpetrators, and … the humiliation of the victims of terrorist offenses or their families' has been covered.[88] In practice, Spanish

en/latest/news/2015/01/france-faces-litmus-test-freedom-expression-dozens-arrested-wake-attacks/; and Ministère de la Justice, 'Infractions commises à la suite des attentats terroristes commis les 7, 8 et 9 janvier 2015' (12 January 2015), http://www.justice.gouv.fr/publication/circ_20150113_infractions_commises_suite_attentats201510002055.pdf, Annex, 3.

[80] Ministère de la Justice, 'Infractions commises' (ibid) 1.

[81] Ibid, 2–3.

[82] See BBC News, 'Charlie Hebdo Attack: Three Days of Terror', *BBC News* (14 January 2015), http://www.bbc.com/news/world-europe-30708237; and Amnesty International, 'France Faces "Litmus Test"' (above n 79).

[83] There were 2,342 recorded incidents of glorification and provocation in 2015 and 1,847 incidents in 2016, 80% of which were public glorification of an act of terrorism: InterStats and Ministère de l'Intérieur, 'Insécurité et délinquance en 2016 : premier bilan statistique' (18 January 2017), available at https://www.interieur.gouv.fr/Interstats/Actualites/Insecurite-et-delinquance-en-2016-premier-bilan-statistique (accessed 6 March 2019), 116. There were 385 convictions in 2015 and 10 in 2014: S Joahny, 'Apologie du terrorisme, un condamné par jour', *Le Journal du Dimanche* (4 September 2016), http://www.lejdd.fr/Societe/Justice/Apologie-du-terrorisme-un-condamne-par-jour-807154.

[84] Le Monde, 'Dieudonné M'Bala M'Bala condamné à deux mois de prison avec sursis', *Le Monde* (18 March 2015), http://www.lemonde.fr/actualite-medias/article/2015/03/18/dieudonne-m-bala-m-bala-condamne-a-deux-mois-de-prison-avec-sursis_4596071_3236.html: 'I feel like Charlie Coulibaly'.

[85] L Imbert, 'Apologie d'actes terroristes : des condamnations pour l'exemple', *Le Monde* (13 January 2015), http://www.lemonde.fr/societe/article/2015/01/13/apologie-d-actes-terroristes-des-condamnations-pour-l-exemple_4555102_3224.html.

[86] See respectively Arts 18(1) and 578 of the Spanish Penal Code (10/1995, available at https://www.boe.es/buscar/act.php?id=BOE-A-1995-25444&tn=1&p=20190302#a578); and Barak-Erez and Sharia (above n 73) 7.

[87] R Minder, 'Crackdowns on Free Speech Rise across a Europe Wary of Terror', *New York Times* (24 February 2016), https://www.nytimes.com/2016/02/25/world/europe/spain-europe-protest-free-speech.html?_r=0; and BBC News, 'What is Eta?' *BBC News* (8 April 2017), http://www.bbc.com/news/world-europe-11183574.

[88] Art 578 was introduced through Organic Law No 7/2000 of 22 December 2000, and it criminalises both the 'glorification or justification' (*el enaltecimiento o la justificación*) of terrorist offences. See Barak-Erez and Sharia (above n 73) 7.

prosecutions and convictions have swept up a motley crew of individuals, forms, and content of expression under this banner.[89] Among the emblematic cases,[90] is that of Alba González Camacho, a twenty-one-year-old who was convicted and sentenced to one year's imprisonment for glorification of terrorism for social media posts. Her tweets included the bizarre promise to 'tattoo myself with the face of the person who shoots [Prime Minister] Rajoy in the neck'.[91] There was no serious suggestion that she incited any crime or intended to, or even that her posts posed any real danger; but the messages were deemed to have 'an ideological content that was highly radicalised and violent'.[92]

Perhaps more curiously still, two puppeteers, Alfonso Lázaro de la Fuente and Raúl García Pérez, were arrested and held in custody for five days for a puppet show that allegedly glorified terrorism.[93] Amidst the general chaotic antics of the show, in which a nun was stabbed with a crucifix by a pregnant witch, a judge hung himself, and a police officer blew them all up, one puppet displayed a banner bearing the sign 'Gora ALKA-ETA' (which translates to 'Up with ETA' and sounds similar to al-Qaeda).[94] It is difficult to see what the show provoked, beyond puzzlement, possible amusement for some, and offence for others.[95] While the puppeteers were eventually released by a judge and the charges dropped,[96] their arrest triggered significant debate as to how conduct such as this could conceivably constitute a crime.[97] As the case of Cassandra Vera highlighted above has shown, the courts have pushed back on evolving practice by noting that 'a penal sanction [was] not appropriate'.[98] But that case is only one of a number brought against artists, musicians, bloggers, and rappers for crimes of expression under broad Spanish legislation.[99]

[89] Between April 2014 and April 2016, 69 people were arrested as part of 'Operation Spider'; 22 were found guilty of glorifying terrorism. See 'Amnesty International Report 2016/17' (above n 66) 337.

[90] See also the Cassandra Vera case discussed above in s I and at n 2.

[91] R Minder, 'In a First for Spain, a Woman Is Convicted of Inciting Terror Over Twitter', *New York Times* (22 February 2014), https://www.nytimes.com/2014/02/23/world/europe/in-a-first-for-spain-a-woman-is-convicted-of-inciting-terror-over-twitter.html.

[92] Minder, 'In a First for Spain' (ibid), quoting the judge in the case. The prosecution relied on background pictures on González Camacho's Twitter account, including of el Grapo, Che Guevara, and Soviet soldiers in Berlin after defeating Nazi Germany.

[93] Associated Press, 'Spanish Investigation into "Terrorism-Praising" Puppet Show Shelved', *Guardian* (29 June 2016), https://www.theguardian.com/world/2016/jun/28/spanish-investigation-terrorism-praising-puppet-show-shelved-eta; and Reuters, 'Spanish Judge Frees Puppeteers Jailed for Glorifying Terrorism', *Guardian* (11 February 2016), https://www.theguardian.com/world/2016/feb/10/spanish-judge-frees-puppeteers-raul-garcia-alfonso-lazaro-basque-eta.

[94] 'Amnesty International Report 2016/17' (above n 66) 337.

[95] G Pasquini, 'Why Is the Spanish Government Afraid of a Puppet Show?' *New Yorker* (1 March 2016), https://www.newyorker.com/news/news-desk/why-is-the-spanish-government-afraid-of-a-puppet-show.

[96] Associated Press, ''Spanish Investigation Shelved' (above n 93).

[97] Pasquini (above n 95); Amnesty International, 'Puppeteers Accused of Glorifying Terrorism', Doc EUR 41/3428/2016 (12 February 2016); Minder, 'Crackdowns on Free Speech Rise' (above n 87).

[98] FJ Pérez, 'Second Spanish Rapper Sentenced to Prison for Praising Terrorism', *El País* (English) (2 March 2018), https://elpais.com/elpais/2018/03/02/inenglish/1519998382_971403.html.

[99] On 21 February 2018, musician Valtonyc Hasel's sentence was upheld by the Spanish Supreme Court. See above n 1. For the case involving his brother, Pablo Hase, see Pérez (ibid).

iii. Incitement and Dissemination in the Netherlands

In the Netherlands, long-established incitement laws have been used to increasingly wide-reaching effect in recent years.[100] In the so-called 'Context Case', several men were convicted by a District Court for the 'terrorist crime' of inciting participation in the armed conflict in Syria through their social media posts.[101] Dutch law limits incitement by the requirement of a 'direct relation … between the incitement and the criminal offence incited', and the Court found that the incitement 'can be direct or indirect'.[102] The incitement laws were broadly interpreted to include 'provoking the thought of an act, trying to establish the opinion that it is desirable or necessary and to rouse the desire to bring it about', which could occur through a 'request, an exhortation, … [or] the expression of high moral appreciation of an act'.[103] There was no requirement 'that incitement has any result' or even that the public has seen the expression: it simply must be accessible to the public, including via the Internet.[104]

The decision provides an interesting indication of the extent to which social media use can form the basis of incitement charges.[105] The Court found that incitement could arise through posts on Twitter,[106] a Facebook profile,[107] or a YouTube channel,[108] even if, as noted above, no one saw them. Complicity to incitement also arose for one co-accused as the editor of a Facebook page on which a post appeared (though messages posted in a private Facebook group did not constitute incitement because they were not publicly accessible).[109] Finally, while 'retweeting' without further comment did not constitute incitement as a 'retweet is not endorsement', this principle did not apply to an endorsement of the original tweet or where 'the retweet fits in with a series of the accused's messages of a similar nature … within a certain period'.[110] Moreover, even if a retweet alone may not constitute incitement, the Court found it can constitute dissemination of inciting material.[111]

[100] Penalties increase by a third where the incitement and dissemination concern a terrorist offence. See Arts 131 and 132 of the Dutch Criminal Code as translated in *Prosecutor v Imane* (above n 50) paras 11.6 and 11.12.

[101] *Prosecutor v Imane* (above n 50) para 11.24. Unlike Belgian courts, Dutch courts refuse to look at the impact of armed conflict and IHL on 'terrorism' allegations.

[102] *Prosecutor v Imane* (above n 50) para 11.7.

[103] Ibid, paras 11.8–11.9.

[104] Ibid, paras 11.9–11.11. Expanding further, the Court noted that 'where the court finds incitement … proved, it will also finds [sic] dissemination … proved' (para 12.2).

[105] See International Crimes Database, 'Prosecutor v Imane B et al' (10 December 2015), http://www.internationalcrimesdatabase.org/Case/3270.

[106] *Prosecutor v Imane* (above n 50) paras 12.62–12.69.

[107] Ibid, paras 12.75–12.79.

[108] Ibid, paras 12.118–12.124.

[109] Ibid.

[110] Ibid, para 11.22; and *Wetboek van Strafrecht* (Criminal Code, Netherlands), Art 131.

[111] *Wetboek van Strafrecht*, Art 132. See, eg, *Prosecutor v Imane* (above n 50) paras 12.54 and 12.56.

iv. Propagandising in Turkey

In Turkey, Article 7(2) of the Anti-Terrorism Law prohibits making 'propaganda on behalf of a terrorist organisation'. The prolific and widespread application of these vague and broad-reaching laws in Turkey in recent months and years has been described in reports from the United Nations, Council of Europe, Organization for Security and Co-operation in Europe (OSCE), and other entities[112] as giving rise to a grave crisis in respect of freedom of expression.[113] Particular concerns were raised by CoE Commissioner for Human Rights Nils Muižnieks as to 'the use of the concept of "incitement to violence", which has been systematically interpreted in a non-ECHR-compliant manner'.[114]

The extensive application of broad-reaching provisions by Turkish prosecutors and courts in a way that targets expression of dissent and criticism – perceived as inherently dangerous threats to the state – demonstrates that the stakes are high. A significant number of cases are 'based on the consideration of certain statements of the accused as coinciding generally with the aims of a terrorist organisation', with devastating impact on political and social debate.[115] The Turkish Ministry of the Interior announced on 24 December 2016 that in the preceding six months, 3710 judicial proceedings had been initiated against social media users. Referred to as 'judicial harassment' by the COE Commissioner, the application of these laws has resulted in the systematic criminal prosecution of academicsournalists, lawyers, human rights defenders, artists, intellectuals, and even opposition parliamentarians on the grounds of their 'provocation' or expression of 'moral support for terrorism'.[116]

[112] See the Parliamentary Assembly of the Council of Europe, Recommendation 2097 (2017), http://assembly.coe.int/nw/xml/XRef/Xref-XML2HTML-en.asp?fileid=23403&lang=en (accessed 29 April 2019); Muižnieks (above n 5); OSCE, 'OSCE Representative Condemns Continued Arrests of Journalists in Turkey, Calls on Authorities to Restore Media Pluralism', press release (31 October 2016), http://www.osce.org/fom/278326 (accessed 31 March 2019); and OSCE, 'OSCE Representative on Freedom of the Media Calls on Turkey to Decriminalize Journalistic Work Following Arrest of *Die Welt* Journalist', press release (1 March 2017), http://www.osce.org/fom/302351.

[113] See, eg, Report of the Special Rapporteur on the promotion and protection of the right to freedom of opinion and expression on his mission to Turkey, A/HRC/35/22/Add.3 (7 June 2017), paras 16 and 17; and the Joint Written Statement submitted by International PEN, the International Press Institute, Reporters Sans Frontiers, nongovernmental organizations in special consultative status, A/HRC/32/NGO/120 (8 June 2016).

[114] Muižnieks (above n 5).

[115] Ibid.

[116] See thousands of arrests and revocation of passports of signatories of the 'Academics for Peace' statements of January 2016. Following presidential condemnation of 'mock academics', criminal investigations were launched based on Art 7(2) of the Anti-Terrorism Law. Other cases include novelists and linguists, such as Aslı Erdoğan and Necmiye Alpay. Cited in Muižnieks (above n 5) para 65. In 2016 the Turkish Parliament lifted the immunities of 139 parliamentarians, subject to pending prosecution for statements deemed to insult the President or other public officials, to constitute terrorist propaganda or incitement to hatred. See Muižnieks (above n 5) para 69 on the alarming 'judicial harassment' of MPs. For updated information, see the website of the Turkey Litigation Support Project: https://www.turkeylitigationsupport.com/ (accessed 31 March 2019).

III. FUNDAMENTAL PRINCIPLES OF LAW

The overview above demonstrates that there is a strong global appetite both for the creation of new 'preventive' offences and for their use in practice. This legislative and prosecutorial proclivity towards preventive use of criminal law must be viewed alongside the general principles of criminal law and international human rights law, considered in turn below, which anticipate and accommodate the preventive use of criminal law but also set down a basic constraining framework.

A. Constraining Principles of Criminal Law

While criminal law is predominantly responsive, its preventive function is neither new nor inherently controversial. Criminal law is at least in part always aimed at preventing or deterring future crime.[117] The 'preventive rationale' is heightened in respect of certain exceptional groups of offences, common in national systems and reflected to an extent in international criminal law, which allow early intervention before the relevant crime is completed.[118] While the preventive function may not be unprecedented, it cannot be assumed that states have unfettered power in pursuing this goal.[119] For the range of crimes of expression, questions arise as to the basis upon which states may punish them, as well as whether the requirements (or constraining principles) of criminal law, set out below, are met.

i. The Harm Principle and Remoteness

A general justification for the intervention of criminal law is that it is responsive to harm caused to a protected value or, at a minimum (and not without controversy), a real and intended risk of such harm. As punishment in turn must correspond to an individual's culpability, it reflects the contribution of the individual to that harm or risk. Sufficient 'normative involvement' of an individual in a wrong ultimately caused by another or in the very least in the deliberate creation of risk of such a wrong, is an essential prerequisite to individual criminal responsibility.[120] Conversely, remoteness is another constraining principle of

[117] N Jareborg, *Essays in Criminal Law* (Stockholm, Iustus Forlag, 1988), cited in A Ashworth and L Zedner, *Preventive Justice* (Oxford, Oxford University Press, 2014) 3: 'The very point of threatening with punishment would be lost if one did not presuppose that the threat has some preventive effect.'

[118] For instigation, the act must be commenced or attempted, and for inchoate offences, which, exceptionally, do not. See also Ashworth and Zedner (ibid) 3.

[119] Ashworth and Zedner (above n 117) p. 8.

[120] For crimes such as terrorist attacks to be imputed to another who, for example, possesses material or makes statements that may be deemed by some to 'glorify' such acts, the original actor must have had 'some form of normative involvement [in the other person's] subsequent choice' to commit a crime and 'the intent to cause the final crime itself'. See Ashworth and Zedner (above n 117) 112, quoting AP Simester and A von Hirsch, *Crimes, Harms, and Wrongs: On the Principles of Criminalisation* (Oxford, Hart Publishing, 2014) 81.

criminal law, such that an individual cannot be prosecuted for speech with no meaningful proximate link to an ultimate wrong.[121]

These principles are reflected in the scope of crimes of expression in international criminal law. Prosecuting crimes of 'instigation', which include urging, soliciting, or inducing,[122] requires that the harm actually arises to the extent that the principal crime 'in fact occurs or is attempted'.[123] In certain circumstances, however, the imperative of harm prevention might be said to justify criminal law's intervention before the harm materialises, through inchoate offences (such as incitement). Put alternately, the clear and overwhelming risk posed by certain conduct justifies the intervention of criminal law before the harm materialises.[124] This exceptional category of crimes has been described by Andrew Ashworth and Lucia Zedner as intending 'to penalise conduct prior to the causing of the wrong or harm, thus authorising official intervention (and hence prevention) before the intended result occurs, where there is intent to cause harm'.[125]

The exceptional nature of such crimes and the risk in question are reflected in the fact that in international criminal law, incitement is criminalised only in respect of genocide. Even then, it is subject to qualifiers that limit its scope and safeguard the nexus between an individual and the harm. Incitement to genocide is criminalised only when it is 'public' and 'direct' – which both the International Law Commission and the ICTR describe as excluding 'vague or indirect suggestions'[126] – and there is intent to cause harm.

In various ways, this contrasts with the contemporary trend towards criminalisation of expression that was illustrated above in section II. On the international level, UNSC Resolution 1624 notably does not refer to any harm or particular level of risk that must arise from the incitement that states were called on to prohibit by law. The European Convention refers loosely to 'caus[ing] a danger that an offence may be committed', firmed up somewhat by the EU Directive's reference to 'manifestly caus[ing] a danger that a terrorist act will be committed'.[127] On the national level, most of the provisions examined

[121] Ashworth and Zedner (above n 117) 109.

[122] UN General Assembly, 'Rome Statute of the International Criminal Court (Last Amended 2010)' (17 July 1998, entered into force 1 July 2002), https://www.refworld.org/docid/3ae6b3a84.html, Art 25(3)(b).

[123] Ibid.

[124] In addition to the overwhelming risk in relation to genocide, another example of the inherent harm or danger rationale arises in certain 'possession' offences where an inherent danger arises from, eg, the possession of explosives.

[125] Ashworth and Zedner (above n 117) 97.

[126] International Law Commission, 'Report of the International Law Commission on the Work of its 48th Session' (1996) A/CN.4/SER.A/1996/Add.l (Part 2) 22. Albin Eser has described directness as less about the individuals incited than about 'excluding indirect influences'. A Eser, 'Individual Criminal Responsibility' in A Cassesse, P Gaeta, and JRWD Jones (eds), *The Rome Statute of the International Criminal Court: A Commentary*, vol 1 (Oxford, Oxford University Press, 2002) 805. The accused must also have intended to bring about the harm (see below).

[127] EC, Proposal for a Council Framework Decision amending Framework Decision 2002/475/JHA on combating terrorism, Doc COM 2007 0650 (6 November 2007), 450.

above explicitly delink the offences from their result – no harm need result, no identifiable person need actually have been incited or encouraged or in any way influenced, and there need have been no intent to cause harm.[128] While a number of national measures refer to the creation of risk and 'danger', in some cases this corresponds to a more abstract danger that attitudes or environments will be influenced, as opposed to a real risk of a particular crime being committed.[129] In practice, in many states around the world, prosecutions relate to speech that apparently created no quantifiable or concrete risk of terrorism but were nonetheless evaluated as constituting 'dangerous' – or perhaps simply unacceptable – speech. In particular, offences of glorification, justification, and apology have on their face only the most tangential or debatable link to future terrorist acts.

These offences fall into the category that Ashworth and Zedner have described as 'pre-inchoate' offences, which seek to criminalise conduct not only before the harm materialises but before it reaches the level of an inchoate offence, with or without requiring proof of intent to cause the eventual harm.[130] These extreme forms of preventive offences that have burgeoned in the counterterrorism context in recent years can be considered 'ad hoc extensions of the criminal law'.[131]

A schism has therefore emerged between evolving practice on the one hand and, on the other hand, the sort of 'direct and immediate' call to violence, with attendant risk, that is associated with incitement in the UN Secretary-General's Report and is reflected in international criminal law and (as noted below) in some human rights jurisprudence.[132] The reason for the more expansive approach is clear enough, reflecting the desire to criminalise the role of incitement in 'creating the environment that nurtures particular acts of terrorism rather than in promoting specific acts'.[133] The extent to which the criminal law *can* do this depends on the essential link between the individual prosecuted and harm caused, or at least risked, such that the individual is punished 'for a harm that s/he has done or risked him or herself', rather than for speculative wrongs that may derive from the potential impact of dangerous ideas on others.[134]

[128] In some cases, the ideas need not have yet been communicated. See, eg, cases in which leaflets were never distributed, but it was still deemed 'propagandising' in Turkey; or, eg, possession prosecutions in the UK (though some judges have insisted on a direct connection between possession and an act of terrorism). F Galli, 'Developments in the Construction of Criminal Legislation: *R v Zafar and Others*' (2008) 172(33) *Justice of the Peace* 532–35.

[129] See discussion of intent below.

[130] Ashworth and Zedner (above n 117) 96: these offences arise in some instances 'before the conduct amounts to ... encouraging or assisting crime' and without requiring that intent to cause or contribute to harm be proved.

[131] Ashworth and Zedner (above n 117) 3 and 98: 'offences aimed at purely preparatory conduct' that 'may be criminalised without the need for proof of an intent to cause harm'.

[132] This corresponds to the test in US jurisprudence. See Barak-Erez and Sharia (above n 73) 14–19.

[133] Y Ronen, 'Terrorism and Freedom of Expression' in B Saul (ed), *Research Handbook on International Law and Terrorism* (Cheltenham, Edward Elgar, 2014) 450.

[134] Ashworth and Zedner have distinguished harm done or risked by the person and 'the possible future acts of ... a third party'. See Ashworth and Zedner (above n 117) 112. For a direct example of being held to account for statements by others, see Saul (above n 44) on Australian laws allowing prosecution of individuals for statements by others within an organisation.

ii. The Mental and Material Elements of an Offence

The most basic requirements of criminal responsibility is that the individual has engaged in *conduct* (contributing to or directed towards harm to a protected value) with the relevant *intent*, creating the essential nexus between an individual and the criminal wrong referred to above. The culpable conduct and intent – *actus reus* and *mens rea*, or the material and mental elements – provide the objective and subjective conditions for punishability. It is worth reflecting on how these basic elements are enshrined in emerging laws and practice in the context of crimes of expression.

As outlined in the previous section, culpable conduct in this context may consist of speech, publishing the ideas of others, tweeting and retweeting, posting images or words, or more vaguely 'making messages available'. The conduct is the expression or dissemination itself. This is accepted for established crimes, such as instigation or direct and public incitement, but the conditions noted above ensure that the criminal law response to what people say, as opposed to what they do, remains exceptional.[135]

While expression may in exceptional circumstances constitute criminal conduct, it is uncontroversial that *thoughts* may not. In accordance with the Roman law principle *cogitationis poenam nemo patitur*,[136] punishment cannot encroach into the private sphere of the individual until such time as the thoughts have been brought, through conduct, 'into the external world'.[137] Many of the current crimes of expression criminalise the expression of thoughts delinked from any 'concrete act' in the external world, beyond the sharing of the thought. As such, crimes of expression lie awkwardly and perhaps perilously in between the penalisation of Orwellian 'thoughtcrimes' and action, in the sense envisaged in criminal law. As such, they require particular caution in the reach of criminal law.

Intent is at the core of criminal law and is the basis for the culpability and legal responsibility of individuals. Albin Eser has suggested that for crimes of expression, recklessness or negligence is not enough, but rather that incitement carries a 'double intent requirement' in respect of his or her own and the principal's conduct.[138] The expression must be directed at causing a principal offender to commit a particular crime, and the instigator must assume that it will be committed.[139] While the crime envisaged need not be 'determined in all its details', the key is that the intent is 'concrete in being directed at a certain crime and perpetrator', such that the wrongdoer anticipates the crime 'in its essential elements and rough outlines'.[140]

[135] There must be a link to a concrete crime commenced or attempted (for instigation) or at least intended and giving rise to risk (for incitement).

[136] 'Nobody endures punishment for thought.' Justinian's *Digest* (48.19.18).

[137] Ashworth and Zedner (above n 117) 110.

[138] Eser (above n 126) 797.

[139] Ibid.

[140] Ibid, 798.

By contrast, for emerging crimes of expression, intent requirements are far from clear.[141] Some require no intent to contribute to or induce or incite a specific crime or indeed any crime at all.[142] Where mental element requirements do appear, they often relate not to an eventual terrorist act but to the intent to engage in the expression itself. For example, in the EU Directive on Combating Terrorism, the public distribution of messages that 'glorify' terrorist acts are criminal if the *distribution* is intentional and causes a danger of an offence being committed; the mental element applies only to distribution, not to the creation of the danger, still less the commission of the actual attack. In pre-inchoate offences, such as in the UK offence of publishing or disseminating statements that are 'likely to be understood ... as a direct or indirect encouragement ... of acts of terrorism',[143] or possession of information 'likely ... to be useful in the commission or preparation of such acts',[144] recklessness would suffice.[145]

iii. Punishment Commensurate with Individual Responsibility

Criminal sanctions must be commensurate with the responsibility of the individual, based on the conduct of the individual, as well as his or her intent.[146] That the punishment cannot be 'collective' or 'objective' is an essential principle of criminal law in legal systems across the globe and is moreover reflected in international law.[147] Punishment must be commensurate not only with the crime but with an individual's role in the crime.[148]

As the previous section of this chapter illustrates, heightened penalties attach to terror-related crimes in many states (including mandatory penalties in some), and crimes of expression associated with terrorism increasingly carry arguably inflated penalties.[149] These penalties reflect assumptions about the gravity of terrorism offences that may not hold up in light of the expanded reach of offences, the remoteness of the accused's conduct from terrorist acts,

[141] Ashworth and Zedner (above n 117) 109–10, questioning the consistency of UK preparatory and pre-inchoate offences with the 'remoteness' test.

[142] See above s II. Unlike SC Resolution 1624, the CoE Convention refers to intent to commit 'a terrorist offence'.

[143] UK Terrorism Act (2006), s 2(3).

[144] Ibid.

[145] Ashworth and Zedner (above n 117) 98.

[146] See, eg, European Parliament, 'An EU Approach to Criminal Law', P7_TA(2012)0208, Resolution of 22 May 2016 on an EU approach to Criminal Law, Doc (2010/2310(INI)) (2013/C 264 E/02) (2012).

[147] See the case at the International Criminal Tribunal for the Former Yugoslavia, *Prosecutor v Tadic*, Case No IT-94-1-A, Appeals Chamber Judgment (15 July 1999) para 186: 'Nobody may be held criminally responsible for acts in which he has not personally engaged or in some way participated.' On the prohibition on collective punishments in IHL, see Article 33 of the Fourth Geneva Convention, Article 75 Additional Protocol I, and Article 6(2) of Additional Protocol II.

[148] *Nulla poene sine lege*. See Art 22, Rome Statute (above n 128); and European Parliament, 'An EU Approach to Criminal Law' (above n 146).

[149] See also Duffy (above n 13) ch 4.

and possible lack of criminal intent. International practice reveals many recent examples of hefty custodial sentences for 'indirect incitement' offences.[150] The apparent justification is the abstract danger that this speech is seen to represent, not the conduct, intent, or culpability of the individuals involved, which raises serious doubts concerning proportionate punishment.

iv. Nullum Crimen and *Basic Rule-of-Law Requirements*

Certainty, precision, and foreseeability are prerequisites for any criminal law, consistent with basic rule-of-law constraints.[151] The principle of *lex certa* requires that criminal law must be sufficiently certain to allow those within a state's jurisdiction to understand the law's limits and modify their behaviour. However, difficulties arise when international and regional frameworks require incitement to terrorism to be criminalised despite the ongoing failure to define 'terrorism' on the international level.[152] This is most striking in UNSC Resolution 1624, which fails to define 'terrorist acts' (or incitement). National definitions of 'terrorism' have also been frequently criticised by international monitoring mechanisms for their breadth and vagueness.[153] When incitement to notions such as 'extremism', which are likewise vague and controversial, is also criminalised, the problem is magnified.[154] With this approach, accessorial offences suffer the same fate as the underlying offence.

In relation to crimes of expression, the definitional deficit is compounded by the lack of clarity in respect of the 'incitement', 'justification', 'encouragement', or 'apology' related offences themselves, as discussed above. What amounts to the Russian law's 'justification' or 'popularisation of terrorist ideas', Israeli law's 'sympathy', Turkish law's 'propagandising', or the unspecified 'dangers' referred to above, is far from clear and foreseeable. The same could be asked of what 'encouragement' means in the United Kingdom if, as the courts have found, it doesn't

[150] See, eg, G Erebara, 'Albania Jails Nine Jihadi Recruiters', *Balkan Insight* (4 May 2016), http://www.balkaninsight.com/en/article/heavy-sentences-spelled-for-albania-jihadi-recruiters-05-04-2016. Russia's Yarovaya amendments of 2016 increased the penalties for 'public justification of terrorism': A Maida, 'Online and on All Fronts: Russia's Assault on Freedom of Expression', *Human Rights Watch* (18 July 2017), https://www.hrw.org/report/2017/07/18/online-and-all-fronts/russias-assault-freedom-expression. In general, Dutch laws increase penalties for terrorism-related crimes by one third, while UK law provides for up to seven years of imprisonment for encouragement. See the UK Terrorism Act (2006), s 1(7).

[151] Ashworth and Zedner (above n 117) 113–14.

[152] Some definitions (eg, the CoE Convention) refer to existing terrorism conventions; others (eg, UNSC Resolution 1624) do not.

[153] Duffy (above n 13) chs 2 and 7.

[154] B Emmerson (Special Rapporteur), 'Report on the Promotion and Protection of Human Rights and Fundamental Freedoms while Countering Terrorism', UN Doc A/HRC/31/65 (22 February 2016) para 21; and UN Human Rights Committee (UNHRC), 'General Comment 34 on Article 19 of the ICCPR', CCPR/C/GC/34 (12 September 2011), https://www2.ohchr.org/english/bodies/hrc/docs/gc34.pdf, para 46.

necessarily involve encouraging anything or anyone in particular.[155] The reason for this is in part linked to what Ashworth and Zedner have cited as the rule-of-law problem arising where laws 'provide for the criminalisation and punishment of conduct that is significantly broader than the wrong it is aimed to prevent'.[156] In these types of offences, 'the conduct specified by the legislation is not its real target but only a proxy for it, or identified as a likely precursor to it'.[157] The result is overly broad offences that do not reflect the harm the law seeks to prevent.

It is a basic rule-of-law principle that criminal law should be strictly applied and restrictively interpreted. It cannot be interpreted by analogy, and any ambiguity should be resolved in favour of the accused.[158] As practice burgeons, we look to courts for strict application of basic principles to ensure respect for rule-of-law constraints, the presumption of innocence, burden of proof,[159] and the overall fairness of the criminal process.[160]

Among these fundamental rule-of-law principles, *ultima ratio* acknowledges the inherently intrusive nature of criminal law and the exceptional powers of the state by ensuring that resort to criminal law is exceptional and must be strictly justified.[161] This is reflected, for example, in the 2012 European Parliament Resolution entitled 'An EU Approach to Criminal Law':

> Whereas in view of its being able by its very nature to restrict certain human rights and fundamental freedoms of suspected, accused or convicted persons, in addition to the possible stigmatising effect of criminal investigations, and taking into account that excessive use of criminal legislation leads to a decline in efficiency, criminal law must be applied as a measure of last resort (*ultima ratio*) addressing clearly defined and delimited conduct, which cannot be addressed effectively by less severe measures and which causes significant damage to society or individuals ...[162]

The principle of liberal criminal law corresponds often to what has been described as the 'culture of executive restraint' in resort to criminal law.[163]

[155] See *Choudary and Rahman*, sentencing remarks (above n 61) 6.

[156] Ashworth and Zedner (above n 117) 113.

[157] Ibid.

[158] See, eg, European Parliament, 'An EU Approach to Criminal Law' (above n 146).

[159] The risk of inverting the burden of proof may arise as courts shift the emphasis to what the accused did not do to demonstrate opposition to terrorism. See *Choudary and Rahman*, sentencing remarks (above n 61).

[160] Questions of evidence and procedure, and their implications, go beyond this short chapter, but it is noted that the breadth and ambiguity of the offences, and the need for broad contextual analysis of facts, means that wide-reaching and potentially prejudicial evidence that may not normally be relevant and admitted is placed before the jury in common law systems. This risks making thought the basis of the crime charged, or at least strongly influential in determinations of guilt, and it risks discrimination.

[161] A Dambrauskienė, 'The Conception of the Ultima Ratio Principle' (2015) 97 *Teisė* 116–34. Feinberg has referred to no other more effective measure or 'less restrictive appropriate alternative': J Feinberg, *Harm to Others* (New York, Oxford University Press, 1984) 26, cited in Ashworth and Zedner (above n 117) 103.

[162] European Parliament, 'An EU Approach to Criminal Law' (above n 146) I.

[163] Anderson (above n 14) 19.

Recent international developments, legislative changes, and in particular decisions in practice to prosecute relatively minor offences suggest that the principle of restraint has been turned on its head.

So far as the rationale for expansive approaches to criminal intervention is preventive, practical or policy considerations arise in relation to its effectiveness as a preventive tool. It has been increasingly recognised in international practice in recent years that coercive counterterrorism laws may be ineffective[164] or, more importantly, counterproductive.[165] As the UN Special Rapporteur on Terrorism and Human Rights recently noted, the primacy that Security Council Resolutions have given to criminal law 'seems a short-sighted and potentially counter-productive approach, especially considering the broader global landscape focused on countering and preventing the "violent extremism that is conducive to terrorism"'.[166] Sweeping large groups of people under the web of criminality, often by employing religious profiling, may generate the resentments and sense of injustice (real or perceived) that recent reports have identified as 'pull factors', attracting younger people in particular to violent extremism and to travel abroad to fight for various terrorist groups.[167] This is one of a number of countervailing factors that must be considered in assessing the justification for the criminal law's intervention.[168] Another is the impact on human rights, to which we now turn.

B. Restraining Principles: Freedom of Expression

Crimes of expression should be consistent with international human rights law, which provides flexible parameters for the lawful criminalisation and prosecution of terrorism-related speech crimes. Prosecuting crimes of expression may have an impact on myriad rights, including the principles of *nullum crimen sine lege* and fair trial, freedom of association, and the rights to religion, equality, and private life. The greatest direct impact is on the right to freedom of expression (and the associated freedoms of thought, association, and assembly), which forms the focus of this section.

[164] See Muižnieks (above n 5) on the diminishing returns from increased resort to criminal law.

[165] The debate on the radicalising influence of some counter-radicalisation policies in the UK is a case in point. See UN High Level report on Threats and Challenges, discussed in Duffy (above n 13) ch 4. For more on counter-radicalisation strategies, see also the chapters in this volume by Aziz Z Huq and Andreas Armborst.

[166] Ní Aoláin (above n 12), referring to Security Council Resolution 2396 (2017) and highlighting the problem of vague inchoate offences.

[167] OSCE Office for Democratic Institutions and Human Rights (ODIHR), 'Countering the Incitement and Recruitment of Foreign Terrorist Fighters: The Human Dimension', background paper for Vienna Counter-Terrorism Expert Conference (30 June–1 July 2015), available at https://www.osce.org/odihr/166646 (accessed 7 March 2019).

[168] Ashworth and Zedner (above n 117) 106: 'Before criminalisation is justified, it must be clear that there are not strong countervailing considerations, such as the absence of harm, the creation of unwelcome social consequences, the curtailment of important rights, and so forth.'

As a starting point, the prevention of terrorism is part of the positive human rights obligations of states to ensure respect for rights within their jurisdictions, as the ECtHR recalled in the recent *Beslan School Siege* case (2017).[169] States are specifically obliged to prohibit propagandising for war,[170] racial hatred,[171] and hate speech more broadly.[172] Preventive measures are therefore required in a range of circumstances, but they must be implemented consistently with human rights law, including freedom of expression, as explicitly reflected in UNSC Resolution 1624, the CoE Convention, and the EU Directive.

Freedom of expression is important in itself as a fundamental right linked to the development of the human person and as a prerequisite to guarantee 'the exercise of all human rights'[173] and the preservation of democracy.[174] This dual rationale is important – and can give rise to tensions. The importance of freedom of speech in a democracy is not predicated on the pro-democratic content of the material or the perceived value of the truth it proclaims. Although it has been suggested for example that 'human rights bodies appear to assume that freedom of expression serves different goals than the unbiased pursuit of truth; indeed they appear to assume a specific truth worthy of protection, namely democracy',[175] this is a provocative proposition. Freedom of expression protects disturbing and offensive speech as well as potentially anti-democratic ideas,[176] as the price society pays for the pluralism 'without which there *is* no democratic society'.[177]

[169] ECtHR, *Tagayeva and Others v Russia*, App 26562/07 (13 April 2017). Russia was in violation for its failure to prevent (as well as to adequately respond to) identifiable threats of terrorism. On the debate around the extent and nature of the positive obligations, which may conflict with other rights, see Lazarus (above n 17).

[170] International Covenant on Civil and Political Rights (ICCPR), Art 20(3).

[171] International Convention on the Elimination of All Forms of Racial Discrimination (CERD), Art 4.

[172] Note that hate speech is a narrower category than, eg, the protection of victims of terrorism, though it can also be subject to abuse. See Muižnieks (above n 5) paras 119–20, reporting abuse of the hate speech rationale by the Turkish state to justify measures against persons deemed to have insulted the religious views of the majority.

[173] UNHRC, 'General Comment 34' (above n 154) para 2; and K Boyle and S Shah, 'Thought, Expression, Association, and Assembly' in D Moeckli, S Shah, and S Sivakumaran (eds), *International Human Rights Law*, 2nd edn (Oxford, Oxford University Press, 2014) 217.

[174] *Handyside v UK* (above n 6) §49: 'Freedom of expression constitutes one of the essential foundations of … [a democratic] society, one of the basic conditions for its progress and for the development of every man.'

[175] Ronen (above n 133) 444.

[176] ECtHR, *Gündüz v Turkey*, Judgment, Application 35071/97 (4 December 2003), where critical commentary on democracy and support for sharia were considered to be part of a necessary debate in a pluralistic society, as it did not call for violence. At the same time, it is potentially relevant to note that in exceptional cases, the ECtHR has held that an application with the purpose of undermining the democratic order or destroying human rights represents an 'abuse of petition' (under Art 17) and is inadmissible. See, eg, *Communist Party of Germany v the Federal Republic of Germany*, Judgment, Application 250/57 (20 July 1957).

[177] *Handyside v UK* (above n 6) para 49, emphasis added.

Nonetheless, the right to free expression is of course subject to limits, even within a cautious, rights-focused approach, and the question, as ever, is where the limits lie. The basic test governing permissible restrictions is enshrined in international treaties,[178] which require that restrictions be prescribed by law, pursue a legitimate aim, and be necessary and proportionate to that aim.[179] Although cases before human rights courts and bodies tend to turn on the final arm – the 'necessity or proportionality' test – each element of this test is relevant to the practice in relation to crimes of expression.

i. The 'Prescribed by Law' Test

Within the European Convention on Human Rights (ECHR) framework, the 'prescribed by law' test requires that a restriction on freedom of expression is enshrined at the relevant time in a sufficiently clear and precise manner to ensure 'adequate accessibility and foreseeability of law, to enable the individual to regulate his conduct in the light of the foreseeable consequences of a given action'.[180] This implies more broadly that the restriction 'should also be compatible with the rule of law' and the relevant Convention principles.[181]

The vagueness and potential breadth of incitement-related offences (including 'glorification,' 'justification/apology', 'making available a message', and causing 'danger') and indeed of the terrorism or extremism to which they are directed have already been discussed above. Human rights courts and bodies deciding individual applications will generally not assess the lawfulness of laws *in abstracto* but instead focus on how they are applied *in concreto*. While the ECtHR has expressed concerns regarding legislative compatibility with the Convention,[182] other entities, such as the CoE Human Rights Commissioner and the United Nations Human Rights Committee (UNHRC) in its state reporting function, have been even more direct and robust concerning the incompatibility of propaganda, glorification, and justifications provisions with the requirement of clarity and specificity.[183]

[178] Art 19 of the International Covenant on Civil and Political Rights (ICCPR); Art 10 of the European Convention on Human Rights; Art 13 of the Inter American Convention on Human Rights; and Art 9 of the African Charter on Human and People's Rights.

[179] For example, Art 10(2) ECHR makes clear the interference must be 'prescribed by law and … necessary in a democratic society, in the interests of [*inter alia*] national security, territorial integrity, or public safety, for the prevention of disorder or crime, [or] for the protection of health or morals.'

[180] *The Observer and Guardian Newspapers v UK* (above n 6) para 62.

[181] *Ekin v France* (above n 6) para 44.

[182] Ibid, paras 58–65.

[183] Muižnieks (above n 5); and UNHRC, 'Concluding Observations' (above n 46).

ii. A Legitimate Aim?

There is little doubt that prevention of crime, including terrorism, is in a broad sense a 'legitimate aim' to be pursued by the state.[184] However, the relevant question here is not whether terrorism prevention is legitimate or even whether particular preventive counterterrorism laws pursue that aim. Rather, what matters is whether the particular restrictions are imposed pursuant to a specified legitimate aim.

It should be considered whether 'indirect incitement' laws, as applied in particular cases, do in fact correspond to any of the legitimate aims set out in, for example, Article 10 of the ECHR. Criminal provisions aimed directly at preventing future terrorist acts fulfil this criterion, potentially serving public order, crime prevention, and/or national security ends. More controversial are those that are justified by reference to the feelings of victims of past crimes. If not linked to preventing crime and preserving public order, the legitimacy of the restrictions must be justified as hate speech.[185]

Given the extent of documented overreach and misuse of terrorism and incitement laws to silence political opposition, there are often serious doubts whether this requirement is met. In practice, courts and bodies tend not to focus on the legitimacy of the aim pursued; the ECtHR may note there is some 'possible' legitimate aim that a measure may pursue, before focusing more rigorously on the necessity and proportionality test.[186] If the Court were to engage more robustly with the 'legitimate aim' criteria, it would enable clearer distinctions to be drawn between restrictions that have no meaningful link to terrorism prevention at all, and those that do but fall foul of the proportionality analysis.[187] A docile approach to this criterion may also risk legitimising false narratives around the purpose of measures. The ECtHR tendency to shy away from the legitimate aim criterion may also contribute to confusion as to the basis on which decisions are being made and the meaning of relevant legal standards such as 'national security' or 'public order'.[188] Understanding the 'legitimate aim' test, including which particular aim is invoked, is also an essential prerequisite to an adequate assessment of the next arm of the test, namely whether restrictions are necessary and proportionate to the particular aim.

[184] In principle it could meet a number of specified grounds, namely national security, public safety, the prevention of disorder or crime, and the protection of health. It corresponds to obligations, as noted above.

[185] See, eg, ECtHR, *Erbakan v Turkey*, Judgment, Application 59405/00 (6 July 2006) para 56.

[186] Eg, *Ekin v France* (above n 6) para 48.

[187] See, eg, the 'judicial harassment' of journalists and civil society actors in Turkey (discussed above). The Court has also rejected over-reaching assertions as to links between speech and the protection of security under the necessity test. See *Ekin v France* (above n 6); ECtHR, *Doner and Others v Turkey*, Judgment, Application 29994/02 (7 March 2017); and ECtHR, *Fatullayev v Azerbaijan*, Judgment, Application 40984/07 (22 April 2010).

[188] Eg, the lack of a definition of 'national security' was noted in *The Observer and Guardian Newspapers v UK* (above n 6).

iii. The Key Criterion: The Necessity and Proportionality Test

Any limitation on freedom of expression must be 'necessary' – pursuant to a 'pressing social need' – and proportionate to the specified legitimate aims.[189] While regional systems vary somewhat,[190] both the ECtHR and its Inter-American counterpart have repeatedly stressed that the necessity and proportionality test is a stringent one to be applied restrictively,[191] with exceptions being 'strictly construed' and 'narrowly interpreted'.[192] The necessity stage of the test must not be misunderstood as a simple large-scale 'balancing' between freedom of expression and other interests such as countering terrorism and security. As the ECtHR has reiterated, 'the choice is not between two conflicting principles but with a principle of freedom of expression that is subject to a number of exceptions which must be narrowly interpreted'.[193] Accordingly, where a dispute arises, the burden of proving that any constraint on expression is permissible falls to the state.[194] Moreover, the test cannot operate so as to undermine the 'essence of the right'.[195]

In practice, ECtHR determinations of necessity and proportionality are acutely driven by each case's particular facts and context. The Court looks at the interference 'in the light of the case as a whole to determine whether the restriction is proportionate, including the content of the impugned statements and the context in which they were made'.[196] As a result, it can be difficult to discern clear principles from the jurisprudence, as legal standards become intertwined with particular facts.[197] This is particularly so in light of the controversial 'margin of appreciation' doctrine, which translates into particular deference on terrorism and security issues, albeit subject to the Court's oversight.[198] In addition,

[189] *Handyside v UK* (above n 6) para 49.

[190] In the Inter-American system, this focus on the necessity of the interference based on the particular content is reflected in the specific rule precluding prior censorship. Art 13(2) of the American Convention on Human Rights includes a virtual ban on all prior censorship; any limitations must be applied subsequent to publication. The only exception to that is if a state of emergency is declared under Art 27.

[191] UNHRC, 'General Comment 34' (above n 154) para 11; Boyle and Shah (above n 173) 226, who cite *Handyside v UK* (above n 6) para 49, as well as IACHR, *Ivcher-Bronstein v Peru* (Series C No 74) (6 June 2001); and ICCPR, Art 19(3).

[192] *Ceylan v Turkey* (above n 6) para 32; *The Observer and Guardian Newspapers v UK* (above n 6) paras 71–72; and ECtHR, *Sunday Times v UK (No 1)*, Judgment, Series A, No 30 (29 March 1979) para 65.

[193] *Sunday Times v UK* (ibid) para 65.

[194] D Kaye (Special Rapporteur), 'Promotion and Protection of the Right to Freedom of Opinion and Expression', UN General Assembly, A/71/373 (6 September 2016), https://www.refworld.org/docid/57fb6b974.html, para 9 (quoting UNHRC, 'General Comment 34' (above n 154) paras 27 and 21).

[195] Ibid.

[196] *Ceylan v Turkey* (above n 6) para 32.

[197] For an example, see ECtHR, *Leroy v France*, Merits and Just Satisfaction, Application 36109/03 (2 October 2008) paras 3–8.

[198] The court assesses whether 'the national authorities applied standards which were in conformity with the principles embodied in Article 10 and, moreover, that they relied on an acceptable assessment of the relevant facts'. *Steel and Morris v UK*, Application 68416/01 (15 February 2005) para 87.

some decisions of the Court and other supranational bodies such as the UNHRC are so minimalist and light on legal reasoning that they provide little meaningful guidance.[199]

For a range of reasons then, human rights jurisprudence does not provide a clear answer to the question of where the line lies for acceptable, or overreaching, restrictions on freedom of expression through criminal law. Nonetheless, a review of case law reveals certain factors that have proved relevant to this assessment and may provide some guidance as to how the skeletal legal framework should be interpreted, case by case, in a challenging and evolving field.

IV. CASE LAW AND THE ANALYSIS OF NECESSITY AND PROPORTIONALITY

A. Justifications for Resorting to Criminal Law

The nature and form of an interference or restriction on rights clearly influence the proportionality analysis. Criminal prosecution is a particularly direct and extreme form of interference, given the implications for the individuals involved, as well as the chilling effect on others. At a minimum, in the necessity and proportionality equation, weightier justifications are required for resort to criminal law than less onerous (noncriminal) measures.

Although supranational courts are reluctant to provide guidance on when criminal prosecution is *per se* unfair,[200] there are also sources in support of the requirement of restraint, consistent with the view of criminal law as *ultimo ratio*, to be strictly justified by the serious nature of the conduct and the lack of appropriate alternative responses.[201] Judge Sergio García Ramírez of the Inter-American Court of Human Rights (IACtHR) has put it in these terms:

> In an authoritarian political milieu, the criminal law solution is used frequently: it is not the last resort; it is one of the first, based on the tendency to 'govern with the penal code in the hand', a proclivity fostered by blatant and concealed authoritarianism and by ignorance, that can think of no better way to address society's legitimate demand for security. The opposite happens in a 'democratic environment': criminalization of behaviours and the use of sanctions are a last resort, turned to only when all others have been exhausted or have proven to be inadequate to punish the most serious

[199] See, eg, HRC, *AK and AR v Uzbekistan* (Communication No 1233/2003), UN Doc CCPR/C/95/D/1233/2003 (2009); 16 IHRR 719 (2009).

[200] One commentator has described fair trial as 'encompass[ing] both the right to a "fair trial" proper as well as the right of the defendant to be tried only in circumstances in which it would be "fair to try" him or her': ALT Choo, *Abuse of Process and Judicial Stays of Criminal Proceedings* (Oxford, Oxford University Press, 2008) 188.

[201] Eg, IACHR, *Humberto Palamara Iribarne v Chile*, Judgment, Series C No135 (22 November 2005); and IACHR, *Ricardo Canese v Paraguay*, Series C No 111 (31 August 2004). See also the Concurring Separate Opinion of Ramirez J in IACHR, *Ulloa v Costa Rica*, Merits, Reparations and Costs, Series C No 107, IHRL 1490, 200, para 16.

> violations of important legal interests. Then, and only then, does a democracy resort to punitive measures: because it is indispensable and unavoidable.[202]

B. 'Incitement to Violence' as a Bright Line

When considering the necessity and proportionality of a particular interference with free speech, including prosecution, courts look to the twin pillars of 'content' and 'context'. The question most consistently asked by bodies, including the ECtHR, is whether the content of the speech, in the particular context, incites violence or amounts to hate speech (which has been recognised only more recently).[203] In this determination, a court may also examine recent events and the amount of time elapsed between the occurrence of events that are the subject of the speech[204] or a history of violence in a particular country or region.[205] In the vast majority of cases concerning restrictions on speech in the terrorism context, incitement to violence constitutes the bright line over which protected speech cannot legally pass. A number of Turkish cases before the ECtHR have turned on this 'essential element', namely whether there was a 'call for the use of violence, armed resistance, or uprising'.[206]

The ECtHR has not defined this incitement to violence, to which it often refers, but jurisprudence indicates what it is *not*. It does not include merely 'hostile', 'negative', or 'acerbic' comments and criticism,[207] as 'the line between virulent or even offensive criticism and incitement must not … be confused'.[208]

[202] *Ulloa v Costa Rica* (ibid). More broadly, see N Mavronicola, 'Crime, Punishment and Article 3 ECHR: Puzzles and Prospects of Applying an Absolute Right in a Penal Context' (2015) 15(4) *Human Rights Law Review* 721–43.

[203] Eg, ECtHR, *Halis Doğan v Turkey (No 2)*, Application 71984/01 (25 July 2006); ECtHR, *Fatullayev v Azerbaijan*, Judgment, Application 40984/07 (22 April 2010); *Sener v Turkey*; *Ozgur Gundem v Turkey*, Application 23144/93, Judgment of 16 March 2000, ECtHR, *Reports 2000-III*; *Surek v Turkey (No 2)*, Application 26682/95; and *Müdür Duman v Turkey*, Judgment, Application 15450/03 (6 October 2015).

[204] For example, in *Lehideux and Isorni*, the Court, referring to remarks made in a eulogy about a French Nazi collaborator, ruled that it is 'inappropriate to deal with such remarks, forty years on, with the same severity as ten or twenty years previously'. ECtHR, *Lehideux and Isorni v France*, Judgment, Application 55/1997/839/1045 (23 September 1998) para 55.

[205] In *Leroy v France* (above n 197), the fact that the cartoon was featured in a publication in the Basque region, an area particularly sensitive to national security threats, was a factor in holding it to be a threat to national security. Similarly, see *Purcell and Others v Ireland*, Decision on Admissibility, Application 15404/89 (16 April 1991).

[206] ECtHR, *Belek and Velioğlu v Turkey*, Judgment, Application 44227/04 (6 October 2015) paras 24–27. This was the 'main factor' to be taken into account in deciding that the interference with the applicants' freedom of expression was not justified.

[207] ECtHR, *Falakaoglu v Turkey*, Judgment, Application 77365/01 (26 April 2005) para 35. See also ECtHR, *Incal v Turkey*, Judgment, Application 22658/93 (9 June 1998); and *Otegi Mondragon v Spain*, Judgment, Application 2034/07 (15 March 2011) para 54.

[208] ECRI, 'Explanatory Memorandum to ECRI General Policy Recommendation No 15 on Combating Hate Speech' CRI(2016)15 (8 December 2015) 59.

The Court has also noted that 'a message of intransigence as to the objectives of a proscribed organisation cannot be confused with incitement to violence or hatred'.[209] The use of particular vocabulary, such as 'resistance', 'struggle,' 'liberation', 'state terrorism', or 'genocide', is not enough to establish incitement.[210] Similarly, expressing support for a leader of a terrorist organisation without further incitement to violence does not suffice.[211] Moreover, the IACtHR has noted that restrictions to speech based on threats to national security cannot be abstract or hypothetical but must involve at least 'a reasonable risk of serious disturbance'.[212]

C. Distinguishing the Content of Impugned Speech from its Source

An important distinction arises between the content of impugned speech, understood in context, and its source. Prosecutions for publishing statements that did not advocate violence on the basis that they were made by a banned organisation have been found to violate Article 10 of the ECHR in a series of Turkish cases,[213] notably *Belek and Velioğlu v Turkey*.[214] By contrast, the prosecution did not exceed the margin of appreciation in the *Surek* case, in part because the letters in question identified individuals and could have incited violence towards them.[215]

It follows that if an opinion expressed by individuals is supported or shared by an illegal organisation, it is not alone sufficient for prosecution. While this seems obvious enough, there have been Turkish prosecutions for aiding and assisting the *Partiya Karkerên Kurdistanê* (Kurdistan Workers Party) (PKK) even though the impugned acts involved publications that promoted Kurdish culture and requests by parents for education in Kurdish (in addition to Turkish) at their local schools.[216] The ECtHR cautioned that 'expressions of opinion that may

[209] ECtHR, *Surek and Ozdemir v Turkey*, Judgment, Applications 23927/94 and 24277/94 (8 July 1999) para 61; ECtHR, *Erdogdu v Turkey*, Judgment, Application 25723/94 (15 June 2000) *Reports 2000-VI*; and *Ceylan v Turkey* (above n 6).

[210] *Ceylan v Turkey* (above n 6) para 34.

[211] ECtHR, *Yalçinkaya and Others v Turkey*, Judgment (24 June 2014) para 34, where the criminal prosecution of an expression of a 'mark of respect' for a leader of a terrorist organisation – in the absence of inciting or endorsing violence – was found to be an unjustifiable limit on free expression.

[212] *Francisco Uson Ramirez v Venezuela*, Judgment, Case 577-05 (20 November 2009), Report No 36/06, Inter-Am Court of Human Rights, OEA/Ser.L/V/II.127 Doc 4 rev 1 (2007), para 89.

[213] ECtHR, *Gözel and Özer v Turkey*, Judgment, Applications 43453/04 and 31098/05 (6 July 2010); and *Belek and Velioğlu v Turkey* (above n 206).

[214] *Belek and Velioğlu v Turkey* (above n 206) paras 5–12.

[215] *Surek and Ozdemir v Turkey* (above n 209).

[216] ECtHR, *Doner v Turkey* (above n 187) paras 107 and 108. Turkey was found to have failed to make a reasonable assessment of the facts and to apply standards in conformity with Art 10. The parents were on trial before a State Security Court for over a year, and although they were ultimately acquitted, there was a violation of Art 10 nonetheless.

have coincided with the aims or instructions of an illegal armed organisation cannot be the guiding criteria'.[217]

D. 'Non-public' Incitement?

The ECtHR has also noted the relevance of the public/private nature of communication, as well as its reach, in determining whether restrictions may be justified as necessary and proportionate. For example, in *Incal v Turkey*, the applicant had been convicted of 'non-public incitement' due to the creation of leaflets that had never been distributed. The Court focused ultimately on the content of the leaflets, which did not incite hatred or violence,[218] but it noted there had been no evidence produced 'of any *concrete action* which might belie the sincerity of the aim declared by the leaflet's authors'.[219] The Court has also criticised Turkey for prosecuting individuals for merely possessing material relating to the PKK.[220] The relevance of the impact, actual and potential, has also been clear in decisions that the criminalisation of poetry could not be justified.[221]

E. Content, Context, and the Link between Incitement and Violence

While jurisprudence points to incitement to violence as the litmus test, a key question is how it should be understood in terms of the requisite immediacy or remoteness between the speech in question and any ensuing violence. The real level of danger presented by speech, in light of who is saying what in which context, is a key question across systems.[222] The importance of the proximate link between the expression and the harm or risk is reflected in a statement by the African Commission of Human and People's Rights:

> The presumption is that a state should not restrict freedom of expression on grounds of national security unless there is (1) a real risk of harm (2) to a legitimate interest and (3) a close causal link between the risk of harm and the expression.[223]

[217] Ibid, para 107.

[218] *Incal v Turkey* (above n 208) para 50: 'virulent' complaints, accusations, and appealing to the population of Kurdish origin to band together and form collectivities to raise political demands could not justify interference.

[219] Ibid, para 51, emphasis added.

[220] *Müdür Duman v Turkey* (above n 203).

[221] ECtHR, *Karatas v Turkey*, Judgment, Application 23168/94 (8 July 1999).

[222] See, eg, the 'Report on Terrorism and Human Rights' of the Inter-American Commission, which refers to factors such as 'the dangers presented by the individual making the speech (military, intelligence, official, private citizen, etc) and the level of influence he or she may have on members of society ...'.

[223] Declaration of Principles on Freedom of Expression in Africa (2002), adopted by the African Commission on Human and Peoples' Rights at its 32nd Ordinary Session, Banjul, Gambia (17–23 October 2002).

The Inter-American Commission on Human Rights (IACHR), the Organization of American States (OAS) Special Rapporteur for Freedom of Expression, and the Office of the UN Commissioner for Human Rights (UNCHR) have lent their voice to the view that the necessity test requires a close and immediate connection between a speech act and violence in order to justify restrictions on free speech. A 2017 joint press release expressing concern over changes to the Honduran penal code on apology and incitement of terrorism acts stated:

> Regarding the incitement to violence – understood as the incitement to commit crimes, the breaking of public order or national security – the IACHR have repeatedly stressed that it must be backed up by actual, truthful, objective and strong proof that the person was not simply issuing an opinion (even if that opinion was hard, unfair, or disturbing) but that the person had the clear intention of committing a crime and the actual, real, and effective possibility of achieving this objective. The criminalisation of speech relating to terrorism should be restricted to instances of intentional incitement to terrorism – understood as a direct call to engage in terrorism which is directly responsible for increasing the likelihood of a terrorist act occurring, or to actual participation in terrorist acts.[224]

This approach mirrors the UN Secretary-General's Report on Resolution 1624.[225] It also reflects the more detailed Johannesburg Principles on National Security, Freedom of Expression and Access to Information (1996), which suggested some years earlier that expression as a threat to national security should only be punished where *intended* to incite imminent violence, *likely* to incite such violence, and where there is a direct and immediate connection between the expression and the likelihood or occurrence of such violence.[226]

Suggesting that the content of speech should involve a direct call to acts of terrorism, intent to commit a crime, and some effect as necessary elements of incitement sits uncomfortably alongside certain decisions of the ECtHR and UNHRC. For example, the UNHRC in *AK and AR v Uzbekistan* decided there was no violation under the International Covenant on Civil and Political Rights (ICCPR) even though the applicants had been convicted for speech that did not advocate violence but did support an unlawful organisation with 'radical religious views'.[227] The purpose of the organisation itself has been described

[224] Joint press release (above n 48). See also the 'Joint Declaration on Freedom of Expression and Countering Violent Extremism' adopted by the Rapporteurs on Freedom of Expression (2016), http://www.ohchr.org/EN/NewsEvents/Pages/DisplayNews.aspx?NewsID=19915&LangID=E (accessed 7 March 2019).

[225] See UN, 'The Protection of Human Rights and Fundamental Freedoms while Countering Terrorism: Report of the Secretary General' (above n 25). See also the discussion above at s II-A.

[226] See the Johannesburg Principles on National Security, Freedom of Expression and Access to Information, UN Doc E/CN.4/1996/39.

[227] *AK and AR v Uzbekistan* (above n 199), concerning the conviction of the two authors for seeking, receiving, and imparting information and 'radical ideas related to Islam' in relation to the Hizb ut-Tahrir organisation, as discussed in H Keller and M Sigron, 'State Security v Freedom of Expression: Legitimate Fight against Terrorism or Suppression of Political Opposition' (2010) 10(1) *Human Rights Law Review* 151–68.

as 'establishing an Islamic caliphate and restoring Islamic piety', and while it has been suggested that such an organisational aim may potentially conflict with the exercise of certain rights under the ICCPR, that is quite distinct from invoking violence. And in any case, 'an in-depth analysis of the threat' was entirely missing from the decision.[228] As a former member of the UNHRC has suggested, the Committee 'settled for succinct views in order to avoid tackling a delicate issue'.[229] This decision was handed down despite the UNHRC's own 'General Comment 34 on Article 19 of the ICCPR' noting that offences, including encouraging, glorifying, or justifying terrorism, 'should be clearly defined to ensure that they do not lead to unnecessary or disproportionate interference with freedom of expression'.[230]

A similar lightening rod for critical reflection is the case of *Leroy v France* at the ECtHR.[231] The applicant had been convicted for complicity in the glorification of terrorism under Article 24 of the French 'Press Law',[232] for a cartoon published shortly after 11 September 2001 in which collapsing buildings carried the caption (mimicking a Sony advertisement) 'We have all dreamt of it … Hamas did it'.[233] The Court looked at the full circumstances of the case, including the choice of wording, the context of the cartoon's publication, and the margin of appreciation available to states to protect themselves from terrorism, concluding that there had been no violation of Article 10.[234] A broad array of factors were cited, including that the cartoon glorified the destruction of the United States by violence, that it was disrespectful to victims of the attack, that the timing of the publication of the cartoon was significant, that it may have encouraged violence and disorder, and that incitement need not be acted upon to constitute an offence.[235] The Court finally emphasised that the modest fine imposed (€1,500) was not a disproportionate penalty given the full context of the case.[236]

This is a striking example of the ECtHR's holistic contextual approach,[237] sketching out myriad factors relevant to its particular assessment of whether a state had overstepped its margin in the concrete case. The need for a broad assessment of content and context notwithstanding, there is a danger of conflating legal standards and the facts of a case. The decision in *Leroy* sits uncomfortably

[228] Keller and Sigron (ibid) 159. For context, see also Human Rights Watch, 'Creating Enemies of the State: Religious Persecution in Uzbekistan' (2004), https://www.hrw.org/sites/default/files/reports/uzbekistan0304.pdf, 48.

[229] Keller and Sigron (above n 227).

[230] UNHRC, 'General Comment 34' (above n 154) para 46.

[231] *Leroy v France* (above n 197). See generally, S Sottiaux, '*Leroy v France*: Apology of Terrorism and the Malaise of the European Court of Human Rights' Free Speech Jurisprudence' (2009) *European Human Rights Law Review* 415–27.

[232] On *Loi sur la liberté de la presse*, see above s II-B, especially text at n 73.

[233] *Leroy v France* (above n 197) paras 3–8.

[234] Ibid, paras 37–39.

[235] Ibid, paras 43–45.

[236] Ibid, paras 11 and 46–47.

[237] *Surek and Ozdemir v Turkey* (above n 209) is another.

alongside the Court's repeated reference to incitement to violence as a key criterion and its insistence on a strict approach to restrictions to speech. The case exposes some potential inconsistency between human rights bodies around the difficult question of permissible restrictions on freedom of expression, at least with regard to the robustness with which they are willing to identify the limits. The UNHCR has often assumed that a threat justifies interference while avoiding clarifying the nature and implications of apparently 'ideological' threats. While the ECtHR deference is a little more understandable given its margin of appreciation doctrine, its case law is just as unhelpful in creating applicable legal standards of broader application. The need for greater clarity and consistency to guide evolving practice around the world and to avoid undermining the essence of the right to free speech is clear. There is likely to be no shortage of opportunities as developing laws and practice make their way to the supranational level.

F. Special Protection for Certain Types or Forms of Expression

While content and context are the key pillars the ECtHR has used to assess permissible restrictions to speech, the form and purpose of the speech is also relevant.

i. Political Speech, the Press, and Human Rights Defenders

Human rights courts and bodies have recalled that there is little scope for restrictions on political speech and the reporting of political issues.[238] The ECtHR has called for particular caution in respect of prosecution of the press[239] and has condemned associated interferences, such as investigation and surveillance of journalists in order to reveal their sources;[240] and limiting access to information for journalists and NGOs has been found to constitute an interference with the exercise of their functions of assisting 'informed public debate' and being 'social "watchdogs"'.[241] Expressions by elected representatives[242] and human rights defenders also deserve diligent protection.

[238] *Surek and Ozdemir v Turkey* (above n 209) paras 57–60.

[239] Ibid; and *The Observer and Guardian Newspapers v UK* (above n 6) paras 79–91.

[240] ECtHR, *Telegraaf Media Nederland Landelijke Media BV and Others v the Netherlands*, Judgment, Application 39315/06 (22 November 2001). The Court held that the objective of the surveillance was to reveal the journalists' sources, and the interference with Art 10 could not be justified on the ground of national security because the relevant law in the Netherlands had not provided appropriate safeguards in respect of the powers of surveillance used against the journalists because the surveillance could be authorised without prior review by an independent body with the power to prevent or terminate the surveillance.

[241] ECtHR, *Társaság A Szabadságjogokért v Hungary*, Judgment, Application 37374/05 (14 April 2009) para 27.

[242] The ECtHR made it clear that '[w]hile freedom of expression is important for everybody, it is especially so for an elected representative of the people'. See Muižnieks (above n 5).

As noted by the African Commission on Human and Peoples' Rights (ACHPR), speech directed towards the promotion and protection of human rights 'is of special value to society and deserving of special protection'.[243] Broadening incitement laws and burgeoning prosecutions of offences of 'justification', 'expressions of sympathy', and '*apologie* for terrorism' have been recognised to stifle political debate on, *inter alia*, the causes, contributing factors, or (in the language of the UN Global Strategy) 'conditions conducive to the spread of terrorism'.[244] The key question is: to what extent does the assertion of alternative political views, however unpalatable to established political doctrine and including such goals as the establishment of 'an Islamic state', also constitute political speech?

ii. Artistic Expression

The ECtHR has noted that freedom of expression 'protects not only the *substance* of the ideas and information expressed but also the *form* in which they are conveyed'.[245] Nonetheless, poetry, comedy, art, and puppetry have increasingly been prosecuted as indirect incitement, as outlined in the earlier sections of this chapter. Given the role of the arts in democratic development, the ECtHR has called for extreme caution:

> Those who create, perform, distribute or exhibit works of art contribute to the exchange of ideas and opinions which is essential for a democratic society … [Hence] the obligation on the state not to encroach unduly on their freedom of expression.[246]

The subjectivity associated with messages conveyed through art is plain. In *Karatas v Turkey*, the applicant had been convicted under antiterrorism legislation for publishing an anthology of poetry that the Court noted 'taken literally … might be construed as inciting readers to hatred, revolt, and the use of violence'.[247] However, 'the fact that they were artistic in nature and of limited impact made them less a call to an uprising than an expression of deep distress in the face of a difficult political situation'.[248] While putting opinions in verse or a newspaper can hardly protect individuals from prosecution, this jurisprudence suggests certain forms of speech deserve particularly careful scrutiny prior to prosecution. This contrasts starkly with the numerous examples of prosecutions of artists, journalists, and political actors, including human rights defenders, across the world today.

[243] ACHPR, *Law Offices of Ghazi Suleiman v Sudan*, Case No 228/99 (29 May 2003) para 52.

[244] The UN global counterterrorism strategy recognises the need to address conditions conducive to the spread of terrorism. See UN General Assembly Resolution on the Global Counter-Terrorism Strategy Review, A/RES/70/291 (19 July 2016), available at https://www.un.org/sc/ctc/news/document/a-res-70-291-the-united-nations-global-counter-terrorism-strategy-review/, para 39.

[245] *Karatas v Turkey* (above n 221) emphasis added. See also *De Haes and Gijsels v Belgium*, Judgment, Application 19983/92 (24 February 1997), Reports 1997-I, 236, para 48.

[246] ECtHR, *Alinak v Turkey*, Judgment, Application 40287/98 (29 March 2005) para 42.

[247] *Karatas v Turkey* (above n 221) paras 49–54

[248] Ibid.

G. The Role of Domestic Courts

The broad contextual approach of the ECtHR in relation to restrictions on speech has been matched by the Court's insistence that domestic courts must also take into account all relevant considerations and context, as well as its assertion that 'automatic repression' of speech crimes is irreconcilable with Article 10. In *Gözel and Özer v Turkey*, for example, the Court found a violation when the nature of the offences enshrined in law provided 'no obligation on domestic courts to carry out a textual or contextual examination of the publication'.[249] This should be noted by governments attempting to develop legislation that automatically represses possession or dissemination of certain material.

H. Penalties

Finally, in determining the proportionality of an interference, the ECtHR considers the nature of the penalties imposed. It is noteworthy that the 'modest fines' imposed in the key cases where no violation was found, such as *Surek I* and *Leroy*, were relevant to the findings that the state was 'within its margin of appreciation' and no breach had occurred.[250] Reliance on limited punitive impact has regrettably sometimes meant that the ECtHR has not gone to the heart of the matter – ie, whether prosecution should have been permissible at all. However, in the *Doner* case it recognised that the process itself may constitute punishment and violation: a finding of a violation due to a criminal process does not wholly depend on a subsequent conviction, still less upon the penalty.[251]

This conclusion reflects the broader principle of criminal and human rights law that penalties must be proportionate to the wrong. Penalties for incitement and other terrorism-related offences increasingly give rise to doubts as to the necessity and proportionality of the resulting punishment, which will fall to be determined over time by human rights courts. As a judge of the IACtHR has noted,

> Classifying behaviors as criminal offenses must be done carefully and by rigorous standards, and the punishment must always be tailored to the importance of the protected interests, the harm done to them or the peril to which they are exposed, and the culpability of the perpetrator.[252]

[249] *Gözel and Özer v Turkey* (above n 213). The Court stated that domestic courts must look at objectives of the media, the right of the public, and 'other dimensions of the surrounding context' before convicting. Automatic offences of publishing statements by banned groups, or possession of information, fell foul of this requirement.

[250] *Surek and Ozdemir v Turkey* (above n 209) paras 63–65.

[251] *Doner v Turkey* (above n 187), where acquittals at the end of a long process did not affect the finding of a violation.

[252] *Ulloa v Costa Rica* (above n 201) separate opinion of Ramirez J.

V. CONCLUSION

An invigorated approach to criminal law has been lauded and promoted as part of a move away from the exceptionalism that has characterised much of the 'war on terror' and towards a rule-of-law approach to counterterrorism. However, exceptionalist tendencies have also emerged in relation to the criminal law, as its preventive potential has been stretched to prosecute 'crimes of expression' that are not necessarily linked in any meaningful way with terrorist acts. The implications of the broadening scope of offences and burgeoning prosecutorial practice – for criminal law, human rights protection, and the effective prevention of terrorism – call for sober reflection.

Criminal responsibility must correspond to individual culpability, based on conduct and intent, as well as to some meaningful link to criminal acts, not to a broader abstract danger, however serious or concerning. Early intervention against attempts, preparatory acts, and forms of conspiracy have all been referred to as 'good practices' consistent with an effective rule-of-law approach to countering terrorism within the criminal justice framework.[253] But when criminal law relies on its preventive function to reach further back and further out, it risks falling foul of the fundamental legal principles upon which its legitimacy depends. Straining the proximate link between an individual and a crime, and loosening requirements of conduct and intent, risk unravelling the basic precepts of criminal law and human rights law, with potential consequences beyond the counterterrorism context.[254]

While much ink has been spilled over the ill-defined nature and amorphous scope of terrorism – and increasingly of 'extremism' – the problems that they present are multiplied by offences that consist of encouraging, justifying, or creating an abstract danger of that ill-defined eventuality. So far as new offences lack clarity and specificity, and existing laws are interpreted expansively in a manner that prejudices the accused, they fall foul of requirements of legality and specificity under both criminal law and IHRL.

So far as the content of speech, understood in context, calls for and creates a real risk of violent acts, criminalisation is likely to be consistent with international human rights standards. Resort to criminal law should, however, be exceptional. Prosecuting the expression and sharing of ideas on the basis that they are offensive and represent a general 'danger' to society is irreconcilable with the essence of the right to free speech. While necessity and proportionality are eminently contextual assessments, and human rights courts have provided

[253] Global Counterterrorism Forum (GCTF), 'Rabat Memorandum on Good Practices for Effective Counterterrorism Practice in the Criminal Justice Sector' (2012), https://www.thegctf.org/Portals/1/Documents/Framework%20Documents/A/GCTF-Rabat-Memorandum-ENG.pdf. See, eg, 'Good Practice 13' on the scope of criminal law, which does not include indirect incitement of the type discussed in this chapter.

[254] Duffy (above n 13) ch 12.

no blueprint (and sometimes little clarity) for the acceptable intervention of criminal law, human rights jurisprudence does highlight the importance of distinguishing incitement to violence from speech that is acerbic, offensive, uncomfortable, or even supportive of banned organisations or undemocratic ideas. These distinctions and the need for a strict approach to justifying interference with freedom of expression required by IHRL, including the particular need for protection of political and artistic expression, are in little evidence in current practice, as demonstrated by this chapter.

Going forward, one of the challenges facing responsible governments and civil society will be to understand the broader implications of these laws and practices. Evidence already points to the 'nefarious targeting' of political opponents[255] and the devastating impact on the press, academic freedom, the arts, human rights and humanitarian organisations, and democratic debate. These laws and practices arise in a global climate in which human rights defenders are under threat in various forms, including through the criminalisation of their work.[256]

Paradoxically, although the recent flurry of legislative activity was sparked off by the Security Council, it jars with some of the principles necessary for effective, long-term counterterrorism as espoused by the United Nations and many others. The UN counterterrorism strategy called for urgent reflection on the 'conditions conducive to the spread of terrorism' almost a decade ago,[257] while the UN Secretary-General's 'Plan of Action on Preventing Violent Extremism' emphasises the importance of creating platforms for and fostering 'dialogue and discussion'.[258] Meanwhile those participating in essential debate on causes, contributors, and sustaining factors risk criminal prosecution in numerous states around the globe. The legislative and prosecutorial trends have prompted growing concerns about effectiveness. Do overextended, sweeping criminal laws lose their expressive value and social opprobrium or indeed become counterproductive?[259] If they fuel the sense of injustice and discrimination recognised as a significant 'pull factor' attracting young people in particular to terrorism,[260]

[255] 'Security Council dictate may be used by states to nefariously target those who disagree with them': Ní Aoláin (above n 12), in relation to the focus on criminal law, as well as inchoate offences, in UNSC Resolution 2178 (2014) and UNSC Resolution 2396 (2017). See also M Scheinin, 'Back to Post-9/11 Panic? Security Council Resolution on Foreign Terrorist Fighters', *Just Security* (23 September 2014), https://www.justsecurity.org/15407/post-911-panic-security-council-resolution-foreign-terrorist-fighters-scheinin/.

[256] Inter-American Commission on Human Rights, 'Criminalization of the Work of Human Rights Defenders', OEA/Ser.L/V/II, Doc 49/15 (31 December 2015), http://www.oas.org/en/iachr/reports/pdfs/criminalization2016.pdf.

[257] Pillar I of the United Nations Global Counter-Terrorism Strategy, A/RES/60/288 (20 September 2006) 2; and UN General Assembly, 'Plan of Action to Prevent Violent Extremism: Report of the Secretary-General', A/70/674 (24 December 2015).

[258] UN, 'Plan of Action to Prevent Violent Extremism' (ibid) para 49(e).

[259] European Parliament, 'An EU Approach to Criminal Law' (above n 146).

[260] See, eg, Emmerson (above n 154) 8–9.

and if they undermine the creation of 'safe environments' for civil society and democratic debate,[261] then they may be at odds with their own preventive rationale.

The role of legislatures, prosecutors, and courts will be crucial as political pressure grows in the face of changing and challenging terrorist threats. Prosecutorial discretion is often cited as a safeguard against broad-reaching laws. However, as Lord Bingham has noted,

> The rule of law is not well served if a crime is defined in terms wide enough to cover conduct which is not regarded as criminal and it is then left to the prosecuting authorities … not to prosecute to avoid injustice.[262]

Courts too will prove critical as laws convert more fully into practice and prosecutions. Criminal courts face the challenge of applying these laws consistently within the rule-of-law framework, prosecuting genuine incitement to violence yet curtailing overreach. Applications to supranational human rights courts will also increase, providing the opportunity for clearer, more robust human rights jurisprudence to guard against overreaching criminal law and to protect freedom of expression at a time of acute vulnerability.

REFERENCES

Amnesty International, 'Amnesty International Report 2016/17: The State of the World's Human Rights' (2017), https://www.amnesty.org.au/wp-content/uploads/2017/02/air201617-english_2016-17.pdf.

——, 'Egypt: 10-Year Prison Term for Insulting President an Outrageous Assault on Freedom of Expression', *Amnesty International* (13 April 2017).

——, 'France Faces "Litmus Test" for Freedom of Expression as Dozens Arrested in Wake of Attacks', *Amnesty International* (16 January 2015).

Anderson, D (UK Independent Reviewer of Terrorism Legislation), 'Shielding the Compass: How to Fight Terrorism without Defeating the Law' (2013), https://terrorismlegislationreviewer.independent.gov.uk/wp-content/uploads/2013/04/SHIELDING-THE-COMPASS1.pdf.

Andreu-Guzmán, F, 'Terrorism and Human Rights No 2', International Commission of Jurists Occasional Paper (March 2003).

Ashworth, A and Zedner, L, *Preventive Justice* (Oxford, Oxford University Press, 2014).

Associated Press, 'Spanish Investigation into "Terrorism-Praising" Puppet Show Shelved', *Guardian* (29 June 2016).

Barak-Erez, D and Sharia, D, 'Freedom of Speech, Support for Terrorism, and the Challenge of Global Constitutional Law' (2011) 2(1) *Harvard National Security Journal* 1–30.

BBC, 'Charlie Hebdo Attack: Three Days of Terror', *BBC News* (14 January 2015).

[261] See UN Security Council, 'Madrid Guiding Principles: A Practical Tool for Member States to Stem the Flow of Foreign Terrorist Fighters', S/2015/939 (23 December 2015), which refers to obligations to 'safeguard the ability of non-governmental actors to operate in a safe environment'.

[262] Cited in Anderson (above n 14).

——, 'Tareena Shakil Jailed for Six Years for Joining IS', *BBC News* (1 February 2016).

——, 'What is Eta?' *BBC News* (8 April 2017).

Berger, JM, 'Promoting Disengagement from Violent Extremism', International Centre for Counter-Terrorism (ICCT) Policy Brief (August 2016), https://icct.nl/wp-content/uploads/2016/08/CVE-Policy-Brief-FINAL.pdf.

Boyle, K and Shah, S, 'Thought, Expression, Association, and Assembly' in D Moeckli, S Shah, and S Sivakumaran (eds), *International Human Rights Law*, 2nd edn (Oxford, Oxford University Press, 2014).

Chachko, E, 'Israel's New Counter-Terrorism Law', *Lawfare* (13 July 2016), https://www.lawfareblog.com/israels-new-counterterrorism-law.

Choo, ALT, *Abuse of Process and Judicial Stays of Criminal Proceedings* (Oxford, Oxford University Press, 2008).

Crown Prosecution Service (UK), 'The Counter-terrorism Division of the Crown Prosecution Service (CPS): Successful Prosecutions since the End of 2006' (10 February 2017), https://www.cps.gov.uk/counter-terrorism-division-crown-prosecution-service-cps-successful-prosecutions-end-2006.

Dambrauskienė, A, 'The Conception of the Ultima Ratio Principle' (2015) 97 *Teisė* 116–34.

Duffy, H, *The War on Terror and the Framework of International Law*, 2nd edn (Cambridge, Cambridge University Press, 2015).

Emmerson, B (Special Rapporteur), 'Report on the Promotion and Protection of Human Rights and Fundamental Freedoms while Countering Terrorism', UN Doc A/HRC/31/65 (22 February 2016).

Erebara, G, 'Albania Jails Nine Jihadi Recruiters', *Balkan Insight* (4 May 2016), http://www.balkaninsight.com/en/article/heavy-sentences-spelled-for-albania-jihadi-recruiters-05-04-2016.

Feinberg, J, *Harm to Others* (New York, Oxford University Press, 1984).

France-Presse, A, 'Spanish Woman Given Jail Term for Tweeting Jokes about Franco-Era Assassination', *Guardian* (30 March 2017).

Frenett, R and Silverman, T, 'Foreign Fighters: Motivations for Travel to Foreign Conflicts' in A de Guttry, F Capone, and C Paulussen (eds), *Foreign Fighters under International Law and Beyond* (The Hague, Springer, 2016).

Front Line Defenders, 'Mohamed Ramadan Sentenced under Counter-Terrorism Law', *Front Line Defenders* (13 April 2017), https://www.frontlinedefenders.org/en/case/mohamed-ramadan-sentenced-under-counter-terrorism-law.

Galli, F, 'Developments in the Construction of Criminal Legislation: *R v Zafar and Others*' (2008) 172(33) *Justice of the Peace* 532–35.

Gilsinan, K, 'Is ISIS's Social-Media Power Exaggerated?' *Atlantic* (23 February 2015).

Global Counterterrorism Forum (GCTF), 'Rabat Memorandum on Good Practices for Effective Counterterrorism Practice in the Criminal Justice Sector' (2012), https://www.thegctf.org/Portals/1/Documents/Framework%20Documents/A/GCTF-Rabat-Memorandum-ENG.pdf.

Gurski, P, *Western Foreign Fighters: The Threat to Homeland and International Security* (Lanham, Rowman and Littlefield, 2017).

Hill, M (UK Independent Reviewer of Terrorism Legislation), 'The Terrorism Acts in 2016: Report on the Operation of the Terrorism Acts 2000 and 2006' (January 2018), https://terrorismlegislationreviewer.independent.gov.uk/wp-content/uploads/2018/01/Terrorism-Acts-in-2016.pdf.

Imbert, L, 'Apologie d'actes terroristes : des condamnations pour l'exemple', *Le Monde* (13 January 2015).

Inter-American Commission on Human Rights, 'Criminalization of the Work of Human Rights Defenders', OEA/Ser.L/V/II, Doc 49/15 (31 December 2015), http://www.oas.org/en/iachr/reports/pdfs/criminalization2016.pdf.

Jareborg, N, *Essays in Criminal Law* (Stockholm, Iustus Forlag, 1988).

Joahny, S, 'Apologie du terrorisme, un condamné par jour', *Le Journal du Dimanche* (4 September 2016), http://www.lejdd.fr/Societe/Justice/Apologie-du-terrorisme-un-condamne-par-jour-807154.

Kaye, D (Special Rapporteur), 'Promotion and Protection of the Right to Freedom of Opinion and Expression', UN General Assembly, A/71/373 (6 September 2016), https://www.refworld.org/docid/57fb6b974.html.

Keller, H and Sigron, M, 'State Security v Freedom of Expression: Legitimate Fight against Terrorism or Suppression of Political Opposition' (2010) 10(1) *Human Rights Law Review* 151–68.

Lazarus, L, 'Positive Obligations and Criminal Justice: Duties to Protect or Coerce?' in L Zedner and JV Roberts (eds), *Principles and Values in Criminal Law and Criminal Justice: Essays in Honour of Andrew Ashworth* (Oxford, Oxford University Press, 2012).

Le Monde, 'Dieudonné M'Bala M'Bala condamné à deux mois de prison avec sursis', *Le Monde* (18 March 2015).

Le Monde and AFP, '1847 délits d'apologie et de provocation au terrorisme enregistrés en 2016', *Le Monde* (19 January 2017).

Le Parisien, 'Dijon: il nomme son Wifi, "Daesh 21", et est condamné à de la prison avec sursis', *Le Parisien* (4 November 2016).

Maida, A, 'Online and on All Fronts: Russia's Assault on Freedom of Expression', *Human Rights Watch* (18 July 2017).

Mavronicola, N, 'Crime, Punishment and Article 3 ECHR: Puzzles and Prospects of Applying an Absolute Right in a Penal Context' (2015) 15(4) *Human Rights Law Review* 721–43.

McGuinness, R, 'French Teen Guilty of "Defending Terrorism" after Naming Wi-Fi Network "Daesh 21"', *Sunday Express* (7 November 2016).

Minder, R, 'Crackdowns on Free Speech Rise across a Europe Wary of Terror', *New York Times* (24 February 2016).

——, 'In a First for Spain, a Woman Is Convicted of Inciting Terror Over Twitter', *New York Times* (22 February 2014).

Muižnieks, N (Council of Europe Commissioner for Human Rights), 'Memorandum on Freedom of Expression and Media Freedom in Turkey', Doc CommDH(2017)5 (15 February 2017).

National Post, 'Don't Criminalize the Glorification of Terrorism, Law Professors Urge Government', *National Post* (22 January 2015).

Ní Aoláin, F, 'The UN Security Council, Global Watch Lists, Biometrics, and the Threat to the Rule of Law', *Just Security* (17 January 2018).

OSCE, 'OSCE Representative Condemns Continued Arrests of Journalists in Turkey, Calls on Authorities to Restore Media Pluralism', press release (31 October 2016), http://www.osce.org/fom/278326 (accessed 31 March 2019).

——, 'OSCE Representative on Freedom of the Media Calls on Turkey to Decriminalize Journalistic Work Following Arrest of Die Welt Journalist', press release (1 March 2017), http://www.osce.org/fom/302351 (accessed 31 March 2019).

OSCE Office for Democratic Institutions and Human Rights (ODIHR), 'Countering the Incitement and Recruitment of Foreign Terrorist Fighters: The Human Dimension', Background paper for Vienna Counter-Terrorism Expert Conference (30 June–1 July 2015), available at https://www.osce.org/odihr/166646 (accessed 7 March 2019).

Pasquini, G, 'Why Is the Spanish Government Afraid of a Puppet Show?' *New Yorker* (1 March 2016).

Pérez, FJ, 'Second Spanish Rapper Sentenced to Prison for Praising Terrorism', *El País* (English) (2 March 2018).

Press Association, 'Security Guard Jailed for Five Years over Tweets Glorifying Isis', *Guardian* (29 April 2016).

Reuters, 'Spanish Judge Frees Puppeteers Jailed for Glorifying Terrorism', *Guardian* (11 February 2016).

Ronen, Y, 'Terrorism and Freedom of Expression' in B Saul (ed), *Research Handbook on International Law and Terrorism* (Cheltenham, Edward Elgar, 2014).

Saul, B, 'Australia and International Counter-Terrorism Law and Practice' in D Rothwell and E Crawford (eds), *International Law in Australia*, 3rd edn (Sydney, Thomson Reuters, 2016).

Scheinin, M, 'Back to Post-9/11 Panic? Security Council Resolution on Foreign Terrorist Fighters', *Just Security* (23 September 2014).

Sottiaux, S, '*Leroy v France*: Apology of Terrorism and the Malaise of the European Court of Human Rights' Free Speech Jurisprudence' (2009) *European Human Rights Law Review* 415–27.

van Ginkel, B, 'Incitement to Terrorism: A Matter of Prevention or Repression?' International Centre for Counter-Terrorism (ICCT) Research Paper (August 2011), https://www.icct.nl/download/file/ICCT-Van-Ginkel-Incitement-To-Terrorism-August-2011.pdf.

Weinstein, S, 'Are we all Terrorists?', *New Internationalist* (1 December 2017), https://newint.org/features/2017/12/01/are-we-all-terrorists.

Zedner, L, 'Pre-Crime and Post-Criminology' (2007) 11(2) *Theoretical Criminology* 261–81.

Part IV

Exceptionalism, Risk, and Prevention

16

Oversight of the State of Emergency in France

MARC-ANTOINE GRANGER*

IN THE MONTHS after 'Red All Saints' Day' ('*Toussaint rouge*') on 1 November 1954, 'disorder', 'permanent insecurity', and 'psychosis' reigned in Algeria.[1] 'Assassinations of Muslims known for their loyalty' were perpetrated by the National Liberation Front (*Front de libération nationale*).[2] The threat of general insurrection haunted people, and the ability of the state to guarantee security was sorely in question. Undeniably, the Government of Edgar Faure could have resorted to the mechanism of martial law in a state of siege (*état de siège*),[3] which allows the transfer of powers to military authorities, including the power vested in civil authorities to maintain order and manage the police, when there is an 'imminent danger resulting from a foreign war or an armed insurrection'.[4] However, the Government (at least officially) rejected the use of this procedure in order to avoid 'significant disruption to the economic development of the country'.[5] In truth, only if the Government had recognised the existence of war between France and Algeria[6] or insurrection in some governmental departments (both of which were politically unthinkable) could it have reasonably declared France in a state of siege.

* The author and editors would like to thank Alix de Zitter for translating the first draft of this chapter.

[1] These terms are from the Explanatory Note of Bill n° 10478 establishing the state of emergency (22 March 1955).

[2] Ibid.

[3] Law of 9 August 1849 on the state of siege, amended by the Law of 3 April 1878 on the state of siege. Article 5 of ordinance n° 2004-1374 of 20 December 2004 on the legislative part of the Defense Code abrogated these two laws. The statutory provisions on the state of siege are now codified under Articles L 2121(1)– L 2121(8) of the Defense Code.

[4] Article L 2121(1) of the Defense Code.

[5] Bill n° 10478 Explanatory Note (above n 1).

[6] It was not until 1999 that the term 'Algerian war' was officially used to refer to the earlier period. See Law n° 99-882 of 18 October 1999 on the replacement of the terms 'operations in North Africa' by 'war in Algeria and battles in Tunisia and Morocco'.

Instead, the Government reached the conclusion that there were 'insufficient legal grounds designed for times of insurrection'.[7] It is in this context that Law n° 55-385 was passed on 3 April 1955, creating instead the legal concept of a 'state of emergency' (*état d'urgence*) and applying it to the Algerian territory.[8] This law survived the end of the Fourth Republic, and indeed, the *Conseil constitutionnel* (Constitutional Council) ruled in 1985 that the Constitution of the Fifth Republic of 4 October 1958 'did not abrogate the Law of 3 April 1955 regarding the state of emergency'.[9]

Unlike both martial law in a state of siege and the exceptional powers of the President of the French Republic, which are provided for respectively under Articles 36 and 16 of the Constitution, the state of emergency does not have a constitutional basis. Twice, in 1993 and 2007, expert committees in vain suggested adding the provisions on the state of emergency into the Constitution.[10] In November 2015, three days after terrorist attacks were perpetrated in Paris, then-President François Hollande, in a speech before Parliament,[11] echoed these suggestions when he proposed a constitutional amendment designed to include the state of emergency.[12] For this purpose, a Constitutional Bill on the protection of the nation was introduced before the National Assembly on 23 December 2015.[13] In addition to adding Article 36(1) to the Constitution, which would have provided for a state of emergency, the Bill would have allowed the legislature to lay down 'the conditions under which a French-born citizen who holds another nationality could be deprived of his/her French nationality when convicted of a crime that constitutes a serious attack to the life of the nation'.[14] After three months of parliamentary

[7] Bill n° 10478 Explanatory Note (above n 1).

[8] Law n° 55-385 of 3 April 1955 instituting a state of emergency and declaring its application in Algeria. Para IV(1) of Art 176 of Law n° 2011-525 of 17 May 2011 on the simplification and improvement of the law modified the title of the Law of 3 April 1955 by replacing the words 'instituting the state of emergency and declaring its application in Algeria' by 'in the state of emergency'.

[9] *Conseil constitutionnel* decision n° 85-187 DC of 25 January 1985, Law on the state of emergency in New Caledonia and Other Territories, para 4.

[10] See 'Propositions pour une révision de la Constitution: rapport du Comité consultatif pour une révision de la Constitution', présidé par le doyen Georges Vedel (La documentation française, 1993); and Comité de réflexion et de proposition sur la modernisation et le rééquilibrage des institutions de la Ve République, 'Une Ve République plus démocratique' (La documentation française, 2007).

[11] Speech of the President of the French Republic before Parliament (16 November 2015), www.assemblee-nationale.fr/14/cri/congres/20154001.asp.

[12] The presidential proposal to revise the Constitution occurred *after* a state of emergency was declared in 14 November 2015. Unlike the Constitutions of other Member States of the European Union, the French Constitution can be amended even during a state of siege or during a state of emergency (L'état d'urgence, Législation comparée, Les documents de travail du Sénat, 2006, www.senat.fr/lc/lc156/lc156_mono.html). Indeed, in Decision n° 92-312 DC of 2 September 1992 on the EU Treaty, the *Conseil constitutionnel* ruled that 'The limitations on the periods during which the Constitution cannot be modified … result from Articles 7, 16, and 89(4) of the Constitution.'

[13] Bill n° 3381 on the amendment of the Constitution regarding the protection of the Nation, registered at the National Assembly on 23 December 2015.

[14] Art 2 of Bill n° 3381 (ibid).

deliberation and disagreement between the National Assembly and the Senate regarding the wording of the text, the President finally decided to 'close the constitutional debate' in early 2016.[15] Thus, the state of emergency remains deprived of a constitutional foundation.

Although it was designed in 1955 to solve the Algerian crisis, the French state of emergency has always had a territorial framework that is much broader than Algeria: it can be 'declared in all or part of the metropolitan territory … or overseas departments'.[16] In other words, the state of emergency was not conceptualised as an exceptional regime applicable only to the situation in Algeria, as evidenced by the explanatory memorandum of the Bill that established it: 'public policy considerations justified … by the situation in Algeria are not the only ones which can be taken into consideration'.[17] During parliamentary debates in 1955, the Minister of Internal Affairs (*Ministre de l'Interieur*) stated:

> The department that was first confronted by what is called … the state of emergency … is the department of civil protection, following the looting which took place in Orléansville after the earthquake.… Therefore, the text that establishes the state of emergency … is necessary … to counter the difficulties modern states face due either to natural calamities or to different origins.[18]

And indeed, while the state of emergency was declared for the first time in Algeria,[19] it was subsequently used on three occasions in other French territories[20] and four times in mainland France.[21] In France, a state of emergency was declared to prevent an airborne operation (referred to as a 'resurrection') on Corsica and on the mainland;[22] then in 1961 in response to the Generals' putsch in Algeria;[23] again in the face of urban riots that started on 27 October 2005

[15] Declaration of the President of the French Republic on the amendment of the Constitution (30 March 2016), http://discours.vie-publique.fr/notices/167000919.html.

[16] Art 1, Law n° 55-385 (above n 8).

[17] Bill n° 10478 Explanatory Note (above n 1).

[18] Maurice Bourgès-Maunoury, Minister of Home Affairs, Summary of the debates before the National Assembly (31 March 1955).

[19] Art 15(1), Law n° 55-385 (above n 8).

[20] A state of emergency was declared in New Caledonia and its territories by Decree ('arrêté') n° 85-35 of 12 January 1985 of the High Commissioner of the French Republic. A state of emergency was declared in the territories of Wallis and Futuna by two Decrees of the Superior Administrator: n°s 117 and 118 (29 October 1986). And a state of emergency was declared in the Windward Isles of French Polynesia by two decrees of the High Commissioner of the Republic: n°s 1214 CAB and 1215 CAB (24 October 1987).

[21] Notably, General de Gaulle also considered declaring a state of emergency in May 1968 but instead dissolved the National Assembly upon the request of his Prime Minister. See the recording of de Gaulle on 30 May 1968, https://fresques.ina.fr/de-gaulle/fiche-media/Gaulle00366/allocution-radiodiffusee-du-30-mai-1968.html.

[22] Art 1, Law n° 58-487 of 17 May 1958.

[23] Decree n° 61-395 of 22 April 1961 on the declaration of the state of emergency; and Decree n° 61-396 of the same day on the application of the state of emergency.

in several hundred municipalities;[24] and most recently, following the Paris terrorist attacks of 13 November 2015.

After its initial adoption of the most recent state of emergency in November 2015,[25] the legislature extended the state of emergency six times, until it officially ended on 1 November 2017.[26] At the time of the first and fourth extensions, the legislature held that it wanted to 'adapt and … modernise some provisions of the 1955 Law' to make the state of emergency as effective as possible in order to prevent further terrorist acts and to strengthen 'the guarantees … regarding the implementation of powers entrusted to the administrative authority'.[27] Article 4(1) was added to the 1955 law:

> The National Assembly and the Senate shall be informed without delay of the measures the Government adopts during the state of emergency. They can request additional information as part of the evaluation and monitoring of these measures.[28]

As a result, in addition to the existing channels of judicial review, there are now some measures of parliamentary control over the state of emergency, largely in response to the threat that emergency powers represent to fundamental rights.

Indeed, 'either in case of imminent danger resulting from serious breaches of the public order or in case of events, which have by their nature or gravity,

[24] Decree n° 2005-1386 of 8 November 2005 on the application of Law n° 55-385; and Decree n° 2005-1387 of 8 November 2005 on the application of Law n° 55-385.

[25] Art 1 of Decree n° 2015-1475 of 14 November 2015 on the application of Law n° 55-385 of 3 April 1955 declaring the state of emergency, from 14 November 2015 at midnight in mainland France and Corsica. Art 1 of Decree n° 2015-1493 of 18 November 2015 extended the application of the state of emergency to Guadeloupe, Guyana, Martinique, Reunion Island, Mayotte, Saint-Barthélémy and Saint-Martin.

[26] Law n° 2015-1501 of 20 November 2015 extended the state of emergency for a duration of three months (from 26 November 2015); Law n° 2016-162 of 19 February 2016 extended it again for three months (from 26 February 2016); Law n° 2016-629 of 20 May 2016 extended it for two more months (from 26 May 2016); and Law n° 2016-987 of 21 July 2016 extended it for six more months (from 21 July 2016). Following the resignation of Prime Minister Manuel Valls on 6 December 2016 and in the absence of a new extension of the state of emergency, the Law n° 2016-987 of 21 July 2016 should have become null as of 22 December 2016, pursuant to Art 4 of the Law n° 55-385 of 3 April 1955 (above n 8): 'The law extending the state of emergency becomes null fifteen clear days after the resignation of the Government or of the dissolution of the National Assembly.' However, Law n° 2016-1767 of 19 December 2016 extended the state of emergency from 22 December 2016 to 15 July 2017. It was specifically extended to cover the election period, which it was anticipated would 'double the threat on the French society': 'First, the multiplication of rallies, public meetings, and voting operations will result in concentrations of the population which represent targets and require security measures. Second, a terror attack during the election period, a period of political debates which can be quite tensed, would have an increased impact and would seriously and directly damage the French democratic and institutional life.' See the Statement of the reasons justifying the adoption of the extension of Law n° 55-385 on the state of emergency, presented on behalf of Prime Minister Bernard Cazeneuve by Bruno Le Roux, Minister of Internal Affairs (National Assembly, 10 December 2016). Finally, Law n° 2017-1154 of 11 July 2017 extended the state of emergency until 1 November 2017.

[27] Explanatory Note on the Bill of Law n° 3225 extending the application of Law n° 55-385 of 18 November 2015.

[28] Art 4(1), Law n° 55-385 (above n 8), as drafted based on Art 2, Law n° 2016-987 (above n 26).

the character of a public calamity',[29] the state of emergency grants the Minister of Internal Affairs and the Prefects extensive powers: for instance, the power to order home searches and raids anywhere and at any time, night or day;[30] to limit the freedom of movement of people and vehicles in certain places and at specific times;[31] to place under house arrest any person who there are serious reasons to believe may represent a threat to security or public order;[32] or to temporarily close theatres, pubs, and meeting places.[33]

All of these measures, some of which require express authorisation,[34] are violations of rights and freedoms, including, for example, the inviolability of homes, the right to privacy, freedom of movement, the right of assembly, and freedom of speech. The French government addressed these issues in a letter to the Secretary General of the European Council on 24 November 2015, indicating that the state of emergency 'may involve derogations to [its] obligations under the Convention'.[35] (The letter was submitted pursuant to Article 15(3) of the European Convention of Human Rights (ECHR) – an Article which itself had been subject to reservation by the French Republic upon ratification of the Convention.[36])

Even during original parliamentary debates on the adoption of the state of emergency in relation to Algeria, the measures faced strong criticism. Some MPs described Law n° 55-385 as 'violating human rights',[37] a 'villainous law',[38] a 'fascist law',[39] and even as 'a law which is worse in some cases than the emergency laws of Vichy'.[40] It was due to such criticisms and to the

[29] Art 1, Law n° 55-385 (above n 8).

[30] Ibid, Art 11.

[31] Ibid, Art 5(1).

[32] Ibid, Art 6.

[33] Ibid, Art 8.

[34] Such is the case of the administrative searches conducted pursuant to the first subparagraph of the first paragraph of Art 11, Law n° 55-385 (above n 8).

[35] Letter of 24 November 2015 addressed to the Secretariat General of the European Council by Jocelyne Caballero on behalf of the permanent representation of France to the European Council.

[36] 'The Government of the Republic, pursuant to Article 64 of the Convention, expresses a reservation to paragraph 1 of Article 15 to the effect that … the circumstances enumerated … by Article 1 of Law n° 55-385 of 3 April 1955 on the declaration of the state of emergency, and which allow the application of the provisions of these texts must be understood as corresponding to the purpose of Article 15 of the Convention.' See the Reservation contained in the instrument of ratification (3 May 1974), www.coe.int/fr/web/conventions/full-list/-/conventions/treaty/005/declarations?p_auth=sC3wH9US&_coeconventions_WAR_coeconventionsportlet_enVigueur=false&_coeconventions_WAR_coeconventionsportlet_searchBy=state&_coeconventions_WAR_coeconventionsportlet_codePays=FRA&_coeconventions_WAR_coeconventionsportlet_codeNature=2.

[37] Georges Marrane, Minutes of the debates of the *Conseil de la République* (1 April 1955).

[38] Louis Namy, Minutes of the debates of the *Conseil de la République* (1 April 1955).

[39] Alice Sportisse, Minutes of the debates of the National Assembly (31 March 1955).

[40] Robert Ballanger, Minutes of the debates of the National Assembly (first session, 31 March 1955).

particularly serious attacks on liberties that the government attempted to 'reason the *raison d'Etat*'[41] (to use Mireille Delmas-Marty's expression) by implementing both judicial and non-judicial oversight mechanisms for the state of emergency.

I. JUDICIAL OVERSIGHT OF THE STATE OF EMERGENCY

> Confronted with the arbitrariness of power, any interested party must be able to find a judge.
>
> Jean-François Henry, *Rubin de Servens* (*Conseil d'État*, 2 March 1962)[42]

Article 16 of the Declaration of the Rights of Man and of the Citizen (1789) sets out the principle of the 'guarantee of rights' (*garantie des droits*). It is precisely because it is part of the rule of law that the state of emergency places important emphasis on the right to judicial remedy. However, the judiciary has only secondary competence: it can play a role only when there has been criminal noncompliance with certain administrative police measures relating to the state of emergency (notably those concerning house arrest)[43] or when judicial proceedings follow administrative police operations (for example, when infringements are detected during administrative searches,[44] baggage searches, or vehicle inspections).[45]

The legality of eight administrative search orders was challenged before the criminal courts on 17 May 2016.[46] In three cases, the courts annulled seizures that had followed administrative searches on the grounds that the search orders had been insufficiently reasoned. However, administrative judges and the *Conseil constitutionnel*, rather than criminal court judges, remain the ones on the front line of litigation involving measures adopted on the basis of Law n° 55-385.[47]

[41] M Delmas-Marty, *Raisonner la raison d'État. Vers une Europe des droits de l'homme* (Paris, PUF, 1989).

[42] Conclusions for the *Conseil d'État* (2 March 1962), *Rubin de Servens* (1962) RDP 310.

[43] Art 13, Law n° 55-385 (above n 8).

[44] See *Cour de cassation*, crim (28 March 2017), n°s 16-85072 and 16-85073.

[45] The last paragraph of Art 8(1), Law n° 55-385 (above n 8) provides, in addition, that the decision to authorise visual inspections, baggage searches, and the inspection of circulating vehicles, stopped or stationed on public roads or in places accessible to the public, shall be transmitted without delay to the public prosecutor.

[46] These figures were communicated to Parliament by the *Direction des affaires criminelles et des grâces* ('Directorate of Criminal Affairs and Pardons') of the Ministry of Justice. See the 'Progress Report on Oversight of the State of Emergency', Meeting of the Law Commission of the National Assembly (17 May 2016), available at http://www2.assemblee-nationale.fr/14/commissions-permanentes/commission-des-lois/controle-parlementaire-de-l-etat-d-urgence/controle-parlementaire-de-l-etat-d-urgence/(block)/27358. See in particular D Raimbourg and J-F Poisson, 'Communication d'étape sur le contrôle de l'état d'urgence' (17 May 2016), http://www2.assemblee-nationale.fr/static/14/lois/communication_2016_05_17.pdf.

[47] Art 4(8), Law n° 2015-1501 (above n 26) removed the jurisdiction of the military courts for crimes and related offences that are subject to the jurisdiction of criminal courts.

The next section examines the mechanisms through which administrative courts can exercise some limited authority over the implementation and continuation of a state of emergency, while the section that follows examines the more extensive oversight powers accorded to the *Conseil constitutionnel* and the *Conseil d'État* with regard to administrative police measures adopted in application of the law on the state of emergency.

A. Oversight of the Declaration of a State of Emergency and its Continued Enforcement

An administrative judge can review: (1) the declaration of a state of emergency; and (2) the presidential decision to keep it in force. Nonetheless, the President of the Republic, acting under Law n° 55-385, cannot be regarded as a mere administrative authority subject to unconstrained judicial review, since the role of administrative judges is also necessarily limited.

i. Oversight of the Declaration of a State of Emergency

Pursuant to Article 2(1) of Law n° 55-385, the President of the Republic is responsible for initiating the declaration of a state of emergency. The President, however, does not act completely independently, since the declaration takes the form of a decree (*arrêté*) adopted by the Council of Ministers and countersigned by the Prime Minister and the competent ministers.[48] This decree determines the territorial constituency or constituencies in which the state of emergency enters into force.

This presidential decision to declare a state of emergency is likely to be challenged before the administrative courts. This was implicitly held by the *Conseil d'État* in *Rolin et Boisvert* (2006)[49] in relation to the decree of 8 November 2005, which declared a state of emergency following urban violence that had started on 27 October 2005 in hundreds of French communities.[50] Unlike the decision of the President to invoke the exceptional powers of Article 16 of the Constitution,[51] the decision to declare a state of emergency does not correspond to either of the two categories identified as an 'act of government' (namely, an act relating to the relations between the executive and Parliament or an act relating to the relations between the Government and a foreign state or international organisation[52]). Consequently, the declaration of a state of emergency is subject to review by the administrative court.

[48] Art 19, Constitution of 4 October 1958.

[49] *Conseil d'État*, Assembly (24 March 2006) *Rolin et Boisvert*, n° 286834.

[50] Decree n° 2005-1386 of 8 November 2005 on the application of Law n° 55-385 of 3 April 1955.

[51] *Conseil d'État*, Assembly (2 March 1962) *Rubin de Servens et autres*, n°s 55049 and 55055, *Recueil des décisions du Conseil d'État, statuant au contentieux* (*rec*) 143.

[52] On this point, see the commentary on *Conseil d'État* (19 February 1875) *Prince Napoléon* in M Long et al, *Les grands arrêts de la jurisprudence administrative*, 21st edn (Paris, Dalloz, 2017) 16.

However, the true extent of judicial authority over a declaration of a state of emergency remains relatively uncertain. Such oversight is constrained first because it is exercised in relation to the presidential decision to *end* a state of emergency (see further below). Second, the President's discretionary power to declare a state of emergency rests on the competence to qualify a situation as an 'imminent peril' or a 'public calamity'. Could a mere administrative judge exercise complete oversight in such situations without undermining the separation of powers?

Beyond this relative uncertainty, another restriction on judicial authority to overrule a decree declaring a state of emergency should be noted. Due to the 'distinctive characteristics of the regime' defined by Law n° 55-385,[53] an administrative judge has jurisdiction over the legality of a presidential decree only if no law has been passed to extend the state of emergency.[54] This means that the possibility of challenging a declaration of a state of emergency is narrow since, pursuant to Article 2, last paragraph, of Law n° 55-385, the intervention of the legislature is necessary in any case to maintain the state of emergency beyond twelve days from its declaration. Of course, the law extending the state of emergency can be referred to the *Conseil constitutionnel* pursuant to Article 61, paragraph 2, of the Constitution (optional and *a priori* control of the constitutionality of ordinary laws). However, if the state of emergency does not have a constitutional basis, the *Conseil constitutionnel* seized of such a law cannot perhaps assess whether the conditions for the application of the state of emergency are met. Ultimately, once a law of prorogation has been adopted, the administrative judge can only adjudicate on the decision of the President regarding early termination of the state of emergency.

ii. Continued Enforcement of the State of Emergency

In 2005, 2015, 2016, and 2017, the laws extending the state of emergency allowed the President of the Republic the possibility of ending the state of emergency before the expiration date set by Parliament.[55] This power reflects both the principle of 'formal parallelism' and the inherently temporary nature of a state of

[53] *Rolin et Boisvert* (above n 49).

[54] The *Conseil d'État* has justified this by explaining that such a law would 'ratify the initial decision' to declare a state of emergency. The use of the term 'ratification' is questionable insofar as the legislature does not just confirm the initial decision by the President to declare a state of emergency but must also check whether the conditions imposed by Law n° 55-385 are still met. In that respect, see *Conseil d'État*, Ordinance (27 January 2016) *Ligue des droits de l'homme et autres*, n° 396220. For further discussion on this issue, see D Baranger, 'Quel 'État de droit'? Quels contrôles? Le juge des référés et le maintien en vigueur de l'état d'urgence' (2016) 2 *RFDA* 355–64.

[55] Art 3, Law n° 2005-1425 of 18 November 2005 extending the application of Law n° 55-385 of 3 April 1955; Art 3, Law n° 2015-1501 (above n 26); Unique Article, III, Law n° 2016-162 (above n 26); Single Article, II, Law n° 2016-629 (above n 26); Article 1, III, Law n° 2016-987 (above n 26); Art 1, Law n° 2016-1767 (above n 26); and Article 1, III, Law n° 2017-1154 (above n 26).

emergency. In fact, it was a Presidential decree in January 2006 that ended the state of emergency that had been extended for a period of three months starting on 21 November 2005.[56] However, this power to terminate the state of emergency has not always been a prerogative of the President. The Law of 7 August 1955 extending the state of emergency for a period of six months in Algeria entrusted this power to the Government rather than to the President.[57] After all, initially the declaration of the state of emergency was a legislative prerogative,[58] and in a parliamentary system, the Government is naturally responsible before the Parliament. In the light of this, some authors have suggested entrusting both the declaration and the suspension of the state of emergency to the Prime Minister and the government.[59] However, the likelihood of this 'pious wish' is small insofar as the Fifth Republic is a presidential regime in which the President leads the executive power,[60] 'ensures the respect of the Constitution [... and ...] the proper functioning of public authorities and the continuity of the State'.[61]

In any case, in 2005 and again in 2016, the *juge des référés* (judge of interim measures) of the *Conseil d'État* agreed to hear submissions aimed at allowing the President of the Republic to end the state of emergency (with a decree adopted by the Council of Ministers) before the expiration date prescribed by the law of extension or, at the very least, to have the possibility to re-examine the situation.[62] The *Conseil* ruled that 'the silence of the law on the conditions of exercise of this power cannot be interpreted, in the light of the fact that a system of exceptional powers has effects which, in a state governed by the rule of law, are inherently limited in time and space, to avoid a review by the judge of the legality'.[63]

The control exercised here by the judge is limited in order to protect the 'broad discretionary power' of the President of the Republic to 'exercise or not the power conferred to him by the law to end the state of emergency before the expiry of the prescribed period'.[64] It is therefore unlikely that any *juge des référés* of the *Conseil d'État* would order the President to re-examine a situation or enjoin him to end the state of emergency. In 2005,

[56] Art 1, Decree n° 2006-2 of 3 January 2006 ending the application of Law n° 2005-1425 (above n 55).

[57] Art 1(2), Law n° 55-1080 of 7 August 1955 on the state of emergency in Algeria.

[58] On this historical aspect, see A Heymann-Doat, 'L'état d'urgence, un régime juridique d'exception pour lutter contre le terrorisme?' (2016) (38)1 *Archives de politique criminelle* 59–74, 68; and F Rolin, 'L'état d'urgence' in B Mathieu (ed), *Cinquantième anniversaire de la Constitution française* (Paris, Dalloz, 2008) 613.

[59] D Baranger, 'L'état d'urgence dans la durée' (2016) 3 *RFDA* 447–54.

[60] de Gaulle, 'Discours de Bayeux', speech (16 June 1946), http://www.charles-de-gaulle.org/wp-content/uploads/2017/03/Discours-de-Bayeux-16-juin-1946.pdf.

[61] Art 5(1), Constitution of 4 October 1958.

[62] *Conseil d'État*, ord (9 December 2005), *Mme Allouache et autres*, n° 287777; and *Ligue des droits de l'homme et autres* (above n 54).

[63] *Mme Allouache et autres* (ibid); and *Ligue des droits de l'homme et autres* (above n 54).

[64] *Conseil d'État*, *Ligue des droits de l'homme et autres* (above n 54).

a *juge des référés* held that 'it could not be validly argued that the President has, in the exercise of his extended discretion, taken a decision which would be vitiated by unlawfulness, when ... the circumstances which justified the declaration of urgency have changed significantly.'[65] In 2016, the same judge ruled that the President had not committed a serious and manifestly unlawful interference with a fundamental freedom when he failed to adopt a decree to end the state of emergency. Decisive factors in the decision included the attacks perpetrated on and after 13 November 2015, France's involvement in large-scale external military operations (OPEX) aimed at 'striking bases from which terrorist operations are prepared, organised and financed',[66] and the fact that measures adopted under the state of emergency 'help to prevent imminent dangers to which the country is exposed'.[67]

All in all, both the declaration of a state of emergency and the decision of the President of the Republic not to end it can be challenged before the administrative courts. However, the actual capacity of judges to rule on these highly political decisions is questionable. While a judge may not be in a position of authority over the choice of the President either to declare a state of emergency or not to end it, the existence of some oversight may nonetheless provide incentive for restraint on the part of the President. In the end, however, the limited powers of oversight when it comes to decisions on the declaration and termination of a state of emergency stand in contrast to the extensive powers to review and control administrative police measures that are adopted as part of the state of emergency. These powers will be discussed in the following section.

B. Oversight of Administrative Police Measures

There are extensive powers of oversight for administrative police measures adopted in application of the state of emergency in France. Recent rulings by the *Conseil constitutionnel* (discussed further below) have affirmed these powers, which are also exercised traditionally by administrative courts.

Unsurprisingly, Law n° 55-385 was not subject to constitutional review during the Fourth Republic, since constitutional review was largely 'symbolic'.[68] Even during the Fifth Republic, constitutional review of the law on the state of emergency was adopted only at a late stage. Ordinance n° 60-372 of 15 April 1960 would have allowed for review of the constitutionality of Law n° 55-385.[69]

[65] *Conseil d'État, Mme Allouache et autres* (above n 62).

[66] *Conseil d'État, Ligue des droits de l'homme et autres* (above n 54).

[67] Ibid.

[68] George Vedel, quoted in L Favoreu et al (eds), *Droit constitutionnel*, 21st edn (Paris, Dalloz, 2018) 329.

[69] Ordinance n° 60-372 of 15 April 1960 modifying some provisions of Law n° 55-385 of 3 April 1955 on the state of emergency.

However, the lack of express legislative ratification of the ordinance meant that referral to the *Conseil constitutionnel* was not possible. In contrast, the New Caledonia State of Emergency Law was referred to the *Conseil constitutionnel* in 1985, but the Court did not take the opportunity to consider the constitutionality of Law n° 55-385.

First, the *Conseil constitutionnel* has limited the situations in which it undertakes review of a law that has already been adopted:

> If the constitutional regularity of the terms of a promulgated law can be usefully challenged during the adoption of the law which modifies, supplements or affects its application, the same does not apply when it comes to a mere application of that law.[70]

Then the Court held that the New Caledonia State of Emergency Law was a mere application of Law n° 55-385 and declined to review the constitutionality of that law.[71]

The adoption of the Law of 20 November 2015 extending the application of Law n° 55-385 on the state of emergency and reinforcing the effectiveness of its provisions gave rise to the hope of a referral to the *Conseil constitutionnel* to consider the constitutionality of Law n° 55-385. This hope was quickly dashed by Prime Minister Manuel Valls during parliamentary debates when he stated, 'It is always risky to refer a law to the *Conseil constitutionnel*.'[72] In response to similar comments made by Minister of Justice Pascal Clément in 2005, the President of the *Conseil constitutionnel*, Pierre Mazeaud, countered that 'Respect for the Constitution is not a risk but a duty.'[73] Despite the truth of that statement, the Law of 20 November 2015 was not referred to the *Conseil constitutionnel*.

i. Recent Rulings by the Conseil constitutionnel *Regarding Oversight of Emergency Measures*

Nine recent 'priority rulings on constitutionality' (known as *questions prioritaires de constitutionnalité* (QPC)) have allowed *a posteriori* review of the constitutionality of laws.[74] Consequently, specific provisions of Law n° 55-385 have been referred to the *Conseil constitutionnel*, most notably those concerning

[70] Decision n° 85-187 DC (above n 9) para 10.

[71] Ibid.

[72] Minutes of Senate debates (20 November 2015).

[73] The subject was the institution of a harsh regime of 'judicial surveillance' over offenders with a high recidivism risk (including, for example, surveillance through electronic tagging). See P Mazeaud, 'L'erreur', Institut de France Colloquium (25–26 October 2006), https://www.conseil-constitutionnel.fr/sites/default/files/as/root/bank_mm/pdf/Conseil/erreur.pdf.

[74] Art 61(1), Constitution of 4 October 1958, as amended by Art 29, Constitutional Law n° 2008-724 of 23 July 2008 on the modernisations of the institutions of the Fifth Republic.

house arrest,[75] search and administrative seizures,[76] control of meetings and public places,[77] identity checks, baggage searches and vehicle visits,[78] specific protected areas in which the residence of people is regulated,[79] and other restrictions on residence. Without detailing the various decisions rendered in relation to these issues, a few important points should be made.

Firstly, the *Conseil constitutionnel* confirmed that police measures adopted within the framework of a state of emergency are not subject to judicial supervision (ie, from public prosecutors or judges). This conclusion rests on a restrictive conception of the notion of individual freedom. Constitutional jurisprudence has historically distinguished between administrative and judicial policing, 'mapping' the relationship between constitutionally guaranteed rights and freedoms and policing measures.[80] If a police measure is determined to have an administrative nature (in distinction to those with a judicial nature), the *Conseil constitutionnel* infers the application of different standards of constitutional limits, regardless of the object of the measure (eg, identity checks, police custody, search of vehicles) and regardless also of the fundamental rights and liberties at issue. Administrative police measures remain 'solely the responsibility of the executive power'.[81] This means that, unlike judicial police measures, they do not have to be placed 'under the direction or supervision of a judicial authority'.[82] However, when an administrative police measure restricts individual freedom (ie, deprives an individual of freedom), Article 66 of the Constitution mandates judicial supervision of the measure.[83] In contrast, if no infringement of individual freedom is involved, there is no legislative obligation to provide for judicial supervision. In the cases mentioned above that related to house arrest and administrative searches,

[75] *Conseil constitutionnel*, decision n° 2015-527 QPC (22 December 2015), *M Cédric D (Assignations à résidence dans le cadre de l'état d'urgence)*; and *Conseil constitutionnel*, decision n° 2017-624 QPC (16 March 2017), *M Sofiyan I (Assignations à résidence dans le cadre de l'état d'urgence II)*.

[76] *Conseil constitutionnel*, decision n° 2016-536 QPC (19 February 2016), *Ligue des droits de l'homme (Perquisitions et saisies administratives dans le cadre de l'état d'urgence)*; *Conseil constitutionnel*, decision n° 2016-567/568 QPC (23 September 2016), *M Georges F et autre (Perquisitions administratives dans le cadre de l'état d'urgence II)*; and *Conseil constitutionnel*, decision n° 2016-600 QPC (2 December 2016), *M Raïme A (Perquisitions administratives dans le cadre de l'état d'urgence III)*.

[77] *Conseil constitutionnel*, decision n° 2016-535 QPC (19 February 2016), *Ligue des droits de l'homme (Police des réunions et des lieux publics dans le cadre de l'état d'urgence)*.

[78] *Conseil constitutionnel*, décision n° 2017-677 QPC (1 December 2017), *Ligue des droits de l'Homme (Contrôles d'identité, fouilles de bagages et visites de véhicules dans le cadre de l'état d'urgence)*.

[79] *Conseil constitutionnel*, décision n° 2017-684 QPC (11 January 2018), *Associations La cabane juridique / Legal Shelter et autre (Zones de protection ou de sécurité dans le cadre de l'état d'urgence)*.

[80] M-A Granger, *Constitution et sécurité intérieure. Essai de modélisation juridique*, Prix de thèse du Conseil constitutionnel (Paris, LGDJ, 2011) 41.

[81] *Conseil constitutionnel*, decision n° 2005-532 DC (19 January 2006), *Loi relative à la lutte contre le terrorisme et portant dispositions diverses relatives à la sécurité et aux contrôles frontaliers*, para 5.

[82] Ibid.

[83] Art 66, Constitution of 4 October 1958: 'No one shall be arbitrarily detained. The Judicial Authority, guardian of the freedom of the individual, shall ensure compliance with this principle in the conditions laid down by statute.'

the *Conseil constitutionnel* concluded that such measures do not affect individual freedom and are therefore exempt from judicial supervision.

This conclusion is unsurprising with regard to house arrest, since the *Conseil constitutionnel* had already held that administrative restrictions on the residency of foreigners unable to leave the country immediately[84] do not fall within the scope of Article 66 of the Constitution.[85] Likewise, in Decision n° 2015-527 QPC of 22 December 2015, the *Conseil constitutionnel* held that the Minister of Internal Affairs can impose residency requirements within a determined vicinity without involving a deprivation of individual freedom within the meaning of Article 66.[86] For the *Conseil constitutionnel*, a person under house arrest is not comparable to a person detained or held in police custody, and the law expressly prohibits the creation of 'camps where people under house arrest would be detained'.[87] The *Conseil constitutionnel* furthermore held that the Minister of Internal Affairs can confine a person to house arrest within a specified geographic location for a period not exceeding twelve hours per twenty-four hours without triggering the deprivation of freedom that would require the protection of judicial oversight.[88] However, the *Conseil constitutionnel* formulated interpretative reservations on this point, holding that more than twelve hours of house arrest in a twenty-four-hour period constitutes a custodial measure that is subject to judicial authority.[89]

The *Conseil constitutionnel* gave no indication why the twelve-hour threshold was chosen instead of, for example, an eight-hour threshold, as was suggested during parliamentary debates. At that time, the rapporteur of the *Commission des lois de l'Assemblée nationale* (Committee on the Laws of the National Assembly) declared that even eight hours of house arrest should be considered 'administrative detention, which pursuant to Article 66 of the Constitution [...] should be ruled upon by a judge'.[90]

Regarding administrative searches, which may take place during the day or the night and cover any place, including domiciles, the *Conseil constitutionnel* likewise held that they 'do not affect individual freedom' and are therefore not subject to judicial oversight.[91] This conclusion is unsurprising since the *Conseil constitutionnel* no longer links the principle of inviolability of domiciles to Article 66 of the Constitution.[92] Instead, the *Conseil* merely reiterated that, pursuant to Law

[84] Art L 561(2), Code of Entry and Residence of Aliens and the Right to Asylum (CESEDA).

[85] *Conseil constitutionnel*, decision n° 2011-631 DC (9 June 2011), *Loi relative à l'immigration, à l'intégration et à la nationalité*, para 68.

[86] *Conseil constitutionnel*, decision n° 2015-527 QPC (above n 75) para 5.

[87] Art 6(4), Law n° 55-385 (above n 8).

[88] *Conseil constitutionnel*, decision n° 2015-527 QPC (above n 75) para 6.

[89] Ibid.

[90] JJ Urvoas, Debates of the National Assembly (19 November 2015).

[91] *Conseil constitutionnel*, decision n° 2016-536 QPC (above n 76) para 4.

[92] See, for instance, *Conseil constitutionnel*, decision n° 2013-357 QPC (29 November 2013), *Société Wesgate Charters Ltd (Visite des navires par les agents des douanes)*, paras 6 and 7; and *Conseil constitutionnel*, decision n° 2013-679 DC (4 December 2013), *Loi relative à la lutte contre la fraude fiscale et la grande délinquance économique et financière*, paras 38 and 39.

n° 55-385, the public prosecutor must be informed without delay of the decision ordering any search and must afterwards receive a report of the search.

Secondly, in spite of widespread concerns surrounding the implementation of a national state of emergency, the *Conseil constitutionnel* has appeared reluctant to exercise its right to scrutinise measures likely to be adopted within the framework of the state of emergency. This reticence has resulted in sanctions for only measures that manifestly and disproportionately infringe rights and freedoms. These include the legislative provisions allowing the Minster of Internal Affairs and the Prefect to temporarily shut down theatres, licensed drinking establishments, and meeting facilities in areas within which the state of emergency has been declared. The *Conseil constitutionnel* held that the provisions in question do not demonstrate a manifestly unbalanced conciliation between, on the one hand, the right of collective expression of ideas and opinions and entrepreneurial freedom and, on the other hand, the constitutional principle of safeguarding public order.[93]

Similarly, the minimalist oversight exercised by the *Conseil constitutionnel* is reflected in its decision regarding the constitutionality of searches ordered by the Minister of Internal Affairs or the Prefect pursuant to Law n° 55-385.[94] Nonetheless, the *Conseil constitutionnel* has rendered seven decisions of partial or total censure regarding specific searches conducted under the emergency framework,[95] notably some involving seizure and preservation of data.

Thirdly, in the context of terrorist attacks, the *Conseil constitutionnel* has tried to clarify the legal framework of certain police measures adopted during the state of emergency. First, the *Conseil* filled a legislative gap by specifying the circumstances that may justify an administrative search at night. In that regard, it held that such a search must be justified 'by urgency or the impossibility of carrying it out during the day'.[96] The *Conseil* also specified that the decision ordering a search and the conditions for its implementation 'must be justified and proportionate to the reasons justifying the measure and in particular to the circumstances leading to the declaration of a state of emergency'.[97] The *Conseil* also clarified the time limits in relation to house arrests; temporary closures of theatres, licensed drinking establishments and meeting facilities; and measures prohibiting meetings. If a measure is set to expire at the end of a declared state of emergency,[98] the *Conseil constitutionnel* held that in the event of a further prorogation of the state of emergency, the measure cannot be automatically extended without

[93] *Conseil constitutionnel*, decision n° 2016-535 QPC (above n 77) paras 10 and 13.

[94] *Conseil constitutionnel*, decision n° 2016-536 QPC (above n 76) para 12.

[95] *Conseil constitutionnel*, decisions n° 2016-536 QPC (above n 76); n° 2016-567/568 QPC (above n 76); n° 2016-600 QPC (above n 76); n° 2017-624 QPC (above n 75); n° 2017-635 QPC (9 June 2017); n° 2017-677 QPC (above n 78); and n° 2017-684 QPC (above 79).

[96] *Conseil constitutionnel*, decision n° 2016-536 QPC (above n 76) para 10.

[97] Ibid.

[98] Art 14, Law n° 55-385 (above n 8).

being renewed.[99] Lastly, and above all, the *Conseil constitutionnel* clarified the office of the administrative judge with regard to administrative police measures adopted as part of the state of emergency.[100] On four occasions, it has indicated that administrative judges are responsible for ensuring that such measures are 'appropriate, necessary and proportionate to the purposes pursued'.[101] Therefore, administrative judges maintain oversight of the proportionality of police measures taken in application of the law on the state of emergency.

Ultimately, the role of the *Conseil constitutionnel* in providing for oversight of administrative police measures adopted in the context of the state of emergency has not been surprising. While maintaining a minimalist approach to oversight, the *Conseil constitutionnel* has provided some guidance on the legal framework of some police measures and on the scope of the administrative judge's role with regard to those measures.

ii. Substantive Oversight and Rapid Judicial Intervention

Recent administrative case law on the subject has brought about two major changes to the legal framework of states of emergency in France. The first is an expansion of substantive oversight of administrative police measures. The second is the introduction of a mechanism whereby a judge of interim measures can intervene quickly in cases involving emergency measures that directly infringe fundamental freedoms.[102]

Oversight 'on the cheap',[103] as used to be performed by an administrative judge, has been replaced by complete control over proportionality, along the lines of the classic jurisprudence in *Benjamin*.[104] The most important aspects of this evolution are worth reflecting on. Beginning with the *Dame Bourokba*

[99] *Conseil constitutionnel*, decision n° 2015-527 QPC (above n 75) para 13; and *Conseil constitutionnel*, decision n° 2016-535 QPC (above n 77) para 9.

[100] Pursuant to the first paragraph of Article 14(1), Law n° 55-385 (above n 8), police measures 'taken on the basis of this law are subject to the supervision of the administrative courts under the conditions laid down by the Code of Administrative Justice'.

[101] *Conseil constitutionnel*, decision n° 2015-527 QPC (above n 75) para 12; *Conseil constitutionnel*, decision n° 2016-535 QPC (above n 77) para 8; *Conseil constitutionnel*, decision n° 2016-536 QPC (above n 76) para 10; and *Conseil constitutionnel*, decision n° 2017-624 QPC (above n 75) para 18.

[102] Another salient feature of the recent decisions of the administrative courts is the increased rigour with which they treat the subject of compatibility between domestic emergency legislation and international conventions. See *Conseil d'État*, ord, 9 December 2005, *Mme Allouache et autres* précitée; and *Rolin et Boisvert* (above n 49). In the face of accusations that Law n° 55-385 infringes the European Convention on Human Rights, the administrative courts now provide substantial justification for their decisions. See *Conseil d'État*, 11 December 2015, *MC Domenjoud*, n° 395009). See further X Dupré de Boulois and L Milano, 'Jurisprudence administrative et Convention européenne des droits de l'homme' (2016) *RFDA* 769.

[103] This expression is borrowed from X Domino (Maître des requêtes of the *Conseil d'État*), 'Assignations à résidence en état d'urgence' (2016) *RFDA* 105.

[104] *Conseil d'État* (19 May 1933) *Benjamin, rec* 541.

decision in 1955 (the same year that Law n° 55-385 was enacted),[105] the *Conseil d'État* exercised only very limited control over the state-of-emergency decisions taken by administrative authorities. In that particular case, in order to assess the lawfulness of a decision by the Prefect prohibiting Mrs Bourokba from residing within a certain locale (*department*), the *Conseil* considered only whether that decision was taken 'for reasons outside the scope' of Law n° 55-385.[106] As Professor Roland Drago pointed out at the time,

> By this formula … the *Conseil d'État* holds that the measures adopted during a state of emergency are discretionary. The judge may annul those measures only for formal error or a misuse of power without being able to assess the substantive lawfulness of the act'.[107]

However, during the state of emergency in New Caledonia, the *Conseil* specifically considered whether the administrative authority had committed a manifest error of assessment when it adopted administrative policing measures through an application of Law n° 55-385. In the 1985 decision *Mme Dagostini*, the *Conseil* ruled that 'when [the administrative authority] found that the conduct of Mrs Dagostini … justified a measure refusing entry or stay, it did not vitiate its decision of manifest error of assessment'.[108] Finally, in the *Rolin et Boisvert* decision of 2006,[109] the *Conseil* exerted its strongest authority ('*contrôle le plus poussé*') yet by imposing a standard of strict proportionality.[110]

Recent decisions of the administrative courts confirm the direction of this evolution. Administrative judges now impose a three-part standard that focuses on the suitability, necessity, and proportionality of administrative police measures. A case in point is the 2015 referral decision and contentious opinion of the *Conseil d'État* in QPC No 2015-527.[111] In that case, the *Conseil* indicated that administrative judges now exercise 'complete oversight' ('*entier contrôle*') over the administrative police measures adopted on the basis of Law n° 55-385.[112] For instance, with regard to house arrest, in a judgment of 19 May 2016, the Marseille Administrative Court of Appeal held that the threat to public order and public security posed by the claimant's activities, who was closely connected to a radical Salafi imam, was sufficient to justify his house arrest.[113] The Court noted that the defendant under house arrest had been to Schaerbeck (Belgium)

[105] *Conseil d'État* (16 December 1955) *Dame Bourokba*, *rec* 596.

[106] Ibid.

[107] R Drago, Note on *Conseil d'État* (16 December 1955) *Dame Bourokba* (1956) *Dalloz* 396.

[108] *Conseil d'État* (25 July 1985) *Mme Dagostini*, n° 68151, *rec* 226.

[109] *Rolin et Boisvert* (above n 49).

[110] C Landais and F Lenica, 'Contentieux de la légalité de l'état d'urgence' (2006) *AJDA* 1033. See also J-M Sauvé in D Raimbourg and J-F Poisson, 'Report n° 3784 on the Parliamentary Control of the State of Emergency', *Commission des lois constitutionnelles, de la législation et de l'administration générale de la République*, National Assembly, (25 May 2016) 18.

[111] *Conseil d'État* (11 December 2015) n° 395009.

[112] Ibid.

[113] Administrative Court of Appeal (CAA) of Marseille (19 May 2016) n° 16MA00655.

and in the vicinity of Molenbeek, both known to be home to many radical Islamists. The Court also took into account the fact that the defendant had been held in custody by the police, and during a search at his home, the police had found 195 cell phones, 209 USB sticks, material for learning foreign languages, as well as numerous train tickets confirming his trips to France, Belgium, and Germany.

In its opinion (‘*avis contentieux*’) *Napol et Thomas* of 6 July 2016, the *Conseil d’État*, responding to judicial questions from two administrative tribunals, also stated, ‘It is for the judge to exercise full control’ over the reasons justifying an administrative search order ‘in order to ensure … that the ordered measure was adapted, necessary and proportionate to its purpose in the specific circumstances which led to the declaration of a state of emergency’.[114] Further,

> This review is carried out in the light of the factual situation prevailing at the date on which the measure was taken, having regard to the information available to the administrative authority at that time. In that regard, subsequent events, in particular the results of the search, have no impact.[115]

This reliance on proportionality when reviewing administrative police measures is, however, ‘very ineffective’ since such a measure has often already ‘exhausted its effects’: the search was carried out, the meeting could not be held, the performance was cancelled, etc.[116] Fortunately, as a result of the Law of 30 June 2000 on summary proceedings before the administrative courts,[117] litigants are now able to petition a judge of interim measures to take appropriate measures, which are in principle provisional,[118] ‘as soon as possible’.[119] Accordingly, the judge of interim measures is now responsible for rapid and vigilant monitoring of administrative police measures adopted in the context of a state of emergency. As of 15 September 2016, administrative tribunals had considered 207 interim measures related to administrative police actions taken during the state of emergency; and on appeal, the *Conseil d’État* had held 46 summary hearings.[120]

[114] *Conseil d’État*, Opinion (6 July 2016) *M Napol et M Thomas*, n°s 398234 and 399135.

[115] Ibid.

[116] F Julien-Laferrière, ‘L’état d’urgence: un danger potentiel pour les libertés’ (2016) 145 *Les petites affiches* 12.

[117] Law n° 2000-597 of 30 June 2000 on the application for interim measures before administrative jurisdictions.

[118] The principle was established by Article L 511-1, Code of Administrative Justice. However, it has many limitations. In particular, the administrative courts introduced an exception to petitions for the protection of fundamental liberties (*référé-liberté*) since ‘when no provisional measure is capable of satisfying this requirement, in particular when the input deadlines or the nature of the breach block this action, (the judge) may order the person who is the author to take any action likely to safeguard the effective exercise of the fundamental freedom in question.… This applies in particular when the infringement results from a prohibition whose effects are themselves temporary or limited in time.’ See *Conseil d’État*, ord (30 March 2007) n° 304053.

[119] Art L 511-1, Code of Administrative Justice: ‘Le juge des référés statue par des mesures qui présentent un caractère provisoire. Il n'est pas saisi du principal et se prononce dans les meilleurs délais.’

[120] These figures were communicated by the President of the Administrative Jurisdiction Division of the *Conseil d’État*: B Stirn, ‘Lutte contre le terrorisme, état d’urgence et État de droit’, Conference at the Institut d’études politiques d’Aix-en-Provence (21 September 2016), http://www.conseil-etat.fr/Actualites/Discours-Interventions/Lutte-contre-le-terrorisme-etat-d-urgence-et-Etat-de-droit.

Recourse by litigants to emergency procedures, in particular the ability to petition for protection of fundamental liberties (*référé-liberté*) as provided by Article L 521(2) of the Code of Administrative Justice, has allowed administrative judges to intervene quickly in cases involving emergency measures. Upon a petition for protection of fundamental liberties, a judge has forty-eight hours to rule and, if necessary, the power to order all measures necessary to safeguard any fundamental freedom that has been 'seriously and manifestly breached' by public authorities.[121]

A petition for protection of fundamental liberties thus offers litigants a very efficient legal remedy – although such petitions are not applicable to all administrative police measures taken in the context of a state of emergency. Nor are they always effective at mitigating the impacts of administrative searches, many of which are immediate. In the case of an emergency petition involving house arrest, however, the *Conseil d'État* has explicitly ruled that the requirement of urgency is presumed to be satisfied:

> Having regard to its object and effect, in particular to the restrictions on the freedom of movement, an administrative decision ordering the house arrest of an individual pursuant to Article 6 of [Law n° 55-385], affects in principle, except in particular circumstances, seriously and immediately the situation of an individual, such as to create a situation of urgency justifying that the administrative judge of interim measures may order within a very short period of time a protective and provisional safeguard measure, if the other conditions laid down in that Article are fulfilled.[122]

On 21 July 2016, the law extending the application of the state of emergency enshrined this interpretation by inserting into Law n° 55-385 'The condition of urgency is presumed to be satisfied when challenging judicially through the mechanism of interim measure a house arrest.'[123] Since the condition of urgency is presumed to be fulfilled, it is then for the judge of interim measures to determine whether the house arrest in question involves a serious and manifestly unlawful infringement of a fundamental freedom. In addition to considering the way in which the house arrest was undertaken, the judge must also check for 'the existence of serious reasons to believe that the behaviour of the person under house arrest constitutes a threat to security and public order'.[124]

In this respect, the judge of interim measures exercises oversight by requiring detailed information justifying the house arrest. For example, the judge of

[121] Art L 521(2) CJA. 'Fundamental liberty' is an autonomous notion that can be interpreted broadly by the judge.

[122] *Conseil d'État* (11 December 2015) *M J Domenjoud*, n° 394989; *M L Gauthier*, n° 394990; *M C Verrier*, n° 394991; *M P Boilleau*, n° 394992; *Mme M Saiter*, n° 394993; *Mme S Crochet*, n° 395002, and *M C Domenjoud*, n° 395009.

[123] Art 6, Law n° 2016-987 (above n 26). By aiming at any 'judicial proceedings for interim measures', the legislature has negligently extended the scope of the presumption, which is now applicable, for example, to the petition for suspension (*référé-suspension*) of Art L 521-1 CJA. On this specific point, see, O Le Bot, 'Prorogation de l'état d'urgence et mesures de lutte antiterroriste' (2016) *AJDA* 1914.

[124] *Conseil constitutionnel*, decision n° 2015-527 QPC (above n 75) para 15.

interim measures of the *Conseil d'État* was able to suspend an order of house arrest on the grounds that 'the evidence produced by the Minister of Internal Affairs did not sufficiently justify' that the individual was a radical Islamist.[125] In particular, it was established that the presence of the litigant in the vicinity of the domicile of a person under special protection was justified by a visit to his mother, who lived in the immediate vicinity, and that the litigant under house arrest had not taken photographs of police facilities but rather used his mobile phone, which was held in front of his face, in 'speaker' mode because he had kept his helmet on his head while stopping his scooter. The effectiveness of this approach to safeguarding rights has been borne out by the fact that on occasion, when a judge of interim measures has begun to consider a petition, the Minister of Internal Affairs has pre-emptively responded by modifying the terms of the house arrest[126] or even repealing the house arrest order.[127]

The Law of 21 July 2016 expanded the role of judges of interim measures.[128] In order to avert the possibility that the *Conseil constitutionnel* might declare evidence seized during an administrative search as inadmissible, the legislature made the use of such data conditional upon authorisation by a judge of interim measures.[129] In such circumstances, the judge must make a decision within forty-eight hours of the date of the referral regarding the lawfulness of a seizure and the request to make use of any evidence thereby obtained. In the event of a refusal by the judge of interim measures and subject to an appeal to the *Conseil d'État*, the data obtained through the search shall be destroyed, and documents seized shall be returned to their owner.

This new power granted to judges of interim measures substantially expands their role while at the same time confirming them as the guardians of freedoms. Indeed, in addition to the traditional powers of suspension and injunction, a judge of interim measures now has the exceptional power of authorisation, which runs counter to the usual practice of judges intervening only *ex post* because of the principle of prerequisite (*principe du préalable*). Indeed, as of 26 October 2016, administrative tribunals had made use of this authority for eighty decisions, including seventy general authorisations, partial authorisations, withdrawal authorisations, and eight rejected applications. On appeal, the *Conseil d'État* considered five cases, upholding the initial refusal decision in one case.[130]

By way of illustration, the case law makes clear, for example, that maintaining communications with people who have left for Syria and Iraq as jihadists

[125] *Conseil d'État*, ord (22 January 2016) n° 396116.
[126] See for examples, *Conseil d'État*, ord (6 January 2016) n° 395622.
[127] See for examples, *Conseil d'État*, ord (24 February 2016) n° 397235.
[128] Law n° 2016-987 (above n 26).
[129] Art 11, I(7) Law n° 55-385 (above n 8).
[130] These figures were communicated in D Raimbourg and J-F Poisson, 'Information Report n° 4281 on Parliamentary Control of the State of Emergency', Constitutional Law Commission, National Assembly (6 December 2016) 57.

justifies an authorisation to use seized computer data.[131] In contrast, such an authorisation cannot be granted for files seized from the mobile phone of a person searched simply because the files contain 'elements in Arabic that could not be exploited immediately'.[132]

In any event, this new power on the part of judges of interim measures to authorise the use of computer data has placed additional strain on the administrative justice system, especially since the work of the Administrative Court of Appeals has already increased as a result of disputes arising from state-of-emergency measures. Given that seventy per cent of magistrates on administrative tribunals and administrative courts of appeal report that they suffer from their working conditions,[133] the likely outcome of this expansion in power is even greater delays in the processing of appeals.

In the end, any measure now taken on the basis of Law n° 55-385 is likely to be reviewed by either an administrative judge or the *Conseil constitutionnel.* As a result, it is no longer true that, as Government Commissioner René Rivet stated in his conclusions to the *Clef* case in 1925, the police do not expect 'to see their actions frustrated by permanent threats of contentious complications'.[134] As will be discussed in the next section, this change has also been accompanied by the institutionalisation of non-judicial oversight of internal security forces acting within the framework of the state of emergency.

II. NON-JUDICIAL OVERSIGHT OF THE STATE OF EMERGENCY

Forms of non-judicial oversight over the state of emergency are numerous. For example, one has only to look at the opinion of the *Conseil d'État* (acting as counsel to the Government) on a bill extending the state of emergency or amending Law n° 55-385;[135] at numerous appeals lodged by human rights groups such as the League of Human Rights before both the administrative court and the *Conseil constitutionnel*; or at the advice given by the National Consultative

[131] *Conseil d'État*, ord (23 August 2016) n° 402571.

[132] *Conseil d'État*, ord (5 September 2016) n° 403026.

[133] S Gouès in Report n° 3784 (above n 110) 39.

[134] R Rivet, conclusions on *Conseil d'État* (13 March 1925) *Clef* (1925) RDP 276.

[135] See for instance the Opinions of the *Conseil d'État* on 2 February, 18 July, and 8 December 2016. In particular, in its Opinion of 18 July 2016, the *Conseil d'État* recognised: 'In view of the nature of the attack in Nice … the present situation qualifies itself as an "imminent peril resulting from serious breaches of the public order" within the meaning of Article 1 of Law n° 55-385 of 3 April 1955 on the state of emergency.' However, the *Conseil d'État* warned public authorities that 'renewals of the state of emergency cannot be perpetual and that a state of emergency must remain temporary.' See Opinion of 18 July 2016 by the Internal Affairs Department (*section de l'intérieur*) of the *Conseil d'État* on the bill extending the application of the Law n° 55-385 of 3 April 1955 on the state of emergency and modifying some of its provisions.

Commission on Human Rights to public authorities.[136] However, two forms of non-judicial oversight that have developed during the Fifth Republic deserve particular attention: parliamentary oversight (established in 2015); and the Rights Defender (*Défenseur des droits*), whose role was instituted under the 2008 constitutional revision.

A. Parliamentary Oversight: The Ongoing Role of the Law Commissions

The November 2015 addition of Article 4(1) to Law nº 55-385 set out the principle of parliamentary oversight of the state of emergency in France.[137] This unprecedented and permanent form of oversight centres around the Law Commissions of the National Assembly and the Senate, which have fully embraced their new prerogative.

The institution of parliamentary scrutiny of the state of emergency was initially discussed during the parliamentary debates on the Law of 18 November 2005 extending the application of the state of emergency.[138] In particular, the Rapporteur of the Law Commission of the Senate indicated his wish for Parliament 'to be associated with the control and implementation of the state of emergency'.[139] The system ultimately adopted at that time, however, fell short of true parliamentary oversight, only allowing Parliament to be informed of the decision of the President of the Republic to end the state of emergency before the expiry of the time limit under the law of prorogation.[140]

Ten years later during parliamentary debates on the law of 20 November 2015, which sought not only to extend the application of the state of emergency but also to increase the effectiveness of its provisions,[141] the question of parliamentary control re-emerged. The Rapporteur of the Law Commission of the National Assembly advocated for the establishment of 'close and constant Parliamentary oversight of the measures adopted and enforced by the executive power in times of crisis that by definition contain limitations of rights and freedoms'.[142] His argument that 'everyone should have access to complete data to grasp the nature of the state of emergency' led to the inclusion of Article 4(1) – the first real form of parliamentary oversight of the state of emergency.[143] Accordingly, the Government must now inform the National Assembly and the

[136] See for instance CNCDH, 'Opinion on the Monitoring of the State of Emergency' (18 February 2016), https://www.legifrance.gouv.fr/affichTexte.do?cidTexte=JORFTEXT000032107678&categorieLien=cid.

[137] Art 4, Law n° 2015-1501 (above n 26).

[138] Law n° 2005-1425 (above n 55).

[139] J-J Hyest, Senate Debates (16 November 2005).

[140] Art 3, Law n° 2005-1425 (above n 55).

[141] Law n° 2015-1501 (above n 26).

[142] J-J Urvoas, National Assembly Debates (18 November 2015).

[143] Report n° 3784 (above n 110).

Senate 'without delay' of all measures adopted under the framework of the state of emergency. Moreover, since the enactment of Law of 21 July 2016 extending the application of the state of emergency and measures to strengthen the fight against terrorism,[144] administrative authorities must transmit 'without delay' to both assemblies a copy of all acts adopted in application of the state of emergency. In addition, both assemblies 'may request any additional information in the context of the monitoring and evaluation of these measures'.[145]

These recent steps mark an innovative leap forward in the parliamentary practice of the Fifth Republic, since 'never before had any chamber performed similar investigation activities'.[146] The new authority includes real-time monitoring of the measures taken in the context of the state of emergency and is carried out in addition to the conventional *ex post* oversight of the government's actions under Article 24 of the Constitution.

As an innovative development in French democratic governance, Parliament's right to scrutinise measures implemented by the executive during the state of emergency may end up testing the constitutional principle of the separation of powers. In Portugal, Article 162(b) of the Constitution provides *expressis verbis* for parliamentary monitoring of a state of emergency (*estado de emergencia*), and the Government therefore submits to the Assembly of the Republic (unicameral Parliament) detailed reports on measures taken under the state of emergency.[147] In contrast, the French Constitution does not provide expressly for parliamentary oversight of the application of the state of emergency. Moreover, it is significant to note that the current provisions of Article 4(1) of Law n° 55-385 were included in the draft adopted by the National Assembly, which constitutionalised the state of emergency;[148] yet the Law of 20 November 2015 was not referred to the *Conseil constitutionnel* (see discussion above). The *Conseil*'s *a priori* authority to rule on questions of constitutionality means that the legality of these new forms of parliamentary oversight may yet be challenged.

Nonetheless, in the National Assembly and in the Senate, the Law Commissions also exercise *a priori* competence with regard to issues of security and civil liberties.[149] The Commissions have been careful to preserve the rights of the opposition. On 25 November 2015, a few days after the addition of Article 4(1), the Law Commission of the Senate delegated some oversight power to a monitoring committee composed of six senators in order to allow all the political

[144] Art 2(1), Law n° 2016-987 (above n 26).

[145] Art 4(1), Law n° 55-385 (above n 8).

[146] J-J Urvoas, National Assembly Debates (2 December 2015).

[147] Art 17, Organic Law n° 44 of 30 September 1986 (modified) on the 'state of siege' (*estadode sítio*) and the 'state of emergency' (*estado de emergência*). See the note on comparative law of the Senate on the state of emergency regimes (March 2016), https://www.senat.fr/lc/lc264/lc264.pdf, 59–60.

[148] Constitutional Bill n° 3381 (above n 13).

[149] See in particular Art 36(18), Rules of Procedure of the National Assembly.

groups to be represented.[150] Shortly after, the Law Commission of the National Assembly likewise entrusted the tasks of daily monitoring, tracking, and supervision of the state of emergency to two co-rapporteur deputies, including a member of the opposition party. In order to involve representatives of all groups in this monitoring mission, regular meetings of the Committee's bureau were organised.[151]

The Law Commission of the National Assembly, at the invitation of its President, decided for the first time to authorise commissions of enquiry pursuant to Article *5ter* of the Ordinance of 17 November 1958 on the functioning of parliamentary assemblies. It therefore has considerable powers, including to hear persons under oath,[152] to carry out on-the-spot checks, and to request all information likely to facilitate its mission.[153] Additionally, sanctions (fines or imprisonment) may be imposed in cases of refusal to appear,[154] nondisclosure of information,[155] or false testimony.[156] On 10 December 2015, the Law Commission of the Senate likewise moved to authorise regular commissions of enquiry regarding the state of emergency.

In its oversight capacity, the Law Commission of the National Assembly also decided to combine 'a follow-up of data on the implementation of the state of emergency' with 'a more in-depth reflection on certain themes and certain facts'.[157] In an unprecedented move, it published the comprehensive statistical data provided by the Government regarding the police measures adopted in application of the state of emergency. A table listing the administrative measures taken from 22 July 2016 to 8 December 2016, for example, shows that during this period, ninety-six house arrests were carried out and thirteen sites or meeting venues were closed as part of the state of emergency. Another table presents the judicial follow-up of the measures taken during the state of emergency from 22 July 2016 to 6 December 2016: 384 administrative searches resulted in 55 judicial proceedings on a wide range of 'violations' (including weapon trafficking, drug trafficking, visa violations, noncompliance with health regulations, etc).

Notwithstanding the large amount of important information provided by the statistics, conclusions about the overall effectiveness of state-of-emergency

[150] M Mercier (UDI-UC-Rhône), Special Rapporteur, É Assassi (CRC-Seine-Saint-Denis); E BenBassa (Écolo-Val-de-Marne); J Mézard (RDSE-Cantal); A Richard (Socialiste et républicain-Val-d'Oise); and C Troendlé (Les Républicains-Haut-Rhin).

[151] 'Intermediary Communication (*communication d'étape*) on the Control of the State of Emergency', meeting of the Law Commission of the National Assembly (16 December 2015), http://www2.assemblee-nationale.fr/static/14/lois/communication_2015_12_16.pdf.

[152] Art 6(II)(3), Ordinance n° 58-1100 of 17 November 1958 on the functioning of the parliamentary assemblies.

[153] Ibid, Art 6(II)(2).

[154] Ibid, Art 6(III)(1).

[155] Ibid, Art 6(III)(2).

[156] Ibid, Art 6(III)(4).

[157] J-J Urvoas, National Assembly Debates (2 December 2015).

measures can as yet be only tentative.[158] In order to obtain further detailed information on the conditions of implementation of certain specific administrative police measures taken in application of the state of emergency (including administrative searches and house arrests), the co-rapporteurs of the Law Commission have sent several letters to the Minister of Internal Affairs. As of 14 October 2016, sixty-eight letters had been sent, and the Ministry had replied to each of them.[159] The Law Commission has supplemented this information with field trips and by conducting several hearings, including with the heads of the intelligence and security services, the vice-president of the *Conseil d'État*, the President of the litigation section of the *Conseil*, the trade unions representatives of the administrative judges, the central director of the judicial police of the Ministry of Internal Affairs, and the Director of Criminal Affairs and Pardons of the Ministry of Justice.

The progress and findings of the co-rapporteurs of the Law Commission are reported to all members of the Commission and published on the website of the National Assembly. As a result, as early as 13 January 2016, the Law Commission was able to note a 'gradual termination of administrative measures' insofar as 'the main targets and objectives have been addressed', 'the effect of surprise has largely faded, and the people concerned have also fully prepared themselves to face possible administrative measures'.[160] As far as administrative searches are concerned, it was noted:

> [Administrative searches] constituted a particularly vigorous shock … on a movement difficult to characterise as strictly delinquent or strictly radicalised but which can appear as fertile soil to welcome and support terrorist networks. [The searches] will have made it possible to refine the knowledge of the functioning of this movement while fighting ordinary crimes.[161]

In their communication of 17 May 2016, the co-rapporteurs of the Law Commission advised the legislature not to renew the authorisation to carry out administrative searches at the next extension of the application of the state of emergency.[162] A few days later, when Law n° 2016-629 extended the state of

[158] On this issue, see G Fenech and S Pietrasanta, 'Report n° 3922', Inquiry Commission on the Measures Taken by the State to Fight Terrorism Since 7 January 2015 (5 July 2016) 264; and Raimbourg and Poisson, 'Report n° 4281' (above n 130) 118–19.

[159] See the table on the monitoring of mail sent to the Government (14 October 2016), http://www2.assemblee-nationale.fr/14/commissions-permanentes/commission-des-lois/controle-parlementaire-de-l-etat-d-urgence/controle-parlementaire-de-l-etat-d-urgence/(block)/27425.

[160] 'Intermediary Communication on the Control of the State of Emergency', meeting of the Law Commission of the National Assembly (13 January 2016), http://www2.assemblee-nationale.fr/static/14/lois/communication_2016_01_13.pdf.

[161] Raimbourg and Poisson, 'Report n° 4281' (above n 130) 209.

[162] 'Intermediary Communication on the Control of the State of Emergency', meeting of the Law Commission of the National Assembly (17 May 2016), http://www2.assemblee-nationale.fr/static/14/lois/communication_2016_05_17.pdf.

emergency for a period of two months, it did not include the power to order administrative searches.[163]

With regard to house arrests, the report from the co-rapporteurs of the National Assembly on 6 December 2016 suggested specifying that in principle 'a person may not be under house arrest more than eight months over a period of twelve months'.[164] Two weeks later, Law n° 2016-1767 again extended the state of emergency until 15 July 2017 but specified that 'from the declaration of the state of emergency and for its entire duration, the same person may not be placed under house arrest for a total period equivalent to more than twelve months'.[165]

In the Senate, the State of Emergency Monitoring Committee established by the Law Commission has also been regularly informed of the number of administrative police measures taken under the law on the state of emergency. However, this data has not been published on the Senate website, which contains links only to two letters addressed to the Ministry of Internal Affairs requesting details on the judicial consequences of administrative searches, and on the decree of 1 December 2015 of the Prefect of the Pas-de-Calais (which delimited the zone of protection and certain house arrests).[166]

While the lack of public reporting from the Senate Committee may appear at first glance to reveal a weaker commitment to oversight in comparison with the National Assembly co-rapporteurs, the Committee has held numerous hearings of security actors (including the Prefect of Paris Police and the Paris Public Prosecutor) and associations or persons whose role is to defend public freedoms (eg, the President of the National Consultative Commission on Human Rights). These hearings have provided in-depth examinations of police measures taken within the framework of the state of emergency. Moreover, in order to inform the Law Commission and Senate on the appropriateness of further extensions of the state of emergency, the Committee has made several communications regarding the number of administrative police measures, appeals, etc, which are accessible online.

B. The Rights Defender

In addition to the parliamentary oversight provided by the Law Commissions of the National Assembly and Senate, the newly created position of Rights Defender further expands the avenues for non-judicial oversight of the state of emergency in France. Following the success of the Ombudsperson in Spain,[167]

[163] Law n° 2016-629 (above n 26).

[164] Raimbourg and Poisson, 'Report n° 4281' (above n 130) 126.

[165] Art 2(I), Law n° 2016-1767 (above n 26).

[166] See https://www.senat.fr/commission/loi/comite_etat_durgence/lettres_thematiques_rapporteur_etat_durgence.html (last accessed 4 March 2019).

[167] Comité de réflexion (above n 10) 95.

the Committee for Reflection and Proposal on the Modernisation and Rebalancing of the Institutions of the Fifth Republic (*le comité de réflexion et de proposition sur la modernisation et le rééquilibrage des institutions de la Vème République*) in 2007 proposed changing the name of the Mediator of the Republic (*Médiateur de la République*) to 'Defender of Fundamental Rights' (*Défenseur des droits fondamentaux*).[168] Subsequently, the 2008 amendments to the Constitution included a title XI*bis* dedicated to the 'Rights Defender' (*Défenseur des droits*). Article 71(1) assigns to the Rights Defender the ambitious mission of

> ensuring the due respect of rights and freedoms by state administrations, territorial communities, public legal entities, as well as by all bodies carrying out a public service mission or by those that the Institution Act decides fall within his/her remit.[169]

This 'administrative authority whose independence finds its basis in the Constitution'[170] is appointed by the President of the Republic for a non-renewable six-year term.[171]

The creation of the position of Rights Defender responded to a desire to rationalise the institutional landscape of non-judicial protection of freedoms. In that sense, the Rights Defender replaced four earlier independent administrative authorities, namely the Mediator of the Republic, the Child Advocate, the High Authority for Combating Discrimination (*La haute autorité de lutte contre les discriminations*), and the National Security Ethics Commission (*Commission nationale de déontologie de la sécurité*). Thus, the Rights Defender is responsible for 'defending and promoting the best interests and rights of the child enshrined in the law or in international commitments ratified or approved by France',[172] 'fighting discrimination',[173] and 'ensuring the respect of ethics by persons carrying out security activities on the territory of the Republic'.[174]

It was within the scope of these missions that the Rights Defender received sixty referrals between November 2015 and September 2016 on specific measures taken in application of the law on the state of emergency, including thirty-eight search-and-seizure cases and nineteen relating to house arrest.[175] During the same period, the Rights Defender was also involved in twenty-two other instances that were indirectly linked to the state of emergency (for example,

[168] Ibid, 92–93.
[169] Art 71(1)(i), Constitution of 4 October 1958.
[170] *Conseil constitutionnel*, Decision n° 2011-626 DC (29 March 2011), *Loi organique relative au Défenseur des droits*, para 5.
[171] Art 71-1(4), Constitution of 4 October 1958.
[172] Art. 4(2), Organic Law No 2011-333 of 29 March 2011 on the Rights Defender.
[173] Ibid, Art 4, 3°.
[174] Ibid, Art 4, 4°.
[175] Le Défenseur des droits, 'Summary of the Claims on the State of Emergency Received as of 9 September 2016' (9 November 2016), http://archive.wikiwix.com/cache/?url=http%3A%2F%2Fwww.defenseurdesdroits.fr%2Ffr%2Factus%2Factualite-du-droit%2Fbilan-des-reclamations-relatives-l%27etat-d%27urgence-recues-par-le-defenseur.

an unfair dismissal claim concerning an employee's facial hair).[176] At the end of the investigation of these cases, the Rights Defender was able 'to settle very concrete situations, such as the adjustment of some house arrests in order to take into account a number of objective constraints such as school timetables',[177] as well as to issue specific recommendations on administrative police measures within the context of the state of emergency.

Two sets of recommendations in particular are worth noting. First, on 26 February 2016, the Rights Defender made general recommendations on the use of police and national gendarmerie forces when they intervene in premises where children are present.[178] Citing reports about 'the execution of searches in the middle of the night and in the presence of children, sometimes very young, without any precaution being taken' and traumatising incidents in which sleeping children were woken from their beds by armed police officers, the Rights Defender recommended, among other things, that 'information on the presence of children at the scene of the intervention should be systematically communicated to law enforcement authorities in order for them to take it into account when preparing the operation'.[179] It was also recommended that the police and national gendarmerie forces designate a person on their team responsible for the protection of minors present during each intervention. This person could, for example, isolate him/herself with the minors so they do not witness the intervention. For hooded units such as the 'RAID' (*Recherche, Assistance, Intervention, Dissuasion*) and the 'GIGN' (*Groupes d'Intervention de la Gendarmerie Nationale*), the Rights Defender advised that 'as far as possible, hoods must be removed to talk to young children'.[180]

In a memorandum of 16 March 2016, the Rights Defender was pleased to note that the Minister of Internal Affairs had apparently followed the recommendations insofar as asking the internal security forces 'to ascertain whether young children would be present and to adapt intervention plans accordingly'.[181] In addition, on the heels of these recommendations, the *Conseil d'État* in its opinion for *Napol et Thomas* stated:

> During a search, it is important to respect the dignity of persons and to pay particular attention to the situation of children who might be present. The use of force or coercion shall be strictly limited to what is necessary for the conduct of the operation and the protection of persons.[182]

[176] Ibid.
[177] J Toubon, 'Le Défenseur des droits, un contre-pouvoir ?' (2016) *Constitutions* 213.
[178] Le Défenseur des droits, 'General Recommendations on the Use of Police and Gendarmerie Forces When They Intervene in Premises Where Children Are Present' (26 February 2016), https://juridique.defenseurdesdroits.fr/doc_num.php?explnum_id=14344.
[179] Ibid.
[180] Ibid.
[181] Raimbourg and Poisson, 'Report n° 4281' (above n 130) 48–49.
[182] *Napol et Thomas* (above n 114).

A second set of recommendations were made by the Rights Defender in May 2016. These involved the implementation of administrative searches and compensation pertaining to damages suffered therein.[183] In particular, the Rights Defender' recommended that law enforcement officials should systematically provide copies of search orders to the persons concerned. This proposal received legislative endorsement with the Law of 21 July 2016.[184] The Rights Defender also recommended 'facilitating the access to the right of compensation by providing for exceptional compensation for damages made by administrative police measures taken in application of the state of emergency'.[185] This was in direct response to a November 2015 circular from the Minister of Internal Affairs regarding state liability during the course of the state of emergency. While state liability was acknowledged 'to presuppose the existence of gross negligence', the circular stated:

> For law enforcement agents to break down a door or to cause property damages should not in itself constitute gross negligence when these interventions are justified in order to fight terrorism or prevent breaches of public order within the framework of the state of emergency.[186]

The recommendations of the Rights Defender found a welcome extension in the opinion *Napol et Thomas*, where the *Conseil d'État* declared, 'Any fault committed in the execution of searches ordered on the basis of Law n° 55-385 may engage the responsibility of the State.'[187] Therefore, state responsibility for damages caused during the material execution of administrative searches may be engaged for simple misconduct, not only for gross negligence.

In the same opinion, the *Conseil d'État* stated that in order to determine whether simple misconduct resulted from the execution of a search, a judge must take into account the 'conduct of the persons present at the time of the search and the difficulties of administrative actions in the particular circumstances which led to the declaration of the state of emergency'.[188] In addition, the *Conseil d'État* provided numerous guidelines on the conditions in which search operations are to be carried out, clarifying in particular issues related to night searches, the use of force, and damage to property. First, the *Conseil d'État* recalled what the *Conseil constitutionnel* held in decision No 2016-536 QPC:[189] 'The search

[183] Le Défenseur des droits, 'General Recommendations on the Implementation of Administrative Searches and the Compensation of Individuals in Connection to the Application of the State of Emergency' (26 May 2016), https://juridique.defenseurdesdroits.fr/doc_num.php?explnum_id=14685.

[184] Art 5(3), Law n° 2016-987 (above n 26).

[185] 'Recommendations on Administrative Searches and Compensation' (above n 183).

[186] Minister of Internal Affairs, 'Administrative Searches in Application of the State of Emergency', circular (25 November 2015).

[187] *Conseil d'État*, Opinion, (above n 114).

[188] *Napol et Thomas* (above n 114).

[189] *Conseil constitutionnel*, n° 2016-536 QPC (above n 76) para 10.

of a house at night must be justified by urgency or the impossibility of doing it during the day.'[190] Then the *Conseil d'État* held:

> Unless there are serious reasons to believe that the occupier(s) of the premises are likely to react to the search by dangerous behaviour or to destroy or conceal material elements, the voluntary opening of the searched premises shall be sought and force may be used to enter *only as a last resort*.[191]

Moreover, according to the *Conseil d'État*, officers conducting a search are required 'to ensure the respect of the dignity of the persons' and to use force or coercion only if it is 'necessary for the conduct of the operation and the protection of persons'.[192] Lastly, the *Conseil d'État* pointed out that 'damage to property must be strictly proportionate to the purpose of the operation', and 'all deteriorations should be justified by the search of elements relevant to the purpose of the search'.[193] In practice, by May 2016, only twenty-two contentious claims had been made, with a total potential compensation amount reaching a little over €224,000.[194]

All in all, the role of the Rights Defender in informing and directing claimants to the remedies available to them, together with the specific recommendations that have been incorporated into administrative police measures, means that the Rights Defender has become a strong 'counter-power'[195] to executive overreach during the state of emergency.

III. CONCLUSION

Ultimately, the state of emergency does not operate outside the rule of law – as evidenced by the numerous forms of judicial and non-judicial oversight that have been outlined in this chapter. Despite these checks and forms of oversight, however, a state of emergency cannot be maintained indefinitely: by definition, it is a temporary response to an 'imminent peril resulting from serious breaches of public order'.[196] If the declaration of a state of emergency was necessary following the terrorist attacks perpetrated on French soil in 2015, its maintenance for almost two years must nonetheless be interrogated. Undeniably, though, the threat posed by terrorism is persistent and important. As pointed out by the head of the Anti-Terrorist Coordination Unit (*Unité de coordination de la lutte anti-terroriste*, 'UCLAT'), 'We have not seen anything yet: unfortunately,

[190] *Napol et Thomas* (above n 114).
[191] Ibid, emphasis added.
[192] Ibid.
[193] Ibid.
[194] Raimbourg and Poisson, 'Report n° 4281' (above n 130) 54.
[195] Toubon (above n 177).
[196] Art 1, Law n° 55-385 (above n 8).

the worst is yet to come.'[197] In that respect, it makes sense to develop sustainable means of fighting terrorism. This is the 'collateral impact' of the recent state of emergency in France.

A clear example of this sort of ancillary development is the authorisation of night searches in case of emergency and for preliminary investigations of terrorist offences under the Law of 3 June 2016.[198] Even more recently, the 'Collomb' Law of 30 October 2017[199] has incorporated into common law a 'lite' state of emergency, that is to say, a version that is slightly less restrictive of freedoms. The roots of these new powers for the administrative police authorities in France can nonetheless be traced to Law n° 55-385. But terrorism cannot be eradicated or even held at bay by an increase of police powers alone. An effective response to terrorism must be global in perspective. In particular, education, robust integration policies, and the fight against inequality are more important than ever if we are to see, as the Universal Declaration of Human Rights states, 'the advent of a world in which human beings shall enjoy freedom of speech and belief and freedom from fear and want'.

REFERENCES

Baranger, D, 'L'état d'urgence dans la durée' (2016) 3 *RFDA* 447–54.

——, 'Quel 'État de droit'? Quels contrôles? Le juge des référés et le maintien en vigueur de l'état d'urgence' (2016) 2 *RFDA* 355–64.

de Gaulle, C, 'Discours de Bayeux', speech (16 June 1946), http://www.charles-de-gaulle.org/wp-content/uploads/2017/03/Discours-de-Bayeux-16-juin-1946.pdf.

Delmas-Marty, M, *Raisonner la raison d'État. Vers une Europe des droits de l'homme* (Paris, PUF, 1989).

Domino, X (Maître des requêtes of the Conseil d'État), 'Assignations à résidence en état d'urgence' (2016) *RFDA* 105.

Drago, R, 'Note on *Conseil d'État* (6 December 1955) *Dame Bourokba*' (1956) *Dalloz* 396.

Dupré de Boulois, X and Milano, L, 'Jurisprudence administrative et Convention européenne des droits de l'homme' (2016) *RFDA* 769.

Dutheillet de Lamothe, L and Odinet, G, 'L'urgence dans tous ses états' (2016) *AJDA* 247.

——, 'Perquisitions le Conseil d'État fouille dans ses classiques' (2016) *AJDA* 1635.

Favoreu, L, et al (eds), *Droit constitutionnel*, 21st edn (Paris, Dalloz, 2018).

Granger, M-A, *Constitution et sécurité intérieure. Essai de modélisation juridique*, Prix de thèse du Conseil constitutionnel (Paris, LGDJ, 2011).

Heymann-Doat, A, 'L'état d'urgence, un régime juridique d'exception pour lutter contre le terrorisme?' (2016) (38)1 *Archives de politique criminelle* 59–74.

[197] L Garnier (Anti-Terrorist Coordination Unit) in Report n° 3784 (above n 110).

[198] Art 1, 2°, b, Law n° 2016-731 of 3 June 2016 reinforcing the fight against organised crime, terrorism and their financing, and improving the efficiency and the guaranties of criminal procedures.

[199] Law n° 2017-1510 of 30 October 2017 reinforcing internal security and the fight against terrorism.

Julien-Laferrière, F, 'L'état d'urgence: un danger potentiel pour les libertés' (2016) 145 *Les petites af-fiches* 12.

Landais, C and Lenica, F, 'Contentieux de la légalité de l'état d'urgence' (2006) *AJDA* 1033.

Le Bot, O, 'Prorogation de l'état d'urgence et mesures de lutte antiterroriste' (2016) *AJDA* 1914.

Le Défenseur des droits, 'General Recommendations on the Implementation of Administrative Searches and the Compensation of Individuals in Connection to the Application of the State of Emergency' (26 May 2016), https://juridique.defenseurdesdroits.fr/doc_num.php?explnum_id=14685.

——, 'General Recommendations on the Use of Police and Gendarmerie Forces When They Intervene in Premises Where Children Are Present' (26 February 2016), https://juridique.defenseurdesdroits.fr/doc_num.php?explnum_id=14344.

Long, M, et al, *Les grands arrêts de la jurisprudence administrative*, 21st edn (Paris, Dalloz, 2017).

Mazeaud, P, 'L'erreur', Institut de France Colloquium (25–26 October 2006), https://www.conseil-constitutionnel.fr/sites/default/files/as/root/bank_mm/pdf/Conseil/erreur.pdf.

Raimbourg, D and Poisson, J-F, 'Communication d'étape sur le contrôle de l'état d'urgence' (17 May 2016), http://www2.assemblee-nationale.fr/static/14/lois/communication_2016_05_17.pdf.

——, 'Report n° 3784 on Parliamentary Control of the State of Emergency', Constitutional Law Commission, National Assembly (25 May 2016).

——, 'Report n° 4281 on Parliamentary Control of the State of Emergency', Constitutional Law Commission, National Assembly (6 December 2016).

Rolin, F, 'L'état d'urgence' in B Mathieu (ed), *Cinquan-tième anniversaire de la Constitution française* (Paris, Dalloz, 2008).

Sauvé, J-M, 'L'état d'urgence ne peut être renouvelé indéfiniment', *Le Monde* (18 November 2016).

Stirn, B, 'Lutte contre le terrorisme, état d'urgence et État de droit', Conference at the Institut d'études po-litiques d'Aix-en-Provence (21 September 2016), available at www.conseil-etat.fr.

Toubon, J, 'Le Défenseur des droits, un contre-pouvoir ?' (2016) *Constitutions* 213.

17

Bounded Factuality: The Targeted Killing of Salah Shehadeh and the Legal Epistemology of Risk

SHIRI KREBS

I. INTRODUCTION

On 22 July 2002, the Israeli Air Force dropped a one-tonne bomb on the home of Salah Shehadeh, who was then the head of the Operational Branch of Hamas in Gaza. The attack on Shehadeh's home in Gaza City resulted in the death of Shehadeh himself; his assistant, Zaher Saleh Nassar; Shehadeh's wife, Laila Khamis Shahadeh; and their fifteen-year-old daughter, Iman Salah Shahadeh. Eleven other civilians were also killed in the attack, seven of them children. One hundred and fifty bystanders were injured.[1]

Six years later, Israeli Prime Minister Ehud Olmert was pressured by the Israeli Supreme Court to establish a Special Investigatory Commission to investigate the attack, its circumstances, the relevant decision-making processes, and the availability of alternatives. Three years after that (nine years after the attack), a detailed report was finally published.[2] The information detailed in the Shehadeh Commission Report offers an intimate window into the decision-making processes concerning targeted killing operations and a rare look into the sensitive fact-finding process that serves as a basis for targeted killing operations.

[1] The names and further details about the victims are elaborated in s IV below. See also A Meyerstein, 'Case Study: The Israeli Strike against Hamas Leader Salah Shehadeh' (19 September 2002) *Crimes of War Magazine*; and I Rosenzweig and Y Shany, 'Special Investigatory Commission Publishes Report on Targeted Killing of Shehadeh' (2011) 27 *Terrorism and Democracy*.

[2] Special Investigatory Commission, 'Report on the Targeted Killing of Salah Shehadeh' [in Hebrew] (27 February 2011), http://www.pmo.gov.il/SiteCollectionDocuments/PMO/32communication/spokemes/reportshchade.pdf [hereafter 'Shehadeh Commission Report']. For an English summary of the Report's main findings, see Rosenzweig and Shany (ibid); and Israel Ministry of Foreign Affairs, 'Salah Shehadeh Special Investigatory Commission', English summary of the Shehadeh Commission Report (27 February 2011), https://mfa.gov.il/MFA/AboutIsrael/State/Law/Pages/Salah_Shehadeh-Special_Investigatory_Commission_27-Feb-2011.aspx (last accessed 5 February 2019).

Analysis of the Report reveals the potential impact of legal norms and legal processes on risk assessments and interpretation of intelligence information. In trying to explain, for example, how 'missing information became positive information' about the absence of civilians at the site of the attack, the Report illustrates how legal fact-finding processes are distorted by organisational culture and personal biases. 'Groupthink', compartmentalisation, and security-oriented institutional goals may together result in the development of fact-finding processes that are focused on satisfying domestic and international law and that inevitably lead to the production of facts that comply with the legal requirements.

By focusing on cognitive and organisational biases influencing fact-finders in the context of targeted killing decision-making, this chapter engages with and further advances a growing literature that adopts a behavioural approach to international law.[3] This approach explores the implications of human behaviour for international law and is based on empirical observations, focusing on actual rather than assumed behaviour.[4] Its central concept is the idea of bounded rationality, which recognises that human cognitive capacities are not perfect but rather limited by a variety of cognitive, emotional, and social (or group-based) biases.[5] Accordingly, the main contribution of the behavioural approach to international law is to shed light on a variety of systemic biases in individual and group decision-making processes within various contexts of international law.[6] To penetrate deeper into legal decision-making and untangle the socio-psychological biases affecting it, this chapter focuses on fact-finding processes in the context of targeted killing decision-making, including the production and interpretation of intelligence information. Specifically, the chapter identifies some of the legal rules governing targeted killings as a source of bias ('law-fulfilling prophecy') that shapes information-gathering and interpretation practices.

The term 'targeted killing' refers to the intentional and premeditated use of lethal force by state actors against suspected terrorists who are specifically identified in advance.[7] The legality of targeted killing operations and,

[3] See, eg, T Broude, 'Behavioral International Law' (2015) 163(4) *University of Pennsylvania Law Review* 1099–157, 1152–53; and G Sitaraman and D Zionts, 'Behavioral War Powers' (2015) 90 *New York University Law Review* 516–88.

[4] Broude (ibid) 112–13.

[5] D Kahneman, 'Maps of Bounded Rationality: Psychology for Behavioral Economics' (2003) 93(5) *American Economic Review* 1449–75.

[6] Sitaraman and Zionts (above n 3) 520; Broude (above n 3) 1150; and M Milanovic, 'Establishing the Facts about Mass Atrocities: Accounting for the Failure of the ICTY to Persuade Target Audiences' (2015) 47 *Georgetown Journal of International Law* 1321–78.

[7] P Alston, 'Report of the Special Rapporteur on Extrajudicial, Summary or Arbitrary Executions', UN Human Rights Council, A/HRC/14/24/Add.6 (28 May 2010) 5. For other definitions, see N Melzer, *Targeted Killings in International Law* (Oxford, Oxford University Press, 2008) 4–5; C Downs, '"Targeted Killings" in an Age of Terror: The Legality of the Yemen Strike' (2004) 9(2) *Journal of Conflict and Security Law* 277–94, 280; and D Kretzmer, 'Targeted Killing of Suspected Terrorists: Extra-Judicial Executions or Legitimate Means of Defence?' (2005) 16(2) *European Journal of International Law* 171–212, 176.

specifically, the conditions under which such operations are permissible are unclear and contested.[8] Legal practitioners and scholars have argued passionately about the body of law to be applied: international human rights law or international humanitarian law?[9] They have also argued about the proper interpretation of substantive norms: who constitutes a legitimate target; whether 'direct participation' includes membership in a terrorist organisation or whether it necessitates involvement in certain activities; whether it is lawful to target a suspected terrorist at any time and place; and whether there are any temporal or geographical restrictions to targeted killing operations.[10]

Somewhat less debated and underexplored (partly due to lack of available information) are the facts and circumstances justifying the use of lethal force against named individuals without trial.[11] It may be easier, especially for lawyers, to debate the legal framework; but regardless of the exact interpretation of the legal rules, the legality of *all* targeted killing operations rests upon the facts of any particular case, the credibility of the evidence, and the satisfaction of the relevant burden of proof. This chapter turns the spotlight on the legal facts used to support targeting decisions – their production, interpretation, and role in targeting decision-making processes.

The chapter begins in section II with an overview of the challenges to legal fact-finding during armed conflict. Section III introduces the concept of 'bounded factuality' in targeting decision-making and offers an interdisciplinary analysis of the distortions and limitations of targeting decision-making processes. The studies surveyed in this section include literature on organisational culture in the intelligence community, biased risk assessments, and misjudgements of facts. Section IV then illustrates some of these dynamics using the report of the Israeli Special Investigatory Commission on the targeted killing of Salah Shehadeh.[12] Based on a comprehensive interdisciplinary analysis of studies in law, psychology,

[8] In another article, I have surveyed the conflicting legal sources and offered a comprehensive analysis of the many disagreements and open questions concerning targeted killing law: S Krebs, 'Reducing Uncertainty in Targeted Killing Decision-Making' (2018) 44 *Florida State University Law Review* 943–93. See also MN Schmitt, 'Extraterritorial Lethal Targeting: Deconstructing the Logic of International Law' (2013) 52 *Columbia Journal of Transnational Law* 77–112, 78, arguing that 'in particular, pundits often ask the wrong questions or answer the right ones by reference to the wrong body of law. The result is growing confusion, as analytical errors persist and multiply.' See also R Chesney, 'Who May Be Killed? Anwar al-Awlaki as a Case Study in the International Legal Regulation of Lethal Force' in MN Schmitt (ed), *Yearbook of International Humanitarian Law: Volume 13, 2010* (The Hague, TMC Asser Instituut, 2011) 5: 'The use of lethal force in response to terrorism … has been the subject of extensive scholarship, advocacy, and litigation over the past decade … Yet we remain far from consensus.'

[9] Chesney (ibid) 29–38; and S Vité, 'Typology of Armed Conflicts in International Humanitarian Law: Legal Concepts and Actual Situations' (2009) 873 *International Review of the Red Cross* 69–94.

[10] Chesney (above n 8) 44.

[11] See the chapter in this volume by Liora Lazarus on the way secrecy in law undermines critical scholarship.

[12] Shehadeh Commission Report (above n 2).

sociology, and political science, as well as on the primary documents released by the Shehadeh Commission, section V offers several recommendations designed to improve fact-finding and enhance risk assessments.

II. LEGAL FACT-FINDING AND TARGETING DECISION-MAKING

A. The Contingent Nature of Legal Facts

Truth is a fundamental objective of all adjudication.[13] Two of the working assumptions of the practice of adjudication are that accuracy in fact-finding constitutes a precondition for just decisions;[14] and fact-finding is a neutral practice,[15] aimed at ascertaining an objective 'truth'.[16] However, there is an inescapable tension between accuracy in fact-finding and some of the legal rules governing legal fact-finding. In fact, legal fact-finding is set to produce a contingent version of reality, as it adheres to legal rules and processes that frame the story, infuse it with meaning, and dictate how the relevant facts are construed.

Ontologically, law provides norms and rules that construct reality in a specific manner, and this legal reality or 'legal truth' may differ from non-legal constructions of reality.[17] Terms such as 'genocide', 'civilian', 'terrorist', 'torture', and 'responsibility' have unique meanings as legal terms, and they potentially have other meanings outside the law, within political, ethical, or moral discourses. When we adopt legal discourse to interpret reality and determine the truth, our findings relate to the legal reality, which may be very different from the moral, ethical, or political interpretation of reality.[18] For example, a legal finding that

[13] M Damaska, 'Truth in Adjudication' (1997) 49 *Hastings Law Journal* 289–308, 301; and L Laudan, *Truth, Error, and Criminal Law: An Essay in Legal Epistemology* (Cambridge, Cambridge University Press, 2006) 1. See also the US Federal Rules of Evidence, Rule 102.

[14] Damaska (ibid) 289 and 292.

[15] KL Scheppele, 'Just the Facts, Ma'am: Sexualized Violence, Evidentiary Habits, and the Revision of Truth' (1992) 37 *New York Law School Law Review* 123.

[16] For example, the International Criminal Tribunal for the former Yugoslavia (ICTY) prides itself in producing an 'undeniable truth', as well as 'creating a historical record, combatting denial and preventing attempts at revisionism'. See the UN International Criminal Tribunal for the Former Yugoslavia webpage 'Achievements', http://www.icty.org/en/about/tribunal/achievements (accessed 26 October 2018). Similarly, Christof Heyns (UN Special Rapporteur on extrajudicial, summary, or arbitrary executions and member of the UN Independent Investigation on Burundi) stated, 'It is crucial to ascertain [the disputed facts] in an indisputable manner.' C Heyns, 'Enhanced Interactive Dialogue on Burundi', Human Rights Council (22 March 2016), https://www.refworld.org/pdfid/5728500c4.pdf.

[17] MS Moore, 'Legal Reality: A Naturalist Approach to Legal Ontology' (2002) 21(6) *Law and Philosophy* 619–705, 632: 'we thus can expect no precision in how to combine the very general moral, historical, scientific, and semantic facts that make a legal interpretation correct.' See also JM Balkin, 'The Proliferation of Legal Truth' (2003) 26(1) *Harvard Journal of Law and Public Policy* 5–16, 7: 'law's truth is not the only truth, and law's vision of reality is not the only reality.'

[18] Balkin (ibid) has argued that law's power to enforce its vision of the world can clash with other practices of knowledge and with other forms of truth.

a government employee is not responsible for torturing a detainee depends on the legal interpretation and meanings of both 'torture' and 'responsibility'. Applying a moral interpretation, our findings concerning the existence of or responsibility for torture may be different. Additionally, legal reality is often binary, coercing complex reality into simplified categories such as 'combatant' or 'civilian', thus losing information that could have been meaningful if a spectrum approach rather than binary categorisation was in force.[19]

Epistemologically, legal fact-finding determines questions of fact based on legal conventions, procedures, and rules of evidence that guide us in our decisions regarding what is considered 'true'. First, these rules carve the boundaries of the story itself by limiting the universe of facts that are included in the legal account of 'what happened'. Only facts that are specifically relevant to establishing legal truth, such as causes of death or intent of the perpetrator, are included. Other facts relating to, for example, the roots of the conflict, social processes of dehumanisation, or acts committed outside the temporal or geographical jurisdiction of the legal institution conducting the fact-finding efforts, are excluded.

Second, legal epistemology further restructures the story by determining the weight, reliability, sufficiency, and admissibility of the relevant facts. Legal rules determine the value and strength of the information collected, preferring some facts over others. While many of these rules are designed to promote an accurate account of events,[20] they nonetheless make choices concerning how to construct reality. Moreover, some rules of evidence and legal procedures depart from the goal of ascertaining the truth and favour other purposes, such as protecting national security, deterring police misconduct, or even controlling the direction of errors. These rules determine how facts should be treated and interpreted, what the required burden of proof is, and which evidence should be suppressed (because it is considered hearsay, because the information is privileged, because it was obtained unlawfully, or because of several other reasons). Either way, law requires us to determine 'what happened' while ignoring important facts that describe some aspects of the events in question.

The ontological and epistemological questions concerning legal fact-finding cannot all be answered within the scope of this chapter. Rather, this brief and general introduction serves to demonstrate the contingent nature of legal fact-finding, as well as to introduce some of the main challenges facing any project of legal fact-finding. As security crises tend to amplify some of the main concerns regarding legal fact-finding, this chapter focuses on the challenges to legal fact-finding in the context of armed conflict.

[19] Sherwin has explored more generally the clash between law's demand for truth and justice and the modem mind's demand for closure and certainty, leading lawyers and processes of adjudication to simplify reality by leaving the 'messy things' out: RK Sherwin, 'Law Frames: Historical Truth and Narrative Necessity in a Criminal Case' (1994) 47(1) *Stanford Law Review* 39–83, 40–41.

[20] US Federal Rules of Evidence, Rule 102.

B. Challenges to Legal Fact-Finding During Armed Conflict

During armed conflicts fact-finding becomes more challenging than in peaceful times or regarding issues not related to security concerns. Some of these challenges are unique to the judicial or executive fact-finding processes, while others relate to dissemination and assimilation of facts.

First, legal fact-finding during armed conflict or concerning security matters is meaningfully constrained by concrete legal rules, such as the state secrets doctrine and security privileges, which by definition limit the available facts included in the fact-finding process.[21] Second, restrictive legal procedures such as *ex parte* and *in camera* proceedings further constrain fact-finding concerning security matters.[22] Third, security considerations often influence judicial decision-making by promoting deference to security agencies and executive decision-makers,[23] who may be subject to the phenomenon of groupthink,[24] consequently be overconfident, and tend towards the overestimation of risk.[25] Fourth, while determining what happened in in the context of an armed conflict, legal fact-finding efforts may be compromised by cognitive and emotional biases, including cognitive consistency, motivated reasoning, and denial.[26]

[21] D Barak-Erez and M Waxman, 'Secret Evidence and the Due Process of Terrorist Detentions' (2009) 48(3) *Columbia Journal of Transnational Law* 3, 5; and SH Cleveland, 'Hamdi Meets Youngstown: Justice Jackson's Wartime Security Jurisprudence and the Detention of "Enemy Combatants"' (2005) 68(4) *Albany Law Review* 1127–44, 1132–34. Cf the chapter in this volume by Liora Lazarus.

[22] Barak-Erez and Waxman (ibid) 21; and H Stewart, 'Is Indefinite Detention of Terrorist Suspects Really Constitutional?' (2005) 54 *University of New Brunswick Law Journal* 235, 245.

[23] D Kretzmer, *The Occupation of Justice: The Supreme Court of Israel and the Occupied Territories* (Albany, State University of New York Press, 2002) 118; and R Kitai-Sangero, 'The Limits of Preventive Detention' (2009) 40 *McGeorge Law Review* 903–34, 912.

[24] The concept of groupthink is used to explain deficient decision-making dynamics resulting in flawed decisions in group environments. Groupthink dynamics proliferate within small, cohesive groups and during times of great stress. See D Badie, 'Groupthink, Iraq, and the War on Terror: Explaining US Policy Shift toward Iraq' (2010) 6(4) *Foreign Policy Analysis* 277–96, 280–81 and 285. For a different explanation, see GS McNeal, 'Targeted Killing and Accountability' (2014) 102 *Georgetown Law Journal* 681–794, 755–58. See also IL Janis, *Groupthink: Psychological Studies of Policy Decisions and Fiascoes*, 2nd edn (Boston, Wadsworth, 1982) 9; and MA O'Connor, 'The Enron Board: The Perils of Groupthink' (2003) 71 *University of Cincinnati Law Review* 1233–319, 1258.

[25] R Jervis, 'War and Misperception' (1988) 18(4) *Journal of Interdisciplinary History* 675–700, 688; and E Kahana, 'Analyzing Israel's Intelligence Failures' (2005) 18(2) *International Journal of Intelligence and CounterIntelligence* 262–79, 274.

[26] For literature concerning cognitive consistency and confirmation bias, see L Ross and A Ward, 'Psychological Barriers to Dispute Resolution' in MP Zanna and JM Olson (eds), *Advances in Experimental Social Psychology*, Vol 27 (San Diego, Academic Press, 1995) 263–64. For literature concerning motivated cognition, see D Kahan, 'Foreword: Neutral Principles, Motivated Cognition, and Some Problems for Constitutional Law' (2012) 125(1) *Harvard Law Review* 1–77, 19. For literature concerning denial, see S Cohen, *States of Denial: Knowing about Atrocities and Suffering* (Malden, Polity Press, 2013) 6. Fact-finders may further be influenced by the false-positive–false-negative bias, meaning a mistake will only be discovered if a dangerous person is set free, but not if he or she is targeted or continues to be preventively detained. See Kitai-Sangero (above n 23) 909; and G Van Harten, 'Weaknesses of Adjudication in the Face of Secret Evidence' (2009) 13(1) International Journal of Evidence and Proof 1–27, 1.

Fifth, some security measures challenge fact-finding, as they involve predictions of future occurrences rather than descriptions of past events.[27] For example, while deciding cases concerning preventative measures such as security detentions or targeted killings, decision-makers are tasked with making predictions and calculating probabilities about the future. Sixth, some facts seem easily severable from value judgments: eg, 'were there traces of Sarin gas in the blood of the victims?' However, in security matters it is often the case that crucial facts consist of complex social evaluation: 'How dangerous is the suspect?' 'How reliable is the intelligence?'[28] Seventh, the combination of all of these challenges puts legal fact-finding during armed conflict at risk of defactualisation or mistreatment of facts. As legal practitioners and judges are not typically trained to make factual determinations, and as significant information is excluded from the fact-finding process, they tend to do what they are uniquely qualified to do: make normative evaluations and interpretations.[29]

Finally, these various limitations on accuracy in legal fact-finding unavoidably challenge not only the process of legal fact-finding itself but also the receptiveness of various audiences to the findings or outcomes of a fact-finding process. Public receptiveness to legal fact-finding is further compromised by a variety of socio-psychological dynamics, including cognitive consistency and biased assimilation of new information,[30] confirmation bias,[31] motivated cognition,[32] and collective memories and beliefs,[33] which may trigger distortion or rejection of threatening information.

[27] For more general discussion of these challenges, see Damaska (above n 13) 299.

[28] Ibid, 299–300.

[29] David Faigman has argued, for example, that legal fact-finding in the constitutional context is flawed, as the US Supreme Court approaches factual questions as a matter of normative legal judgment rather than as a separate inquiry aimed at information gathering. DL Faigman, 'Normative Constitutional Fact-Finding: Exploring the Empirical Component of Constitutional Interpretation' (1991) 139 *University of Pennsylvania Law Review* 541–613, 544–45, 547, and 549.

[30] According to cognitive consistency theories, human cognition is substantially affected by mutual interaction among pieces of psychological knowledge. Mounting evidence further demonstrates processes of biased assimilation of new information, meaning people tend to interpret subsequent evidence so as to maintain their initial beliefs. C Lord, L Ross, and M Leper, 'Biased Assimilation and Attitude Polarization: The Effects of Prior Theories on Subsequently Considered Evidence' (1979) 37(11) *Journal of Personality and Social Psychology* 2098–109; D Simon, CJ Snow, and SJ Read, 'The Redux of Cognitive Consistency Theories: Evidence Judgments by Constraint Satisfaction' (2004) 86(6) *Journal of Personality and Social Psychology* 814–37.

[31] The term 'confirmation bias' connotes the seeking or interpretion of evidence in ways that are partial to existing beliefs, expectations, or hypotheses in hand. See RS Nickerson, 'Confirmation Bias: A Ubiquitous Phenomenon in Many Guises' (1998) 2(2) *Review of General Psychology* 175–220.

[32] Ziva Kunda has explained that a motivation to arrive at particular conclusions may affect reasoning through reliance on a biased set of cognitive processes (strategies for accessing, constructing, and evaluating beliefs) that are considered most likely to yield the desired conclusion. There is considerable evidence that people are more likely to arrive at conclusions that they want to arrive at, but their ability to do so is constrained by their ability to construct seemingly reasonable justifications for these conclusions. Z Kunda, 'The Case for Motivated Reasoning' (1990) 108(3) *Psychological Bulletin* 480–98.

[33] Societal beliefs and collective memories are cognitions that are shared by society members on topics and issues that are of special concern for the particular society and that contribute to the

Because legal fact-finding during armed conflict is uniquely challenging, it is important to understand these limitations and, when possible, to consider alternatives to current practices of legal fact-finding. The remainder of this chapter will explore these challenges within the context of targeted killing decision-making processes and will offer ways to better account for failures and mistakes, as well as alternative processes to enhance fact-finding.

III. 'BOUNDED FACTUALITY' IN TARGETING DECISIONS

Following the general discussion of the challenges to fact-finding efforts during armed conflict, this section focuses on a specific fact-finding process conducted to assess threat, risk, and collateral damage, for the purpose of targeted killing decision-making.

A. Intelligence and the Risk of Error

When successful, a targeted killing operation is an irreversible measure. Unlike detention regimes, it is designed to kill, not capture. The legality of this deadly measure depends on the factual circumstances of each case and rests mainly on the availability of intelligence information concerning the severity of the security threat, the activities of the targeted individual, the existence or inexistence of feasible less harmful measures, and the anticipated collateral damage. It is not the 'heat of the battle' or immediate eyesight evidence that drives the killing decision-making process but rather a rational and calculated decision-making process that is based on secret information that the targeted individual cannot challenge or object to.

Therefore, the legality of a targeted killing operation is heavily dependent upon the quality, breadth, and reliability of the intelligence on which it is based.[34] How well that information is documented, how closely that information is scrutinised and by whom are key factors in any assessment of targeted killing operations.[35] Social psychology studies have long demonstrated that individuals tend to search and absorb information that is in line with their core social beliefs, while omitting or distorting contradictory information.[36] The construction and evaluation of information in social settings is influenced

sense of uniqueness of the society's members. See D Bar-Tal, 'Societal Beliefs in Times of Intractable Conflict: The Israeli Case' (1998) 9(1) *International Journal of Conflict Management* 22–50, 25–26; and D Bar-Tal, 'Collective Memory of Physical Violence: Its Contribution to the Culture of Violence' in E Cairns and MD Roe (eds), *The Role of Memory in Ethnic Conflict* (London, Palgrave Macmillan, 2003) 77.

[34] Alston (above n 7) 25; and the Shehadeh Commission Report (above n 2).

[35] McNeal (above n 24) 719–20.

[36] See the references for cognitive consistency and confirmation bias above in n 26.

by prior beliefs, ideologies, and interests,[37] as well as by group identities and commitments.[38] Those tasked with preventing catastrophic terrorist attacks therefore interpret associated risk differently than those tasked with preserving personal liberties. Paul Slovic, Baruch Fischhoff, and Sarah Lichtenstein al have found that subjective judgements are a major component of any risk assessment, whether made by experts or lay people.[39] They have specifically pointed out the problem of overconfidence, finding that experts think they can estimate failure rates with much greater precision than is actually the case.[40]

Some common ways in which experts misjudge factual information and associated risks are (i) the failure to consider the ways in which human errors can influence technological systems; (ii) the failure to anticipate human response to safety measures; and (iii) insensitivity to how technological systems function as a whole.[41] While analysing intelligence failures with regard to Iraqi weapons of mass destruction (WMDs), Robert Jervis has found that many of the intelligence community's judgements were stated with overconfidence, assumptions were insufficiently examined, and assessments were based on previous judgements without carrying forward the uncertainties.[42]

Legal evaluations of risks associated with targeted killings (such as collateral damage assessments) are also prone to expert bias on two levels: first, by intelligence agents as they collect and analyse information; and, second, by lawyers as they interpret and evaluate the intelligence information presented to them.

Overconfidence becomes an even greater problem in the counterterrorism context due to the aversion of decision-makers to the risks associated with terrorism.[43] While governments and their security agencies normally exhibit risk-neutral attitudes in their decision-making, decision-makers within security agencies tend to be risk-averse because of the dire nature and potentially catastrophic consequences of terrorism attacks.[44] Indeed, overconfidence in

[37] I Maoz et al, 'Reactive Devaluation of an "Israeli" vs "Palestinian" Peace Proposal' (2002) 46(4) *Journal of Conflict Resolution* 515–46, 543.

[38] DM Kahan et al, 'They Saw a Protest: Cognitive Illiberalism and the Speech–Conduct Distinction' (2012) 64 *Stanford Law Review* 851–906. See also L Eden, *Whole World on Fire: Organizations, Knowledge and Nuclear Weapons Destruction* (Ithaca, Cornell University Press, 2004) 37–60.

[39] P Slovic et al, 'Facts and Fears: Understanding Perceived Risk' in RC Schwing and WA Albers (eds), *Societal Risk Assessment: How Safe is Safe Enough?* (New York, Plenum Press, 1980).

[40] Ibid. See also Sitaraman and Zionts (above n 3) 534–35, discussing 'fundamental attribution error'.

[41] Slovic et al (above n 39) 187.

[42] R Jervis, 'Reports, Politics, and Intelligence Failures: The Case of Iraq' (2006) 29(1) *Journal of Strategic Studies* 3–52, 14 and 22.

[43] L Huddy et al, 'Threat, Anxiety, and Support of Antiterrorism Policies' (2005) 49(3) *American Journal of Political Science* 593–608. Similarly, Jessica Stern has described the post-2001 US policy responses to bioterrorism as evidence of 'dreaded risk bias'. J Stern, 'Dreaded Risk and the Control of Biological Weapons' (2002) 27(3) *International Security* 89–123.

[44] MG Stewart, BR Ellingwood, and J Mueller, 'Homeland Security: A Case Study in Risk Aversion for Public Decision-Making' (2011) 15(5/6) *International Journal of Risk Assessment and Management* 367–86, 370.

one's decisions goes hand in hand with overestimation of risk.[45] Analysing Israeli intelligence failures, Ephraim Kahana has emphasised the inherent problem of overestimation of threats within the Israeli intelligence community.[46] The urgency of many targeted killing decisions, the danger associated with nonaction, and groupthink dynamics within security organisations add to the risks of individual and institutional biased interpretation of information.[47]

i. Risk of Error Assessing Potential Risk to Civilians

In 2013 President Barak Obama declared, 'Before any strike is taken, there must be near certainty that no civilians will be killed or injured – the highest standard we can set.'[48] Indeed, it is well accepted that 'every effort must be made to minimize collateral damage'.[49] But how is the anticipated collateral damage being assessed? Gregory McNeal has described at length a highly sophisticated and automated process involving software (FAST-CD) that predicts the anticipated effects of particular weapons on certain targets. The weapons-effect data contained in FAST-CD is based on empirical data gathered in field tests, probability, historical observations from weapons employed on the battlefield, and physics-based computerised models for collateral damage estimates.[50] Casualty estimates are also based on standardised methods, including McNeal's 'Population Density Reference Table', which lists data from the intelligence community and estimates the population density during day, night, and special events.[51]

While these methods help to standardise the targeted killing decision-making process and to minimise certain types of human error, they are nonetheless imperfect and prone to different kinds of errors. First, the data is limited by the quantity and reliability of the intelligence information collected.[52] Naturally, security agencies spend time, effort, and resources on collecting real-time intelligence on their targets and their whereabouts. However, the data suggests that intelligence on anticipated collateral damage may be less robust, and a significant portion of this data stems from algorithm-based assessments based on general probabilities calculations rather than on real-time assessments. These calculations do not take into account last-minute changes in operational environments

[45] GD Koblentz, 'Predicting Peril or the Peril of Prediction? Assessing the Risk of CBRN Terrorism' (2011) 23(4) *Terrorism and Political Violence* 501–20, 511.

[46] Kahana (above n 25) 274. Somewhat similarly, Jervis has pointed out that states are prone to exaggerate the reasonableness of their own positions and the hostile intent of others. Jervis, 'War and Misperception' (above n 25) 688.

[47] See Badie (above n 24) 280–81 and 285; and the brief discussion of groupthink above at n 24.

[48] B Obama, 'Remarks by the President at the National Defense University', Fort McNair, Washington, DC (23 May 2013), available at https://obamawhitehouse.archives.gov/the-press-office/2013/05/23/remarks-president-national-defense-university.

[49] AN Guiora, 'Determining a Legitimate Target: The Dilemma of the Decision Maker' (2012) 47(2) *Texas International Law Journal* 315–35.

[50] McNeal (above n 24) 741.

[51] Ibid, 751.

[52] Ibid, 742.

or the reliability of the data.[53] The accuracy and reliability of collateral damage calculations are further challenged by the fact that suspected terrorists tend to change their locations frequently, making it harder to collect reliable intelligence on the anticipated collateral damage in real time.[54]

Second, such complicated collateral damage calculations create an illusion of robustness, as they appear to account for a great deal of information. However, a large amount of information does not necessarily mean that it is reliable and accurate for the exact time and method of the operation, and the complexity of calculations may obscure the inherent uncertainty and incompleteness of the data.[55] Additionally, the focus on numerical calculations of anticipated harm may engender dehumanisation of the prospective 'collateral damage', as flesh-and-blood people are reduced to meaningless numbers. (McNeal, for example, has mentioned that on average each drone strike in Pakistan has killed between 0.8 and 2.5 civilians.[56])

Similar to collateral damage calculations, the evaluation of 'feasible' precautions against civilian harm depends on the availability of intelligence information about a concrete target and his or her surroundings.[57] Careful examination of such information is necessary to determine whether the targeting state did everything feasible beforehand to ensure correct identification of the target and target location, to choose appropriate means, and to assess the anticipated collateral damage.

The cognitive and organisational biases described above are notable in the counterterrorism context generally, but they may particularly affect assessments of feasible precautions and alternative methods during targeted killing decision-making processes. Specifically, overestimation of the threat posed by a target, coupled with overconfidence in this assessment of threat, may motivate decision-makers to rule out less harmful measures because such measures may decrease the chances of success in eliminating the threat. Additionally, the level of tolerance within the relevant society for military casualties may bias the assessment of feasible precautions. Often, when alternatives are considered, risks to one's soldiers or civilians dominate the decision-making process and influence the risk assessment process and the consideration of alternate courses of action.[58]

[53] Ibid, 740–45. Additionally, concrete fact-finding practices – such as requiring 'positive information' as to the presence of civilians (mentioned in the Shehadeh Commission Report) – generate biased interpretations of the available information. See the discussion in s IV-C below.

[54] See s IV below.

[55] This risk is further enhanced by the tendency to bury internal disagreements within the security organisations concerning the factual framework rather than flagging such disagreements for the decision-makers. See the discussion in s IV-C below.

[56] McNeal (above n 24) 755.

[57] Melzer (above n 7) 365.

[58] TW Smith, 'Protecting Civilians … or Soldiers? Humanitarian Law and the Economy of Risk in Iraq' (2008) 9(2) *International Studies Perspectives* 144–64; and MA Khalidi, '"The Most Moral Army in the World": The New "Ethical Code" of the Israeli Military and the War on Gaza' (2010) 39(3) *Journal of Palestine Studies* 6–23.

ii. Intelligence, Institutions, and Inescapable Errors

In her 2009 book *Spying Blind*, Amy Zegart pointed out that attributing intelligence failures to individuals is dangerous because it can gloss over the institutional constraints and forces that create situations in which it is likely that people will make poor decisions.[59] She found that institutional weaknesses in both the US Central Intelligence Agency (CIA) and Federal Bureau of Investigation (FBI) were at the heart of the intelligence failure concerning the 9/11 attacks. Specifically, she pointed at flawed information-sharing schemes, deficiencies in the intelligence community's system for prioritising collection and analysis of intelligence, and inadequate personnel (regarding both the number of intelligence officers required to collect and analyse large volumes of information and their ability to translate data from other languages).[60]

Moreover, Zegart found that recommendations – both before and after 9/11 – to improve these critical intelligence deficiencies in CIA structure prioritisation processes, human intelligence capabilities, and personnel systems were not implemented. Reforms from within ran into resistance from entrenched routines and a firmly established organisational culture, while external reforms generated opposition or indifference from key political players.[61] The nature of organisations and the fragmentation of the intelligence community hindered any attempts to adapt, even after a failure as catastrophic as September 11. She therefore concluded that while the constraints that hinder adaptation in US intelligence agencies might be mitigated, these constraints can never be eliminated entirely.[62]

Analysing intelligence failures concerning Iraqi weapons of mass destruction and reviewing the three main official reports that investigated the failures,[63] Jervis also concluded in 2006 that intelligence errors are ultimately inescapable.[64] Focusing on inherent biases and social structures in the intelligence community, he argued that while the US and UK reports conveyed a great deal of information,

[59] AB Zegart, *Spying Blind: The CIA, the FBI, and the Origins of 9/11* (Princeton, Princeton University Press, 2009) 6–7.

[60] AB Zegart, 'September 11 and the Adaptation Failure of US Intelligence Agencies' (2005) 29(4) *International Security* 78–111, 103–4.

[61] Ibid, 105–7.

[62] Ibid, 109.

[63] Jervis reviewed: Select Committee on Intelligence (US Senate), 'Report on the US Intelligence Community's Prewar Intelligence Assessments on Iraq' (7 July 2004), available at https://fas.org/irp/congress/2004_rpt/ssci_iraq.pdf, Lord Butler of Brockwell (Chair, UK House of Commons Committee), 'Review of Intelligence on Weapons of Mass Destruction: Report of a Committee of Privy Councillors to the House of Commons' [the 'Butler Report'] (14 July 2004); and Commission on the Intelligence Capabilities of the United States Regarding Weapons of Mass Destruction, 'Report to the President of the United States' (31 March 2005), available at https://fas.org/irp/offdocs/wmd_report.pdf.

[64] Jervis, 'Reports, Politics, and Intelligence Failures' (above n 42). See also Kahana (above n 25) 274.

they were neither intellectually satisfactory nor effective for improving intelligence:

> I think we can be certain that the future will see serious intelligence failures, some of which will be followed by reports like these. Reforms can only reduce and not eliminate intelligence errors, and in any event there is no reason to expect that the appropriate reforms will be put in place. Perhaps a later scholar will write a review like this one as well.[65]

The failures surrounding both 9/11 and WMDs in Iraq were at least to some extent influenced by a unique set of political circumstances, and both Zegart's and Jervis's critiques focused on organizational constraints within a broader political scheme. But their examples are nonetheless illustrative with regard to the entrenched organizational culture they have identified within intelligence communities and institutions. The organizational constraints, biases, and resistance to change that were at the heart of both the 9/11 and Iraq intelligence failures are also present in smaller-scale intelligence fact-finding processes, including those employed in the context of targeted killings.

B. Inherent Risks for Civilians

Targeted killing operations entail many risks to innocent civilians, which are intensified by the very nature of terrorism and the legal responses to it. First, being 'the weapon of the weak',[66] terrorism contravenes the international humanitarian legal principle of distinction by putting civilians at risk. By definition, terrorists target civilians and direct their attacks at random individuals. This deliberate victimisation of innocent civilians creates a public outcry for revenge and promotes political receptiveness to measures that may also put enemy civilians at risk.[67]

Second, terrorist organisations act in clandestine ways and often find shelter in loosely governed civilian areas.[68] To escape accountability, they do not wear uniforms and make efforts to blend in with the civilian population.[69] Sometimes they even use civilians purposefully, as voluntary or involuntary human shields, thus increasing tremendously the risk to civilians.[70] Therefore, any counterterrorism measure will face difficulties in avoiding collateral damage and protecting innocent bystanders.[71]

[65] Jervis, 'Reports, Politics, and Intelligence Failures' (above n 42) 48.

[66] M Crenshaw, 'The Long View of Terrorism' (2014) 113(759) *Current History* 40–42.

[67] M Abrahms, 'Why Terrorism Does Not Work' (2006) 31(2) *International Security* 42–78.

[68] CCB Kittner, 'The Role of Safe Havens in Islamist Terrorism' (2007) 19(3) *Terrorism and Political Violence* 307–29.

[69] Crenshaw (above n 66).

[70] MN Schmitt, 'Human Shields in International Humanitarian Law' (2008) 47(2) *Columbia Journal of Transnational Law* 292–338, 294–96.

[71] McNeal (above n 24) 714.

Third, as terrorists hide among civilians, the risk of failed or mistaken identification increases. According to interviews with military officials conducted by McNeal, seventy per cent of unintended civilian casualties in targeted killing operations in Afghanistan and Iraq were attributable to mistaken identification.[72] This means that terrorist tactics increase the risk to innocent civilians from targeted killing operations.

Fourth, the process of categorising civilians into legitimate and illegitimate targets for lethal attacks may in itself pose a risk to civilians. Classifying civilians into binary legal categories requires clear 'yes' or 'no' answers. In reality, terrorism is rather a spectrum of activities and engagement, and individuals' involvement in terrorism may change overtime and move from one point to another on this spectrum.[73] Separate from the question of whether a specific individual may lawfully be killed is the question of how kill lists are made. McNeal found that kill lists are essentially based on value judgements concerning an individual's contribution to the enemy group, focusing on her value to the group's ability to conduct operations, the depth of her involvement (the time between her death and its impact on the enemy group), the time it will take the enemy group to recuperate from her death, and the impact of her death on the overall operative capacity of the enemy group.[74] Such complex predictions and evaluations are obviously imprecise and imperfect, especially as they tend to be made by those responsible for state security, and therefore tend to be risk-averse when it comes to terrorism prevention. Additionally, once the list is set, various cognitive and institutional biases, including confirmation bias, may come into play to reassert previously made decisions and undermine or misinterpret potentially meaningful new information.[75]

The following section will examine these inherent challenges to risk assessment and fact-finding in targeted killing decision-making processes, using the Israeli Special Investigatory Commission on the targeted killing of Salah Shehadeh as the basis for the discussion.

[72] Ibid, 738.

[73] A Pedahzur and A Perliger, 'The Changing Nature of Suicide Attacks: A Social Network Perspective' (2006) 84(4) *Social Forces* 1987–2008. With regard to Al Qaeda, McNeal has stated that it can be understood best as a decentralised social network and is therefore resistant to the loss of any one node. See McNeal (above n 24).

[74] McNeal (above n 24) 715.

[75] Various studies in psychology have established that confirmation bias may impact the interpretation and analysis of data in various contexts, including forensic science. For example, Kassin et al have found that because forensic analysis is always coupled with some level of subjective human judgment, confirmation bias, as well as additional psychological biases, may affect analysis of data. Specifically, they have found that confessions and other types of information can set into motion forensic confirmation biases that corrupt lay witness perceptions and memories, as well as the judgements of experts in various domains of forensic science. SM Kassin, IE Dror, and J Kukucka, 'The Forensic Confirmation Bias: Problems, Perspectives, and Proposed Solutions' (2013) 2(1) *Journal of Applied Research in Memory and Cognition* 42–52.

IV. THE ISRAELI INVESTIGATION OF THE TARGETED KILLING OF SALAH SHEHADEH

Salah Shehadeh was head of the Operational Branch of Hamas in Gaza and was accused by Israel of having killed large numbers of Israeli military personnel and civilians.[76] On 22 July 2002, the Israeli Air Force dropped a one-tonne bomb on Shehadeh's house in Gaza City. In addition to killing Shehadeh, his wife, Laila, their teenage daughter, Iman Salah, and Shehadeh's assistant, Zaher Saleh Nassar, the attack killed eleven other civilians: 27-year-old Iman Hassan Matar was killed in a nearby tin shack, together with her five children – eleven years old Alaa Muhammad Matar, five years old Dunia Rami Matar, four years old Muhammad Raed Matar, two years old Aiman Raed Matar, and Dina Raed Matar, who was not even a year old when she died; twenty-two years old Muna Fahmi al-Huti and her two young children – five years old Subhi Mahmoud and three years old Muhammad Mahmoud – were killed in the nearby 'garage house'; forty-two years old Yusef Subhi Ali a-Shawa was killed in one of the tin shacks; and sixty-seven years old Khader Muhammad a-Sa'idi was fatally wounded while walking in the street. 150 civilian bystanders were injured.[77]

A. The Establishment of the Commission

Due to the extensive collateral damage of the operation, the Israel Defense Forces (IDF) conducted internal investigations, but the IDF Military Advocate General (MAG) eventually decided not to initiate criminal investigations. In response, several human rights organisations and individuals submitted a petition to the Israeli Supreme Court, sitting as the High Court of Justice (HCJ), demanding it reverse the MAG decision and open a criminal investigation.[78] During the Court hearings, the State accepted the Court's suggestion to establish an independent and objective investigatory commission to investigate the circumstances of the operation and the severe collateral damage inflicted on innocent civilians.[79]

On 23 January 2008, then-Prime Minister Olmert appointed the Special Investigatory Commission to examine the targeted killing operation directed against Shehadeh. The Commission was instructed to review the circumstances of the attack and the availability of effective alternatives. It was also authorised to recommend administrative and disciplinary measures or the initiation of criminal proceedings against the relevant actors. The Commission was composed of three members: Zvi Inbar, the former MAG and Legal Advisor

[76] Shehadeh Commission Report (above n 2).

[77] Meyerstein (above n 1).

[78] *Yoav Hess and Others v the Judge Advocate General and Others*, HCJ 8794/03 (23 December 2008), unofficial English translation available at http://www.adh-geneve.ch/RULAC/pdf_state/HCJ-decision-8794-03-1-.pdf.

[79] Ibid.

of the Knesset (the Israeli Parliament); retired Major General Yitzhak Eitan, former Commander of the IDF Central Command; and Yitzhak Dar, the former head of the Operations Department at the Israel Security Agency (ISA).

Soon after the announcement of the appointment of the Commission members, the petitioners submitted new arguments, opposing the decision to appoint only members with military and security experience.[80] On 23 August 2008, the HCJ finally rejected the petition, holding that there was no defect in the formation of the Commission.[81] The Court emphasised that none of the Commission members were at the time serving in any state security or military agencies. The Court further stated that the scepticism regarding the objectivity of the Commission was completely unfounded, especially 'at this preliminary stage, in which the Commission had not yet finished its job and had not reached any conclusions'.[82] On 31 August 2009, the Commission's chairperson, Advocate Inbar, passed away and was replaced by retired Supreme Court Justice Tova Strasberg-Cohen.

B. The Report

On 27 February 2011, the Shehadeh Commission published its final report.[83] The Report began with an analysis of the security situation that existed from the beginning of the Second Intifada (September 2000) up to the targeted killing of Shehadeh in July 2002.[84] The Commission characterised this period as an 'armed conflict' and noted that during these two years, many Palestinian terrorist attacks took place within Israel, causing the death of 474 Israelis and injuring 2,649.[85]

The Report then described the role that each governmental authority plays in a targeted killing operation. The ISA, as the authority that initiates targeted killing operations, is responsible for gathering the relevant intelligence and for mapping the surroundings of the target area in order to facilitate evaluation of anticipated collateral damage (ie, uninvolved civilians and civilian objects that might be damaged from the attack).[86] The IDF is the authority that usually executes the attack. The IDF Operations Department is responsible for ensuring that the intended target is a legitimate target and for exploring the feasibility of detaining the targeted individual or using a less lethal measure that would attain the same goal of preventing the intended target from continuing terrorist activity. After receiving the necessary authorisations to implement the operation,

[80] Ibid.
[81] Ibid.
[82] Ibid, para 13.
[83] Shehadeh Commission Report (above n 2).
[84] Ibid, 21–24.
[85] Ibid, 21.
[86] Ibid, 25.

the method of attack is chosen to ensure the operation's success while minimising the anticipated collateral damage (which must remain non-excessive). Apart from authorisation from the head of the ISA and the IDF Chief of General Staff, the operation must also be approved by the Prime Minister and the Minister of Defense.[87]

With regard to the normative framework, the Commission declared that international humanitarian law (IHL) was the relevant legal framework and pointed out that IHL allows for attacks on military targets and on combatants and civilians taking direct part in hostilities, provided that such attacks also meet the requirements of distinction and proportionality.[88] The Report referred to several additional principles that should be considered when ordering a targeted killing operation: the exceptionality of the measure; the use of targeted killing only against persons who are either committing or commissioning terrorist attacks; reliance on solid, accurate, and reliable intelligence regarding the likely continuance of the designated target's participation in terrorist activities; the use of targeted killing as a preventive measure rather than as a punitive measure; the exhaustion of less lethal alternatives; minimisation of damage to uninvolved civilians; and use of targeted killing only in areas where the IDF does not have actual control.[89] The Report further stressed four requirements stemming from the Israeli Supreme Court's landmark 2006 case concerning the legality of targeted killings:[90] (a) accurate and reliable information should be gathered about the identity and classification of the civilians who take direct part in hostilities; (b) all feasible efforts should be made to use less lethal measures; (c) the principle of proportionality must be observed, and the harm to uninvolved civilians must not be excessive; and (d) an investigatory committee should be established to investigate any operation that results in exceptional outcomes.[91]

Applying the normative legal framework to the specific circumstances of the Shehadeh operation, the Commission determined that Shehadeh was indeed a legitimate target, as a civilian who had directly participated in hostilities. The Commission also found that there were no lesser means (such as detaining him) available, since Shehadeh took shelter in a very densely populated refugee camp in Gaza, and any operation to detain him would have endangered the lives of IDF soldiers.[92]

The Report then elaborated on the internal processes and the role that each military or security authority played in preparing the targeted killing of Shehadeh.

[87] Ibid, 26–27.

[88] Ibid, 34–37.

[89] Ibid, 31.

[90] *Public Committee Against Torture in Israel v Government of Israel*, HCJ 769/02, 57(6) Israel SC 285 (13 December 2006), available at http://elyon1.court.gov.il/files_eng/02/690/007/A34/02007690.a34.pdf, paras 40–46 and 59.

[91] Shehadeh Commission Report (above n 2) 43.

[92] Ibid, 55–60.

The ISA was in charge of surveillance of Shehadeh and was responsible for planning the operation.[93] All the information was brought to Yuval Diskin, the Deputy Head of the ISA, who was the ISA authority responsible for targeted killings. Diskin's recommendation to approve Shehadeh as a legitimate target was submitted to Avi Dichter, the Head of the ISA, and was then presented to Moshe Yaalon, then Chief of General Staff, who consulted with the IDF authority responsible for targeted killings, the Deputy Chief of General Staff Gabi Ashkenazi, as well as with members of the highest political echelons: then-Minister of Defense Benjamin Ben-Eliezer and then-Prime Minister Ariel Sharon.[94]

After receiving all of the relevant authorisations, the ISA began tracking Shehadeh's location. Knowing he was wanted by the Israeli authorities, Shehadeh used seven hideouts and continually moved between them. Throughout this time, several alternative plans to target Shehadeh were abandoned, due to a low-success assessments and high risk to IDF soldiers and civilians in the area (twice due to positive information concerning the presence of Shehadeh's daughter).[95] According to the Report, Israel security services cancel operations when there is positive information about the presence of children who might be physically endangered by the attack.[96]

A few days before the operation, Shehadeh was located in an apartment in a two-story building in a densely populated refugee camp in northern Gaza. According to the information available at the time, the ground floor was used as a warehouse, and the upper floor was used as a residence.[97] The method of attack chosen was the dropping of a one-tonne bomb from the air. According to the Shehadeh Commission Report, this method of attack was chosen for two reasons: its high probability of success and low risk to IDF forces. The Commission also noted that the alternative of using two half-tonne bombs had been considered but was rejected because the probability of success was too low and because there was a higher risk that one of the bombs would miss the target and kill many uninvolved civilians.[98]

Ultimately, the Commission concluded that the decision to approve the operation was legitimate, the risk of harming Shehadeh's daughter notwithstanding.[99] With regard to Shehadeh's assistant, Zahar Natzer, the Commission found him to be a legitimate target on his own, and the anticipated death of Shehadeh's wife was considered proportionate collateral damage. The Commission nonetheless concluded that the death of Shehadeh's daughter, as well as the other eleven civilian fatalities, was disproportionate and excessive,

[93] Ibid, 61.
[94] Ibid, 62.
[95] Ibid, 68.
[96] Ibid, 70.
[97] Ibid, 63.
[98] Ibid, 64.
[99] Ibid, 65, 69, and 98.

even when taking into consideration the significant amount of risk Shehadeh's continuous terrorist activities presented to the citizens of Israel.[100] However, the Commission accepted the Israeli authorities' claims that this disproportionate outcome was not anticipated, and had such an outcome been anticipated, the operation would not have been carried out.[101]

The Commission examined the information-gathering process that led to the belief that the collateral damage would be less extensive than it was, and concluded that the intelligence that was presented before the decision-makers was incomplete.[102] It also found that at one point in the process, the absence of information as to the presence of people in the vicinity of the house was presented as information to the effect that there were no people in that area.[103] The Commission determined that the failure of intelligence with respect to the presence of uninvolved civilians in close proximity to Shehadeh stemmed from two main factors: (a) the resources that were devoted to discovering his whereabouts (and not the surroundings of this area); and (b) the concern that if Israeli intelligence agencies were to attempt to retrieve information regarding others in the area, Shehadeh would understand that his hideout was not secure. Therefore, it concluded that the balance between military necessity and protection of uninvolved civilians was inappropriate, and this led to a disproportionate (yet unanticipated) outcome.[104]

Based on its analysis, the Commission found no reason to suspect that a crime (or any violation of relevant international humanitarian or Israeli law) was committed by any of the persons involved in the planning, authorisation, and implementation of the targeted killing operation.[105] The Commission emphasised that the mere fact that civilians were inadvertently killed did not render the operation unlawful or a war crime, and that the reasonableness and legality of the operation should be considered on the basis of the available ex ante information, even if it turned out that the information was false.[106] The Commission was therefore satisfied with the fact that all of the relevant state bodies had conducted internal inquiries and that the process was subsequently improved in order to avoid outcomes of this nature in the future.[107]

In its recommendations, the Commission stated that the rules of international humanitarian law should be better embedded within the daily work of the security services; that the principle of proportionality should be strictly implemented according to the circumstances of each case; and that written guidelines

[100] Ibid, 71.
[101] Ibid, 67 and 72.
[102] Ibid, 78.
[103] Ibid, 79.
[104] Ibid, 81.
[105] Ibid, 103–6.
[106] Ibid, 47.
[107] Ibid, 105.

on the legal, ethical, normative, and moral principles concerning targeted killing operations should be formulated. Moreover, it expressed the opinion that the ISA should strengthen its intelligence efforts regarding collateral damage to the uninvolved civilian population.[108] The Commission also recommended that all relevant interactions, communications, and decisions preceding a targeted killing operation be documented and that the relevant documentation be preserved for future investigation if needed.[109]

The Commission's general recommendations to the security authorities are significant, as they highlight some procedural issues that can and should be improved, and they represent an important contribution to the advancement of transparency in the context of targeted killing operations. Nonetheless, the Commission's work and conclusions should be taken with some reservations and will be examined more closely below.

C. Bounded Factuality, Intelligence, and Risk of Error

i. Deference to Security Agencies

The Shehadeh Commission Report was based on information that was submitted to the Special Investigatory Commission by the IDF, ISA, and the Air Force. The information was accepted by the Commission in its entirety despite the fact that these bodies were clearly interested parties in the investigation. The Commission did not find any of their testimony unconvincing, even when parts were inherently inconsistent. The Commission did not critically challenge any of the positions presented by the security agencies.

In some instances, the complete and overwhelming acceptance of the security agencies' position defies plain logic and starkly contradicts other pieces of evidence. For example, while elaborating on Shehadeh's terrorist activity – a description that could be a 'cut and paste' from the information provided by the relevant security agencies – the Commission accepted as fact the assertion that Shehadeh was personally responsible for all of the Israeli terrorism casualties, including deaths and injuries, from July 2001 until Shehadeh's own death in July 2002.[110] The Commission's description in fact appears as a 'cut-and-paste' copy of the text provided to them. Incidents were not specified, details were not presented, and no other external sources were mentioned. Nor was there any reference to fragmentation amongst Hamas leadership or to other terror organisations that were operating in Gaza at the time. Another example can be found in the Commission's acceptance of the IDF claim that the method of dropping a one-tonne bomb on Shehadeh's house was chosen, among other reasons,

[108] Ibid, 107.
[109] Ibid, 108.
[110] Ibid, 21 and 55–59.

to reduce collateral damage (in comparison with the alternative of using two half-tonne bombs instead).[111] To support this finding, the Commission added that indeed, the one-tonne bomb was accurate in hitting Shehadeh's house, and that the damage to the surroundings was caused not by the impact of the bomb itself but rather by its shock wave (as if that was not a natural anticipated outcome of the hit).[112] The Commission also accepted as an uncontested fact the claim that the operation was conducted at night in order to minimise risk to civilians. This claim sharply contradicted other pieces of information suggesting that people were actually living in tin shacks and thus would most probably be sleeping in their beds at such time. (The evidence also suggested that the tin shacks would sustain the most severe collateral damage.)

ii. 'Failure is an Orphan'

While acknowledging that the disproportionate outcome resulted from severe intelligence failures (including misrepresentation of existing information), the Commission concluded that the targeted killing of Shehadeh was nonetheless lawful. It determined that the operation was a legitimate attack against a person who had participated directly in hostilities and that the 'unfortunate harm' caused by the attack was *unintentional* and *unpredictable* and was not the result of disrespect for human life. The Commission therefore determined that none of the involved security and political decision-makers violated either Israeli or international criminal law. It exonerated all of those involved in the attack from any criminal, administrative, or even ethical responsibility. The 'mistakes' were attributed to an isolated intelligence failure caused by 'incorrect assessments and mistaken judgments'.[113] The Commission refrained from attributing these 'failures', 'incorrect assessments', and 'mistakes' to any of the relevant decision-makers, and no one was held responsible for any of them.

While it certainly could be the case that no specific individual was responsible for committing specific international or domestic crimes, the Shehadeh Commission did not examine the possibility there might nonetheless have been violations of the IHL principles of proportionality and precaution. Unfortunately, the Commission did not separate between the relevant facts, deviation from the applicable legal norms, and the possible legal implications of such deviation.

iii. The Requirement of 'Positive Information'

In dealing with the death of Shehadeh's daughter in the attack, the Commission adopted the State's position that her death was not anticipated by any

[111] Ibid, 63–64.
[112] Ibid, 65.
[113] Israel Ministry of Foreign Affairs, English summary of the Shehadeh Commission Report (above n 2).

of the relevant decision-makers.[114] In adopting this view, the Commission entirely ignored the testimony of the Deputy Head of ISA, who had objected to carrying out the operation as planned based specifically on his concerns that Shehadeh's daughter was with Shehadeh. In dismissing this testimony, the Commission stated that without positive information that the child was actually present in the house, it was legitimate to assume she wasn't there and therefore to carry on with the operation.[115] This supposed need for positive information as to the presence of civilians, together with the acceptance of the intelligence agency's decision not to focus its efforts on investigating the surroundings of the target clearly led to an unacceptable outcome. Moreover, it altogether vitiates the principle of precaution. The requirement of positive information concerning the presence of civilians generates an interpretive tool that has far-reaching consequences concerning fact-finding practices and the meaning of intelligence information: it transforms the absence of facts about the presence of civilians into existing facts about the absence of civilians.

iv. The Treatment of Internal Disagreements

The decision to carry out the Shehadeh operation despite the evidence that suggested innocent civilians might get hurt was not unanimous. On 19 July 2002, the Deputy Director of the ISA held a meeting of both ISA and Air Force personnel concerning the planned operation. In the meeting, the intelligence information was presented, and various scenarios were discussed. In the discussion, the Air Force representatives estimated that the surroundings would suffer severe damage and that the greatest damage – even if the attack were to hit the target precisely as planned – would be caused to the nearby tin shacks and garage house. While the garage house was believed to be empty at night, the assessment indicated there would be at least several wounded and dead in the tin shacks.[116]

At this point, two senior ISA members advocated opposing options. The Head of Operations Division suggested a different course of action so as to minimise collateral damage and to prevent the anticipated harm to uninvolved civilians; while the Head of the Southern Region insisted that the operation should proceed as planned (because he believed that attacking at night would minimise the harm to uninvolved civilians). At the end of that meeting, the Deputy Head of the ISA decided not to proceed with the operation as planned but rather continue gathering intelligence in order to come up with an alternative ground operation that would better protect innocent civilians.[117]

[114] Shehadeh Commission Report (above n 2) 67.
[115] Ibid, 69.
[116] Ibid, 73.
[117] Ibid, 74.

Immediately afterwards, the Head of the Southern Region appealed this decision to the Director of the ISA, who upheld the appeal and reversed the decision, determining that the operation would be carried out as planned. His decision was based on several considerations, all focused on state security: (1) the scope, frequency, and severity of terrorist attacks against Israel had increased; (2) the probability of finding a practical alternative was low, and the consultations that would have to be conducted with regard to the potential new plan might thwart the killing of the target altogether.[118]

Later that day, the IDF Head of Operations Branch held another meeting, where the ISA representatives presented the planned operation. At the end of this meeting, the IDF Head of Operations Branch recommended postponing the operation until the tin shacks were evacuated. Then a final meeting was held at the IDF Chief of Staff's office. The discussion focused on the potential harm to residents of the tin shacks. The Deputy Chief of Staff, as well as the Head of the IDF Operations Branch, objected to the proposed plan and recommended waiting and, in the meantime, gathering more information. The Head of the ISA recommended carrying on with the operation as planned. At the end of this meeting, the IDF Chief of Staff decided to approve the operation as planned. His decision was based on the belief that the garage house would be empty and the assumption that the risk of killing a few civilian bystanders was proportional to the enormous damage anticipated from future terrorist attacks planned by Shehadeh.[119]

Between 19 July, when the final decision to carry out the operation was made, and July 22, when the attack took place, the operation was postponed several times due to conclusive evidence concerning the presence of Shehadeh's daughter and other children in the vicinity.[120]

These internal deliberations demonstrate the different approaches to precaution: one approach would be to err on the side of caution and to treat uncertainty as evidence that civilians will be harmed, unless conclusively proven otherwise. This approach motivates the state to conduct the necessary investigations to clarify the situation and to positively find out the possible implications of an attack. This was the approach adopted by the Deputy Head of the ISA and by the IDF Head of Operations Branch. A different approach would be to ignore uncertainty and to consider only 'positive information' that the relevant agencies come across in deciding the appropriate course of action. This approach reduces the state's burden to investigate to a minimum and contradicts the very concept of precaution. Nonetheless, this was the approach adopted by the Head of the ISA and the IDF Chief of Staff (as well as, later on, by the Shehadeh Commission). By adopting such a narrow approach to precaution,

[118] Ibid, 74–75.
[119] Ibid, 76.
[120] Ibid.

the Shehadeh Commission paved the way for decision-makers to ignore inconclusive information that does not coincide with their agenda, without the need to investigate further and obtain more information.

More importantly, these internal disagreements within the Israeli security agencies concerning the factual framework and the proper interpretation of intelligence information further emphasise the uncertainty concerning relevant facts and the intrinsic difficulty of making conclusive factual determinations concerning risks to civilians. The fact that such internal disagreements are typically buried within security organisations and are not transparent to political decision-makers increases the tendency of such decision-makers to accept the security narrative as the only acceptable interpretation of a complicated and often uncertain reality.

v. Limited Political Oversight

Political oversight of military and security agencies is crucial for maintaining and upholding the principle of precaution. While security agencies are focused on narrow security considerations, the political leadership considers a wider range of considerations, including foreign affairs and diplomatic interests, economic interests, and humanitarian interests.

The Report of the Shehadeh Commission reveals a troubling deference to security experts on the part of Israeli political leaders. The responsible minister, the Minister of Defense, testified that he largely left the decision to his military secretary and that he trusted the ISA and military experts. In fact, the Minister of Defense was abroad and did not personally participate in any of the relevant meetings. He was briefed by his military secretary by telephone before approving the operation. The brief did not include information on the existence of alternatives, the danger to residents of the tin shacks, or the disagreements between senior officials of the ISA and IDF.[121] (The Prime Minister could not provide testimony to the Commission due to his medical condition.)

The information gathered by the Shehadeh Commission concerning the role of the political leadership in targeted killing decision-making reveals another important weakness of the fact-finding process. Political oversight is currently handicapped by the lack of any meaningful tools to challenge the security narrative. First, it is clear that information-gathering by intelligence agencies focuses on the target and his or her whereabouts rather than on anticipated harm to civilians. Second, as discussed above, the absence of information concerning the presence of civilians is treated as information about their absence. Third, disagreements about interpretation of intelligence are buried within each organisation and are not carried forward. As a result, civilian decision-makers are presented with a coherent narrative that appears to justify targeting.

[121] Ibid, 82–83.

Alternatives, disagreements, and uncertainties concerning the meaning of the intelligence information are not presented and discussed in a meaningful way that would allow civilian decision-makers to challenge the military decision or decide to take a different course of action. Under such conditions, it is no wonder that the political leadership views this oversight responsibility as a formality rather than real engagement with the data and any proposed plan. The oversight function of civilian decision-makers can be an important one in the context of targeted killings, but only if any absences of concrete information, internal disagreements concerning interpretation of intelligence information, and alternative courses of action are brought forward.

vi. Law-Fulfilling Prophecy

The Shehadeh Commission went to great lengths to explain 'how did it happen, that with all of the sensitivity and awareness to prevent harming civilians, especially children, that such unexpected collateral damage could occur?'[122] While emphasising that the result was unexpected, unintended, and not the responsibility of any specific individual, the Commission did concede that 'at some point, the missing information became positive information that the garage house and tin shacks were uninhabited'.[123]

However, a thorough inspection of the evidence that was in front of the Commission suggests that the information which the Commission characterised as 'missing' was not missing at all. In fact, the military fact-finding process produced several aerial photos and source information indicating that civilians were living in the tin shacks next to Shehadeh's residence. Additional evidence suggested that Shehadeh's daughter was with him. Intelligence analysts could also employ their familiarity with the area and common sense, to determine that civilians were likely going to be present at the site of the attack. In other parts of its Report, the Commission itself mentioned the common knowledge that the area was densely populated, as well as aerial photos showing water tanks and satellite dishes on the roofs of the tin shacks. It also mentioned the air force estimations concerning severe collateral damage to the tin shacks and their inhabitants.[124] So how did it happen that (non-missing) information about the presence of civilians turned into information about their absence?

One possible explanation is that the need to meet the legal proportionality standard, which focuses on *anticipated* damage, may motivate intelligence analysts and security-oriented decision-makers to see empty buildings in the middle of a densely populated refugee camp. Groupthink, compartmentalisation, and security-oriented institutional goals may all join

[122] Ibid, 77.
[123] Ibid, 79.
[124] Ibid, 78.

in to develop fact-finding practices that produce facts that are consistent with the legal requirements. In this case, it seems that fragmentation within the security organisations enabled ISA decision-makers to selectively pick and choose intelligence information provided by the air force and military, in order to fit with the legal requirements. The growing frustration within the agency regarding previous targeting plans that had been cancelled due to the presence of civilians also meant that ISA decision-makers were motivated to disregard any information suggesting that bystanders would be harmed under the new plan.

In fact, the plans to kill Shehadeh were postponed several times due to 'positive information' about the presence of his daughter and other civilians in the area. The 22 July attack too had been cancelled initially by the Deputy Head of the ISA, for similar reasons. His decision was determined to be based on 'uncertain' information and therefore overruled, but the truth is that the information on the anticipated absence of Shehadeh's daughter was likewise 'uncertain' – arguably even more so than the information about her possible presence. By requiring 'positive information' ascertaining the presence of civilians at the time and place of the attack, ISA decision-makers were able to give the available facts the desired meaning – a meaning that seemed consistent with the legal proportionality requirement and made the anticipated collateral damage low enough to lawfully proceed with the operation.

V. IMPROVING FACT-FINDING IN TARGETING DECISION-MAKING

The information gathered by the Shehadeh Commission reveals several disturbing patterns concerning fact-finding in the context of targeted killing decision-making. Fact-finding efforts were channelled to the whereabouts of Shehadeh rather than to the anticipated harm to bystanders in the vicinity of the attack; information concerning likely inhabitants in the tin shacks, including evidence of satellite dishes and water tanks on the roofs, was ignored or interpreted as 'inconclusive'; and the 'absent' information about the inhabitancy of the shacks was interpreted to mean that the shacks were uninhabited. The missing facts about the presence of civilians were not regarded as a gap in knowledge but rather interpreted as existing facts about the absence of civilians. Similarly, internal disagreements concerning the interpretation of the available data were not highlighted, and once one interpretation was adopted, all prior disagreements were silenced so as not to disturb the consistency and strength of the chosen narrative. Before the civilian decision-makers signed off on the plan for the attack, they were presented with a coherent narrative that minimised uncertainties and filled in missing information with interpreted conclusions rather than concrete facts.

It should therefore not be all that surprising that information about the presence of civilians turned into 'facts' about their absence. However, it should be concerning. This fact-finding process, for all of its limitations, is the basis for life-and-death decisions – not only with regard to intended targets but also, as the Shehadeh case clearly demonstrates, with regard to potentially large numbers of civilians in surrounding areas. Accordingly, this section proposes several recommendations to improve the fact-finding practices of such targeted-killing operations and thereby move from a culture of 'bounded factuality' to a culture of transparent fact-finding.

A. Acknowledging the Problem

It is essential to acknowledge the limitations on legal fact-finding during armed conflicts. Likewise, it is necessary to consider how motivated reasoning, psychological biases, and organisational cultures may all impact the interpretation of intelligence during targeting decision-making processes.

B. Enhancing Fact-Finding and Improving Political Oversight

To improve some of the problems identified above, inter-agency communications should embrace both information-sharing and a norm of robust deliberation over the interpretation of such information. Missing or lacking information should be highlighted, along with internal disagreements concerning interpretation of data. Internal disagreements within the intelligence community should be brought before the political leadership, who bears the final responsibility for targeting decisions and must be able to exercise meaningful oversight over the security agencies.

Additionally, the burden of proof required to justify a suggested targeting operation should be further unpacked and clarified by decision-makers, including the methodology used to determine the level of certainty attached to the final narrative. Similarly, the 'positive information' requirement should be replaced with a duty to err on the side of caution, as well as to conduct further fact-finding as necessary to complement inconclusive, missing, or unreliable information.

C. Independent *Ex Ante* and *Ex Post* Review

A rigorous inter-agency review process should be established, with the goal of offering alternative interpretation of intelligence information, assessing its credibility, weight, and possible meanings. Similar to the idea of 'red teams' in investigative journalism, this process – which after all may end with a decision to kill a specific individual without trial – should include members external to the intelligence-gathering teams who are able and willing to trace the sources of interpreted or analysed information and make determinations concerning missing information and the need to gather more evidence before they endorse a targeting decision.

Additionally, an independent ex post review committee that is capable of challenging the security agencies and of conducting effective ex post review should be established. The committee should be permanent and independent, and should be empowered to ex post review the decision to target an individual, the processes that were undergone, and the design and execution of the actual operation. The committee should not be limited to former military officials and security experts but rather include members from various backgrounds, such as those who have served in the public defender's office or civil society organizations. The committee must be authorised to review not only security agency decisions but also policies and oversight mechanisms related to other state officials. While conducting ex post review of targeted killing operations, such a committee should be empowered to recommend initiating criminal investigations in appropriate cases, or whether reparations should be paid by the state. Finally, the work of such a committee should be made public in a timely manner (with minimal necessary redactions to protect sources and intelligence methods) in order to further increase transparency.

D. Distinguishing between Brute Facts, Empirical Predictions, Value Judgements, and Legal Facts

Targeting decisions are supposed to be based on facts: facts regarding the impact of the chosen weapon, facts about the presence of civilians nearby, facts concerning the dangerousness of the target, facts about the existence of feasible alternatives. However, not all facts are created equal. Some are brute facts: the weight of the bomb, the distance between the target site and other buildings, the number of casualties afterwards. Other facts are inferences and predictions drawn from data, such as levels of threat or the feasibility of alternatives. And yet another type of facts are value judgements, such as the excessiveness of the harm to some civilians in comparison to the gain in security for the population at large. Some facts concern the past, while others are predictions about the future. Will civilians be present? Will the target be involved in future attacks? And some facts are "legal facts," such as the categorisation of casualties into 'combatants' and 'civilians', the 'proportionality' of 'collateral damage', and the liability of those involved in a targeted killing operation.

Fact-finding processes that form the basis of targeted killing decisions, including the process that led to the killing of Salah Shehadeh, do not tend to distinguish between different types of facts. Similar levels of proof and certainty may be attributed to various types of facts, and fact-finders tend to disregard the unique empirical challenges raised by each type of fact.[125] Improving fact-finding processes in the context of targeted killings therefore requires developing a sensitivity to the different types of facts. Fact-finders should clearly distinguish between brute facts, interpretations, and predictions, and they should attribute varying levels of certainty and reliability to the information accordingly. This would allow decision-makers to review the brute facts and enable review teams to offer alternative interpretations of these facts. It would also enable the identification of truly missing information (in contrast to wrongly interpreted information), and decision-makers could then explicitly consider whether more information is necessary before giving a green light for something as serious as a targeted killing operation.

Moreover, while collecting brute facts and making relevant predictions and interpretations based on these facts is mainly the task of fact-finders, value judgments (such as deciding what constitutes disproportionate collateral damage) entail moral, ethical, and legal considerations and should therefore ultimately be the responsibility of people who have expertise in these areas rather than expertise in security. The distinction between fact-finding and value judgments may also contribute to future accountability measures in the context of targeted killing, particularly with regard to identifying the sources of intelligence failures and mistakes.

VI. CONCLUSION

Governments around the world target and kill individuals to prevent them from committing terrorist attacks or other atrocities.[126] They use this method secretly, sometimes without even taking responsibility for such operations and without making most of the relevant information public. What are the criteria for targeting individuals? What amount of evidence is required to make targeting decisions? What are the procedures to identify mistakes and avoid misuse of this method? And how are basic facts being analysed and assessed?

This chapter has aimed to shed light on the legal fact-finding processes that are at the heart of targeting decision-making. By focusing on the unique challenges to legal fact-finding during armed conflicts, it has sought to explain how organisational structures and psychological biases may lead to intelligence failures and skew legal analysis in favour of permitting questionable targeting operations. Analysis of the Israeli Shehadeh Commission illustrates how a domestic

[125] MD Risinger, 'Searching for Truth in the American Law of Evidence and Proof' (2013) 47(3) *Georgia Law Review* 801–36. See also MS Moore, 'The Plain Truth about Legal Truth' (2003) 26(1) *Harvard Journal of Law and Public Policy* 23–47, 24–26 (distinguishing between propositions of fact, general law, interpretation, value, and logic).

[126] Melzer (above n 7) 9–10.

investigatory body might be held captive by a national security narrative and interpret information accordingly. In stark contrast to the many paragraphs in the Shehadeh Commission Report about the suffering of the Israeli population as a result of terrorist attacks, the Report's information regarding the damage done to Palestinian civilians and their property as a direct result of the Shehadeh killing was short and laconic, containing only two figures – the number of civilians killed and the number of those injured. The description of the impoverished and densely populated refugee camp where the attack took place was limited to the potential security threats that it created for IDF soldiers; the damage to nearby houses and civilian properties was not mentioned at all; and the names of the innocent bystanders who were killed in the street or trapped under the ruins of their homes were completely absent. To the Commission, they were nothing more than unanticipated 'collateral damage'.

Adopting a different approach to fact-finding, as suggested in this chapter, could have led decision-makers and investigators to identify concrete errors and pinpoint exactly when and how inconclusive, partial, and uncertain information was transformed into brute 'facts' – facts that that ultimately served as the basis for a lethal military operation that took the lives of thirteen innocent bystanders.

REFERENCES

Abrahms, M, 'Why Terrorism Does Not Work' (2006) 31(2) *International Security* 42–78.

Alston, P, 'Report of the Special Rapporteur on Extrajudicial, Summary or Arbitrary Executions', UN Human Rights Council, A/HRC/14/24/Add.6 (28 May 2010).

Badie, D, 'Groupthink, Iraq, and the War on Terror: Explaining US Policy Shift toward Iraq' (2010) 6(4) *Foreign Policy Analysis* 277–96.

Balkin, JM, 'The Proliferation of Legal Truth' (2003) 26(1) *Harvard Journal of Law and Public Policy* 5–16.

Barak-Erez, D and Waxman, M, 'Secret Evidence and the Due Process of Terrorist Detentions' (2009) 48(3) *Columbia Journal of Transnational Law* 3.

Bar-Tal, D, 'Collective Memory of Physical Violence: Its Contribution to the Culture of Violence' in E Cairns and MD Roe (eds), *The Role of Memory in Ethnic Conflict* (London, Palgrave Macmillan, 2003).

——, 'Societal Beliefs in Times of Intractable Conflict: The Israeli Case' (1998) 9(1) *International Journal of Conflict Management* 22–50.

Broude, T, 'Behavioral International Law' (2015) 163(4) *University of Pennsylvania Law Review* 1099–157.

Chesney, R, 'Who May Be Killed? Anwar al-Awlaki as a Case Study in the International Legal Regulation of Lethal Force' in MN Schmitt (ed), *Yearbook of International Humanitarian Law: Volume 13, 2010* (The Hague, TMC Asser Instituut, 2011).

Cleveland, SH, 'Hamdi Meets Youngstown: Justice Jackson's Wartime Security Jurisprudence and the Detention of "Enemy Combatants"' (2005) 68(4) *Albany Law Review* 1127–44.

Cohen, S, *States of Denial: Knowing about Atrocities and Suffering* (Malden, Polity Press, 2013).

Commission on the Intelligence Capabilities of the United States Regarding Weapons of Mass Destruction, 'Report to the President of the United States' (31 March 2005), available at https://fas.org/irp/offdocs/wmd_report.pdf.

Crenshaw, M, 'The Long View of Terrorism' (2014) 113(759) *Current History* 40–42.

Damaska, M, 'Truth in Adjudication' (1997) 49 *Hastings Law Journal* 289–308.

Downs, C, '"Targeted Killings" in an Age of Terror: The Legality of the Yemen Strike' (2004) 9(2) *Journal of Conflict and Security Law* 277–94.

Eden, L, *Whole World on Fire: Organizations, Knowledge and Nuclear Weapons Destruction* (Ithaca, Cornell University Press, 2004).

Faigman, DL, 'Normative Constitutional Fact-Finding: Exploring the Empirical Component of Constitutional Interpretation' (1991) 139 *University of Pennsylvania Law Review* 541–613.

Guiora, AN, 'Determining a Legitimate Target: The Dilemma of the Decision Maker' (20121) 47(2) *Texas International Law Journal* 315–35.

Heyns, C, 'Enhanced Interactive Dialogue on Burundi', Human Rights Council (22 March 2016), https://www.refworld.org/pdfid/5728500c4.pdf.

Huddy, L, Feldman, S, Taber, C, and Lahav, G, 'Threat, Anxiety, and Support of Antiterrorism Policies' (2005) 49(3) *American Journal of Political Science* 593–608.

Janis, IL, *Groupthink: Psychological Studies of Policy Decisions and Fiascoes*, 2nd edn (Boston, Wadsworth, 1982).

Jervis, R, 'Reports, Politics, and Intelligence Failures: The Case of Iraq' (2006) 29(1) *Journal of Strategic Studies* 3–52.

——, 'War and Misperception' (1988) 18(4) *Journal of Interdisciplinary History* 675–700.

Kahan, D, 'Foreword: Neutral Principles, Motivated Cognition, and Some Problems for Constitutional Law' (2012) 125(1) *Harvard Law Review* 1–77.

Kahan, DM, Hoffman, DA, Evans, D, Braman, D, and Rachlinski, JJ, 'They Saw a Protest: Cognitive Illiberalism and the Speech–Conduct Distinction' (2012) 64 *Stanford Law Review* 851–906.

Kahana, E, 'Analyzing Israel's Intelligence Failures' (2005) 18(2) *International Journal of Intelligence and CounterIntelligence* 262–79.

Kahneman, D, 'Maps of Bounded Rationality: Psychology for Behavioral Economics' (2003) 93(5) *American Economic Review* 1449–75.

Kassin, SM, Dror, IE, and Kukucka, J, 'The Forensic Confirmation Bias: Problems, Perspectives, and Proposed Solutions' (2013) 2(1) *Journal of Applied Research in Memory and Cognition* 42–52.

Khalidi, MA, '"The Most Moral Army in the World": The New "Ethical Code" of the Israeli Military and the War on Gaza' (2010) 39(3) *Journal of Palestine Studies* 6–23.

Kitai-Sangero, R, 'The Limits of Preventive Detention' (2009) 40 *McGeorge Law Review* 903–34.

Kittner, CCB, 'The Role of Safe Havens in Islamist Terrorism' (2007) 19(3) *Terrorism and Political Violence* 307–29.

Koblentz, GD, 'Predicting Peril or the Peril of Prediction? Assessing the Risk of CBRN Terrorism' (2011) 23(4) *Terrorism and Political Violence* 501–20.

Krebs, S, 'Reducing Uncertainty in Targeted Killing Decision-Making' (2018) 44 *Florida State University Law Review* 943–93.

Kretzmer, D, *The Occupation of Justice: The Supreme Court of Israel and the Occupied Territories* (Albany, State University of New York Press, 2002).

——, 'Targeted Killing of Suspected Terrorists: Extra-Judicial Executions or Legitimate Means of Defence?' (2005) 16(2) *European Journal of International Law* 171–212.

Kunda, Z, 'The Case for Motivated Reasoning' (1990) 108(3) *Psychological Bulletin* 480–98.

Laudan, L, *Truth, Error, and Criminal Law: An Essay in Legal Epistemology* (Cambridge, Cambridge University Press, 2006).

Lord Butler of Brockwell (Chair, UK House of Commons Committee), 'Review of Intelligence on Weapons of Mass Destruction: Report of a Committee of Privy Councillors to the House of Commons' [the 'Butler Report'] (14 July 2004).

Lord, C, Ross, L, and Leper, M, 'Biased Assimilation and Attitude Polarization: The Effects of Prior Theories on Subsequently Considered Evidence' (1979) 37(11) *Journal of Personality and Social Psychology* 2098–109.

McNeal, GS, 'Targeted Killing and Accountability' (2014) 102 *Georgetown Law Journal* 681–794.

Melzer, N, *Targeted Killings in International Law* (Oxford, Oxford University Press, 2008).

Meyerstein, A, 'Case Study: The Israeli Strike against Hamas Leader Salah Shehadeh', *Crimes of War Magazine* (19 September 2002).

Milanovic, M, 'Establishing the Facts about Mass Atrocities: Accounting for the Failure of the ICTY to Persuade Target Audiences' (2015) 47 *Georgetown Journal of International Law* 1321–78.

Maoz, I, et al, 'Reactive Devaluation of an "Israeli" vs "Palestinian" Peace Proposal' (2002) 46(4) *Journal of Conflict Resolution* 515–46.

Moore, MS, 'Legal Reality: A Naturalist Approach to Legal Ontology' (2002) 21(6) *Law and Philosophy* 619–705.

——, 'The Plain Truth about Legal Truth' (2003) 26(1) *Harvard Journal of Law and Public Policy* 23–47.

Nickerson, RS, 'Confirmation Bias: A Ubiquitous Phenomenon in Many Guises' (1998) 2(2) *Review of General Psychology* 175–220.

O'Connor, MA, 'The Enron Board: The Perils of Groupthink' (2003) 71 *University of Cincinnati Law Review* 1233–319.

Obama, B, 'Remarks by the President at the National Defense University', Fort McNair (Washington, DC, 23 May 2013), available at https://obamawhitehouse.archives.gov/the-press-office/2013/05/23/remarks-president-national-defense-university.

Pedahzur, A and Perliger, A, 'The Changing Nature of Suicide Attacks: A Social Network Perspective' (2006) 84(4) *Social Forces* 1987–2008.

Risinger, MD, 'Searching for Truth in the American Law of Evidence and Proof' (2013) 47(3) *Georgia Law Review* 801–36.

Rosenzweig, I and Shany, Y, 'Special Investigatory Commission Publishes Report on Targeted Killing of Shehadeh' (2011) 27 *Terrorism and Democracy*.

Ross, L and Ward, A, 'Psychological Barriers to Dispute Resolution' in MP Zanna and JM Olson (eds), *Advances in Experimental Social Psychology, Vol 27* (San Diego, Academic Press, 1995).

Scheppele, KL, 'Just the Facts, Ma'am: Sexualized Violence, Evidentiary Habits, and the Revision of Truth' (1992) 37 *New York Law School Law Review* 123.

Schmitt, MN, 'Extraterritorial Lethal Targeting: Deconstructing the Logic of International Law' (2013) 52 *Columbia Journal of Transnational Law* 77–112.

——, 'Human Shields in International Humanitarian Law' (2008) 47(2) *Columbia Journal of Transnational Law* 292–338.

Select Committee on Intelligence (US Senate), 'Report on the US Intelligence Community's Prewar Intelligence Assessments on Iraq' (7 July 2004), available at https://fas.org/irp/congress/2004_rpt/ssci_iraq.pdf.

Sherwin, RK, 'Law Frames: Historical Truth and Narrative Necessity in a Criminal Case' (1994) 47(1) *Stanford Law Review* 39–83.

Simon, D, Snow, CJ, and Read, SJ, 'The Redux of Cognitive Consistency Theories: Evidence Judgments by Constraint Satisfaction' (2004) 86(6) *Journal of Personality and Social Psychology* 814–37.

Sitaraman, G and Zionts, D, 'Behavioral War Powers' (2015) 90 *New York University Law Review* 516–88.

Slovic, P, Fischhoff, B, and Lichtenstein, S, 'Facts and Fears: Understanding Perceived Risk' in RC Schwing and WA Albers (eds), *Societal Risk Assessment: How Safe is Safe Enough?* (New York, Plenum Press, 1980).

Smith, TW, 'Protecting Civilians ... or Soldiers? Humanitarian Law and the Economy of Risk in Iraq' (2008) 9(2) *International Studies Perspectives* 144–64.

Stern, J, 'Dreaded Risk and the Control of Biological Weapons' (2002) 27(3) *International Security* 89–123.

Stewart, H, 'Is Indefinite Detention of Terrorist Suspects Really Constitutional?' (2005) 54 *University of New Brunswick Law Journal* 235.

Stewart, MG, Ellingwood, BR, and Mueller, J, 'Homeland Security: A Case Study in Risk Aversion for Public Decision-Making' (2011) 15(5/6) *International Journal of Risk Assessment and Management* 367–86.

Van Harten, G, 'Weaknesses of Adjudication in the Face of Secret Evidence' (2009) 13(1) *International Journal of Evidence and Proof* 1–27.

Vité, S, 'Typology of Armed Conflicts in International Humanitarian Law: Legal Concepts and Actual Situations' (2009) 873 *International Review of the Red Cross* 69–94.

Zegart, AB, 'September 11 and the Adaptation Failure of US Intelligence Agencies' (2005) 29(4) *International Security* 78–111.

——, *Spying Blind: The CIA, the FBI, and the Origins of 9/11* (Princeton, Princeton University Press, 2009).

18

Countering Terrorism and Violent Extremism: The Security–Prevention Complex

ANDREAS ARMBORST

I. INTRODUCTION

OVER THE PAST decade, the field of counterterrorism has stretched into areas of civil society that traditionally did not deal with the prevention of terrorism. Today, it is not only the police and the military that fight terrorism but society as a whole: teachers, parents, mosques, municipal workers, social workers, tech companies, and bloggers are involved in the prevention of radicalisation. The expansion of the counterterrorism and counterextremism domain is the consequence of a paradigm shift that addresses the root causes of terrorism rather than just combatting it with military means. And although these approaches may be less controversial in terms of human rights when compared to extreme counterterrorism measures – such as targeted killings and extraordinary renditions, the scale of these new practices make critical reflection necessary.

Security practices are never neutral. All such practices implicitly or explicitly define something or someone as a threat to security, even if this framing becomes more subtle as the counterterrorism complex involves a growing number of professional groups. There are at least two mechanisms through which the state expands security into additional sectors: incentives and regulations. In the rapidly growing field of countering violent extremism (CVE), we can observe both. For example, there are financial incentives for nongovernmental organisations (NGOs) and municipalities to apply for funding and implement CVE practices.[1] In contrast, a state can impose statutory duties on those institutions that it sees as indispensable partners for its CVE strategy. For example, there are statutory

[1] For a list of grantees of federal funds in this field, see a minor interpellation to the German federal parliament, *Deutscher Bundestag* (21 March 2018), http://dipbt.bundestag.de/doc/btd/19/013/1901349.pdf.

duties for teachers in the United Kingdom to report signs of radicalisation among their students. In Germany, legislators have introduced a bill that make it mandatory for social media companies to delete hate speech and extremist content.[2]

To further illustrate mechanisms through which states expand security, this chapter presents some of the current developments in counterterrorism in Germany and considers them in the context of security and human rights. The section below presents three terms that are key to this chapter: security, terrorism, and CVE. Section III describes three legal approaches to counterterrorism in Germany and some of their implications for civil liberties. Section IV then examines the expansion of counterterrorism practices into other realms of public life, in particular Germany's recent 'national strategy to prevent extremism and promote democracy', which was introduced in July 2016 under the aegis of the Federal Ministry of Family Affairs. Reflecting on the programmes and measures associated with the strategy, the section points out some opportunities to alleviate tensions between security and human rights.

II. TERRORISM, SECURITY, AND COUNTERING VIOLENT EXTREMISM

Can we prevent terrorism by countering violent extremism? And does this approach alleviate the seeming strain between security on the one hand and human rights on the other? Before addressing these questions, three key terms must be defined.

A. Security

Security encompasses numerous discourses, policies, and actions, and these days it appears as a dominant and omnipresent concern. Yet without further specification, the term has little descriptive or analytical value. From a linguistic point of view, 'security' is a floating signifier, an arbitrary description of any state. From a constructivist point of view, security is not an empirical fact but rather a discursive one:

> It may be grammatically correct to use the term 'security' as a noun that is the subject of a sentence, but it is dangerous to go on to the assumption that security actually exists even as a fuzzy concept.... [A]ll we can know about security is what people do in its name ...[3]

Sociologists further nuance the term by proposing that 'security' is not only a linguistic wildcard but also ontologically and epistemically subjective.[4] In other words,

[2] Netzwerkdurchsuchungsgesetz ('Network Enforcement Act'); also Gesetz zur Verbesserung der Rechtsdurchsetzung in sozialen Netzwerken – NetzDG from 1 September 2017.

[3] M Valverde, 'Questions of Security: A Framework for Research' (2011) 15(1) *Theoretical Criminology* 3–22, 5.

[4] J Searle, *The Construction of Social Reality* (London, Penguin, 1996) 8.

there is no universal yardstick to determine at which particular point security may be absent. The status 'secure/insecure' carries no information if it does not refer to something experienceable. It could be a description of virtually anything and everything, including social, political, medical, technological, and military conditions.[5]

A straightforward solution would be to define security as the absence of threats. But then the burden of meaning bears on the word 'threat' (or danger), and not surprisingly, this also appears to be linguistically and empirically vacant, as David Garland has observed:

> Dangers are dangers for someone – for specific individuals or groups or species, under certain conditions – nothing is dangerous as such. On the other hand, anything and everything has the potential to become a danger to something or someone. All that is required is that there are interests or values that the thing may adversely affected.[6]

At first glance, security seems to be a self-evident and objective fact; at second glance it seems to be just the opposite. Semantic analysis cannot enlighten us any further than that.

If we accept then that security is a highly contingent social construct, we can start to study 'what people do in its name' and the consequences of such actions for other people. In this regard it might be helpful to think of different *regimes* of security:[7] cybersecurity, information technology (IT) security, maritime security, environmental security, homeland (domestic) security, human security, urban security, and so on. Security regimes interact and interfere with each other. Professional elites lay out rules, standards, technical or academic descriptions of what constitutes security within their regime and what constitutes threats to this status. They take action to preserve or restore security within their domain. The pursuit of security in one domain can mean a threat to security in another: if we define security as the physical integrity and self-determination of individuals, then the criminal justice system threatens the security of deviant people in order to protect the interests of others. In reaction to a threat from one security regime, individuals may take action to protect their particular interests: for example, they may engage technical protection such as messenger encryption in order to counter surveillance, or they may undertake legal action or have legal protection insurance.

[5] Jeremy Waldron has made the point that security is not binary (present/absent) but rather a gradual state and 'a matter of more or less'. See J Waldron, *Torture, Terror and Trade-Offs: Philosophy for the White House* (Oxford, Oxford University Press, 2010). See also L Lazarus, 'The Right to Security' in R Cruft, MS Liao, and M Renzo (eds), *Philosophical Foundations of Human Rights* (Oxford, Oxford University Press, 2015) 439.

[6] D Garland, 'The Rise of Risk' in R Ericson and A Doyle (eds), *Risk and Morality* (Toronto, Toronto University Press, 2003) 51.

[7] The notion of 'regime' is borrowed from international relations, but I use it here with a slightly different intention. See RO Keohane, 'The Demand for International Regimes' (1982) 36(2) *International Organization* 325–55.

This overlap of various security regimes means that the establishment of domestic security affects the protection of civil liberties. A citizen can misuse his or her civil liberties to harm other citizens (not necessarily de jure, but de facto). Extremist groups such as white supremacists (ab)use their right to free speech to slur other groups (immigrants, non-whites, etc). Offensive language and agitation can stretch the boundaries of free speech and has become a hot-button issue in the context of social media. This can put the state into a quandary in which neither the protection of free speech nor the rights of targeted social groups can be perfectly attained. Andrew Ashworth and Lucia Zedner have examined the 'paradox of liberty' with regard to this dilemma.[8] The point is to illustrate the many mechanisms through which the 'attainment of security' can adversely affect people's interests. Because this dilemma to some extent is unavoidable, we need to be clear about the 'hierarchy of rights': '… if security constitutes such an essential element of all other rights, then let us secure those rights in the first instance, instead of deploying the language of security to arrive at their protection.'[9]

Another option to reconcile security and civil liberties is to attain security through approaches that do not infringe other rights (or at least do so to a lesser extent). The aim of CVE, through non-repressive and non-statutory means (education, community work, etc), is not to clash with civil liberties and human rights in the ways that more extreme forms of counter terrorism do. However, the prevention framework introduces its own tensions, which will be discussed below.

B. Terrorism

Whereas security is linguistically a 'floating signifier', terrorism has been described as an 'essentially contested concept'.[10] The most distinguishable attribute of terrorism appears to be the controversy around its definition rather than a particular type of violent action. Constructivists therefore conclude that terrorism is just a 'political claim' without any other empirical manifestation in the real world: 'The term terrorism creates the false impression that the action it describes represents a special or unique phenomenon.'[11] The terminological

[8] A Ashworth and L Zedner, *Preventive Justice* (Oxford, Oxford University Press, 2014) 257.

[9] Lazarus (above n 5) 441.

[10] F Collier, FD Hidalgo, and AO Maciuceanu, 'Essentially Contested Concepts: Debates and Applications' (2006) 11(3) *Journal of Political Ideologies* 211–46; W Gallie, 'Essentially Contested Concepts' (1956) 56(1) *Proceedings of the Aristotelian Society* 167–98; and L Weinberg, A Pedahzur, and S Hirsch-Hoefler, 'The Challenges of Conceptualizing Terrorism' (2004) 16(4) *Terrorism and Political Violence* 777–94.

[11] J Hayes, 'Is the Concept of Terrorism Still Useful?', International Relations and Security Network paper, ETH Zurich Center for Security Studies (23 January 2015), http://www.css.ethz.ch/en/services/digital-library/publications/publication.html/187968, 1.

debate notwithstanding, we can tackle the issue of terrorism from the opposite direction. That is, by asking whether there is within the behavioural range of political violence some distinctive action that empirically justifies treating this action as a separate category of political violence.[12]

In public discourse, terrorism is often described as the ultimate threat to security. Indeed, terrorism is an abnormal type of crime, not so much for the human losses and economic damage that it causes but for the reaction of the state that it triggers. In response to ordinary crime, the state tends to apply existing criminal law; in response to terrorism, the state often *changes* criminal law.[13] Ordinary crimes, regardless of how despicable or how enormous, do not have as great an impact on the evolution and application of law:

> [P]erhaps the most draconian and burgeoning preventive laws are those presented as countering the potentially catastrophic harms inflicted by terrorist attacks. Within the criminal law these includes specific terrorism offences of possession, preparatory offences, crimes of publication and dissemination of inflammatory material, and offences of association with and support for terrorist organisations.[14]

The notion of terrorism touches on legal doctrine and even legal philosophy.[15] It has facilitated the 'preventive turn' in penal policy,[16] and states throughout the world bend the rule of law when fighting against terrorism. This includes preventive and pretrial detention, extraordinary rendition, and torture of terrorist suspects, to name the most obvious examples.[17]

However, not even the most oppressive state apparatus has been successful in eradicating terrorism entirely. A state may establish a monopoly on the 'legitimate' use of force, but even totalitarian states find it virtually impossible to monopolise the use of force altogether. Terrorists seek to demonstrate just this. For some groups, killing indiscriminately is the preferred choice to demonstrate how powerless the regime actually is.[18] The German sociologist Heinrich Popitz described this as the paradox of power: the *ultima ratio* for the exercise of power – killing – is an option for everyone at any time.[19]

[12] A Armborst, 'Conceptualizing Political Violence of Non-state Actors in International Security Research' in A Kruck and A Schneiker (eds), *Researching Non-state Actors in International Security: Theory and Practice* (London, Routledge, 2017).

[13] For example, by introducing new offences such as § 129a StGB in response to attacks of the Red Army Faction; or § 129b StGB in response to the 9/11 attacks.

[14] Ashworth and Zedner (above n 8) 4.

[15] L Lazarus and BJ Goold, 'Introduction' in BJ Goold and L Lazarus (eds), *Security and Human Rights* (Oxford, Hart Publishing, 2007).

[16] H Carvalho, *The Preventive Turn in Criminal Law* (Oxford, Oxford University Press, 2017); and T Müller, *Präventiver Freiheitsentzug als Instrument der Terrorismusbekämpfung* (Berlin, Duncker & Humblot, 2011).

[17] L Sonderegger, *Die Rückkehr der Folter? Anwendung von Zwang bei der Vernehmung im deutschen und US-amerikanischen Recht* (Berlin, Dunker & Humblot, 2012).

[18] For example, al Qaeda in Iraq used this strategy of terror during the Civil War in Iraq (2006–10).

[19] H Popitz, *Phänomene der Macht: Autorität – Herrschaft – Gewalt – Technik* (Tübingen, Mohr Siebeck, 1992).

C. Countering Violent Extremism (CVE)

Fortunately, governments have more options than just killing terrorists. Counter-terrorism can be broadly divided into approaches from five domains: military, diplomacy, intelligence, criminal justice, and the emerging field of CVE.[20] Most CVE programs implicitly or explicitly incorporate a public health model of preventive healthcare, which identifies three broad areas of prevention: primary prevention focuses on long-term and population-based measures directed at extremists (eg, education); secondary prevention addresses groups and individuals with known risks for violent extremism (eg, outreach for youths who are vulnerable to radicalisation); and tertiary prevention encompasses reactive measures, such as rehabilitation and reintegration of those who have actively supported extremist groups.[21]

As early as 2002, when most other people were thinking about military and quasi-military solutions to terrorism, John Braithwaite, an early advocate for CVE practice, recommended 'a web of controls to prevent terrorism'.[22] He has proposed that primary, secondary, and tertiary prevention constitute a more sustainable CVE strategy than the US 'war on terror'. The stated rationale of the war on terror was to permanently neutralise the threat of so-called jihadi terrorism through swift and decisive military action. Fifteen years later, the war on terror has not accomplished this goal. In 2015, the White House stated in its National Security Strategy that CVE is 'more important than our capacity to remove terrorists from the battlefield'.[23] The emerging field of CVE thus marks a strategic shift in national and international strategies to prevent terrorism.

Two interrelated motivating factors likely underlie this shift. First, governments of liberal democracies can no longer ignore public fears regarding the 'surveillance state'. A variety of whistle-blowers (Julian Assange, Chelsea Manning, Edward Snowden, and hundreds of anonymous individuals) have facilitated this development, although these revelations did not resonate in public discourse and policy as much as one might expect. Some governments have even 'understood, normalized and accepted the surveillance practices of the [US National Security Agency (NSA)]'.[24] Following the Snowden revelations

[20] A Pedahzur and M Ranstorp, 'A Tertiary Model for Countering Terrorism in Liberal Democracies: The Case of Israel' (2001) 13(2) *Terrorism and Political Violence* 1–26; J Braithwaite, 'Thinking Critically about the War Model and the Criminal Justice Model for Combatting Terrorim', Law and Society Association Panel Finding Ground between Traditional Adversaries (September 2002), https://papers.ssrn.com/sol3/papers.cfm?abstract_id=330500; and J Braithwaite, 'Regulating Terrorism' in B Forst, J Greene, and J Lynch (eds), *Criminologists on Terrorism and Homeland Security* (Oxford, Oxford University Press, 2011).

[21] S Harris-Hogan, K Barelle, and A Zamnit, 'What is Countering Violent Extremism? Exploring CVE Policy and Practice in Australia' (2016) 8(1) *Behavioral Sciences of Terrorism and Political Aggression* 6–24.

[22] Braithwaite, 'Thinking Critically' (above n 20) 31.

[23] White House, 'National Security Strategy of the United States' (February 2015), https://obamawhitehouse.archives.gov/sites/default/files/docs/2015_national_security_strategy_2.pdf, ii.

[24] D Murakami Wood and S Wright, 'Before and After Snowden' (2015) 13(2) *Surveillance and Society* 132–38, 137.

in June 2013 the German government invoked (among other arguments) the threat of terrorism to defend surveillance practices of the NSA[25] but subsequently reassessed its own counterterrorism practices, probably with future election outcomes in mind.

Second, governments can no longer uphold the promise to create security by assassinating terrorists and by means of mass surveillance. A wave of attacks inspired by the Islamic State in Europe has shown the limits of the military and intelligence approach to prevent terrorism. Even the arguments of those who were willing to sacrifice liberal rights for expanded counterterrorism measures must recognise the famous statement attributed to Benjamin Franklin: 'Those who would give up essential liberty to purchase a little temporary safety deserve neither liberty nor safety.'[26]

To what extent the emergence of CVE programmes is related to public scrutiny of security services remains an open question. More obviously, CVE has emerged due to the limited capability of security services to address the social origins and root causes of terrorist behaviour.[27] The root cause debate has inspired national and international CVE programmes such as the UK Prevent Strategy,[28] the US Strategic Implementation Plan for Empowering Local Partners to Prevent Violent Extremism,[29] the European programme Preventing Terrorism and Countering Violent Extremis and Radicalization,[30] the UN Plan of Action to Prevent Violent Extremism,[31] the German Strategy for Prevention of Extremism and Promotion of Democracy,[32] and a German National Prevention Programme (NPP) against Islamist Extremism.[33]

[25] M Schulze, 'Patterns of Surveillance Legitimization: The German Discourse on the NSA Scandal' (2015) 13(2) *Surveillance and Society* 197–217, 206.

[26] B Franklin (1755) quoted in BA Arrigo (ed), *The Sage Encyclopedia of Surveillance, Security, and Privacy* (Thousand Oaks, Sage, 2018) 408.

[27] T Bjørgo (ed), *Root Causes of Terrorism* (New York, Routledge, 2005).

[28] Secretary of State for the Home Department (UK), '*Prevent* Strategy', Cm 8092 (June 2011), https://assets.publishing.service.gov.uk/government/uploads/system/uploads/attachment_data/file/97976/prevent-strategy-review.pdf. For discussion of the UK Prevent Strategy, see also the chapter in this volume by Aziz Z Huq.

[29] White House, 'Strategic Implementation Plan for Empowering Local Partners to Prevent Violent Extremism in the United States' (October 2016), https://www.dhs.gov/sites/default/files/publications/2016_strategic_implementation_plan_empowering_local_partners_prev.pdf.

[30] Organization for Security and Co-operation in Europe (OSCE), Secretariat (2014) 'Preventing Terrorism and Countering Violent Extremism and Radicalization that Lead to Terrorism: A Community-Policing Approach' (March 2014) (OSCE, Vienna), available at https://www.osce.org/atu/111438.

[31] United Nations General Assembly, 'Plan of Action to Prevent Violent Extremism', A/70/674 (24 December 2015).

[32] Federal Government (Germany), 'Federal Strategy to Prevent Extremism and Promote Democracy' (adopted July 2016), available in English at https://www.bmfsfj.de/blob/115448/cc142d640b37b7dd76e48b8fd9178cc5/strategie-der-bundesregierung-zur-extremismuspraevention-und-demokratiefoerderung-englisch-data.pdf.

[33] Ministry of the Interior (Germany), 'Nationales Präventions-programm gegen islamistischen Extremismus' (2017), available at https://www.bmi.bund.de/SharedDocs/downloads/DE/veroeffentlichungen/themen/sicherheit/praeventionsprogramm-islamismus.html.

Although CVE aims to address risk factors and root causes of terrorism through non-coercive means, issues of rights inevitably arise. Crime prevention always carries the risk of stigmatising innocent people as criminals. For example, many practitioners in school-based violence prevention programmes explain that schools are often reluctant to implement crime prevention programmes because it implies that there is a crime problem in their schools. Likewise, CVE practices can create the impression that the focal individuals or communities are a threat to security.

Another sensitive issue of CVE is its intrinsically political nature. There usually are identifiable and potentially legitimate grievances at the core of the ideologies that CVE deals with. When authorities seek to become involved in political and religious education, it is crucial that they do not discourage critical thinking in the process. After all, the hallmark of a liberal society is free speech, whether it is radical or otherwise. Terrorism studies veteran Brian Jenkins has pointed out how critical such policies can be:

> As authorities push upstream to intervene before terrorist-related crimes are committed, we have to be careful to avoid patrolling ideologies. What seems to be a sensible preventive measure can slide into policing beliefs.[34]

A related point of concern is that CVE measures in Germany do not explicitly lay out concrete objectives. Accordingly, there are no binding criteria to decide, for example, at which point a person may be considered successfully deradicalised. This makes CVE practices arbitrary to some extent, and commentators have expressed constitutional concerns in this regard.[35]

III. APPROACHES TO COUNTERTERRORISM IN GERMANY: PROSECUTION, PREVENTION, AND PRE-PREVENTION

Roughly speaking, three legal frameworks regulate domestic security in Germany.[36] First, German criminal law, which includes the penal code (*Strafgesetzbuch*, or StGB) and the criminal procedure code (*Strafprozeßordnung*, or StPO), uses instruments of criminal investigation and sanction. Second, *Gefahrenabwehrecht* (law for the defence against threats) regulates police interventions to prevent immanent threats. More recently, a third legal approach to preventing terrorism through intervention by the security services has emerged: the so-called

[34] BM Jenkins, BBH Hoffman, and M Crenshaw, 'How Much Really Changed about Terrorism on 9/11?' Atlantic (11 September 2016), https://www.theatlantic.com/international/archive/2016/09/jenkins-hoffman-crenshaw-september-11-al-qaeda/499334/.

[35] K Leimbach, A Mathiesen, and BD Meier, 'Prävention von Radikalsierung und extremistischer Gewalt' (2017) 29(4) *Neue Kriminalpolitik* 413–23.

[36] For a collection of laws relevant to security, see WR Schenke, K Graulich, and J Ruthig, *Sicherheitsrecht des Bundes* (München, Beck, 2019).

Gefahrenvorsorgerecht.[37] Because it increases the level of proactivity, it can be translated and described as 'pre-prevention'.[38]

These frameworks aim to protect public order through repressive and preventive means, by defining in more or less precise terms 'security' and 'security threats'. As such, they are an example of a security regime – a system of rules, definitions, standards, and procedures that give contour to the otherwise vacant term 'security'. However, the (implicit) definition of security and security threats within these frameworks is circular: security is the absence of threats to legally protected goods.[39] This passes the burden of definition from 'security' to 'threats' to 'legally protected goods'. Legally protected goods, in turn, are defined as 'legally recognised interests'.[40] Hypothetically, any interest can achieve the status of a legally protected good as soon as it becomes a matter of security and is therefore eligible to be protected through criminal law.[41] The definitional regress brings us right back to the initial question: what is security and what threatens this status?

The potential boundlessness of the meaning of 'security' enables a potentially infinite expansion of security practices: 'since there is nothing that could not be perceived or declared as a threat, anything can become the target of prevention.'[42] For this reason, the German penal law has a self-restricting mechanism. Its primary focus is crimes that have already been committed, not the prevention of future crimes. The penal system is structured in this way so that the state cannot exploit the inherently vague meaning of 'threat' to justify arbitrary usage of the intrusive instruments of criminal investigation.[43] These legal mechanisms tame the state and its potential ambition to securitise everything.

Like few other crimes, terrorism challenges this doctrine. Germany is caught in a particularly salient dilemma between ensuring the security of its citizens and protecting the rights of suspected terrorists. Every constitutional democracy has to ensure both protection of its citizens against harmful conduct of other citizens (Hobbes) and protection against unlawful interventions of the

[37] Müller (above n 16) 69.

[38] In the German legal literature *Gefahrenabwehr* is also referred to as *Pävention I*, whereas *Gefahrenvorsorge* is referred to as *Prävention II*. See, for example, V Chalkiadaki, *Gefährderkonzepte in der Kriminalpolitik. Rechtsvergleichende Analyse der deutschen, französischen und englischen Ansätze* (Wiesbaden, Springer, 2017) 27.

[39] In German legal discourse, 'legally protected goods' are those individual and public interests that are protected by laws. See D Dubber, 'Theories of Crime and Punishment in German Criminal Law' (2005) 53(3) *American Journal of Comparative Law* 679–707; and CC Lauterwein, *The Limits of Criminal Law: A Comparative Analysis of Approaches to Legal Theorizing* (New York, Routledge, 2016).

[40] G Jakobs, *Rechtsgüterschutz? Zur Legitimation des Strafrechts* (Paderborn, Ferdinand Schöningh, 2012) 22.

[41] S Schick, 'Buchrezension' (2014) 4 *Zeitschrift für Internationale Strafrechtsdogmatik* 195–98.

[42] U Bröckling, 'Vorbeugen ist besser … Zur Soziologie der Prävention' (2008) 1 *Behemoth: A Journal on Civilisation* 38–48, 39 (my translation).

[43] Chalkiadaki (above n 38).

state (Locke). Because the German penal doctrine imposes definite limits on prevention,[44] it is not the most effective instrument to exercise crime prevention. Terrorism is a painful reminder of this dilemma.

This is not to say that German penal law has no preventive function at all, but jurisprudential assumptions about its preventive effects hardly work in the case of many terrorism offences. There are four theoretical assumptions about the preventive effects of criminal punishment: the assumption of general deterrence (*negative Generalprävention*) is least likely to work for politically and religiously motivated actors who are willing to make sacrifices for their cause and take repression by the state for granted if not as encouragement for their actions.[45] According to the second assumption (*positive Generalprävention*), applying the law upholds people's confidence in the validity of norms despite the fact that these norms are constantly being violated.[46] Without such general confidence, no one would be willing to play by the rules. Generally, this preventive effect is stronger the more common the incriminated action (eg, tax fraud and parking violations). For terrorism, the preventive effect of *positive Generalprävention* is weak. Terrorism is too rare and too enormous that it would be necessary to remind people that it is prohibited. Unlike more frequently occurring crimes, terrorist acts do not tend to undermine general confidence in the validity of law because people take for granted that killing innocent people indiscriminately is not an action that is tacitly accepted by others.

Whereas penal measures presumably have low preventive impact at the societal level, they can have impact at the individual level. Penal sanctions limit the ability of individuals to commit acts of terrorism – a feature referred to as negative special prevention (*negative Spezialprävention*). But also in the pretrial stage, detention can prevent terrorism. When authorities have accumulated sufficient evidence that an individual or a group is close to executing an act of terrorism, they can detain suspects in order to prevent imminent attacks. Compared to their counterparts in the United States and Britain, German authorities can use pretrial custody as a preventive means for shorter periods.[47] Tim Müller has critically reviewed the following types of preventive detention as an instrument for counterterrorism in Germany: different varieties of police custody

[44] M Steinsiek, *Terrorabwehr durch Strafrecht? Verfassungsrechtliche und strafrechtssystematische Grenzen der Vorfeldkriminalisierung*, Hannoversches Forum der Rechtswissenschaften Bd. 39 (Baden-Baden, Nomos Publishing, 2012).

[45] D Black, 'Terrorism as Social Control' in M Deflem (ed), *Terrorism and Counter-Terrorism: Criminological Perspectives* (Amsterdam, Emerald, 2004).

[46] In sociological theory this is called 'counterfactual stability', referring to the ability of social systems to uphold expectations despite the fact that they constantly clash with experience (*contra factum*). In this regard, terrorism is not a counterfactual event because people make the (correct) assumption that acts of terrorism rarely occur (in Western societies). See N Luhmann, *Das Recht der Gesellschaft* (Berlin, Suhrkamp, 1993).

[47] See S Forster, *Freiheitsbeschränkung für mutmaßliche Terroristen. Eine Analyse der Terrorismusgesetzgebung des Vereinigten Königreichs* (Berlin, Dunckler & Humblot, 2010) 151–61; and Chalkiadaki (above n 38) 231.

(*Polizeigewahrsam*), which has a maximum of two weeks;[48] custody prior to deportation (*Abschiebehaft*), which has a maximum of eighteen months; pretrial detention (*Untersuchungshaft*), up to six months with the possibility of consecutive extension). Post-trial detention can be prison sentence (*Freiheitsstrafe*) and detention to prevent reoffending (*Sicherhungsverwahrung*), which is unlimited.[49] Taking into account the fact that many terrorist organisations involve recruitment of young people, juvenile detention (*Jugendarrest*) can be added to this list.

But even more than deterrence and incapacitation, German penal law is inspired by the ideal of rehabilitation (*positive Spezialprävention*). There are gaps between this ideal and how it is put into practice, especially with regard to the rehabilitation of those classified as Islamists; German penal institutions have more experience with desistence programmes designed for right-wing extremists. Since the prison system can be an 'incubator'[50] and 'petri dish' for radicalisation,[51] and given the growing number of offenders classified as Islamists, this development is crucial for domestic security in Germany and other countries. Among all preventive functions assumed by the German penal law, it can be argued that rehabilitative measures have the strongest potential to actually prevent terrorism in the long run.

Within German criminology there is animated discussion about whether the punitive turn, diagnosed by Garland within the United States and Britain, has also taken place in Germany.[52] What seems certain is that there has been a preventive turn in German penal law. Originating in environmental criminal law,[53] terrorism is another crucial driver of this development: it has facilitated a doctrinal shift from retributive to preventive penal law in Germany by creating new statutory offences for acts that do not *per se* threaten the public order or other legally protected goods.[54] These are referred to as acts that create dangers for legally protected goods (*Gefährdungsdelikte*). As such they are *mala prohibita*, meaning culpable preparatory action with the potential (and intention) to cause harm, rather than *mala in se*, ie, culpable action that actually has caused harm.

[48] The federal state of Bavaria recently proposed suspending any time restrictions of the *Unterbindungsgewahrsam* (inhibition detention) for so-classified Islamists. This, however, is more likely a PR stunt rather than a likely future development.

[49] Müller (above n 16). Confusingly, *Sicherhungsverwahrung* can literally be translated as 'preventive detention', but in German criminal law it refers to the prevention of reoffending through custody after regular prison sentence, when a person is deemed too dangerous to be released.

[50] MS Hamm, *The Spectacular Few: Prisoner Radicalization and the Evolving Terrorist Threat* (New York, New York University Press, 2013) 46.

[51] Prison chaplain in New Folsom, cited in Hamm (ibid) 118.

[52] H Kury and E Shea (eds), *Punitivity: International Developments* (Bochum, Brockmeyer, 2011).

[53] K Seelmann, 'Risikostrafrecht: Die "Risikogesellschaft" und ihre "symbolische Gesetzgebung" im Umwelt-und Betäubungsmittelstrafrecht' (1992) 75(4) *Kritische Vierteljahresschrift für Gesetzgebung und Rechtswissenschaft* 452–71.

[54] Such as formation and membership of a terrorist organisation under § 129 a and b StGB. See Müller (above n 16).

Despite this development, the legal threshold for repressive means of prevention in Germany remains relatively high, in particular in comparison with the United Kingdom.[55] The legal division between repression (through penal law) and prevention (through *Gefahrenabwehrrecht*) is another particularity of the German legal system. Prevention and the more recent trend of pre-prevention have considerably lower legal hurdles because they encompass regulations within the police law of the country's sixteen federal states, which can be applied without the reasonable suspicion of a past crime.[56] The difference between prevention and pre-prevention is that the police can become active not only when someone immanently threatens security but also when someone creates or is involved in conditions that can lead to a threat of security.

The trend of proactivity in preventive law mirrors the development in the repressive penal code, namely to expand the reach of the law to antecedent events, that is, events that are not dangerous as such but have the potential to create dangers. Some German legal scholars therefore speak of a third approach to governing domestic security in Germany. This third pillar can be described as pre-prevention (*Gefahrenvorsorge*), which has been criticised for building the basis of a 'prevention state',[57] and 'Hyperpreventionalism',[58] meaning a state characterised by its relentless efforts to prevent crime at the cost of privacy and other constitutional rights.

Preventive and investigative measures (be they repressive, preventive, or pre-preventive) can suspend individual rights, such as informational self-determination (*Informationelle Selbstbestimmung*). These measures differ in their level of intrusiveness and have different thresholds before they can be legally invoked. The more proactive a measure is, the larger the group of potentially affected people. The fear of human right activists and privacy advocates is that by steadily increasing the level of proactivity in terrorism prevention, private citizens are increasingly monitored by ever more subtle means (video surveillance, dragnet policing, telecommunication data retention, and so on).[59]

CVE as a means of prevention seems to be the consequential extension of this development. Especially in the case of primary prevention (eg, in education) the maximum level of proactivity seems to have been reached. Addressing people with preventive measures who do not even remotely constitute a threat to security is of course the inherent logic of prevention. By shifting the preventive regime from security services to NGOs, communities, and the education sector, CVE practices are theoretically less coercive – though not necessarily less

[55] See Forster (above n 47).

[56] Müller (above n 16) 27.

[57] S Huster and K Rudolph (eds), *Vom Rechtsstaat zum Präventionsstaat* (Frankfurt, Suhrkamp, 2008); and H Prantl, 'Der große Rüssel', *Süddeutsche Zeitung* (19 May 2010).

[58] G Frankenberg, *Staatstechnik: Perspektiven auf Rechtsstaat und Ausnahmezustand* (Frankfurt, Suhrkamp, 2010).

[59] See S Egbert and B Paul, 'Editorial: Auf dem Weg in die Pre-Crime Society? Analysen zur Vorfeldorientierung in Alltagskontexten' (2018) 2 *Kriminologisches* (special issue) 87–89.

intrusive. After all, the expansion of security practices, whether in legal, social, or educational spheres, may always have unintended consequences. The role of CVE programmes in resolving the tensions between liberty and security in the German context will be explored further in the next section.

IV. DOMESTIC PREVENTION OF VIOLENT EXTREMISM IN GERMANY

In the summer of 2016, following recommendations in the UN 'Plan of Action to Prevent Violent Extremism',[60] the German federal government announced a 'Federal Strategy to Prevent Extremism and Promote Democracy'.[61] The strategy stresses that traditional security services are only one part of a comprehensive response to violent extremism:

> Ultimately, anti-democratic phenomena must also be countered using all the means available to the constitutional state. This includes the banning of associations, the precise observation of the extremist scene by the security forces and the criminal prosecution of people who have committed crimes.[62]

Although the report affirms the role of the police and intelligence services, the subtext is that prevention of extremism must take place predominantly within civil society. Tellingly, the strategy was released under the aegis of the Ministry for Family Affairs. It builds upon seven hundred already existing, publicly funded grantees and covers different manifestations of extremism, including right-wing extremism, left-wing extremism, Islamist extremism, Islamophobia, antisemitism, antiziganism, homophobia, and transphobia. The main activities are political education, intercultural learning, engagement of NGOs, counselling, monitoring and intervention, and social media campaigns.

The strategy does not explicitly refer to the public health model with its three areas of prevention (primary, secondary, and tertiary), but this typology can be used to structure the wide-ranging initiative. A 2017 survey of German CVE programmes found at least 721 individual projects.[63] Three quarters of these initiatives addressed right-wing extremism; four per cent left-wing extremism; and fourteen per cent Islamist extremism. Some projects addressed different forms of extremism at the same time, and some addressed extremism without specifying any particular type. Notably, some projects deliberately addressed

[60] UN General Assembly (above n 31).

[61] 'Federal Strategy to Prevent Extremism and Promote Democracy' (above n 32). See also B Said and H Fouad, 'Countering Islamist Radicalisation in Germany: A Guide to Germany's Growing Prevention Infrastructure', International Centre for Counter-terrorism (ICCT) Policy Brief (September 2018), https://icct.nl/publication/countering-islamist-radicalization-in-germany-a-guide-to-germanys-growing-prevention-infrastructure/.

[62] 'Federal Strategy to Prevent Extremism and Promote Democracy' (above n 32) 11–12.

[63] F Gruber and S Lützinger, 'Extremismusprävention in Deutschland – Erhebung und Darstellung der Präventionslandschaft. Bundeskriminalamt' (Wiesbaden, Federal Criminal Police Office (BKA), 2017). The actual number of initiatives is higher. Gruber and Lützinger have identified almost 2000 CVE projects, but for their analysis, they obtained sufficient information for only 721.

issues of Islamism, Islamophobia, and antisemitism together, as these forms of extremism are often part of a process of co-radicalisation.[64]

Like traditional security measures, CVE practices cover a continuum of proactivity. Primary prevention addresses distal factors that may cause radicalisation within a broad target group. This could be, for example, intercultural learning in elementary school or religious education. Secondary prevention addresses groups or individuals with known risk factors for violent extremism. For example, the extensive national network of counselling services provides help to active members of the salafi and jihadi-salafi milieu and their families and peers (eg, Hayat and the Violence Prevention Network VPN). Finally, tertiary prevention addresses those who are fully radicalised, for instance through therapeutic or social work with convicted offenders.

Primary prevention accounts for 44 per cent of German CVE interventions,[65] whereas only six per cent of programmes can be considered tertiary prevention – by specifically addressing individuals who show manifest signs of radicalisation, such as having committed a politically motivated crime. Another interesting statistic is the number of civil- and state-operated initiatives: 336 initiatives have been identified as independently operated by NGOs, while 385 programmes are governmental (either federal or state-level).[66]

Even at this early stage in the implementation of the national strategy, it is worth considering what the German case tells us about the triad of security, terrorism, and CVE. While the title of the plan refers to 'preventing extremism' and 'promoting democracy', the ultimate goal is to prevent terrorism and to increase security. The national strategy aims to do so by using non-coercive CVE means alongside the traditional penal and legal processes of the police and intelligence services. German CVE therefore appear to be a genuine effort to balance repressive and preventive measures. The Ministry of Family Affairs, which leads the CVE strategy, and its independent research body, the German Youth Institute (DJI), traditionally have a very sceptical stance in regard to state security practices and can be seen as an institutional counterbalance to them.

From a conceptual point of view the question is whether these emerging practices securitise new sectors of society or whether they socialise security. The first part of the question refers to what Stanley Cohen described as net-widening – the expansion of social control through the involvement of non-state actors in law enforcement.[67] But perhaps this apparent trend can also be seen the other

[64] D Pratt, 'Islamophobia as Reactive Co-radicalization' (2015) 26(2) *Islam and Christian–Muslim Relations* 205–18.

[65] Gruber and Lützinger (above n 63) 13.

[66] Ibid, 30.

[67] S Cohen, *Visions of Social Control: Crime, Punishment and Classification* (Cambridge, Polity Press, 1985).

way around: non-state actors and NGOs are gaining influence in a field traditionally dominated by the state, and in so doing, they bring in their own approaches, mentalities, and professional skills.

V. CONCLUSION

This chapter has described a strategic shift from repression to prevention of terrorism in Germany. It has argued that while increasing the level of proactivity of police and intelligence measures may exacerbate longstanding tensions between individual rights and civil liberties. CVE has been situated as an alternative means of dealing with a key dilemma of government: how to effectively protect citizens from terrorism while preserving hard-fought liberal achievements at the same time. Nevertheless, CVE is not an end in itself, and CVE practices must be accountable to standards of effectiveness and fairness in order to justify public spending.

It is also crucial to anticipate the consequences of the preventive turn in penal law. Creating new statutory offences targeting those who have not caused harm but only have the *potential* to cause harm (*Gefährdungsdelikte*) could in fact simply create more criminals. Especially in the case of offences related to terrorism, those who are convicted are thereafter labelled not just criminals but terrorists. This can have far-reaching consequences for their opportunities to reintegrate into society. Despite their criminal conduct, many individuals who are found *de jure* to be terrorists do not pose a direct threat to security – but time in custody may change that. For example, prison experience could increase the credibility of an extremist among his/her peers. Penalising and relentlessly prosecuting certain activities as terrorist crimes put a significant number of people through the prison system with unknown consequences for both their personal level of radicalisation as well as the spread of ideology within the prison system. Depending on the effectiveness of offender rehabilitation and deradicalisation programmes, prisons can be a cooling pond or a boiler.

While section III described the structural limitations of using the criminal justice system alone to prevent terrorism, section IV showed how Germany has circumvented some of these obstacles by adopting preventive strategies that are carried out by institutions outside the criminal justice system. These CVE approaches raise other issues, such as the stigmatisation of already vulnerable groups. CVE may also elicit fears that it represents an insidious expansion of existing state security practices into new areas of civil society. But there is also an alternative view to this trend – one that sees the German CVE enterprise as a process in which non-state actors will increasingly participate in the national security game as new stakeholders and may eventually change its rules.

REFERENCES

Armborst, A, 'Conceptualizing Political Violence of Non-state Actors in International Security Research' in A Kruck and A Schneiker (eds), *Researching Non-state Actors in International Security: Theory and Practice* (London, Routledge, 2017).

Arrigo, BA (ed), *The Sage Encyclopedia of Surveillance, Security, and Privacy* (Thousand Oaks, Sage, 2018).

Ashworth, A and Zedner, L, *Preventive Justice* (Oxford, Oxford University Press, 2014).

Bjørgo, T (ed), *Root Causes of Terrorism* (New York, Routledge, 2005).

Black, D, 'The Geometry of Terrorism' (2004) 22(1) *Sociological Theory* 14–25.

——, 'Terrorism as Social Control' in M Deflem (ed), *Terrorism and Counter-terrorism: Criminological Perspectives* (Amsterdam, Emerald, 2004).

Braithwaite, J, 'Regulating Terrorism' in B Forst, J Greene, and J Lynch (eds), *Criminologists on Terrorism and Homeland Security* (Oxford, Oxford University Press, 2011).

——, 'Thinking Critically about the War Model and the Criminal Justice Model for Combatting Terrorim', Law and Society Association Panel *Finding Ground between Traditional Adversaries* (September 2002), https://papers.ssrn.com/sol3/papers.cfm?abstract_id=330500.

Bröckling, U, 'Vorbeugen ist besser … Zur Soziologie der Prävention' (2008) 1 *Behemoth: A Journal on Civilisation* 38–48.

Carvalho, H, *The Preventive Turn in Criminal Law* (Oxford, Oxford University Press, 2017).

Chalkiadaki, V, *Gefährderkonzepte in der Kriminalpolitik. Rechtsvergleichende Analyse der deutschen, französischen und englischen Ansätze* (Wiesbaden, Springer, 2017).

Cohen, S (1985) *Visions of Social Control: Crime, Punishment and Classification* (Cambridge, Polity Press).

Collier, F, Hidalgo, FD, and Maciuceanu, AO, 'Essentially Contested Concepts: Debates and Applications' (2006) 11(3) *Journal of Political Ideologies* 211–46.

Dubber, D, 'Theories of Crime and Punishment in German Criminal Law' (2005) 53(3) *American Journal of Comparative Law* 679–707.

Egbert, S and Paul, B, 'Editorial: Auf dem Weg in die Pre-Crime Society? Analysen zur Vorfeldorientierung in Alltagskontexten' (2018) 2 *Kriminologisches* (special issue) 87–89.

Federal Government (Germany), 'Strategy to Prevent Extremism and Promote Democracy' (adopted July 2016), available in English at https://www.bmfsfj.de/blob/115448/cc142d640b37b7dd76e48b8fd9178cc5/strategie-der-bundesregierung-zur-extremismuspraevention-und-demokratiefoerderung-englisch-data.pdf.

Forster, S, *Freiheitsbeschränkung für mutmaßliche Terroristen. Eine Analyse der Terrorismusgesetzgebung des Vereinigten Königreichs* (Berlin, Dunckler & Humblot, 2010).

Frankenberg, G, *Staatstechnik: Perspektiven auf Rechtsstaat und Ausnahmezustand* (Frankfurt, Suhrkamp, 2010).

Gallie, W, 'Essentially Contested Concepts' (1956) 56(1) *Proceedings of the Aristotelian Society* 167–98.

Garland, D, *The Culture of Control: Crime and Social Order in Contemporary Society* (Oxford, Oxford University Press, 2001).

——, 'The Rise of Risk' in R Ericson and A Doyle (eds), *Risk and Morality* (Toronto, Toronto University Press, 2003).

Goold, BJ and Lazarus, L (eds), *Security and Human Rights* (Oxford, Hart Publishing, 2007).

Gruber, F and Lützinger, S, 'Extremismusprävention in Deutschland – Erhebung und Darstellung der Präventionslandschaft. Bundeskriminalamt' (Wiesbaden, Federal Criminal Police Office (BKA), 2017).

Hamm, MS, *The Spectacular Few: Prisoner Radicalization and the Evolving Terrorist Threat* (New York, New York University Press, 2013).

Harris-Hogan, S, Barelle, K, and Zamnit, A, 'What is Countering Violent Extremism? Exploring CVE Policy and Practice in Australia' (2016) 8(1) *Behavioral Sciences of Terrorism and Political Aggression* 6–24.

Hayes, J, 'Is the Concept of Terrorism Still Useful?', International Relations and Security Network paper, ETH Zurich Center for Security Studies (23 January 2015), http://www.css.ethz.ch/en/services/digital-library/publications/publication.html/187968.

Huster, S and Rudolph, K (eds), *Vom Rechtsstaat zum Präventionsstaat* (Frankfurt, Suhrkamp, 2008).

Jakobs, G, *Rechtsgüterschutz? Zur Legitimation des Strafrechts* (Paderborn, Ferdinand Schöningh, 2012).

Jenkins, BM, Hoffman, B and Crenshaw, M, 'How Much Really Changed about Terrorism on 9/11?' *Atlantic* (11 September 2016), https://www.theatlantic.com/international/archive/2016/09/jenkins-hoffman-crenshaw-september-11-al-qaeda/499334/.

Keohane, RO, 'The Demand for International Regimes' (1982) 36(2) *International Organization* 325–55.

Kury, H and Shea, E (eds), *Punitivity: International Developments* (Bochum, Brockmeyer, 2011).

Lauterwein, CC, *The Limits of Criminal Law: A Comparative Analysis of Approaches to Legal Theorizing* (New York, Routledge, 2016).

Lazarus, L, 'The Right to Security' in R Cruft, MS Liao, and M Renzo (eds), *Philosophical Foundations of Human Rights* (Oxford, Oxford University Press, 2015).

Lazarus, L and Goold, BJ, 'Introduction' in BJ Goold and L Lazarus (eds), *Security and Human Rights* (Oxford, Hart Publishing, 2007).

Leimbach, K, Mathiesen, A, and Meier, BD, 'Prävention von Radikalsierung und extremistischer Gewalt' (2017) 29(4) *Neue Kriminalpolitik* 413–23.

Luhmann, N, *Das Recht der Gesellschaft* (Berlin, Suhrkamp, 1993).

Ministry of the Interior (Germany), 'Nationales Präventions-programm gegen islamistischen Extremismus' (2017), available at https://www.bmi.bund.de/SharedDocs/downloads/DE/veroeffentlichungen/themen/sicherheit/praeventionsprogramm-islamismus.html.

Müller, T, *Präventiver Freiheitsentzug als Instrument der Terrorismusbekämpfung* (Berlin, Duncker & Humblot, 2011).

Murakami Wood, D and Wright, S, 'Before and After Snowden' (2015) 13(2) *Surveillance and Society* 132–38.

Organization for Security and Co-operation in Europe (OSCE), 'Preventing Terrorism and Countering Violent Extremism and Radicalization that Lead to Terrorism: A Community-Policing Approach' (March 2014), available at https://www.osce.org/atu/111438.

Pedahzur, A and Ranstorp, M, 'A Tertiary Model for Countering Terrorism in Liberal Democracies: The Case of Israel' (2001) 13(2) *Terrorism and Political Violence* 1–26.

Popitz, H, *Phänomene der Macht: Autorität – Herrschaft – Gewalt – Technik* (Tübingen, Mohr Siebeck, 1992).

Prantl, H, 'Der große Rüssel', *Süddeutsche Zeitung* (19 May 2010).

Pratt, D, 'Islamophobia as Reactive Co-radicalization' (2015) 26(2) *Islam and Christian–Muslim Relations* 205–18.

Said, B and Fouad, H, 'Countering Islamist Radicalisation in Germany: A Guide to Germany's Growing Prevention Infrastructure', International Centre for Counter-terrorism (ICCT) Policy Brief (September 2018), https://icct.nl/publication/countering-islamist-radicalization-in-germany-a-guide-to-germanys-growing-prevention-infrastructure/.

Schenke, WR, Graulich, K, and Ruthig, J, *Sicherheitsrecht des Bundes* (München, Beck, 2019).

Schick, S, 'Buchrezension' (2014) 4 *Zeitschrift für Internationale Strafrechtsdogmatik* 195–98.

Schulze, M, 'Patterns of Surveillance Legitimization: The German Discourse on the NSA Scanda' (2015) 13(2) *Surveillance and Society* 197–217.

Searle, J (1996) *The Construction of Social Reality* (London, Penguin).

Secretary of State for the Home Department (UK), '*Prevent* Strategy', Cm 8092 (June 2011), https://assets.publishing.service.gov.uk/government/uploads/system/uploads/attachment_data/file/97976/prevent-strategy-review.pdf.

Seelmann, K, 'Risikostrafrecht: Die "Risikogesellschaft" und ihre "symbolische Gesetzgebung" im Umwelt-und Betäubungsmittelstrafrecht' (1992) 75(4) *Kritische Vierteljahresschrift für Gesetzgebung und Rechtswissenschaft* 452–71.

Sonderegger, L, *Die Rückkehr der Folter? Anwendung von Zwang bei der Vernehmung im deutschen und US-amerikanischen Recht* (Berlin, Dunker & Humblot, 2012).

Steinsiek, M, *Terrorabwehr durch Strafrecht? Verfassungsrechtliche und strafrechtssystematische Grenzen der Vorfeldkriminalisierung*, Hannoversches Forum der Rechtswissenschaften Bd. 39 (Baden-Baden, Nomos Publishing, 2012).

United Nations General Assembly, 'Plan of Action to Prevent Violent Extremism', A/70/674 (24 December 2015).

Valverde, M 'Questions of Security: A Framework for Research' (2011) 15(1) *Theoretical Criminology* 3–22.

Waldron, J (2010) *Torture, Terror and Trade-Offs: Philosophy for the White House* (Oxford, Oxford University Press).

Weinberg, L, Pedahzur, A, and Hirsch-Hoefler, S, 'The Challenges of Conceptualizing Terrorism' (2004) 16(4) *Terrorism and Political Violence* 777–94.

White House, 'National Security Strategy' (February 2015), https://obamawhitehouse.archives.gov/sites/default/files/docs/2015_national_security_strategy_2.pdf.

——, 'Strategic Implementation Plan for Empowering Local Partners to Prevent Violent Extremism in the United States' (October 2016), https://www.dhs.gov/sites/default/files/publications/2016_strategic_implementation_plan_empowering_local_partners_prev.pdf.

19

Security and Human Rights in the Context of Forced Migration

DAVID IRVINE AND TRAVERS McLEOD*

I. INTRODUCTION

IN THEIR OPENING to the first edition of this book in 2007, Liora Lazarus and Benjamin Goold lamented how, post-9/11, the words 'security' and 'human rights' had 'come to connote an almost insuperable opposition'.[1] More than a decade on, proponents of security and human rights are still often perceived to sit in opposing trenches. Forced migration is another context in which this opposition plays out. By forced migration, we mean migratory movements of people in the most vulnerable of circumstances: the movement of asylum seekers, refugees, stateless and trafficked persons.[2] These forms of migration are proving the most difficult for governments to manage and raise complex challenges within both national and international communities.

We live in an era of unprecedented displacement. Ongoing crises around the world over the past decade, not least in Syria, Afghanistan, and Myanmar, have pushed global numbers of forced migrants to a record high.[3] 'Security' concerns about people on the move range from real to irrational. Politicians have stoked unease about such movements. In March 2017, Hungarian

* An earlier version of this paper was presented at the third meeting of the Asia Dialogue on Forced Migration (ADFM) in Kuala Lumpur in September 2016. It has benefited from the feedback received from participants at that meeting, as well as research support from the ADFM Secretariat and Caitlin McCaffrie.

[1] L Lazarus and B Goold, 'Introduction: Security and Human Rights – The Search for a Language of Reconciliation' in BJ Goold and L Lazarus (eds), *Security and Human Rights* (Oxford, Hart Publishing, 2007) 1.

[2] For background information, see Asia Dialogue on Forced Migration (ADFM) materials (available at the Centre for Policy Development website: cpd.org.au/intergenerational-wellbeing/asia-dialogue-on-forced-migration/) and the T20 Dialogue on Forced Migration (http://www.t20germany.org/forced-migration/).

[3] UNHCR, 'Global Trends: Forced Displacement in 2017' (June 2017), http://www.unhcr.org/globaltrends2017/.

Prime Minister Viktor Orban described European refugee policy in the wake of the Syrian civil war as the 'Trojan horse' of terrorism.[4] The same words were used in a similar context by Donald Trump in November 2015 during his US presidential campaign.[5] On 27 January 2017, after he had become President, Trump issued an executive order on 'Protecting the Nation from Foreign Terrorist Entry'.[6] Pursuant to the Order, the US Refugee Admissions Program was suspended for 120 days. Immigration was also limited from seven Muslim-majority countries for 90 days, and Syrian refugees were suspended from entering the country indefinitely. The Order, which was swiftly halted by litigation, then revised twice by the Trump Administration before ultimately being upheld in June 2018 by the US Supreme Court,[7] has given effect to Trump's campaign promise to institute 'extreme vetting' for refugees.

In this hostile environment, human rights and security advocates are often pitted against each other. Effective responses to human displacement have been stymied by a degree of unreality that afflicts arguments emanating from both the 'security' and the 'human rights' camps. In practice, the arguments and responses have proved difficult to disentangle. Advocates on both sides have found it difficult to adapt to the new context, scale, and proximity of mass displacement. The parameters have changed. States have a duty to accept and protect forced migrants, especially refugees, in accordance with international obligations and conventions. At the same time, they have a duty to protect the security of their citizens. This chapter argues that these duties and obligations can be integrated more effectively by improving collaborative registration and identification practices.

The first edition of this book did not devote much space to the relationship between security and human rights in the context of forced migration. Didier Bigo and Elspeth Guild made passing reference in their chapter on surveillance to 'the increasingly easy exchange of data between "competent" agencies at transnational level and the existence of zones of detention that, in the name of the fight against terrorism and illegal migration, block the cross-border movement of persons in need of refuge'.[8] Kent Roach spoke of the use of

[4] P Donahue and I Wishart, 'Merkel, Orban Clash on Refugees, Laying Bare European Disunity', *Bloomberg* (30 March 2017), https://www.bloomberg.com/politics/articles/2017-03-30/merkel-orban-clash-on-refugees-laying-bare-european-disunity.

[5] Fox News, 'Donald Trump: Refugees Could Be the Ultimate Trojan Horse', *Fox News* (17 November 2015), http://video.foxnews.com/v/4619147765001/?#sp=show-clips.

[6] The full text of Executive Order 13769 is available at https://www.whitehouse.gov/the-press-office/2017/01/27/executive-order-protecting-nation-foreign-terrorist-entry-united-states. An additional executive order on the same subject was issued on 6 March 2017 following litigation challenging the constitutionality of the first, followed by a presidential proclamation issued on 24 September 2017 further revising the executive order. See https://www.whitehouse.gov/presidential-actions/presidential-proclamation-enhancing-vetting-capabilities-processes-detecting-attempted-entry-united-states-terrorists-public-safety-threats/.

[7] *Trump v Hawaii*, 17-965, 585 US __ (2018), https://www.supremecourt.gov/opinions/17pdf/17-965_h315.pdf.

[8] D Bigo and E Guild, 'The Worst-Case Scenario and the Man on the Clapham Omnibus' in Goold and Lazarus (eds) (above n 1) 99.

immigration law as antiterrorism law within United Nations Security Council Resolution 1373, adopted shortly after 9/11, which directed states to 'ensure, in conformity with international law, that refugee status is not abused by the perpetrators, organisers or facilitators' of terrorism.[9] Neil MacFarlane suggested that 'human security' may become the lens through which rights are privileged within a security discourse, although this was in the context of the nascent 'Responsibility to Protect' doctrine.[10]

The nature of the forced migration challenge demonstrates the importance of approaches that reveal how protecting security and human rights can be complementary, not contradictory. Unless managed more effectively, forced migration will have permanent and intensifying impacts across the globe for states, regions, and individuals. In this chapter, we argue that close examination of the security and human rights dimensions of forced migration reinforces the interplay between them: they are not opposite sides of the coin but rather integrated and interdependent. Perceived security concerns can be overly narrow – largely about *who* is on the move – and underplay the significant effects of protracted processing systems and poor integration, which ultimately deny basic rights and in turn become the source of further security concerns. Similarly, human rights advocates emphasise the right to move, the central principle of *non-refoulement*,[11] and the importance of alternatives to detention, but often overlook how more efficient and effective security measures can expedite processing, improve community confidence, and enhance the protection of rights.

Borrowing from Jeremy Waldron and drawing on the second-track Asia Dialogue on Forced Migration, we contend that more dignified, durable, and effective governance structures can be built if security is integrated with human rights and if advocates update their arguments to fit the current context of forced migration. Failure to do so will only erode rights for individuals and exacerbate security concerns. The need for better regional information cooperation and national identification and registration systems is one example of where an integrated approach can deliver security and humanitarian dividends.

II. WHAT IS SECURITY?

'We should be clear about what we are looking for.'[12] Writing in 2006 on 'Safety and Security', Waldron criticised the lack of time devoted by academics,

[9] K Roach, 'Sources and Trends in Post-9/11 Anti-terrorism Laws' in Goold and Lazarus (eds) (above n 1). See also UN, Security Council Resolution 1373 (2001), S/RES/1373 (2001), https://www.unodc.org/pdf/crime/terrorism/res_1373_english.pdf, para 2(g).

[10] SN MacFarlane, 'Human Security and the Law of States' in Goold and Lazarus (eds) (above n 1).

[11] *Non-refoulement* refers to the obligation not to force a refugee or asylum seeker to return to a country in which he/she is liable to be subjected to persecution. See Art 33, Refugee Convention 1951.

[12] J Waldron, 'Safety and Security' (2006) 85(2) *Nebraska Law Review* 454–507, 459.

practitioners, and people in general to the question of what security means. Waldron was particularly scathing of political philosophers. He said it was 'shocking to discover how little attention' had been paid to the topic of security, describing it as a 'disgraceful gap in political philosophy' made worse by Thomas Hobbes's declaration that attaining security was the *raison d'être* of political enterprise.[13] The first duty of government – its 'litmus test' – is indeed the protection of its citizens. The way security is established, however, can be just as important, especially for democracies. The wars in Afghanistan and Iraq over the past two decades have revealed that 'those who viewed the attainment of security solely as a function of military action alone were mistaken'.[14] Security under the rule of law becomes essential – not just the establishment of security but *how* it is achieved and whether it can be legitimately sustained on a long-term basis.[15] When it can, security is imbued with a 'deeper understanding of human freedom'.[16] It becomes, as Ian Loader has described, 'a central value of the good society'.[17]

Wherever it is found, security is best understood as 'a complex and structured function of individual safety',[18] although it has broader and deeper characteristics than mere physical safety.[19] Security 'is fundamental to our thinking about legitimacy', wrote Waldron, describing it as 'deceptively simple on the surface' but 'quite complex underneath'.[20] To some extent, the 'security and safety of citizens living within our community is just as much a human right as the other civil liberties of individual citizens'.[21] The interdependent relationship between the two is distorted when 'partisans of security just like partisans of liberty identify important aspects of our way of life that they want to emphasise, but they emphasise them in different ways and in light of different concerns'.[22] Where one right or claim or goal is impacted by the treatment of another, analysis of '*whose* liberty' and '*whose* security is being enhanced or diminished'

[13] Ibid, 456 and 502. See also the chapter in this volume by Chetan Bhatt.

[14] P Chiarelli and P Michaelis, 'Winning the Peace: The Requirement for Full Spectrum Operations' (1993) 47(2) *Military* Review 4–17.

[15] T McLeod, *Rule of Law in War: International Law and United States Counterinsurgency in Iraq and Afghanistan* (Oxford, Oxford University Press, 2015) 20–24, 116–32, and 163–94.

[16] Lazarus and Goold, 'Introduction' (above n 1) 19; and S Fredman, 'The Positive Right to Security' in Goold and Lazarus (eds) (above n 1) 322–23.

[17] Lazarus and Goold, 'Introduction' (above n 1) 30. See also 9.

[18] Waldron (above n 12) 502.

[19] Ibid, 461–64.

[20] Ibid, 502.

[21] D Irvine, 'Balancing National Security and Civil Rights', speech given at S Rajaratnam School of International Studies, 10th Asia–Pacific Programme for Senior National Security Officers (11 April 2016). Note, however, observations on the lack of clarity with which a 'right to security' is often asserted and therefore contested. See further L Lazarus, 'Mapping the Right to Security' in Goold and Lazarus (eds) (above n 1) 326–29; and L Lazarus, 'The Right to Security' in R Cruft, M Liao, and M Renzo (eds), *The Philosophical Foundations of Human Rights* (Oxford, Oxford University Press, 2015).

[22] Waldron (above n 12) 505.

becomes paramount.[23] Andrew Ashworth has described this process as 'structured engagement' with the substance of human rights and security claims.[24]

Sufficient frameworks and mechanisms to integrate security and human rights, and the capability to implement such mechanisms effectively, can ensure security mechanisms 'do not become a menace to our civil liberties', as they have been elsewhere.[25] They may also reveal, as Ashworth has suggested, 'that certain rights are more subject to the claims of security than others'.[26] Lazarus and Goold have explained their vision of this sort of structured engagement as follows:

> By ensuring that there are clear, or at least identifiable standards, standards by which evidence for such actions can be judged by the judiciary and (where appropriate) the public at large, we improve the chances not only of there being a meaningful discussion between different sides of the security debate, but also that members of the executive can be held accountable for their actions. Equally, human rights cannot simply be held up as trumps without a clear and rigorous exposition of the exact protections to which such rights give rise and the reasons such protections cannot be weakened in the face of security claims. There is, in short, an onus on all sides of the security and rights debate to make clear, structured and accessible arguments.[27]

III. SECURITY AND HUMAN RIGHTS IN PRACTICE: FORCED MIGRATION

In what follows, we accept the challenge set by the first edition for researchers and practitioners to consider how security and human rights interact in practice:

> It is not enough to assert rights as a good in themselves by reference to metaphysical arguments that transcend social reality. Rights advocates must show how rights can work in practice, how the rule of law can be maintained, why the integrity of the law matters and how rights-regarding institutions can be shown to work even when facing our most perilous social challenges.[28]

We do so from quite different perspectives: one as a former diplomat and head of intelligence charged with countering terrorism; the other with a research and policy background in international relations and international law. Our contribution examines part of the interaction between security and human rights in the field of forced migration, with a particular focus on identification systems. Attempting such a task given the subject matter can be like

[23] Ibid, 503.
[24] See A Ashworth, 'Security, Terrorism and the Value of Human Rights' in Goold and Lazarus (eds) (above n 1).
[25] Irvine (above n 21).
[26] Lazarus and Goold, 'Introduction' (above n 1) 16–17.
[27] Ibid, 17.
[28] Ibid, 12.

'walking a tightrope'.[29] It is perhaps more fraught when a contribution is made jointly. To assist, we draw on deliberations of the Asia Dialogue on Forced Migration (ADFM), with which both of us have been closely involved.[30]

A. The Asia Dialogue on Forced Migration (ADFM)

Established in August 2015, the ADFM has brought members together to reconcile security and human rights considerations as part of the ADFM objective to pursue more effective, dignified, and durable policy approaches to forced migration. The ADFM has convened seven times (in Australia, Thailand, Malaysia, Indonesia, and the Philippines) and comprises over thirty-five experts from government, nongovernment, policy, and academic institutions from countries including Australia, Bangladesh, Canada, Indonesia, Malaysia, Myanmar, New Zealand, the Philippines, and Thailand, together with individuals from the office of the United Nations High Commissioner for Refugees (UNHCR) and the International Organization for Migration (IOM).

ADFM members have agreed that unless forced migration is properly managed, it will have intensifying negative impacts on countries across the Asia-Pacific region. A collective, coordinated response to challenges associated with both sudden and ongoing episodes of displacement, regardless of their cause, is vital. Furthermore, any discussion of 'forced migration' must cover, to a greater or lesser extent, related issues such as protection, durable solutions, irregular migration (whether by land or sea), economic migration, migrant smuggling, trafficking, statelessness, sudden displacement, resettlement, and integration.[31] The capabilities, policies, standards, and regional structures that respond to these issues must also be considered.

B. Forced Migration in the Asia-Pacific

The Asia-Pacific region is home to the largest undocumented flow of migrants and the largest number of refugees and displaced people in the world.[32] The number of registered refugees and asylum seekers, however, is much lower than those displaced. For example, beginning 25 August 2017, more than 720,000 Rohingya refugees from Rakhine State, Myanmar fled across the border into neighbouring

[29] Ibid, 13.

[30] The ADFM is convened by four regional policy institutes: the Centre for Policy Development, Australia; the Institute of Human Rights and Peace Studies at Mahidol University, Thailand; the Institute of Strategic and International Studies, Malaysia; and the Centre for Political Studies at the Indonesian Institute of Sciences.

[31] See the statement agreed at the first ADFM meeting, available at https://cpd.org.au/2015/10/first-regional-dialogue-meeting-on-forced-migration-in-the-asia-pacific/.

[32] See the International Organization for Migration webpage 'Asia and the Pacific': http://www.iom.int/asia-and-pacific. See also T McLeod, 'Patient Policy-Making for a Region on the Move', *Inside Story* (30 October 2017), http://insidestory.org.au/patient-policy-making-for-a-region-on-the-move/.

Bangladesh. As of 31 October 2018, a total of 24,874 persons had been verified through the government of Bangladesh and UNHCR joint verification exercise.[33] There were 97,345 verified refugees in Thailand,[34] and 161,140 refugees and asylum seekers registered with UNHCR in Malaysia.[35]

The movement of regular and irregular labour migrants is the Asia-Pacific region's most significant form of migration. For example, Thailand and Malaysia host up to three and six million migrant workers respectively, many of whom have 'undocumented' status.[36] These flows are largely uncontrolled and raise associated problems of trafficking, smuggling, forced labour, criminal syndicates, and money laundering. They affect the integrity of borders and immigration regimes and can overwhelm state capacities to respond. At an individual level, large numbers of irregular migrants trying to find work and working illegally can result in high levels of disenfranchisement and poverty, leading to criminal behaviour, trafficking and exploitation, and social unrest.[37] Often irregular labour migrant flows are mixed with refugees and stateless persons in need of protection. These large, mixed flows of people moving irregularly and often not tracked through official channels, can be a source of insecurity in the countries in which they move and the temporary camps in which they are housed.[38]

IV. FORCED MIGRATION AND HUMAN RIGHTS

Forced migration of whatever category imposes international legal and moral obligations on countries of haven to treat the victims of forced migration with compassion, generosity, and respect, as well as to provide practical support. Very often, advocates point to the United Nations Convention Relating to the Status of Refugees (1951) as the baseline for action; and recent Global Compacts, which have been backed by an overwhelming majority of countries, do suggest a normative shift.[39] Yet in some regions, particularly Southeast Asia, many countries are not party to the 1951 Refugee Convention. Another

[33] See Inter Sector Coordination Group (ISCG), 'Situation Report Data Summary: Rohingya Crisis' (1 November 2018), https://reliefweb.int/sites/reliefweb.int/files/resources/iscg_situation_report_01_nov_2018_data_summary.pdf.

[34] UNHCR, 'RTG/MOI-UNHCR Verified Refugee Population' (30 September 2018), https://www.unhcr.or.th/sites/default/files/u11/Thailand_Myanmar%20Border_Refugee%20Population%20Overview_%20Sept%202018.pdf.

[35] UNHCR, 'Figures at a Glance in Malaysia' (August 2018), http://www.unhcr.org/en-au/figures-at-a-glance-in-malaysia.html (accessed 11 February 2019).

[36] Asia Dialogue on Forced Migration, 'Rohingya Case Study', ADFM Second Meeting Briefing Paper (January 2016), https://cpd.org.au/wp-content/uploads/2016/02/Track-II-Participant-Pack-2-9-Feb.pdf.

[37] See, for example M Caballero-Anthony, 'Managing Migration in Southeast Asia' in M Curley and S Wong (eds), *Security and Migration in Asia: The Dynamics of Securitisation* (London, Routledge, 2008) 169.

[38] See World Bank, *Forcibly Displaced: Toward a Development Approach Supporting Refugees, the Internally Displaced, and Their Hosts* (Washington, DC, World Bank, 2017) xi, 31, 50, 58–59, and 84.

[39] See information about the 1951 Refugee Convention at http://www.unhcr.org/1951-refugee-convention.html; regarding the Global Compact for Safe, Orderly, and Regular Migration (GCM)

significant event in recent years has been the development by the Association of Southeast Asian Nations (ASEAN) of the ASEAN Convention Against Trafficking in Persons, Especially Women and Children (ACTIP), which entered into force in March 2017.[40] Concrete measures taken to tackle trafficking and forced labour are also evident in the US State Department annual 'Trafficking in Persons' report, California's Anti-Trafficking legislation, the UK Modern Slavery Act 2015; and the Australian Modern Slavery Act 2018.[41]

Notwithstanding the obligations placed on nation states by international conventions and by the UN Guiding Principles on Internal Displacement,[42] it is a political reality that national governments are obliged to take several competing factors into account in deciding how to treat the subject of forced migration. Some of these are legislated.[43] Other relevant factors include cost; security and safety concerns; in-country arrangements for refugees and other forced migrants; and public acceptance of immigration and refugees. These factors influence government decisions on whether and how to grant temporary haven, to provide permanent protection, or to extend work rights and other social benefits.[44]

An especially relevant political reality that governments of receiving countries must consider is the willingness of their general publics to accept immigration of any kind, including immigration by refugee status.[45] While granting temporary first asylum in countries of first flight is often automatic, in response to a mass influx, the public perception in developed countries is typically that those who are accepted as refugees or trafficked and stateless persons eventually become

(2018), see the IOM webpage, https://www.iom.int/global-compact-migration; and regarding the Global Compact on Refugees (2018), see UN General Assembly, 'Report of the UN High Commissioner for Refugees, Part II: Global Compact on Refugees', A/73/12 (Part II) (2 August 2018).

[40] See the text and additional information about the ACTIP at https://asean.org/asean-convention-against-trafficking-in-persons-especially-women-and-children/.

[41] For the US 'Trafficking in Persons' report, see https://www.state.gov/j/tip/rls/tiprpt/. For more on trafficking in California, see KD Harris (AG), 'The State of Human Trafficking in California', California Department of Justice report (2012), https://oag.ca.gov/sites/all/files/agweb/pdfs/ht/human-trafficking-2012.pdf; and the California Department of Justice human trafficking website: https://oag.ca.gov/human-trafficking. For the Modern Slavery Act in the UK and Australia, see respectively http://www.legislation.gov.uk/ukpga/2015/30/contents/enacted and https://www.legislation.gov.au/Details/C2018A00153.

[42] United Nations Commission on Human Rights, 'Guiding Principles on Internal Displacement', E/CN.4/1998/53/Add.2 (11 February 1998), https://www.ohchr.org/en/issues/idpersons/pages/standards.aspx.

[43] See, for example, the Migration Act 1958 (Cth), s 36; and M Kenny, 'Explainer: How Australia Decides Who Is a Genuine Refugee', *Conversation* (23 February 2017).

[44] See K Long, 'When Refugees Stopped Being Migrants: Movement, Labour and Humanitarian Protection' (2013) 1(1) *Migration Studies* 4–26.

[45] See further P Ueffing, F Row, and C Mulder, 'Differences in Attitudes Toward Immigration Between Australia and Germany: The Role of Immigration Policy' (2015) 40(4) *Comparative Population Studies* 437–64. See also P Legrain, 'Even When They're Wrong, They're Right', *openDemocracy* (27 October 2017), https://www.opendemocracy.net/philippe-legrain/even-when-they-re-wrong-they-re-right; J Kosho, 'Media Influence on Public Opinion Attitudes toward the Migration Crisis' (2016) 5(5) *International Journal of Scientific and Technology Research* 86–91.

permanent settlers.[46] Justified or not, this perception has prompted concern: in Europe regarding refugees from Syria and North Africa; in the United States, Canada, and Australia about 'illegal immigration' and refugee intakes.[47] Public perception is also an issue in countries of transit and first asylum in Africa and the Middle East, as well as in South and Southeast Asia.[48]

Governments must be responsive to these concerns. In many countries, acceptance of immigration or protection for forced migrants is based on a 'compact' – an unwritten understanding between the government and the governed, namely that the government will regulate the volume of immigrants and persons offered protection in accordance with broad criteria, and that the community will welcome and support those who are offered protection. In 2011, Paul Kelly described how the 'politics of people movement' in Australia 'originate in this enduring 1945 compact between the Chifley government and the nation'.[49] Similarly, in 2001, Mary Crock wrote about how the 'expectation that the government controls the immigration process' is 'part of the Australian culture'.[50]

The broad criteria governments might use as part of this process include:

- the ability of the economy and society to absorb such people, temporarily or permanently;
- the nature and character of the immigrants or temporary entrants and their impact on civil society; and
- the preservation of national security, public order, and community harmony.

While such criteria are difficult to measure and constantly up for debate, there is nevertheless often community expectation that the government will apply them in determining migration intake levels. For example, in countries that accept and resettle large numbers of refugees (such as Australia, Canada, and the United States), there continues to be a general public acceptance of immigration and of refugees, provided that governments demonstrate they remain in control of

[46] See, for example, K Murphy, 'Voters Back Deportation of Asylum Seekers if Refugee Claims Fail: Guardian Essential Poll', *Guardian* (30 May 2017); and R Nickel and D Ljunggren, 'Almost Half of Canadians Want Refugees Illegally Crossing into Canada Deported: Poll', *Reuters* (20 March 2017).

[47] See, for example, Legrain, 'Even When They're Wrong' (above n 45). Cf A Markus, 'Mapping Social Cohesion: The Scanlon Foundation Surveys' (2017), https://www.monash.edu/__data/assets/pdf_file/0009/1189188/mapping-social-cohesion-national-report-2017.pdf, 52–53.

[48] See H Dempster and K Hargrave, 'Understanding Public Attitudes towards Refugees and Migrants', Chatham House Working Paper 512 (June 2017).

[49] See P Kelly, *The March of Patriots: The Struggle for Modern Australia* (Melbourne, Melbourne University Publishing, 2011) 188: 'It is conceivably the most powerful political compact in Australia's history.' See also S Ozdowski, 'Australia's Multiculturalism: Success or Not?', address to the Sydney Institute (9 March 2016); and T Moran and L Kamener, 'We've Lost the Knack of Finding Jobs for Refugees', *Australian* (20 February 2017): 'Over time, the social compact that supports a large immigration program could fray. That's a cost that a diverse, open and prosperous Australia cannot afford.'

[50] M Crock, 'Contract of Compact: Skilled Migration and the Dictates of Politics and Ideology' (2001) 16 *Georgetown Immigration Journal* 135.

their borders and can mitigate potential threats against security, public safety, and public wellbeing.[51] The Scanlon Foundation Mapping Social Cohesion Survey has tracked public attitudes toward immigration in Australia over eleven years. The 2018 results found that 52 per cent of Australians still view levels of immigration as 'about right' or 'too low'. Agreement with statements such as 'multiculturalism has been good for Australia' remains high at 85 per cent.[52] These findings place Australia among the most accepting nations in the world in terms of public attitudes toward migrants and refugees.[53]

Comparable attitudes can be seen in some Asian countries. In 2016, Bangladesh was ranked sixteenth most 'accepting' country in the Gallup 'Migrant Acceptance Index', the highest ranked Asian country surveyed.[54] A 2014 Gallup Poll found relatively high levels of public sympathy in several Asian countries toward immigrants who have fled persecution or who lack political and religious freedoms: 58–62 per cent of those polled in Indonesia expressed sympathy; 63–70 per cent in Malaysia; and 73–79 per cent in Vietnam.[55] Efforts such as Migration Works in Malaysia and the Saphan Siang (Bridge of Voices) campaign in Thailand promote social cohesion and more positive attitudes towards migrant workers.[56] Other indicators point towards perceptions of refugees in Asia that are more positive than in other regions. A November 2015 Essential survey found that 80 per cent of respondents in India, 75 per cent in Vietnam and 72 per cent in China agreed with providing social protection and work rights to refugees – much higher percentages than in the United States (55 per cent) and the United Kingdom (53 per cent).[57]

Globally, prevailing public perceptions and attitudes towards migrants, including forced migrants, can change quickly. Gallup polling recorded 52 per cent of Europeans desiring lower immigration levels in December 2015, whereas only

[51] See Markus (above n 47) 52–53 (on Australian and Canadian attitudes); and S Telhami, 'American Attitudes on Refugees from the Middle East', *Brookings* (13 June 2016). See further K Coté-Boucher, 'Bordering Citizenship in "An Open and Generous Society": The Criminalization of Migration in Canada' in S Pickering and J Ham (eds), *The Routledge Handbook on Crime and International Migration* (London, Routledge, 2014).

[52] Markus (above n 47) 1–3.

[53] Ibid, 53–55.

[54] N Esipova, J Fleming, J Ray, 'New Index Shows Least, Most Accepting Countries for Migrants', *Gallup* (23 August 2017), https://news.gallup.com/poll/216377/new-index-shows-least-accepting-countries-migrants.aspx.

[55] N Esipova, J Ray, A Pugliese, and D Tsabutashvili, 'How the World Views Migration', International Organization for Migration (2015), http://publications.iom.int/system/files/how_the_world_gallup.pdf, 11; and M McAullife, 'Resolving the Policy Conundrums: Enhancing Protection in Southeast Asia', Trans-Atlantic Council on Migration and the Migration Policy Institute (January 2016) 16 and 35.

[56] More information available from the Migration Works website (http://migrationworks.org) and the Saphan Siang website (http://www.saphansiang.org).

[57] International Trade Union Confederation (ITUC), 'ITUC Frontlines Poll – Special Topic: Refugees' (November 2015), http://www.ituc-csi.org/IMG/pdf/ituc_1510_res_omnibus_frontlines_refugee_report_09112015.pdf.

34 per cent worldwide wanted immigration to decrease.[58] Such perceptions are fuelled by economic insecurity, concerns for community and personal safety, real or imagined threats to social and cultural values, and fears that migration is uncontrolled.[59] Prejudice towards migrants may be more pronounced if their mode of arrival is perceived to be illegal or irregular, especially when these issues are politicised or when new arrivals fail to integrate quickly into the life and society of the receiving country.[60]

V. FORCED MIGRATION AND SECURITY

Forced migration is a symptom of security threats and is itself a source of insecurity. Reasons for movement include armed conflict, civil unrest, natural, environmental, chemical or nuclear disaster, famine, and land development projects.[61] The security environment of the Asia-Pacific is in flux, and as a case in point, forced migration movements in the region are largely multi-causal.[62] Conventional threats like interstate conflict and civil war continue, as does the risk of nuclear proliferation. Newer risks are also posed by terrorism, cybersecurity threats, and pandemics. Many of these threats at any given time may force individuals to move internally or internationally.

A. Security in the Asia-Pacific

The Asia-Pacific population is becoming older, less equal, and more peripatetic. While more traditional threats to security such as political unrest and civil war continue to play a role, climate change, global economic downturns, and rising inequality also increasingly contribute to forced migration in the region.[63]

[58] N Esipova, A Pugliese, and J Ray, 'Europeans Most Negative Towards Immigration', *Gallup* (16 October 2015), http://www.gallup.com/poll/186209/europeans-negative-toward-immigration.aspx?g_source=Asia-Pacific%20Immigration&g_medium=search&g_campaign=tiles.

[59] See Dempster and Hargrave (above n 48); and Telhami (above n 51).

[60] M Sunpuwan and S Niyomsilpa, 'Perception and Misperception: Thai Public Opinions on Refugees and Migrants from Myanmar' (2012) 21(1) *Journal of Population and Social Studies* 47–58, 47–48; and H McHugh-Dillion, '"If They Are Genuine Refugees, Why?" Public Attitudes towards Unauthorised Arrivals in Australia', Foundation House (April 2015), http://www.foundationhouse.org.au/wp-content/uploads/2015/07/Public-attitudes-to-unauthorised-arrivals-in-Australia-Foundation-House-review-2015.pdf.

[61] More information is available at the website of the International Association for the Study of Forced Migration: http://iasfm.org.

[62] Norwegian Refugee Council and Internal Displacement Monitoring Centre, 'Global Overview 2015: People Internally Displaced by Conflict and Violence' (May 2015), http://www.internal-displacement.org/sites/default/files/inline-files/20150506-global-overview-2015-en.pdf, 56–58.

[63] See further A Missirian and W Schlenker, 'Asylum Applications Respond to Temperature Fluctuations' (2017) 358(6370) *Science* 1610–14; Australian Department of Defence, 'Written Submission to Senate Standing Committee on Foreign Affairs, Defence and Trade Inquiry into the Implications

Many non-traditional threats are often aggregated under the term 'human security'.[64] Human security is, broadly, about a community of people having the ability and capacity to meet their economic, social, cultural, and political needs, which enables individuals to fully develop their human potential.[65] Regional and national security is weakened when human security is undermined or compromised.

Climate change is one of the major non-traditional factors that now affect human security and will profoundly affect the displacement of persons in the Asia-Pacific. With its mixture of developed and developing nations, Asia is the frontline of climate challenges.[66] It has more than ninety per cent of the world's exposure to tropical cyclones and is home to the top five countries situated in low-lying coastal areas (classified by population): Bangladesh, China, Vietnam, India, and Indonesia.[67] Populations in these areas are highly susceptible to storms, flooding, and climate induced sea-level rises.[68] The effects of climate migration are already being felt, with the Asian Development Bank estimating that over forty-two million people were displaced between 2010 and 2011 due to 'sudden-onset climate related and extreme weather events'.[69] Failure of any of Asia's five major river systems, whether induced by human activity or climate change, could severely impact regional agriculture and be the catalyst for further forced migration. Among climate change experts, the question is not *if* climate change will prompt another mass migration event, but *when*.[70]

of Climate Change for Australia's National Security' (August 2017); and R Sturrock and P Ferguson, 'The Longest Conflict: Australia's Climate Security Challenge', Centre for Policy Development (June 2015).

[64] See Part III of the first edition of this volume, especially Macfarlane (above n 10); and JM Welsh, 'The Responsibility to Protect: Securing the Individual in International Society' in Goold and Lazarus (eds) (above n 1).

[65] UN General Assembly, 'Resolution Adopted on 16 September 2005: 2005 World Summit Outcome', A/RES/60/1, http://www.un.org/en/development/desa/population/migration/generalassembly/docs/globalcompact/A_RES_60_1.pdf, para 143; and United Nations Human Security Unit, 'Strategic Plan: 2014–2017' (2014), https://www.unocha.org/sites/dms/HSU/HSU%20Strategic%20Plan%202014-2017%20Web%20Version.pdf, 18. See also Macfarlane (above n 10).

[66] Intergovernmental Panel on Climate Change, *Climate Change 2014: Impacts, Adaptation and Vulnerability (Part A: Global and Sectoral Aspects)* (Cambridge, Cambridge University Press, 2014) 373.

[67] Intergovernmental Panel on Climate Change, *Climate Change 2014: Impacts, Adaptation and Vulnerability (Part B: Regional Aspects)* (Cambridge, Cambridge University Press, 2014) 1346.

[68] P Christoff and R Eckersley, 'No Island Is an Island: Security in a Four Degree World' in P Christoff (ed), *Four Degrees of Global Warming: Australia in a Hot World* (Oxford, Routledge, 2014) 191.

[69] Asian Development Bank, 'Addressing Climate Change and Migration in Asia and the Pacific: Final Report', Manila Asian Development Bank (March 2012), 3.

[70] See Intergovernmental Panel on Climate Change (IPCC), 'Global Warming of 1.5 °C', special report (2018), available at https://www.ipcc.ch/sr15/; and D Ionesco, D Mokhnacheva, and F Gemenne, 'The Atlas of Environmental Migration', International Organization for Migration (2017), https://www.iom.int/sites/default/files/about-iom/gender/Atlas-of-Environmental-Migration.pdf.

B. Forced Migrants and Security

As the opening to this chapter highlighted, security considerations have become prevalent in debates about refugees and migration more broadly. Research since the first edition of this book has illustrated the extent to which immigration has become increasingly subject to 'securitisation' or, as Alison Gerard and Sharon Pickering have described it, 'crimmigration'.[71] Mary Bosworth and Mhairi Guild have identified a growing tendency for asylum seekers and refugees to be situated within 'discourses of criminalisation in government policy and legislation, in the media, and in public and community discussions'.[72]

The association of asylum seekers and refugees with questions of security reveals the common perception that some refugees pose a security risk. A 2017 World Bank study noted that opinion leaders in six host countries (Ethiopia, Jordan, Kenya, Lebanon, Turkey, and Uganda) 'suspected refugee camps of being breeding grounds for radicalisation and arms transfer, while viewing successful assimilation of refugees into urban areas as a potential breach of public security'.[73] A 2016 Pew Research Centre survey of ten European nations found that more than fifty per cent of respondents in eight of these countries believed 'incoming refugees increase the likelihood of terrorism in their country'.[74] A 2016 Brookings survey found that fifty-nine per cent of Americans would support the United States taking more refugees from the Middle East *if* they were screened for security risks.[75] Respondents were likely unaware that, according to the UNHCR, refugees are already 'the most heavily screened and vetted' of 'all the categories of persons entering the US'.[76]

While there is little evidence to suggest refugees, including those entering the United States, pose any greater security threat than other groups of migrants, governments have to deal with these public perceptions about new arrivals.[77] It is key to the current Australian compact.[78] Arguments that compare the relative

[71] See further A Gerard and S Pickering, 'Crimmigration: Criminal Justice, Refugee Protection and the Securitisation of Migration' in H Bersot and B Arrigo (eds), The Routledge Handbook of International Crime and Justice Studies (London, Routledge, 2013).

[72] See M Bosworth and M Guild, 'Governing through Migration Control: Security and Citizenship in Britain' (2008) 48(6) *British Journal of Criminology* 703–19, 703–4. See further S Pickering and J Ham (eds), *The Routledge Handbook on Crime and International Migration* (New York, Routledge, 2014).

[73] World Bank (above n 34) 58–59.

[74] R Wike, B Stokes, and K Simmons, 'Europeans Fear Wave of Refugees Will Mean More Terrorism, Fewer Jobs', Pew Research Center Report (11 July 2016), http://www.pewglobal.org/2016/07/11/europeans-fear-wave-of-refugees-will-mean-more-terrorism-fewer-jobs/.

[75] Telhami (above n 51).

[76] A Altman, 'This Is How the Syrian Refugee Screening Process Works, *Time* (17 November 2015), http://time.com/4116619/syrian-refugees-screening-process.

[77] See also AP Schmid, 'Links between Terrorism and Migration: An Exploration', International Centre for Counter-Terrorism Research Paper (May 2016), http://icct.nl/wp-content/uploads/2016/05/Alex-P.-Schmid-Links-between-Terrorism-and-Migration-1.pdf, 4 and 44.

[78] On this point, see the remarks made by Duncan Lewis, Director of the Australian Security Intelligence Organisation (ASIO), on 25 May 2017 in the Australian Senate, denying there was a link

threat of forced migrants to other existing threats miss this point. Assuring the public that refugees are properly vetted has become one way of maintaining public support for their acceptance. It is vital that this vetting process is as efficient as possible.

Although immediate risks posed by refugees can dominate public and policy conversations, greater security issues can arise if resettlement and integration of refugees and other migrants are done poorly. Recent research suggests a lack of attentiveness to effective settlement services may generate greater security risks over the long term.[79] This problem will be more pronounced if 'refugees are treated as a short-term humanitarian problem rather than as a long-term integration challenge'.[80] Indeed, perceptions that forced migrants are a security risk are often motivated by concerns about longer-term radicalisation of migrants. Those concerns are in turn generated in part by the pace of integration into communities. If settlement services are not effective, with adequate investment so that refugees can rebuild their lives, new arrivals may be held in a poorer light.[81]

Recent analysis suggests greater security threats arise because of poor settlement services, not because of *who* is on the move. In Australia, only a small proportion of visa applicants are rejected on national security or character grounds.[82] That does not, however, obviate the need for careful security and character checking, in accordance with community expectations and the compact on immigration. Robust security checks built into status determinations are a necessary condition for greater community confidence.

We have attempted to set out above the reasons why forced migration is a symptom of security threats and can itself be a source of insecurity. Regardless of whether one is in the 'security camp' or the 'human rights camp', it must be acknowledged that some forced migrants may pose a non-trivial security risk. That risk, however small, necessitates conscientious decisions by intelligence

between refugees and terrorism: Attorney-General's Portfolio (Australia), *Budget Estimates 2017–18*, Hansard Transcript (25 May 2017), https://www.aph.gov.au/Parliamentary_Business/Senate_Estimates/legconctte/estimates/bud1718/AGD/index. See also Australian Broadcasting Corporation (ABC), 'Refugee Program Is Not the Source of Terrorism in Australia: Lewis', *RN Breakfast* (ABC Radio, 31 May 2017), http://www.abc.net.au/radionational/programs/breakfast/refugee-program-is-not-the-source-of-terrorism-v1/8574768.

[79] Schmid (above n 77).

[80] D Byman, 'Do Syrian Refugees Pose a Terrorism Threat?' *Markaz*, Brookings Institution blog (27 October 2015), https://www.brookings.edu/2015/10/27/do-syrian-refugees-pose-a-terrorism-threat/.

[81] H Sherrell, 'Settling Better: Reforming Refugee Employment and Settlement Services', Centre for Policy Development (February 2017); and P Legrain, 'Step Up: How to Get Refugees into Work Quickly', Open Political Economy Network (OPEN) Report (August 2017), http://www.opennetwork.net/step-get-refugees-work-quickly/.

[82] Personal observations of D Irvine based on experience in government. See also Duncan Lewis remarks (above n 78); and Australian Department of Home Affairs, 'Visa Statistics', https://www.homeaffairs.gov.au/research-and-statistics/statistics/visa-statistics/visa-cancellation (last accessed 19 February 2019).

and law enforcement agencies that integrate respect for civil liberties and human rights with the imperative to collect and assess intelligence that enables government to meet its first obligation: the protection of the community. Effective completion of this task goes unnoticed, whereas one failure can threaten the viability and public support for longstanding and otherwise successful immigration systems.[83]

VI. SECURITY AND RIGHTS AS COMPLEMENTARY, NOT CONTRADICTORY

During its third meeting, in Kuala Lumpur in September 2016, the ADFM focused on the real and perceived security threats generated by forced migration. ADFM members determined that better management of these threats could reduce their likelihood, improve community confidence in the management of forced migrant movements, and encourage a larger number of countries to participate in establishing more effective, durable, and dignified regional architecture on forced migration.

As explained earlier, the Asia-Pacific region has the largest undocumented flow of migrants and the largest number of refugees and displaced people in the world. There can be no doubt that there is a particular security threat in not knowing who is in one's territory. ADFM deliberations in Kuala Lumpur concluded that responding to the challenge of identification and registration of forced migrants in a predictable and coordinated way would facilitate positive security and human rights outcomes for the governments, communities, and individuals involved.

Security concerns about forced migrants around the world often boil down to one important question: *who* is on the move? This question is fundamental to determining refugee status. The 1951 Refugee Convention obliges countries to assess claims based on the criterion of a 'well-founded fear of persecution'.[84] The Convention also allows for a national government to refuse entry or residence to someone when there are reasonable grounds to regard that person as a danger to national security or if that person, having been convicted of a particularly serious crime, constitutes a danger to the community of that country.[85] In practice, however, determining who is on the move is much easier said than done.

Consider, for example, the current humanitarian crisis impacting the Rohingya people in Myanmar, many of whom have fled reported acts of genocide

[83] See Irvine (above n 21).

[84] Art 1, 1951 Refugee Convention, as amended by the 1967 Protocol Relating to the Status of Refugees: a refugee being a person, outside of his country, who has a 'well-founded fear of being persecuted for reasons of race, religion, nationality, membership of a particular social group or political opinion'.

[85] Art 33, 1951 Refugee Convention (ibid).

in Rakhine State and are now settled temporarily in camps in Cox's Bazar, Bangladesh.[86] The Rohingya are generally understood to be stateless refugees but have not been recognised as such by Bangladesh, which is not a signatory to the 1951 Refugee Convention or to either of the international Statelessness Conventions of 1954 and 1961. Nevertheless, Bangladesh has accepted the Rohingya in large numbers according to their own criteria. By keeping their borders open and not immediately deporting or repatriating them, Bangladesh immigration officials have in effect made a judgement that at the very least the Rohingya refugees have a plausible or *prima facie* case for special treatment on humanitarian grounds. Bangladesh has also made a judgement that it will not grant a status that would enable the Rohingya migrants to settle permanently in that country.

A Rohingya individual in this scenario has two options: (i) to first seek refugee or another status from an appropriate authority (eg, the UNHCR, IOM, or the government of Bangladesh), wait until the application is accepted, and then settle in Bangladesh, be voluntarily repatriated to Myanmar, or be resettled (permanently or temporarily) in a third country (legal entry); or (ii) to seek alternative means of travel (land, sea, or air) to a preferred destination without prior approval by relevant authorities. In either case, any third country must determine the individual's status – including whether he/she is a genuine refugee – based on an assessment of the individual's identity, his/her claims of persecution or fear of persecution, and available information concerning conditions in the individual's country of origin.

In practice, these options require an individual to undergo two or three assessment processes run by different authorities, each requiring him/her to provide information in order to support his/her claim, including proof of identity, a narrative justifying the claim to refugee status, and other documentary evidence. Each process will be conducted according to the priorities of each particular agency, whether it is a national immigration department or an international organisation. Different countries and agencies may give less consideration to issues that are important to final-destination countries. Moreover, personal circumstances may change (for example, marriage or childbirth) in the time that elapses between these independent and often unconnected processes. The involvement of traffickers, smugglers, or other agents in facilitating movement or access to work may generate multiple identity cards of varying authenticity and recognised official status, while genuine documentation may be lost or otherwise inaccessible. For many Rohingya, for example, documents indicating land ownership or citizenship have been destroyed or confiscated. This means that decision-makers in each country often start their own processes from scratch, further prolonging the entire ordeal for the individual in question.

[86] US Department of State, 'Documentation of Atrocities in Northern Rakhine State' (August 2018), https://www.state.gov/documents/organization/286307.pdf; and International Crisis Group, 'Myanmar's Rohingya Crisis Enters a Dangerous New Phase', Asia Report No 292 (7 December 2017), available at https://www.crisisgroup.org/asia/south-east-asia/myanmar/292-myanmars-rohingya-crisis-enters-dangerous-new-phase.

While national governments usually have systematic processes and procedures for evaluating claims for refugee status and assessing the potential threat represented by individuals, those processes are often inhibited by the need to rely solely on interviews (often in a different language) with a claimant or with other refugees who may have some knowledge of the claimant. Security and character-checking is also hindered by insufficient cooperation, information-sharing, recordkeeping, and standardisation of security criteria between international agencies, intermediary countries, and countries of eventual settlement. Seeking corroborative information from the country of origin may be logistically impossible or even prohibited, the situation in Rakhine State, Myanmar being a case in point.

The paucity of information available and the deficiencies in processes between states and international agencies make decision-making more difficult. Importantly, it also means that claimants are left for longer in limbo in an unsatisfactory, halfway state of transit (with potentially significant personal and emotional consequences). The result is often that countries of final destination must make national security judgements based on insufficient or unreliable information. In most cases, the consequences of giving a claimant the benefit of the doubt on security or character issues may not be a cause for concern, but the nature of terrorism and the consequences of serious and organised crime are such that some destination countries are unwilling to accept the risk, given their own commitments to national security, public order, and social cohesion. This unwillingness is compounded by the reflexive misperception by some members of the public, often stoked by popular media, that certain classes of immigrants bring with them an increased risk of terrorism.[87] In the face of this low-risk but high-consequence equation, governments remain concerned not to betray their side of the national 'immigration compact'.[88]

A. Confidence in the System: Assessing Claims Fairly and Efficiently

As we have explained, public confidence in the security screening process for refugees and forced migrants is essential to ensure public acceptance of immigration. A receiving country will want to satisfy itself that an applicant for entry (of any type, not just on humanitarian grounds) will not threaten national security in terms of espionage, sabotage, or politically motivated violence; and will not seek to exercise improper political influence. The receiving country will

[87] See Kosho (above n 45) 86–91; and Legrain, 'Even When They're Wrong' (above n 45). For a critical examination of the common conflation of Islam with terrorism, see the chapter in this volume by Aziz Huq.

[88] See K Connolly, 'Angela Merkel Defends Germany's Refugee Policy after Attacks', *Guardian* (29 July 2016). Note also how these domestic considerations impacted negotiations of Global Compacts on Refugees, and on Safe, Orderly, and Regular Migration: S Martin and E Ferris, 'Border Security, Migration Governance and Sovereignty' (2017) 7(3) *Migration Policy Practice* 12–15.

also want to be assured that the applicant will not conduct serious or organised criminal activities – for which the principal test has been conviction for a crime involving a prison sentence of one year or longer (an arbitrary, one-dimensional, and unreliable guide).

In recent times, entrance on international humanitarian grounds has relied on necessarily subjective judgements by authorities and agencies, including the UNHCR. The tendency has been towards broad and inclusive interpretation of these criteria.[89] Determination of refugee status is made more difficult where, as is increasingly the case, decision-makers are unable to verify claims or even the true identity of claimants for humanitarian visas under the Refugee Convention. Making inquiries in a country of origin in order to determine whether *non-refoulement* is relevant may itself give rise to *refugee sur place* claims. As the Rohingya example above suggests, such inquiries may introduce the risk of persecution on return or may result in adverse impacts to family members who remain in the country of origin.

Article 33(2) of the Refugee Convention allows for a country to deny entrance to someone who would otherwise be protected by the *non-refoulement* principle if there are 'reasonable grounds' to consider that person 'a danger to the security of the country'. In practice, only a small number of such rejections occur.[90] Those claimants denied entry on these grounds have a range of options, all unpalatable to them: (i) to return to their country of origin when political conditions change favourably there; (ii) to remain in transit camps in the hope that a destination country will eventually accept them; or (iii) to seek to integrate into life in the transit country (assuming that they allowed to do so).

A second series of policy decisions must be made by states about the treatment and management of people who are granted some form of temporary or permanent entry (either prior to or after determination of refugee status). These policy decisions will be affected by the national capacity to provide the basic necessities of life and social services (food, housing, health, education, and employment services); possible prior relationships between groups of migrants and the local population; and mainstream narratives about potential security threats to the community. Each of these criteria for public acceptance of immigration has nuances that can change according to national circumstances and the public mood.

The criteria and methodology for assessing refugee status, security and character threats, and communal harmony issues should not differ according to the method of arrival. Risk assessment should be no different whether a person arrives by regular or irregular means, as a claimant for refugee status,

[89] See J Hathaway and W Hicks, 'Is There a Subjective Element in the Refugee Convention's Requirement of "Well-Founded Fear"?' 2005 26(2) *Michigan Law Review* 505–62; and G Goodwin-Gill, 'International Law, Refugees, and Forced Migration' in E Fiddian-Qasmiyeh, G Loescher, K Long, and N Sigona (eds), *Oxford Handbook of Refugee and Forced Migration Studies* (Oxford, Oxford University Press, 2014).

[90] See references listed above at n 82.

as a trafficked person, or as a stateless person (although if someone is stateless, the process may well be more difficult). Identifying opportunities to build security features into the identification and registration processes would alleviate some state and community concerns. The ability of assessment processes to improve documentation and underpin a more confident understanding of who is within a country's borders and the risks that they do or do not pose will be important.

B. ADFM Recommendations

Stronger cooperation between the countries of first flight, international agencies, and leading resettlement countries would assist in managing the presence and movement of refugees and other forced migrants. Such cooperation could be organised through formal agreements and memorandums of understanding between countries and agencies, setting out the objectives, principles, and details of enhanced cooperation on migrant flows. Cooperation on addressing security and character issues will not be achieved in the absence of improvement on the broader issue of cooperation between the UNHCR and affected countries to control and manage the flows of refugees. To this end, the ADFM Secretariat has made several recommendations to countries in the Asia-Pacific region.

In the main, the ADFM recommendations are for governments in the region to intervene at the earliest point whenever displacement occurs in order to ensure the joint registration and identification of forced migrants. This requires governments, international agencies, and intelligence organisations to develop robust, functional systems to collect, coordinate, and share this information. Moreover, the collection and sharing of such information would need to be consistent with emerging best practice, including that relating to biometric data and the vulnerability of forced migrants. The ADFM has also advocated for governments in the Asia-Pacific region to work collectively to explore alternatives to detention for forced migrants. It has requested the intergovernmental Bali Process on People Smuggling, Trafficking in Persons and Related Transnational Crime to include on its agenda regular discussion of the broader medium- to long-term security considerations arising from protracted displacement in the region, consistent with the 2016 Bali Declaration.[91]

Several recommendations were endorsed in Colombo, Sri Lanka in November 2016 by Bali Process senior officials as part of their 'Review of the Response to the Andaman Sea Situation'.[92] The Review also encouraged countries to develop functional joint identification, screening, and registration systems. The Colombo meeting also established a Task Force on Planning and Preparedness

[91] See the Bali Process website: https://www.baliprocess.net/.

[92] Bali Process, 'Review of Region's Response to Andaman Sea Situation of May 2015', https://www.baliprocess.net/UserFiles/baliprocess/File/Review%20of%20Andaman%20Sea_Final_Bali%20Process%20AHG%20SOM_16%20Nov%202016.pdf (November 2016).

comprised of operational-level governmental officials who are responsible at the national level for developing these joint identification, screening, and registration systems.

Understandably, states wish to preserve their sovereignty and control over their own national affairs. However, the benefits of coordination and sharing responsibilities are considerable, and they will enhance the ability of countries to manage what is a transnational problem in an effective and humane way. To this end, identity-checking could be done more systematically, efficiently, and collaboratively by countries in the region. Reforms could include early checking of international police records and, where possible and consistent with *non-refoulement* and refugee protection principles, with the country of origin. The Regional Support Office of the Bali Process could facilitate protocols for standardised reception and interviewing procedures applicable at each point in the journey to refugee status, along with requirements on the nature of information to be obtained from claimants. The protocols would outline proper recording by authorities of information and documentation provided by claimants, and procedures for sharing information obtained in the preceding phases with final-destination countries.

These measures require considerable coordination between international agencies, NGOs, and affected countries. They also require close cooperation between immigration, law enforcement, and intelligence agencies of affected countries, as well as a commitment to building capability in those countries that are presently facing challenges in managing refugee flows effectively and humanely. Cooperation on the dual issues of establishing refugee status and evaluating character and security risk may require legislative change in some countries. Confidence and cooperation may be further enhanced if affected countries could reach agreement on numbers or quotas of refugees from a given region, to work closely on arranging the voluntary, safe, and dignified return or repatriation of persons who do not meet the criteria for protection, and to assist jointly in the management and sustenance of claimants in countries of first flight. Leading resettlement countries could also direct assistance to alleviate the burden of housing, subsistence costs, and processing refugees in those countries.

VII. CONCLUSION

Security is not the 'meta-principle upon which all rights rest'.[93] Any right to security, as Sandra Fredman argued in the first edition, is best understood as being embedded in a deeper understanding of human freedom, one that must involve reciprocal benefits and opportunities.[94] We have attempted to clarify

[93] Lazarus and Goold, 'Introduction' (above n 1). See also Lazarus, 'Mapping the Right to Security' (above n 21).

[94] Cf L Lazarus, 'Mapping the Right to Security' (above n 21) 326–29.

the relationship between rights and security in the context of forced migration. We have provided a practical example of where security and rights considerations might be reconciled through effective and humane assessment of refugee claims. Security, law and order, community safety, and public confidence are important issues for governments to consider when people are moving across borders irregularly. At the same time, humanitarian concerns must be of similar priority for governments. A necessary condition for governments to attend effectively to these issues is the ability to determine *who* is in their country. Current identification and registration processes for forced migrants, however, have been inhibited by difficulties in verifying identity, incorrect and incomplete information provided by individuals, a lack of coordination within and between affected countries, and the absence of collaborative systems.

By instituting reforms to make the process systematic and efficient, we suggest that governments can more effectively deal with the perception of security threats associated with forced migration, improve public confidence in the management of forced migration, and generate improved economic and social outcomes for communities and individuals. The benefits of coordination and sharing of responsibilities are considerable, and they will enhance the ability of countries to manage what is a transnational problem in an effective and humane way.

One humanitarian benefit of improved identification and registration is reducing the protracted nature of processing and resettlement, and the diminished rights and livelihoods available during that time. Reforms should not focus solely on *who* is moving but rather consider how forced migrants fare once they arrive and are settled in receiving countries. Greater resources and research devoted to resettlement may enhance the rights and opportunities available to forced migrants and lead to their more successful absorption into the national fabric of settlement countries.[95] Settlement and employment outcomes must improve in order to strengthen community cohesion and avert alienation. Governments, international agencies, business, and civil society cannot effectively address the unprecedented flow of forced migrants without turning their attention to these issues, particularly during times of slow economic growth. Without doing so, we risk falling into the 'security as physical safety' trap, in practice as much as in theory. The effectiveness of settlement services, emerging best practice, and the relationship of settlement services with longer-term security threats and the realisation of individual rights, must be regularly examined and can help to sharpen understanding on how security and rights claims can be complementary, not contradictory.

[95] See further J Shields, J Drolet, and K Valenzuela, 'Immigration Settlement and Integration Services and the Role of Non-profit Service Providers: A Cross-National Perspective on Trends, Issues and Evidence', RCIS Working Paper 2016/1 (February 2016); Sherrell (above n 81); Legrain, 'Step Up' (above n 81); P Mares, *Not Quite Australian: How Temporary Migration is Changing the Nation* (Melbourne, Text Publishing, 2016); and C Dauvergne, *The New Politics of Immigration and the End of Settler Societies* (Cambridge, Cambridge University Press, 2016) 124–49.

REFERENCES

Altman, A, 'This Is How the Syrian Refugee Screening Process Works, *Time* (17 November 2015).

Ashworth, A, 'Security, Terrorism and the Value of Human Rights' in BJ Goold and L Lazarus (eds), *Security and Human Rights* (Oxford, Hart Publishing, 2007).

Asia Dialogue on Forced Migration (ADFM), 'Rohingya Case Study', ADFM Second Meeting Briefing Paper (January 2016), https://cpd.org.au/wp-content/uploads/2016/02/Track-II-Participant-Pack-2-9-Feb.pdf.

Asian Development Bank, 'Addressing Climate Change and Migration in Asia and the Pacific: Final Report', Manila Asian Development Bank (March 2012).

Australian Broadcasting Corporation (ABC), 'Refugee Program Is Not the Source of Terrorism in Australia: Lewis', *RN Breakfast* (ABC Radio, 31 May 2017), http://www.abc.net.au/radionational/programs/breakfast/refugee-program-is-not-the-source-of-terrorism-v1/8574768.

Australian Department of Defence, 'Written Submission to Senate Standing Committee on Foreign Affairs, Defence and Trade Inquiry into the Implications of Climate Change for Australia's National Security' (August 2017).

Bali Process, 'Review of Region's Response to Andaman Sea Situation of May 2015' (November 2016), https://www.baliprocess.net/UserFiles/baliprocess/File/Review%20of%20Andaman%20Sea_Final_Bali%20Process%20AHG%20SOM_16%20Nov%202016.pdf.

Bigo, D and Guild, E, 'The Worst-Case Scenario and the Man on the Clapham Omnibus' in BJ Goold and L Lazarus (eds), *Security and Human Rights* (Oxford, Hart Publishing, 2007).

Bosworth, M and Guild, M, 'Governing through Migration Control: Security and Citizenship in Britain' (2008) 48(6) *British Journal of Criminology* 703–19.

Byman, D, 'Do Syrian Refugees Pose a Terrorism Threat?' *Markaz*, Brookings Institution blog (27 October 2015), https://www.brookings.edu/2015/10/27/do-syrian-refugees-pose-a-terrorism-threat/.

Caballero-Anthony, M, 'Managing Migration in Southeast Asia' in M Curley and S Wong (eds), *Security and Migration in Asia: The Dynamics of Securitisation* (London, Routledge, 2008).

Chiarelli, P and Michaelis, P, 'Winning the Peace: The Requirement for Full Spectrum Operations' (1993) 47(2) *Military Review* 4–17.

Christoff, P and Eckersley, R, 'No Island Is an Island: Security in a Four Degree World' in P Christoff (ed), *Four Degrees of Global Warming: Australia in a Hot World* (Oxford, Routledge, 2014).

Connolly, K, 'Angela Merkel Defends Germany's Refugee Policy after Attacks', *Guardian* (29 July 2016).

Coté-Boucher, K, 'Bordering Citizenship in "An Open and Generous Society": The Criminalization of Migration in Canada' in S Pickering and J Ham (eds), *The Routledge Handbook on Crime and International Migration* (London, Routledge, 2014).

Dauvergne, C, *The New Politics of Immigration and the End of Settler Societies* (Cambridge, Cambridge University Press, 2016).

Dempster, H and Hargrave, K, 'Understanding Public Attitudes towards Refugees and Migrants', Chatham House Working Paper 512 (June 2017).

Donahue, P and Wishart, I, 'Merkel, Orban Clash on Refugees, Laying Bare European Disunity', *Bloomberg* (30 March 2017), https://www.bloomberg.com/politics/articles/2017-03-30/merkel-orban-clash-on-refugees-laying-bare-european-disunity.

Esipova, N, Fleming, J, and Ray, J, 'New Index Shows Least, Most Accepting Countries for Migrants', *Gallup* (23 August 2017), https://news.gallup.com/poll/216377/new-index-shows-least-accepting-countries-migrants.aspx.

Esipova, N, Pugliese, A, and Ray, J, 'Europeans Most Negative Towards Immigration', *Gallup* (16 October 2015), http://www.gallup.com/poll/186209/europeans-negative-toward-immigration.aspx?g_source=Asia-Pacific%20Immigration&g_medium=search&g_campaign=tiles.

Esipova, N, Ray, J, Pugliese, A and Tsabutashvili, D, 'How the World Views Migration', International Organization for Migration (2015), http://publications.iom.int/system/files/how_the_world_gallup.pdf.

Fox News, 'Donald Trump: Refugees Could Be the Ultimate Trojan Horse', *Fox News* (17 November 2015), http://video.foxnews.com/v/4619147765001/?#sp=show-clips.

Fredman, S, 'The Positive Right to Security' in BJ Goold and L Lazarus (eds), *Security and Human Rights* (Oxford, Hart Publishing, 2007).

Gerard, A and Pickering, S, 'Crimmigration: Criminal Justice, Refugee Protection and the Securitisation of Migration' in H Bersot and B Arrigo (eds), *The Routledge Handbook of International Crime and Justice Studies* (London, Routledge, 2013).

Goodwin-Gill, G, 'International Law, Refugees, and Forced Migration' in E Fiddian-Qasmiyeh, G Loescher, K Long, and N Sigona (eds), *Oxford Handbook of Refugee and Forced Migration Studies* (Oxford, Oxford University Press, 2014).

Goold, BJ and Lazarus, L (eds), *Security and Human Rights*, 1st edn (Oxford, Hart Publishing, 2007).

Harris, KD (AG), 'The State of Human Trafficking in California', California Department of Justice report (2012), https://oag.ca.gov/sites/all/files/agweb/pdfs/ht/human-trafficking-2012.pdf.

Hathaway, J and Hicks, W, 'Is There a Subjective Element in the Refugee Convention's Requirement of "Well-Founded Fear"?' 2005 26(2) *Michigan Law Review* 505–62.

Intergovernmental Panel on Climate Change (IPCC), *Climate Change 2014: Impacts, Adaptation and Vulnerability (Part A: Global and Sectoral Aspects)* (Cambridge, Cambridge University Press, 2014).

——, *Climate Change 2014: Impacts, Adaptation and Vulnerability (Part B: Regional Aspects)* (Cambridge, Cambridge University Press, 2014).

——, 'Global Warming of 1.5°C', special report (2018), available at https://www.ipcc.ch/sr15/.

International Crisis Group, 'Myanmar's Rohingya Crisis Enters a Dangerous New Phase', Asia Report No 292 (7 December 2017), available at https://www.crisisgroup.org/asia/south-east-asia/myanmar/292-myanmars-rohingya-crisis-enters-dangerous-new-phase.

International Trade Union Confederation (ITUC), 'ITUC Frontlines Poll – Special Topic: Refugees' (November 2015), http://www.ituc-csi.org/IMG/pdf/ituc_1510_res_omnibus_frontlines_refugee_report_09112015.pdf.

Inter Sector Coordination Group (ISCG), 'Situation Report Data Summary: Rohingya Crisis' (1 November 2018), https://reliefweb.int/sites/reliefweb.int/files/resources/iscg_situation_report_01_nov_2018_data_summary.pdf.

Ionesco, D, Mokhnacheva, D, and Gemenne, F, 'The Atlas of Environmental Migration', International Organization for Migration (2017), https://www.iom.int/sites/default/files/about-iom/gender/Atlas-of-Environmental-Migration.pdf.

Irvine, D, 'Balancing National Security and Civil Rights', speech given at S Rajaratnam School of International Studies, 10th Asia–Pacific Programme for Senior National Security Officers (11 April 2016).

Kelly, P, *The March of Patriots: The Struggle for Modern Australia* (Melbourne, Melbourne University Publishing, 2011).

Kenny, M, 'Explainer: How Australia Decides Who Is a Genuine Refugee', *Conversation* (23 February 2017).

Kosho, J, 'Media Influence on Public Opinion Attitudes toward the Migration Crisis' (2016) 5(5) *International Journal of Scientific and Technology Research* 86–91.

Lazarus, L, 'Mapping the Right to Security' in BJ Goold and L Lazarus (eds), *Security and Human Rights* (Oxford, Hart Publishing, 2007).

——, 'The Right to Security' in R Cruft, M Liao, and M Renzo (eds), *The Philosophical Foundations of Human Rights* (Oxford, Oxford University Press, 2015).

Lazarus, L and Goold, B, 'Introduction: Security and Human Rights – The Search for a Language of Reconciliation' in BJ Goold and L Lazarus and B Goold (eds), *Security and Human Rights* (Oxford, Hart Publishing, 2007).

Legrain, P, 'Even When They're Wrong, They're Right', *openDemocracy* (27 October 2017), https://www.opendemocracy.net/philippe-legrain/even-when-they-re-wrong-they-re-right.

——, 'Step Up: How to Get Refugees into Work Quickly', Open Political Economy Network (OPEN) Report (August 2017), http://www.opennetwork.net/step-get-refugees-work-quickly/.

Long, K, 'When Refugees Stopped Being Migrants: Movement, Labour and Humanitarian Protection' (2013) 1(1) *Migration Studies* 4–26.

MacFarlane, SN, 'Human Security and the Law of States' in BJ Goold and L Lazarus (eds), *Security and Human Rights* (Oxford, Hart Publishing, 2007).

Mares, P, *Not Quite Australian: How Temporary Migration is Changing the Nation* (Melbourne, Text Publishing, 2016).

Markus, A, 'Mapping Social Cohesion: The Scanlon Foundation Surveys' (2017), https://www.monash.edu/__data/assets/pdf_file/0009/1189188/mapping-social-cohesion-national-report-2017.pdf.

Martin, S and Ferris, E, 'Border Security, Migration Governance and Sovereignty' (2017) 7(3) *Migration Policy Practice* 12–15.

McAullife, M, 'Resolving the Policy Conundrums: Enhancing Protection in Southeast Asia', Trans-Atlantic Council on Migration and the Migration Policy Institute (January 2016).

McLeod, T, 'Patient Policy-Making for a Region on the Move', *Inside Story* (30 October 2017), http://insidestory.org.au/patient-policy-making-for-a-region-on-the-move/.

——, *Rule of Law in War: International Law and United States Counterinsurgency in Iraq and Afghanistan* (Oxford, Oxford University Press, 2015).

McHugh-Dillion, H, '"If They Are Genuine Refugees, Why?" Public Attitudes towards Unauthorised Arrivals in Australia', Foundation House (April 2015), http://www.foundationhouse.org.au/wp-content/uploads/2015/07/Public-attitudes-to-unauthorised-arrivals-in-Australia-Foundation-House-review-2015.pdf.

Missirian, A and Schlenker, W, 'Asylum Applications Respond to Temperature Fluctuations' (2017) 358(6370) *Science* 1610–14.

Moran, T and Kamener, L, 'We've Lost the Knack of Finding Jobs for Refugees', *Australian* (20 February 2017).

Murphy, K, 'Voters Back Deportation of Asylum Seekers if Refugee Claims Fail: Guardian Essential Poll', *Guardian* (30 May 2017).

Nickel, R and Ljunggren, D, 'Almost Half of Canadians Want Refugees Illegally Crossing into Canada Deported: Poll', *Reuters* (20 March 2017).

Norwegian Refugee Council and Internal Displacement Monitoring Centre, 'Global Overview 2015: People Internally Displaced by Conflict and Violence' (May 2015), http://www.internal-displacement.org/sites/default/files/inline-files/20150506-global-overview-2015-en.pdf.

Ozdowski, S, 'Australia's Multiculturalism: Success or Not?', address to the Sydney Institute (9 March 2016).

Roach, K, 'Sources and Trends in Post-9/11 Anti-terrorism Laws' in BJ Goold and L Lazarus (eds), *Security and Human Rights* (Oxford, Hart Publishing, 2007).

Schmid, AP, 'Links between Terrorism and Migration: An Exploration', International Centre for Counter-Terrorism Research Paper (May 2016), http://icct.nl/wp-content/uploads/2016/05/Alex-P.-Schmid-Links-between-Terrorism-and-Migration-1.pdf.

Sherrell, H, 'Settling Better: Reforming Refugee Employment and Settlement Services', Centre for Policy Development (February 2017).

Shields, J, Drolet, J, and Valenzuela, K, 'Immigration Settlement and Integration Services and the Role of Nonprofit Service Providers: A Cross-National Perspective on Trends, Issues and Evidence', RCIS Working Paper 2016/1 (February 2016).

Sturrock, R and Ferguson, P, 'The Longest Conflict: Australia's Climate Security Challenge', Centre for Policy Development (June 2015).

Sunpuwan, M and Niyomsilpa, S, 'Perception and Misperception: Thai Public Opinions on Refugees and Migrants from Myanmar' (2012) 21(1) *Journal of Population and Social Studies* 47–58.

Telhami, S, 'American Attitudes on Refugees from the Middle East', *Brookings* (13 June 2016).

Ueffing, P, Row, F, and Mulder, C, 'Differences in Attitudes Toward Immigration Between Australia and Germany: The Role of Immigration Policy' (2015) 40(4) *Comparative Population Studies* 437–64.

United Nations, 'Security Council Resolution 1373', S/Res/1373 (2001), https://www.unodc.org/pdf/crime/terrorism/res_1373_english.pdf.

United Nations General Assembly, 'Resolution Adopted on 16 September 2005: 2005 World Summit Outcome', (A/RES/60/1), http://www.un.org/en/development/desa/population/migration/generalassembly/docs/globalcompact/A_RES_60_1.pdf.

United Nations High Commissioner for Refugees (UNHCR), 'Global Trends: Forced Displacement in 2015' (June 2016), https://s3.amazonaws.com/unhcrsharedmedia/2016/2016-06-20-global-trends/2016-06-14-Global-Trends-2015.pdf.

United Nations Human Security Unit, 'Strategic Plan: 2014–2017' (2014), https://www.unocha.org/sites/dms/HSU/HSU%20Strategic%20Plan%202014-2017%20Web%20Version.pdf.

US Department of State, 'Documentation of Atrocities in Northern Rakhine State' (August 2018), https://www.state.gov/documents/organization/286307.pdf.

Waldron, J, 'Safety and Security' (2006) 85(2) *Nebraska Law Review* 454–507.

Welsh, JM, 'The Responsibility to Protect: Securing the Individual in International Society' in Benjamin Goold and Liora Lazarus (eds), *Security and Human Rights* (Oxford, Hart Publishing, 2007).

Wike, R, Stokes, B, and Simmons, K, 'Europeans Fear Wave of Refugees Will Mean More Terrorism, Fewer Jobs', Pew Research Center Report (11 July 2016), http://www.pewglobal.org/2016/07/11/europeans-fear-wave-of-refugees-will-mean-more-terrorism-fewer-jobs/.

World Bank, *Forcibly Displaced: Toward a Development Approach Supporting Refugees, the Internally Displaced, and Their Hosts* (Washington, DC, World Bank, 2017).

Index

Introductory Note

References such as '178–79' indicate (not necessarily continuous) discussion of a topic across a range of pages. Wherever possible in the case of topics with many references, these have either been divided into sub-topics or only the most significant discussions of the topic are listed. Because the entire work is about 'security' and 'human rights', the use of these terms (and certain others which occur constantly throughout the book) as an entry point has been minimised. Information will be found under the corresponding detailed topics.

9/11 3–4, 11–14, 183–84, 204–7, 211–12, 236, 245–48, 334–36
rights after 248–50
abduction 194–95
absolute authority 34, 268–70
abstract danger 361, 364, 380
abuses 160, 162, 168, 180, 182, 196, 200, 205–7
human rights 12, 182, 205
transnational counterterrorism 185, 188, 194, 196, 205, 207
academic freedom 2, 148–51, 171, 381
academic scholarship 147–48, 160, 173
academic scrutiny 12, 151, 163, 171–73
academics 12, 14, 147–48, 150–54, 156–57, 160–61, 197, 200
legal 12, 151–52, 159, 172
accountability 12–13, 151, 167, 171–73, 179–98, 200–207
agents of 181–82, 203
corporate 203
definition of 180–85, 204, 207
democratic 168
domestic state mechanisms 186–93
instruments 182, 190, 194, 207
legal 12, 148, 152
legislative 190–91, 206
limited forms of 206–7
measures 172, 180–81, 189–90, 193, 200, 204–5, 449
taxonomy of 180, 205
mechanisms 179–207
non-state mechanisms 198–204
processes 185–86, 189–90, 199, 201, 206
as requiring of explanations and justifications 181–85
retrospective, *see* retrospective accountability
state 165, 172
supranational state mechanisms 193–98
taxonomy of mechanisms and processes 185–86
transnational 179, 185, 192, 196, 204, 206
for transnational counterterrorism 179, 183–85, 196, 204
accusations, anonymous 307, 310–11, 319
ACLU (American Civil Liberties Union) 168
activism, civil society 224–25
actors 4, 18, 31, 163, 198, 314, 324, 334
multiple 183, 185, 190
non-state 179–80, 182, 185, 197–99, 204–5, 207, 227–29, 468–69
security 181, 184, 413
social 227
state 64–65, 88–89, 171, 182, 184, 205, 339, 422
state and non-state 13, 179–80, 182, 193, 212, 229
adequacy 190, 281–82
ADFM, *see* Asia Dialogue on Forced Migration
administrative authorities 392, 395, 404–5, 410, 414
administrative courts 17, 286, 395, 398, 404–5, 408
administrative detention 99, 401
administrative judges 394–96, 403–4, 406, 408, 412
administrative measures 17, 411–12
administrative police measures 394–95, 412–13, 415–17
oversight 398–408

administrative searches 394, 400–402, 405–7, 411–13, 416
advocacy groups, civil society 180, 185, 199, 205–7
affiliation 79, 306
religious 80, 218
Afghanistan 10, 57, 69, 80, 188, 193, 473, 476
agencies 54–55, 134, 182, 190, 227, 283, 488, 490–91
foreign 192–93, 204
intelligence 3, 82, 216, 277, 286–87, 444, 467–68, 492
international 489, 491–93
law enforcement 290, 292, 487
security 179, 181, 192, 204–5, 429–30, 440, 444, 447–48
watchdog 191–92
airports 108, 125, 127–32, 136
al Qaeda 77, 79–81, 94, 227, 270, 336
Algeria 42, 389–91, 393, 397
aliens, enemy 99–100
American Civil Liberties Union, *see* ACLU
Amnesty International 85, 186, 193, 199, 202, 223–24, 237, 285
anonymity 14–15, 154, 201, 273, 298, 307–8, 311, 313–20
during trial 309–13
impact of 308, 318
measures 314, 318
prior to trial 306–9
for victims 297–320
witness 307, 310, 313, 316, 319
anonymous accusations 307, 310–11, 319
anonymous statements 315, 317
anonymous testimony 306, 310, 313, 315, 317–18
anonymous victim participation 15, 305, 307–8, 311–13, 316–17, 319
anonymous witness statements 309–11
anonymous witnesses 15, 305–6, 308–11, 313–19
inadmissibility of 317, 319
anticipated collateral damage 428, 430–31, 436–37, 446
anticipated harm 431, 442, 444, 446
anti-pluralism 55
anti-riot law 241–42, 252
antisemitism 8, 467–68
apologie 347–49, 353–55, 378
apology 351, 353, 355, 361, 364, 375
archives 147, 166–67, 172
archival integrity 163, 166–67, 169
archival material 162, 167, 172
Arendt, Hannah 262, 265–66, 268, 331
armed conflict 314, 324, 335–36, 339–40, 425–28, 436, 447, 449
challenges to legal fact-finding during 423, 426
high-intensity 317
non-international, *see* NIACs
under international humanitarian law 335–39
armed groups 324, 336–38
armed resistance 324, 337, 372
arrest 37, 108, 116, 133, 223, 234, 355–56
house 17, 393–94, 400–402, 404, 406–7, 411–15
artistic expression 378, 381
artists 356, 358, 378
ASEAN (Association of Southeast Asian Nations) 480
Asia 216, 237, 482, 484
Southeast 479, 481
Asia Dialogue on Forced Migration (ADFM) 473, 478, 487, 491
recommendations 491–92
Asia-Pacific region 483–84, 487, 491
forced migration 478–79
security 483
assessment
processes 488, 491
risk 130, 314, 422–24, 429, 431, 434, 490
Association of Southeast Asian Nations (ASEAN) 480
asylum 38, 327, 330
political 323, 327, 331
seekers 99, 102–3, 128, 130, 136, 139, 478–79, 485
temporary first 480–81
atrocities 38, 43, 100, 261, 263, 323, 327, 331
attacks 245, 252–53, 297, 336–37, 421–22, 435–38, 441–43, 445–46
large-scale 252–54
proportionate 331, 336
terrorist, *see* terrorist attacks
Australia 53, 125, 216, 333, 336, 478, 481–82, 486
Austria 2, 10, 56, 66, 82, 85, 89, 290–92
authoritarian regimes 62, 113, 323, 326–27, 331, 334, 337, 339–40
authorities 141–42, 246–47, 270–71, 436, 462, 464, 488, 490
administrative 392, 395, 404–5, 410, 414
judicial 107, 283, 290, 396, 400–401

legal 152, 158, 224, 229, 338
national 276–78, 281
authority
absolute 34, 268–70
political 267–70

backlash
anti-immigration 211–12, 216
nationalist 211–29
bad faith 172–73
balance 36, 38, 160–61, 239–40, 259–60, 289, 305–6, 308
image of 27, 37
metaphor of 239, 249
Bangladesh 59, 212, 220–21, 478–79, 482, 484, 488
Bayrou Memo 67–68
Belgium 2, 66, 85, 291, 326, 353, 404–5
beliefs 60–62, 85, 88, 90–91, 93, 235–36, 243, 245
religious 61, 67, 83, 86
best practice, emerging 491, 493
biases 18, 160, 422, 431–33
organisational 422, 431
psychological 447, 449
bikinis 54, 57, 71
bilateral extradition treaties 328, 331
binaries 57, 71, 183, 425, 434
biometric data 134, 491
biopolitical surveillance 131
bioterrorism 247
black sites 194, 196, 199, 203, 205
blogs 133, 200, 350
bombs 251, 253–54, 297, 438, 441, 448
half-tonne 438, 441
nuclear 251–52
one-tonne 421, 435, 438, 440–41
border agents/officers 126–27, 129, 132, 140
border controls 129, 137
as counterterrorism 102–5
border surveillance 127, 131, 141
borders 11, 101–4, 125–30, 133–42, 211, 478–79, 482, 488
land 131, 136
national 216, 219, 326
boundaries 14, 35, 54, 158, 267, 271, 425, 458
cultural 54–55
of legality 158–59
bounded factuality 18, 421–50
in targeting decisions 428–34
Britain, *see* **United Kingdom**
British Muslims 84, 87, 117
burkini 10, 54–57, 59, 69–71
bystanders 421, 433, 435, 443, 450
civilian 435, 443

caliphate, Islamic 353, 376
Canada 133–34, 180, 187–88, 192–93, 198, 216, 478, 481
courts 187–88
government 138, 187–88, 191–92
Canada Border Services Agency (CBSA) 134
capacity 6, 17–18, 20, 110, 148, 160, 220, 229
institutional 220
operative 434
caricature 6, 63–64, 67–70
casualties 216, 236, 245, 253, 314, 339, 430, 448
catastrophe 242, 248–50
Central European University 150–51
Central Intelligence Agency, *see* **CIA**
Charter of Fundamental Rights of the EU 14, 277, 279–80, 283, 285, 293
children 63, 67, 261, 415, 435, 438, 443, 445
China 205–6, 340, 482, 484
CIA (Central Intelligence Agency) 3, 168, 193–97, 199, 205, 432
citizens
dual 100, 105
ideal 10, 68, 70
naturalised 99–100, 105, 117
ordinary 153, 251, 276, 278, 291, 293
safe 133, 141
citizenship 9, 11, 40, 111, 116–17, 119, 129–31, 141
deprivation of 4, 88, 99, 104, 109, 118
rights 11, 99–119, 261
status 99, 116–17, 131
civil liberties 58, 106, 262, 456, 458, 469, 476–77, 487
civil society 18, 20, 185–86, 198, 200–201, 205, 269, 381–82
activism 224–25
advocacy groups 180, 185, 199, 205–7
groups 180, 186, 193–95, 197–98, 201–4, 224
civilians 330–31, 336–41, 424–25, 430–31, 433–35, 437–39, 441–48, 450
absence of 422, 442, 446
bystanders 435, 443
decision-makers 444–46
innocent 328, 335, 433–35, 442
risk to 433–34, 444
uninvolved 436–40, 442

CJEU (Court of Justice of the European Union) 13–15, 275–77, 279–81, 283–86, 288–89, 291–94
  and right to privacy 276–81
classified information 155, 192, 198
climate change 216, 483–84
closed material proceedings (CMPs) 109, 114, 154–55, 171–73
CMPs, *see* **closed material proceedings**
CoE, *see* **Council of Europe**
coercion 6, 81–82, 86, 182, 223, 415, 417
  state 86, 91
coercive interrogation 250
coercive powers 9, 206, 262
coercive remedies 183–84
cognitive consistency 426–27
collateral damage 428, 430–31, 433, 435, 439, 441, 445, 448–50
  anticipated 428, 430–31, 436–37, 446
  calculations 431
collective interests 235, 238–40, 246
collective memories 166, 427–28
Commission Nationale de l'Informatique et des Libertés 286
communications 215, 276, 290, 374, 412–13, 440
  contents of 285, 289
  electronic 276, 287
community confidence 475, 486–87
compensation 163, 165, 191, 416–17
competing interests 281, 293, 315, 324
competing rights 313–19
complex relationships 102, 142, 227
compliance 219–20, 226, 280, 336
  securing 222–23, 226
complicity 188–89, 191, 193, 196, 202, 206, 350, 357
conduct 180–82, 184, 189–90, 192, 348–50, 362–65, 380, 415–17
  criminal 333, 362, 469
  security 198, 200
confidence
  community 475, 486–87
  public 489, 493
confidential material 302, 304
conflict 29–31, 67, 105, 147, 240, 312–13, 337, 340
  armed, *see* armed conflict
Conseil constitutionnel 287–88, 390, 394–96, 398–403, 407–8, 410, 416
consent 128, 134, 138, 278, 280, 301
consistency, cognitive 426–27
constitutional courts 2, 66, 164, 289–91, 293
constitutional rights 4, 228, 259, 466
constitutionalism 1, 3, 16
constitutionality 241, 291, 396, 398–99, 402, 410
constitutions 220, 228, 290–91, 390, 395–97, 399–401, 410, 414
constraints 20, 117, 157, 370, 432
  organizational 433
contestation 9, 32, 56, 77, 79, 92, 148, 160
control 54, 56, 180–83, 185, 189, 204–5, 397–98, 491–92
  immigration 125, 132, 260
  parliamentary 392, 409
controversy 149, 168, 221–23, 359, 458
convictions 114, 116, 240, 242, 315, 317, 352, 355–56
cooperation 111, 192, 196, 216, 309, 338, 491–92
  transnational 323, 332, 335–36, 338
cooperative repression 335, 340
coordination 179, 417, 492–93
co-radicalisation 468
co-rapporteurs 411–13
core functions 12, 137, 159
corporate accountability 203
corporations 180, 186, 200, 203–6, 222–23
costs 93–94, 135, 139, 155, 240, 245, 248, 294
  of security 10, 20, 92–93
Council of Europe (CoE) 194–95, 197, 347–48, 358
countering violent extremism, *see* **CVE**
counter-power 17, 417
counter-radicalisation 81–82, 85–86
counterterrorism 31, 36, 38, 90–93, 101–5, 117–19, 204–6, 455–56
  activities 12, 184, 188–89, 192, 197, 203, 205
  critique 90–94
  curtailing citizenship rights and mobility as 105–14
  immigration and border controls as 102–5
  laws 15–16, 78–79, 82, 100, 102, 323–24, 335–36, 338–40
  limits of old critiques 90–91
  new paths for critical inquiry 91–94
  policies 10, 80–82, 90, 103, 154, 215, 275, 289
  powers 84, 200, 294
  practices 38, 302, 346, 456, 461
  soft and hard 77–94

transnational 12, 179–80, 182–85, 187–89, 192–93, 197, 205, 329
transnational abuses 185, 188, 194, 196, 205, 207
Counterterrorism and Security Act (CTSA) 106–9, 111–13, 117
Counter-Terrorism Committee (CTC) 333, 335
countries of first flight 491–92
countries of origin 489–90, 492
Court of Justice of the European Union, *see* **CJEU**
courts 170–71, 184–89, 192–94, 275–79, 283–85, 290–91, 326–28, 369–74, 376–79
administrative 17, 286, 395, 398, 404–5, 408
constitutional 2, 66, 164, 289–91, 293
domestic 186–88, 193, 198, 282, 289, 293, 379
human rights 40, 44, 368, 377, 379–80, 382
supranational 193, 197, 371
crimes 251–52, 276–78, 326–27, 350–51, 359–60, 362–63, 375, 463–64
domestic 251–52, 317, 441
of expression 343–82
international 298, 331
of mobility 105
ordinary 251, 332, 412, 459
organised 489
terrorist 169, 340, 351, 357, 363, 462, 469
transnational 135, 491
war 163, 331, 336–38, 439
criminal conduct 333, 362, 469
criminal cooperation treaties 325, 329, 332
criminal intent 349, 364
criminal investigations 85, 88, 202, 365, 435, 448, 462–63
criminal justice system 18, 313, 457, 469
criminal law 15–16, 18–19, 240, 343–46, 359–66, 371, 380–81, 459
constraining principles of 359–66
domestic 116, 252, 332
international 15, 305, 317, 320, 331, 345, 350, 359–61
intervention 359–60, 381
responses 324, 346–47, 362
criminal offences 111, 134, 282, 348–50, 353, 357
criminal procedures 117, 289, 305, 462
criminal process 102–3, 365, 379
criminal responsibility 163, 344, 359, 362, 380
criminal tribunals, 298, 300–301, 303, 305–10, 313–14, 316–17, 319
criminalisation 15–16, 330–32, 336–40, 344–46, 348–49, 360–61, 365–66, 374–75
crimmigration 99, 131, 485
Crown Prosecution Service, *see* **CPS**
CSIS (Canadian Security Intelligence Service) 134, 192
CTC (Counter-Terrorism Committee) 333, 335
CTSA, *see* **Counterterrorism and Security Act**
culpability 165, 359, 362, 364, 379–80
culture 17, 54, 59, 89, 92, 236, 243, 447
boundaries 54–55
corporate 223
organisational 422–23, 432, 447
popular 236, 246
custody 193, 233, 244–45, 356, 405, 465, 469
police 400–401, 464
CVE (countering violent extremism) 18–19, 455–56, 458, 460–62, 466, 468–69
practices 455, 460, 462, 466, 468–69

danger 252, 348–49, 360–61, 363–64, 374, 457, 465–66, 487
abstract 361, 364, 380
grave 206, 252
real 201, 356
data
biometric 134, 491
collection 14–15, 275–93
exchange 474
personal 15, 128, 275, 280, 282, 289
protection 277–93
retained 283, 285, 292
retention 14–15, 275–93, 466
security 203, 277
transfers 280–82
Data Protection Directive 278, 280–81
Data Retention and Investigatory Powers Act (DRIPA) 283–86
Data Retention Directive 14, 276–79, 282, 284, 289, 293
death 30, 245, 268, 421, 425, 434, 436, 440–41
penalty 329
decision-makers 427, 429, 431, 439, 441–42, 444, 447, 449–50
civilian 444–46
political 441, 444

decision-making, processes 18, 421–23, 428, 430–31, 434, 447
deep secrets 153–61, 167, 173
defence 215, 218, 246–47, 298, 301–3, 305–6, 309–12, 316
preparation 300, 314
rights 215, 300–303, 305–6, 308–11, 319–20
defendants 15, 160, 162, 244, 299–300, 316, 404–5
rights of 15, 304, 306, 308
degrading treatment 30–31, 118
dehumanisation 29, 34, 38–39, 41, 425, 431
demarcation 9, 33, 35, 332, 340
democracies 201, 204, 293–94, 323, 327, 367, 372, 456
liberal 1, 5, 13, 20, 212, 214, 259, 262
democratic accountability 168
democratic society 151, 344, 367, 378
deportation 102–4, 118, 139, 225, 234, 346, 465
deprivation of citizenship 4, 88, 99, 104, 109, 118
destination countries 280, 489–90
detainees 224, 226, 233, 249, 251, 425
detention 4–5, 102–4, 187–88, 190–91, 193, 201–2, 252–53, 464–65
administrative 99, 401
immigration 191, 217
indefinite 4–5, 245, 250
practices 187, 226
pretrial 459, 464–65
preventive 37, 248, 252, 464
secret 195, 202, 205
Digital Rights Ireland 276–77, 279–80, 282, 284–86, 288–89, 291–92, 294
dignity 9–10, 34–35, 42–43, 45–46, 235–38, 240–42, 249–50, 252
reaffirming 42–46
diplomatic representations 187–88
direct incitement 16, 345, 348–50
Directives
on Combating Terrorism 349, 363
Data Protection 278, 280–81
Data Retention 14, 276–79, 282, 284, 289, 293
e-Privacy 278, 285
disclosure 104, 134, 162, 170–71, 201, 302, 315
discretion, prosecutorial 309, 334, 382
discretionary powers 396–97
discrimination 11, 67, 93, 137, 277, 329, 381, 414
religious 67, 78, 90
displacement 29, 32, 236, 244, 478, 484, 491
forced 216
internal 480
disproportionate outcomes 439, 441
dissent 14–15, 44, 163, 218, 273, 333, 358
distribution, difficulties with 27, 36–38
distributive justice 10, 93–94
dogma 77, 79, 81, 83, 85, 87, 89, 91
domestic courts 186–88, 193, 198, 282, 289, 293, 379
domestic crimes 251–52, 317, 441
domestic security 179, 458, 462, 465–66
domestic terrorism 93, 334
DRIPA, *see* **Data Retention and Investigatory Powers Act**
dual-status victim participants/ witnesses 304–5, 309, 313
duties 31, 163, 166–67, 169, 172, 325, 331–32, 474
Dworkin, Ronald 13, 45, 151, 183, 234–44, 248–54
defence of rights as trumps 252–53
theory of rights revolution 239–43
dynamic integrity 10, 45–46

early intervention 86, 359, 380
ECHR (European Convention on Human Rights) 40–41, 43, 45, 103, 108, 111–14, 316, 368–69
economic development 6, 389
economic exclusion 10, 93
economic power 212, 220
ECtHR, *see* **European Court of Human Rights**
education 11, 59, 67, 82, 238, 458, 460, 466
higher 149–50
religious 462, 468
effective enforcement 30, 279
effective prevention 30, 380
effectiveness 29–30, 158, 221, 399, 407, 409, 411, 469
Egypt 59, 194, 202, 205–6, 216, 343
electronic communications 276, 287
emergency 389–91, 397–99, 401–3, 405, 409, 411, 413, 415–18
conditions 7, 17
powers 2, 17, 84–85, 88, 93, 102, 228, 234

public 29, 103, 243
state of 16–17, 85, 234, 288, 390–400, 402–6, 408–18
emerging best practice 491, 493
employment 133–34, 137, 139, 493
encouragement 351–53, 364, 464
encroachment 64, 289
enemies 35, 37, 101, 266, 326, 340
of the state 11, 101, 118
enemy aliens 99–100
enforcement 217, 225–26, 264, 279, 293, 299, 395–96, 415–16
effective 30, 279
engagement 17–18, 346, 434, 445, 467, 477
e-Passports 126
e-Privacy Directive 278, 285
equal moral status 29, 42–43, 45
equality 90, 204, 235–36, 238, 240, 242, 249–50, 300
of arms 32, 303, 309
Equator Banks 219–20
Equator Principles 212, 219–21, 229
errors 83, 125, 130, 425, 428, 430, 440–41, 449
human 429–30
intelligence 18, 432–33
manifest 404
ETA (Euskadi Ta Azkatasuna) 355–56
European Convention on Human Rights, *see* **ECHR**
European Court of Human Rights (ECtHR) 40–41, 43, 164–65, 193–96, 302, 315–16, 367–70, 372–79
European Parliament 150, 193–96, 205, 282, 365
European Union 81, 197, 215–16, 275–78, 280, 282, 285, 293
Data Protection Directive 278, 280–81
Data Retention Directive 14, 276–79, 282, 284, 289, 293
Directive on Combating Terrorism 349, 363
e-Privacy Directive 278, 285
evaluation 157–58, 161, 207, 392, 428, 431, 434, 436
normative 152, 171, 427
evidence 117, 166–70, 300–302, 304–5, 309–17, 407, 440–43, 445–46
historical 162–63
secret 4, 109, 148
ex post oversight 410
ex post review 182, 447–48
exceptional powers 16, 365, 390, 395, 397, 407
exceptional protective measures 298, 310, 319
exceptionalism 1, 16–17, 380, 387
exclusion 9, 93, 110, 112, 117–18, 129–31, 139–40, 309
economic 10, 93
pre-emptive 15, 319
temporary 101, 106, 109–10, 115–16
executive measures 114, 185, 346
executive orders 113, 217–18, 474
executive power 2, 5, 225, 397, 400, 409
executive watchdogs 180, 184, 192–93, 198, 205, 207
executives 64, 186, 191–93, 197–98, 218, 286
exercise of power 227, 266, 459
exile 116
internal 113–14, 117
existential threats 9, 29
expansive offences 16, 344
expeditious trial 305, 308
expertise 152, 161, 200, 449
exposure 20, 155, 162, 179, 184, 190, 194, 199
public 184, 200
expression 240–41, 347, 349, 351, 355–58, 360, 362–63, 373–78
artistic 378, 381
crimes of 343–82
freedom of 204, 344, 352, 366–68, 370–71, 374–75, 377–78, 381–82
of ideas 16, 344
of othering 10, 46
religious 58, 66, 85
extirpation 78, 83, 94
Islam as object of 88–90
extradition 103, 188, 194, 323, 325–27, 329–32, 334–35, 339
political offence exception 323–31, 334, 339–41
extraordinary measures 248, 252
extraordinary renditions 5, 99, 104, 190, 196, 199, 455, 459
extraterritorial jurisdiction 111, 329–30, 334
extremism 53, 57, 59, 68, 70–71, 364, 460–61, 467–69
Islamist 71, 461, 467
religious 10, 53–59
right-wing 7–8, 465, 467

secular 53–59, 71
violent 261, 366, 455, 457, 459–61, 463, 465, 467–69

Facebook 203, 279, 355, 357
fact-finders 422, 448–49
fact-finding 424, 426–28, 434, 446–47, 449–50
legal 18, 422–28, 447, 449
practices 442, 446–47
processes, sensitive 421
facts
brute 448–49
relevant 147, 302, 424–25, 441, 444
factuality, bounded 18, 421–50
failures, intelligence 429, 432–33, 439, 441, 449
fair trial 114, 118, 162, 300–301, 311–12, 315, 320, 323
rights 15, 114, 173, 300, 313, 316, 319
fairness 197, 249, 299–300, 304, 312, 365, 469
faith 10, 39, 77–78, 81, 83, 91, 117, 225
bad 172–73
family life 108, 111, 113–14, 118, 263
fear 267–70
of mass terrorism 249, 252–54
of violence 267–68
Federal Bureau of Investigation (FBI) 203, 432
federal government 59, 134, 224
fees 132, 136
final-destination countries 488, 492
financial institutions 198, 204, 219, 227
First Amendment 201, 218, 239
floating signifiers 456, 458
force
lethal 2, 5, 18, 422–23
use of 264, 415–16, 459
forced displacement 216
forced labour 479–80
forced migrants 19, 473–74, 480–82, 486–87, 489, 491, 493
forced migration 19, 473–93
in Asia-Pacific 478–79
and human rights 479–83
and security 483–87
forced relocation 101, 106, 113–15
foreign fighters 80, 100–101, 105, 112, 114–16, 118, 291, 345
foreign governments 325–27, 331, 339–40
foreign nationals 100, 103, 117, 217, 327
foreign states 189, 202, 325–27, 335, 338, 340, 395
foreigners 35, 40–41, 63, 99, 105, 247, 251, 401
foreseeability 16, 159, 290, 364, 368
Foucault, Michel 138, 262, 264, 266
France 66–67, 70, 82, 84–85, 292–93, 353–55, 389, 391
Conseil constitutionnel 287–88, 390, 394–96, 398–403, 407–8, 410, 416
continued enforcement of state of emergency 396–98
declaration of a state of emergency 395–96, 398, 402, 405, 417
judicial oversight 394–408
Law Commissions 409–13
Loi sur le renseignement 286–88
National Assembly 390–92, 401, 409–13
non-judicial oversight 17, 394, 408–17
oversight of administrative police measures 398–408
parliamentary oversight 409–10, 413
Rights Defender 17, 409, 413–17
Senate 391–92, 409–11, 413
state of emergency 2, 288, 389–418
Franko Aas, Katja 130–31, 141
free speech 238–39, 241–42, 372, 377, 380, 458, 462
restrictions on 347, 375
freedom 65–67, 108–9, 118, 241–42, 249–50, 393, 400–402, 406–7
academic 2, 148–51, 171, 381
of expression 204, 344, 352, 366–68, 370–71, 374–75, 377–78, 381–82
fundamental 20, 333, 365, 398, 403, 406
individual 64, 400–401
personal 278, 292–94
political 239, 339–40
religious 66–67, 86, 482
sexual 89
of speech 89, 367, 393, 418
French Muslims 85, 89, 93
Freud, Sigmund 263–64
functions 69–70, 91, 223, 226, 229, 240, 244, 246
core 12, 137, 159
preventive 359, 380, 464–65
fundamental freedoms 20, 333, 365, 398, 403, 406
fundamental liberties 333, 406
fundamental principles 116, 195, 201, 281
incitement 359–71

Gaza 421, 435, 437–38, 440
genocide 331, 340, 360, 373, 424, 487
Germany 6, 10, 30, 56, 289–90, 456, 461–66, 469
  approaches to counterterrorism 462–67
  CVE (countering violent extremism) 467–69
globalisation 135, 211–12
  and human rights 213–15
glorification of terrorism 343, 347–52, 354–56, 361, 368, 376
goods, protected 463, 465
governance 62, 127, 167, 205, 262, 264, 267, 270
governmentality 86, 90, 264
governments 138–41, 191–92, 239–41, 326–27, 339–40, 389–90, 480–81, 493
  foreign 326–27, 331, 339–40
  national 14, 105, 480, 487, 489
Greer, Steven 30–31
grievances 39–40, 91
  legitimate 339, 462
gross negligence 416
Guantanamo Bay 4, 184, 187–88, 224, 226, 246
guidance 62, 171, 263, 371, 403
guilt 238, 307–8

habeas corpus 4, 184, 187–88
harbinger theory 236, 242, 245–48, 250, 252–53
Harcourt, Bernard 90–91
harm 242, 252–53, 359–62, 365, 374, 379, 465, 469
  anticipated 431, 442, 444, 446
  principle 359
hate speech 367, 369, 372, 456
headscarves 46, 66–70
higher education 149–50
historical evidence 162–63
history 42, 71, 147, 150, 155, 160, 166, 168–69
Hobbes, Thomas 13, 267–70, 463
hostilities 104, 118, 324, 336–38, 437, 441
house arrest 17, 393–94, 400–402, 404, 406–7, 411–15
HRC, *see* **Human Rights Committee**
human dignity, *see* **dignity**
human error 429–30
human rights
  abuses 12, 182, 205
  attacks on 41–43
  bodies 367, 377
  commitment to 16, 19, 39
  courts 40, 44, 368, 377, 379–80, 382
  crisis in human rights buy-in 39–42
  embedding norms beyond the state 219–28
  and forced migration 479–83
  foundations of 29, 34
  and globalisation 213–15
  individual 213–14
  jurisprudence 361, 371, 381–82
  language 10, 64, 66, 69, 71, 213
  norms 2–3, 211–12, 216, 219, 223, 225–26, 228
  and security 8, 18, 70, 212, 254, 259–60, 262, 267
  threat to 10, 211–12
  violations 66, 165–66, 252
Human Rights Committee (HRC) 164, 333, 352
Human Rights Watch 150, 186, 193, 199, 202, 223–24
human security 260–61, 457, 475, 484
humanitarian law 165–66
humanitarian visas 490
humanity 33, 35, 38, 41–42, 168, 218, 237, 331
Hungary 2, 150
hybrid criminal tribunals 298, 300–301, 303, 305–10, 313–14, 316–17, 319

ICCPR, *see* **International Covenant on Civil and Political Rights**
ICJ, *see* **International Commission of Jurists**
ICRC, *see* **International Committee of the Red Cross**
ICTR (International Criminal Tribunal for Rwanda) 350, 360
ICTY (International Criminal Tribunal for the former Yugoslavia) 314–18
ideal citizens 10, 68, 70
ideal men 66
ideal society 60, 62, 69–70
ideal world 62–65, 68, 70, 228
identification 19, 302, 312, 434, 449, 487, 491, 493
  joint 491–92
identity 9, 11, 53, 55, 139, 141–42, 306–7, 309–12
  Islamic 78, 80, 84
  management 129–30
  multiple 10, 55, 71
  Muslim 10, 79, 83, 85, 87, 92

national 11, 142
religious 53, 77–81, 83, 85–87, 89, 91, 93
ideologies 71, 86, 429, 462, 469
IDF (Israel Defense Forces) 435–38, 440, 444
IHRL, *see* **international human rights law**
ill treatment 29, 31–32, 40–41, 329
illegitimate violence 13, 262, 265
imagination, political 13, 115
immigrants 458, 481–82, 489
illegal 36
immigration 78, 82, 102, 104, 136–37, 140, 480–83, 485–86
anti-immigration backlash 211–12, 216
control 125, 132, 260
detention 191, 217
laws 4, 99, 102–4, 117, 211, 475
officers 112, 125–26, 132
public acceptance of 480, 489–90
regulations 224–25
and security 11, 136, 140
status 104, 127, 129, 134–35
imprisonment 102, 107, 112, 114, 252, 343, 352–53, 356
impunity 4, 166, 323, 327, 330
in camera proceedings 170, 426
incentives 324, 337–38, 341, 398, 455
inchoate offences 360–61
incitement 347–48, 350–52, 354, 357, 360–62, 364, 372–77, 379
case law and analysis of necessity and proportionality 371–79
content, context and link with violence 374–77
direct 16, 345, 348–50
and domestic courts 379
France and Spain 353–56
fundamental principles 359–71
indirect, *see* indirect incitement
international legal measures against 347–50
justifications for resorting to criminal law 371–72
national practice 350–58
Netherlands 357
non-public 374
penalties 379
special protection for certain forms of expression 377–78
Turkey 358
United Kingdom 352–53
to violence 344, 358, 372–75, 377, 382
inclusion 1–21, 82, 170, 305, 409
indefinite detention 4–5, 245, 250
India 216, 482, 484
indirect incitement 343–82
offences 16, 350, 364
practice 347–58
individual freedom 64, 400–401
individual liberty 115, 118, 237
individual responsibility 344, 359
punishment commensurate with 363–64
individual security 6, 101, 261, 267
Indonesia 59, 478, 482, 484
inequalities 9, 11, 128, 137, 141–42, 215, 418, 483
information 134–35, 153–58, 160–61, 197–98, 427–32, 438–41, 443–47, 491–92
available 423, 488
classified 155, 192, 198
detailed 200, 285, 406, 412
intelligence 216, 228, 422, 428–31, 442, 444–47
leaked 155, 195
missing 422, 445–46, 448–49
partial 153, 155–56
personal 11, 134, 138, 277, 308
positive 422, 438, 441–43, 445–47
relevant 153, 160, 171, 449
secret 160–61, 182, 189, 191–93, 196, 198, 200, 204–7
uncertain 446, 450
unreliable 447, 489
inhumanity 32–33, 36, 42, 46
injunctions 217, 407
injustices 168, 228, 340, 366, 381–82
innocence 116, 277, 282, 292, 300, 307–8, 365
innocent civilians 328, 335, 433–35, 442
insecurity 1, 20, 60, 62–63, 65, 479, 483, 486
instigation 16, 345, 360, 362
institutional capacity 220
institutions 211–12, 219, 225, 228–29, 325, 327, 414, 432–33
financial 198, 204, 219, 227
formal 212, 225–27, 229
multilateral 214, 216
non-state 185, 195–96, 206, 212, 219, 225–26, 228–29
state 180, 198, 204, 206, 212, 220, 228–29, 326
insurrection 389–90
integration 55, 67, 82, 475, 478, 486

integrity 27, 42, 45–46, 172, 303, 306, 477, 479
archival 163, 166–67, 169
dynamic 10, 45–46
intelligence 117–18, 160, 168, 427–28, 430, 432, 439–40, 486–87
agencies/services 3, 82, 216, 277, 286–87, 444, 467–68, 492
errors 18, 432–33
information 216, 228, 422, 428–31, 442, 444–47
interpretation 444, 447
reliable 431, 437
and risk of error 428–33
intent 41, 241, 298, 348–49, 351, 360–64, 375, 380
criminal 349, 364
intercultural learning 467–68
interests 13, 15, 281, 283, 303–4, 307, 340, 457
collective 235, 238–40, 246
competing 281, 293, 315, 324
legitimate 14, 309, 324, 374
personal 302–3
victim 304, 309
interference 37, 108–9, 114, 277, 293, 370–71, 377, 379
interim measures 405–7
judge of 397, 403, 405–8
internal displacement 480
internal exile 113–14, 117
international agencies 489, 491–93
International Commission of Jurists (ICJ) 223, 225
International Committee of the Red Cross (ICRC) 16, 335, 337
international community 179, 298, 326, 329, 332, 473
International Covenant on Civil and Political Rights (ICCPR) 316, 331, 375–76
international criminal law 15, 305, 317, 320, 331, 345, 350, 359–61
International Criminal Tribunal for Rwanda (ICTR) 350, 360
International Criminal Tribunal for the former Yugoslavia, *see* **ICTY**
international human rights law (IHRL) 27–28, 298–300, 305, 314, 320, 346, 359, 380–81
international humanitarian law 16, 163, 324, 334–35, 340, 423, 437, 439
international institutions 13, 211–12, 215, 225–26
International Labour Organization (ILO) 220
international law 27, 202–3, 227, 298–99, 325, 331–34, 337, 422
International Organization for Migration (IOM) 478, 488
international peace 65, 297, 299
international standards 206, 305
international terrorism 114, 129, 275, 278, 293, 298, 320, 334
internationalism 211–12
interpretation 31–32, 43, 305, 422–23, 427, 444, 446–47, 449
of intelligence information 444–45, 447
interrogation 17, 104, 147, 168, 238, 253
coercive 250
intervention 82, 118, 325, 396, 415–16, 462, 467
early 86, 359, 380
intolerance 71
intransigence, state 225–26
intrusions 126, 135, 279, 335
invasions 134, 261, 264
illegal 7
investigations 78–79, 81, 199, 201, 281–82, 303, 309, 440
criminal 85, 88, 202, 365, 435, 448, 462–63
investigative journalism 12, 182, 193, 199, 205, 447
investigative media 195, 200, 205–7
inviolability 393, 401
IOM, *see* **International Organization for Migration**
Iran 10, 57, 59, 69, 217
Iraq 7, 80, 100–101, 104, 188, 217, 264, 433–34
Ireland 280–81, 291
Northern 37, 102, 106
IS, *see* **Islamic State**
ISA (Israel Security Agency) 436–38, 440, 442–44, 446
ISIS 7, 58, 100–101, 104, 115, 117, 353
Islam 10–11, 55, 58–59, 71, 77–81, 83, 86, 88–94
as object for reform 86–88
as object of extirpation 88–90
radical 88, 99
as signal and proxy for risk 83–86
symbols of 86, 92
varied uses 83–90
Islamic caliphate 353, 376
Islamic identity 78, 80, 84

Islamic law 62–65
Islamic religiosity 83, 85
Islamic State 77, 79–81, 94, 100, 106, 270, 345, 352–53
Islamism 80, 465, 468
Islamist extremism 71, 461, 467
Islamists 87, 465
Islamophobia 8, 20, 55, 217, 467–68
Israel 5, 430
  targeted killing of Salah Shehadeh 435–46
  Shehadeh Commission 18, 421, 423–24, 434–36, 438, 440–41, 443–46, 448, 450
  Supreme Court 421, 435, 437
Israel Defense Forces, *see* **IDF**
Israel Security Agency, *see* **ISA**
Israeli Special Investigatory Commission 18, 423, 434
Italy 106, 194, 289

jihadists 107, 116, 118, 275, 355, 407
joint identification 491–92
journalists 12, 14, 156, 199–200, 344, 377–78
  investigative 12, 199, 205
judges 305–6, 308, 311, 314, 353, 397–98, 400–401, 404–7
  administrative 394–96, 403–4, 406, 408, 412
  of interim measures 397, 403, 405–8
  pretrial 301–12, 318
  STL 300, 304–5
judicial authority 107, 283, 290, 396, 400–401
judicial oversight 286, 394–408
judicial police 400, 412
judicial proceedings 303, 358, 394, 411
judicial review 187, 189, 226, 228, 278, 286, 392, 395
judicial supervision 400–401
judiciary 17, 62, 186–87, 205, 283, 299, 394, 477
jurisdiction, extraterritorial 111, 329–30, 334
jurisprudence 222, 236, 239, 302, 370, 372, 378
  human rights 361, 371, 381–82
justice 65, 214–15, 228, 276, 278, 281, 302, 304
  distributive 10, 93–94
  open 12, 159, 169, 172–73
  procedural 302
justified limits on rights 238, 241, 248, 253

Kadi v Commission 214, 218
Kant, Immanuel 240, 267, 269–70
killings, targeted 2, 5, 18, 154, 156, 245, 247, 421–50
kinetic underclass 139
knowledge 12, 151–53, 155–56, 158, 166, 206, 247, 252

labels 40, 42, 100, 118, 140
land borders 131, 136
landing cards 132–33
language 11, 17, 55–56, 61, 64, 69, 83, 140
  human rights 10, 64, 66, 69, 71, 213
  of Islamic law 62, 64
  legal 62, 64, 70
  religious 57, 68
  of security 56–57, 71, 458
Law Commissions 409–13
law enforcement agencies 290, 292, 487
lawmakers 69–70, 282, 288, 293
lawyers 12, 112, 242, 304, 306, 344, 423, 429
leaders 2, 222–23, 373
leadership, political 444–45, 447
leakers 180, 182, 186, 197, 200–201, 205
Lebanon 297–301, 307, 309, 313–15, 317–20, 485
legal academics 12, 151–52, 159, 172
legal accountability 12, 148, 152
legal authority 152, 158, 224, 229, 338
legal fact-finding 18, 422–28, 447, 449
legal framework 281, 313, 319, 323, 347, 402–3, 423, 462
legal norms 212, 221–22, 226–27, 422, 441
legal pluralism 226–27, 229
legal positivism 183
legal processes 152, 154, 422, 468
legal representation 110, 308
legal secrets 147, 153–60
legal standards 369–70, 376–77
legal status 13, 130, 222, 226
legality 227, 229, 394, 396–97, 422–23, 428, 437, 439
  boundaries of 158–59
  non-state 228
legislation 62, 106–7, 148, 192, 291, 293, 344, 365
  rights-restrictive 292, 294
legislative accountability 190–91, 206
legislative committees 180, 184, 189–90, 193
legislative drift 290, 293
legislatures 186, 189–92, 194–97, 200, 205, 207, 390, 392

legitimacy 2, 71, 155, 195, 222, 346, 353, 369
  moral 10, 92
legitimate aims 369
legitimate grievances 339, 462
legitimate interests 14, 309, 324, 374
legitimate rebellions 332
legitimate targets 423, 436–38
lethal force 2, 5, 18, 422–23
lethal measures 436–37
liberal democracies 1, 5, 13, 20, 212, 214, 259, 262
liberal democratic polity 266
liberal political philosophy 262, 267–68
liberal rights 264, 461
liberal state 10, 14, 92, 263
liberalism 2–3, 20, 92–93, 262
liberation 54, 237, 329, 373
liberty 37–38, 41, 100, 113, 260, 268, 270–71, 461
  individual 115, 118, 237
  and security 27, 37–38
Libya 217
limited powers 62, 299, 398
listing process for UNSC 1267 186–87, 193, 197–98
litigation 187–89, 193, 217, 237, 394, 474
Luban, David 33–34, 37

Malaysia 478–79, 482
managed return 109, 112, 115
management 55, 129, 151, 262, 264, 487, 490, 492–93
marginalised groups 10, 118
martial law 389–90
mass surveillance 14, 180, 197, 203, 205, 207, 286, 293
mass terrorism 13, 242, 250–52, 254
  fears of 13, 248, 249, 252–54
material, archival 162, 167, 172
McNeal, Gregory 430–31, 434
measures
  executive 114, 185, 346
  extraordinary 248, 252
  interim 405–7
  police 400, 402–3, 411, 413
  preventive 11, 79, 367, 437, 462, 466, 468
  protective 298, 301, 305–7, 312, 314–17, 319–20
  punitive 372, 437
  rectifying 302, 311
  security, *see* security measures
media 38, 41, 180, 185–86, 190, 195, 197–201, 204–7
  investigative 195, 200, 205–7
  social 343, 345, 352, 458, 467
  traditional 200
memories, collective 166, 427–28
metadata 154, 247, 276–78, 282, 287, 289
migrant flows 89, 479, 491
migrants 20, 90, 103, 482–83, 486
  forced 19, 473–74, 480–82, 486–87, 489, 491, 493
  undesirable 89, 139
migration 77, 127–28, 136, 140–41, 473, 479, 483, 485
  economic 478
  forced, *see* forced migration
military objectives 336–37
military targets 336, 437
minorities 80, 84, 87, 93–94, 118, 260, 340
  Muslim 66, 92
misconduct 180–82, 184, 188, 195, 201, 416, 425
missing information 422, 445–46, 448–49
mistakes, ***see*** **errors**
mobile phones 407–8
mobility 11, 101, 104–5, 115, 117–18, 129, 138–39, 141
  crimes of 105
  rights 11, 101, 139
monitoring 223, 226, 392, 410, 467
  daily 411
moral ambiguity 154–55
moral legitimacy 10, 92
moral status 27, 46, 154
  equal 29, 42–43, 45
  privileged 214
morality, public 69
Morocco 66, 68
motivations, political 103, 334
Muller, Benjamin 127, 131, 133, 135, 138, 141
multilateral institutions 214, 216
multiple identities 10, 55, 71
multi-stakeholder regimes 220–21
Muslim identity 10, 79, 83, 85, 87, 92
Muslim minorities 66, 92
Muslim women 10, 53–71
Muslim-majority countries 217, 474
Muslims 10, 57, 59, 61, 77–79, 81, 83–88, 90–94
  American 88, 94
  British 84, 87, 117

French 85, 89, 93
as problem 78–83
Myanmar 217, 473, 478, 487–89

National Assembly 390–92, 401, 409–13
national authorities 276–78, 281
national governments 14, 105, 480, 487, 489
national identity 11, 142
national laws 220, 278, 325–26, 328, 330, 333, 335–39
national security 117–18, 217–18, 228, 260–61, 369, 375, 486–87, 489
agendas 211, 229
interests of 108, 114
and nationalism 215–18
policy 99, 216, 224
powers 226, 228
threat to 104, 234, 373, 375
National Security Agency, *see* **NSA**
nationalism 8, 13, 20, 211–12, 215, 219, 229
and national security 215–18
nationalist backlash 211–29
nationalist politics 216–17, 219, 229
nationality 5, 40, 104, 111, 390
natural law 267–68, 270
necessity 16, 31, 64, 69, 169, 264, 369–72, 379–80
strict 314–15
negligence 362
gross 416
Netherlands 81, 89, 92, 292, 353
incitement and dissemination 357
New York Times 200, 238
NEXUS programme 11, 131, 133–35, 137–40, 360, 362
NGOs (non-governmental organisations) 65, 195, 213, 220, 223, 227, 455, 466–69
NIACs (non-international armed conflicts) 324, 336–38
Nigeria 59
non-citizens 35, 102, 104, 117, 128, 130, 141
nondisclosure 298, 302, 308, 318, 411
non-discrimination 90, 92, 323
non-governmental organisations, *see* **NGOs**
non-international armed conflicts, *see* **NIACs**
non-intervention 325, 327, 331
non-judicial oversight 17, 394, 408–17
non-public incitement 374
non-residents 126, 141
non-state actors 179–80, 182, 185, 197–99, 204–5, 207, 227–29, 468–69
non-state institutions 185, 195–96, 206, 212, 219, 225–26, 228–29
non-state mechanisms 180, 185–86, 190, 212, 223, 225
nonviolent protest 15, 333, 339
normative evaluations 152, 171, 427
norms 28–30, 32, 45, 152, 165, 227, 424, 464
anti-torture 44–45
human rights 2–3, 211–12, 216, 219, 223, 225–26, 228
legal 212, 221–22, 226–27, 422, 441
Northern Ireland 37, 102, 106
NSA (National Security Agency) 200, 246–47, 460
nuclear bombs 251–52
nuclear terrorism 246, 331
nullum crimen 364, 366
NYPD (New York Police Department) 83–84

Obama Administration 201, 247
objectives, military 336–37
obligations, positive 30–31, 367
offences 330, 332–33, 348–50, 352–54, 359–61, 363–65, 376, 378–80
expansive 16, 344
inchoate 360–61
mental and material elements 362–63
pre-inchoate 361, 363
preventive 347, 359, 361
terrorism 333–34, 340, 348–49, 355, 363, 459, 464
offenders 325, 328–29, 362, 465
non-political 328
political 323, 325, 327, 330, 335
Ombudsperson, UNSC Resolution 1267 186, 198, 204
open justice 12, 159, 169, 172–73
opposition, political 299, 369
oppression 20, 43, 166, 324, 327, 331
oppressive regimes 327, 334
orders, executive 113, 217–18, 474
ordinary crimes 251, 332, 412, 459
organisational biases 422, 431
organisational culture 422–23, 432, 447
Organization for Security and Co-operation in Europe, *see* **OSCE**
organisational constraints 433
OSCE (Organization for Security and Co-operation in Europe) 358
othering 9–10, 27–45, 135
expressions of 10, 46
politics of 39, 41–43, 45–46

radical 9, 27, 29, 34
systemic 35, 46
and torture 33–36
outsiders 8–9, 130, 153
oversight
of administrative police measures 398–408
ex post 410
judicial 286, 394–408
non-judicial 17, 394, 408–17
parliamentary 409–10, 413
political 18, 444
powers 395, 398, 410
of French state of emergency 389–418

pain 33–34, 201
infliction of 33
Pakistan 80, 188, 431
parliamentary control 392, 409
parliamentary debates 116, 391, 393, 399, 401, 409
parliamentary oversight 409–10, 413
partial information 153, 155–56
passports 107, 110, 118, 125, 129, 133, 138, 141; *see also* **travel documents**
seizure 107–8, 110
patriotism 263–64
peace 61–62, 65, 67, 263–65, 267–68, 270, 298, 338
international 65, 297, 299
peaceful politics 264–67
penalties 132, 166, 363, 379
incitement 379
perceptions 80, 238, 253, 481–83, 486, 493
public 293, 480–82, 485
of terrorism 236, 248
permanent residents 126, 131, 133, 138
permanent review bodies 185–86, 192
perpetrators 35, 202–3, 314, 323, 326, 349, 355, 362
persecution 39, 329–32, 482, 487–88, 490
political 103, 327, 329
personal data 15, 128, 275, 280, 282, 289
personal freedoms 278, 292–94
personal information 11, 134, 138, 277, 308
personal interests 302–3
persuasion 181, 183, 185
petitions 66, 405–7, 435–36
Philippines 478
photos 57
aerial 445
published 355
physical safety 313, 319, 476
physical security 301–2, 306, 308, 314, 317
physical violence 56, 428
pluralism 55, 57, 71, 151, 223, 344, 367
legal 226–27, 229
police 84, 106–7, 112, 115–16, 405, 408, 415, 466–69
custody 400–401, 464
judicial 400, 412
measures 400, 402–3, 411, 413
administrative 394–95, 398–408, 412–13, 415–17
New York Police Department (NYPD) 83–84
powers 238, 418
policymakers 103, 115, 181, 293
political asylum 323, 327, 331
political authority 267–70
political debates 13, 378
political decision-makers 441, 444
political discourse 6, 128, 235–36, 259–60
political freedom 239, 339–40
political imagination 13, 115
political leadership 444–45, 447
political motivation 103, 334
political offences 325–27, 330, 334, 338
political offenders 323, 325, 327, 330, 335
political opposition 299, 369
political oversight 18, 444
political persecution 103, 327, 329
political philosophy 228, 476
liberal 262, 267–68
political power 8, 83, 228, 268
political rebels 326, 339
political resistance 15–16
criminalisation of 332–35
violent 323–41
political speech 377–78
political violence 38, 102, 266, 324–25, 329, 334–35, 459
politicians 20, 93, 115, 254, 473
politics 137, 139, 141, 235, 239, 262, 264–66, 270
nationalist 216–17, 219, 229
of othering 39, 41–43, 45–46
peaceful 264–67
security 6, 8
and violence 262, 264–65, 267, 269
popular culture 236, 246
populism 1, 20, 150, 218
right-of-centre 11, 20, 77, 82, 94
security 1, 8–9, 20–21
populist rhetoric 150, 341

positive information 422, 438, 441–43, 445–47
positive law 28, 239, 267, 269
positive obligations 30–31, 367
positivism 183, 239
legal 183
power(s) 17, 103–4, 106–8, 113, 182, 262–67, 392–94, 396–98
broad 286, 308
coercive 9, 206, 262
counterterrorism 84, 200, 294
discretionary 396–97
emergency 2, 17, 84–85, 88, 93, 102, 228, 234
exceptional 16, 365, 390, 395, 397, 407
executive 2, 5, 225, 397, 400, 409
exercise of 227, 266, 459
limited 62, 299, 398
new 407–8, 418
oversight 395, 398, 410
police 238, 418
security 184, 196, 200
to seize travel documents 107–9
separation of 396, 410
stop-and-search 45, 87
pragmatism 44
predictions 17, 183, 427, 434, 448–49
pre-emptive exclusion 15, 319
pre-inchoate offences 361, 363
prejudice 35, 307–8, 312, 380, 483
pre-legislative scrutiny 106, 108
preliminary rulings 280, 284, 291
pre-prevention 18, 462–63, 466
prescribed by law test 368
pretrial 303, 306–9, 319
detention 459, 464–65
phase 310, 319, 464
prevention 16, 65, 82, 275, 282, 455, 460–64, 466–67
effective 30, 380
primary 460, 466, 468
secondary 460, 468
terrorism 16, 291, 346, 348, 367, 369, 466, 469
tertiary 460, 468
preventive detention 37, 248, 252, 464
preventive measures 11, 79, 367, 437, 462, 466, 468
preventive offences 347, 359, 361
preventive rationale 359, 382
primary prevention 460, 466, 468
priority of prosecution 115, 117
prisoners 38, 40, 44, 189, 202
prisons, secret 12, 179, 193, 196
privacy 14–15, 273, 275–76, 278–79, 281–83, 289, 291, 466
in Europe 282–92
rights 14, 118, 128, 134, 275–82, 285, 288, 291–93
and security 275–94
and trusted traveller programmes 129–35
private regulators 223, 225
private sector 179, 198, 280
private violence 6, 10, 93
privilege 136–41
proactivity 463, 466, 468–69
probative value 301, 310–11
procedural protections 115, 119
procedural safeguards 4, 14, 108, 244
proceedings 159, 281, 283–84, 302–3, 306–7, 309–10, 312, 314
in camera 170, 426
closed 45, 115
closed material 109, 114, 154–55, 171–73
in camera 170, 426
judicial 303, 358, 394, 411
legal 12, 154, 159
Special Tribunal for Lebanon (STL) 301, 304, 307, 319
processes, iterative 180, 185–86, 196, 200
profiling 39, 85, 91–93, 277
racial 91, 204
religious 78, 90, 366
proof 103, 137, 163, 251–52, 361, 365, 423, 425, 447–48
propaganda 67, 80, 94, 358, 368
propagandising 344, 364, 367
in Turkey 358
property 241–42, 263, 331, 416–17, 450
damage 326, 334
proportionality 16, 18, 109, 370–72, 379–80, 403–5, 437, 439
analysis 184, 369, 371
strict 404
test 368–70
proportionate attacks 331, 336
proportionate punishment 114, 364
prosecution 182–83, 199, 201, 305–6, 311, 344–46, 372–73, 377–79
priority of 115, 117
prosecutorial discretion 309, 334, 382
prosecutors 300, 311, 334, 355, 382
public 400, 402
protected goods 463, 465

protection 9–11, 244–45, 282, 306–7, 406, 458, 475–79, 481
data 277–83, 286, 291–93
procedural 115, 119
special 377–78, 407
of victims 314–15
protective measures 298, 301, 305–7, 312, 314–17, 319–20
exceptional 298, 310, 319
provocation 67, 350–51, 354–55, 358
public 348–49
psychological biases 447, 449
public acceptance of immigration 480, 489–90
public confidence 489, 493
public discourse 221, 459–60
public emergency 29, 103, 243
public exposure 184, 200
public life 85, 266, 456
public morality 69
public order 369, 392–93, 402, 404, 406, 416–17, 463, 465
public perceptions 293, 480–82, 485
public prosecutors 400, 402
public provocation 348–49
public safety 108, 115, 242, 245, 482
public scrutiny 18, 109, 155, 461
public security 404, 485
public spaces 55–56, 67
publicity 182, 185, 197, 200, 203–5, 207
punishment 105, 115, 194, 204, 359, 362–63, 365, 379
commensurate with individual responsibility 363–64
proportionate 112, 114, 364
purity 56–59

QPC (*questions prioritaires de constitutionnalité*) 399, 401, 404, 416
qualified rights 45, 114

racial profiling 91, 204
racism 40, 42, 55
radical Islam 88, 99
radical othering 9, 27, 29, 34
radicalisation 81, 100, 105, 114, 455–56, 460, 465, 468–69
Rakhine State 478, 488–89
rapporteur 401, 409, 422
rationality 60, 90
reasonable suspicion 108, 466
rebellion 270, 324–26, 331
legal death of 323–41
legitimate 332
rebels 269, 334, 340
political 326, 339
recklessness 362–63
reconciliatory approaches 313, 317
recruitment 81, 101, 104, 118, 345, 465
rectifying measures 302, 311
redress 12, 29, 180–82, 184–85, 188–89, 198, 204–5, 207
reforms 19, 78, 83, 86, 91, 117, 432–33, 492–93
Islam as object for 86–88
refugee status 102–4, 475, 479–80, 487–90, 492
refugees 19, 128, 130, 216–17, 473–74, 479–82, 485–86, 488–92
Rohingya 478, 488
Syrian 474
Registered Traveller Service 132–33
regulation 10, 78, 88, 132, 215, 220, 283, 294
regulatory regimes 221, 223, 225
rehabilitation 105, 460, 465, 469
reliability 163, 425, 428, 430–31, 449
reliable intelligence 431, 437
religion 9, 25, 54, 56–57, 70–71, 79, 88, 135
religiosity 57, 70
Islamic 83, 85
religious affiliation 80, 218
religious beliefs 61, 67, 83, 86
religious discrimination 67, 78, 90
religious education 462, 468
religious expression 58, 66, 85
religious extremism 10, 53, 59
religious freedoms 66–67, 86, 482
religious identity 53, 77–81, 83, 85–87, 89, 91, 93
religious language 57, 68
religious profiling 78, 90, 366
relocation, forced 101, 106, 113–15
remedies, coercive 183–84
remoteness 16, 359, 363, 374
rendition 180–81, 183, 189–91, 194–97, 199, 202–3, 205, 207
extraordinary 5, 99, 104, 190, 196, 199, 455, 459
victims 4, 193
representation, legal 110, 308
representations, diplomatic 187–88
repression 323–24, 326, 332, 334, 338–39, 464, 466, 469
cooperative 335, 340

resettlement 19, 478, 486, 493
countries 491–92
residence 137, 139, 400, 438, 487
residents, permanent 126, 131, 133, 138
resilience 1–21, 118
resistance 3, 16, 56, 87, 94, 331, 340, 432–33
armed 324, 337, 372
political 15–16, 323, 331–32, 335, 339–40
sites of 54, 219
resources 19, 91, 128, 205, 331, 430, 439, 493
restrictive security measures 11, 214
retained data 283, 285, 292
retention 107, 275–79, 281–83, 285, 287, 289, 291, 293
data 14–15, 275–93, 466
periods 276–77, 289, 291, 293
retrospective accountability 12, 160–63, 166, 169, 173
and secrecy 160–71
return, managed 109, 112, 115
review 172–73, 182, 187–88, 299, 395, 397–99, 448–49, 491
ex post 182, 447–48
judicial 187, 189, 226, 228, 278, 286, 392, 395
rhetoric, populist 150, 341
right-of-centre populism 11, 20, 77, 82, 94
rights
after 9/11 248–50
Carter to Bush 243–45
citizenship 11, 99–119, 261
competing 313–19
constitutional 4, 228, 259, 466
defence 215, 300–303, 305–6, 308–11, 319–20
defendant 15, 304, 306, 308
human, *see* human rights
justified limits on 238, 241, 248, 253
liberal 264, 461
of membership and mobility 104, 115
mobility 11, 101, 139
natural 267, 270
privacy 14, 118, 128, 134, 275–82, 285, 288, 291–93
qualified 45, 114
revolution 237, 239, 243
and security 8–9, 13, 128, 234–35, 249–50, 259, 267, 493
as complementary not contradictory 487–92
as trumps 233–54
to truth 12, 163–67, 169, 172–73
victim 299, 301–2, 304, 312–13
and violence 262
witness 310
women's 55, 58
Rights Defender 17, 409, 413–17
rights revolution 239–43
rights-restrictive legislation 292, 294
right-wing extremism 7–8, 465, 467
right-wing terrorism 8
riot 241–42, 252–53
risk
assessment 130, 314, 422–24, 429, 431, 434, 490
to civilians 433–34, 444
factors 462, 468
Rohingya 478, 487–88, 490
rule of law 6, 16–17, 20, 151–52, 159–61, 172, 227, 268–69
Russia 2, 205–6, 216, 340, 353

safe citizens 133, 141
Safe Harbour scheme 14, 279–81, 293
safeguards 277–78, 285, 300, 305, 307, 315, 317, 323
procedural 4, 14, 108, 244
safety 56, 59, 133, 135–36, 251, 261, 476, 480
physical 313, 319, 476
public 108, 115, 242, 245, 482
workplace 221
salafi-jihadi ideologies 261, 270–71
sanctions 179–85, 188, 191, 194, 196, 204–7, 215, 263
satellite dishes 445–46
Saudi Arabia 10, 57–58, 69
scholarship 12, 147–48, 157, 161, 167, 173, 234
academic 147–48, 160, 173
legal 158, 161
and secrecy 148–52
schools 67, 71, 462
Schrems v Data Protection Commissioner 276, 279–81, 294
screening 132, 136, 491–92
security 129, 489
scrutiny 12, 126, 153, 157, 161–62, 165–67, 169, 173
academic 12, 151, 163, 171–73
future 171–73
pre-legislative 106, 108
public 18, 109, 155, 461
state 91, 128

search orders 394, 416
searches 84–85, 104, 107, 400, 402, 405, 407, 415–18
administrative 394, 400–402, 405–7, 411–13, 416
baggage 394, 400
secondary prevention 460, 468
secrecy 147–49, 153–55, 157, 159–61, 165, 169, 171–73, 193
as meta-paradigmatic challenge 147–73
moral ambiguity of 154–55
and retrospective accountability 160–71
and scholarship 148–52
shallow 153–55
secret detentions 195, 202, 205
secret evidence 4, 109, 148
secret information 160–61, 182, 189, 191–93, 196, 198, 200, 204–7
secret law 147, 154
secret prisons 12, 179, 193, 196
secrets
deep 153–61, 167, 173
legal 147, 153–60
shallow 153–57, 159
secular extremism 53–59, 71
secularism 2, 57, 59, 66, 70–71, 82
secure society 63, 65, 68–69, 267–68
secure world 60, 62–63, 65–67, 70
securitarianism 275, 289, 293–94
securitisation 6, 10, 83, 87, 127, 129–30, 138, 142
securitised states 36, 43, 58
security
actors 181, 184, 413
agencies 179, 181, 192, 204–5, 429–30, 440, 444, 447–48
attainment of 313, 458, 476
conduct 198, 200
costs 10, 20, 92–93
data 203, 277
definition of 456–58, 475–77
demands of 1, 19, 279
discourses 260–61, 475
domestic 179, 458, 462, 465–66
and forced migration 483–87
human 260–61, 457, 475, 484
and human rights 8, 18, 70, 212, 254, 259–60, 262, 267
and immigration 11, 136, 140
individual 6, 101, 261, 267
language of 56–57, 71, 458
and liberty 27, 37–38
measures 4, 102, 304, 427, 468
restrictive 11, 214
perfect 60, 62, 65, 294
physical 301–2, 306, 308, 314, 317
policies 62, 87–88, 92–94, 100, 191, 216, 246
politics 6, 8
populism 1, 8–9, 20–21
powers 184, 196, 200
practices 271, 455, 463, 467
and privacy 275–94
and privilege 136–41
public 404, 485
regimes 214–15, 457–58, 463
right to 259, 492
and rights 8–9, 13, 128, 234–35, 249–50, 259, 267, 493
as complementary not contradictory 487–92
risks 79, 83, 87, 319, 485–86, 492
services 106–7, 112, 116, 190, 200, 211, 461–62, 466
and suprarationality 59–61
as trump 250–54
security–prevention complex 455–69
segregation 66–67, 238
self-incrimination 112
self-preservation 267, 269
self-representation 305, 320
separation of powers 396, 410
serious crimes 277–78
settlement 65, 84, 489, 493
countries 19, 493
shallow secrecy 153–57, 159
Shehadeh, Salah 18, 421, 423, 434–35, 448
Shehadeh Commission 421, 423–24, 434–36, 438, 440–41, 443–46, 448, 450
slavery 2, 34–36, 45, 150, 168, 213
Snowden revelations 179, 203, 460
social actors 227
social chaos 57–58
social contract 264, 269
social media 343, 345, 352, 458, 467
companies 203, 456
posts 356–57
social order 64, 67, 264, 269
social processes 266, 425
social sorting 11, 128–29, 140, 142
social standards 219–20
social workers 82, 455
society
democratic 151, 344, 367, 378
ideal 60, 62, 69–70
secure 63, 65, 68–69, 267–68

socioeconomic status 11, 135, 140
sorting, social 11, 128–29, 140, 142
Southeast Asia 479, 481
sovereign power 13, 142
sovereignty 130, 268–69, 325, 331, 492
Spain 343, 353, 355, 413
Special Tribunal for Lebanon (STL) 15, 297–311, 313, 315, 317–20
  criteria for reconciling competing rights and security 313–19
  judges 300, 304–5
  jurisdiction 306, 311, 314
  proceedings 301, 304, 307, 319
  security and human rights at 298–305
  Statute (STLS) 297–98, 300, 302, 305, 307, 312, 314, 316
specificity 278, 306, 368, 380
spirit thievery 34, 36
standards 249, 251, 278, 280, 282, 285, 457, 477–78
  human rights 15–16, 46, 314, 317, 380
state accountability 165, 172
state actors 64–65, 88–89, 171, 182, 184, 205, 339, 422
state coercion 86, 91
state institutions 180, 198, 204, 206, 212, 220, 228–29, 326
state intransigence 225–26
state of emergency 16–17, 85, 234, 288, 390–400, 402–6, 408–18
  France 2, 288, 389–418
state of siege 389–90
state power 6, 13, 81, 211, 228, 271, 339
state responsibility 317, 416
state scrutiny 91, 128
state surveillance 4, 9, 14–15, 233, 294
state violence 13, 266
stateless persons 118, 473, 478–80, 491
status 11, 13, 128–29, 139, 149–50, 457, 463, 488
  citizenship 99, 116–17, 131
  immigration 104, 127, 129, 134–35
  legal 13, 130, 222, 226
  moral, *see* moral status
  refugee 102–4, 475, 479–80, 487–90, 492
  socioeconomic 11, 135, 140
  victim participant 303, 308
STL, *see* **Special Tribunal for Lebanon**
stop-and-search powers 45, 87
student visas 125–26
subjective judgements 429, 490
subjectivity 86, 378
Sudan 217
supervision 400, 411
  judicial 400–401
suprarational logic 60–61
suprarational world 66, 70
suprarationality
  in religious and secular laws 61–66
  and security 59–61
surveillance
  biopolitical 131
  mass 14, 180, 197, 203, 205, 207, 286, 293
  state 4, 9, 14–15, 233, 294
  technologies 14, 127
suspected terrorists 35, 37, 101, 103, 216, 248, 422–23, 431
suspicion 10, 64, 79, 83, 85, 90, 108, 116, 155–56
  criteria of 10, 90
  reasonable 108, 466
Sweden 285, 335
  legislation 279, 284–85
Syria 66, 80, 100–101, 104, 191, 216–17, 473, 481
Syrian refugees 474

targeted killings 2, 5, 18, 154, 156, 245, 247, 421–50
  fact-finding in decision-making 446–49
  inherent risks for civilians 433–34
  intelligence and risk of error 428–33
  Israeli investigation of Salah Shehadeh 435–44
  legal fact-finding and targeting decision-making 424–28
targeting decisions 423, 447–49
  bounded factuality in 428–34
targets
  legitimate 423, 436–38
  military 336, 437
teachers 82, 86–87, 150, 455–56
temporary exclusion 101, 106, 109–10, 115–16
Temporary Exclusion Orders, *see* **TEOs**
temporary first asylum 480–81
tensions 115, 211, 214–15, 236, 456, 458, 467, 469
TEOs (**Temporary Exclusion Orders**) 109–12, 114
terror, war on 27, 38, 99, 102, 154, 233, 380, 460

terrorism, see also *Introductory Note*
in armed conflict under international humanitarian law 335–39
definition of 458–59
domestic 93, 334
glorification of 343, 347–52, 354–56, 361, 368, 376
incitement to 347–48, 364
international 114, 129, 275, 278, 293, 298, 320, 334
mass 13, 242, 250–52, 254
nuclear 246, 331
offences 333–34, 340, 348–49, 355, 363, 459, 464
perceptions of 236, 248
prevention 16, 291, 346, 348, 367, 369, 466, 469
right-wing 8
threat of 104, 235, 250–51, 253, 461
terrorist attacks 17, 100–101, 114, 214, 437, 443, 450, 459
terrorists 41, 113, 324–25, 327–29, 349–50, 353, 459–60, 469
potential 106, 109
suspected 35, 37, 101, 103, 216, 248, 422–23, 431
tertiary prevention 460, 468
testimony 301, 310, 312–14, 316, 318, 440, 442, 444
anonymous 306, 310, 313, 315, 317–18
Thailand 219–20, 478–79, 482
threats 10–11, 67–71, 104–5, 114–18, 211–12, 252–53, 430–31, 462–63
existential 9, 29
external 139, 238
to national security 104, 234, 373, 375
perceived 67, 266
political 150
potential 64, 69, 119, 212, 253, 482, 489
security 7, 109, 455, 457, 462–63, 466, 485–87, 493
tolerance 1, 71, 195, 218, 344, 431
torture 9, 27–46, 191, 193–94, 205–6, 243, 250–52, 424–25
absolute prohibition of 4, 9, 27–32, 36, 45–46, 312
and othering 33–36
anti-torture norm 44–45
victims 34, 36, 165
totalitarian states 268, 459
TPIMs (Terrorism Prevention and Investigation Measures) 113–14
trafficked persons 473, 491
trafficking 478–80, 491
transfers, data 280–82
transnational accountability 179, 185, 192, 196, 204, 206
transnational cooperation 323, 332, 335–36, 338
transnational counterterrorism 12, 179–80, 182–85, 187–89, 192–93, 197, 205
abuses 185, 188, 194, 196, 205, 207
accountability mechanisms for 179–207
conventions 329–32
transnational crime 135, 491
transparency 155, 159, 171, 200, 203–4, 440, 448
travel bans 2, 89, 184, 187
travel documents, powers to seize 107–9
travellers 108, 126–29, 131–32, 137, 140
low-risk 128, 137
trusted 11, 128–29, 132, 134–36, 138–42
trial
in absentia 300
expeditious 305, 308
fair, *see* fair trial
unfair 327, 329
Trojan horses 58–59, 125–41, 474
Trump, Donald 32, 168, 201, 206, 216, 259, 474
trusted traveller programmes (TTPs) 11, 125–42
and threat to privacy 129–35
truth 151, 163–66, 267, 269–70, 302–3, 367, 389, 424–25
right to 12, 163–67, 169, 172–73
TTPs, *see* **trusted traveller programmes**
Tunisia 66, 68–69
Turkey 59, 66, 68, 70, 150, 344, 372–74, 378–79
propagandising in 358
Twitter 350, 353, 356–57

UK Border Force 132
uncertainty 78–79, 241, 429, 431, 443–45
underclass, kinetic 139
undesirable migrants 89, 139
unfair trial 327, 329
UNHCR (United Nations High Commissioner for Refugees) 377, 478–79, 485, 488, 490
United Kingdom 44–45, 99–103, 109–10, 125–26, 132–34, 188–91, 215–17, 282–83
Counterterrorism and Security Act (CTSA) 106–9, 111–13, 117

Data Retention and Investigatory Powers Act (DRIPA) 283–86
encouragement offences 352–53
government 44, 103–4, 109, 111, 162, 187, 286
Independent Reviewer of Terrorism Law 87
Registered Traveller service 11, 128, 131–33, 135–36, 139–40

United Nations 65, 81, 180, 216, 323, 358, 381
Security Council 102–5, 186–87, 214–15, 297, 299, 332–35, 338, 340
UNSC Resolution 1267 listing process 186–87, 193, 197–98
UNSC Resolution 1267 Ombudsperson 186, 198, 204

United Nations High Commissioner for Refugees, *see* **UNHCR**

United States 1–2, 81, 188–91, 200–201, 211–12, 214–18, 280, 481–82
Federal Bureau of Investigation (FBI) 203, 432
First Amendment 201, 218, 239
National Security Agency (NSA) 158, 200, 246–47, 460
Safe Harbour scheme 14, 279–81, 293

unpredictability 60, 63, 254

unreliable information 447, 489

'us' and 'them' narratives 38–39

value judgements 427, 434, 448–49

veils 58–59, 66, 83

victim participants 298, 301, 303–8, 311–12, 318
active 307
anonymous 15, 305, 308, 311, 317, 319
dual-status 309
lawyers 304, 306
non-anonymous 308

victim participation 302–4, 307–9, 312–13, 319

victim states 326, 331, 335

victim witnesses 15, 301, 312, 315

victims 5–6, 33–35, 66–68, 165, 169, 189, 195, 349
anonymity for 297–320
interests 304, 309
rendition 4, 193
rights 299, 301–2, 304, 312–13
torture 34, 36, 165

Vietnam 264, 482, 484

violence 7, 241, 259–71, 324–28, 331–32, 334–35, 339–41, 372–76
fear of 267–68
illegitimate 13, 262, 265
incitement to 344, 358, 372–75, 377, 382
physical 56, 428
political 38, 102, 266, 324–25, 329, 334–35, 459
and politics 262, 264–65, 267, 269
private 6, 10, 93
state 13, 266

violent extremism 261, 366, 455, 457, 459–61, 463, 465, 467–69

violent political resistance 323–41

visas 125, 127, 129, 133
humanitarian 490
student 125–26

vulnerable groups 13, 20, 469

war crimes 163, 331, 336–38, 439

watchdog(s)
agencies 191–92
executive 180, 184, 192–93, 198, 205, 207
NGO 220

whistleblowers 12, 173, 180, 186, 198–201, 291, 460

witness anonymity 307, 310, 313, 316, 319

witness rights 310

witness statements, anonymous 309–11

witnesses 15, 298–302, 304–7, 309–12, 314, 316–19, 415
victim 15, 301, 312, 315

women 54–55, 57, 59, 66–70, 83, 247, 340
Muslim 10, 53–61, 66–67, 69–71
non-ideal 66, 68
non-Muslim 54, 56
rights 55, 58

workplace safety 221

World Bank 219–20, 485

World University Service 149

xenophobia 20, 55, 211–12

Yemen 217